Issues for Debate in Human Rights
Selections from *CQ Researcher*

CQ PRESS

A Division of SAGE
Washington, D.C.

CQ Press
2300 N Street, NW, Suite 800
Washington, DC 20037
Phone: 202-729-1900; toll-free, 1-866-4CQ-PRESS (1-866-427-7737)
Web: www.cqpress.com

Contents
Annotated Contents
Preface
Contributors

International Human Rights Institutions and Humanitarian Intervention

Annotated Contents

INTERNATIONAL HUMAN RIGHTS INSTITUTIONS AND HUMANITARIAN INTERVENTION

Human Rights Issues

Human-rights advocates are voicing disappointment with what they have seen so far of President Barack Obama's approach to human-rights issues when forming U.S. foreign policy. They applaud Obama for working to restore U.S. influence on human rights by changing President George W. Bush's policies on interrogating and detaining terrorism suspects. However, they also see evidence that the Obama administration is reluctant to challenge authoritarian governments for clamping down on political dissidents or rigging elections. For example, these critics complain that Obama should not have tried to curry favor with the Chinese government by postponing a meeting with the Dalai Lama until after the president visited China in November 2009. Administration officials insist Obama is devoted to human rights and democratization and cite, among other moves, the decision to join the United Nations Human Rights Council. Conservative critics, however, say the council is a flawed institution and the United States should have stayed out.

World Peacekeeping

After the United Nations arose from the ashes of the Holocaust, the world's collective vow "Never again" seemed ironclad and irrevocable. As part of its effort to prevent future wars and genocides, the U.N. began to station peacekeepers around the globe, beginning in 1948 in Jerusalem. But the peace-keeping missions have had limited success. Now, prompted by the horror of the killings in Rwanda and Darfur, and before that in Bosnia, the world body has adopted a controversial new concept—the Responsibility to Protect doctrine—designed to stop future catastrophes. Known as R2P, it holds that the world community has a moral duty to halt genocide—even inside a sovereign country. Detractors call R2P legal imperialism, and even its defenders admit that the rhetoric has not yet translated into meaningful aid for Darfur. Other international alliances, including NATO and the European and African unions, have stepped up to provide military muscle to keep the peace in other hotspots in the meantime.

Human Trafficking and Slavery

From the villages of Sudan to the factories, sweatshops and brothels of India and South Asia, slavery and human trafficking still flourish. Some 27 million people worldwide are held in some form of slavery, forced prostitution or bonded labor. Some humanitarian groups buy captives' freedom, but critics say that only encourages slave traders to seize more victims. Meanwhile, nearly a million people are forcibly trafficked across international borders annually and held in captivity. Even in the United States, thousands of women and children from overseas are forced to become sex workers. Congress recently strengthened the Trafficking Victims Protection Act, but critics say it is still not tough enough and that certain U.S. allies that harbor traffickers are treated with "kid gloves" for political reasons.

Women's Rights

Women around the world have made significant gains in the past decade, but tens of millions still face significant and often appalling hardship. Most governments now have gender-equality commissions, electoral gender quotas and laws to protect women against violence. But progress has been mixed. A record number of women now serve in parliaments, but only 14 of the world's 193 countries currently have elected female leaders. Globalization has produced more jobs for women, but they still constitute 70 percent of the world's poorest inhabitants and 64 percent of the world's illiterate. Spousal abuse, female infanticide, genital mutilation, forced abortions, bride-burnings, acid attacks and sexual slavery remain pervasive in some countries, and rape and sexual mutilation have reached epic proportions in the war-torn Democratic Republic of the Congo. Experts say without greater economic, political and educational equality, the plight of women will not improve, and society will continue suffering the consequences.

Aiding Refugees

Some 42 million people worldwide have been uprooted by warfare or other violence, including 16 million refugees who are legally protected because they left their home countries. Most live in refugee camps and receive aid from the United Nations or other agencies but cannot work or leave the camps without special permission. Another 26 million people who fled violence are not protected by international treaties because they remain in their home countries. The number of such "internally displaced persons" (IDPs) has risen in the last decade, largely due to wars in Africa, Iraq, Afghanistan and Colombia. Millions of IDPs live in harsh conditions, and many receive no aid. Some critics say the U.N. High Commissioner for Refugees should do much more for IDPs, but the agency already faces severe budget shortfalls and bleak prospects for more donations from wealthy nations. Meanwhile, scientists warn that the number of people displaced by natural disasters—now about 50 million a year—could rise dramatically in coming years due to climate change.

Rescuing Children

The numbers are grim: every day more than 25,000 children under age 5—the equivalent of 125 jetliners full of youngsters—die from hunger, poverty or easily preventable illnesses such as diarrhea and malaria. Millions of others are abandoned, trafficked into prostitution, forced into armed conflict or used as child laborers—mostly in sub-Saharan Africa, Asia and Eastern Europe. While governments and nongovernmental organizations struggle to help, aid cutbacks due to the world economic crisis could trigger 200,000–400,000 additional child deaths each year. Meanwhile, experts and policy makers disagree over how best to combat AIDS among children and whether more foreign aid would do more harm than good. Others question whether the United States should ratify the U.N. Convention on the Rights of the Child. The United States is the only nation besides Somalia that hasn't adopted the treaty.

HUMAN RIGHTS AND CONFLICT
Closing Guantánamo

President Obama on his second full day in office ordered the closing of the Guantánamo detention camp within a year. The facility at the U.S. Naval Station in Cuba has been controversial ever since President George W. Bush decided in late 2001 to use it to hold suspected enemy combatants captured in Afghanistan and elsewhere. Both Obama and Republican candidate John McCain promised during the presidential campaign to close the facility if elected. But that poses many difficult issues in regard to the camp's remaining 241 prisoners. The government wants to send many to other countries—with few takers so far—but worries that some may resume hostile activities against the United States. Some may be brought to the United States for trial, but those prosecutions would raise a host of uncharted legal issues. Meanwhile, opposition already has surfaced to any plans for housing detainees in the United States, and human-rights advocates worry the Obama administration may continue to back some form of preventive detention for suspected terrorists.

Torture Debate

Countries around the globe—including the United States—are using coercive interrogation techniques that critics say amount to torture in the fight against terrorism. Despite international laws banning the practice, authoritarian nations have long abused prisoners and dissidents, and a handful of democracies have used torture in recent decades against what they considered imminent threats. Republican presidential candidates said they would authorize torture to prevent impending terrorist attacks. U.S. soldiers in Iraq say they would torture suspects to save the lives of their comrades. Human-rights advocates worry the use of torture by the United States is legitimizing its use globally and destroying America's moral authority to speak out against regimes that abuse prisoners in far worse ways. U.S. officials credit "enhanced interrogation" methods with averting terrorist attacks. But many experts say information gained by torture is unreliable.

Child Soldiers

Since the mid-1990s, the world has watched in horror as hundreds of thousands of children and young teenagers have participated in nearly 50 wars, mostly in Africa and Asia. Children as young as 5 or 6 have served in combat, and thousands of abducted young girls have been forced into sexual slavery. Some terrorist groups strap explosive-rigged vests onto children and use them as suicide bombers. Others have been recruited, sometimes forcibly, into the official armed forces or paramilitary units of several dozen countries. U.N. treaties prohibit the use of child soldiers, and the Security Council "names and shames" persistent violators. But only four former guerrilla commanders have been convicted by international tribunals, and some human-rights advocates urge more aggressive prosecution of perpetrators. However, some peace negotiators say threats of prosecution can obstruct cease-fire negotiations and prolong the fighting. In the United States, where children under 18 serve in the military in non-combat roles, Congress is considering laws to combat the use of child soldiers overseas.

REGIONAL ISSUES
Human Rights in China

When the curtain rose on the Summer Olympics in Beijing in August 2008, China eagerly showcased its hypersonic economic growth and its embrace of what it calls the "rule of law." But 19 years after its bloody suppression of protesters in Tiananmen Square, China also displayed its human-rights record for all to judge. Human-rights advocates say the sheen of Chinese progress and prosperity hides repression and brutality by the Chinese Communist Party, including the violent repression of pro-independence protesters in Tibet, forced abortions stemming from China's one-child policy and the trampling of basic freedoms of speech, religion and assembly. Chinese government officials say their nation of 1.3 billion people has made huge strides on the legal and human-rights fronts and that the West has no business interfering in China's internal affairs.

Crisis in Darfur

More than two years after government and rebel fighters signed a peace agreement in Sudan, violence is still rampant in Darfur. At least 2.4 million people have been displaced and up to 400,000 have died since 2003. And observers say the situation is getting worse. Rebel groups have splintered into more than a dozen warring factions, bandits are attacking relief workers and drought threatens to make the coming years among the deadliest in Darfur's history. Despite pressure from religious and human-rights groups, the international community seems unable—or unwilling—to find a lasting solution. In 2008, a year after the U.N. authorized the world's largest peace-keeping force in Darfur, only 37 percent of the authorized personnel had been deployed, and no military helicopters had been provided. The International Criminal Court indicted Sudanese President Omar Hassan al-Bashir on charges of genocide, but some fear this will trigger more violence than justice. Some say China, Sudan's largest trading partner and arms supplier, should pressure Sudan to end the violence.

The Troubled Horn of Africa

Plagued by conflict, poverty and poor governance, the Horn of Africa is arguably the most troubled part of the world's poorest continent. In desperately poor Somalia, an 18-year civil war has forced more than a million people from their homes, leaving behind a safe haven for pirates and, possibly, Islamic terrorists. In Ethiopia, an increasingly authoritarian, Western-backed government has jailed opposition leaders and clamped down on the press and human-rights activists. In tiny Eritrea, a government that once won the admiration of legions of Western diplomats and journalists for its self-sufficiency and discipline has become an isolated dictatorship. The recent withdrawal of Ethiopian troops from Somalia and the election of a moderate leader to the country's transitional government have raised international hopes that the lawlessness there will be brought under control. But Somalia's new government faces an insurgency from radical Islamists and worldwide pressure to stop the increasingly aggressive pirates who terrorize cargo ship crews off Somalia's coast and find refuge in its seaside villages.

Preface

Is the Obama administration making human rights enough of a priority? Are the world's nations doing enough to end human trafficking and slavery? Are crackdowns on basic freedoms in China increasing? These questions—and many more—are at the heart of debates in the area of international human rights. Students must first understand the facts and contexts of these and other issues if they are to analyze and articulate well-reasoned positions.

The first edition of *Issues for Debate in Human Rights* includes twelve reports by *CQ Researcher*, an award-winning weekly policy brief that explains difficult concepts and provides balanced coverage of competing perspectives. Each article analyzes past, present and possible political maneuvering and is designed to promote in-depth discussion and further research to help readers formulate their own positions on crucial international issues.

This collection is organized into three subject areas: humanitarian institutions and intervention, human rights and conflict and regional issues—to cover a range of topics found in most human-rights courses. Citizens, journalists and business and government leaders also can turn to the collected articles to become better informed on key issues, actors and policy positions.

CQ RESEARCHER

CQ Researcher was founded in 1923 as Editorial Research Reports and was sold primarily to newspapers as a research tool. The magazine was renamed and redesigned in 1991 as *CQ Researcher*. Today, students are its primary audience. While still used by hundreds of journalists and newspapers, many of which reprint portions of the reports, the *Researcher*'s main subscribers are high school, college and public libraries. In 2002, the *Researcher* won the American Bar Association's coveted Silver Gavel award for magazine excellence for a series of nine reports on civil liberties and other legal issues.

Researcher staff writers—all highly experienced journalists—sometimes compare the experience of writing a *Researcher* report to drafting a college term paper. Indeed, there are many similarities. Each report is as long as many term papers—about 11,000 words—and is written by one person without any significant outside help. One of the key differences is that writers interview leading experts, scholars and government officials for each issue.

Like students, staff writers begin the creative process by choosing a topic. Working with the *Researcher*'s editors, the writer identifies a controversial subject that has important public policy implications. After a topic is selected, the writer embarks on one to two weeks of intense research. Newspaper and magazine articles are clipped or downloaded, books are ordered and information is gathered from a wide variety of sources, including interest groups, universities and the government. Once the writers are well informed, they develop a detailed outline, and begin the interview process. Each report requires a minimum of ten to fifteen interviews with academics, officials, lobbyists and people working in the field. Only after all interviews are completed does the writing begin.

CHAPTER FORMAT

Each issue of *CQ Researcher*, and therefore each selection in this book, is structured in the same way. Each begins with an overview, which briefly summarizes the areas that will be explored in greater detail in the rest of the chapter. The next section chronicles important and current debates on the topic under discussion and is structured around a number of key questions, such as "Should U.S. companies in China push for human-rights reforms?" and "Should Guantánamo detainees be prosecuted in civilian courts?" These questions are usually the subject of much debate among practitioners and scholars in the field. Hence, the answers presented are never conclusive but instead detail the range of opinion on the topic.

Next, the "Background" section provides a history of the issue being examined. This retrospective covers important legislative measures, executive actions and court decisions that illustrate how current policy has evolved. Then the "Current Situation" section examines contemporary policy issues, legislation under consideration and legal action being taken. Each selection concludes with an "Outlook" section, which addresses possible regulation and court rulings, as well as domestic and international government initiatives.

Each report contains features that augment the main text: two to three sidebars that examine issues related to the topic at hand, a pro versus con debate between two experts, a chronology of key dates and events and an annotated bibliography detailing major sources used by the writer.

CUSTOM OPTIONS

Interested in building your ideal CQ Press Issues book, customized to your personal teaching needs and interests? Browse by course or search for specific topics or issues from our online catalog of *CQ Researcher* issues at http://custom.cqpress.com.

ACKNOWLEDGMENTS

We wish to thank many people for helping to make this collection a reality. Tom Colin, managing editor of *CQ Researcher*, gave us his enthusiastic support and cooperation as we developed this first edition of *Issues for Debate in Human Rights*. He and his talented staff of editors and writers have amassed a first-class library of *Researcher* reports, and we are fortunate to have access to that rich cache.

Some readers may be learning about *CQ Researcher* for the first time. We expect that many readers will want regular access to this excellent weekly research tool. For subscription information or a no-obligation free trial of *Researcher,* please contact CQ Press at www.cqpress.com or toll-free at 1-866-4CQ-PRESS (1-866-427-7737).

We hope that you will be pleased by the first edition of *Issues for Debate in Human Rights.* We welcome your feedback and suggestions for future editions. Please direct comments to Elise Frasier, Acquisitions Editor for International Relations and Comparative Politics, College Publishing Group, CQ Press, 2300 N St. NW, Suite 800, Washington, D.C. 20037, or efrasier@cqpress.com.

—The Editors of CQ Press

Contributors

Thomas J. Colin, managing editor of *CQ Researcher*, has been a magazine and newspaper journalist for more than 30 years. Before joining Congressional Quarterly in 1991, he was a reporter and editor at the Miami Herald and National Geographic and editor in chief of Historic Preservation. He holds a bachelor's degree in English from the College of William and Mary and in journalism from the University of Missouri.

Kathy Koch, assistant managing editor of *CQ Researcher*, specializes in education and social policy issues. She has freelanced in Asia and Africa for various U.S. newspapers, including The Christian Science Monitor and USA Today. She also covered environmental legislation for CQ Weekly and reported for newspapers in South Florida. She graduated in journalism from the University of North Carolina at Chapel Hill.

Associate Editor **Kenneth Jost** graduated from Harvard College and Georgetown University Law Center, where he is an adjunct professor. He is the author of The Supreme Court Yearbook and editor of The Supreme Court from A to Z (both CQ Press). He was a member of the *CQ Researcher* team that won the 2002 American Bar Association Silver Gavel Award.

Thomas J. Billitteri is a freelance journalist in Fairfield, Pa., who has more than 30 years' experience covering business, nonprofit institutions and related topics for newspapers and other publications. He has written previously for *CQ Researcher* on teacher education, parental rights and mental-health policy. He holds a BA in English and an MA in journalism from Indiana University.

John Felton is a freelance journalist who has written about international affairs and U.S. foreign policy for nearly 30 years. He covered foreign affairs for the Congressional Quarterly Weekly Report during the 1980s, was deputy foreign editor for National Public Radio in the early 1990s and has been a freelance writer specializing in international topics for the past 15 years. His most recent book, published by CQ Press, is The Contemporary Middle East: A Documentary History. He lives in Stockbridge, Mass.

Karen Foerstel is a freelance writer who has worked for the Congressional Quarterly Weekly Report and Daily Monitor, The New York Post and Roll Call, a Capitol Hill newspaper. She has published two books on women in Congress—Climbing the Hill: Gender Conflict in Congress and The Biographical Dictionary of Women in Congress. She currently lives and works in London. She has worked in Africa with ChildsLife International, a nonprofit that helps needy children around the world, and with Blue Ventures, a marine conservation organization that protects coral reefs in Madagascar.

Lee Michael Katz has been a senior diplomatic correspondent for USA Today, the International Editor of UPI and an independent policy journalist who has written lengthy articles on foreign policy, terrorism and national security. He has reported from more than 60 countries. He holds an MS from Columbia University and has traveled frequently with the U.S. Secretary of State.

Robert Kiener is an award-winning writer whose work has appeared in the London Sunday Times, The Christian Science Monitor, The Washington Post, Reader's Digest, Time Life Books, Asia Inc. and other publications. For more than two decades he lived and worked as an editor and correspondent in Guam, Hong Kong and England and is now based in the United States. He frequently travels to Asia and Europe to report on international issues. He holds an MA in Asian Studies from Hong Kong University and an M.Phil. in International Relations from Cambridge University.

David Masci specializes in social policy, religion and foreign affairs. Before joining *CQ Researcher* as a staff writer in 1996, he was a reporter at CQ's Daily Monitor and CQ Weekly. He holds a BA in medieval history from Syracuse University and a law degree from The George Washington University.

Jason McLure is a correspondent for Bloomberg News and Newsweek based in Addis Ababa, Ethiopia. He previously worked for Legal Times in Washington, D.C., and in Newsweek's Boston bureau. His reporting has appeared in The Economist, Business Week, the British Journalism Review and National Law Journal. His work has been honored by the Washington, D.C., chapter of the Society for Professional Journalists, the Maryland-Delaware-District of Columbia Press Association and the Overseas Press Club of America Foundation. He has a master's degree in journalism from the University of Missouri.

Seth Stern is a legal-affairs reporter at the CQ Weekly Report. He has worked as a journalist since graduating from Harvard Law School in 2001, including as a reporter for The Christian Science Monitor in Boston. He received his undergraduate degree at Cornell University's School of Industrial and Labor Relations and a master's degree in public administration from Harvard's Kennedy School of Government. He is co-authoring a biography of Supreme Court Justice William J. Brennan Jr.

Human Rights Issues

By Kenneth Jost

Excerpted from the CQ Researcher. Kenneth Jost. (October 30, 2009). "Human Rights Issues." *CQ Researcher*, 909-932.

Human Rights Issues

BY KENNETH JOST

THE ISSUES

As a young boy, Tenzin Gyatso, the 14th Dalai Lama, received a gift in his Tibetan homeland from President Franklin D. Roosevelt: a gold watch showing the phases of the moon and the days of the week.

Nearly seven decades later, the leader of the Tibetan government in exile as well as the spiritual leader of Tibetan Buddhists had the watch with him in 2007 as another U.S. president, George W. Bush, bestowed on him the Congressional Medal of Freedom.

When he visited Washington in early October, however, the 74-year-old Buddhist monk was less warmly received by the current president, Barack Obama. To avoid offending the Chinese government over its political and cultural struggles with Tibetan dissidents, Obama decided to postpone a personal meeting with the Dalai Lama until after the president's visit to China in November.

Administration officials insisted that deferring what has been since 1991 a regular drop-in at the White House was no slight. They noted that the postponement had been agreed to in meetings between the Dalai Lama's advisers and one of Obama's closest aides, Valerie Jarrett, in advance of the monk's weeklong visit to Washington in early October.

The Dalai Lama himself brushed off any hint of hurt feelings from the postponement. In an Oct. 7 interview, he told CNN's Wolf Blitzer that he considered Obama "sympathetic" to the

The Dalai Lama says he is not upset about not meeting with President Obama during his visit to Washington in early October. Obama postponed meeting with the Tibetan leader to avoid offending the Chinese government over its treatment of Tibetan dissidents; the meeting will occur after Obama visits China in November. Human rights advocates see the postponement as a sign of weakness in the administration's support for human rights and democratization.

Getty Images/Ralph Orlowski

Tibetan cause and expected the president to raise the issue with Chinese leaders during his mid-November visit. "More serious discussion is better than just a picture, so I have no disappointment," he said. [1]

Human rights advocates, however, see the postponement as a mistake in itself and a troubling sign of weakness in the Obama administration's approach in promoting human rights and democratization in other countries. "It plays into the narrative that the administration will defer to power rather than principle," says Tom Malinowski, Washington director for Human Rights Watch.

"That obviously sends a message," says Elisa Massamino, chief executive officer of Human Rights First. "Decisions like that can be very powerfully damaging to the solidarity with the people who we claim to be standing with."

Obama cheered human rights advocates with the steps he took in his first days in office to scrap some of the controversial detention and interrogation policies that his predecessor, Bush, had adopted to deal with suspected terrorists following al Qaeda's Sept. 11, 2001, attacks on the United States. "You can't overstate the importance of that in terms of sending a signal to our own people and to the rest of the world that the United States is going to return to taking those commitments to fundamental human rights seriously," says Massamino.

In the months since then, however, human rights advocates on the political left and political right have been finding more to fault than to praise in Obama's dealings with countries viewed as human rights violators.

"They haven't yet come up with a consistent approach to human rights as to what they're trying to get in human rights as opposed to what they're trying to get country by country," says Jennifer Windsor, executive director of Freedom House, an older group generally seen as more conservative than such newer organizations as Human Rights First and Human Rights Watch. "I sort of wonder why it's taking them so long," Windsor says. "They keep on apologizing."

"So far, his administration has been characterized by a marked turning away

Global Freedom Declines for Third Year

Global freedom suffered its third consecutive year of decline in 2008, according to the annual survey by Freedom House. Overall, the human rights monitoring and advocacy organization rated 89 countries with a total population of 3.1 billion as free, 62 countries with 1.4 billion people as partly free and 42 countries with 2.3 billion people as not free.

Notable developments during the year, according to the report, included declines in Russia and in the non-Baltic countries of the former Soviet Union; stagnation in the Middle East and North Africa and substantial reversals for democracy in sub-Saharan Africa. The group also voiced disappointment with China's failure to improve its human rights situation during the year it hosted the Summer Olympic Games.

Among countries of particular importance to the United States, Iraq was credited with registering a small gain because of ebbing violence and reduced political terror, while Afghanistan was moved from partly free to not free because of "rising insecurity and increasing corruption and inefficiency in government institutions."

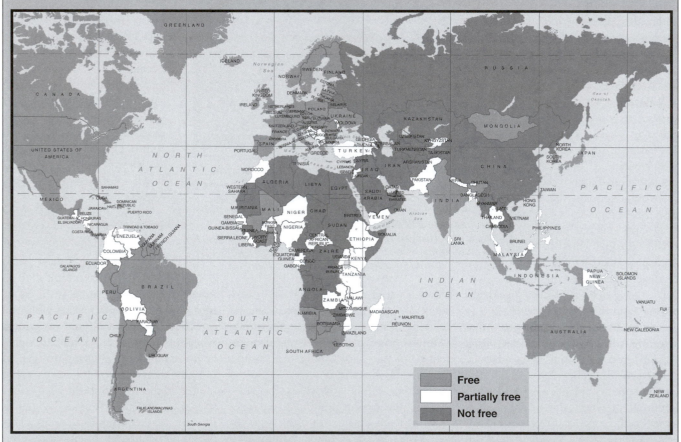

Source: "Freedom in the World 2009," Freedom House, www.freedomhouse.org/template.cfm?page=363&year=2009

from interest in human rights and democracy that has been a feature of United States foreign policy since the presidency of Jimmy Carter," says Joshua Muravchik, a fellow at the Foreign Pol-

icy Institute at Johns Hopkins University's School of Advanced and International Studies in Washington and a leading neoconservative expert on human rights.

Grumbling about the president's human rights record was already widespread before Obama became the unanticipated recipient on Oct. 9 of this year's Nobel Peace Prize. In selecting

Obama, the Norwegian Nobel Committee said he had created "a new atmosphere of international politics," adding, "Democracy and human rights are to be strengthened." [2]

A few hours later, Obama said he was "surprised" and "humbled" by the award. "I do not feel that I deserve to be in the company of so many transformative figures that have been honored by this prize," he said. But Obama said he would accept the award as "a call to action to confront the common challenges of the 21st century."

The reaction to the award in the United States and around the world was decidedly mixed. "Too early," said Lech Walesa, the Polish labor leader and later prime minister who was the 1983 Nobel laureate. But other previous winners applauded the selection. In a congratulatory letter, the Dalai Lama, the 1989 laureate, told Obama that the Nobel committee "has rightly noted your efforts towards a world without nuclear weapons and your constructive role in environmental protection."

Within the United States, Democrats and some Republicans voiced approval of the selection, but many GOP politicians were unenthusiastic to negative. Much of the reaction among mainstream media commentators and bloggers was skeptical, even from some liberals. (See "At Issue," p. 925.)

The divisions over the peace prize mirror experts' evaluations of Obama's contributions on human rights issues after nine months in office. "The jury is still out, but I think the Obama administration is headed in the right direction," says David Kaye, head of the International Human Rights Clinic at UCLA Law School and a former State Department official under Presidents Bill Clinton and George W. Bush.

But Michael Mandelbaum, director of the foreign policy program at Johns Hopkins, says the administration has downplayed human rights. "They very conspicuously backed away from the strong advocacy of rights, from putting

Obama: Democracy Is a Human Right

President Obama has stressed the importance of democracy and human rights in four recent speeches to international audiences, beginning with a widely hailed address at Cairo University in June. Human rights groups say they are encouraged by Obama's remarks but are looking for more concrete actions from the administration to support democratization and civil society movements.

"America does not presume to know what is best for everyone, just as we would not presume to pick the outcome of a peaceful election. But I do have an unyielding belief that all people yearn for certain things: the ability to speak your mind and have a say in how you are governed; confidence in the rule of law and the equal administration of justice; government that is transparent and doesn't steal from the people; the freedom to live as you choose. These are not just American ideas; they are human rights. And that is why we will support them everywhere."
— remarks at Cairo University, Cairo, Egypt, June 4, 2009

"The arc of history shows us that governments which serve their own people survive and thrive; governments which serve only their own power do not. Governments that represent the will of their people are far less likely to descend into failed states, to terrorize their citizens, or to wage war on others. Governments that promote the rule of law, subject their actions to oversight, and allow for independent institutions are more dependable trading partners. And in our own history, democracies have been America's most enduring allies, including those we once waged war with in Europe and Asia — nations that today live with great security and prosperity."
— remarks at the New Economic School graduation, Moscow, July 7, 2009

"America will not seek to impose any system of government on any other nation — the essential truth of democracy is that each nation determines its own destiny. What we will do is increase assistance for responsible individuals and institutions, with a focus on supporting good governance — on parliaments, which check abuses of power and ensure that opposition voices are heard; on the rule of law, which ensures the equal administration of justice; on civic participation, so that young people get involved; and on concrete solutions to corruption like forensic accounting, automating services, strengthening hotlines, and protecting whistle-blowers to advance transparency and accountability."
— remarks to the Ghanaian Parliament, Accra, July 11, 2009

"Democracy cannot be imposed on any nation from the outside. Each society must search for its own path, and no path is perfect. Each country will pursue a path rooted in the culture of its people and in its past traditions. And I admit that in the past America has too often been selective in its promotion of democracy. But that does not weaken our commitment, it only reinforces it. There are basic principles that are universal; there are certain truths which are self-evident — and the United States of America will never waver in our efforts to stand up for the right of people everywhere to determine their own destiny."
— remarks to United Nations General Assembly, New York, Sept. 23, 2009

Source: The White House, www.whitehouse.gov/the_press_office

that at the center of their policies and putting that at the center of their rhetoric," he says.

The United States took the lead after World War II in the adoption of international human rights agreements, but human rights took a back seat to global power politics during the tensest years of the Cold War. In the late 1970s, however, President Jimmy Carter made human rights an explicit centerpiece of U.S. foreign policy. Every president since then has continued the stated commitment to human rights, though in markedly different ways. [3]

President George W. Bush continued to voice support for human rights and used his second inaugural address in 2005 to put promoting democracy at the center of his foreign policy goals. The results of Bush's policies — in Iraq, the Mideast and the rest of the world — are disputed. Whatever Bush's final legacy may be, many experts and advocates say Obama is shaping his approach to the issues in conscious distinction with Bush's more aggressive approach. "They are almost afraid to speak out against human rights abuses in any country because it's going to be like Bush," says Freedom House's Windsor.

Admirers note that Obama has given four major foreign policy speeches reaffirming U.S. support for human rights, most recently at the United Nations General Assembly. (See box, p. 913.) They also point out that Obama appointed two longtime human rights advocates to pivotal posts at the State Department. Harold Hongju Koh, a former Yale Law School dean, is serving as the department's legal adviser; Michael Posner, the longtime head of Human Rights First, was confirmed in late September as assistant secretary of state for human rights, democracy and labor. "These two guys are really, really committed to a value-driven, human rights-oriented U.S. foreign policy," UCLA's Kaye says.

The admirers acknowledge, however, and critics emphasize that Obama has also sought to "engage" with several countries with deplorable human rights records, including Egypt, Syria, Iran and Myanmar (formerly Burma). Muravchik accuses Obama of "a rush to have new and friendly relations with a whole series of the most cruel and dictatorial regimes."

The debate over Obama's policies takes place against what Freedom House describes in its most recent annual report as the third consecutive year of decline in global freedom. The report credits Bush — and his two predecessors, Clinton and his father George H. W. Bush — with helping promote positive developments for democracy since the end of the Cold War. But it also points to "a turnaround in democracy's fortunes" in Bush's second term and points to "the lack of . . . durable gains" in the Middle East and North Africa as "a major disappointment for American policy." [4] (See map, p. 912.)

Apart from the changes in the post-9/11 interrogation and detention policies, Obama's most concrete action to date is the decision to join the United Nations Human Rights Council, a U.N. forum reconstituted in 2006 that the Bush administration pointedly boycotted. As with Obama's moves on anti-terrorism policies, reactions to the decision divide along ideological lines: Liberals support the move; conservatives do not. (See sidebar, p. 916.)

Obama's trip to China will be closely watched for new clues on how human rights fits in with other U.S. interests — economic, diplomatic, strategic — in dealing with countries with less than exemplary human rights records.

As the president prepares for the trip, here are some of the major questions that human rights watchers are debating:

Is the Obama administration deemphasizing human rights in U.S. foreign policy?

In a visit to China and other Asian countries in February, Secretary of State Hillary Rodham Clinton raised eyebrows among human rights advocates by appearing to put rights issues below other U.S. concerns. In comments to the traveling press corps, Clinton said the United States would continue pressing China on Tibet, Taiwan and free-speech issues, but added, "Our pressing on those issues can't interfere with the global economic crisis, the global climate change crisis and the security crisis."

Human rights groups complained in advance about signals that human rights issues were to be downgraded on the trip. "Extremely disappointed," said Amnesty International USA. Today, many human rights advocates continue to question Clinton's statement. "We're not going to talk about human rights until we solve global warming and the economic crisis?" asks Muravchik, the Johns Hopkins fellow. "That gives them a pretty large margin of impunity." [5]

Beyond U.S.-China relations, the administration appears to be basing its human rights policies on a view that private diplomacy is more effective than public rhetoric in encouraging authoritarian governments to turn away from repressive policies. Human rights advocates on the left and right disagree.

"They're saying they want to achieve real gains and to engage in order to get something accomplished," says Freedom House's Windsor. "In the past, we have not seen quiet diplomacy work."

"It's not enough to say we're going to talk with people," says Massamino of Human Rights First. "It's not an end in itself."

A former Bush administration official goes further. "It seems clear to me that the Obama administration has no human rights policy," Elliott Abrams, deputy national security director for democracy in Bush's second term and now a senior fellow with the Council on Foreign Relations, tells the conservative *FrontPageMagazine.com*. "That is, while in some inchoate sense they would like respect for human rights to grow around the world, as all Americans would, they have no actual policy to achieve that goal — and they subordinate it to all their other policy goals." [6]

Other human rights advocates, however, say the criticism is overblown. "The administration understandably wanted to distinguish itself from what it saw as the [Bush administration's] overly messianic and at times aggressive and hectoring approach toward these issues," says Human Rights Watch's Malinowski. "The narrative of Bush cared and Obama doesn't," he adds, "is extraordinarily simplistic and misguided."

Thomas Carothers, vice president for studies at the Carnegie Endowment for International Peace in Washington, also says the criticism of Obama's policies is exaggerated. "The idea that we've suddenly gone soft on Russia, on China and so forth tends to be a bit of an overstatement," he says.

Still, Malinowski says human right advocates have cause for concern. Obama's apparent approach, he says, "can easily be interpreted and to some extent is being interpreted by the permanent foreign policy bureaucracy at the State Department as an argument for engaging [repressive] governments without pressure, without sanctions, without a significant emphasis on what [bureaucrats] dismiss as moral issues."

Muravchik, the Johns Hopkins fellow, says the administration's approach reflects a wrongheaded effort to differentiate Obama's policies from Bush's. "There was an obvious opening in keeping with his desire to be critical of Bush's legacy to say that in this area Bush pronounced good ideas but didn't deliver," Muravchik says. "Instead, he's said that Bush was on the wrong track in essence by telling other governments how to behave."

Obama's engagement strategy, Muravchik concludes, "necessarily involves a downgrading if not betrayal of human rights." Other human rights watchers, however, are prepared to suspend judgment to see what results are achieved by the approach reflected, for example, in Clinton's comments on China.

"A charitable reading of that is that we need to find new tactics; we're not going to engage in a Kabuki dance; that's not getting results," says Massamino of Human Rights First.

"There's a lot to be said for the idea that in pushing a human rights agenda,

Secretary of State Hillary Rodham Clinton visits with South African soldiers assigned to U.N. peacekeeping duties in the Democratic Republic of the Congo during her weeklong visit to war-torn Africa in August. Earlier in the year she was criticized for saying human rights should not "interfere" with U.S.-China relations.

sometimes and in some places and with some countries it's better to push it quietly," says UCLA professor Kaye. "Over time, it may be that the Obama administration will either see that working or will see it not working. In those situations where they see it not working, they may move the disagreements from the private channels to the more public ones.

"It's too early to conclude that they are sacrificing the human rights agenda for some Kissingerian realpolitik," he concludes, referring to Henry Kissinger, who served as secretary of state under Presidents Richard M. Nixon and Gerald R. Ford. "I don't think that's what's happening."

Is the Obama administration reducing U.S. support for democratization in other countries?

President Obama used one of his first major foreign policy speeches abroad to reaffirm to his Egyptian audience and the broader Muslim world the United States' support for promoting democracy. Democratic principles such as freedom, equality and rule of law "are not just American ideas," Obama said in the June 4 address in Cairo. "They are human rights. And that is why we will support them everywhere."

Obama made no reference in the speech, however, to the repressive policies of his host, Egyptian President Hosni Mubarak. In advance, he even rejected a reporter's suggestion to describe Mubarak as "authoritarian." And when Obama hosted the Egyptian leader at the White House on Aug. 18, the subject of democracy was unmentioned in public comments. [7]

The on-again, off-again invocation of the democracy message leaves human rights advocates less than satisfied. "President Obama could have been more explicit," says Malinowski, the Human Rights Watch director in Washington. "It's important that the president's private messages to leaders like Mubarak be emphasized with public messages. I agree that was a missed opportunity."

Former Bush administration official Abrams bluntly criticized Obama for selecting Cairo as the site of the earlier address and then omitting any mention of human rights in the joint press availability with Mubarak at the White House. "Democracy activists in Egypt have been abandoned," he said in the *FrontPageMagazine.com* interview.

Muravchik, the Johns Hopkins fellow, is similarly critical of Obama's delayed

Report on Abuses in Gaza Sparks Concern

Critics see anti-Israel tilt by U.N. Human Rights Council.

Israel launched a three-week air and ground assault on Gaza in December 2008 aimed at stopping Palestinian militants from firing missiles at civilian targets across the border. During and after the invasion, the ruling Hamas government in Gaza charged that Israeli forces had committed war crimes by wantonly attacking Palestinian civilians. [1]

Now, a respected South African jurist has found both sides responsible for endangering civilians during the conflict. In a report commissioned by the United Nations Human Rights Council, Judge Richard Goldstone recommends that Israel and Gaza conduct their own investigations of human rights abuses by their side during the fighting. If no investigations are forthcoming within six months, Goldstone wants the U.N. Security Council to turn the dispute over to the International Criminal Court. [2]

Goldstone's report has drawn critical reactions from both sides. Israel has condemned Goldstone, who is Jewish, for furthering what they perceive to be the council's constant berating of the Jewish state. [3] Many Israelis complain that complying with the investigation would be fruitless because the council is already biased against them.

While Hamas has lauded Goldstone for denouncing Israeli military tactics and agreed to investigate some portions of the report, the rival Palestinian Authority originally decided to defer action, citing an inadequate number of people needed to support an investigation. However, after facing criticism for their decision, the authority requested that the U.N. conduct a special session on the conflict.

Several prominent human rights organizations, specifically Amnesty International and Human Rights Watch, have defended the report for calling attention to rights abuses. The U.N.'s top human rights official, Navi Pillay, has offered her endorsement, as well.

The report has focused worldwide attention on the Human Rights Council, a 47-nation body created in 2006 to replace a larger U.N. human rights forum widely denounced as ineffective. Critics said the earlier U.N. Commission on Human Rights was unsuccessful at prosecuting nations that violated human rights and showed poor judgment in allowing countries with questionable human rights records, including China and Russia, to be members. Under President George W. Bush, the United States criticized the commission and refused to join the council.

President Obama changed the policy, however, and the United States joined the council in May 2009. Critics say the council is still fundamentally flawed and inordinately critical of Israel. But human rights groups are applauding the shift. They say that U.S. involvement and an altered structure will help bring human rights abusers to justice.

The council has enacted a new, periodic review of all 192 U.N. member states in order to monitor human rights conditions in every state. Council members are chosen by the U.N. General Assembly instead of by the Economic and Social Council, which was previously in charge of elections. Additionally, a complaints procedure allows individuals and organizations to bring potential violations to the attention of the council. [4]

Proponents of the council say the changes signal a vast improvement over the commission, but many claim that a disproportionate amount of time continues to be spent on Israel's alleged human rights violations while others, such as Sudan, face little investigation. The council has appointed an independent expert to monitor Sudan and asked the country to remedy human rights violations but has taken no disciplinary action against the government. [5]

During its three-year existence, the council has passed a resolution on freedom of expression that prohibits limiting expression

response to evidence of irregularities in the Iranian presidential election in June. "Obama was so devoted to this course of making friends with the dictators that he refused for the first week to say or do anything to encourage the Iranian people," Muravchik says. "After a week went by, it was clear that his stand was untenable in terms of the views of the Iranian people, the American people and the stands of some other Western leaders. So he spoke out, which was all to the good but quite belated."

To democratization expert Carothers, Obama's speech represents a recasting of the Bush administration's approach to promoting democracy. "He set out an alternative rhetorical framework that emphasizes that we will not impose democracy on others, that we recognize that different kinds of democracy exist and that we will be sure not to equate elections with democracy," Carothers says.

Carothers says Obama's approach will be "more appealing to people in many parts of the world." But he adds, "It is clear that this administration is not going to make democracy promotion a major emphasis of its policy."

In Egypt, the administration seems to be trying to heal the rift in U.S.-Egyptian relations, which were seen to have suffered in the Bush years because of his administration's criticisms of Egypt's record on human rights. The Bush policies were widely credited, however, with encouraging some liberalization by the Mubarak government.

Today, human rights advocates say repressive policies are returning in Egypt just as U.S. support for democratization efforts is lagging. "Despite the president's speech, there's been little indication that the Egyptian government's

in order to protect religion. It has examined the continuing conflict in Gaza and passed resolutions aimed at remedying rights violations in Myanmar (formerly Burma) and the Democratic Republic of the Congo (DRC), particularly those involving women and children.

Many cite the ability of the United States to broker the freedom of expression resolution with Egypt as a sign that the council is enacting positive change. However, critics still claim that the council shows favoritism towards some countries, with bloc voting by region significantly furthering that bias. Specifically, the Arab countries and many of the African countries vote together on resolutions, making it difficult to pass those that allow the examination of rights violations in places like the DRC.

The Goldstone report has again brought these criticisms to the surface. In the special session requested by the Palestinian Authority, the council endorsed the report, a move that allows the investigation to be taken before the U.N. Security Council. This is the seventh of 12 sessions in the past year involving Israel — another indication many say, of the rights council's bias against Israel. The United States voted against the report and has veto power over the Security Council's agenda, making it unlikely the investigation will travel that far. China and Russia voted for the report but have since indicated their opposition to involving the Security Council. [6]

Last month, speaking in Geneva, U.S. Assistant Secretary for Democracy, Human Rights and Labor Michael Posner and State Department legal adviser Harold Hongju Koh expressed hope that U.S. involvement in the council would help to create a non-political U.N. body able to support victims and prosecute rights violators. [7] But the United States and Israel have expressed concern that the Goldstone report and proceedings within the rights council demonstrate a political bias against Israel and do not focus enough on human rights violations by the Palestinians.

In a 24-page assessment, Freedom House gives the council mixed ratings, with a passing grade only on the use of so-called special rapporteurs and failing grades on adoption of resolutions on urgent human rights crises. The organization specifically criticizes the council for a "disproportionate" number of resolutions critical of Israel. More broadly, the report concludes that democratic countries on the council have failed to counter the "considerable resources" devoted by a "small but active group" of non-democratic countries to limiting the council's effectiveness in protecting human rights. [8]

— *Emily DeRuy*

[1] For background, see Irwin Arieff, "Middle East Peace Prospects," *CQ Global Researcher*, May 2009, pp. 119-148.

[2] See "Human Rights in Palestine and Other Occupied Arab Territories: Report of the United Nations Fact-Finding Mission on the Gaza Conflict," Sept. 25, 2009, www2.ohchr.org/english/bodies/hrcouncil/docs/12session/A-HRC-12-48.pdf. See Christiane Amanpour, "A Look at the Allegations of Israeli and Hamas War Crimes," CNN International, Sept. 30, 2009, for interviews with Judge Goldstone and former U.S. Secretary of State Madeleine Albright.

[3] See Amir Mizroch, "Grappling with Goldstone," *The Jerusalem Post*, Sept. 18, 2009, p. 9.

[4] See "The Human Rights Council," The U.N. Human Rights Council, www2. ohchr.org /english/bodies/hrcouncil/ for full description of council structure.

[5] "Human Rights Council Establishes Mandate of Independent Expert on Sudan for One Year," U.N. Human Rights Council, June 18, 2009, www. unhchr.ch/huricane/huricane.nsf/view01/91B0E40B4256A0C3C12575D90071224 5?opendocument. For background, see Karen Foerstel, "Crisis in Darfur," *CQ Global Researcher*, September 2008, pp. 248-270.

[6] See Neil MacFarquhar, "U.N. Council Endorses Gaza Report," *The New York Times*, Oct. 16, 2009, www.nytimes.com/2009/10/17/world/middleeast/17nations.html ?_r=1&scp=1&sq=Goldstone%20report%20&st=cse.

[7] "Geneva Press Briefing by Harold Hongju Koh and Michael Posner," United States Mission, Sept. 28, 2009, http://geneva.usmission.gov/2009/09/28/koh-posner/.

[8] See "The U.N. Human Rights Council Report Card: 2007-2009," Freedom House, Sept. 27, 2009, www.freedomhouse.org/uploads/special_report/84.pdf.

human rights record is at all a concern to this administration or that they're willing to put any material support or diplomatic heft in order to get a reversal of the deteriorating situation in Egypt," says Freedom House's Windsor.

U.S. aid to democratization programs in Egypt, including funding for civil society groups, fell from $55 million in fiscal 2008 to $20 million in the current fiscal year. The Obama administration is proposing a modest increase to $25 million for the current year.

Overall, the administration is requesting $2.81 billion for democratization programs for fiscal 2010, an increase of $234 million, according to an analysis by Freedom House. "To their credit, they actually kept democracy and human rights levels up," says Windsor. [8]

Windsor says U.S. support for pro-democracy groups is important because of the resistance by authoritarian countries to outside aid. "Over the last three to four years, there's been a backlash by governments to make sure that no 'color revolution' occurs in their own country," she says, referring to the pro-democracy "Orange Revolution" in Ukraine and "Rose Revolution" in Georgia.

"We think neither the Bush administration nor the Obama administration has fully stood up for the right to cross-border help to fulfill human rights," Windsor continues.

In Egypt, a U.S. embassy official insisted in response to criticism from Egyptian activists that U.S. support continues. "We may have changed tactics, but our commitment to democracy and human rights promotion in Egypt is steadfast," an embassy official said in an e-mailed response to a reporter's questions. [9] But Carothers says human rights issues generally are getting only limited attention as the administration deals with other major foreign policy problems in Iraq, Iran and Afghanistan.

"They have been very busy with the major crises on their hands and have neither articulated nor begun to implement any kind of broad approach on human rights," Carothers says. "These are really pressing, and human rights seems to be of secondary concern."

Was President Obama right to have the United States join the United Nations Human Rights Council?

When a Danish newspaper published a full page of satirical depictions of the Prophet Muhammad in 2005, Muslim leaders around the world denounced the publication as a defamation of Islam. Many called on the Danish government to take legal action against the newspaper. A Danish prosecutor found no basis for proceeding against the newspaper, however. And many leaders and commentators in Europe and the United States criticized the Muslim response as a threat to freedom of expression.

The dispute exemplified the tension between many Muslims and much of the rest of the world over how to reconcile free speech with freedom of religion. Now, the United States and predominantly Muslim Egypt have joined in sponsoring a broad U.N. reaffirmation of freedom of expression that condemns religious intolerance but significantly omits any legal sanctions for criticizing religion or specific faiths.

The freedom of expression resolution, adopted Oct. 2 by consensus by the United Nations Human Rights Council, marked the first significant accomplishment by the United States since the Obama administration's decision to join the still-new U.N. forum. The Bush administration had refused to join the council after it was created in 2006 to replace the U.N. Commission on Human Rights, which was widely criticized as weak and ideologically polarized. [10]

Many human rights advocates say the passage of the freedom of expression resolution demonstrates the Obama administration was right to join the council. "The United States was successful in reaching out to Egypt," says Neil Hicks, senior adviser on U.N. issues for Human Rights First. By omitting any reference to defamation of religion, the resolution means that "there will no longer be an effort to weaken protection of freedom of expression in the name of protecting religion," Hicks says.

Other human rights advocates, however, are troubled by passages in the resolution critical of the rising incidence of religious intolerance and stereotyping. The resolution has "some very good language and some problematic language," says Paula Schriefer, director of advocacy at Freedom House, who follows U.N. issues. "There's some question whether this foray has been completely successful."

Hicks acknowledges the resolution is only "a step in the right direction" and may not end the dispute. Like most human rights advocates, however, including Freedom House, Hicks applauds the U.S. decision to participate in the council. "Our hope is that with U.S. membership there will be a concerted effort to stand up for democratic values in the council," Hicks says. "We're waiting for that to happen."

Some conservative human rights watchers, however, say the United States should have stayed out. "It was a token of the Bush administration's devotion to human rights that it would refuse to wade into this cesspool," says Johns Hopkins fellow Muravchik. "It is a great pity that the Obama administration has reversed that."

To join the council, the United States won election by 167 of the 192 members of the U.N. General Assembly in balloting in May. Among the 14 other countries elected were five with checkered human rights records, including two major powers, China and Russia; the regional power Saudi Arabia; and two smaller countries, Cameroon and Cuba. [11]

The U.N. Commission on Human Rights, the predecessor forum, had drawn criticism for being open to membership by — and domination by — human rights violators. In an effort to remedy the problem, membership in the new council requires an absolute majority of votes from the General Assembly rather than election from a regional bloc.

Proponents say the council is also stronger because all U.N. members will be subject to a "universal periodic review" of their records on rights issues, with council members up for review first. The commission had no procedure for reviewing human rights conditions in every country, Hicks says.

Supporters say membership by human rights violators is inevitable, but U.S. membership will strengthen the democratic bloc within the council. "Without United States leadership, other democratic countries rarely stand up effectively for human rights," says Human Rights Watch's Malinowski. "And repressive countries tend to band together quite effectively."

Mandelbaum at Johns Hopkins faults both the council and its predecessor for an anti-Israel bias. "They spend all their time persecuting the only country in the Middle East that takes human rights seriously: Israel," he says. Israel, which is not a member of the council, strongly criticized a report commissioned by the council that acused Israeli forces of human rights abuses during the invasion of Gaza launched in December 2008. (*See sidebar, p. 916*.)

Hicks agrees that the U.N. rights bodies have been guilty of "over-concentration on the Israeli-Palestinian situation," but he says that council actions adopting country-specific resolutions on Myanmar and Congo this year have shown some signs of reduced geographic-bloc voting.

In any event, most human rights experts applaud the Obama administration's decision to join the council. "The United States goes into these

Continued on p. 920

Chronology

1945-1990s

U.S. takes lead in establishing United Nations, writing international human rights law; U.S. support for democracy tempered by Cold War rivalry with communist bloc.

1945
United Nations established.

1948
Universal Declaration of Human Rights adopted by the U.N.

1950s
U.S. supports coups to oust leftist regimes in Guatemala, Iran; blocks unified election in Vietnam; sends no aid to anti-communist revolt in Hungary.

1960s
U.S. role in Vietnam War escalates; U.S. takes no action as Soviet Union crushes reform movement in Czechoslovakia.

1975
Vietnam War ends with fall of Saigon government, reunification under communist regime. . . . Helsinki Accords signed; Soviet bloc agrees to respect human rights.

1977-1981
President Jimmy Carter puts human rights at center of U.S. foreign policy.

1980s
U.S. support for right-wing regimes in Central America, contras in Nicaragua widely criticized in U.S., elsewhere; U.S. aid helps oust authoritarian leaders in Philippines, Haiti.

1989
Berlin Wall falls; Eastern European countries throw off communist governments; Cold War ends.

1990s
Human rights machinery institutionalized at United Nations: U.N. high commissioner for human rights created; war crimes tribunals established in former Yugoslavia, Rwanda.

———— • ————

2001-Present

Bush administration war on terror policies criticized, democracy promotion legacy questioned; Obama administration criticized for downplaying human rights.

2001
President George W. Bush launches invasion of Afghanistan for harboring al Qaeda after Sept. 11, 2001, attacks on U.S.; prepares aggressive policies to detain, interrogate "enemy combatants."

2002
U.S. opens prison camp for suspected terrorists at Guantánamo Bay Naval Base in Cuba; move widely criticized in Muslim world and by some European allies. . . . International Criminal Court established; U.S. declines to participate.

2003
U.S.-led invasion of Iraq topples Saddam Hussein; with U.S. support, parliamentary elections, referendum on new constitution held in 2005.

2004
U.S. labels killings of civilians in Sudan's Darfur province "genocide." . . . With U.S. backing, Hamid Karzai elected president of Afghanistan; parliamentary elections follow in 2005.

2005
Bush, in second inaugural address, promises U.S. support for democracy "in every nation and culture."

2006
U.S. declines to participate in newly created United Nations Human Rights Council.

2008
Bush prepares to leave office with democracy, human rights legacy sharply debated.

January-March 2009
Barack Obama inaugurated; repudiates Bush policies on detention and interrogation; promises to close Guantánamo within year (January). . . . Secretary of State Hillary Rodham Clinton draws fire for saying human rights should not "interfere" with U.S.-China relations (February). . . . U.S. signs U.N. petition favoring decriminalization of homosexual conduct (March). . . .

April-June 2009
U.S. wins election to U.N. Human Rights Council; administration signals support for U.N. convention to eliminate discrimination against women (May). . . . Obama says U.S. will support human rights "everywhere"; U.N. Ambassador Susan Rice indicates administration support for U.N. pact on children's rights (June).

July-September 2009
Clinton visits war-torn Congo during Africa visit (August). . . . Obama tells U.N. General Assembly U.S. has "too often been selective" in promoting democracy (September).

October 2009
Human Rights Council adopts freedom of expression resolution; endorses report opposed by U.S. that accuses Israel of targeting civilians in Gaza; U.S. critics say stance shows need to pull out of council. . . . Clinton, others unveil new policy on Sudan/Darfur; "carrots and sticks" approach criticized by some.

Clinton Vows Opposition to Violence Against Gays

'Killing campaign' in Iraq goes unpunished, rights group says.

The victim was taken from his parents' Baghdad home late one evening in April by four armed, masked men, who shouted insults as they dragged him away. His body was found in a garbage dump in the neighborhood the next day, his genitals cut off and a piece of his throat ripped out.

The victim's offense: He was gay. Three weeks later, when Human Rights Watch investigators spoke with the victim's 35-year-old partner, he struggled to speak. "In Iraq, murderers and thieves are respected more than gay people," he said. [1]

The incident was part of the group's report, published in August, which describes a "killing campaign" by "death squads" that swept through Iraq in the early months of 2009. The campaign was concentrated in Baghdad's Sadr City, the stronghold of supporters of the anti-American Shiite cleric Moktada al-Sadr, but killings also were reported in other cities.

The killings were done "with impunity," according to the report, based on three weeks of on-site interviews by Scott Long, director of Human Rights Watch's LGBT Rights Project, and a second investigator. Iraqi police and security forces did little to investigate or try to halt the killings, the report said. No arrests or prosecutions had been announced when the report was published.

Iraq is one of many countries where violence against lesbian, gay, bisexual or transgender persons occurs and goes unpunished or is even abetted by authorities. In many others, LGBT persons are subject to harassment, intimidation and even prosecution because of their sexual orientation or gender identity. In Senegal, nine people, including the head of an AIDS service organization, were arrested in December 2008 and given long prison sentences the next month, purportedly for engaging in homosexual conduct. [2]

Now, Secretary of State Hillary Rodham Clinton is promising that the United States will do more to track and oppose violence in other countries against LGBT persons. "Where it happens anywhere in the world, the United States must speak out against it and work for its end," Clinton said in a Sept. 11 speech to the Roosevelt Institute in New York City, where she was receiving the institute's Four Freedoms Medal. [3]

Despite widespread criticism of President Obama for allegedly downplaying human rights, LGBT rights advocates are giving the administration positive marks for increased attention to those issues after eight years of general neglect under President George W. Bush. "They've been very open to the dialogue," says Michael Guest, senior counselor at the Council for Global Equality, a coalition founded in 2008 to work for LGBT rights around the world.

Guest notes that the Obama administration decided in March to support a United Nations petition sponsored by France and the Netherlands calling for decriminalization of homosexual conduct. The Bush administration had taken no position on the resolution, now supported by 67 countries. Guest served as ambassador to Romania in the second Bush administration until his resignation in 2007 over the lack of spousal benefits and privileges for his partner.

In her speech, Clinton promised to give increased attention to violence against the LGBT community in the State Department's annual country-by-country reports on human rights. The most recent report, published in February and compiled during the Bush administration, includes what Guest calls the most detailed listing of LGBT rights violations to date. Among the incidents in 2008 noted were the murder of a transgender activist in Honduras, imprisonment in Egypt of men suspected

Continued from p. 918

things recognizing that the council is not a perfect body," says UCLA's Kaye. "Rather than sitting outside and complaining, it's now inside the tent." ■

BACKGROUND

'Unalienable' Rights

As the first of the United States' founding documents, the Declaration of Independence affirmed a belief in the "unalienable" human rights of "life, liberty, and the pursuit of happiness" and the democratic principle of "consent of the governed." Those beliefs have remained central American ideals ever since. In the 20th century, the United States put its military and diplomatic might behind efforts to promote democracy and human rights — with limited success after World War I, somewhat more after World War II. Human rights remained a talking point during the Cold War but often took a back seat to geopolitics in the conflicts with two communist powers: the Soviet Union and China. [12]

The American Revolution succeeded in part because of aid from France. The young Republic turned a deaf ear in the 1820s, however, to pleas for help in the Greek war of independence. Then-Secretary of State John Quincy Adams said the United States was a "well-wisher to the freedom and independence of others," but "champion and vindicator only of her own." In the century's two major external wars — with Mexico (1846-1848) and Spain (1898) — the United States claimed to be spreading democracy, but the conflicts were aimed, in fact, at continental expansion and imperial conquest, respectively. [13]

of being HIV-positive and extensive discrimination in India against gays and lesbians in education and employment. [4]

The United States raised the issue of violence and rights violations against LGBT persons on Oct. 8 at a meeting of the Organization for Security and Co-operation in Europe, a regionwide human rights forum. Earlier, a U.S. representative had noted concern about the refusal in some countries to grant permits for pro-LGBT "pride" parades. Guest says increased U.S. attention to documenting LGBT issues is important because problems often go unreported. "LGBT communities in many countries are extremely marginalized, and social and cultural norms are such that nobody complains," he says.

Long also applauds the administration's statements on LGBT rights but says more concrete actions are needed. "What we're still looking for is action at the embassy level in countries where egregious things are going on," he says.

As one example, Long points to Uganda, where legislation was introduced in parliament in early October to tighten an existing prohibition on homosexual conduct by making any advocacy of or information about homosexuality a crime. [5] Long notes that Uganda received substantial funding under the Bush administration's AIDS initiative. "It will be a test of the Obama administration to see if it uses its leverage to oppose this bill,

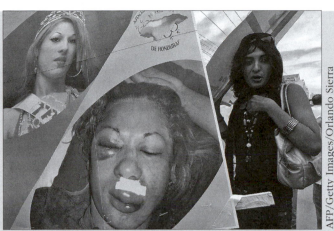

LGBT activists in Tegucigalpa, Honduras, protest the murder of a transgender activist on May 15, 2009. Secretary of State Hillary Clinton has promised to give increased attention to violence against the LGBT community.

AFP/Getty Images/Orlando Sierra

which would be devastating to gays and lesbians," he says.

In its report on the Iraq killings, Human Rights Watch calls on the United States and U.S.-led multinational forces in Iraq to assist Iraqi authorities in investigating the killings and vetting and training Iraqi police on human rights issues with "no exceptions for sexual orientation and gender expression or identity." Long sees no action thus far on either of the recommendations. "It's not clear the embassy has done anything," he says.

— Kenneth Jost

[1] "They Want Us Exterminated," Human Rights Watch, August 2009, www.hrw.org/en/reports/2009/08/16/they-want-us-exterminated. The report does not identify the victim and uses a pseudonym for his partner.

[2] See Donald G. McNeil Jr., "Senegal: Where AIDS Efforts Are Often Praised, Prison for Counselors Is a Surprise," *The New York Times,* Jan. 20, 2009, p. D6.

[3] The full text is on the State Department's Web site: www.state.gov/secretary/rm/2009a/09/129164.htm. The one-paragraph reference drew coverage only in LGBT media. See Rex Wockner, "Clinton Says U.S. Will Fight Anti-Gay Violence Worldwide," *Windy City Times* (Chicago), Sept. 23, 2009.

[4] "2008 Country Reports on Human Rights Practices," U.S. State Department, Feb. 25, 2009, www.state.gov/g/drl/rls/hrrpt/2008/index.htm. See also "U.S. Government Documents Trend of Severe Human Rights Abuse Against LGBT People," Council for Global Equality, February 2009, www.globalequality.org/storage/cfge/documents/dos_human_rights_report_2008_analysis.pdf.

[5] See "Rights Groups Challenge Uganda's New Same-Sex Proposal," Voice of America English Service, Oct. 16, 2009.

As an emergent global power, the United States entered World War I with an explicit goal to "make the world safe for democracy." President Woodrow Wilson envisioned a postwar order founded on national self-determination with peace maintained by the League of Nations. With the United States out after the Senate's refusal to ratify the Versailles Treaty, the League was weakened from birth. The newly independent nations of Central and Eastern Europe mutated into dictatorships in the 1920s and '30s. And an isolationist-minded United States did nothing during the Spanish Civil War to prevent Francisco Franco's fascists from ousting a democratic government.

World War II brought a renewed commitment to human rights and democracy from the United States. Before the U.S. entry into the war, President Franklin D. Roosevelt in January 1941 identified four freedoms — freedom of speech and expression, freedom of religion, freedom from want and freedom from fear — as fundamental to people "everywhere in the world." Roosevelt's major wartime partner, British Prime Minister Winston Churchill, vowed in October 1942 that the war would end with "the enthronement of human rights." Like Wilson before him, Roosevelt envisioned a postwar order of national self-determination, including decolonization by wartime allies Britain and France. Decolonization proceeded only slowly over the next two decades, however. And the postwar settlement with the Soviet Union, an ally in the war, left Moscow in effective control of Eastern Europe.

As the war ended, the United States took the lead role in establishing an institutional and legal infrastructure intended to preserve the peace while promoting human rights. The charter of the newly created United Nations declared the goal of promoting "human rights and fundamental freedoms for all." As a member of the U.S. delegation, Eleanor Roosevelt, the late president's widow, helped create and became the first head of the U.N. Commission on Human Rights. And the commission organized the drafting of the Universal Declaration of Human Rights, adopted by the U.N. General Assembly on Dec. 10, 1948. The treaty's 30 articles detail individual rights that are to serve "as a common standard of achievement for all peoples and all nations."

Hopes for a worldwide flourishing of human rights fell victim to the Cold War. As UCLA's Kaye points out, the ideological conflict with the Soviet Union forced the United States to struggle between devotion to human rights and pursuit of other geopolitical interests. Republican and Democratic presidents alike often resolved the conflict by supporting U.S. allies despite poor records on human rights and democracy. During the Chinese civil war, U.S. support for the Nationalist leader Chiang Kai-shek failed to prevent the communist takeover in 1949, which made Asia — like Europe — a major locus of ideological conflict with the United States and its allies.

A combination of ideological and economic interests led the United States during this period to organize coups that replaced leftist, democratically elected governments with right-wing U.S. allies in such countries as Iran (1953), Guatemala (1954) and Chile (1973). After the French defeat in Vietnam in 1954, the United States divided the nation rather than allow an election likely to have been won by the communist leader Ho Chi Minh. The United States did nothing, however, when Hungarians revolted against

the communist government in 1956 or when Czechoslovakians rose up against their communist rulers in 1968. By then, the United States was bogged down in the Vietnam War, which ended in 1975 with the country unified under communist rule.

Rights Commitments

The end of the Vietnam War coincided with other developments that helped give human rights new prominence both domestically and internationally. The Soviet Union and its Eastern European satellites joined with the United States and Western Europe in 1975 in the historic Helsinki

Palestinian youths throw stones at Israeli soldiers near the West Bank town of Hebron on Oct. 12, 2009. The United States has opposed a U.N. Human Rights Council report that accuses Israel of targeting Palestinian civilians in Gaza.

AFP/Getty Images/Hazem Bader

Accords, which committed all signatories to respect for human rights. In the United States, President Carter's election and four years in office left a lasting legacy of human rights as a central theme in U.S. foreign policy for future presidents, Republicans and Democrats alike. Then in the 1990s the fall of the Soviet Union and the end of the Cold War allowed

human rights to be given greater priority in comparison to other national interests in the formation of U.S. foreign policy.

The Helsinki Accords — technically, the Final Act of the Conference on Security and Co-operation in Europe — were signed by the United States, Canada, the Soviet Union and all European countries but two (Albania and Andorra). They committed all of the countries to "respect for human rights and fundamental freedoms, including the freedom of thought, conscience, religion or belief." In signing the agreement, the Soviet Union won the West's recognition of postwar borders, but with the proviso that they could be changed by peaceful means. The Soviet Union and the West remained at odds over how to define rights, but the accords spawned the creation of "Helsinki watch" monitoring groups that helped focus attention on alleged abuses.

Democrat Carter won election over Republican Gerald R. Ford in 1976 largely because of Ford's pardon of former President Richard M. Nixon for the Watergate scandal. In keeping with his moralistic approach to domestic and foreign issues alike, Carter promised in his campaign to make human rights a centerpiece of U.S. foreign policy. He institutionalized that commitment in his first year in office by creating in the State Department the Bureau of Human Rights and Humanitarian Affairs (now, the Bureau of Human Rights, Democracy and Labor). With the 30th anniversary of the Universal Declaration of Human Rights in 1978, Carter vowed again to make human rights central to U.S. policy as long as he was president. In the next year,

Secretary of State Warren Christopher told a congressional committee that the United States had contributed to the atmosphere that enabled civilian regimes to replace military rulers in several countries and release political prisoners in some others.

With the election of the conservative Republican Ronald Reagan in 1980, rights issues became a sharp partisan divide in the United States. Democrats criticized Reagan for a renewed hard line in relations with the Soviet Union and for support of right-wing, rights-abusing regimes in El Salvador and Guatemala and right-wing rebels in Nicaragua. Under Reagan, however, U.S. aid to democratic movements abroad was institutionalized with the establishment of the National Endowment for Democracy as a publicly funded, privately operated entity. And by his second term Reagan was being credited with a turnaround on human rights exemplified by the U.S. backing of the successful ouster of two authoritarian U.S. allies: Ferdinand Marcos in the Philippines and Jean-Claude Duvalier in Haiti.

The dissolution of the Soviet Union and the ouster of communist regimes throughout Eastern Europe came with stunning suddenness during the presidency of George H. W. Bush. Reagan's admirers credit the downfall to his hard-line stance, but they and less-partisan observers also say the communist regimes failed because of the failure of communism itself. Whatever the causes, the events opened the door to opportunities for democratization and liberalization. Two decades later, Russia remains under critical scrutiny on rights issues, but many of the Eastern European countries are credited with successful transitions to democratic, rights-respecting governments.

Despite the easing of East-West tensions and a professed commitment to human rights, President Clinton was seen by rights advocates as falling short in some actions — for example, in delink-ing rights and trade with China and moving slowly to confront the humanitarian crises in the Rwanda conflict and in the wars in the former Yugoslavia. UCLA professor Kaye notes, however, that Democrat Clinton had to contend with a Republican-controlled House for six of his eight years in office and a GOP-controlled Senate for four.

The 1990s saw great progress, however, in the institutionalization of rights machinery at the United Nations, beginning in 1993 with the creation of the position of High Commissioner for Human Rights. Despite continuing controversy for its alleged anti-Israel bias, the Commission on Human Rights became an invaluable source of information by increase the use of so-called special rapporteurs to investigate and report on conditions in individual countries and in broad areas such as arbitrary detention, child prostitution and violence against women. The U.N. Security Council also approved the creation of war crimes tribunals for the Balkan and Rwandan conflicts, even as a U.N.-sponsored conference was drafting a treaty to create a permanent International Criminal Court (ICC). Concerned with possible prosecution of U.S. service members, however, the United States was one of seven countries to vote against approval of the treaty in the U.N. General Assembly in 1998.

Rights Dichotomies

President Bush's record on human rights was sharply disputed during his eight years in the White House and remains sharply disputed today. Bush's admirers say the wars in Afghanistan and Iraq brought human rights improvements in both countries; critics say rights conditions in both countries continue to be unsatisfactory. The opposing camps similarly disagree on the detention and interrogation policies that Bush adopted in his "war on terror." Even Bush's critics concede, however, that his administration took positive steps on some human right fronts unconnected with the post-9/11 events.

Bush adopted an aggressive legal strategy after the Sept. 11, 2001, attacks on the United States to apprehend, detain and interrogate suspected al Qaeda members and sympathizers. Most notably, he claimed that the Geneva Conventions did not apply to the "enemy combatants" rounded up in Afghanistan and elsewhere and that they could be held at the Guantánamo Bay Naval Base in Cuba outside jurisdiction of federal courts. Both claims stirred strong opposition from European allies and from human rights groups within and outside the United States. Both claims were also rejected by the Supreme Court, which held in a series of cases that the Guantánamo detainees were protected by the Geneva Conventions' so-called Common Article 3 and that they could use federal habeas corpus petitions to challenge the legality of their imprisonment.

Bush mixed national security objectives with human rights goals in the wars both in Afghanistan and in Iraq. Admirers see human rights gains. "There are free elections in Iraq," says Johns Hopkins professor Mandelbaum. "Women go to school in Afghanistan."

In its most recent annual report issued in February 2009, however, Human Rights Watch is sharply critical of rights conditions in each. In Iraq, the government — described as resting on a narrow ethnic and sectarian base — is blamed for widespread torture and abuse of detainees. The report says girls and women are subject to gender-based violence; gays and lesbians are also subject to violence "by state and non-state actors." In Afghanistan, the government — described as weak and riddled with corruption — is faulted for taking no action on a justice-and-reconciliation plan adopted in 2006. Education for girls continues to lag, the report says, because of violence in some regions and social pressures elsewhere.

While criticizing Bush for taking "backward" steps on the war on terror, UCLA's Kaye says his presidency should not be viewed "as purely a dark period" on human rights issues. As one example, he notes the administration's decision in 2004 to accuse the Sudanese government of genocide in the rebellious province of Darfur. The administration also contributed to an international peacekeeping force and opposed a suspension of the ICC warrant against Sudan's president, Omar Hassan al-Bashir, for allegedly overseeing genocide in Darfur. Kaye also praises Bush for expanding U.S. programs to combat HIV/AIDS abroad. Bush won congressional approval for a $15 billion anti-AIDS initiative in 2003; as it was set to expire in 2008 he signed a five-year, $48 billion expansion. Kaye also gives Bush credit for tackling other global issues, such as human trafficking.

The Bush administration had less interest, however, in international human rights treaties. Most notably, the administration strongly opposed ratification of the treaty creating the ICC. Clinton had signed the treaty in 2000 but deferred asking the Senate to ratify it until after the court was in operation. Once the court began operations in 2002, however, Bush said he would not ask for ratification unless U.S. service members were exempted from possible prosecutions. Kaye notes that Bush also did not push for U.S. action on other international human rights covenants, including the Convention on the Rights of the Child and the Convention on the Elimination of All Forms of Discrimination Against Women. In its report, Human Rights Watch also cites the U.S. opposition to the U.N. Human Rights Council as an example of the Bush administration's "arrogant approach to multilateral institutions."

During his campaign, Obama strongly criticized the Bush administration's anti-terrorism policies as having lowered respect for the United States around the world. In his acceptance speech at the Democratic National Convention on Aug. 27, 2008, he promised to "restore our moral standing." He also vowed to "build new partnerships to defeat the threats of the 21st century: terrorism and nuclear proliferation, poverty and genocide, climate change and disease."

As president, Obama moved quickly to redeem one of his promises by reversing some of Bush's anti-terror policies in his first week in office. He scrapped legal opinions that had questioned the applicability of the Geneva Conventions to suspected terrorists, shuttered the Central Intelligence Agency's secret prisons and set a one-year deadline for closing the Guantánamo prison camp.

In a series of foreign policy addresses from June through September, Obama also sought to reengage with the international community on a wide range of issues, including democracy and human rights. In his June 4 speech in Cairo, Obama pointedly underlined for the Muslim world the importance of religious tolerance and women's rights. In Ghana on July 11, he faulted post-colonial Africa for too much corruption and too little good governance. A few days earlier in Moscow, however, Obama steered clear of any direct criticism of Russia's restrictions on political freedoms. And his Sept. 23 speech to the U.N. General Assembly included only a single paragraph on democracy — but with the significant admission that the United States "has too often been selective in its promotion of democracy." ■

CURRENT SITUATION

Rights Policies in Flux

The Obama administration shows signs of becoming more active on international human rights issues, but it continues to draw mixed reactions from human rights groups and experts.

In the weeks since Obama's address to the U.N. General Assembly, the administration has unveiled a new strategy aimed at easing the humanitarian crisis in the Sudanese province of Darfur and implementing the 2005 peace accord between the country's predominantly Arab North and Christian and animist South. The administration has also strongly protested the Sept. 28 massacre and mass rapes of political protesters in the West African nation of Guinea, called for investigation of possible abuses during Sri Lanka's now-ended civil war and protested the arrest of a prominent human rights lawyer in Syria.

UCLA professor Kaye applauds the new Sudan policy for use of "benchmarks" to judge the government's compliance with the requested actions, but he adds, "The jury's still out." He says the statements on Guinea, Sri Lanka and Syria are "important signals" of the administration's human rights policy, but more action is needed. "One should hope that the statements of opposition and outrage are followed up by diplomatic moves," he says.

Johns Hopkins fellow Muravchik questions what he calls "the softer line" toward the Sudan government. Like Kaye, he views the U.S. stances on Guinea, Sri Lanka and Syria as unexceptional. The United States has "nothing at stake in Guinea or Sri Lanka," Muravchik says, "and issuing a protest about the arrest of a human rights lawyer is a fairly routine and mild thing to do."

The Sudan policy, announced by Clinton on Oct. 19, represents a conscious effort to find a balance between a hard-line approach emphasizing punitive sanctions and a refusal to deal with Sudanese President Bashir and a more conciliatory stance combining positive incentives and engagement with Bashir's government. [14]

Continued on p. 926

At Issue:

Does President Obama deserve the Nobel Peace Prize for 2009?

BEN COHEN
EDITOR, THEDAILYBANTER.COM

WRITTEN FOR *CQ RESEARCHER*, OCT. 25, 2009

*a*lthough Obama has governed as a centrist, one can't help but think that he is turning a very heavy ship ever so slowly leftwards, and that deep down, his heart lies far further to the left than he would like to let on. There is little doubt that Obama would, if he could, enact the extension of equal rights to gays, end the war in Iraq and Afghanistan, reconcile the Israelis and Palestinians and seriously reform the financial system.

The truth is, however, that a country taken over by special interests cannot be turned around quickly.

It is true that Obama has largely failed to deliver on all the above. But then again, he has only been in power for 11 months. And there has been progress — the engagement with the Middle East, multilateralism as the first option rather than the last, substantially increased unemployment benefits, cheaper student loans, a commitment (on paper at least) to reducing carbon dioxide emissions and a rebranding of America abroad.

Does this warrant a Nobel Peace Prize? Yes, and here's why.

The United States became a feared and despised state under the rule of the George W. Bush administration. The brazen disregard for global opinion, the trampling of international law and the overt environmental destruction were hallmarks of a presidency determined to project American power at all costs. With one election, the world forgave — and almost forgot — the tragic Bush years as a young, black president who spoke of hope rather than hatred, and cooperation rather than force, swept into power.

This monumental shift cannot and must not be underestimated.

Obama's Peace Prize was not necessarily given to him for what he has accomplished. It was given to him for what he can accomplish. As South African Archbishop Desmond Tutu put it:

"It is an award that speaks to the promise of President Obama's message of hope."

Hope will not fix the environment, stop the wars in Afghanistan and Iraq or prevent bankers from stealing all of our money.

Obama can certainly do better, much better than he is doing now. But it is too early to cast judgment, and he deserves time to make the changes he promised.

Obama has won the most prestigious prize for contributions to humanity in the world.

Now he must earn it.

ERICK ERICKSON
EDITOR-IN-CHIEF, REDSTATE.COM

WRITTEN FOR *CQ RESEARCHER*, OCT. 26, 2009

*i*n July 2006, speaking to schoolchildren, Betty Williams, the Nobel Peace Prize winner from Northern Ireland, said she would "love to kill George W. Bush." This year's recipient, Barack Obama, has yet to encounter a problem for which blaming Bush is not a solution. He fits the Nobel Peace Prize mold, which by and large is determined by a committee that runs an affirmative-action program giving preference to those people who view world peace as an absence of American influence — extra points to Americans who hate the American ideal.

Like Al Gore and Jimmy Carter before him, Barack Obama has done nothing to further peace in our time but has repudiated strong American leadership. The Nobel committee, possessed by the spirit of former British Prime Minister Neville Chamberlain, has descended to farcically awarding prizes for prospective peace that will never come and global warming fixes that will never work, but will make Al Gore a very rich man.

The Peace Prize long ago ceased to have any relevance to anyone outside the left. Awarding the prize to Yasser Arafat, who had the blood of thousands on his hands, was akin to awarding a safe-driving certificate to Ted Kennedy. The only thing the prize now stands for is approval from the anti-American European left. We should hope the president of the United States would pause to consider that, but as he did not, we can be sure he agrees.

In fact, in Barack Obama's short tenure as president he has done his best to apologize for perceived American abuses of power and arrogance, backpedaled on key issues of national security and flirted with some of the most kleptocratic, tyrannical regimes in modern history. Siding with tyrants over the democracy-loving people of Honduras, giving lip service to freedom as Iranians were gunned down in the streets of Tehran and coddling up to our Chinese bankers have ingratiated the man with those who have always been offended by the last 10 words of "The Star Spangled Banner." If that merits a peace prize, most Americans would probably prefer war.

The prospective peace the Nobel committee hopes for will not come. It is as illusory as the pot of gold at the end of the rainbow. Barack Obama's vanity will, however, compel him to pursue it. We can be sure his peace will be America's loss.

Continued from p. 924

The six-year-long crisis in Darfur — part of the turmoil in Africa's largest country spanning more than two decades — has defied peacekeeping and mediation efforts by the international community. Government-aided militias are blamed for killing at least 350,000 people; more than 2.4 million people have been displaced, most of them living in refugee camps that depend on international humanitarian groups for food and other supplies. In his campaign, Obama had called for strong sanctions against Bashir's government.

Darfur advocacy groups are voicing guarded optimism about the new approach. Jerry Fowler, president of the Washington-based Save Darfur Coalition, said the policy was similar to the "balance of incentives and pressures" that the group had been calling for. But he said the policy would not succeed without "substantial presidential leadership."

From a critical perspective, however, Bret Stephens, a *Wall Street Journal* columnist, mocked the administration's "menu of incentives and disincentives" in the policy. "It's the kind of menu Mr. Bashir will languidly pick his way through till he dies comfortably in his bed," Stephens wrote. [15]

On Guinea, Clinton registered a strong protest over the killing of more than 150 demonstrators in the capital of Conakry opposing the military government of Capt. Moussa "Dadis" Camara. There were also reports of dozens of rapes — including mass rapes and sexual mutilation of the victims — by government soldiers. Clinton on Oct. 7 denounced the brutality and violence as "criminality of the greatest degree" and called on Camara to step down. She also dispatched William Fitzgerald, deputy assistant secretary of state for African affairs, to Guinea to deliver the protest. [16]

The State Department's report on Sri Lanka, issued on Oct. 22, detailed alleged atrocities by both sides in the now-ended insurgency by a militant Tamil group seeking to create a separate homeland on the South Asian island nation. The report, requested by Congress, described as credible allegations that the government had targeted civilians and that the Tamil United Liberation Front had recruited children for the fighting. The report called for a full investigation by the government. "A very important part of any reconciliation process is accountability," State Department spokesman Ian Kelly said. [17]

On Syria, the administration joined Britain, France and international human rights groups in calling for the release of the prominent lawyer and former judge Haitham Maleh, who has been jailed since his Oct. 14 arrest. Maleh, 78, has opposed Syria's Baathist government and called for lifting the state of emergency it imposed after taking power in 1963. The arrest is "the latest Syrian action in a two-year crackdown on lawyers and civil society activists," the State Department said. [18]

The flurry of new statements "doesn't change the picture much," says Muravchik. "It's always true that any U.S. administration will be on the side of human rights if there is no cost to it in the coin of other U.S. foreign policy goals," he explains. "The problem that every administration faces is that insofar as we use some of our political influence and capital to press for human rights, we necessarily create frictions with governments that abuse human rights that make it harder for us to do other kinds of business with them."

Rights Treaties in Limbo

The Obama administration is signaling support for ratifying two long-pending United Nations-sponsored treaties on women's rights and children's rights, but Senate action is in doubt because of continued opposition from social conservatives and others.

The United States is all but alone in failing to join the two treaties: the Convention on the Elimination of All Discrimination Against Women and the Convention on the Rights of the Child. Besides the United States, only six other countries have failed to ratify the treaty on sex discrimination: Iran, Nauru, Palau, Somalia, Sudan and Tonga. Somalia is the only other country not to have approved the children's rights charter. [19]

The United States signed both treaties during Democratic administrations, but Republican opposition in Congress — fueled by opposition from social conservatives — has prevented the Senate ratification needed to give the treaties force of law. Now, the Obama administration says it wants both treaties ratified, but it has not set a timetable for moving on either one.

Social conservatives say both treaties pose threats to traditional family roles in the United States and to states' prerogatives on social issues. Some critics also question the treaties' practical effect since the signatories include any number of countries with poor human rights records. But human rights groups and other social welfare advocates say U.S. support for the treaties is important both symbolically and in practice. But they reject warnings that the treaties would impinge on private family arrangements.

The treaty on women's rights — sometimes known by the acronym CEDAW — was completed in 1979 and signed by the United States the next year while Carter was president. The Senate Foreign Relations Committee held hearings on the treaty in 1988, 1990, 1994 and 2002.

President Clinton submitted the treaty for ratification in 1994 with reservations on some issues including paid maternity leave and combat assignments for women. In the face of GOP opposition, Clinton never pressed for a Senate floor vote. Under

Democratic control, the Foreign Relations Committee again recommended ratification in 2002, but the Bush administration opposed the treaty, and no floor vote was held.

In her confirmation hearing, U.N. Ambassador Rice said the administration considered the women's rights treaty "a priority." The treaty was included in May on a list of those recommended for action, but no action has been taken. Conservative groups continue to denounce the treaty. "It's the Equal Rights Amendment on steroids," says Wendy Wright, head of Concerned Women for America. Among other provisions, opponents complain of one that calls for nations to work to eliminate "stereotyped roles for men and women." [20]

The Reagan and George H. W. Bush administrations played a part in negotiating the children's rights pact but never signed it because of concern about its impact on U.S. law. The Clinton administration signed the treaty in 1995, but did not seek Senate ratification. The George W. Bush administration actively opposed the treaty.

Obama voiced concern during his campaign about the U.S. failure, along with Somalia, to approve the treaty. In a classroom session with schoolchildren in New York City in June, Rice said officials are actively discussing "when and how it might be possible to join." Again, no concrete action has been taken.

Conservative groups strongly oppose the pact. Stephen Groves, a fellow at the Heritage Foundation, a conservative think tank in Washington, says the treaty would give a U.N. body "a say over how children in American should be raised, educated or disciplined." [21]

The Obama administration's receptiveness to multilateral rights accords is viewed as a positive by human rights groups, but Human Rights Watch's Washington director Mali-nowski says political considerations still shape the ratification strategies. "They're rightly starting with the ones on which there's the most consensus," he says. Johns Hopkins fellow Muravchik questions the value of the charters. "I wouldn't say they are empty exercises, but their importance is quite secondary," he says.

On a more contentious issue, Human Rights Watch is urging the administration to move away from Bush's strong opposition to the ICC and instead "develop a constructive relationship" with the tribunal. Without joining the court, the group says the United States can lend assistance to investigations and prosecutions. It also wants the administration to oppose provisions passed by Congress in 2002 that, among other things, prohibited U.S. participation in peacekeeping missions unless U.S. service members were granted immunity from possible war crime prosecutions before the tribunal. So far, the administration has backed the ICC's prosecution of Sudan's President Bashir but has not outlined a general policy toward the court. ■

OUTLOOK

Waiting for Results

When President Obama arrives in Beijing in mid-November, he will be seeking to enlist China's help in dealing with some of the United States' most pressing issues, including nuclear proliferation, climate change and the global economic slowdown. Despite a newly published report by the joint Congressional-Executive Commission criticizing China for increased repression in some areas, however, U.S. experts expect human rights to be low on the agenda for Obama's visit.

"Elevating human rights . . . is not going to serve U.S. interests at this point," says Elizabeth Economy, director of Asia studies for the Council on Foreign Relations, a New York-based think tank.

The administration's critics, particularly partisan conservatives, accuse Obama of an across-the-board downgrading of human rights. Administration officials, however, depict the president as fully committed to promoting human rights abroad.

"The president's policy on these issues is clear," State Department legal adviser Koh told reporters at a Sept. 29 briefing in Geneva during a U.N. Human Rights Council session. "He promotes human rights through engagement. He promotes human rights through diplomacy. He promotes human rights through efforts to find common ground. And he's prepared to do this in both bilateral and multilateral settings."

Some experts see logic in the administration's apparent preference for engagement over confrontation but still warn about the risks of a perceived weakening of U.S. opposition to abusive practices. Obama "believes that solving foreign policy problems requires engaging with America's adversaries and ending the lecturing (and hectoring) tone of his predecessor," writes James Goldgeier, a senior fellow with the Council on Foreign Relations and a professor of political science and international affairs at George Washington University.

The strategy "might seem to make sense," Goldgeier continues. "Unfortunately, it sends a signal to repressive regimes that no one is going to call them to account for their human rights violations. And those fighting for freedom in their home countries may soon worry that the United States is no longer their champion." [22]

Johns Hopkins professor Mandelbaum is less convinced that the administration has merely shifted tactics on human rights issues without reducing their priority as a foreign policy goal. "No administration wants to say that it is downgrading human rights, so of course that's what they would say," Mandelbaum remarks. "Maybe they'll turn out to be correct."

Some of the administration's tactical choices are evidently open to debate, such as the decision to defer Obama's meeting with the Dalai Lama until after the China trip. Economy calls it a mistake. "The Dalai Lama is a global leader," she says. "Deciding to meet with him is unrelated to the China issue."

But Douglas Paal, a China expert at the Carnegie Endowment for International Peace who was on the National Security Council staff under Presidents Reagan and George H. W. Bush, calls the decision "a reasonable choice." "Tibet is at the head of China's core interests," he says. "Taking note of that, the administration doesn't want to have a debate about meeting with the Dalai Lama."

In a detailed report published on Oct. 16, the Congressional-Executive Commission on China finds increased repression in Tibet and the predominantly Uighur Xinjiang province along with increased harassment of human rights lawyers and advocates throughout the country. On Tibet, the report recommends that the United States urge China to open a dialogue with the Dalai Lama. It also calls on the government to increase aid to non-governmental organizations (NGOs) for programs to aid Tibetans. [23]

In other sections, the report similarly urges a mix of government-to-government pressure along with concrete steps by the U.S. government and NGOs. The commission, created in 2000, includes nine senators, nine House members and five executive branch appointees. The Obama administration's seats on the commission are vacant; the administration has been slow in filling many executive branch slots.

With a full plate of major international crises and a challenging domestic agenda, the Obama administration is understandably hard-pressed to find time and resources to devote to human rights issues that — as in Sudan — present difficult and complex policy choices. Clinton, however, took time in August for a weeklong trip to Africa that included meetings with rape victims and visiting a refugee camp in the war-torn Democratic Republic of the Congo. [24] And in a visit to Russia in October, the secretary of state used a speech to university students to urge Moscow to open the political system. As *The New York Times*' reporter noted, "Mrs. Clinton spoke far more forcefully about human rights and the rule of law than she did on a trip to China earlier this year." [25]

With U.S. influence on other nations' internal policies necessarily limited, the likely impact of Clinton's Africa tour or Moscow speech is easily doubted. Human rights groups, however, believe the United States has made a difference in the past. Now, they are waiting with some impatience and skepticism to see whether the Obama administration will devote enough time, attention and resources to make a difference again.

"I keep hearing from the administration an interest in focusing on results," says Human Rights First Executive Director Massamino. "That's how I think they ought to be judged." ∎

Notes

[1] Quoted in "Dalai Lama Shrugs Off Apparent Snub by Obama," Reuters, Oct. 8, 2009. For earlier coverage, see John Pomfret, "Obama's Meeting With the Dalai Lama Is Delayed," *The Washington Post*, Oct. 5, 2009, p. A1. The story notes that since 1991 three U.S. presidents — George H. W. Bush, Bill Clinton, and George W. Bush — have had a total of 10 meetings with the Dalai Lama at the White House; all were private photo opportunities except the Congressional Medal of Freedom ceremony in 2007. For background on China and Tibet, see Thomas J. Billitteri, "Human Rights in China," *CQ Researcher*, July 25, 2008, pp. 601-624; Brian Beary, "Separatist Movements," *CQ Global Researcher*, April 2008, pp. 85-114.

[2] The official press release is at http://nobelprize.org/nobel_prizes/peace/laureates/2009/press.html.

[3] For previous coverage, see Peter Katel, "Exporting Democracy," *CQ Researcher*, April 1, 2005, pp. 269-292; and in *Editorial Research Reports*: Kenneth Jost, "Human Rights," Nov. 13, 1998, pp. 977-1000; Mary H. Cooper, "Human Rights in the 1980s," July 19, 1985, pp. 537-556; and Richard C. Schroeder, "Human Rights Policy," May 18, 1979, pp. 361-380.

[4] See Arch Puddington, "Freedom in the World 2009: Setbacks and Resilience," Freedom House, July 2009, www.freedomhouse.org/template.cfm?page=130&year=2009. Puddington is Freedom House's director of research.

[5] Clinton is quoted in "Clinton: human rights

About the Author

Associate Editor **Kenneth Jost** graduated from Harvard College and Georgetown University Law Center. He is the author of the *Supreme Court Yearbook* and editor of *The Supreme Court from A to Z* (both *CQ Press*). He was a member of the *CQ Researcher* team that won the American Bar Association's 2002 Silver Gavel Award. His previous reports include "Closing Guantánamo" and "The Obama Presidency" (with *CQ Researcher* staff). He is also author of the blog *Jost on Justice* (http://jostonjusticeblogspot.com).

can't interfere with other crises," CNN, Feb. 22, 2009; Amnesty International's statement can be found at www.amnestyusa.org/document.php?id=ENGUSA20090220001&rss=iar#. For coverage, see Mark Landler, "Clinton Paints China Policy With a Green Hue," *The New York Times*, Feb. 22, 2009, p. A8.

[6] Jamie Glazov, "Obama's Human Rights Disaster," *FrontPageMagazine.com*, Aug. 25, 2009, http://frontpagemag.com/readArticle.aspx?ARTID=36042.

[7] The text of the president's address in Cairo can be found on the White House Web site: www.whitehouse.gov/the_press_office/Remarks-by-the-President-at-Cairo-University-6-04-09/. For analysis, see Peter Baker, "Following a Different Map to a Similar Destination," *The New York Times*, June 9, 2009, p. A10. The text of Obama's and Mubarak's Aug. 18 remarks to reporters is on the White House Web site: www.whitehouse.gov/the_press_office/Remarks-by-President-Obama-and-President-Mubarak-of-Egypt-during-press-availability/.

[8] "Making Its Mark: An Analysis of the Obama Administration FY2010 Budget for Democracy and Human Rights," Freedom House, July 2009, www.freedomhouse.org/uploads/FY2010Budget Analysis.pdf. For figures on Egypt, see Sudarsan Raghavan, "Egyptian Reform Activists Say U.S. Commitment Is Waning," *The Washington Post*, Oct. 9, 2009, p. A14.

[9] Quoted in *ibid.*

[10] The text of the resolution can be found on the U.N. Council on Human Rights' Web site: www2.ohchr.org/english/bodies/hrcouncil/12session/docs/A_HRC_RES_12_16_AEV.pdf. For coverage of the council's action, see Frank Jordans, "UN rights body approves US-Egypt free speech text," The Associated Press, Oct. 2, 2009. For background, see Warren Hoge, "As U.S. Dissents, U.N. Approves a New Council on Rights Abuse," *The New York Times*, March 16, 2006, p. A3.

[11] See Neil MacFarquhar, "U.S. Joins Rights Panel After Vote in the U.N.," *The New York Times*, May 13, 2009, p. A5. The other countries elected to the council were Bangladesh, Djibouti, Jordan, Kyrgyzstan, Mauritius, Mexico, Nigeria, Senegal and Uruguay.

[12] Background drawn from previous *CQ Researcher* reports, footnote 3. See also Robert L. Maddex (ed.), *International Encyclopedia of Human Rights: Freedoms, Abuses, and Remedies* (2000).

[13] Adams quoted in Joshua Muravchik, *Exporting Democracy: Fulfilling America's Destiny* (1991), p. 19.

[14] For the State Department's background paper, see www.state.gov/r/pa/prs/ps/2009/oct/130676.htm. For background, see Karen Foerstel, "Crisis in Darfur," *CQ Global Researcher*, September 2008, pp. 243-270.

[15] Bret Stephens, "Does Obama Believe in Human Rights?" *The Wall Street Journal*, Oct. 20, 32009, p. A19.

[16] "Clinton: Violence in Guinea 'Criminal,' " The Associated Press, Oct. 7, 2009.

[17] "Report to Congress on Incidents During the Recent Conflict in Sri Lanka," U.S. Department of State, Oct. 22, 2009, www.state.gov/documents/organization/131025.pdf. For coverage, see "U.S. Details Possible Sri Lanka Civil War Abuses," Reuters, Oct. 7, 2009.

[18] "U.S. Says Syria Should Release 78-Year-Old Dissident," Reuters, Oct. 24, 2009.

[19] Background drawn from two Congressional Research Service reports, both by Luisa Blanchfield: "The United Nations Convention on the Elimination of All Forms of Discrimination Against Women," Aug. 7, 2009, http://assets.opencrs.com/rpts/R40750_20090807.pdf; "The United Nations Convention on the Rights of the Child: Background and Policy Issues," Aug. 5, 2009, http://assets.opencrs.com/rpts/R40484_20090805.pdf.

[20] Wright quoted in David Crary, "Discord likely over ratifying women's rights pact," The Associated Press, March 7, 2009.

[21] Quoted in Robert Kiener, "Rescuing Children," *CQ Global Researcher*, October 2009, p. 265.

[22] See "Critics say Obama is punting on human rights. Agree or disagree," *The Arena*, www.politico.com/arena/archive/obama-human-rights.html. The online forum hosted by *Politico* included comments from eight other experts and political activists.

[23] "Congressional-Executive Commission on China," Annual Report 2009, Oct. 10, 2009, www.cecc.gov/pages/annualRpt/annualRpt09/CECCannRpt2009.pdf.

[24] See Jeffrey Gettleman, "A Flash of Pique After a Long Week in a Continent Full of Troubles," *The New York Times*, Aug. 13, 2009, p. A8.

[25] Mark Landler, "In Russia, Clinton Urges Russia to Open Its Political System," *The New York Times*, Oct. 15, 2009, p. A6.

FOR MORE INFORMATION

Council on Foreign Relations, 58 East 68th St., New York, NY 10065; (212) 434-9400; www.cfr.org. Nonprofit organization that operates a think tank, sponsors task forces, and publishes *Foreign Affairs*, a leading journal of global politics.

Council for Global Equality, 1220 L St., N.W., Suite 100-450, Washington, DC 20005-4018; (202) 719-0511; www.globalequality.org. Brings together international human rights activists, foreign policy experts, LGBT leaders, philanthropists and corporate officials to encourage a strong American voice on human rights concerns impacting LGBT communities worldwide.

Freedom House, 1301 Connecticut Ave., N.W., 6th Floor, Washington, DC 20036; (202) 296-5101; www.freedomhouse.org. Works to advance the worldwide expansion of political and economic freedom through international programs and publications, including annual country reports.

Heritage Foundation, 214 Massachusetts Ave., N.E., Washington, DC 20002; (202) 546-4400; www.heritage.org. Public policy research institute promoting conservative positions on free enterprise, limited government and a strong national defense.

Human Rights First, 333 Seventh Ave., 13th Floor, New York, NY 10001-5108; (212) 845-5200; www.humanrightsfirst.org. Nonprofit international human rights organization promoting laws and policies that advance universal rights and freedoms.

Human Rights Watch, 350 Fifth Ave., 34th floor, New York, NY 10118-3299; (212)-290-4700; www.hrw.org. Leading independent organization dedicated to defending human rights around the world through objective investigations of abuses and strategic, targeted advocacy.

Bibliography

Selected Sources

Books

Muravchik, Joshua, *Exporting Democracy: Fulfilling America's Destiny*, AEI (American Enterprise Institute) Press, 1991.

With the Cold War ending, a leading neoconservative author laid out the case for an active U.S. role in promoting democracy in other countries. Includes notes.

Traub, James, *The Freedom Agenda: Why America Must Spread Democracy (Just Not the Way George Bush Did)*, Farrar Straus and Giroux, 2008.

As George W. Bush's presidency was ending, journalist Traub argued that aid to civil-society organizations focused on political liberalization, economic modernization and social welfare is the best way for the United States to promote democracy abroad. Includes six-page note on sources.

Articles

Bolton, John, "Israel, the U.S., and the Goldstone Report," *The Wall Street Journal*, Oct. 19, 2009, p. A19.

The former U.S. ambassador to the United Nations argues that the U.N. Human Rights Council's approval of the report by South African jurist Richard Goldstone critical of Israel's conduct during the Gaza war shows that the Obama administration made a mistake in joining the body and should now withdraw.

Carothers, Thomas, "The Democracy Crusade Myth," *The National Interest online*, July 1, 2007, www.national interest.org/PrinterFriendly.aspx?id=14826.

A leading democratization expert at the Carnegie Endowment for International Peace says that despite pro-democracy rhetoric, the Bush administration actually gave traditional security and economic interests priority over promoting democracy abroad.

Krauthammer, Charles, "Three Cheers for the Bush Doctrine," *Time*, March 14, 2005, p. 28.

The conservative columnist argues that President Bush's plan for democratization has sparked free elections in numerous countries.

Kristof, Nicholas D., "What to Do About Darfur," *The New York Review of Books*, July 2, 2009, www.ny-books.com/articles/22771.

The New York Times foreign affairs columnist, in reviewing several books on the crisis in Sudan's Darfur province, calls the Obama administration's approach to the crisis inadequate but only a start. The article was written before the administration's announcement in October of a new "carrots and sticks" policy toward Sudan aimed at easing the Darfur crisis and fully implementing the 2006 accord that ended the Sudanese civil war.

Risen, Clay, "Does Human Rights Talk Matter?" *The New Republic*, Feb. 24, 2009, www.tnr.com/blog/the-plank/does-human-rights-talk-matter.

The article argues that Secretary of State Hillary Rodham Clinton gave a green light to rights abusers throughout the world with her statement that China's human rights violations would not interfere with U.S.-China relations. Risen is a free-lance writer and managing editor of *Democracy: A Journal of Ideas.*

Reports and Studies

"Annual Report 2009," Congressional-Executive Commission on China, Oct. 10, 2009, www.cecc.gov/pages/annual Rpt/annualRpt09/CECCannRpt2009.pdf.

A commission established to monitor human rights and the rule of law in China finds that the country's continued use of repression undermines its stated international commitments to create a more open society. The 468-page report calls on the U.S. government to monitor Chinese progress in turning the principles outlined in the National Human Rights Action Plan of 2009 into tangible results.

"2008 Country Reports on Human Rights Practices," U.S. Department of State, Feb. 25, 2009, www.state.gov/g/drl/rls/hrrpt/2008/index.htm.

The State Department's congressionally mandated country reports on human rights practices points to three overarching trends during 2008: "a growing worldwide demand for greater personal and political freedom; governmental efforts to push back on those freedoms, and further confirmation that human rights flourish best in participatory democracies with vibrant civil societies."

"Freedom in the World 2009," Freedom House, July 2009, www.freedomhouse.org/template.cfm?page=363&year=2009.

The organization's annual survey, covering 193 countries and 16 territories, finds a third consecutive yearly decline in global freedom. In an overview, the group's research director says the United States and other democracies face "serious challenges" in confronting "a forceful reaction" by authoritarian governments against democratic reformers and outside assistance for democratization.

"World Report 2009," Human Rights Watch, www.hrw.ort/world-report-2009.

The group's 19th annual review, covering human rights practices in more than 90 countries, opens with an essay by Executive Director Kenneth Roth arguing that intergovernmental discussions of human rights have recently been dominated by "human rights spoilers" — countries and leaders opposed to enforcement of human rights.

The Next Step:

Additional Articles from Current Periodicals

Gays

Londo, Ernesto, "Gay Men Targeted in Iraq, Report Says," *The Washington Post*, **Aug. 17, 2009, p. A6.**

The Iraqi government must do more to protect gay men who are being targeted by militias, Human Rights Watch.

Riley, Michael, "Polis Takes Iraq to Task Over Attacks on Gays," *Denver Post*, **April 9, 2009, p. A1.**

Rep. Jared Polis, D-Colo., is an openly gay member of Congress who toured Iraq to investigate the treatment of gays.

Sly, Liz, "Gays Being Targeted and Killed in Iraq, Groups Say," *Los Angeles Times*, **Aug. 18, 2009, p. A19.**

A London-based group supporting gays in Iraq says 87 killings have occurred so far in 2009 related to anti-gay sentiments.

Global Crises

Burns, Robert, "Obama Sets New Policy to Nudge Sudan Toward Peace," The Associated Press, Oct. 19, 2009.

The Obama administration has outlined a new policy that provides incentives for the Sudanese government to end violence in Darfur.

Klug, Foster, "Obama Postpones Meeting With Dalai Lama," *News Journal* **(Delaware), Oct. 6, 2009.**

President Obama has decided not to meet with the Dalai Lama to discuss human rights in China until first meeting with President Hu Jintao in Beijing.

Mann, William C., "Obama's Policy on Darfur Lacks Clarity, Advocates Say," *The Boston Globe*, **June 20, 2009, p. 4.**

Human rights groups fear for the survival of 2.5 million Darfurians in refugee camps if the Obama administration doesn't commit to plans to ensure their security.

Nuechterlein, Donald, "Human Rights Take Back Seat to Realpolitik," *Saginaw* **(Michigan)** *News*, **March 8, 2009.**

Human rights are not as important to U.S. interests as vital economic and strategic considerations in dealing with China.

Goldstone Report

Boudreaux, Richard, "War Crimes in Gaza Reported," *Los Angeles Times*, **Sept. 16, 2009, p. A19.**

The deaths of nearly 1,400 Palestinians in Gaza during the 22-day Israeli offensive amounted to war crimes — and possible crimes against humanity — according to U.N. investigator Judge Richard Goldstone.

Cumming-Bruce, Nick, "U.N. Investigator Presents Report on Gaza War," *The New York Times*, **Sept. 30, 2009, p. A3.**

The lead U.N. investigator for the Gaza conflict says the lack of accountability for war crimes in the region has reached a crisis point.

Sanders, Edmund, "Fact-Finding Mission in Gaza Faces Skeptics," *Los Angeles Times*, **June 29, 2009, p. A14.**

A United Nations panel investigating war crimes in Gaza has been labeled as biased by Israelis, while Palestinians believe any inquiries won't amount to much.

U.N. Human Rights Council

Guest, Iain, "Obama's Moment on Human Rights," *The Christian Science Monitor*, **Dec. 10, 2008, p. 9.**

U.S. membership in the Human Rights Council would give hope to moderate governments yearning for a stronger U.N. human rights program.

Higgins, Alexander G., "U.N. Chief Urges U.S. to Join Human Rights Body," *Lewiston* **(Idaho)** *Morning Tribune*, **Dec. 13, 2008.**

U.N. Secretary-General Ban Ki-moon has urged the United States to play a more active role in the United Nations' protection of human rights by joining the Human Rights Council.

Holmes, Kim R., "Liberty Forum Better Than U.N. Rights Council," *The Washington Times*, **Dec. 25, 2008, p. A4.**

The Human Rights Council has become a protection racket for the world's worst human rights abusers.

Lynch, Colum, "U.S. to Seek Seat on U.N. Human Rights Council," *The Washington Post*, **April 1, 2009, p. A2.**

The Obama administration is seeking to enter a new era of engagement in American foreign policy by seeking a seat on the U.N. Human Rights Council.

CITING *CQ RESEARCHER*

Sample formats for citing these reports in a bibliography include the ones listed below. Preferred styles and formats vary, so please check with your instructor or professor.

MLA STYLE

Jost, Kenneth. "Rethinking the Death Penalty." CQ Researcher 16 Nov. 2001: 945-68.

APA STYLE

Jost, K. (2001, November 16). Rethinking the death penalty. *CQ Researcher, 11,* 945-968.

CHICAGO STYLE

Jost, Kenneth. "Rethinking the Death Penalty." *CQ Researcher,* November 16, 2001, 945-968.

WORLD PEACEKEEPING

BY LEE MICHAEL KATZ

Excerpted from the CQ Global Researcher. Lee Michael Katz. (April 2007). "World Peacekeeping." *CQ Global Researcher*, 75-100.

World Peacekeeping

BY LEE MICHAEL KATZ

THE ISSUES

As the United Nations marked Holocaust Commemoration Day this year, the world's failure to stop the deaths and devastation in Darfur made the occasion far more urgent than the usual calendar exercise.

New Secretary-General Ban Ki-moon had to deliver his remarks on videotape, pointedly noting he was on his way to Ethiopia for an African Union summit focusing on ending the carnage against black Africans in western Sudan. Just weeks after taking office, the head of the world body said he was strongly committed to this message: "We must apply the lessons of the Holocaust to today's world." [1]

Elderly Holocaust survivors in the audience served as visible witness before delegates of the international body that rose out of the ashes of World War II's Nazi evils. But it was clear that more than 60 years later, the lessons had not been fully learned.

"I still weep today" at the memories of those, including her father and brother, who were marched to the gas chambers at Auschwitz, said Simone Veil, a well-known French Holocaust survivor.

But she also pointed to slaughter that happened decades afterward and is still happening today. While those who survived hoped the pledge "Never Again" would ring true, Veil said, sadly their warnings were in vain. "After the massacres in Cambodia, it is Africa that is paying the highest price in genocidal terms," she said, in a call for action to stop the killings in Darfur. An estimated 200,000 have been killed, countless women raped and 2 million made homeless as armed Arab militia

A Polish soldier from the European Union Force supporting the U.N. mission in the Democratic Republic of the Congo participates in training for hostage-rescue operations at the EUFOR base in Kinshasa. A French helicopter hovers above.

AFP/Getty Images/Marco Longari

known as janjaweed prey on vulnerable villagers.

The laments about a lack of life-saving action continue despite the fact that the United Nations has endorsed, at least in principle, a new concept to keeping the peace in the 21st century called the Responsibility to Protect. At its heart is the fundamental notion that the world has a moral obligation to intervene against genocide.

This includes using military force if necessary, even when the deaths are taking place inside a sovereign nation as in the 1994 ethnic massacre in Rwanda. A reduced U.N. force in the African nation did not physically try to stop the slaughter by Hutus in Rwanda of 800,000 fellow Rwandans — mainly Tutsis but also moderate Hutus — in a matter of weeks. Traditionally, such intervention would be seen as off-limits inside a

functioning state, especially a member of the United Nations.

So the notion of the Responsibility to Protect "is very significant because it removes an excuse to turn a blind eye to mass atrocities," says Lee Feinstein, a former U.S. diplomat and author of a 2007 Council on Foreign Relations report on R2P, as the concept is known. [2] Such excuses went "unchallenged" until recently, he says. "If the U.N. is serious about this — and there are questions — this is a big deal." But a decade after Rwanda, the deaths, displacement and widespread rapes in Darfur have been ongoing even after the Responsibility to Protect was endorsed by the U.N. General Assembly in 2005 and in a Security Council resolution a year later.

"Darfur is another Rwanda," said Paul Rusesabagina, whose actions to save 1,268 refugees from genocide were made famous by the movie "Hotel Rwanda." [3] "Many people are dying every day. The world is still standing by watching," he said. "History keeps repeating itself — and without teaching us a lesson."

Secretary-General Ban must make the Responsibility to Protect his top priority if there is hope to stem mass killings in the future, Feinstein argues. That contradiction between the promise of the Responsibility to Protect and the situation in Darfur is what Ban faces in leading the world body.

Ban has cited Responsibility to Protect as at least one of his priorities, noting its unfulfilled promise. "We must take the first steps to move the Responsibility to Protect from word to deed," Ban declared. [4]

But, like his predecessors, Ban wields only moral authority as the leader of

Major Worldwide Peacekeeping Operations

The African Union, European Union Force, NATO and United Nations combine for 24 peacekeeping forces deployed around the world. The U.N. has 15 missions, with the most recent deployment being a police force in Timor-Leste in 2006.

Peacekeeping Missions

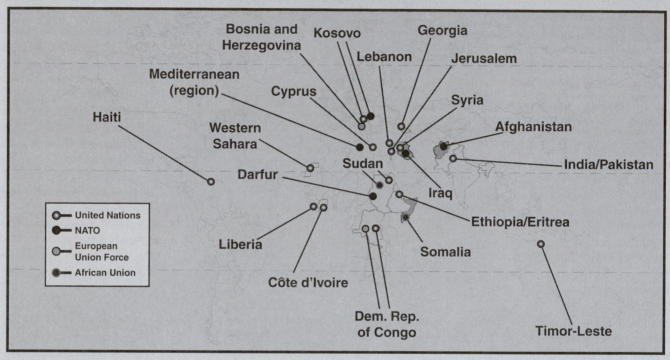

Legend:
- ○ United Nations
- ● NATO
- ◐ European Union Force
- ◉ African Union

Map labels: Bosnia and Herzegovina, Kosovo, Georgia, Lebanon, Jerusalem, Mediterranean (region), Cyprus, Syria, Haiti, Afghanistan, Western Sahara, India/Pakistan, Darfur, Sudan, Iraq, Liberia, Ethiopia/Eritrea, Somalia, Côte d'Ivoire, Dem. Rep. of Congo, Timor-Leste

Sources: African Union, Delegation of the European Commission to the USA, NATO, United Nations Department of Peacekeeping Operations

the world body. There is no standing U.N. army to back up his pronouncements. "He doesn't have troops to send," says the Secretary-General's spokeswoman Michele Montas. "What the Secretary-General can do besides an advocacy role is limited."

Though U.N. peacekeeping forces have taken on an increasingly aggressive posture in recent years, the U.N. system of relying on donated troops doesn't offer the speed or military capability for invading a country to force an end to murders. Nor is it likely countries that traditionally contribute troops would rush to put their soldiers in harm's way, notes Jean-Marie Guéhenno, U.N. Undersecretary General in charge of peacekeeping operations. "If they feel they are going to have to shoot their

way in, it's no more peacekeeping. Sometimes, it may be necessary," Guéhenno says candidly in an interview, "but it will have to be done by other organizations."

NATO, possibly the African Union (with outside logistical help and equipment) and ad hoc "coalitions of the willing" nations are the likely global candidates for any truly muscular interventions to stop the slaughter of innocents.

But even for U.N. peacekeepers, fast-moving events can foster a combat atmosphere. Today's peacekeeping faces the dangers of unrest or battle from Latin America to Africa.

Such threats have spawned a new term that has taken root in 21st-century U.N. operations: "robust peacekeeping." Modern U.N. forces may have attack he-

licopters and Special Forces, "the type of military capabilities you would not have traditionally associated with peacekeeping operation, "Guéhenno notes.

"We're not going to let an armed group unravel a peace agreement that benefits millions of people," he says. The peacekeeping chief sounds more like a general threatening overwhelming force rather than a diplomat cautious of its implications. "So we'll hit hard on those spoilers," he promises. Guéhenno cited Congo as an example, but there are others.

Peacekeeping forces today face rapidly changing situations. In Somalia, Ethiopian troops conducted a successful invasion by New Year's 2007, well before peacekeepers could be deployed to stop the fighting. But attacks continued to rock Mogadishu, the capital, and emergency peacekeeping plans intensified.

In Lebanon last year, the deadly aftermath of Israel-Hezbollah battles brought the need for the U.N. to ramp up a large peacekeeping force extraordinarily quickly.

Guéhenno's U.N. peacekeeping department has its hands full as it is, trying to keep up with worldwide demand for troops, police and civilian advisors. Much like Microsoft dominates the computer world, the United Nations is by far the dominant brand in peacekeeping.

With more than 100,000 troops, police and civilian officials in 18 peace missions around the world, the United Nations has the largest amount of peacekeepers deployed since the organization's founding in 1945. That total could exceed 140,000 depending on the strength of any new missions in Somalia and Darfur. Former Secretary-General Kofi Annan warned before he left office: "U.N. peacekeeping is stretched as never before."

Traditionally, impoverished nations are major troop contributors, in part because the payments they receive help them economically. Bangladesh, Pakistan and India each had about 9,000-10,000 troops in U.N. peacekeeping forces in 2006. Jordan, Nepal, Ethiopia, Ghana Uruguay, Nigeria and South Africa were also major troop contributors. [5]

Although peacekeeping advocates argue peacekeeping is a bargain compared to the cost of all-out war, peacekeeping on a global scale does not come cheap. The approved U.N. 2006-2007 budget is more than $5 billion.

Peacekeeping is paid for by a special assessment for U.N. members weighted on national wealth and permanent Security Council member status. The United States pays the largest share of peacekeeping costs: 27 percent (though congressional caps on payment have resulted in lower payments in recent years). [6] Other top contributors include Japan, Germany, the United Kingdom,

France, Italy, China, Canada, Spain and South Korea. [7]

But peacekeeping operations often are hampered by having to run deeply into the red. In November 2006, peacekeeping arrears totaled $2.2 billion.

U.N. peacekeeping is also hobbled by the built-in logistical problem of having to cobble each mission together after Security Council authorization.

Ban Ki-moon, right, new secretary-general of the United Nations, gets a briefing in January 2007 at the United Nations Organization Mission in the Democratic Republic of the Congo in Kisangani, where he laid a wreath for fallen peacekeepers.

Plans for standing U.N. military forces have never gotten off the ground. But U.N. police are starting to take "baby steps," starting with dozens of officers for a permanent force, says senior U.N. police official Antero Lopes.

In recent years, U.N. peacekeeping officials have made inroads to daunting logistical problems by maintaining pre-positioned materiel in staging area in Italy, notes former New Zealand Ambassador Colin Keating. But there is still a great need for equipment. "You can't just go down to Wal-Mart and buy a bunch of APCS" — armored personnel carriers, he says.

Other regional organizations involved in keeping the peace, with efforts ranging from armed intervention

to watching over ballot boxes, include:

- **North Atlantic Treaty Organization (NATO):** The military alliance of 26 countries, including the United States, has 75,000 troops worldwide responsible for some of the more muscular interventions, such as the aftermath of the war in Afghanistan, where it has a force of 30,000.

- **African Union (AU):** Established in 2001, the 53-nation coalition has a 7,000-man force in Darfur, including many Rwandans. Another AU contingent of 8,000 has been in Mogadishu since March 6.

- **European Union (EU):** Its troops have taken over Bosnian peacekeeping with a force of 7,000. The EU's broader peacekeeping plans include creation of a long-discussed rapid-reaction force of 60,000. But EU foreign policy chief Javier Solana notes that despite those bold aims, the organization has been depending on a softer "mixture of civilian, military, economic, political and institution-building tools." [8]

U.N. Provides Half of Peacekeeping Forces

With 82,751 personnel spread among 15 missions worldwide, the United Nations contributes over 50 percent of the world's peacekeeping forces.

Organization	Personnel	Missions	Nations Contributing Personnel
United Nations	82,751	15	114
NATO	55,000	5	37 (includes 11 NATO allies)
African Union	15,000	2	10
European Union Force	8,500	2	34 (includes 10 non-EU nations)
Organization for Security and Co-operation in Europe	3,500	19	56
Multinational Force & Observers	1,687	1	11

Sources: African Union, Delegation of the European Commission to the USA, Multinational Force & Observers, NATO, OSCE, United Nations Department of Peacekeeping Operations

- **Organization for Security and Co-operation in Europe (OSCE):** The 56-member group, working on a non-military level, has more than 3,000 OSCE officers in 19 locations from Albania to Uzbekistan. Their activities are aimed at encouraging political dialogue and supporting post-conflict resolution. [9]
- **Multinational Force and Observers (MFO):** It has about 1,700 troops from the United States and 10 other countries stationed on the Egyptian side of the Israeli-Sinai border.

As an abstract concept, global peacekeeping seems like a reasonable and virtuous response to global problems. Who better than neutral referees to keep fighters apart? Indeed, under the 1948 International Convention on the Prevention and Punishment of the Crime of Genocide, the United States and other participating countries are obliged "to prevent and punish" genocide. But forceful military intervention is clouded by questions that range from national sovereignty to international political will along with such practical issues as troop supply and logistics in remote corners of the world.

Increasingly, the Holocaust-related lesson seems to be the notion that the international community has a moral obligation — and indeed a right — to enter sovereign states to stop genocide and other human rights violations.

The Responsibility to Protect concept was detailed in a 2001 report by the International Commission on Intervention and State Sovereignty (ICISS), co-chaired by Algerian diplomat Mohamed Sahnoun and former Australian Foreign Minister Gareth Evans, now head of the non-governmental International Crisis Group, dedicated to stopping global conflict. "There is a growing recognition that the issue is not the 'right to intervene' of any State, but the 'Responsibility to Protect' of every State," the report said. [10]

By 2006, writes Evans in a forthcoming book, "the phrase 'Responsibility to Protect' was being routinely used, publicly and privately, by policymakers and commentators almost everywhere whenever the question was debated as to what the international community should do when faced with a state committing atrocities against its own people, or standing by allowing others to do so. [11]

More important, he points out, the concept was formally and unanimously adopted by the international community at the U.N. 60th Anniversary World Summit in September 2005. References to the Responsibility to Protect concept have also appeared in Security Council resolutions, including one calling for action in Darfur.

But R2P remains a sensitive concept, and the reference to U.N. military action in the 2005 World Summit document is very carefully couched: "We are prepared to take collective action, in a timely and decisive manner . . . on a case-by-case basis . . . as appropriate, should peaceful means be inadequate and national authorities are manifestly failing to protect their populations from genocide, war crimes, ethnic cleansing and crimes against humanity." [12]

As a rule, national sovereignty has been a hallowed concept at the United Nations, and what countries did within their own borders was considered their own business.

"The traditional view of sovereignty, as enabling absolute control of everything internal and demanding immunity from external intervention, was much reinforced by the large increase in U.N. membership during the decolonization era," Evans said at Stanford University on Feb. 7, 2007. "The states that joined were all newly proud of their identity, conscious in many cases of their fragility and generally saw the non-intervention norm as one of their few defenses against threats and pressures from more powerful international actors seeking to promote their own economic and political interests."

Given that history, if nations back up the R2P endorsement at the U.N. with action, it will represent a dramatic shift in policy.

Will the new "Responsibility to Protect" doctrine actually translate into international protection for the people of Darfur? That question has yet to be answered.

Meanwhile, in the wake of the international community's discussion of new powerful action, here are some of the questions being asked about the future of global peacekeeping:

Will the world support the Responsibility to Protect doctrine?

Judging by the inaction in Darfur in the face of highly publicized pleas from groups around world, the R2P is off to an inauspicious start. "Darfur is the first test of the Responsibility to Protect," says Feinstein, "and the world failed the test."

Echoes of the world's continuing failure to protect its citizens from mass murder reverberated off of the green marble podium in the cavernous U.N. General Assembly Hall this year. "It is a tragedy that the international community has not been able to stop new horrors in the years since the Holocaust," General Assembly President Sheikha Haya Al Khalifa of Bahrain stated. [13] "This makes it all the more important that we remember the lessons of the past so that we do not make the same mistakes in the future."

Yet the Responsibility to Protect concept faces a number of daunting challenges, from potential Third World opposition to the appetite and physical ability of Western nations to intervene. Allan Rock, Canada's ambassador to the United Nations, who advanced the Responsibility to Protect resolution at the world body, said in 2001 that the doctrine was, "feared by many countries as a Trojan horse for the interveners of the world looking for justification for marching into other countries." [14]

Indeed, commented Hugo Chávez, president of Venezuela and nemesis of the United States, "This is very suspicious. Tomorrow or sometime in the future, someone in Washington will say that the Venezuelan people need to be protected from the tyrant Chávez, who is a threat. They are trying to legalize imperialism within the United Nations, and Venezuela cannot accept that." [15]

In Sudan, the shifting conditions of

An African Union peacekeeping soldier stands guard in the village of Kerkera in Darfur, a western province of Sudan, where government-sponsored troops and a militia of Arab horsemen known as "Janjaweed" have been conducting a campaign of devastation against black tribes.

President Omar Hassan Ahmad al-Bashir to allow U.N. troops into Darfur has deterred them as of mid-April 2007.

Like Chávez, al-Bashir has said such a force would be tantamount to an invasion and warned that it could become a fertile ground for Islamic jihadists. Al Qaeda leader Osama bin Laden has already weighed in, urging resistance to any U.N. intervention in Sudan. [16]

And Libyan leader Muammar Qaddafi, far less of a pariah to the West than before, but still prone to inflammatory statements, told Sudanese officials last November, "Western countries and America are not busying themselves out of sympathy for the Sudanese people or for Africa but for oil and for the return of colonialism to the African continent. Reject any foreign intervention." [17]

With a lineup like that against U.N. deployment, cynics might say, there must be good reason to do so. In Darfur, however, the R2P doctrine has become bogged down by practical considerations: The geographical area to be protected is vast, and both the vul-

nerable population and predatory attackers are in close proximity.

But, says Chinua Akukwe, a Nigerian physician and former vice chairman of the Global Health Council, "The U.N. and its agencies must now think the unthinkable — how to bypass murderous governments in any part of the world and reach its suffering citizens in a timely fashion." [18]

Nicole Deller, program advisor for the pro-protection group Responsibility to Protect, says the careful wording of the R2P concept document has given pause to many countries. They remember the disastrous day when 18 Americans died in Mogadishu, Somalia in 1993 — memorialized in the book and movie "Black Hawk Down" — that gave both the United Nations and the United States a black eye. "A lot of that is still blowback from Somalia," she says.

But among African nations there appears an evolution of thinking about sovereignty. Ghana's representative to the United Nations, Nana Effah-Aptenteng, confirmed that change when he told a U.N. audience that African states "have an obligation to intervene in the affairs of another state when its people are at risk." [19]

This is further reflected in the AU Constitutive Act, which recognizes the role of African nations to intervene in cases of genocide. [20]

The Sudanese government, whose oil reserves have given them political and commercial leverage in resisting calls for an end to the slaughter, has reacted by changing the subject. When asked about his country facing possible international military action under The Responsibility to Protect for turning a blind eye to death and destruction in Darfur, Abdalmahmood Abdalhaleem, Sudan's U.N. ambassador, instead turns to resentment of the U.S. role in Iraq and

Israel's actions in Lebanon last summer. "Why didn't they intervene when people in Iraq were slaughtered and people in Lebanon were bombarded and infrastructure destroyed?" he asks. "Why didn't they intervene there?"

The international community, either at the United Nations or elsewhere, is far from having a standard on when to intervene to stop violence or even genocide. But some attempts have been made to come up with questions that can help arrive at an answer. According to the International Commission on Intervention and State Sovereignty, five basic conditions are needed to trigger an intervention by U.N. or other multinational forces:

- **Seriousness of Harm** — Is the threatened harm to state or human security of a kind, and suf-

ficiently clear and serious, to justify the use of military force? In the case of internal threats, does it involve genocide and other large-scale killing, "ethnic cleansing" or serious violations of international humanitarian law?

- **Proper Purpose** — Is the primary purpose of the proposed military action clearly to halt or avert the threat in question, whatever other motives may be in play?

- **Last Resort** — Has every non-military option for meeting the threat in question been explored, with reasonable grounds for believing lesser measures will not succeed?

- **Proportional Means** — Are the scale, duration and intensity of the planned military action the mini-

When Peacekeepers Prey Instead of Protect

U.N. seeking more women officers

The U.N. has been stung in recent years by reports that male peacekeeping soldiers have preyed on women — often girls under age 18 — in vulnerable populations.

In Congo, U.N. officials admit that a "shockingly large" number of peacekeepers have bought sex from impoverished young girls, including illiterate orphans, for payments ranging from two eggs to $5.

What's more, some peacekeeping missions reportedly covered-up the abuse, as well as the children that have been born as their result. Between January 2004 and November 2006, 319 peacekeeping personnel worldwide were investigated for sexual misconduct, U.N. officials say, with 144 military and 17 police sent home and 18 civilians summarily dismissed. [1]

"I am especially troubled by instances in which United Nations peacekeepers are alleged to have sexually exploited minors and other vulnerable people, and I have enacted a policy of 'zero tolerance' towards such offences that applies to all personnel engaged in United Nations operations," Secretary-General Kofi Annan said in March 2005. He also instituted a mandatory training course for all peacekeeping candidates to address the issues.

"You get [these abuses] not just with peacekeepers but with soldiers in general, and it gets worse the further they are from home and the more destitute the local population," says Richard Reeve, a research fellow at Chatham House, a London-based think tank. "The UN will never get rid of the problem, but they are really dealing with it and putting changes into practice." [2]

Now the U.N. is sending women instead of men on certain

U.N. troop and police peacekeeping missions. The first all-female police unit, from India, recently was sent to Liberia, where peacekeepers had been accused of trading food for sex with teenagers. [3] Cases of misconduct by women police are "almost non-existent," says Antero Lopes, a senior U.N. police official.

The head of the new unit, Commander Seema Dhundia, says its primary mission is to support the embryonic Liberia National Police (LNP), but that the presence of female troops will also raise awareness of and respect for women in Liberia, and in peacekeeping. "Seeing women in strong positions, I hope, will reduce the violence against women," she says. [4]

"We plead for nations to give us as many woman police officers as they can," says Lopes. Another advantage of the all-female unit in Liberia is that it is trained in crowd control, Lopes says, shattering a barrier in what had been seen as a male domain. "It is also a message to the local society that women can perform the same jobs as men."

The U.N. is aggressively trying to recruit more female peacekeepers, from civilian managers to foot soldiers to high-ranking officers. "Our predominantly male profile in peacekeeping undermines the credibility of our efforts to lead by example," Jean-Marie Guéhenno, head of the U.N. peacekeeping department, told the Security Council.

That message was not always heard. A decade ago, peacekeeping consultant Judith Stiehm, a professor of political science at Florida International University, was hired by the U.N. to write a pamphlet on the need for women in peacekeeping. Today she says it was a show effort. "I don't think they even really distributed it," Stiehm says. But pushed by the only female peacekeeping mission head, the issue eventually became U.N. policy.

Security Council Resolution 1325, passed in 2000, "urges the secretary-general" to expand the role of women in field operations, especially among military observers and police.

"The little blue pamphlet and the impetus behind it brought about this very important resolution," Stiehm says, "which is not being implemented, but it's on the books." In fact, "less than 2 per cent and 5 per cent of our military and police personnel, respectively, are women," Guéhenno told the Security Council.

Beyond the issue of sexual abuse, the role of women soldiers is important in nations where substantial contact between unrelated men and women is prohibited by religion or custom. "Military men just cannot deal with Arab women — that's so culturally taboo," Stiehm notes, but military women can gather information.

Because the United Nations' peacekeeping forces represent more than 100 countries, cultural variations make a big difference in both the prominence of women and what behavior is acceptable, according to Stiehm. "It is very uneven," she says and "dependant very much on who heads the mission."

Stiehm points to Yasushi Akashi, a Japanese U.N. official in the early 1990s. When confronted with charges of sexual abuse of young girls by troops in his Cambodian mission, "Akashi's reaction was, 'Boys will be boys,' " she says.

In another case, Stiehm recalls arguing with her boss over trying to prevent troops from having sex with underage women. "He didn't see anything wrong with it," she says.

The U.N. is now trying to short-circuit the different-cultures argument with a "Duty of Care" code that pointedly states: "These standards apply to all peacekeepers irrespective of local customs or laws, or the customs or laws of your own country."

Moreover, Stiehm says, "Peacekeepers have an obligation to do better."

Bebiche is one of hundreds of internally displaced persons forced to flee warfare in eastern Democratic Republic of Congo. Countless women and girls there have been brutalized by unprecedented sexual violence, and they have few options for existence but to pursue survival sex.

[1] "U.N. will enforce 'zero tolerance' policy against sexual abuse, peacekeeping official says." U.N. News Centre, Jan. 5, 2007. www.un.org/apps/news/storyAr.asp?NewsID=21169&Cr=sex&Cr1=abuse&Kw1=SExual+Exploitation&Kw2=&Kw3=

[2] Quoted in Tristan McConnell, "All female unit keeps peace in Liberia," *The Christian Science Monitor online*, March 21, 2005; http://news.yahoo.com/s/csm/20070321/ts_csm/ofemmeforce_1.

[3] Will Ross, "Liberia gets all-female peacekeeping force," BBC News, Jan. 31, 2007, http://news.bbc.co.uk/2/hi/africa/6316387.stm.

[4] *Ibid.*

mum necessary to achieve the objective of protecting human life?

• **Balance of Consequences** — Is there a reasonable chance of the military action being successful . . . with the consequences of action unlikely to be worse than the consequences of inaction?

Certainly Darfur's miseries meet many of the conditions, but not all, Evans says. Questions remain whether all non-military options have been exhausted, and there are "hair-raisingly difficult" logistical concerns to consider as well as high potential for civilian injuries, Evans says.

Thus, the R2P is not necessarily a green light for unfettered military action, according to Feinstein and others. "This is not a question of sending in the Marines or even the blue helmets" of the United Nations, he says, pointing out that the doctrine is most effective in bringing international political pressure to bear before conditions lead to mass killings.

Are regional peacekeepers effective?

While the United Nations leads peacekeeping forces around the world, it does not maintain a standing armed force designed to initiate military interventions. When robust military operations are needed, the U.N. can authorize other actors to respond, such as better-equipped or more willing regional organizations such as NATO, the European Union or the African Union, or a combination of those multinational forces. The R2P doctrine, in fact, specifies that U.N.-authorized military action be done "in cooperation with relevant regional organizations as appropriate."

"The U.N. culture is still very much against doing coercive types of operations," says French defense official Catherine Guicherd, on loan to the International Peace Academy in New York, "whereas the NATO culture goes very much in the other direction."

Two current regional operations — the NATO mission in Kosovo and the AU forces in Darfur — reflect the realities of such missions. NATO, working in its European backyard, has been largely effective. The AU, operating in a much larger area with fewer troops and less equipment and support, has been struggling.

At the beginning of 2007, there were 16,000 NATO troops from 36 mostly European nations stationed with the

U.N. peacekeeping force in Kosovo, the Albanian-majority Serbian province seeking autonomy from Belgrade. There is a global alphabet of cooperation in Kosovo. The NATO "KFOR" forces coordinate closely with 2,700 personnel of the U.N. Interim Administration Mission — known as UNMIK — which in turn employs another 1,500 men and women from the EU and OSCE.

Two Israeli journalists who reported from Kosovo in 2002 described an atmosphere of tension and uncertainty and called the force of agencies "a massive and complex multinational presence signaling the commitment of the international community to restoring order and rebuilding civil institutions in this troubled region." [21]

But NATO's toughest deployment has been in Afghanistan, with about 32,000 troops contributing to what is called the International Security Assistance force (ISAF), which provides military support for the government of President Hamid Karzai. More than 100 peacekeepers died in Afghanistan in 2006. And 2007 brought more casualties.

"It's very bloody, much worse than NATO ever dreamed," says Edwin Smith, a professor of law and international relations at the University of Southern California and author of *The United Nations in a New World Order.*

"But this is a fundamental test of their ability to engage in peacekeeping and extraterritorial operations outside of their treaty-designated area," Smith continues. "If it turns out that they cannot play this function, then one wonders how do you justify NATO's continued existence?"

In Africa, European troops also may have to fight a psychological battle stemming from the colonial legacy. It is commonly held that many Africans resent non-African peacekeepers coming to enforce order. Perhaps a more pressing reason, observes Victoria K. Holt, a peacekeeping expert at the Stimson Center in Washington, is that a NATO or U.N. force under a powerful man-

A Swedish peacekeeper checks weapons seized in Kosovo. About 17,000 NATO-led peacekeepers in so-called KFOR missions are responsible for peace and security in the rebellious Albanian-dominated Serbian province. In 1999 NATO forces bombed the area to end ethnic cleansing by the Serbs.

date "would be better equipped and thus, more effective and a challenge to what is happening on the ground."

The notoriously fickle government of Sudan has indicated it would be willing to accept only a hybrid AU-U.N. force. The U.N. should be limited to a "logistical and backstopping role," Ambassador Abdalhaleem says.

The AU can muster troops, but handling logistics and equipment in a huge and remote area such as Darfur is a major problem for even the best-equipped and trained forces. But the AU began 2007 with only 7,000 troops in Darfur, an area the size of France, and with limited equipment, according to Robert Collins, an Africa expert at the University of California-Santa Barbara, who has visited the war-torn nation over the past 50 years.

"They just don't have the helicopters," he says. "They don't have the big planes to fly in large amounts of supplies.

They're just a bunch of guys out there with a couple of rifles trying to hold off a huge insurgency. It doesn't work."

Besides Darfur, the AU has sent peacekeepers to a few other African hotspots, in effect adopting the underpinnings of the Responsibility to Protect by moving to establish its own African Standby Force. Slated to be operational by 2010, the force would have an intelligence unit and a "Continental Early Warning System" to monitor situations that can potentially spark mass killings. The force would be capable of responding to a genocidal situation within two weeks. [22]

Whether such an African force will be able to live up to its optimistic intent poses another big question: Would it receive continuing outside financial help from the West?

African officials and experts report the biggest problem facing AU peacekeeping is funding, particularly in Sudan. "This is . . . one of the worst humanitarian disasters in the world, yet only five donors seem to be properly engaged," said Haroun Atallah, chief executive of Islamic Relief. "All rich countries must step up their support urgently if the disaster of Darfur isn't to turn into an even worse catastrophe." [23]

Should peace-building replace peace-keeping?

In the past, U.N. peacekeeping focused mainly on keeping warring nations apart while they negotiated a peace pact. Now, U.N. peacekeepers increasingly are being called in as part of complex cooperative efforts by regional military organizations, local military, civilians and police to rebuild failed governments.

Some say the shift is inevitable. More than military might is needed for successful peacekeeping, NATO Secretary-General Jaap de Hoop Scheffer noted last year. During a Security Council meeting to highlight cooperation between the United Nations and regional security organizations, he said he had learned "some important lessons," including the

Continued on p. 86

Chronology

1940s-1950s

Founding of U.N. promises peace in the postwar world. First peacekeeping missions are deployed.

1945
United Nations is founded at the end of World War II "to save succeeding generations from the scourge of war."

1948
First U.N. mission goes to Jerusalem following Arab-Israeli War.

1949
U.N. observers monitor the struggle over Kashmir following the creation of India and Pakistan.

1950
Security Council approves a U.N. "police action" in Korea.

1956
United Nations Emergency Force is established during the Suez Crisis involving Egypt, Israel, Britain and France.

1960s

Death of U.N. secretary-general in Congo causes U.N. to avoid dangerous missions.

1960
U.N. Secretary-General Dag Hammarskjold dies in an unexplained plane crash during a U.N. intervention in Congo by U.N. peacekeepers; the mission fails to bring democracy.

1964
U.N. peacekeepers are sent to keep peace between Greeks and Turks on divided Cyprus; the mission continues.

1970s

Cambodian genocide occurs unhindered.

1974
U.N. Disengagement Force is sent to the Golan Heights after fighting stops between Israel and Syria.

1975
Dictator Pol Pot kills more than 1 million Cambodians. U.N. and other nations fail to act.

1978
U.N. monitors withdrawal of Israeli troops from Lebanon.

1980s

Cold War barrier to bold U.N. actions begins to crumble.

1988
U.N. peacekeeping mission monitors ceasefire between Iran and Iraq.

1989
Fall of Berlin Wall symbolizes collapse of Soviet empire and Cold War paralysis blocking U.N. agreement.

1990s

Security Council confronts Iraq. Failures in Bosnia, Somalia, dampen enthusiasm to stop Rwanda killing.

1990
Iraqi leader Saddam Hussein invades Kuwait and defies Security Council demand for withdrawal.

1991
U.N.-authorized and U.S.-led international coalition expels Iraq from Kuwait. . . . U.N. peacekeeping mission is sent to El Salvador.

1992
U.N. Protection Force fails to stop killings in Bosnian civil war.

1993
Ambitious U.N. peace operation fails to restore order in Somalia.

1994
U.N. peacekeepers are unable to stop the massacre of more than 800,000 Rwandans.

1995
U.N. peacekeepers in the Bosnian town of Srebrenica are disarmed and left helpless by Serb forces.

1999
NATO takes military action against Serbia.

2000s-Present

U.N. mounts successful peace-building mission in Liberia.

2003
U.N. peacekeeping mission in Liberia begins to keep peace.

2005
U.N. General Assembly endorses Responsibility to Protect concept at World Summit.

2006
Security Council endorses Responsibility to Protect but intervention in killings in Darfur region is stalled by Sudan's government.

April 9, 2007
U.N. Secretary-General Ban Ki-moon calls for "a global partnership against genocide" and upgrades the post of U.N. Special Adviser for the Prevention of Genocide — currently held by Juan E. Méndez of Argentina — to a full-time position.

Continued from p. 84

need for each organization to play to its strengths and weaknesses.

"NATO offers unparalleled military experience and capability," Scheffer said, "yet addressing a conflict requires a coordinated and coherent approach from the outset. Clearly defined responsibilities . . . are indispensable if we are to maximize our chances of success." [24]

So is post-conflict follow-through. The United Nations has set up a Peacebuilding Commission to follow up after conflicts have been quelled.

Because peacekeeping now often takes place inside nations rather than between them, the United Nations is typically charged not only with trying to keep the peace but also "with building up the basics of a state," notes Guéhenno. "That's why peacekeeping can never be the full answer. It has to be complemented by a serious peace-building efforts.

"Today, we have a completely different situation" from in the past, Guéhenno explains, referring to the world's growing number of so-called failed states. "You have a number of countries around the world that are challenged by internal divides. They don't have the capacity to maintain law and order."

But peacekeeping consultant Judith Stiehm, a professor of political science at Florida International University, sees a contradiction between peace-keeping and peace-building. "That's what gets them in trouble," she says. "You've got guys wearing military uniforms and their missions are very civilian. And once you add the mission of protection, you're not neutral anymore. Some people think of you as the enemy, and it muddies the waters. You can't have it both ways."

Roland Paris, an associate professor of political science at Canada's University of Ottawa, sees inherent cultural flaws, including Western colonialism, in peace-building. "Peace-building operations seek to stabilize countries that have recently experienced civil wars," he wrote. "In pursuing this goal, however, international peace-builders have promulgated a particular vision of how states should organize themselves internally, based on the principles of liberal democracy and market-oriented economics.

"By reconstructing war-shattered states in accordance with this vision, peace-builders have effectively 'transmitted' standards of appropriate behavior from the Western-liberal core . . . to the failed states of the periphery. From this perspective, peace-building resembles an

U.N. Police Face Difficult Challenges

Small problems can escalate quickly

In Timor-Leste (formerly East Timor), a country still raw from decades of fighting for independence, Antero Lopes knew that promptly dealing with a stolen chicken was crucial.

As acting police commissioner for the U.N. mission in the tiny East Asian nation in 2006, he discovered that in such a tense environment, overlooking even a petty crime like a marketplace theft could have serious consequences. "Friends and neighbors are brought in, many of them veterans of Timor's bloody struggles, and suddenly you have an intercommunity problem with 200 people fighting 200 people," he say from U.N. headquarters in Manhattan, where he is now deputy director of U.N. Police Operations. [1]

United Nations police were sent to the former Portuguese colony last year to restore order in the fledgling state. Timor-Leste gained independence from Indonesia in 2002 following a long struggle, but an outbreak of death and violence that uprooted more than 150,000 people prompted the Timorese government to agree to temporarily turn over police operations to the U.N., which called it "the first ever such arrangement between a sovereign nation and the U.N." [2]

The U.N.'s Timorese role reflects how U.N. police have become "a critical component" of the institution's peacekeeping efforts, notes Victoria K. Holt, a senior associate at The Henry L. Stimson Center in Washington and co-director of its Future of Peace Operations program. The U.N. now recognizes "you just can't go from military to civilian society. You have to have

something in between."

A critical role for police wasn't always a given, says Holt, author of *The Impossible Mandate? Military Preparedness, the Responsibility to Protect and Modern Peace Operations.* For much of the United Nations' nearly 60-year peacekeeping history, she says, the lack of a major police role was "one of the biggest gaps. They actually now have a whole police division that didn't exist a number of years ago."

The role and size of the U.N. police effort has grown dramatically in recent years. "Peace operations are increasingly using significant numbers of police to handle security tasks," according to the U.N.'s 2006 Annual Review of Global Peace Operations. Led by the United Nations, the number of police peacekeepers worldwide has tripled since 1998 to about 10,000.

Lopes says that although he is a university-trained police manager with experience ranging from anti-crime to SWAT teams, he is also accustomed to operating in environments without the "same legal framework" one finds in Europe.

He was deployed in Bosnia, for example, while the civil war still raged there in the 1990's. "If you really like these kinds of [policing] challenges," he notes, "you can get addicted."

Balkan violence may not be over, however. The U.N. mission in Kosovo — the Albanian-majority Serbian province seeking autonomy from Belgrade — is bracing for violence, with the disputed area's future set to be decided this year. Already, news of an impending Kosovo independence plan has triggered violent demon-

strations. After U.N. police fired rubber bullets into a crowd of demonstrators in February, killing two people, the U.N. mission there pulled out. [3]

Outside of Kosovo (where the European Union plans to take over police responsibility), the major U.N. police presences are in Haiti and countries in Africa. In Africa, U.N. police missions are hampered by the African Union's lack of proper resources. "In many missions, we find even the lack of simple uniforms," Lopes says, not to mention operable radios, police cars or other basic police equipment.

In Sudan's troubled Darfur, any new police commitment would first focus on "stabilization" of the lawless situation, he says. However, he points out, while U.N. police must not compromise on basic law-enforcement tenets, they still must adapt to local customs in working with local authorities.

So Lopes finds it important to play the role of empathetic psychologist as well as tough global cop.

"This is an issue of local ownership," he says. "We must also read what is in their hearts and minds."

[1] U.N. News Service, December 2006.

[2] *Ibid.*

[3] The Associated Press, "Albanians protest UN Kosovo plan," *Taipei Times*, Feb. 12, 2007, p. 6.

updated (and more benign) version of the *mission civilisatrice*, the colonial-era belief that the European imperial powers had a duty to 'civilize' dependent populations and territories." [25]

But despite an ongoing debate, one part of the formula for the near future seems set: The U.N. has increasingly relied on deploying police to help rebuild a society as part of its peacekeeping efforts around the globe. In fact, as "an interim solution," the global U.N. cops have become the actual police force of such nations as East Timor, Haiti and in Kosovo. "We provide a measure of law and order and security that creates the political window to build up a state," Guéhenno says.

U.N. police realize they are operating in a very different environment. "Now we are a significant pillar in helping the good-governance effort," says Lopes, deputy police advisor in the U.N. Department of Peacekeeping Operations, sounding like a bureaucrat as well as a sheriff.

The Portuguese-born Lopes, who has served as police commissioner for the U.N. mission in East Timor, calls such a heavy U.N. role "a revolution" in the way the United Nations intervenes in internal conflicts. "What we are actually doing is a mixture of peace-keeping and peace-building," he explains. "We are hoping that with good governance — promoting elections and democratized policing — problems will be reduced."

Now, Lopes says, "our role is really to restore the rule of law as opposed to the rule of might."

"It will increasingly be a necessary feature of peace operations," predicts activist Deller. "Just separating factions and establishing elections alone isn't a sustainable model."

But so far, the result in Timor-Leste (the former East Timor) has "been a real disappointment," Deller says. She cites the "re-emergence of conflict," with the U.N. having to come back to try and restore security in the fledgling nation. (*See sidebar, p. 86.*)

Keating, the former New Zealand ambassador to the U.N., believes that without peace-building, "it's very easy to have all these peace-keeping missions out there like Band-Aids," masking deep wounds underneath. He cites the example of "insufficient stickability" in Haiti, where six different U.N. peace operations have sought to hold together the fractured nation since 1995. [26]

"You take your eye off the ball, and before you know it you're back where you started," Keating says.

The latest U.N. Stabilization Mission in Haiti began on June 1, 2004, with the mandate to provide a stable and secure environment, but some Haitian critics say the peacekeepers have behaved more like occupiers.

Alex Diceanu, a scholar at Canada's McMaster University, claims the Haiti operation "has become complicit in the oppression of Haiti's poor majority." For many Haitians, the operation has seemed more like "a foreign occupation force than a United Nations peacekeeping mission," he said. "The few journalists that have reported from these areas describe bustling streets that are

U.N. troops and police are now willing to battle warlords to try and build a democratic political foundation in the impoverished Caribbean nation, Guéhenno says. "This notion of protection of civilians," he says, "that's a change between yesterday's peacekeeping and today's peace-keeping."

Impoverished Haiti is a tough case, but the United Nations can claim suc-

"It's a very ambitious thing," he says. "What they're really trying to do is take countries and put them back together again. That's a very difficult thing to do." ■

BACKGROUND

Late Arrival

The ancient Romans had a description for their effort to pacify their 3-million-square-mile empire: Pax Romana, the Roman Peace. It lasted for more than 200 years, enforced by the Roman legions. [29]

The Hanseatic League in the 13th and 14th centuries arguably was the first forerunner of modern peacekeeping. Without a standing army or police force, the German-based alliance of 100 northern towns stifled warfare, civic strife and crime within its domain, mostly by paying bribes. [30]

For French Emperor Napoleon Bonaparte, peacekeeping was subordinate to conquest, and the extensive colonial empires of the great powers in the 19th century were more intent on exploiting natural resources than on peacekeeping.

In one rare instance, France, inspired by a romantic age in Europe, sent "peacekeepers" to Greece during the Greek revolt against the Turks in 1831 and ended up in tenuous circumstances between two Greek factions competing to fill the power vacuum. [31]

Perhaps the first example of multinational action against a common threat was in 1900 during the Boxer Rebellion in China, when a 50,000-strong force from Japan, Russia, Britain, France, the United States, German, Italy and Austro-Hungary came to protect the international community in Beijing from the Boxer mobs. [32]

The 20th century, ruptured by two world wars, saw few attempts at peace-

Brazilian blue helmets of the United Nations' peacekeeping force in Haiti help Haitian police keep order in the capital, Port-au-Prince, after a fire that ravaged 50 stores in June 2004.

U.N. Photo/Daniel Morel

quickly deserted as terrified residents hide from passing U.N. tanks." [27]

Armed battles are taking place in Haiti, where U.N. forces have taken casualties as they continue to battle heavily armed gangs for control of Haiti's notorious slums. Exasperated by an infamous warlord's hold on 300,000 people in a Port-au-Prince slum called *Cite Soleil*, U.N. troops took the offensive in February 2007. Almost one-tenth of the 9,000-man Haiti force took the battle to the streets, reclaiming control in a block-by-block battle. Thousand of shots were fired at the peacekeepers. [28]

cess in building democracy after civil wars in Liberia and Congo, Keating says, where missions are still ongoing. Finding a "sustainable solution" to get people to live together "ain't easy" for the United Nations, he adds. "They can make a huge difference, but it's a commitment involving many years" to rebuild civilian institutions.

Indeed, notes the legendary Sir Brian Urquhart, a former U.N. undersecretary-general and a leading pioneer in the development of international peacekeeping, "The challenges are far weightier than the U.N. peacekeeping system was ever designed for.

making. In 1919, at the end of World War I — "the war to end all wars" — the international community established the League of Nations to maintain peace. But as World War II approached, the fledgling world body floundered, discredited by its failure to prevent Japanese expansion into China and by Italy's conquest of Ethiopia and Germany's annexation of Austria. [33]

The United Nations was born in 1945 from the rubble of World War II and the ultimate failure of the League of Nations. Britain's Urquhart notes that the U.N.'s most critical task was to prevent doomsday — war between the Soviet Union and the United States. "During the Cold War," he says, "the most important consideration . . . was to prevent regional conflict from triggering an East-West nuclear confrontation."

German Navy Captain Wolfgang Schuchardt joined his once-divided nation's military in the midst of the Cold War, in 1968. "We had a totally different situation then," he recalls. "We had [certain] positions and those were to be defended" against the Soviet Union. Now, priorities have changed and Schuchardt works on strategic planning for the U.N.'s peace-keeping operation in Lebanon, one of the Middle East's most volatile areas.

The United Nations established its first peace-keeping observer operation to monitor the truce that followed the first Arab-Israeli war in 1948. Based in Jerusalem, it proved ineffective in the long term, unable to prevent the next three major Arab-Israeli wars.

In 1949 the United Nations deployed a peace-keeping observer mission to a similarly tense India and Pakistan, then quarreling over a disputed area of Kashmir.

When communist North Korea invaded South Korea in 1950, the U.N.'s forceful response was unprecedented. The Korean War was actually fought under the U.N. flag, with troops from dozens of nations defending South Korea.

But the war was authorized through a diplomatic fluke. The Soviet Union,

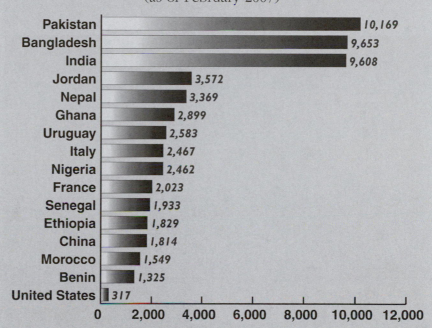

Developing Countries Provide Most Peacekeepers

Developing nations provide the most manpower to U.N. peacekeeping forces. Pakistan, Bangladesh and India were providing half of the U.N.'s nearly 58,000 personnel in early 2007.

U.N. Peacekeeping Forces by Country
(as of February 2007)

Country	Personnel
Pakistan	10,169
Bangladesh	9,653
India	9,608
Jordan	3,572
Nepal	3,369
Ghana	2,899
Uruguay	2,583
Italy	2,467
Nigeria	2,462
France	2,023
Senegal	1,933
Ethiopia	1,829
China	1,814
Morocco	1,549
Benin	1,325
United States	317

Source: "Ranking of Military and Police Contributions to UN Operations," Department of Peacekeeping Operations, United Nations, February 28, 2007

which would have vetoed the American-led invasion, was boycotting the Security Council when the vote to take U.N. action in Korea arose. [34]

As a child, Secretary-General Ban Ki-moon saw the U.N. in action. "As I was growing up in a war-torn and destitute Korea, the United Nations stood by my people in our darkest hour," he recalled. "For the Korean people of that era, the United Nations flag was a beacon of better days to come." [35]

During the Suez Crisis in 1956, the U.N. deployed forces to Egypt, where President Gamal Abdel Nassar had nationalized the Suez Canal, an international waterway that had long been linked to British and French interests. An Israeli invasion and a secretly planned

joint French-British air action combined to confront Egypt, then a client state of the Soviet Union. The move brought East-West tensions to a boil.

To cool the situation, Canada's secretary of state for external affairs, Lester Pearson, suggested sending a U.N. Emergency Force to Egypt. The troops had to be rounded up in a week, but their distinctive light-blue berets had not arrived. So Urquhart had surplus army helmets spray-painted. U.N. peacekeepers henceforth would be recognized around the world as "the blue helmets." [36]

Eventually, pressure from the United States forced Britain, France and Israel to withdraw from the canal. Pearson won the Nobel Prize for his efforts.

U.N. Photo/Maher Attar

Sometimes they fight to keep the peace. In Marrakeh, Lebanon, a French soldier of the United Nations' peacekeeping contingent exchanges gunfire with insurgents of the Shiite militia movement, AMAL.

Congo Quagmire

In the early 1960s U.N. peacekeepers became embroiled in chaos in the fractious, newly created nation of Congo. After gaining independence from Belgium, Congo erupted when strongman Joseph Mobuto seized power, and Prime Minister Patrice Lumumba was assassinated. The struggle quickly turned into a proxy Cold War battle between the United States and the Soviet Union for influence in the region. [37]

Sweden's Dag Hammarskjold, then the U.N. secretary-general, saw in the Congo crisis "an opportunity for the United Nations to assert itself as the world authority in controlling and resolving major international conflicts," writes Poland's Andrzej Sitkowski. "It was his determination, personal com-

mitment and effort which launched the clumsy ship of the organization full speed into the stormy and uncharted waters of Congo. He knew how to start the big gamble, but could not have known how and where it would end." [38]

While shuttling around Congo, a territory the size of Western Europe, Hammarskjold died in a plane crash that was "never sufficiently explained," Sitkowski continues. "It is a tragedy that his commitment and talents were applied, and, ultimately, laid waste in what he himself called a political bordello with a clutch of foreign madams."

The Congo mission cost the lives of 250 peacekeepers but yielded tepid results. Forty years later, U.N. peacekeepers would be back in the country, now known as the Democratic Republic of the Congo.

Other operations have successfully stabilized long-running disputes. In 1964 a U.N. force was deployed to stand between Greece and Turkey over a divided Cyprus. The operation began in 1964, but the island is still divided, and the U.N. force is still present. [39]

During the Cold War stalemate, U.N. peacekeeping had limited goals. As a result, however, it missed the opportunity (some would say moral duty) to stop Cambodian dictator Pol Pot's reign of genocidal terror against his own people. Well more than a million died in Cambodia's "killing fields," where piles of victims' skulls on display to visitors still mark that dark era. Yet the United Nations didn't enter Cambodia until years after the killing ended. [40]

During the 1980s, according to some observers, the United Nations was often stalemated while the Soviet Union and the United States fought over influence at the U.N., and peacekeeping's modest aims reflected the times. "I don't think it was ever designed for victory," Urquhart says. "The peacekeeping business was designed to freeze a potentially very dangerous situation until you got around to negotiating. It was quite successful in that."

Failed Missions

The fall of the Berlin Wall in 1989 heralded the end of the Cold War between the United States and the Soviet Union, as well as an extraordinarily promising start for U.N. action.

In 1991, the Security Council authorized the Persian Gulf War coalition that dislodged Iraqi troops from Kuwait. Though it wasn't fought under a U.N. flag, as in Korea, the first Gulf War demonstrated the U.N.'s clear exercise of military action over words.

Saddam Hussein's 1991 invasion of Kuwait was an unprovoked action by a sovereign nation against another, and clearly prohibited by the U.N. charter.

Continued on p. 92

At Issue:

Does the world community have a "responsibility to protect"?

GARETH EVANS
PRESIDENT, INTERNATIONAL CRISIS GROUP
FORMER CO-CHAIR, INTERNATIONAL COMMISSION ON INTERVENTION AND STATE SOVEREIGNTY

FROM A SPEECH AT STANFORD UNIVERSITY, FEB. 7, 2007

*w*hile the primary responsibility to protect its own people from genocide and other such man-made catastrophes is that of the state itself, when a state fails to meet that responsibility . . . then the responsibility to protect shifts to the international community. . . .

The concept of the "responsibility to protect" [was] formally and unanimously embraced by the whole international community at the U.N. 60th Anniversary World Summit in September 2005 . . . reaffirmed . . . by the Security Council in April 2006, and begun to be incorporated in country-specific resolutions, in particular on Darfur. . . .

But old habits of non-intervention died very hard. Even when situations cried out for some kind of response — and the international community did react through the U.N. — it was too often erratically, incompletely or counter-productively, as in Somalia in 1993, Rwanda in 1994 and Srebrenica in 1995. Then came Kosovo in 1999, when the international community did, in fact, intervene as it probably should have, but did so without the authority of the Security Council. . . .

It is one thing to develop a concept like the responsibility to protect, but quite another to get any policy maker to take any notice of it. . . . We simply cannot be at all confident that the world will respond quickly, effectively and appropriately to new human catastrophes as they arise, as the current case of Darfur is all too unhappily demonstrating. . . .

As always . . . the biggest and hardest piece of unfinished business [is] finding the necessary political will to do anything hard or expensive or politically sensitive or seen as not directly relevant to national interests. . . . We can . . . always justify [the] responsibility to protect . . . on hard-headed, practical, national-interest grounds: States that can't or won't stop internal atrocity crimes are the kind of rogue . . . or failed or failing states that can't or won't stop terrorism, weapons proliferation, drug and people trafficking, the spread of health pandemics and other global risks.

But at the end of the day, the case for responsibility to protect rests simply on our common humanity: the impossibility of ignoring the cries of pain and distress of our fellow human beings. . . . We should be united in our determination to not let that happen, and there is no greater or nobler cause on which any of us could be embarked.

AMBASSADOR ZHENMIN LIU
DEPUTY PERMANENT REPRESENTATIVE PERMANENT MISSION OF THE PEOPLE'S REPUBLIC OF CHINA TO THE UNITED NATIONS

FROM A STATEMENT BEFORE THE U.N. SECURITY COUNCIL, DEC. 4, 2006

*t*he important Security Council Resolution 1674 . . . sets out comprehensive provisions pertaining to the protection of civilians in armed conflict . . . . What is needed now is effective implementation. . . .

First, in accordance with the Charter of the United Nations and international humanitarian law, the responsibility to protect civilians lies primarily with the Governments of the countries concerned. While the international community and other external parties can provide support and assistance . . . they should not infringe upon the sovereignty and territorial integrity of the countries concerned, nor should they enforce intervention by circumventing the governments of the countries concerned.

Second, it is imperative to make clear differentiation between protection of civilians and provision of humanitarian assistance. Efforts made by humanitarian agencies in the spirit of humanitarianism to provide assistance to the civilians affected by armed conflicts . . . should . . . at all times abide by the principles of impartiality, neutrality, objectivity and independence in order to . . . avoid getting involved in local political disputes or negatively affecting a peace process.

Third, to protect civilians, greater emphasis should be placed on prevention as well as addressing both symptoms and root causes of a conflict. Should the Security Council . . . manage to effectively prevent and resolve various conflicts, it would successfully provide the best protection to the civilians. . . . The best protection for civilians is to provide them with a safe and reliable living environment by actively exploring methods to prevent conflicts and effectively redressing the occurring conflicts.

While discussing the issue of protection of civilians in armed conflict, the concept of "responsibility to protect" should continue to be approached with caution by the Security Council. The World Summit Outcome last year gave an extensive and very cautious representation of "the responsibility to protect populations from genocide, war crimes, ethnic cleansing and crimes against humanity." . . . Since many member States have expressed their concern and misgivings in this regard, we believe, it is, therefore, not appropriate to expand, willfully interpret or even abuse this concept. . . .

Finally, we hope that . . . full consideration will be taken of the specific characteristics and circumstances of each conflict so as to adopt appropriate measures with a view to effectively achieving the objective of protecting civilians.

U.S., Japan Pay Most U.N. Peacekeeping Costs

The United States and Japan account for nearly two-thirds of the funds contributed by industrial nations to support the various peacekeeping missions at the United Nations. The U.S. share alone is about 38 percent of the total.

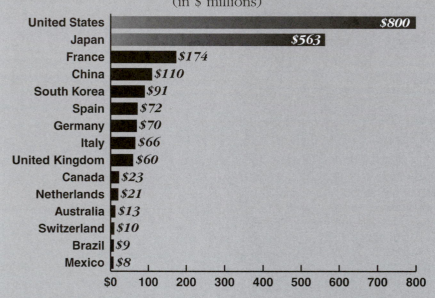

U.N. Peacekeeping Contributions in 2006
(in $ millions)

United States	$800
Japan	$563
France	$174
China	$110
South Korea	$91
Spain	$72
Germany	$70
Italy	$66
United Kingdom	$60
Canada	$23
Netherlands	$21
Australia	$13
Switzerland	$10
Brazil	$9
Mexico	$8

Source: "2006 Status of Contributions to the Regular Budget, International Tribunals, Peacekeeping Operations and Capital Master Plan," United Nations

Continued from p. 90

"I always tell my students," notes international law Professor Smith, "that Saddam was the one guy on Earth dumb enough to do precisely the thing the United Nations was established to prevent."

Heady from that success, U.N. member states sought to transform the new post-Cold War cooperation into a dramatic expansion of United Nations peacekeeping. But its efforts were met by mixed results, and well-known bloody failures in the 1990s when it tried to intervene in critical situations in Africa and Bosnia.

In Somalia, on Africa's eastern horn, ultimately failed peacekeeping efforts led to the rise of warlord Mohamed Farah Aidid and the deaths of 18 U.S. soldiers in the infamous First Battle of Mogadishu. The book and film, "Black Hawk Down," told how a U.S. helicopter was shot down and the bodies of American soldiers were dragged through the streets. The battle left 700 Somalis dead along with a Malaysian and two Pakistanis. [41] Somalia would end up lapsing in lawlessness, and the psychological ramifications of the Somalia debacle still haunt the specter of tough peacekeeping operations. The 1994 Rwandan genocide occurred in central Africa, far from the power centers and concerns of Western aid agencies. The international community, the Clinton administration and the United Nations were all slow to respond, and ineffectual when they did. Canada led U.N. peacekeeping troops in Rwanda, but the reduced force was not authorized or likely able to intervene to prevent the killings.

Former Canadian General Romeo Dallaire, who headed U.N. peace-keeping forces during the Rwandan genocide in 1994, has written the best-selling *Shake Hands with the Devil* in which he criticizes the U.N.'s approach to the conflict. "I have been taking the position from the start that the United Nations is nothing but the front man in this failure," Dallaire states in a BBC interview. "The true culprits are the sovereign states that influence the Security Council, that influence other nations into participating or not." [42]

Bosnia was also a symbol of peacekeeping helplessness. U.N. peacekeepers carved out what they called "safe havens" to protect civilians against the euphemistically called practice of "ethnic cleansing." "Unfortunately, that only created an illusion of safety in an area where there wasn't safety at all," says former New Zealand Ambassador Keating. "That's because there wasn't sufficient personnel."

International expert Smith argues the U.N.'s Bosnia effort was doomed from the start. "They planned it as a humanitarian exercise," he says. "They planned not to use force. And they hamstrung themselves."

The most public example of the United Nations' inability to bring protection or peace, he notes, was when lightly armed Dutch peacekeeping troops were held hostage by Bosnian Serb forces in Srebrenica in July 1995, and turned over thousands of Bosnian Muslims in exchange for the release of 14 Dutch soldiers. The Serbs eventually massacred some 8,000 Bosnian Muslim men and boys in Srebrenica. Photographs of the hapless Dutch were flashed around the world as visible proof that U.N. peacekeepers lacked the ability to defend even themselves.

The Somali and Bosnian experiences were diplomatic, military and humanitarian disasters. "There was no clear operational doctrine for the kinds of things they were doing," says Keating, who served on the U.N. Security Council during that bleak period. "So they made it up as they went along."

Successful Missions

A U.N. mission that helped bring Namibia to independence in 1989 is often cited as a major peacekeeping success story. The U.N. negotiated a protocol allowing the peaceful withdrawal of Marxist rebels from the South-West African Peoples Organization (SWAPO) and Cuban and South African troops.

"Never before had the U.N. devised a peace and independence plan supported by such a web of political agreements, institutional arrangements and administrative buildup," writes Sitkowski, who served with the operation.

In Liberia, a watershed election in 2005 — monitored by the United Nations, the European Union and the Economic Community of West African States — appears to have ended decades of turmoil and violence and translated "security gains into meaningful, political and economic progress," according to the U.N.-supported *Annual Review of Global Peace Operations*. [43]

Liberia's newly elected president, Ellen Johnson-Sirleaf, has become increasingly visible on the world stage. An economist and former U.N. development official with a Harvard master's degree, she has earned the nickname "Iron Lady" for her ability to do tough jobs normally undertaken by "strongmen" in Africa. [44]

"Our peace is so fragile," she said, "that we need a continuation of the U.N. peacekeeping force for at least three to four years, until our own security forces have been restructured and professionalized." [45]

Since 2005 the United Nations' first all-female peacekeeping unit, 103 women from India, has been stationed in Liberia. (*See sidebar, p. 82.*) "The women have quickly become part of Monrovia's urban landscape in their distinctive blue camouflage fatigues and flak jackets," said *The Christian Science Monitor.* "They guard the Ministry of Foreign Affairs, patrol the streets day and night, control crowds at rallies and soccer games and

The first all-female U.N. force, more than 100 policewomen from India, arrives at Liberia's Roberts International Airport in Monrovia on Jan. 30, 2007. The women will spend at least six months in Liberia, a nation emerging from years of brutal civil war.

respond to calls for armed backup from the national police who, unlike the Indian unit, do not carry weapons." [46] ■

CURRENT SITUATION

Force Expansion

The Security Council voted on Jan. 11, 2007, to set up a modest political mission in Nepal to oversee a disarmament and cease-fire accord between the government and former Maoist rebels. [47]

The action came after a spate of significant growth for robust U.N. peacekeeping operations. During the last six months of 2006, the Security Council sent peacekeepers to maintain peace in southern Lebanon, prepare East Timor for reconciliation and stem the violence in Darfur. This built on rapid growth in the numbers and size of peace operations in recent years.

Secretary-General Ban wants to create a new office from the United Nations' 700-person peacekeeping department. It would focus entirely on supporting field operations and provide "a clear line of command, point of responsibility and accountability for field support," says U.N. spokeswoman Montas. That effort would bolster the R2P concept, she says, which is "to protect as rapidly as possible."

Montas points to the confusion and hesitation of the dark moments in the 1990s. "The U.N. had that painful experience of Rwanda and the former Yugoslavia," she says. "Things will have to be done better."

But Ban's peacekeeping reform efforts have been met with hesitation by the General Assembly, leading one European envoy to warn of "death by a thousand meetings." [48]

A major challenge looming for U.N. peacekeeping is the expansion of the force itself. With a potential 40 percent increase in the number of peacekeepers looming in 2007, the Security Council may have to cut short existing operations. That would be a mistake, says former Ambassador Keating. "Leave too early," he says, "chances are you'll be back again in five years."

China and Sudan

In Sudan, mistrust has complicated efforts to get more peacekeeping troops to curb the horrors of Darfur. Sudan's regime, seen as both hostile and uncooperative by the West, is equally suspicious about U.N. involvement.

Sudan's U.N. Ambassador Abdalhaleem accuses Western nations of withholding support for the African Union

Jasmina Zukic, a Muslim who lost 16 family members in the Balkans war, prays at the cemetery in Potocari, Bosnia, where she is waiting for the arrival and reburial of the remains of 610 Bosnian Muslim men, discovered in a mass grave on July 9, 2005. Local Serbs had killed more than 8,000 men and boys under the eyes of U.N. peacekeepers from The Netherlands.

in order to promote U.N. peacekeepers. "Their objective is to make it weak because their objective is to bring blue helmets in Darfur," he charges.

On Feb. 7, during the first visit ever by a Chinese leader to Sudan, President Hu Jintao asked Sudan's President Omar al-Bashir to give the United Nations a bigger role in trying to resolve the conflict in Darfur. Hu also said China wanted to do more business with its key African ally, according to Sudan state media reports.

Beijing has at least a two-fold strategy in courting Africa: political interest in

influencing the 50-plus nations in Africa and a commercial interest in fueling its increasingly voracious economic engine with Sudanese oil and the continent's plentiful natural resources. [49]

Hu had been under Western pressure to do more to use his clout as Sudan's largest oil customer and international investor to push it to accept U.N. peacekeepers in Darfur.

A month later al-Bashir continued his defiance, telling an Arab League meeting in Riyadh, Saudi Arabia, that the proposed U.N.-AU force would be "a violation of Sudan's sovereignty and

a submission by Sudan to outside custodianship." [50]

Arab leaders have been asked to step in to pressure Bashir. After a two-hour meeting with al-Bashir, Saudi Arabian King Abdullah and high-level Arab League and AU representatives, U.N. Secretary-General Ban told reporters, "I think we made progress where there had been an impasse. The king's intervention very much supported my position."

By April 4, as news broke that five AU peacekeepers had been killed in Darfur, Britain and the United States said they were drafting a U.N. resolution to

impose financial sanctions and a possible "no-fly" zone over Darfur to punish Sudan's continued intransigence. Secretary-General Ban asked that a sanction vote be delayed to give him time for more negotiations planned in Africa and New York. [51]

On April 15, Saudi officials said Bashir told King Abdullah that an agreement had been reached for the hybrid AU-U.N. force. But given Bashir and Sudan's record of seeming to cooperate — and then pulling back after reports of agreement — the situation will be uncertain until more peacekeepers are actually in place in Darfur.

Meanwhile, China announced a new military cooperation deal with Sudan, a move one U.N. diplomat described as "pre-emptive." China appeared to be rushing to sign as many deals as possible with Sudan before economic and military sanctions are imposed on Khartoum, he said. [52]

Before Hu's February trip, Western observers, including Deller of the group Responsibility to Protect, had described China as "the great obstructer" in efforts to resolve the Darfur crisis.

Not surprisingly, Hen Wenping, director of African studies at the Chinese Academy of Sciences in Beijing, defended communist China's approach to Darfur: "China's strategy remains the same, and as always, it used quiet diplomacy to keep a constructive engagement, rather than waving a stick." [53]

Traditionally, none of the five permanent, veto-wielding members of the U.N. Security Council contributes many U.N. peacekeeping troops, since their influence in world affairs would compromise their neutrality. But China, one of the five, has emerged as a newly enthusiastic supporter of peacekeeping.

"China firmly supports and actively participates in U.N. peacekeeping operations," said Chinese Ambassador to the U.N. Zhang Yishan in late February. "Up till now, China's contribution in terms of personnel to 15 U.N. peacekeeping operations has reached the level of more than 5,000, and as we speak, there are about 1,000 Chinese peacekeepers serving in 13 mission areas." [54]

"China could flood the market of U.N. peacekeeping if they wanted to," French defense official Guicherd remarks. "Just like they are flooding other markets."

Afghanistan and Beyond

European nations responded tepidly last winter when the U.S.-led alliance in Afghanistan called for more NATO troops, frustrating the Bush administration and NATO officials. The alliance had sought more troops to combat an expected offensive by Taliban insurgents, and top officials warned of dire consequences if European nations didn't deliver. Frustrating NATO military efforts even more, Germany, France and Italy restricted the number of their troops taking part in the heavy fighting in southeastern Afghanistan, where the insurgency has shown its greatest strength. [55]

"I do not think it is right to talk about more and more military means," said German Defense Minster Franz Josef Jung. "When the Russians were in Afghanistan, they had 100,000 troops and didn't win."

Nonetheless, the German cabinet voted in February to send at least six Tornado jets to the front for surveillance operations against the Taliban. "Without security there is no reconstruction," said a chastened Jung, "and without reconstruction there's no security." [56]

The cost of continued combat duty in Afghanistan may influence the debate among NATO nations. Afghanistan has given the NATO organization "their very first taste of significant ground combat," says international law Professor Smith. "They're suffering casualties in ways they had not anticipated. NATO states are beginning to see people coming home in body bags and are wondering why they are involved at all."

Failure in Afghanistan could affect NATO's desire to project its military might in any new peacekeeping operations beyond Europe. "In the long run, there will be enough uncertainty in the world that members of NATO will understand that they must remain capable to some extent, but how far they are willing to stretch themselves will remain under consideration and debate," Smith adds.

Meanwhile, NATO intervention to serve as a buffer between Israel and the Palestinians remains a future possibility, but French defense official Guicherd says NATO is linked too closely with U.S. policy. Given the tension and the acute anti-Americanism in the region, she says, "it wouldn't be a very good idea for the time being." [57]

But NATO member Turkey could provide an entré into the Middle East, points out Smith. Turkey enjoys good relations with Israel and is a majority-Muslim country whose troops might be more acceptable to Arab populations. Smith calls it an "interesting idea. . . . Turkey has NATO [military] capabilities. They might actually play a meaningful role."

As *Turkish Daily News* columnist Hans De Wit put it, "The current situation in the Middle East is, in fact, a perfect chance for Turkey to show its negotiating skills, since its has good relations with all countries in this region.

"But somehow, its image as a former conqueror doesn't help. Turkey has done a terrible job in convincing the world that its intentions . . . are sincere; that it can bring mediation to the region and can be a stabilizer of importance." [58] ∎

OUTLOOK

Is the World Ready?

As the still-uncertain response to Darfur indicates, countries around the world and at the United Nations are not rushing to every emergency call. "The international community has to prove that it is willing to step into difficult situations — and it may yet again," says former New Zealand Ambassador Keating. "But I wouldn't assume that it would every time."

The high ideals and bold aims articulated by the Responsibility to Protect doctrine may be tempered not only by whether the world has the will to send troops in to halt a massacre but also by whether there will be enough troops.

While it strives to play an increasing role around the world, NATO may be tied down at home. Kosovo is set to receive some form of U.N.-decreed independence from a reluctant Serbia, but the Balkans could again be rocked by the kind of bloody ethnic violence that marked the 1990s.

Such renewed ethnic hostility could challenge the NATO stabilization force, requiring the alliance to bolster its troop counts in Kosovo — and slow NATO efforts to export its peacekeeping influence elsewhere.

As the R2P concept takes root, however, pressure may increase for the kind of muscular intervention that only military forces like NATO troops can deliver.

"The right of an individual to live is a higher priority, at least in theory, than the right of states to do as they please," says former U.S. diplomat Feinstein. "Something important is happening in theory, and practice is lagging very far behind."

More than just words will be needed to make the Responsibility to Protect viable, says U.N. spokeswoman Montas. "The political will has to be there," she says, "and the political will has to come from the Security Council."

There is plenty of military might around the world to translate "theory into reality," according to former Australian foreign minister Evans. "The U.N. is feeling desperately overstretched . . . but with the world's armed services currently involving some 20 million men and women in uniform (with another 50 million reservists, and 11 million paramilitaries)," he observes, "it hardly seems beyond the wit of man to work out a way of making some of that capacity available . . . to prevent and react to man-made catastrophe." [59]

For many people, U.N. police official Lopes says, "We are the last port before Hell."

Having served on the Security Council during the Rwanda bloodbath, former Ambassador Keating knows all too well the limitations of U.N. action. Each case is weighed on "its own particular location in time as well as geography — and whether or not the resources are physically available to undertake the task that's envisaged," he says.

In Darfur, for example, there is the additional problem of mistakenly harming civilians, he says, so the council must weigh the "kind of scenario in which the bad guys and the good guys are almost stuck together." That's "one of the daunting things that's confronting any action with respect to Sudan — being "realistic" about the situation," he says.

"It's unforgivable, really, when you think about the 'Never Again' statements" made after the Holocaust, Keating says, "but the reality is at the moment there's no willingness to do it."

Peacekeeping expert Holt, at the Stimson Center, calls peacekeeping "an enduring tool," even though "it's always criticized for falling short of our hopes. But we keep turning back to it.

"A lot of these lessons are learnable and fixable," she adds. Peacekeeping continues to evolve, it's a moving exercise," with very real global stakes. "Millions of people's lives remain in the balance if we don't get this right." ■

Notes

[1] Speech by Ban Ki-moon on Jan. 29, 2007, delivered as a video message.

[2] Feinstein's comments on the civilian and military issues involved in the right to protect can be found at the Council on Foreign Relations Web site: www.cfr.org/publication/12458/priority_for_new_un_secretarygeneral.html?breadcrumb=%2Fpublication%2Fby_type%2Fnews_release%3Fid%3D328.

[3] Quoted in Lee Michael Katz, "The Man Behind The Movie," *National Journal*, April 22, 2006.

[4] From U.N. Secretary-General Ban Ki-moon's address to the Center for Strategic and International Studies in Washington, D.C., Jan. 16, 2007.

[5] U.N. Department of Peacekeeping Operations, "Fact Sheet," May 2006.

[6] "Peacekeeping and Related Stabilization Operations," CRS Report for Congress, Congressional Research Service, July 13, 2006.

[7] U.N. Department of Peacekeeping Operations, *op. cit.*

[8] Quoted in "From Cologne to Berlin and Beyond — Operations, Institutions and Capabilities," address to European Security and Defense Policy Conference, Jan. 29, 2007.

[9] Organization for Security and Co-operation in Europe (OSCE); www.osce.org/activities.

[10] "The Responsibility to Protect," Report of the International Commission on Intervention and State Sovereignty, December 2001, p. VII.

[11] Gareth Evans, *The Responsibility to Protect: The New Global Moral Compact* (forthcoming, 2007).

[12] "World Summit Outcome," U.N. General Assembly, 60th Session, Sept. 20, 2005, Item 39, p. 31.

[13] Quoted in United Nations summary of Holocaust Commemoration speeches, Jan. 29, 2007.

[14] Quoted in Luiza Ch. Savage, "Canada's 'Responsibility to Protect' Doctrine Gaining Ground at the UN, *Maclean's*, July 18, 2005.

[15] "Chávez Criticizes U.N. Reform in Speech," The Associated Press, Sept. 17, 2005.

[16] Luiza Ch. Savage, *op. cit.*; and Paul Reynolds, "Western Pressure Fails to Move Sudan," BBC Online, Oct. 23, 2006; http://news.bbc.co.uk/2/hi/africa/6076698.stm.

[17] Quoted in "Gadhafi: U.N. Darfur Force is Ruse to Grab Sudan's Oil," Reuters, Nov. 20, 2006, Global Research online; www.globalresearch.ca/index.php?context=viewArticle&code=20061120&articleId=3934.

[18] Chinua Akukwe, "Why the Darfur Tragedy Will Likely Occur Again," July 28, 2004, Worldpress.org; www.worldpress.org/Africa/1905.cfm.

[19] William G. O'Neill, "The Responsibility to Protect," *The Christian Science Monitor*, Sept. 28, 2006; www.csmonitor.com/2006/0928/p0928/p09s01-coop.html. O'Neill is senior adviser to the Brookings Institution Project on Internal Displacement.

[20] African Union, *Protocol Relating to the Establishment of the Peace and Security Council of the African Union* (Durban: African Union, July 2002).

[21] David Newman and Joel Peters, "Kosovo as the West Bank, Macedonia as Israel," commentary, *Ha'aretz*, Oct. 30, 2002.

[22] For an analysis of the problems and potential of an African peacekeeping force, see World Politics Watch; www.worldpoliticswatch.com/article.aspx?id=429.

[23] "Aid Agencies Urge Donor Support for African Union Mission in Darfur," *Oxfam America* Online, July 20, 2006; www.oxfamamerica.org/.

[24] See United Nations Security Council Meeting on cooperation with regional organizations, Sept. 20, 2006, http://daccessdds.un.org/doc/UNDOC/PRO/N06/528/73/PDF/N065287.pdf?OpenElement.

[25] Roland Paris, from *Review of International Studies*, British International Studies Association (2002), pp. 637-656.

[26] Center for International Cooperation, *Annual Review of Global Peace Operations*, February 2006; www.cic.nyu.edu.

[27] Alex Diceanu, "For Many Haitians, MINUSTAH Has Been Closer to a Foreign Occupation Force than a U.N. Peacekeeping Mission,"

About the Author

Lee Michael Katz has been a senior diplomatic correspondent for *USA Today*, the International Editor of UPI, and an independent policy journalist who has written lengthy articles on foreign policy, terrorism, and national security. He has reported from more than 60 countries. He holds an MS from Columbia and has traveled frequently with the U.S. Secretary of State.

Peace Magazine, April 2006; www.globalpolicy.org/security/issues/haiti/2006/04better.htm.

[28] Marc Lacey, "U.N. Troops Fight Haiti Gangs One Battered Street at a Time," *New York Times*, Feb. 10 2007, p. A1.

[29] See *World History*, McDougal Litell (2005).

[30] *Encyclopedia Britannica* online; http://concise.britannica.com/ebc/article-9039167/Hanseatic-League.

[31] David Brewer, *The Greek War of Independence: The Struggle for Freedom from Ottoman Oppression and the Birth of the Modern Greek Nation* (2001).

[32] Naval Historical Center, "The Boxer Rebellion and the U.S. Navy, 1900-1901"; www.history.navy.mil/faqs/faq86-1.htm.

[33] For background, see www.answers.com/topic/league-of-nations.

[34] For background, see www.historylearningsite.co.uk/korea.htm.

[35] Quoted in "Ban Ki-moon calls on new generation to take better care of Planet Earth than his own," U.N. News Centre, March 1, 2007; www.un.org/apps/news/story.asp?NewsID=21720&Cr=global&Cr1=warming.

[36] James Traub, interviewed on "Fresh Air," National Public Radio, Oct. 31, 2006.

[37] For a summary of the Congo's ongoing war, see Simon Robinson and Vivienne Walt, "The Deadliest War In The World," *Time*, May 28, 2006; www.time.com/time/magazine/article/0,9171,1198921-1,00.html.

[38] Adrzej Sitkowski, *UN Peacekeeping Myth and Reality* (2006).

[39] For background on the Congo crisis, see Justin Pearce, "DR Congo's Troubled History," BBC Online, Jan. 16, 2001; http://news.bbc.co.uk/1/hi/world/africa/1120825.stm.

[40] The Cambodia Genocide Project at Yale University includes a definition of genocide as well as information on a Responsibility to Protect Initiative at Yale University Online; www.yale.edu/cgp/.

[41] For a detailed account of the Somalia action, see Mark Bowden, "Black Hawk Down: An American War Story", *The Philadelphia Enquirer*, Nov. 16, 1997.

[42] Interview with BBC, "Eyewitness: UN in Rwanda 1994," Sept. 6, 2000, news.bbc.co.uk.

[43] *Annual Review of Global Peace Operations 2006*, op. cit.

[44] For background, see http://africanhistory.about.com/od/liberia/p/Sirleaf.htm.

[45] Quoted in "Liberia's New President," News Hour Online, March 23, 2006; www.pbs.org/newshour/bb/africa/jan-june06/liberia_3-23.html.

[46] Tristan McConnell, "All female unit keeps

FOR MORE INFORMATION

African Union, P.O. Box 3243, Addis Ababa, Ethiopia; (251)-11-551-77-00; www.africa-union.org. Promotes cooperation among the nations of Africa.

European Union Force, Rue de la Loi, 175 B-1048 Brussels, Belgium; (32-2)-281-61-11; www.consilium.europa.eu. Military detachments currently in Bosnia and Herzegovina and the Democratic Republic of the Congo.

International Commission on Intervention and State Sovereignty, 125 Sussex Dr., Ottawa, Ontario K1A 0G2; www.iciss.ca. Independent commission established by the Canadian government that promotes humanitarian intervention.

International Crisis Group, 149 Avenue Louise, Level 24, B-1050 Brussels, Belgium; +32-(0)-2-502-90-38; www.crisisgroup.org. Non-governmental organization using field-based analysis and high-level advocacy to prevent violent conflict worldwide.

Multinational Force and Observers, +39-06-57-11-94-44; www.mfo.org. International peacekeeping force on Sinai Peninsula monitoring military build-up of Egypt and Israel.

North Atlantic Treaty Organization, Blvd. Leopold III, 1110 Brussels, Belgium; +32-(0)-2-707-50-41; www.nato.int. Safeguards NATO member countries via military and political means.

Organization for Security and Co-operation in Europe, Kaerntner Ring 5-7, 1010 Vienna, Austria; +43-1-514-36-0; www.osce.org. World's largest regional security organization serves as a forum for political negotiations and decision-making in conflict prevention and crisis management.

Responsibility to Protect, 708 Third Ave., 24th Fl., New York, NY 10017; (212) 599-1320; www.responsibilitytoprotect.org. Advocacy group working to protect vulnerable populations from war crimes and crimes against humanity.

United Nations Department of Peacekeeping Operations, 760 U.N. Plaza, New York, NY 10017; (202) 963-1234; www.un.org/Depts/dpko/dpko. Responsible for all U.N. peacekeeping missions mandated by the Security Council.

peace in Liberia," *The Christian Science Monitor* online, March 21, 2005; http://news.yahoo.com/s/csm/20070321/ts_csm/ofemmeforce_1.

[47] Warren Hoge, "World Briefing: Asia: Nepal: U.N. Creating New Political Mission," *The New York Times*, Jan. 24, 2007.

[48] Evelyn Leopold, "U.N. Chief's Reform Plans May Be Stalled in Meetings," Reuters, Feb. 5, 2007.

[49] Alfred de Montesquiou, "Chinese president tells Sudan counterpart he must do more for peace in Darfur," The Associated Press, Feb. 2, 2007.

[50] Quoted in Warren Hoge, "Arabs and U.N. Chief Press Sudan's Leader to End Darfur Crisis," *The New York Times*, March 29, 2007, p. A5.

[51] See Colum Lynch, "U.N. Chief Seeks to Delay Sanctions Against Sudan," *The Washington Post*, April 3, 2007, p. A15.

[52] *Ibid.*

[53] Howard W. French, with Fan Wexin, "Chinese Leader to Visit Sudan for Talks on Darfur Con-

flict," *The New York Times* online, Jan. 25, 2007.

[54] Statement by Ambassador Zhang Yishan at the 2006 Session of the Special Committee on Peacekeeping Operations, United Nations, Feb. 27, 2006. Full statement available at www.fmprc.gov.cn/ce/ceun/eng/xw/t237291.htm.

[55] Michael Abramowitz, "Afghanistan Called 'Key Priority' For NATO," *The Washington Post*, Nov. 30, 2006.

[56] Kate Connolly, "Germany beefs up Afghan presence with six fighter jets," *The Guardian* Online, Feb. 8, 2007; full story at www.guardian.co.uk/afghanistan/story/0,,2008088,00.html.

[57] For background, see Samuel Loewenberg, "Anti-Americanism," *CQ Global Researcher*, March 2007, pp. 51-74.

[58] Hans A. H.C. DeWit, "Turkey Needs Confidence, Not Fear," *Turkish Daily News* Online, Feb. 16, 2007; www.turkishdailynews.com.tr/article.php?enewsid=66304.

[59] Evans, *op. cit.*

Bibliography

Selected Sources

Books

Cassidy, Robert, *Peacekeeping In The Abyss: British and American Peacekeeping Doctrine and Practice after the Cold War*, **Praeger, 2004.**

A Special Forces officer and international relations scholar examines and compares U.S. military efforts in Somalia and British operations in Bosnia in an effort to understand which military cultural traits and force structures are more suitable and adaptable for peace operations and asymmetric conflicts.

Danieli, Yael, *Sharing The Front Line And The Back Hills: Peacekeepers Humanitarian Aid Workers And The Media In The Midst Of Crisis*, **Baywood, 2002.**

A clinical psychologist who is co-founder of the Group Project for Holocaust Survivors and Their Children gives voice to the victims of traumatic hotspots such as Kosovo, Haiti and Burundi.

Franke, Volker, ed., *Terrorism and Peacekeeping, New Security Challenges*, **Praeger, 2005.**

An associate professor of international studies at McDaniel College presents numerous case studies in order to examine the challenges to national security policymakers posed by peacekeeping and terrorism.

Johnstone, Ian, ed., *Annual Review of Global Peace Operations 2006*, **Lynne Rienner Publishers, 2006.**

A senior U.N. official and former senior associate at the International Peace Academy examines U.N. missions around the world; includes numerous statistics and also frank observations on peacekeeping's failures and limitations.

Luck, Edward, *The U.N. Security Council: Practice and Promise*, **Routledge, 2006.**

A Columbia University professor and longtime U.N. watcher examines the Security Council's roller-coaster history of military enforcement and sees a "politically awkward division of labor" between major powers and developing countries.

Sitkowski, Adrzej, *U.N. Peacekeeping Myth and Reality*, **Praeger Security International, 2006.**

A veteran U.N. official reflects on peacekeeping operations with a very critical eye; includes an inside look at serving in Namibia, regarded as a model of U.N. success.

Smith, Michael G., with Moreen Dee, *Peacekeeping In East Timor: The Path To Independence*, **International Peace Academy Occasional Series, Lynne Rienner Publishers, 2003.**

"General Mike" Smith, who led the U.N. force in East Timor, concludes broadly there are no "templates" for peacekeeping and that lessons from previous missions were not fully learned.

Traub, James, *The Best Intentions: Kofi Annan and the UN in the Era of American World Power*, **Farrar, Straus and Giroux, 2006.**

A *New York Times* reporter critically portrays U.N. operations through the eyes and staff machinations of the recently departed secretary-general.

Articles

Dalder, Ivo, and James Goldgeiger, "Global NATO," *Foreign Affairs*, **September/October, 2006, p. A1.**

The authors argue that expanding NATO membership, even beyond Europe, can boost the security organization's new peacekeeping role.

Katz, Lee Michael, "The Man Behind The Movie," *National Journal*, **April 22, 2006.**

In an interview, Paul Rusesabagina, the real-life Hotel Rwanda manager, offers a witness to genocide's first-hand perspective, finding the U.N. "useless" in Rwanda.

Lacey, Marc, "U.N. Troops Fight Haiti Gangs One Battered Street at a Time," *The New York Times*, **Feb. 10 2007, p. A1.**

A look at "Evans," a gang leader who controls the slums and lives of 300,000 people in Haiti's Port-au-Prince — and U.N. peacekeeping troops' attempts to take him down.

Reports and Studies

"Darfur and Beyond: What Is Needed To Prevent Mass Casualties," Council on Foreign Relations, January 2007.

A carefully timed report suggests actions that should be taken by the new U.N. secretary-general, NATO, the European and African unions and the United States to prevent future genocides.

"The Responsibility To Protect," Report Of The International Commission On Intervention and State Sovereignty, December 2001.

Diplomats from Australia to Russia provide the intellectual underpinnings of The Responsibility to Protect in this landmark report. Because of the report's timing, it doesn't address the aftermath of the Sept. 11, 2001, attacks in depth.

"The Responsibility To Protect: The U.N. World Summit and the Question of Unilateralism," *The Yale Law Journal*, **March 2006.**

This cautious look at The Responsibility to Protect argues that it limits military action to narrow and extreme circumstances and can be used as a pretext to invade another nation.

The Next Step:

Additional Articles from Current Periodicals

Peace Building

"Thai Government Sets Up Management Policy for Peace-Building in Thailand's Southernmost Provinces," *Thai Press Reports*, June 6, 2005.

In an effort to streamline security operations for peace building in southern Thailand, the government has set up a Committee on Southern Border Provinces Peace-Building Policy.

Murithi, Tim, and Helen Scanlon, "Building Peace When War is Over," *Business Day* **(South Africa), Nov. 8, 2006.**

Burundi and Sierra Leone were selected as the first test cases for the U.N. Peacebuilding Commission, which emphasizes international post-conflict reconstruction.

Purohit, Raj, and José Ramos Horta, "A UN Role in Timor Leste," *The Boston Globe*, **July 4, 2006, p. A11.**

Peace-building processes must pay attention to a nation's need to feed, govern, employ and heal itself, but the world failed to offer sufficient assistance to Timor-Leste.

Regional Peacekeeping

"Pinch that Minister!; Australia and the Island-States," *The Economist*, **Oct. 28, 2006, p. 51.**

Manasseh Sogavare, prime minister of the Solomon Islands, presented a plan to reduce Australia's part in the Regional Assistance Mission to his country.

"Security Council Backs Regional Peacekeeping Force for Somalia," Agence France-Presse, Dec. 6, 2006.

The U.N. has backed a U.S.-drafted resolution that endorses the deployment to Somalia of a peacekeeping mission manned by 8,000 troops from the east African regional Inter-Governmental Authority on Development.

Simamora, Adianto P., "ASEAN Conflict Resolution Mechanisms Needed," *Jakarta Post*, **Feb. 25, 2004.**

Indonesian Minister of Foreign Affairs Hassan Wirayuda said that current security challenges warrant the establishment of an ASEAN regional peacekeeping force.

Responsibility to Protect

"UN Says International Community Not Doing Enough in Strife-Torn Areas," *Press Trust of India*, **Dec. 1, 2006.**

The top aid official at the U.N. has accused the international community of not living up to its responsibilities to protect people in strife-torn areas such as Iraq and Gaza.

"Will They Be Rescued?," *The Economist*, **Sept. 23, 2006, p. 51.**

On the eve of the 61st U.N. General Assembly, 32 member states held events persuading their governments to rec-

ognize a responsibility to protect civilians of Darfur.

Akosile, Abimbola, "Adequate Global Protection, Whose Responsibility?" *This Day* **(Nigeria), Sept. 26, 2006.**

A World Federalist Movement meeting in Abuja raised suggestions on the application of the Responsibility to Protect principle to specific crises.

Gyau Orhin, Isabella, "A Call to Duty," *Public Agenda* **(Ghana), Feb. 19, 2007.**

Ghana's role in international peacekeeping is paramount, given that President John Kufuor is now the African Union chairman.

Sexual Exploitation

"UN Security Council Moves Against Peacekeepers," Panafrican News Agency (Ethiopia), June 3, 2005.

Proper investigation and subsequent punishment of U.N. peacekeepers have been ordered by the Security Council in what is believed to have been sexual abuse of local populations in the Democratic Republic of the Congo.

Lynch, Colum, "Report on Abuse Urges DNA Tests for Peacekeepers," *The Washington Post*, **March 25, 2005, p. A15.**

A report to the U.N. proposes DNA tests for peacekeepers to determine whether they have sexually abused women while on a mission.

Thakur, Ramesh, "Action Must Be Taken Against Peacekeeper Sexual Predators," *Yomiuri Shimbun* **(Japan), March 6, 2006.**

If the United Nations is to maintain its human rights credibility, peacekeepers committing sexual abuse in its name must face investigation and prosecution.

CITING CQ GLOBAL RESEARCHER

Sample formats for citing these reports in a bibliography include the ones listed below. Preferred styles and formats vary, so please check with your instructor or professor.

MLA STYLE

Flamini, Roland. "Nuclear Proliferation." CQ Global Researcher 1 Apr. 2007: 1-24.

APA STYLE

Flamini, R. (2007, April 1). Nuclear proliferation. *CQ Global Researcher*, 1, 1-24.

CHICAGO STYLE

Flamini, Roland. "Nuclear Proliferation." *CQ Global Researcher*, April 1, 2007, 1-24.

Voices From Abroad:

INTERNATIONAL CRISIS GROUP BRUSSELS SEPT. 2006

"Darfur simply does not matter"

"The sad reality is that Darfur simply does not matter enough, and Sudan matters too much, for the international community to do more to stop the atrocities. Much as governments in Europe and the U.S. are disturbed by what is happening in Darfur — and they genuinely are — almost without exception they are not prepared to commit their troops on the ground in Sudan. . . . The issue is problematic for the U.S. because it has a close intelligence relationship with the Sudanese government in its war on terror."

KOFI ANNAN SECRETARY-GENERAL, UNITED NATIONS MARCH 2005

"Policy of zero tolerance"

"I am especially troubled by instances in which United Nations peacekeepers are alleged to have sexually exploited minors and other vulnerable people, and I have enacted a policy of 'zero tolerance' towards such offences that applies to all personnel engaged in United Nations operations. I strongly encourage Member States to do the same with respect to their national contingents."

CENTRE FOR RESEARCH ON GLOBALIZATION CANADA MAY 2006

"Third World intervention"

"We in the West tend to believe that if a white developed country is sending troops to the Third World, it must be a good thing. But until we can envision a situation where Third World intervention against the U.S. or other great powers is realistic and possible, the 'Responsibility to Protect' exists simply as a tool for 'us' in the West to continue subjugating and running the affairs of other countries. Those who would have us intervene in Sudan on the basis of combating unrest under the 'Responsibility to Protect' would have us face the ridiculous situation, as in Kosovo, of 'needing' to violate a country's sovereignty as a result of the West having previously violated it."

WALDEN BELLO EXECUTIVE DIRECTOR, FOCUS ON THE GLOBAL SOUTH (BANGKOK) JAN. 2006

"Dump humanitarian intervention"

"We must forcefully delegitimize this dangerous doctrine of humanitarian intervention to prevent its being employed again in the future against candidates for great power intervention like Iran and Venezuela. Like its counterpart concept of 'liberal imperialism,' there is only one thing to do with the concept of humanitarian intervention: dump it."

OXFORD RESEARCH GROUP UNITED KINGDOM APRIL 2004

"Intervention should be widened"

"Can a universally acceptable humanitarian doctrine still be articulated and defended by the international community? We believe that for the sake of humanity, the answer has to be yes. But this will require civil society doing more to hold governments to account, and building transparency and trust into the processes that lead to a decision to go to war. It will require a return to and further development of the concepts of the ICISS report on 'The Responsibility to Protect.' . . . The understanding of 'intervention' should be widened to include methods of conflict prevention and resolution other than the use of military force."

NOZIZWE MADLALA-ROUTLEDGE DEPUTY MINISTER OF HEALTH, SOUTH AFRICA JULY 2004

"Current approach pays lip service"

"The current U.N. approach entails merely disarming combatants and does not address the dismantling of war economies and effectively re-integrating ex-combatants into society, which is at the root of the problem. The approach pays lip service to gender equality by not taking cognisance of the specific needs of women ex-combatants or the violation of the rights of women by peacekeepers. . . . The delay between the start of peacekeeping operations and the start of peace-building and socio-economic development interventions reduces the ability to absorb combatants into the formal economy and to dismantle the war economy."

WOMEN'S RIGHTS

BY KAREN FOERSTEL

Excerpted from the CQ Global Researcher. Karen Foerstel. (May 2008). "Women's Rights." *CQ Global Researcher*, 115-147.

Women's Rights

BY KAREN FOERSTEL

THE ISSUES

She was 17 years old. The blurry video shows her lying in a dusty road, blood streaming down her face, as several men kick and throw rocks at her. At one point she struggles to sit up, but a man kicks her in the face forcing her back to the ground. Another slams a large, concrete block down onto her head. Scores of onlookers cheer as the blood streams from her battered head. [1]

The April 7, 2007, video was taken in the Kurdish area of northern Iraq on a mobile phone. It shows what appear to be several uniformed police officers standing on the edge of the crowd, watching while others film the violent assault on their phones.

The brutal, public murder of Du'a Khalil Aswad reportedly was organized as an "honor killing" by members of her family — and her uncles and a brother allegedly were among those in the mob who beat her to death. Her crime? She offended her community by falling in love with a man outside her religious sect. [2]

According to the United Nations, an estimated 5,000 women and girls are murdered in honor killings each year, but it was only when the video of Aswad's murder was posted on the Internet that the global media took notice. [3]

Such killings don't only happen in remote villages in developing countries. Police in the United Kingdom estimate that up to 17,000 women are subjected to some kind of "honor"-related violence each year, ranging from forced marriages and physical attacks to murder. [4]

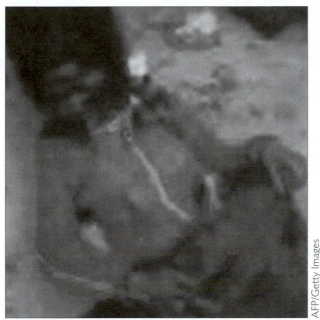

Iraqi teenager Du'a Khalil Aswad lies mortally wounded after her "honor killing" by a mob in the Kurdish region of Iraq. No one has been prosecuted for the April 2007 murder, even though a cell-phone video of the incident was posted on the Internet. Aswad's male relatives are believed to have arranged her ritualistic execution because she had dated a boy from outside her religious sect. The United Nations estimates that 5,000 women and girls are murdered in honor killings around the globe each year.

AFP/Getty Images

But honor killings are only one type of what the international community calls "gender based violence" (GBV). "It is universal," says Taina Bien-Aimé, executive director of the New York-based women's-rights group Equality Now. "There is not one country in the world where violence against women doesn't exist."

Thousands of women are murdered or attacked around the world each day, frequently with impunity. In Guatemala, where an estimated 3,000 women have been killed over the past seven years, most involving some kind of misogynistic violence, only 1 percent of the perpetrators were convicted. [5] In India, the United Nations estimates that five women are burned to death each day by husbands upset that they did not receive sufficient dowries from their brides. [6] In Asia, nearly 163

million females are "missing" from the population — the result of sex-selective abortions, infanticide or neglect.

And since the 1990s some African countries have seen dramatic upsurges in rapes of very young girls by men who believe having sex with a virgin will protect or cure them from HIV-AIDS. After a 70-year-old man allegedly raped a 3-year-old girl in northern Nigeria's commercial hub city of Kano, Deputy Police Chief Suleiman Abba told reporters in January, "Child rape is becoming rampant in Kano." In the last six months of 2007, he said, 54 cases of child rape had been reported. "In some cases the victims are gang-raped." [7]

Epidemics of sexual violence commonly break out in countries torn apart by war, when perpetrators appear to have no fear of prosecution. Today, in Africa, for instance, UNICEF says there is now a "license to rape" in eastern regions of the Democratic Republic of the Congo, where some human-rights experts estimate that up to a quarter of a million women have been raped and often sexually mutilated with knives, branches or machetes. [8] Several of the Congolese rapists remorselessly bragged to an American filmmaker recently about how many women they had gang-raped. [9]

"The sexual violence in Congo is the worst in the world," said John Holmes, the United Nations under secretary general for humanitarian affairs. "The sheer numbers, the wholesale brutality, the culture of impunity — it's appalling." [10]

In some cultures, the female victims themselves are punished. A report by the Human Rights Commission of Pakistan found that a woman is gang-raped every eight hours in that

Only Four Countries Offer Total Equality for Women

Costa Rica, Cuba, Sweden and Norway receive the highest score (9 points) in an annual survey of women's economic, political and social rights. Out of the world's 193 countries, only 26 score 7 points or better, while 28 — predominantly Islamic or Pacific Island countries — score 3 or less. The United States rates 7 points: a perfect 3 on economic rights but only 2 each for political and social rights. To receive 3 points for political rights, women must hold at least 30 percent of the seats in the national legislature. Women hold only 16.6 percent of the seats in the U.S. Congress. The U.S. score of 2 on social rights reflects what the report's authors call "high societal discrimination against women's reproductive rights."

Status of Women's Rights Around the Globe

What the Ratings Mean:

7-9	Offer the most equality for women
4-6	Offer moderate equality for women
0-3	Offer the least equality for women
	Data not available

Source: Cingranelli-Richards Human Rights Dataset, http://ciri.binghamton.edu/, based on Amnesty International's annual reports and U.S. State Department annual Country Reports on Human Rights. The database is co-directed by David Louis Cingranelli, a political science professor at Binghamton University, SUNY, and David L. Richards, an assistant political science professor at the University of Memphis.

country. Yet, until recently, rape cases could not be prosecuted in Pakistan unless four Muslim men "all of a pious and trustworthy nature" were willing to testify that they witnessed the attack. Without their testimony the victim could be prosecuted for fornication and alleging a false crime, punishable by stoning, lashings or prison. [11] When the law was softened in 2006 to allow judges to decide whether to try rape cases in Islamic courts or criminal courts, where such witnesses are not required, thousands took to the streets to protest the change. [12]

Honor killings are up 400 percent in Pakistan over the last two years, and Pakistani women also live in fear of being blinded or disfigured by "acid attacks" — a common practice in Pakistan and a handful of other countries — in which attackers, usually spurned suitors, throw acid on a woman's face and body.

But statistics on murder and violence are only a part of the disturbing figures on the status of women around the globe. Others include:

- Some 130 million women have undergone female genital mutilation, and another 2 million are at risk every year, primarily in Africa and Yemen.
- Women and girls make up 70 percent of the world's poor and two-thirds of its illiterate.
- Women work two-thirds of the total hours worked by men but earn only 10 percent of the income.
- Women produce more than half of the world's food but own less than 1 percent of the world's property.
- More than 500,000 women die during pregnancy and childbirth every year — 99 percent of them in developing countries.
- Two million girls between the ages of 5 and 15 are forced into the commercial sex market each year. [13]
- Globally, 10 million more girls than boys do not attend school. [14]

Despite these alarming numbers, women have made historic progress in some areas. The number of girls receiving an education has increased in the past decade. Today 57 percent of children not attending school are girls, compared to two-thirds in the 1990s. [15]

And women have made significant gains in the political arena. As of March, 2008, 14 women are serving as elected heads of state or government, and women now hold 17.8 percent of the world's parliamentary seats — more than ever before. [16] And just three months after the brutal killing of Aswad in Iraq, India swore in its first female president, Pratibha Patil, who vows to

Continued on p. 121

Women's Suffering Is Widespread

More than two decades after the U.N. Decade for Women and 29 years after the U.N. adopted the Convention on the Elimination of All Forms of Discrimination against Women (CEDAW), gender discrimination remains pervasive throughout the world, with widespread negative consequences for society.

According to recent studies on the status of women today:

- Violence against women is pervasive. It impoverishes women, their families, communities and nations by lowering economic productivity and draining resources. It also harms families across generations and reinforces other violence in societies.
- Domestic violence is the most common form of violence against women, with rates ranging from 8 percent in Albania to 49 percent in Ethiopia and Zambia. Domestic violence and rape account for 5 percent of the disease burden for women ages 15 to 44 in developing countries and 19 percent in developed countries.
- Femicide — the murder of women — often involves sexual violence. From 40 to 70 percent of women murdered in Australia, Canada, Israel, South Africa and the United States are killed by husbands or boyfriends. Hundreds of women were abducted, raped and murdered in and around Juárez, Mexico, over the past 15 years, but the crimes have never been solved.
- At least 160 million females, mostly in India and China, are "missing" from the population — the result of sex-selective abortions.
- Rape is being used as a genocidal tool. Hundreds of thousands of women have been raped and sexually mutilated in the ongoing conflict in Eastern Congo. An estimated 250,000 to 500,000 women were raped during the 1994 genocide in Rwanda; up to 50,000 women were raped during the Bosnian conflict in the 1990s. Victims are often left unable to have children and are deserted by their husbands and shunned by their families, plunging the women and their children into poverty.
- Some 130 million girls have been genitally mutilated, mostly in Africa and Yemen, but also in immigrant communities in the West.
- Child rape has been on the increase in the past decade in some African countries, where some men believe having sex with a virgin will protect or cure them from HIV-AIDS. A study at the Red Cross children's hospital in Cape Town, South Africa, found that 3-year-old girls were more likely to be raped than any other age group.
- Two million girls between the ages of 5 and 15 are forced into the commercial sex market each year, many of them trafficked across international borders.
- Sexual harassment is pervasive. From 40 to 50 percent of women in the European Union reported some form of sexual harassment at work; 50 percent of schoolgirls surveyed in Malawi reported sexual harassment at school.
- Women and girls constitute 70 percent of those living on less than a dollar a day and 64 percent of the world's illiterate.
- Women work two-thirds of the total hours worked by men and women but earn only 10 percent of the income.
- Half of the world's food is produced by women, but women own only 1 percent of the world's land.
- More than 1,300 women die each day during pregnancy and childbirth — 99 percent of them in developing countries.

Sources: "Ending violence against women: From words to action," United Nations, October, 2006, www.un.org/womenwatch/daw/public/VAW_Study/VAW studyE.pdf; www.womankind.org.uk; www.unfp.org; www.oxfam.org.uk; www.ipu.org; www.unicef.org; www.infant-trust.org.uk; "State of the World Population 2000;" http://npr.org; http://asiapacific.amnesty.org; http://news.bbc.co.uk

Negative Attitudes Toward Women Are Pervasive

Negative attitudes about women are widespread around the globe, among women as well as men. Rural women are more likely than city women to condone domestic abuse if they think it was provoked by a wife's behavior.

| Location | Percentage of women in selected countries who agree that a man has good reason to beat his wife if: | | | | | | Women who agree with: | |
	Wife does not complete housework	Wife disobeys her husband	Wife refuses sex	Wife asks about other women	Husband suspects infidelity	Wife is unfaithful	One or more of the reasons mentioned	None of the reasons mentioned
Bangladesh city	13.8	23.3	9.0	6.6	10.6	51.5	53.3	46.7
Bangladesh province	25.1	38.7	23.3	14.9	24.6	77.6	79.3	20.7
Brazil city	0.8	1.4	0.3	0.3	2.0	8.8	9.4	90.6
Brazil province	4.5	10.9	4.7	2.9	14.1	29.1	33.7	66.3
Ethiopia province	65.8	77.7	45.6	32.2	43.8	79.5	91.1	8.9
Japan city	1.3	1.5	0.4	0.9	2.8	18.5	19.0	81.0
Namibia city	9.7	12.5	3.5	4.3	6.1	9.2	20.5	79.5
Peru city	4.9	7.5	1.7	2.3	13.5	29.7	33.7	66.3
Peru province	43.6	46.2	25.8	26.7	37.9	71.3	78.4	21.6
Samoa	12.1	19.6	7.4	10.1	26.0	69.8	73.3	26.7
Serbia and Montenegro city	0.6	0.97	0.6	0.3	0.9	5.7	6.2	93.8
Thailand city	2.0	0.8	2.8	1.8	5.6	42.9	44.7	55.3
Thailand province	11.9	25.3	7.3	4.4	12.5	64.5	69.5	30.5
Tanzania city	24.1	45.6	31.1	13.8	22.9	51.5	62.5	37.5
Tanzania province	29.1	49.7	41.7	19.8	27.2	55.5	68.2	31.8

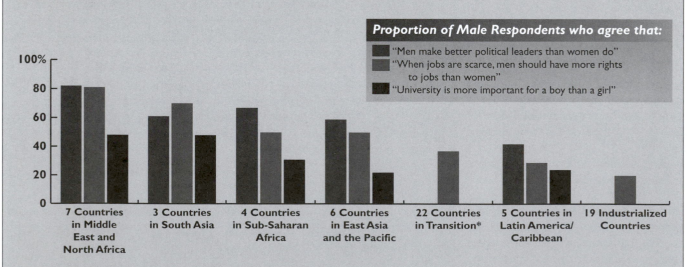

Proportion of Male Respondents who agree that:
- "Men make better political leaders than women do"
- "When jobs are scarce, men should have more rights to jobs than women"
- "University is more important for a boy than a girl"

Categories (x-axis):
7 Countries in Middle East and North Africa; 3 Countries in South Asia; 4 Countries in Sub-Saharan Africa; 6 Countries in East Asia and the Pacific; 22 Countries in Transition*; 5 Countries in Latin America/Caribbean; 19 Industrialized Countries

* Countries in transition are generally those that were once part of the Soviet Union.

Sources: World Heath Organization, www.who.int/gender/violence/who_multicountry_study/Chapter3-Chapter4.pdf; "World Values Survey," www.worldvaluessruvey.org

Continued from p. 119

eliminate that country's practice of aborting female fetuses because girls are not as valued as boys in India. (*See "At Issue," p. 139.*) [17]

Last October, Argentina elected its first female president, Cristina Fernández de Kirchner,* the second woman in two years to be elected president in South America. Michelle Bachelet, a single mother, won the presidency in Chile in 2006. [18] During her inaugural speech Kirchner admitted, "Perhaps it'll be harder for me, because I'm a woman. It will always be harder for us." [19]

Indeed, while more women than ever now lead national governments, they hold only 4.4 percent of the world's 342 presidential and prime ministerial positions. And in no country do they hold 50 percent or more of the national legislative seats. [20]

"Women make up half the world's population, but they are not represented" at that level, says Swanee Hunt, former U.S. ambassador to Austria and founding director of the Women and Public Policy Program at Harvard's Kennedy School of Government.

While this is "obviously a fairness issue," she says it also affects the kinds of public policies governments pursue. When women comprise higher percentages of officeholders, studies show "distinct differences in legislative outputs," Hunt explains. "There's less funding of bombs and bullets and more on human security — not just how to defend territory but also on hospitals and general well-being."

Today's historic numbers of women parliamentarians have resulted partly from gender quotas imposed in nearly 100 countries, which require a certain percentage of women candidates or officeholders. [21]

---

* Isabel Martínez Perón assumed the presidency of Argentina on the death of her husband, Juan Perón, in 1974 and served until she was deposed in a coup d'etat in 1976; but she was never elected.

During the U.N.'s historic Fourth World Conference on Women — held in Beijing in 1995 — 189 governments adopted, among other things, a goal of 30 percent female representation in national legislatures around the world. [22] But today, only 20 countries have reached that goal, and quotas are often attacked as limiting voters' choices and giving women unfair advantages. [23]

Along with increasing female political participation, the 5,000 government representatives at the Beijing conference — one of the largest gatherings in U.N. history — called for improved health care for women, an end to violence against women, equal access to education for girls, promotion of economic independence and other steps to improve the condition of women around the world. [24]

"Let Beijing be the platform from which our global crusade will be carried forward," Gertrude Mongella, U.N. secretary general for the conference, said during closing ceremonies. "The

world will hold us accountable for the implementation of the good intentions and decisions arrived at in Beijing." [25]

But more than 10 years later, much of the Beijing Platform still has not been achieved. And many question whether women are any better off today than they were in 1995.

"The picture's mixed," says June Zeitlin, executive director of the Women's Environment & Development Organization (WEDO). "In terms of violence against women, there is far more recognition of what is going on today. There has been some progress with education and girls.

Spain's visibly pregnant new Defense minister, Carme Chacón, reviews troops in Madrid on April 14, 2008. She is the first woman ever to head Spain's armed forces. Women hold nine out of 17 cabinet posts in Spain's socialist government, a reflection of women's entrance into the halls of power around the world.

But the impact of globalization has exacerbated differences between men and women. The poor have gotten poorer — and they are mostly women."

Liberalized international trade has been a two-edged sword in other ways as well. Corporations have been able to expand their global reach, opening new businesses and factories in developing countries and offering women unprecedented employment and economic opportunities. But the jobs often pay low wages and involve work in dangerous conditions because poor countries anxious to attract foreign investors often are willing to ignore safety and labor protections. [26] And increasingly porous international borders have led to growing numbers of women and girls being forced or sold into prostitution or sexual slavery abroad, often under the pretense that they will be given legitimate jobs overseas. [27]

Numerous international agreements in recent years have pledged to provide women with the same opportunities and protections as men, including the U.N.'s Millennium Development Goals (MDGs) and the Convention on the Elimination of All Forms of Discrimination Against Women (CEDAW). But the MDGs' deadlines for improving the conditions for women have ei-

ther been missed already or are on track to fail in the coming years. [28] And more than 70 of the 185 countries that ratified CEDAW have filed "reservations," meaning they exempt themselves from certain parts. [29] In fact, there are more reservations against CEDAW than against any other international human-rights treaty in history. [30] The United States remains the only developed country in the world not to have ratified it. [31]

"There has certainly been progress in terms of the rhetoric. But there are still challenges in the disparities in education, disparities in income, disparities in health," says Carla Koppell, director of the Cambridge, Mass.-based Initiative for Inclusive Security, which advocates for greater numbers of women in peace negotiations.

"But women are not just victims," she continues. "They have a very unique and important role to play in solving the problems of the developing world. We need to charge policy makers to match the rhetoric and make it a reality. There is a really wonderful opportunity to use the momentum that does exist. I really think we can."

Amidst the successes and failures surrounding women's issues, here are some of the questions analysts are beginning to ask:

Has globalization been good for women?

Over the last 20 years, trade liberalization has led to a massive increase of goods being produced and exported from developing countries, creating

Female Peacekeepers Fill Vital Roles
Women bring a different approach to conflict resolution.

The first all-female United Nations peacekeeping force left Liberia in January after a year's mission in the West African country, which is rebuilding itself after 14 years of civil war. Comprised of more than 100 women from India, the force was immediately replaced by a second female team.

"If anyone questioned the ability of women to do tough jobs, then those doubters have been [proven] wrong," said U.N. Special Representative for Liberia Ellen Margrethe Løj, adding that the female peacekeepers inspired many Liberian women to join the national police force. [1]

Women make up half of the world's refugees and have systematically been targeted for rape and sexual abuse during times of war, from the 200,000 "comfort women" who were kept as sex slaves for Japanese soldiers during World War II [2] to the estimated quarter-million women reportedly raped and sexually assaulted during the current conflict in the Democratic Republic of the Congo. [3] But women account for only 5 percent of the world's security-sector jobs, and in many countries they are excluded altogether. [4]

In 2000, the U.N. Security Council unanimously adopted Resolution 1325 calling on governments — and the U.N. itself — to include women in peace building by adopting a variety of measures, including appointing more women as special envoys, involving women in peace negotiations, integrating gender-based policies in peacekeeping missions and increasing the number of women at all decision-making levels. [5]

But while Resolution 1325 was a critical step in bringing women into the peace process, women's groups say more women should be sent on field missions and more data collected on how conflict affects women around the world. [6]

"Women are often viewed as victims, but another way to view them is as the maintainers of society," says Carla Koppell, director of the Cambridge, Mass.-based Initiative for Inclusive Security, which promotes greater numbers of women in peacekeeping and conflict resolution. "There must be a conscious decision to include women. It's a detriment to promote peace without including women."

Women often comprise the majority of post-conflict survivor populations, especially when large numbers of men have either fled or been killed. In the wake of the 1994 Rwandan genocide, for example, women made up 70 percent of the remaining population.

And female peacekeepers and security forces can fill vital roles men often cannot, such as searching Islamic women wearing burkas or working with rape victims who may be reluctant to report the crimes to male soldiers.

"Women bring different experiences and issues to the table," says Koppell. "I've seen it personally in the Darfur and Uganda peace negotiations. Their priorities were quite different. Men were concerned about power- and wealth-sharing. Those are valid, but you get an entirely different dimension from women. Women talked about security on the ground, security of families, security of communities."

In war-torn countries, women have been found to draw on their experiences as mothers to find nonviolent and flexible ways to solve conflict. [7] During peace negotiations in Northern Ireland, for example, male negotiators repeatedly walked out of sessions, leaving a small number of women at the table. The women, left to their own, found areas of common ground and were able to keep discussions moving forward. [8]

"The most important thing is introducing the definition of security from a woman's perspective," said Orzala Ashraf, founder of Kabul-based Humanitarian Assistance for the Women and Children of Afghanistan. "It is not a man in a uniform standing next to a tank armed with a gun. Women have a broader term — human security — the ability to go to school, receive health care, work and have access to justice. Only by improving these areas can threats from insurgents, Taliban, drug lords and warlords be countered." [9]

The first all-female United Nations peacekeeping force practices martial arts in New Delhi as it prepares to be deployed to Liberia in 2006.

AP Photo/Mustafa Quraishi

[1] "Liberia: UN envoy welcomes new batch of female Indian police officers," U.N. News Centre, Feb. 8, 2008, www.un.org/apps/news/story.asp?NewsID=25557&Cr=liberia&Cr1=.

[2] "Japan: Comfort Women," European Speaking Tour press release, Amnesty International, Oct. 31, 2007.

[3] "Film Documents Rape of Women in Congo," "All Things Considered," National Public Radio, April 8, 2008, www.npr.org/templates/story/story.php?storyId=89476111.

[4] "Ninth Annual Colloquium and Policy Forum," Hunt Alternatives Fund, Jan. 22, 2008, www.huntalternatives.org/pages/7650_ninth_annual_colloquium_and_policy_forum.cfm. Also see Elizabeth Eldridge, "Women cite utility in peace efforts," The Washington Times, Jan. 25, 2008, p. A1.

[5] "Inclusive Security, Sustainable Peace: A Toolkit for Advocacy and Action," International Alert and Women Waging Peace, 2004, p. 15, www.huntalternatives.org/download/35_introduction.pdf.

[6] Ibid., p. 17.

[7] Jolynn Shoemaker and Camille Pampell Conaway, "Conflict Prevention and Transformation: Women's Vital Contributions," Inclusive Security: Women Waging Peace and the United Nations Foundation, Feb. 23, 2005, p. 7.

[8] The Initiative for Inclusive Security, www.huntalternatives.org/pages/460_the_vital_role_of_women_in_peace_building.cfm.

[9] Eldridge, op. cit.

millions of manufacturing jobs and bringing many women into the paid workforce for the first time.

"Women employed in export-oriented manufacturing typically earn more than they would have in traditional sectors," according to a World Bank report. "Further, cash income earned by women may improve their status and bargaining power in the family." [32] The report cited a study of 50 families in Mexico that found "a significant proportion of the women reported an improvement in their 'quality of life,' due mainly to their income from working outside their homes, including in (export-oriented) factory jobs."

But because women in developing nations are generally less educated than men and have little bargaining power, most of these jobs are temporary or part-time, offering no healthcare benefits, overtime or sick leave.

Women comprise 85 percent of the factory jobs in the garment industry in Bangladesh and 90 percent in Cambodia. In the cut flower industry, women hold 65 percent of the jobs in Colombia and 87 percent in Zimbabwe. In the fruit industry, women constitute 69 percent of temporary and seasonal workers in South Africa and 52 percent in Chile. [33]

Frequently, women in these jobs have no formal contract with their employers, making them even more vulnerable to poor safety conditions and abuse. One study found that only 46 percent of women garment workers in Bangladesh had an official letter of employment. [34]

"Women are a workforce vital to the global economy, but the jobs women are in often aren't covered by labor protections," says Thalia Kidder, a policy adviser on gender and sustainable livelihoods with U.K.-based

Oxfam, a confederation of 12 international aid organizations. Women lack protection because they mostly work as domestics, in home-based businesses and as part-time workers. "In the global economy, many companies look to hire the most powerless people because they cannot demand high wages. There are not a lot of trade treaties that address labor rights."

In addition to recommending that countries embrace free trade, Western institutions like the International Monetary Fund and the World Bank during the 1990s recommended that developing countries adopt so-called structural adjustment economic reforms in order to qualify for certain loans and financial support. Besides opening borders to free trade, the neo-liberal economic regime known as the Washington Consensus advocated privatizing state-owned businesses, balancing budgets and attracting foreign investment.

Few Women Head World Governments

Fourteen women currently serve as elected heads of state or government including five who serve as both. Mary McAleese, elected president of Ireland in 1997, is the world's longest-serving head of state. Helen Clark of New Zealand has served as prime minister since 1999, making her the longest-serving female head of government. The world's first elected female head of state was Sirimavo Bandaranaike of Sri Lanka, in 1960.

Current Female Elected Heads of State and Government

Heads of both state and government:

 Gloria Macapagal-Arroyo — President, the Philippines, since 2001; former secretary of Defense (2002) and secretary of Foreign Affairs (2003 and 2006-2007).

 Ellen Johnson-Sirleaf — President, Liberia, since 2006; held finance positions with the government and World Bank.

 Michelle Bachelet Jeria — President, Chile, since 2006; former minister of Health (2000-2002) and minister of Defense (2002-2004).

 Cristina E. Fernández — President, Argentina, since 2007; succeeded her husband, Nestor de Kirchner, as president; former president, Senate Committee on Constitutional Affairs.

 Rosa Zafferani — Captain Regent, San Marino, since April 2008; secretary of State of Public Education, University and Cultural Institutions (2004 to 2008); served as captain regent in 1999; San Marino elects two captains regent every six months, who serve as co-heads of both state and government.

Heads of Government:

 Helen Clark — Prime Minister, New Zealand, since 1999; held government posts in foreign affairs, defense, housing and labor.

 Luísa Días Diogo — Prime Minister, Mozambique, since 2004; held several finance posts in Mozambique and the World Bank.

 Angela Merkel — Chancellor, Germany, since 2005; parliamentary leader of Christian Democratic Union Party (2002-2005).

 Yuliya Tymoshenko — Prime Minister, Ukraine, since 2007; chief of government (2005) and designate prime minister (2006).

 Zinaida Grecianîi — Prime Minister, Moldova, since March 2008; vice prime minister (2005-2008).

Heads of State:

 Mary McAleese — President, Ireland, since 1997; former director of a television station and Northern Ireland Electricity.

 Tarja Halonen — President, Finland, since 2000; former minister of foreign affairs (1995-2000).

 Pratibha Patil — President, India, since 2007; former governor of Rajasthan state (2004-2007).

 Borjana Kristo — President, Bosnia and Herzegovina, since 2007; minister of Justice of Bosniak-Croat Federation, an entity in Bosnia and Herzegovina (2003-2007).

Source: www.guide2womenleaders.com

But according to some studies, those reforms ended up adversely affecting women. For instance, companies in Ecuador were encouraged to make jobs more "flexible" by replacing long-term contracts with temporary, seasonal and hourly positions — while restricting collective bargaining rights.[35] And countries streamlined and privatized government programs such as health care and education, services women depend on most.

Globalization also has led to a shift toward cash crops grown for export, which hurts women farmers, who produce 60 to 80 percent of the food for household consumption in developing countries.[36] Small women farmers are being pushed off their land so crops for exports can be grown, limiting their abilities to produce food for themselves and their families.

While economic globalization has yet to create the economic support needed to help women out of poverty, women's advocates say females have benefited from the broadening of communications between countries prompted by globalization. "It has certainly improved access to communications and helped human-rights campaigns," says Zeitlin of WEDO. "Less can be done in secret. If there is a woman who is condemned to be stoned to death somewhere, you can almost immediately mobilize a global campaign against it."

Homa Hoodfar, a professor of social anthropology at Concordia University in Montreal, Canada, and a founder of the group Women Living Under Muslim Laws, says women in some of the world's most remote towns and villages regularly e-mail her organization. "Globalization has made the world much smaller," she says. "Women are getting information on TV and the Internet. The fact that domestic violence has become a global issue [shows globalization] provides resources for those objecting locally."

But open borders also have enabled the trafficking of millions of women around the world. An estimated 800,000 people are trafficked across international borders each year — 80 percent of them women and girls — and most are forced into the commercial sex trade. Millions more are trafficked within their own countries. [37] Globalization has sparked a massive migration of women in search of better jobs and lives. About 90 million women — half of the world's migrants and more than ever in history — reside outside their home countries. These migrant women — often unable to speak the local language and without any family connections — are especially susceptible to traffickers who lure them with promises of jobs abroad. [38]

And those who do not get trapped in the sex trade often end up in low-paying or abusive jobs in foreign factories or as domestic maids working under slave-like conditions.

But some experts say the real problem is not migration and globalization but the lack of labor protection. "Nothing is black and white," says Marianne Mollmann, advocacy director for the Women's Rights Division of Human Rights Watch. "Globalization has created different employment opportunities for women. Migration flows have made women vulnerable. But it's a knee-jerk reaction to say that women shouldn't migrate. You can't prevent migration. So where do we need to go?" She suggests including these workers in general labor-law protections that cover all workers.

Mollmann said countries can and should hammer out agreements providing labor and wage protections for domestic workers migrating across borders. With such protections, she said, women could benefit from the jobs and incomes promised by increased migration and globalization.

Should governments impose electoral quotas for women?

In 2003, as Rwanda struggled to

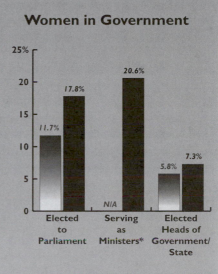

Women Still Far from Reaching Political Parity

Although they have made strides in the past decade, women hold only a small minority of the world's leadership and legislative posts (right). Nordic parliaments have the highest rates of female representation — 41.4 percent — compared with only 9 percent in Arab countries (below). However, Arab legislatures have nearly tripled their female representation since 1997, and some countries in Africa have dramatically increased theirs as well: Rwanda, at 48.8 percent, now has the world's highest percentage of women in parliament of any country. The U.S. Congress ranks 70th in the world, with 89 women serving in the 535-member body — or 16.6 percent.

Women in Government

Elected to Parliament: 11.7% (1997), 17.8% (2008)
Serving as Ministers*: N/A (1997), 20.6% (2008)
Elected Heads of Government/State: 5.8% (1997), 7.3% (2008)

1997 | **2008**

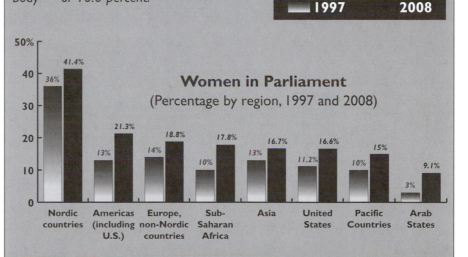

Women in Parliament
(Percentage by region, 1997 and 2008)

Nordic countries: 36% (1997), 41.4% (2008)
Americas (including U.S.): 13% (1997), 21.3% (2008)
Europe, non-Nordic countries: 14% (1997), 18.8% (2008)
Sub-Saharan Africa: 10% (1997), 17.8% (2008)
Asia: 13% (1997), 16.7% (2008)
United States: 11.2% (1997), 16.6% (2008)
Pacific Countries: 10% (1997), 15% (2008)
Arab States: 3% (1997), 9.1% (2008)

* Includes deputy prime ministers, ministers and prime ministers who hold ministerial portfolios.

Sources: Interparliamentarian Union, www.ipu.org/wmn-e/world.htm; State of the World's Children 2007, UNICEF, www.unicef.org/sowc07/; "Worldwide Guide to Women in Leadership" database, www.un.org/womenwatch/daw/csw/41sess.htm.

rebuild itself after the genocide that killed at least 800,000 Hutus and Tutsis, the country adopted an historic new constitution that, among other things, required that women hold at least 30 percent of posts "in all decision-making organs." [39]

Today — ironically, just across Lake Kivu from the horrors occurring in Eastern Congo — Rwanda's lower house of parliament now leads the world in female representation, with 48.8 percent of the seats held by women. [40]

Before the civil war, Rwandan women never held more than 18 percent of parliament. But after the genocide, the country's population was 70 percent female. Women immediately stepped in to fill

Women's Work: From Hauling and Churning . . .

Women's work is often back-breaking and monotonous, such as hauling firewood in the western Indian state of Maharashtra (top) and churning yogurt into butter beside Lake Motsobunnyi in Tibet (bottom). Women labor two-thirds of the total hours worked around the globe each year but earn only 10 percent of the income.

AP Photo/Rajesh Kumar Singh

National Geographic/Getty Images/Melvyn Goldstein

region of the world, primarily through the use of quotas. [42]

But many point out that simply increasing the numbers of women in elected office will not necessarily expand women's rights. "It depends on which women and which positions they represent," says Wendy Harcourt, chair of Women in Development Europe (WIDE), a feminist network in Europe, and editor of *Development*, the journal of the Society for International Development, a global network of individuals and institutions working on development issues. "It's positive, but I don't see yet what it means [in terms of addressing] broader gender issues."

While Afghanistan has mandated that women hold at least 27 percent of the government's lower house seats and at least 17 percent of the upper house, their increased representation appears to have done little to improve women's rights. [43] Earlier this year, a student journalist was condemned to die under Afghanistan's strict Islamic sharia law after he distributed articles from the Internet on women's rights. [44] And nongovernmental groups in Afghanistan report that Afghan women and girls have begun killing themselves in record numbers, burning themselves alive in order to escape widespread domestic abuse or forced marriages. [45]

Having gender quotas alone doesn't necessarily ensure that women's rights will be broadened, says Hoodfar of Concordia University. It depends on the type of quota a government implements, she argues, pointing out that in Jordan, for example, the government has set aside parliamentary seats for the six women who garner the most votes of any other female candidates in their districts — even if they do not win more votes than male candidates. [46] Many small, conservative tribes that cannot garner enough votes for a male in a countrywide victory are now nominating their sisters and wives in the hope that the lower number of votes needed to elect a woman

the vacuum, becoming the heads of households, community leaders and business owners. Their increased presence in leadership positions eventually led to the new constitutional quotas. [41]

"We see so many post-conflict countries going from military regimes to democracy that are starting from scratch with new constitutions," says Drude Dahlerup, a professor of political science at Sweden's Stockholm University who studies the use of gender quotas. "Today, starting from scratch means including women. It's seen as a sign of modernization and democratization."

Both Iraq and Afghanistan included electoral quotas for women in their new constitutions, and the number of women in political office in sub-Saharan Africa has increased faster than in any other

will get them one of the reserved seats. As a result, many of the women moving into the reserved seats are extremely conservative and actively oppose providing women greater rights and freedoms.

And another kind of quota has been used against women in her home country of Iran, Hoodfar points out. Currently, 64 percent of university students in Iran are women. But the government recently mandated that at least 40 percent of university enrollees be male, forcing many female students out of school, Hoodfar said.

"Before, women didn't want to use quotas for politics because of concern the government may try to use it against women," she says. "But women are beginning to look into it and talk about maybe developing a good system."

Quotas can be enacted by constitutional requirements, such as those enacted in Rwanda, by statute or voluntarily by political parties. Quotas also can vary in their requirements: They can mandate the number of women each party must nominate, how many women must appear on the ballot (and the order in which they appear, so women are not relegated to the bottom of the list), or the number of women who must hold government office. About 40 countries now use gender quotas in national parliamentary elections, while another 50 have major political parties that voluntarily use quotas to determine candidates.

Aside from questions about the effectiveness of quotas, others worry about the fairness of establishing quotas based on gender. "That's something feminists have traditionally opposed," says Harcourt.

"It's true, but it's also not fair the way it is now," says former Ambassador Hunt. "We are where we are today through all kinds of social structures that are not fair. Quotas are the lesser of two evils."

Stockholm University's Dahlerup says quotas are not "discrimination

... to Gathering and Herding

While many women have gotten factory jobs thanks to globalization of trade, women still comprise 70 percent of the planet's inhabitants living on less than a dollar a day. Women perform a variety of tasks around the world, ranging from gathering flax in Belarus (top) to shepherding goats in central Argentina (bottom).

against men but compensation for discrimination against women." Yet quotas are not a panacea for women in politics, she contends. "It's a mistake to think this is a kind of tool that will solve all problems. It doesn't solve problems about financing campaigns, caring for families while being in politics or removing patriarchal attitudes. It would be nice if it wasn't neces-

sary, and hopefully sometime in the future it won't be."

Until that time, however, quotas are a "necessary evil," she says.

Do international treaties improve women's rights?

In recent decades, a variety of international agreements have been signed by countries pledging to improve women's lives, from the 1979 Convention for the Elimination of All Forms of Discrimination Against Women to the Beijing Platform of 1995 to the Millennium Development Goals (MDGs) adopted in 2000. The agreements aimed to provide women with greater access to health, political representation, economic stability and social status. They also focused attention on some of the biggest obstacles facing women.

But despite the fanfare surrounding the launch of those agreements, many experts on women's issues say on-the-ground action has yet to match the rhetoric. "The report is mixed," says Haleh Afshar, a professor of politics and women's studies at the University of York in the United Kingdom and a nonpartisan, appointed member of the House of Lords, known as a cross-bench peer. "The biggest problem with Beijing is all these things were stated, but none were funded. Unfortunately, I don't see any money. You don't get the pay, you don't get the job done."

The Beijing Platform for Action, among other things, called on governments to "adjust budgets to ensure equality of access to public sector expenditures" and even to "reduce, as appropriate, excessive military expenditure" in order to achieve the Platform goals.

But adequate funding has yet to be provided, say women's groups. [47] In a report entitled "Beijing Betrayed," the Women's Environment & Development Organization says female HIV cases outnumber male cases in many parts of the world, gender-related violence remains a pandemic and women still make up the majority of the world's poor — despite pledges in Beijing to reverse these trends. [48]

And funding is not the only obstacle. A 2004 U.N. survey revealed that while many countries have enacted laws in recent years to help protect women from violence and discrimination, long-standing social and cultural traditions block progress. "While constitutions provided for equality between women and men on the one hand, [several countries] recognized and gave precedent to customary law and practice in a number of areas . . . resulting in discrimination against women," the report said. "Several countries noted that statutory, customary and religious law coexist, especially in regard to family, personal status and inheritance and land rights. This perpetuated discrimination against women." [49]

While she worries about the lack of progress on the Beijing Platform, WEDO Executive Director Zeitlin says international agreements are nevertheless critical in raising global awareness on women's issues. "They have a major impact on setting norms and standards," she says. "In many countries, norms and standards are very important in setting goals for women to advocate for. We complain about lack of implementation, but if we didn't have the norms and standards we couldn't complain about a lack of implementation."

Like the Beijing Platform, the MDGs have been criticized for not achieving more. While the U.N. says promoting women's rights is essential to achieving the millenium goals — which aim to improve the lives of all the world's populations by 2015 — only two of the eight specifically address women's issues. [50]

One of the goals calls for countries to "Promote gender equality and empower women." But it sets only one measurable target: "Eliminate gender disparity in primary and secondary education, preferably by 2005, and in all levels of education" by 2015. [51] Some 62 countries failed to reach the 2005 deadline, and many are likely to miss the 2015 deadline as well. [52]

Another MDG calls for a 75 percent reduction in maternal mortality compared to 1990 levels. But according to the human-rights group ActionAid, this goal is the "most off track of all the MDGs." Rates are declining at less than 1 percent a year, and in some countries — such as Sierra Leone, Pakistan and Guatemala — maternal mortality has increased since 1990. If that trend continues, no region in the developing world is expected to reach the goal by 2015. [53]

Activist Peggy Antrobus of Development Alternatives with Women for a New Era (DAWN) — a network of feminists from the Southern Hemisphere, based currently in Calabar, Cross River State, Nigeria — has lambasted the MDGs, quipping that the acronym stands for the "Most Distracting Gimmick." [54] Many feminists argue that the goals are too broad to have any real impact and that the MDGs should have given more attention to women's issues.

But other women say international agreements — and the public debate surrounding them — are vital in promoting gender equality. "It's easy to get disheartened, but Beijing is still the blueprint of where we need to be," says Mollmann of Human Rights Watch. "They are part of a political process, the creation of an international culture. If systematically everyone says [discrimination against women] is a bad thing, states don't want to be hauled out as systematic violators."

In particular, Mollmann said, CEDAW has made real progress in overcoming discrimination against women. Unlike the Beijing Platform and the MDGs, CEDAW legally obliges countries to comply. Each of the 185 ratifying countries must submit regular reports to the U.N. outlining their progress under the convention. Several countries — including Brazil, Uganda, South Africa and Australia — also have incorporated CEDAW provisions into their constitutions and legal systems. [55]

Still, dozens of ratifying countries have filed official "reservations" against the convention, including Bahrain, Egypt, Kuwait, Morocco and the United Arab Emirates, all of whom say they will comply only within the bounds of Islamic sharia law. [56] And the United States has refused to ratify CEDAW, with or without reservations, largely because of conservatives who say it would, among other things, promote abortion and require the government to pay for such things as child care and maternity leave. ∎

BACKGROUND

'Structural Defects'

Numerous prehistoric relics suggest that at one time matriarchal societies existed on Earth in which women were in the upper echelons of power. Because early societies did not understand the connection between sexual relations and conception, they believed women were solely responsible for reproduction — which led to the worship of female goddesses. [57]

In more modern times, however, women have generally faced prejudice and discrimination at the hands of a patriarchal society. In about the eighth century B.C. creation stories emerged describing the fall of man due to the weakness of women. The Greeks recounted the story of Pandora who, through her opening of a sealed jar, unleashed death and pain on all of mankind. Meanwhile, similar tales in Judea eventually were recounted in Genesis, with Eve as the culprit. [58]

In ancient Greece, women were treated as children and denied basic rights. They could not leave their houses unchaperoned, were prohibited from being educated or buying or selling land. A father could sell his unmarried daughter into slavery if she lost her virginity before marriage. If a woman was raped, she was outcast and forbidden from participating in public ceremonies or wearing jewelry. [59]

The status of women in early Rome was not much better, although over time women began to assert their voices and slowly gained greater freedoms. Even-

tually, they were able to own property and divorce their husbands. But early Christian leaders later denounced the legal and social freedom enjoyed by Roman women as a sign of moral decay. In the view of the early church, women were dependent on and subordinate to men.

In the 13th century, the Catholic priest and theologian St. Thomas Aquinas helped set the tone for the subjugation of women in Western society. He said women were created solely to be "man's helpmate" and advocated that men should make use of "a necessary object, woman, who is needed to preserve the species or to provide food and drink." [60]

From the 14th to 17th centuries, misogyny and oppression of women took a step further. As European societies struggled against the Black Plague, the 100 Years War and turmoil between Catholics and Reformers, religious leaders began to blame tragedies, illnesses and other problems on witches. As witch hys-

teria spread across Europe — instituted by both the religious and non-religious — an estimated 30,000 to 60,000 people were executed for allegedly practicing witchcraft. About 80 percent were females, some as young as 8 years old. [61]

"All wickedness is but little to the wickedness of a woman," Catholic inquisitors wrote in the 1480s. "What else is woman but a foe to friendship, an unescapable punishment, a necessary evil, a natural temptation, a desirable calamity. . . . Women are . . . instruments of Satan, . . . a structural defect rooted in the original creation." [62]

Indian women harvest wheat near Bhopal. Women produce half of the food used domestically worldwide and 60 to 80 percent of the household food grown in developing countries.

AP Photo/Prakash Hatvalne

Push for Protections

The Age of Enlightenment and the Industrial Revolution in the 18th and 19th centuries opened up job opportunities for women, released them from domestic confines and provided them with new social freedoms.

In 1792 Mary Wollstonecraft published A Vindication of the Rights of

Women, which has been hailed as "the feminist declaration of independence." Although the book had been heavily influenced by the French Revolution's notions of equality and universal brotherhood, French revolutionary leaders, ironically, were not sympathetic to feminist causes. [63] In 1789 they had refused to accept a Declaration of the Rights of Women when it was presented at the National Assembly. And Jean Jacques Rousseau, one of the philosophical founders of the revolution, had written in 1762:

"The whole education of women ought to be relative to men. To please them, to be useful to them, to make themselves loved and honored by them, to educate them when young, to care for them when grown, to counsel them, to make life sweet and agreeable to them — these are the duties of women at all times, and what should be taught them from their infancy." [64]

As more and more women began taking jobs outside the home during the 19th century, governments began to pass laws to "protect" them in the workforce and expand their legal rights. The British Mines Act of 1842, for instance, prohibited women from working underground. [65] In 1867, John Stuart Mill, a supporter of women's rights and author of the book *Subjection of Women*, introduced language in the British House of Commons calling for women to be granted the right to vote. It failed. [66]

But by that time governments around the globe had begun enacting laws giving women rights they had been denied for centuries. As a result of the Married Women's Property Act of 1870 and a series of other measures, wives in Britain were finally allowed to own property. In 1893, New Zealand became the first nation to grant full suffrage rights to women, followed over the next two decades by Finland, Norway, Denmark and Iceland. The United States granted women suffrage in 1920. [67]

One of the first international labor conventions, formulated at Berne, Switzerland, in 1906, applied exclusively to women — prohibiting night work for women in industrial occupations. Twelve nations signed on to it. During the second Berne conference in 1913, language was proposed limiting the number of hours women and children could work in industrial jobs, but the outbreak of World War I prevented it from being enacted. [68] In 1924 the U.S. Supreme Court upheld a night-work law for women. [69]

In 1946, public attention to women's issues received a major boost when the United Nations created the Commission on the Status of Women to address urgent problems facing women around the world. [70] During the 1950s, the U.N. adopted several conventions aimed at improving women's lives, including the Convention on the Political Rights of Women, adopted in 1952 to ensure women the right to vote, which has been ratified by 120 countries, and the Convention on the Nationality of Married Women, approved in 1957 to ensure that marriage to an alien does not automatically affect the nationality of the woman. [71] That convention has been ratified by only 73 countries; the United States is not among them. [72]

In 1951 The International Labor Organization (ILO), an agency of the United Nations, adopted the Convention on Equal Remuneration for Men and Women Workers for Work of Equal Value, to promote equal pay for equal work. It has since been ratified by 164 countries, but again, not by the United States. [73] Seven years later, the ILO adopted the Convention on Discrimination in Employment and Occupation to ensure equal opportunity and treatment in employment. It is currently ratified by 166 countries, but not the United States. [74] U.S. opponents to the conventions claim there is no real pay gap between men and women performing the same jobs and that the

conventions would impose "comparable worth" requirements, forcing companies to pay equal wages to men and women even if the jobs they performed were different. [75]

In 1965, the Commission on the Status of Women began drafting international standards articulating equal rights for men and women. Two years later, the panel completed the Declaration on the Elimination of Discrimination Against Women, which was adopted by the General Assembly but carried no enforcement power.

The commission later began to discuss language that would hold countries responsible for enforcing the declaration. At the U.N.'s first World Conference on Women in Mexico City in 1975, women from around the world called for creation of such a treaty, and the commission soon began drafting the text. [76]

Women's 'Bill of Rights'

Finally in 1979, after many years of often rancorous debate, the Convention on the Elimination of All Forms of Discrimination Against Women (CEDAW) was adopted by the General Assembly — 130 to none, with 10 abstentions. After the vote, however, several countries said their "yes" votes did not commit the support of their governments. Brazil's U.N. representative told the assembly, "The signatures and ratifications necessary to make this effective will not come easily." [77]

Despite the prediction, it took less than two years for CEDAW to receive the required number of ratifications to enter it into force — faster than any human-rights convention had ever done before. [78]

Often described as an international bill of rights for women, CEDAW defines discrimination against women as "any distinction, exclusion or restriction made on the basis of sex which has the effect or purpose of impairing or nullifying the

Continued on p. 132

Chronology

1700s-1800s
Age of Enlightenment and Industrial Revolution lead to greater freedoms for women.

1792
Mary Wollstonecraft publishes *A Vindication of the Rights of Women*, later hailed as "the feminist declaration of independence."

1893
New Zealand becomes first nation to grant women full suffrage.

1920
Tennessee is the 36th state to ratify the 19th Amendment, giving American women the right to vote.

1940s-1980s
International conventions endorse equal rights for women. Global conferences highlight need to improve women's rights.

1946
U.N. creates Commission on the Status of Women.

1951
U.N. International Labor Organization adopts convention promoting equal pay for equal work, which has been ratified by 164 countries; the United States is not among them.

1952
U.N. adopts convention calling for full women's suffrage.

1960
Sri Lanka elects the world's first female prime minister.

1974
Maria Estela Martínez de Perón of Argentina becomes the world's first woman president, replacing her ailing husband.

1975
U.N. holds first World Conference on Women, in Mexico City, followed by similar conferences every five years. U.N. launches the Decade for Women.

1979
U.N. adopts Convention on the Elimination of All Forms of Discrimination against Women (CEDAW), dubbed the "international bill of rights for women."

1981
CEDAW is ratified — faster than any other human-rights convention.

1990s
Women's rights win historic legal recognition.

1993
U.N. World Conference on Human Rights in Vienna, Austria, calls for ending all violence, sexual harassment and trafficking of women.

1995
Fourth World Conference on Women in Beijing draws 30,000 people, making it the largest in U.N. history. Beijing Platform outlining steps to grant women equal rights is signed by 189 governments.

1996
International Criminal Tribunal convicts eight Bosnian Serb police and military officers for rape during the Bosnian conflict — the first time sexual assault is prosecuted as a war crime.

1998
International Criminal Tribunal for Rwanda recognizes rape and other forms of sexual violence as genocide.

2000s
Women make political gains, but sexual violence against women increases.

2000
U.N. calls on governments to include women in peace negotiations.

2006
Ellen Johnson Sirleaf of Liberia, Michelle Bachelet of Chile and Portia Simpson Miller of Jamaica become their countries' first elected female heads of state. . . . Women in Kuwait are allowed to run for parliament, winning two seats.

2007
A woman in Saudi Arabia who was sentenced to 200 lashes after being gang-raped by seven men is pardoned by King Abdullah. Her rapists received sentences ranging from 10 months to five years in prison, and 80 to 1,000 lashes. . . . After failing to recognize any gender-based crimes in its first case involving the Democratic Republic of the Congo, the International Criminal Court hands down charges of "sexual slavery" in its second case involving war crimes in Congo. More than 250,000 women are estimated to have been raped and sexually abused during the country's war.

2008
Turkey lifts 80-year-old ban on women's headscarves in public universities, signaling a drift toward religious fundamentalism. . . . Former housing minister Carme Chacón — 37 and pregnant — is named defense minister of Spain, bringing to nine the number of female cabinet ministers in the Socialist government. . . . Sen. Hillary Rodham Clinton becomes the first U.S. woman to be in a tight race for a major party's presidential nomination.

Continued from p. 130

recognition, enjoyment or exercise by women, irrespective of their marital status, on a basis of equality of men and women, of human rights and fundamental freedoms in the political, economic, social, cultural, civil or any other field."

Ratifying countries are legally bound to end discrimination against women by incorporating sexual equality into their legal systems, abolishing discriminatory laws against women, taking steps to end trafficking of women and ensuring women equal access to political and public life. Countries must also submit reports at least every four years outlining the steps they have taken to comply with the convention. [79]

CEDAW also grants women reproductive choice — one of the main reasons the United States has not ratified it. The convention requires signatories to guarantee women's rights "to decide freely and responsibly on the number and spacing of their children and to have access to the information, education and means to enable them to exercise these rights." [80]

While CEDAW is seen as a significant tool to stop violence against women, it actually does not directly mention violence. To rectify this, the CEDAW committee charged with monitoring countries' compliance in 1992 specified gender-based violence as a form of discrimination prohibited under the convention. [81]

In 1993 the U.N. took further steps to combat violence against women during the World Conference on Human Rights in Vienna, Austria. The conference called on countries to stop all forms of violence, sexual harassment, exploitation and trafficking of women. It also declared that "violations of the human rights of women in situations of armed conflicts are violations of the fundamental principles of international human rights and humanitarian law." [82]

Shortly afterwards, as fighting broke out in the former Yugoslavia and Rwanda, new legal precedents were set to protect women against violence — and particularly rape — during war. In 1996, the International Criminal Tribunal in

Women Suffer Most in Natural Disasters

Climate change will make matters worse.

In natural disasters, women suffer death, disease and hunger at higher rates then men. During the devastating 2004 tsunami in Asia, 70 to 80 percent of the dead were women. [1] During cyclone-triggered flooding in Bangladesh that killed 140,000 people in 1991, nearly five times more women between the ages of 20 and 44 died than men. [2]

Gender discrimination, cultural biases and lack of awareness of women's needs are part of the problem. For instance, during the 1991 cyclone, Bangladeshi women and their children died in higher numbers because they waited at home for their husbands to return and make evacuation decisions. [3] In addition, flood warnings were conveyed by men to men in public spaces but were rarely communicated to women and children at home. [4]

And during the tsunami, many Indonesian women died because they stayed behind to look for children and other family members. Women clinging to children in floodwaters also tired more quickly and drowned, since most women in the region were never taught to swim or climb trees. [5] In Sri Lanka, many women died because the tsunami hit early on a Sunday morning when they were inside preparing breakfast for their families. Men were generally outside where they had earlier warning of the oncoming floods so they were better able to escape. [6]

Experts now predict global climate change — which is expected to increase the number of natural disasters around the world — will put women in far greater danger than men because natural disasters generally have a disproportionate impact on the world's poor. Since women comprise 70 percent of those living on less than $1 a day, they will be hardest hit by climate changes, according to the Intergovernmental Panel on Climate Change. [7]

"Climate change is not gender-neutral," said Gro Harlem Brundtland, former prime minister of Norway and now special envoy to the U.N. secretary-general on climate change. "[Women are] more dependent for their livelihood on natural resources that are threatened by climate change. . . . With changes in climate, traditional food sources become more unpredictable and scarce. This exposes women to loss of harvests, often their sole sources of food and income." [8]

Women produce 60 to 80 percent of the food for household consumption in developing countries. [9] As drought, flooding and desertification increase, experts say women and their families will be pushed further into poverty and famine.

Women also suffer more hardship in the aftermath of natural disasters, and their needs are often ignored during relief efforts.

In many Third World countries, for instance, women have no property rights, so when a husband dies during a natural disaster his family frequently confiscates the land from his widow, leaving her homeless and destitute. [10] And because men usually dominate emergency relief and response agencies, women's specific needs, such as contraceptives and sanitary napkins, are often overlooked. After floods in Bangladesh in 1998, adolescent girls reported high rates of rashes and urinary tract infections because they had no clean water, could not wash their menstrual rags properly in private and had no place to hang them to dry. [11]

"In terms of reconstruction, people are not talking about women's needs versus men's needs," says June Zeitlin, executive director of the Women's Environment and Development Organization, a New York City-based international organization that works for women's equality in global policy. "There is a lack of attention to health care after disasters, issues about bearing children, contraception, rape and vulnerability, menstrual needs — things a male programmer is not thinking about. There is broad recognition that disasters have a disproportionate impact on women. But it stops there. They see women as victims, but they don't see women as agents of change."

Women must be brought into discussions on climate change and emergency relief, say Zeitlin and others. Interestingly, she points out, while women are disproportionately affected by environmental changes, they do more than men to protect the environment. Studies show women emit less climate-changing carbon dioxide than men because they recycle more, use resources more efficiently and drive less than men. [12]

"Women's involvement in climate-change decision-making is a human right," said Gerd Johnson-Latham, deputy director of the Swedish Ministry for Foreign Affairs. "If we get more women in decision-making positions, we will have different priorities, and less risk of climate change." [13]

AP Photo

The smell of death hangs over Banda Aceh, Indonesia, which was virtually destroyed by a tsunami on Dec. 28, 2004. From 70 to 80 percent of the victims were women.

[1] "Tsunami death toll," CNN, Feb. 22, 2005. Also see "Report of High-level Roundtable: How a Changing Climate Impacts Women," Council of Women World Leaders, Women's Environment and Development Organization and Heinrich Boll Foundation, Sept. 21, 2007, p. 21, www.wedo.org/files/Roundtable%20Final%20Report%206%20Nov.pdf.

[2] Ibid.

[3] "Cyclone Jelawat bears down on Japan's Okinawa island," CNN.com, Aug. 7, 2000, http://archives.cnn.com/2000/ASIANOW/east/08/07/asia.weather/index.html.

[4] "Gender and Health in Disasters," World Health Organization, July 2002, www.who.int/gender/other_health/en/genderdisasters.pdf.

[5] "The tsunami's impact on women," Oxfam briefing note, March 5, 2005, p. 2, www.oxfam.org/en/files/bn050326_tsunami_women/download.

[6] "Report of High-level Roundtable," op. cit., p. 5.

[7] "Gender Equality" fact sheet, Oxfam, www.oxfam.org.uk/resources/issues/gender/introduction.html. Also see ibid.

[8] Ibid., p. 4.

[9] "Five years down the road from Beijing: Assessing progress," News and Highlights, Food and Agriculture Organization, June 2, 2000, www.fao.org/News/2000/000602-e.htm.

[10] "Gender and Health in Disasters," op. cit.

[11] Ibid.

[12] "Women and the Environment," U.N. Environment Program, 2004, p. 17, www.unep.org/Documents.Multilingual/Default.asp?DocumentID=468&ArticleID=4488&l=en. Also see "Report of High-level Roundtable," op. cit., p. 7.

[13] Ibid.

the Hague, Netherlands, indicted eight Bosnian Serb police officers in connection with the mass rape of Muslim women during the Bosnian war, marking the first time sexual assault had ever been prosecuted as a war crime. [83]

Two years later, the U.N.'s International Criminal Tribunal for Rwanda convicted a former Rwandan mayor for genocide, crimes against humanity, rape and sexual violence — the first time rape and sexual violence were recognized as acts of genocide. [84]

"Rape is a serious war crime like any other," said Regan Ralph, then executive director of Human Rights Watch's Women's Rights Division, shortly after the conviction. "That's always been true on paper, but now international courts are finally acting on it." [85]

Today, the International Criminal Court has filed charges against several Sudanese officials for rape and other crimes committed in the Darfur region. [86] But others are demanding that the court also prosecute those responsible for the rapes in the Eastern Congo, where women are being targeted as a means of destroying communities in the war-torn country. [87]

Beijing and Beyond

The U.N. World Conference on Women in Mexico City in 1975 produced a 44-page plan of action calling for a decade of special measures to give women equal status and opportunities in law, education, employment, politics and society. [88] The conference also kicked off the U.N.'s Decade for Women and led to creation of the U.N. Development Fund for Women (UNIFEM). [89]

Five years later, the U.N. held its second World Conference on Women in Copenhagen and then celebrated the end of the Decade for Women with the third World Conference in Nairobi in 1985. More than 10,000 representatives from government agencies and NGOs attended the Nairobi event, believed to be the largest gathering on women's issues at the time. [90]

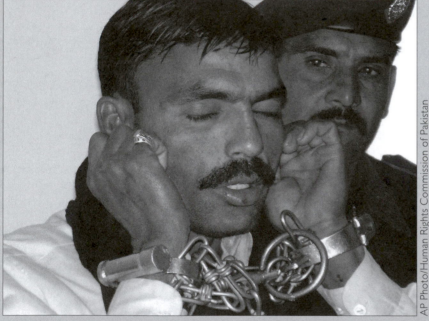

AP Photo/Khalid Tanveer

AP Photo/Human Rights Commission of Pakistan

Honor Killings on the Rise

Women in Multan, Pakistan, demonstrate against "honor killings" in 2003 (top). Although Pakistan outlawed such killings years ago, its Human Rights Commission says 1,205 women were killed in the name of family honor in 2007 — a fourfold jump in two years. Nazir Ahmed Sheikh, a Punjabi laborer (bottom), unrepentantly told police in December 2005 how he slit the throats of his four daughters one night as they slept in order to salvage the family's honor. The eldest had married a man of her choice, and Ahmed feared the younger daughters would follow her example.

Upon reviewing the progress made on women's issues during the previous 10 years, the U.N. representatives in Nairobi concluded that advances had been extremely limited due to failing economies in developing countries, particularly those in Africa struggling against drought, famine and crippling debt. The conference developed a set of steps needed to improve the status of women during the final 15 years of the 20th century. [91]

Ten years later, women gathered in Beijing in 1995 for the Fourth World Conference, vowing to turn the rhetoric of the earlier women's conferences into action. Delegates from 189 governments and 2,600 NGOs attended. More than 30,000 women and men gathered at a parallel forum organized by NGOs, also in Beijing. [92]

The so-called Beijing Platform that emerged from the conference addressed 12 critical areas facing women, from poverty to inequality in education to inadequate health care to violence. It brought unprecedented attention to women's issues and is still considered by many as the blueprint for true gender equality.

The Beijing Conference also came at the center of a decade that produced historic political gains for women around the world — gains that have continued, albeit at a slow pace, into the new century. The 1990s saw more women entering top political positions than ever before. A record 10 countries elected or appointed women as presidents between 1990 and 2000, including Haiti, Nicaragua, Switzerland and Latvia. Another 17 countries chose women prime ministers. [93]

In 2006 Ellen Johnson Sirleaf of Liberia became Africa's first elected woman president. [94] That same year, Chile elected its first female president, Michelle Bachelet, and Jamaica elected Portia Simpson Miller as its first female prime minister. [95] Also that year, women ran for election in Kuwait for the first time. In Bahrain, a woman was elected to the lower house of parliament for the first time. [96] And in 2007, Fernández de Kirchner became the first woman to be elected president of Argentina.

Earlier, a World Bank report had found that government corruption declines as more women are elected into office. The report also cited numerous studies that found women are more likely to exhibit "helping" behavior, vote based on social issues, score higher on "integrity tests," take stronger stances on ethical behavior and behave more generously when faced with economic decisions. [97]

"Increasing the presence of women in government may be valued for its own sake, for reasons of gender equality," the report concluded. "However, our results suggest that there may be extremely important spinoffs stemming from increasing female representation: If women are less likely than men to behave opportunistically, then bringing more women into government may have significant benefits for society in general." [98] ∎

CURRENT SITUATION

Rise of Fundamentalism

Despite landmark political gains by women since the late 1990s, violence and repression of women continue to be daily occurrences — often linked to the global growth of religious fundamentalism.

In 2007, a 21-year-old woman in Saudi Arabia was sentenced to 200 lashes and ordered jailed for six months after being raped 14 times by a gang of seven men. The Saudi court sentenced the woman — who was 19 at the time of the attack — because she was alone in a car with her former boyfriend when the attack occurred. Under Saudi Arabia's strict Islamic law, it is a crime for a woman to meet in private with a man who is not her husband or relative. [99]

After public outcry from around the world, King Abdullah pardoned the woman in December. A government spokesperson, however, said the king fully supported the verdict but issued the pardon in the "interests of the people." [100]

Another Saudi woman still faces beheading after she was condemned to death for "witchcraft." Among her accusers is a man who claimed she rendered him impotent with her sorcery. Despite international protest, the king has yet to say if he will pardon her. [101]

In Iraq, the rise of religious fundamentalism since the U.S. invasion has led to a jump in the number of women being killed or beaten in so-called honor crimes. Honor killings typically occur when a woman is suspected of unsanctioned sexual behavior — which can range from flirting to "allowing" herself to be raped. Her relatives believe they must murder her to end the family's shame. In the Kurdish region of Iraq, the stoning death of 17-year-old Aswad is not an anomaly. A U.N. mission in October 2007 found that 255 women had been killed in Iraqi Kurdistan in the first six months of 2007 alone — most thought to have been murdered by their communities or families for allegedly committing adultery or entering into a relationship not sanctioned by their families. [102]

The rise of fundamentalism is also sparking a growing debate on the issue of women wearing head scarves, both in Iraq and across the Muslim world. Last August Turkey elected a conservative Muslim president whose wife wears a head scarf, signaling the emergence of a new ruling elite that is more willing to publicly display religious beliefs. [103] Then in February, Turkey's parliament voted to ease an 80-year ban on women wearing head scarves in universities, although a ban on head scarves in other public buildings remains in effect.

"This decision will bring further pressure on women," Nesrin Baytok, a member of parliament, said during debate over the ban. "It will ultimately bring us Hezbollah terror, al Qaeda terror and fundamentalism." [104]

But others said lifting the ban was actually a victory for women. Fatma Benli, a Turkish women's-rights activist and lawyer, said the ban on head scarves in public buildings has forced her to send law partners to argue her cases because she is prohibited from entering court wearing her head scarf. It also discourages religiously conservative women from becoming doctors, lawyers or teachers, she says. [105]

Many women activists are quick to say that it is unfair to condemn Islam for the growing abuse against women. "The problem women have with religion is not the religion but the ways men have interpreted it," says Afshar of the University of York. "What is highly negative is sharia law, which is made by men. Because it's human-made, women can unmake it. The battle now is fighting against unjust laws such as stoning."

She says abuses such as forced marriages and honor killings — usually linked in the Western media to Islamic law — actually go directly against the teachings of the Koran. And while the United Nations estimates that some 5,000 women and girls are victims of honor killings each year, millions more are abused and killed in violence unrelated to Islam. Between 10 and 50 percent of all women around the world have been physically abused by an intimate partner in their lifetime, studies show. [106]

"What about the rate of spousal or partner killings in the U.K. or the U.S. that are not called 'honor killings'?" asks Concordia University's Hoodfar. "Then it's only occasional 'crazy people' [committing violence]. But when it's present in Pakistan, Iran or Senegal, these are uncivilized people doing 'honor killings.' "

women from protecting themselves against HIV.

"If you look at all your religions, none will say it's a good thing to beat up or kill someone. They are all based on human dignity," says Mollmann of Human Rights Watch. "[Bad things] are carried out in the name of religion, but the actual belief system is not

Evolving Gender Policies

This past February, the U.N. Convention on the Elimination of All Forms of Discrimination Against Women issued a report criticizing Saudi Arabia for its repression of women. Among other things, the report attacked Saudi Arabia's ban on women drivers and its system of male guardianship that denies women equal inheritance, child custody and divorce rights. [109] The criticism came during the panel's regular review of countries that have ratified CEDAW. Each government must submit reports every four years outlining steps taken to comply with the convention.

The United States is one of only eight countries — among them Iran, Sudan and Somalia — that have refused to ratify CEDAW. [110] Last year, 108 members of the U.S. House of Representatives signed on to a resolution calling for the Senate to ratify CEDAW, but it still has not voted on the measure. [111] During a U.N. vote last November on a resolution encouraging governments to meet their obligations under CEDAW, the United States was the lone nay vote against 173 yea votes. [112]

Getty Images/Paula Bronstein

Pakistani acid attack survivors Saira Liaqat, right, and Sabra Sultana are among hundreds, and perhaps thousands, of women who are blinded and disfigured after being attacked with acid each year in Pakistan, Bangladesh, India, Cambodia, Malaysia, Uganda and other areas of Africa. Liaqat was attacked at age 18 during an argument over an arranged marriage. Sabra was 15 when she was burned after being married off to an older man who became unsatisfied with the relationship. Only a small percentage of the attacks — often perpetrated by spurned suitors while the women are asleep in their own beds — are prosecuted.

And Islamic fundamentalism is not the only brand of fundamentalism on the rise. Christian fundamentalism is also growing rapidly. A 2006 Pew Forum on Religion and Public Life poll found that nearly one-third of all Americans feel the Bible should be the basis of law across the United States. [107] Many women's-rights activists say Christian fundamentalism threatens women's rights, particularly with regard to reproductive issues. They also condemn the Vatican's opposition to the use of condoms, pointing out that it prevents

killing and maiming women."

In response to the growing number of honor-based killings, attacks and forced marriages in the U.K., Britain's Association of Chief Police Officers has created an honor-based violence unit, and the U.K.'s Home Office is drafting an action plan to improve the response of police and other agencies to such violence. Legislation going into effect later this year will also give U.K. courts greater guidance on dealing with forced marriages. [108]

American opponents of CEDAW — largely pro-life Christians and Republicans — say it would enshrine the right to abortion in *Roe v. Wade* and be prohibitively expensive, potentially requiring the U.S. government to provide paid maternity leave and other child-care services to all women. [113] They also oppose requirements that the government modify "social and cultural patterns" to eliminate sexual prejudice and to delete any traces of gender stereotypes in textbooks — such as references to women's lives being primarily in the domestic sector. [114] Many Republicans in Congress also have argued that CEDAW would give too much control over U.S. laws to the United Nations and that it could even require the legalization of prostitution and the abolition of Mother's Day. [115]

The last time the Senate took action on CEDAW was in 2002, when the Senate Foreign Relations Committee, chaired by Democratic Sen. Joseph Biden of Delaware, voted to send the convention to the Senate floor for ratification. The full Senate, however, never took action. A Biden spokesperson says the senator "remains committed" to the treaty and is "looking for an opportune time" to bring it forward again. But Senate ratification requires 67 votes, and there do not appear to be that many votes for approval.

CEDAW proponents say the failure to ratify not only hurts women but also harms the U.S. image abroad. On this issue, "the United States is in the company of Sudan and the Vatican," says Bien-Aimé of Equality Now.

Meanwhile, several countries are enacting laws to comply with CEDAW and improve the status of women. In December, Turkmenistan passed its first national law guaranteeing women equal rights, even though its constitution had addressed women's equality. [116] A royal decree in Saudi Arabia in January ordered an end to a long-time ban on women checking into hotels or renting apartments without male guardians. Hotels can now book rooms to women who show identification, but the hotels must register the women's details with the police. [117] The Saudi government has also said it will lift the ban on women driving by the end of the year. [118]

And in an effort to improve relations with women in Afghanistan, the Canadian military, which has troops stationed in the region, has begun studying the role women play in Afghan society, how they are affected by military operations and how they can assist peacekeeping efforts. "Behind all of these men are women who can help eradicate the problems of the population," said Capt. Michel Larocque, who is working with the study. "Illiteracy, poverty, these things can be improved through women." [119]

In February, during the 52nd session of the Commission on the Status of Women, the United Nations kicked off a new seven-year campaign aimed at ending violence against women. The campaign will work with international agencies, governments and individuals to increase funding for anti-violence campaigns and pressure policy makers around the world to enact legislation to eliminate violence against women. [120]

But women's groups want increased U.N. spending on women's programs and the creation of a single unified agency addressing women's issues, led by an under-secretary general. [121] Currently, four different U.N. agencies address women's issues: the United Nations Development Fund for Women, the International Research and Training Institute for the Advancement of Women (INSTRAW), the Secretary-General's Special Advisor on Gender Issues (OSAGI) and the Division for the Advancement of Women. In 2006, the four agencies received only $65 million — a fraction of the more than $2 billion budget that the U.N.'s children's fund (UNICEF) received that year. [122]

"The four entities that focus on women's rights at the U.N. are greatly under-resourced," says Zeitlin of the Women's Environment & Development Organization. "If the rhetoric everyone is using is true — that investing in women is investing in development — it's a matter of putting your money where your mouth is."

Political Prospects

While the number of women leading world governments is still miniscule compared to their male counterparts, women are achieving political gains that just a few years ago would have been unthinkable.

While for the first time in U.S. history a woman is in a tight race for a major party's nomination as its candidate for president, South America — with two sitting female heads of state — leads the world in woman-led governments. In Brazil, Dilma Rousseff, the female chief of staff to President Luiz Inacio Lula da Silva, is the top contender to take over the presidency when da Silva's term ends in 2010. [123] In Paraguay, Blanca Ovelar was this year's presidential nominee for the country's ruling conservative Colorado Party, but she was defeated on April 20. [124]

And in Europe, Carme Chacón was named defense minister of Spain this past April. She was not only the first woman ever to head the country's armed forces but also was pregnant at the time of her appointment. In all, nine of Spain's 17 cabinet ministers are women.

In March, Pakistan's National Assembly overwhelmingly elected its first female speaker, Fahmida Mirza. [125] And in India, where Patil has become the first woman president, the two major political parties this year pledged to set aside one-third of their parliamentary nominations for women. But many fear the parties will either not keep their pledges or will run women only in contests they are unlikely to win. [126]

There was also disappointment in Iran, where nearly 600 of the 7,000 candidates running for parliament in March were women. [127] Only three won seats in the 290-member house, and they were conservatives who are not expected to promote women's rights. Several of the tallies are being contested. Twelve other women won enough votes to face run-off elections on April 25; five won. [128]

But in some countries, women running for office face more than just tough campaigns. They are specifically targeted for violence. In Kenya, the greatest campaign expense for female candidates is the round-the-clock security required to protect them against rape, according to Phoebe Asiyo, who

Female farmworkers in Nova Lima, Brazil, protest against the impact of big corporations on the poor in March 2006, reflecting the increasing political activism of women around the globe.

served in the Kenyan parliament for more than two decades. [129] During the three months before Kenya's elections last December, an emergency helpdesk established by the Education Centre for Women in Democracy, a nongovernmental organization (NGO) in Nairobi, received 258 reports of attacks against female candidates. [130]

The helpdesk reported the attacks to police, worked with the press to ensure the cases were documented and helped victims obtain medical and emotional support. Attacks included rape, stabbings, threats and physical assaults. [131]

"Women are being attacked because they are women and because it is seen as though they are not fit to bear flags of the popular parties," according to the center's Web site. "Women are also viewed as guilty for invading 'the male territory' and without a license to do so!" [132]

"All women candidates feel threatened," said Nazlin Umar, the sole female presidential candidate last year. "When a case of violence against a woman is reported, we women on the ground think we are next. I think if

the government assigned all women candidates with guns . . . we will at least have an item to protect ourselves when we face danger." [133]

Impunity for Violence

Some African feminists blame women themselves, as well as men, for not doing enough to end traditional attitudes that perpetuate violence against women.

"Women are also to blame for the violence because they are the gatekeepers of patriarchy, because whether educated or not they have different standards for their sons and husbands [than for] their daughters," said Njoki Wainaina, founder of the African Women Development Communication Network (FEMNET). "How do you start telling a boy whose mother trained him only disrespect for girls to honor women in adulthood?" [134]

Indeed, violence against women is widely accepted in many regions of the world and often goes unpunished. A study by the World Health Organization found that 80 percent of women

surveyed in rural Egypt believe that a man is justified in beating a woman if she refuses to have sex with him. In Ghana, more women than men — 50 percent compared to 43 percent — felt that a man was justified in beating his wife if she used contraception without his consent. [135] (*See survey results, p. 120.*)

Such attitudes have led to many crimes against women going unpunished, and not just violence committed during wartime. In Guatemala, no one knows why an estimated 3,000 women have been killed over the past seven years — many of them beheaded, sexually mutilated or raped — but theories range from domestic violence to gang activity. [136] Meanwhile, the government in 2006 overturned a law allowing rapists to escape charges if they offered to marry their victims. But Guatemalan law still does not prescribe prison sentences for domestic abuse and prohibits abusers from being charged with assault unless the bruises are still visible after 10 days. [137]

In the Mexican cities of Chihuahua and Juárez, more than 400 women have been murdered over the past 14 years, with many of the bodies mutilated and dumped in the desert. But the crimes are still unsolved, and many human-rights groups, including Amnesty International, blame indifference by Mexican authorities. Now the country's 14-year statute of limitations on murder is forcing prosecutors to close many of the unsolved cases. [138]

Feminists around the world have been working to end dismissive cultural attitudes about domestic violence and other forms of violence against women, such as forced marriage, dowry-related violence, marital rape, sexual harassment and forced abortion, sterilization and prostitution. But it's often an uphill battle.

After a Kenyan police officer beat his wife so badly she was paralyzed and brain damaged — and eventually

Continued on p. 140

At Issue:

Should sex-selective abortions be outlawed?

NICHOLAS EBERSTADT
HENRY WENDT CHAIR IN POLITICAL ECONOMY,
AMERICAN ENTERPRISE INSTITUTE
MEMBER, PRESIDENT'S COUNCIL ON BIOETHICS

WRITTEN FOR *CQ GLOBAL RESEARCHER*, APRIL 2008

*t*he practice of sex-selective abortion to permit parents to destroy unwanted female fetuses has become so widespread in the modern world that it is disfiguring the profile of entire countries — transforming (and indeed deforming) the whole human species.

This abomination is now rampant in China, where the latest census reports six boys for every five girls. But it is also prevalent in the Far East, South Korea, Hong Kong, Taiwan and Vietnam, all of which report biologically impossible "sex ratios at birth" (well above the 103-106 baby boys for every 100 girls ordinarily observed in human populations). In the Caucasus, gruesome imbalances exist now in Armenia, Georgia and Azerbaijan; and in India, the state of Punjab tallies 126 little boys for every 100 girls. Even in the United States, the boy-girl sex ratio at birth for Asian-Americans is now several unnatural percentage points above the national average. So sex-selective abortion is taking place under America's nose.

How can we rid the world of this barbaric form of sexism? Simply outlawing sex-selective abortions will be little more than a symbolic gesture, as South Korea's experience has shown: Its sex ratio at birth continued a steady climb for a full decade after just such a national law was passed. As long as abortion is basically available on demand, any legislation to abolish sex-selective abortion will have no impact.

What about more general restrictions on abortion, then? Poll data consistently demonstrate that most Americans do not favor the post-*Roe* regimen of unconditional abortion. But a return to the pre-*Roe* status quo, where each state made its own abortion laws, would probably have very little effect on sex-selective abortion in our country. After all, the ethnic communities most tempted by it are concentrated in states where abortion rights would likely be strongest, such as California and New York.

In the final analysis, the extirpation of this scourge will require nothing less than a struggle for the conscience of nations. Here again, South Korea may be illustrative: Its gender imbalances began to decline when the public was shocked into facing this stain on their society by a spontaneous, home-grown civil rights movement.

To eradicate sex-selective abortion, we must convince the world that destrtroying female fetuses is horribly wrong. We need something akin to the abolitionist movement: a moral campaign waged globally, with victories declared one conscience at a time.

MARIANNE MOLLMANN
ADVOCACY DIRECTOR, WOMEN'S RIGHTS DIVISION, HUMAN RIGHTS WATCH

WRITTEN FOR *CQ GLOBAL RESEARCHER*, APRIL 2008

*m*edical technology today allows parents to test early in pregnancy for fetal abnormalities, hereditary illnesses and even the sex of the fetus, raising horrifying questions about eugenics and population control. In some countries, a growing number of women apparently are terminating pregnancies when they learn the fetus is female. The resulting sex imbalance in countries like China and India is not only disturbing but also leads to further injustices, such as the abduction of girls for forced marriages.

One response has been to criminalize sex-selective abortions. While it is tempting to hope that this could safeguard the gender balance of future generations, criminalization of abortion for whatever reason has led in the past only to underground and unsafe practices. Thus, the criminalization of sex-selective abortion would put the full burden of righting a fundamental wrong — the devaluing of women's lives — on women.

Many women who choose to abort a female fetus face violence and exclusion if they don't produce a boy. Some see the financial burden of raising a girl as detrimental to the survival of the rest of their family. These considerations will not be lessened by banning sex-selective abortion. Unless one addresses the motivation for the practice, it will continue — underground.

So what is the motivation for aborting female fetuses? At the most basic level, it is a financial decision. In no country in the world does women's earning power equal men's. In marginalized communities in developing countries, this is directly linked to survival: Boys may provide more income than girls.

Severe gaps between women's and men's earning power are generally accompanied by severe forms of gender-based discrimination and rigid gender roles. For example, in China, boys are expected to stay in their parental home as they grow up, adding their manpower (and that of a later wife) to the family home. Girls, on the other hand, are expected to join the husbands' parental home. Thus, raising a girl is a net loss, especially if you are only allowed one child.

The solution is to remove the motivation behind sex-selective abortion by advancing women's rights and their economic and social equality. Choosing the blunt instrument of criminal law over promoting the value of women's lives and rights will only serve to place further burdens on marginalized and often vulnerable women.

Continued from p. 138

died — media coverage of the murder spurred a nationwide debate on domestic violence. But it took five years of protests, demonstrations and lobbying by both women's advocates and outraged men to get a family protection bill enacted criminalizing domestic violence. And the bill passed only after legislators removed a provision outlawing marital rape. Similar laws have languished for decades in other African legislatures. [139]

But in Rwanda, where nearly 49 percent of the elected representatives in the lower house are female, gender desks have been established at local police stations, staffed mostly by women trained to help victims of sexual and other violence. In 2006, as a result of improved reporting, investigation and response to rape cases, police referred 1,777 cases for prosecution and convicted 803 men. "What we need now is to expand this approach to more countries," said UNIFEM's director for Central Africa Josephine Odera. [140]

Besides criticizing governments for failing to prosecute gender-based violence, many women's groups also criticize the International Criminal Court (ICC) for not doing enough to bring abusers to justice.

"We have yet to see the investigative approach needed to ensure the prosecution of gender-based crimes," said Brigid Inder, executive director of Women's Initiatives for Gender Justice, a Hague-based group that promotes and monitors women's rights in the international court. [141] Inder's group released a study last November showing that of the 500 victims seeking to participate in ICC proceedings, only 38 percent were women. When the court handed down its first indictments for war crimes in the Democratic Republic of the Congo last year, no charges involving gender-based crimes were brought despite estimates that more than 250,000

women have been raped and sexually abused in the country. After an outcry from women's groups around the world, the ICC included "sexual slavery" among the charges handed down in its second case involving war crimes in Congo. [142]

The Gender Justice report also criticized the court for failing to reach out to female victims. It said the ICC has held only one consultation with women in the last four years (focusing on the Darfur conflict in Sudan) and has failed to develop any strategies to reach out to women victims in Congo. [143] ■

OUTLOOK

Economic Integration

Women's organizations do not expect — or want — another international conference on the scale of Beijing. Instead, they say, the resources needed to launch such a conference would be better used to improve U.N. oversight of women's issues and to implement the promises made at Beijing.

They also fear that the growth of religious fundamentalism and neoliberal economic policies around the globe have created a political atmosphere that could actually set back women's progress.

"If a Beijing conference happened now, we would not get the type of language or the scope we got 10 years ago," says Bien-Aimé of Equity Now. "There is a conservative movement, a growth in fundamentalists governments — and not just in Muslim countries. We would be very concerned about opening up debate on the principles that have already been established."

Dahlerup of Stockholm University agrees. "It was easier in the 1990s.

Many people are afraid of having big conferences now, because there may be a backlash because fundamentalism is so strong," she says. "Neo-liberal trends are also moving the discourse about women toward economics — women have to benefit for the sake of the economic good. That could be very good, but it's a more narrow discourse when every issue needs to be adapted into the economic discourse of a cost-benefit analysis."

For women to continue making gains, most groups say, gender can no longer be treated separately from broader economic, environmental, health or other political issues. While efforts to improve the status of women have historically been addressed in gender-specific legislation or international treaties, women's groups now say women's well-being must now be considered an integral part of all policies.

Women's groups are working to ensure that gender is incorporated into two major international conferences coming up this fall. In September, the Third High-Level Forum on Aid Effectiveness will be hosted in Accra, Ghana, bringing together governments, financial institutions, civil society organizations and others to assess whether assistance provided to poor nations is being put to good use. World leaders will also gather in November in Doha, Qatar, for the International Conference on Financing for Development to discuss how trade, debt relief and financial aid can promote global development.

"Women's groups are pushing for gender to be on the agenda for both conferences," says Zeitlin of WEDO. "It's important because . . . world leaders need to realize that it really does make a difference to invest in women. When it comes to women's rights it's all micro, but the big decisions are made on the macro level."

Despite decades of economic-development strategies promoted by Western nations and global financial institutions such as the World Bank, women in many regions are getting poorer. In Malawi, for example, the percentage of women living in poverty increased by 5 percent between 1995 and 2003. [144] Women and girls make up 70 percent of the world's poorest people, and their wages rise more slowly than men's. They also have fewer property rights around the world. [145] With the growing global food shortage, women — who are the primary family caregivers and produce the majority of crops for home consumption in developing countries — will be especially hard hit.

To help women escape poverty, gain legal rights and improve their social status, developed nations must rethink their broader strategies of engagement with developing countries. And, conversely, female activists say, any efforts aimed at eradicating poverty around the world must specifically address women's issues.

In Africa, for instance, activists have successfully demanded that women's economic and security concerns be addressed as part of the continent-wide development plan known as the New Partnership for Africa's Development (NEPAD). As a result, countries participating in NEPAD's peer review process must now show they are taking measures to promote and protect women's rights. But, according to Augustin Wambo, an agricultural specialist at the NEPAD secretariat, lawmakers now need to back up their pledges with "resources from national budgets" and the "necessary policies and means to support women." [146]

"We have made a lot of progress and will continue making progress," says Zeitlin. "But women's progress doesn't happen in isolation to what's happening in the rest of the world. The environment, the global economy, war, peace — they will all have a major impact on women. Women all over world will not stop making demands and fighting for their rights." ∎

Seaweed farmer Asia Mohammed Makungu in Zanzibar, Tanzania, grows the sea plants for export to European companies that produce food and cosmetics. Globalized trade has helped women entrepreneurs in many developing countries improve their lives, but critics say it also has created many low-wage, dangerous jobs for women in poor countries that ignore safety and labor protections in order to attract foreign investors.

AP Photo/Karel Prinsloo

Notes

[1] http://ballyblog.wordpress.com/2007/05/04/warning-uncensored-video-iraqis-stone-girl-to-death-over-loving-wrong-boy/.

[2] Abdulhamid Zebari, "Video of Iraqi girl's stoning shown on Internet," Agence France Presse, May 5, 2007.

[3] *State of the World Population 2000*, United Nations Population Fund, Sept. 20, 2000, Chapter 3, "Ending Violence against Women and Girls," www.unfpa.org/swp/2000/english/ch03.html.

[4] Brian Brady, "A Question of Honour," *The Independent on Sunday*, Feb. 10, 2008, p. 8, www.independent.co.uk/news/uk/home-news/a-question-of-honour-police-say-17000-women-are-victims-every-year-780522.html.

[5] Correspondance with Karen Musalo, Clinical Professor of Law and Director of the Center for Gender & Refugee Studies at the University of California Hastings School of Law, April 11, 2008.

[6] "Broken Bodies, Broken Dreams: Violence Against Women Exposed," United Nations, July 2006, http://brokendreams.wordpress.com/2006/12/17/dowry-crimes-and-bride-price-abuse/.

[7] Various sources: www.womankind.org.uk, www.unfpa.org/gender/docs/studies/summaries/reg_exe_summary.pdf, www.oxfam.org.uk. Also see "Child rape in Kano on the increase," IRIN Humanitarian News and Analysis, United Nations, www.irinnews.org/report.aspx?ReportId=76087.

[8] "UNICEF slams 'licence to rape' in African crisis," Agence France-Press, Feb. 12, 2008.

[9] "Film Documents Rape of Women in Congo," "All Things Considered," National Public Radio, April 8, 2008, www.npr.org/templates/story/story.php?storyId=89476111.

[10] Jeffrey Gettleman, "Rape Epidemic Raises Trauma Of Congo War," *The New York Times*, Oct. 7, 2007, p. A1.

[11] Dan McDougall, "Fareeda's fate: rape, prison and 25 lashes," *The Observer*, Sept. 17, 2006, www.guardian.co.uk/world/2006/sep/17/pakistan.theobserver.

[12] Zarar Khan, "Thousands rally in Pakistan to demand government withdraw rape law changes," The Associated Press, Dec. 10, 2006.

[13] *State of the World Population 2000, op. cit.*

[14] Laura Turquet, Patrick Watt, Tom Sharman, "Hit or Miss?" ActionAid, March 7, 2008, p. 10.

[15] *Ibid.*, p. 12.

[16] "Women in Politics: 2008" map, International Parliamentary Union and United Nations Division for the Advancement of Women, February 2008, www.ipu.org/pdf/publications/wmnmap08_en.pdf.

17 Gavin Rabinowitz, "India's first female president sworn in, promises to empower women," The Associated Press, July 25, 2007. Note: India's first female prime minister was Indira Ghandi in 1966.

18 Monte Reel, "South America Ushers In The Era of La Presidenta; Women Could Soon Lead a Majority of Continent's Population," The Washington Post, Oct. 31, 2007, p. A12. For background, see Roland Flamini, "The New Latin America," CQ Global Researcher, March 2008, pp. 57-84.

19 Marcela Valente, "Cristina Fernandes Dons Presidential Sash," Inter Press Service, Dec. 10, 2007.

20 "Women in Politics: 2008" map, op. cit.

21 Ibid.; Global Database of Quotas for Women, International Institute for Democracy and Electoral Assistance and Stockholm University, www.quotaproject.org/country.cfm?SortOrder =Country.

22 "Beijing Betrayed," Women's Environment and Development Organization, March 2005, p. 10, www.wedo.org/files/gmr_pdfs/gmr2005.pdf.

23 "Women in Politics: 2008" map, op. cit.

24 Gertrude Mongella, address by the Secretary-General of the 4th World Conference on Women, Sept. 4, 1995, www.un.org/esa/gopher-data/conf/fwcw/conf/una/950904201423.txt. Also see Steven Mufson, "Women's Forum Sets Accord; Dispute on Sexual Freedom Resolved," The Washington Post, Sept. 15, 1995, p. A1.

25 "Closing statement," Gertrude Mongella, U.N. Division for the Advancement of Women, Fourth World Conference on Women, www.un. org/esa/gopher-data/conf/fwcw/conf/una/closing.txt.

26 "Trading Away Our Rights," Oxfam International, 2004, p. 9, www.oxfam.org.uk/resources/policy/trade/downloads/trading_rights.pdf.

27 "Trafficking in Persons Report," U.S. Department of State, June 2007, p. 7, www.state. gov/g/tip/rls/tiprpt/2007/.

28 Turquet, et al., op. cit., p. 4.

29 United Nations Division for the Advancement of Women, www.un.org/womenwatch/daw/cedaw/.

30 Geraldine Terry, Women's Rights (2007), p. 30.

31 United Nations Division for the Advancement of Women, www.un.org/womenwatch/daw/cedaw/.

32 "The impact of international trade on gender equality," The World Bank PREM notes, May 2004, http://siteresources.worldbank.org/INT-GENDER/Resources/premnote86.pdf.

33 Thalia Kidder and Kate Raworth, " 'Good Jobs' and hidden costs: women workers documenting the price of precarious employment," Gender and Development, July 2004, p. 13.

34 "Trading Away Our Rights," op. cit.

35 Martha Chen, et al., "Progress of the World's Women 2005: Women, Work and Poverty," UNIFEM, p. 17, www.unifem.org/attachments/products/PoWW2005_eng.pdf.

36 Eric Neumayer and Indra de Soys, "Globalization, Women's Economic Rights and Forced Labor," London School of Economics and Norwegian University of Science and Technology, February 2007, p. 8, http://papers. ssrn.com/sol3/papers.cfm?abstract_id=813831. Also see "Five years down the road from Beijing — assessing progress," News and Highlights, Food and Agriculture Organization, June 2, 2000, www.fao.org/News/2000/000602-e.htm.

37 "Trafficking in Persons Report," op. cit., p. 13.

38 "World Survey on the Role of Women in Development," United Nations, 2006, p. 1, www.un.org/womenwatch/daw/public/World-Survey2004-Women&Migration.pdf.

39 Julie Ballington and Azza Karam, eds., "Women in Parliament: Beyond the Numbers," International Institute for Democracy and Electoral Assistance, 2005, p. 155, www.idea.int/publications/wip2/upload/WiP_inlay.pdf.

40 "Women in Politics: 2008," op. cit.

41 Ballington and Karam, op. cit., p. 158.

42 Ibid., p. 161.

43 Global Database of Quotas for Women, op. cit.

44 Jerome Starkey, "Afghan government official says that student will not be executed," The Independent, Feb. 6, 2008, www.independent.co.uk/news/world/asia/afghan-government-official-says-that-student-will-not-be-executed-778686.html?r=RSS.

45 "Afghan women seek death by fire," BBC, Nov. 15, 2006, http://news.bbc.co.uk/1/hi/world/south_asia/6149144.stm.

46 Global Database for Quotas for Women, op. cit.

47 "Beijing Declaration," Fourth World Conference on Women, www.un.org/womenwatch/daw/beijing/beijingdeclaration.html.

48 "Beijing Betrayed," op. cit., pp. 28, 15, 18.

49 "Review of the implementation of the Beijing Platform for Action and the outcome documents of the special session of the General Assembly entitled 'Women 2000: gender equality, development and peace for the twenty-first century,' " United Nations, Dec. 6, 2004, p. 74.

50 "Gender Equality and the Millennium Development Goals," fact sheet, www.mdgender.net/upload/tools/MDGender_leaflet.pdf.

51 Ibid.

52 Turquet, et al., op. cit., p. 16.

53 Ibid., pp. 22-24.

54 Terry, op. cit., p. 6.

55 "Inclusive Security, Sustainable Peace: A Toolkit for Advocacy and Action," International Alert and Women Waging Peace, 2004, p. 12, www.huntalternatives.org/download/35_introduction.pdf.

56 "Declarations, Reservations and Objections to CEDAW," www.un.org/womenwatch/daw/cedaw/reservations-country.htm.

57 Merlin Stone, When God Was a Woman (1976), pp. 18, 11.

58 Jack Holland, Misogyny (2006), p. 12.

59 Ibid., pp. 21-23.

60 Holland, op. cit., p. 112.

61 "Dispelling the myths about so-called witches" press release, Johns Hopkins University, Oct. 7, 2002, www.jhu.edu/news_info/news/home02/oct02/witch.html.

62 The quote is from the Malleus maleficarum (The Hammer of Witches), and was cited in "Case Study: The European Witch Hunts, c. 1450-1750," Gendercide Watch, www.gendercide.org/case_witchhunts.html.

63 Holland, op. cit., p. 179.

64 Cathy J. Cohen, Kathleen B. Jones and Joan C. Tronto, Women Transforming Politics: An Alternative Reader (1997), p. 530.

65 Ibid.

66 Holland, op. cit, p. 201.

67 "Men and Women in Politics: Democracy Still in the Making," IPU Study No. 28, 1997, http://archive.idea.int/women/parl/ch6_table8.htm.

68 "Sex, Equality and Protective Laws," CQ Researcher, July 13, 1926.

79 The case was Radice v. People of State of New York, 264 U. S. 292. For background, see F. Brewer, "Equal Rights Amendment," Editorial Research Reports, April 4, 1946, available at CQ Researcher Plus Archive, www.cqpress.com.

70 "Short History of the CEDAW Convention," U.N. Division for the Advancement of Women, www.un.org/womenwatch/daw/cedaw/history.htm.

71 U.N. Women's Watch, www.un.org/womenwatch/asp/user/list.asp-ParentID=11047.htm.

72 United Nations, http://untreaty.un.org/ENG-LISH/bible/englishinternetbible/partI/chapter XVI/treaty2.asp.

73 International Labor Organization, www.ilo.org/public/english/support/lib/resource/subject/gender.htm.

74 Ibid.

75 For background, see "Gender Pay Gap," CQ Researcher, March 14, 2008, pp. 241-264.

76 "Short History of the CEDAW Convention" *op. cit.*

77 "International News," The Associated Press, Dec. 19, 1979.

78 "Short History of the CEDAW Convention" *op. cit.*

79 "Text of the Convention," U.N. Division for the Advancement of Women, www.un.org/womenwatch/daw/cedaw/cedaw.htm.

80 Convention on the Elimination of All Forms of Discrimination against Women, Article 16, www.un.org/womenwatch/daw/cedaw/text/econvention.htm.

81 General Recommendation made by the Committee on the Elimination of Discrimination against Women No. 19, 11th session, 1992, www.un.org/womenwatch/daw/cedaw/recommendations/recomm.htm#recom19.

82 See www.unhchr.ch/huridocda/huridoca.nsf/(Symbol)/A.CONF.157.23.En.

83 Marlise Simons, "For First Time, Court Defines Rape as War Crime," *The New York Times*, June 28, 1996, www.nytimes.com/specials/bosnia/context/0628warcrimes-tribunal.html.

84 Ann Simmons, "U.N. Tribunal Convicts Rwandan Ex-Mayor of Genocide in Slaughter," *Los Angeles Times*, Sept. 3, 1998, p. 20.

85 "Human Rights Watch Applauds Rwanda Rape Verdict," press release, Human Rights Watch, Sept. 2, 1998, http://hrw.org/english/docs/1998/09/02/rwanda1311.htm.

86 Frederic Bichon, "ICC vows to bring Darfur war criminals to justice," Agence France-Presse, Feb. 24, 2008.

87 Rebecca Feeley and Colin Thomas-Jensen, "Getting Serious about Ending Conflict and Sexual Violence in Congo," Enough Project, www.enoughproject.org/reports/congoserious.

88 "Women; Deceived Again?" *The Economist*, July 5, 1975.

89 "International Women's Day — March 8: Points of Interest and Links with UNIFEM," UNIFEM New Zealand Web site, www.unifem.org.nz/IWDPointsofinterest.htm.

90 Joseph Gambardello, "Reporter's Notebook: Women's Conference in Kenya," United Press International, July 13, 1985.

91 "Report of the World Conference to Review and Appraise the Achievements of the United Nations Decade for Women: Equality Development and Peace," United Nations, 1986, paragraph 8, www.un.org/womenwatch/confer/nfls/Nairobi1985report.txt.

92 U.N. Division for the Advancement of Women, www.un.org/womenwatch/daw/followup/background.htm.

93 "Women in Politics," Inter-Parliamentary Union, 2005, pp. 16-17, www.ipu.org/PDF/publications/wmn45-05_en.pdf.

94 "Liberian becomes Africa's first female president," Associated Press, Jan. 16, 2006, www.msnbc.msn.com/id/10865705/.

95 "Women in the Americas: Paths to Political Power," *op. cit.*, p. 2.

96 "The Millennium Development Goals Report 2007," United Nations, 2007, p. 12, www.un.org/millenniumgoals/pdf/mdg2007.pdf.

97 David Dollar, Raymond Fisman, Roberta Gatti, "Are Women Really the 'Fairer' Sex? Corruption and Women in Government," The World Bank, October 1999, p. 1, http://siteresources.worldbank.org/INTGENDER/Resources/wp4.pdf.

98 *Ibid.*

99 Vicky Baker, "Rape victim sentenced to 200 lashes and six months in jail; Saudi woman punished for being alone with a man," *The Guardian*, Nov. 17, 2007, www.guardian.co.uk/world/2007/nov/17/saudiarabia.international.

100 Katherine Zoepf, "Saudi King Pardons Rape Victim Sentenced to Be Lashed, Saudi Paper Reports," *The New York Times*, Dec. 18, 2007, www.nytimes.com/2007/12/18/world/middleeast/18saudi.html.

101 Sonia Verma, "King Abdullah urged to spare Saudi 'witchcraft' woman's life," *The Times* (Of London), Feb. 16, 2008.

102 Mark Lattimer, "Freedom lost," *The Guardian*, Dec. 13, 2007, p. 6.

103 For background, see Brian Beary, "Future of Turkey," *CQ Global Researcher*, December, 2007, pp. 295-322.

104 Tracy Clark-Flory, "Does freedom to veil hurt women?" *Salon.com*, Feb. 11, 2008.

105 Sabrina Tavernise, "Under a Scarf, a Turkish Lawyer Fighting to Wear It," *The New York Times*, Feb. 9, 2008, www.nytimes.com/2008/02/09/world/europe/09benli.html?pagewanted=1&sq=women&st=nyt&scp=96.

106 Terry, *op. cit.*, p. 122.

107 "Many Americans Uneasy with Mix of Religion and Politics," The Pew Forum on Religion and Public Life, Aug. 24, 2006, http://pewforum.org/docs/index.php?DocID=153.

108 Brady, *op. cit.*

109 "Concluding Observations of the Committee on the Elimination of Discrimination against Women: Saudi Arabia," Committee on the Elimination of Discrimination against Women, 40th Session, Jan. 14-Feb. 1, 2008, p. 3, www2.ohchr.org/english/bodies/cedaw/docs/co/CEDAW.C.SAU.CO.2.pdf.

110 Kambiz Fattahi, "Women's bill 'unites' Iran and US," BBC, July 31, 2007, http://news.bbc.co.uk/2/hi/middle_east/6922749.stm.

111 H. Res. 101, Rep. Lynn Woolsey, http://thomas.loc.gov/cgi-bin/bdquery/z?d110:h.res.00101.

112 "General Assembly Adopts Landmark Text Calling for Moratorium on Death Penalty," States News Service, Dec. 18, 2007, www.un.org/News/Press/docs//2007/ga10678.doc.htm.

113 Mary H. Cooper, "Women and Human Rights," *CQ Researcher*, April 30, 1999, p. 356.

114 Christina Hoff Sommers, "The Case against Ratifying the United Nations Convention on the Elimination of All Forms of Discrimination against Women," testimony before the Senate Foreign Relations Committee, June 13, 2002, www.aei.org/publications/filter.all,pubID.15557/pub_detail.asp.

115 "CEDAW: Pro-United Nations, Not Pro-Woman" press release, U.S. Senate Republican Policy Committee, Sept. 16, 2002, http://rpc.senate.gov/_files/FOREIGNje091602.pdf.

116 "Turkmenistan adopts gender equality law," BBC Worldwide Monitoring, Dec. 19, 2007.

117 Faiza Saleh Ambah, "Saudi Women See a Brighter Road on Rights," *The Washington Post*, Jan. 31, 2008, p. A15, www.washingtonpost.com/wp-dyn/content/article/2008/01/30/AR2008013003805.html.

118 Damien McElroy, "Saudi Arabia to lift ban on women drivers," *The Telegraph*, Jan. 1, 2008.

119 Stephanie Levitz, "Lifting the veils of Afghan women," *The Hamilton Spectator* (Ontario, Canada), Feb. 28, 2008, p. A11.

120 "U.N. Secretary-General Ban Ki-moon Launches Campaign to End Violence against Women," U.N. press release, Feb. 25, 2008, http://endviolence.un.org/press.shtml.

121 "Gender Equality Architecture and U.N. Reforms," the Center for Women's Global Leadership and the Women's Environment and Development Organization, July 17, 2006, www.wedo.org/files/Gender%20Equality%20Architecture%20and%20UN%20Reform0606.pdf.

122 Bojana Stoparic, "New-Improved Women's Agency Vies for U.N. Priority," Women's eNews, March 6, 2008, www.womensenews.org/article.cfm?aid=3517.

123 Reel, *op. cit.*

124 Eliana Raszewski and Bill Faries, "Lugo, Ex Bishop, Wins Paraguay Presidential Election," Bloomberg, April 20, 2008.

125 Zahid Hussain, "Pakistan gets its first woman Speaker," *The Times* (of London), March 20, p. 52.

126 Bhaskar Roy, "Finally, women set to get 33% quota," *Times of India*, Jan. 29, 2008.

[127] Massoumeh Torfeh, "Iranian women crucial in Majlis election," BBC, Jan. 30, 2008, http://news.bbc.co.uk/1/hi/world/middle_east/7215272.stm.

[128] "Iran women win few seats in parliament," Agence-France Presse, March 18, 2008.

[129] Swanee Hunt, "Let Women Rule," *Foreign Affairs*, May-June 2007, p. 109.

[130] Kwamboka Oyaro, "A Call to Arm Women Candidates With More Than Speeches," Inter Press Service, Dec. 21, 2007, http://ipsnews.net/news.asp?idnews=40569.

[131] Education Centre for Women in Democracy, www.ecwd.org.

[132] *Ibid.*

[133] Oyaro, *op. cit.*

[134] *Ibid.*

[135] Mary Kimani, "Taking on violence against women in Africa," *AfricaRenewal*, U.N. Dept. of Public Information, July 2007, p. 4, www.un.org/ecosocdev/geninfo/afrec/vol21no2/212-violence-aganist-women.html.

[136] Correspondence with Karen Musalo, Clinical Professor of Law and Director of the Center for Gender & Refugee Studies, University of California Hastings School of Law, April 11, 2008.

[137] "Mexico and Guatemala: Stop the Killings of Women," Amnesty International USA Issue Brief, January 2007, www.amnestyusa.org/document.php?lang=e&id=engusa20070130001.

[138] Manuel Roig-Franzia, "Waning Hopes in Juarez," *The Washington Post*, May 14, 2007, p. A10.

[139] Kimani, *op. cit.*

[140] *Ibid.*

[141] "Justice slow for female war victims," *The Toronto Star*, March 3, 2008, www.thestar.com/News/GlobalVoices/article/308784p.

[142] Speech by Brigid Inder on the Launch of the "Gender Report Card on the International Criminal Court," Dec. 12, 2007, www.icc-women.org/news/docs/Launch_GRC_2007.pdf

[143] "Gender Report Card on the International Criminal Court," Women's Initiatives for Gender Justic, November 2007, p. 32, www.icc-women.org/publications/resources/docs/GENDER_04-01-2008_FINAL_TO_PRINT.pdf.

[144] Turquet, *et al., op. cit.*, p. 8.

[145] Oxfam Gender Equality Fact Sheet, www.oxfam.org.uk/resources/issues/gender/introduction.html.

[146] Itai Madamombe, "Women push onto Africa's agenda," *AfricaRenewal*, U.N. Dept. of Public Information, July 2007, pp. 8-9.

FOR MORE INFORMATION

Equality Now, P.O. Box 20646, Columbus Circle Station, New York, NY 10023; www.equalitynow.org. An international organization working to protect women against violence and promote women's human rights.

Global Database of Quotas for Women; www.quotaproject.org. A joint project of the International Institute for Democracy and Electoral Assistance and Stockholm University providing country-by-country data on electoral quotas for women.

Human Rights Watch, 350 Fifth Ave., 34th floor, New York, NY 10118-3299; (212) 290-4700; www.hrw.org. Investigates and exposes human-rights abuses around the world.

Hunt Alternatives Fund, 625 Mount Auburn St., Cambridge, MA 02138; (617) 995-1900; www.huntalternatives.org. A private foundation that provides grants and technical assistance to promote positive social change; its Initiative for Inclusive Security promotes women in peacekeeping.

Inter-Parliamentary Union, 5, Chemin du Pommier, Case Postale 330, CH-1218 Le Grand-Saconnex, Geneva, Switzerland; +(4122) 919 41 50; www.ipu.org. An organization of parliaments of sovereign states that maintains an extensive database on women serving in parliaments.

Oxfam International, 1100 15th St., N.W., Suite 600, Washington, DC 20005; (202) 496-1170; www.oxfam.org. Confederation of 13 independent nongovernmental organizations working to fight poverty and related social injustice.

U.N. Development Fund for Women (UNIFEM), 304 East 45th St., 15th Floor, New York, NY 10017; (212) 906-6400; www.unifem.org. Provides financial aid and technical support for empowering women and promoting gender equality.

U.N. Division for the Advancement of Women (DAW), 2 UN Plaza, DC2-12th Floor, New York, NY 10017; www.un.org/womenwatch/daw. Formulates policy on gender equality, implements international agreements on women's issues and promotes gender mainstreaming in government activities.

Women's Environment & Development Organization (WEDO), 355 Lexington Ave., 3rd Floor, New York, NY 10017; (212) 973-0325; www.wedo.org. An international organization that works to promote women's equality in global policy.

About the Author

Karen Foerstel is a freelance writer who has worked for the Congressional Quarterly *Weekly Report* and *Daily Monitor*, *The New York Post* and *Roll Call*, a Capitol Hill newspaper. She has published two books on women in Congress, *Climbing the Hill: Gender Conflict in Congress* and *The Biographical Dictionary of Women in Congress*. Her most recent *CQ Global Researcher* was "China in Africa." She has worked in Africa with ChildsLife International, a nonprofit that helps needy children around the world, and with Blue Ventures, a marine conservation organization that protects coral reefs in Madagascar.

Bibliography

Selected Sources

Books

Holland, Jack, *Misogyny: The World's Oldest Prejudice*, Constable & Robinson, 2006.

The late Irish journalist provides vivid details and anecdotes about women's oppression throughout history.

Stone, Merlin, *When God Was a Woman*, Harcourt Brace Jovanovich, 1976.

The book contends that before the rise of Judeo-Christian patriarchies women headed the first societies and religions.

Terry, Geraldine, *Women's Rights*, Pluto Press, 2007.

A feminist who has worked for Oxfam and other nongovernmental organizations outlines major issues facing women today — from violence to globalization to AIDS.

Women and the Environment, UNEP, 2004.

The United Nations Environment Programme shows the integral link between women in the developing world and the changing environment.

Articles

Brady, Brian, "A Question of Honour," *The Independent on Sunday*, Feb. 10, 2008, p. 8.

"Honor killings" and related violence against women are on the rise in the United Kingdom.

Kidder, Thalia, and Kate Raworth, " 'Good Jobs' and hidden costs: women workers documenting the price of precarious employment," *Gender and Development*, Vol. 12, No. 2, p. 12, July 2004.

Two trade and gender experts describe the precarious working conditions and job security experienced by food and garment workers.

Reports and Studies

"Beijing Betrayed," Women's Environment and Development Organization, March 2005, www.wedo.org/files/gmr_pdfs/gmr2005.pdf.

A women's-rights organization reviews the progress and shortcomings of governments in implementing the commitments made during the Fifth World Congress on Women in Beijing in 1995.

"The Millennium Development Goals Report 2007," United Nations, 2007, www.un.org/millenniumgoals/pdf/mdg2007.pdf.

International organizations demonstrate the progress governments have made — or not — in reaching the Millennium Development Goals.

"Trafficking in Persons Report," U.S. Department of State, June 2007, www.state.gov/documents/organization/82902.pdf.

This seventh annual report discusses the growing problems of human trafficking around the world.

"The tsunami's impact on women," Oxfam briefing note, March 5, 2005, www.oxfam.org/en/files/bn050326_tsunami_women/download.

Looking at how the 2004 tsunami affected women in Indonesia, India and Sri Lanka, Oxfam International suggests how governments can better address women's issues during future natural disasters.

"Women in Politics," Inter-Parliamentary Union, 2005, www.ipu.org/PDF/publications/wmn45-05_en.pdf.

The report provides detailed databases of the history of female political representation in governments around the world.

Ballington, Julie, and Azza Karam, "Women in Parliament: Beyond the Numbers," International Institute for Democracy and Electoral Assistance, 2005, www.idea.int/publications/wip2/upload/WiP_inlay.pdf.

The handbook provides female politicians and candidates information and case studies on how women have overcome obstacles to elected office.

Chen, Martha, Joann Vanek, Francie Lund, James Heintz, Renana Jhabvala and Christine Bonner, "Women, Work and Poverty," UNIFEM, 2005, www.unifem.org/attachments/products/PoWW2005_eng.pdf.

The report argues that greater work protection and security is needed to promote women's rights and reduce global poverty.

Larserud, Stina, and Rita Taphorn, "Designing for Equality," International Institute for Democracy and Electoral Assistance, 2007, www.idea.int/publications/designing_for_equality/upload/Idea_Design_low.pdf.

The report describes the impact that gender quota systems have on women's representation in elected office.

Raworth, Kate, and Claire Harvey, "Trading Away Our Rights," Oxfam International, 2004, www.oxfam.org.uk/resources/policy/trade/downloads/trading_rights.pdf.

Through exhaustive statistics, case studies and interviews, the report paints a grim picture of how trade globalization is affecting women.

Turquet, Laura, Patrick Watt and Tom Sharman, "Hit or Miss?" ActionAid, March 7, 2008.

The report reviews how governments are doing in achieving the U.N.'s Millennium Development Goals.

The Next Step:

Additional Articles from Current Periodicals

Globalization

**"World Bank Chief Says Globalization Must Be 'Inclusive,' "
Agence France-Presse, Oct. 11, 2007.**
World Bank President Robert Zoellick says globalization must involve participation from women in developing countries, indigenous peoples and the rural poor in order to effectively combat poverty.

Parekh, Angana, "Gender Issues and Globalisation," Business Line (India), June 29, 2007.
The author reviews the book *Urban Women in Contemporary India*, which says many Indian feminists oppose globalization because they say it leads to the feminization of poverty and commoditization of women.

Widiadana, Rita A., "Many Women Lagging in Job Market," Jakarta Post (Indonesia), April 30, 2007.
Globalization is having both positive and negative effects on the economic growth, job creation and employment of women in Indonesia.

Peacekeeping

Kimanuka, Oscar, "Women Keep Peace Better," East African (Kenya), March 27, 2007.
Officials hope using female peacekeepers will help reduce incidents of rape and other abuses perpetrated by their male counterparts.

McConnell, Tristan, "All-Female Unit Keeps Peace in Liberia," The Christian Science Monitor, March 21, 2007, p. 6.
More than 100 Indian women have been sent to Liberia as the first all-female U.N. peacekeeping unit.

Thompson, Tanya, "How Women Can Help Give Peace a Chance," The Scotsman (Scotland), March 27, 2008.
The inclusion of women in peacekeeping forces improves the success of an operation, because it can defuse male-dominated stand-offs.

Political Rights

"Democracy and Women's Representation in JS," United News of Bangladesh, June 11, 2007.
The Election Commission in Bangladesh is attempting to have women make up at least one-third of every tier of every political party.

"Encouraging Women Leaders," Vanguard (Nigeria), March 6, 2007.
Better education has emphasized the importance of female involvement in Nigeria's government, where token positions are reserved for women.

Hunt, Swanee, "Let Women Rule," Foreign Affairs, May/June 2007, p. 109.
Women have largely closed the gender gap in health and education, but the gap remains large when it comes to the highest political representation.

McMinn, Joanna, "A Society that Still Marginalises Women in Public and Political Life," Irish Times, March 8, 2007.
Equal political representation for women in Ireland would bring about social changes with far-reaching benefits for everyone.

Violence

"Violence Against Women Should Be Prevented," Hewad (Afghanistan), Sept. 4, 2007.
Despite the establishment of the Women's Affairs Ministry in Afghanistan, violence against women has increased in rural areas.

"War's Other Victims," The Economist, Dec. 8, 2007.
The number of women and girls subjected to sexual violence has often been overlooked amid the number of people who have died from conflicts around the world.

Brown, DeNeen L., "The Brutal Truth," The Washington Post, April 8, 2008, p. C1.
A filmmaker finds no remorse among rapists in the Democratic Republic of the Congo — where tens of thousands of women have been raped and mutilated over the past decade.

Mushonga, Netsai, "Don't Use 'Culture' to Oppress Women," Zimbabwe Standard, April 23, 2006.
The Women's Coalition of Zimbabwe has called on policymakers to pass the Domestic Violence Bill, but many view the measure as undermining the country's culture.

CITING *CQ GLOBAL RESEARCHER*

Sample formats for citing these reports in a bibliography include the ones listed below. Preferred styles and formats vary, so please check with your instructor or professor.

MLA STYLE
Flamini, Roland. "Nuclear Proliferation." CQ Global Researcher 1 Apr. 2007: 1-24.

APA STYLE
Flamini, R. (2007, April 1). Nuclear proliferation. *CQ Global Researcher*, 1, 1-24.

CHICAGO STYLE
Flamini, Roland. "Nuclear Proliferation." *CQ Global Researcher*, April 1, 2007, 1-24.

Voices From Abroad:

JASVINDER SANGHERA
Director of Karma Nirvana, A women's project and refuge in Derby, England

Police don't understand honor killing

"The women who ring us for support have said, 'We've been to the police and they don't understand and they're sending us back.' Honor-based violence is far more complex than 'typical' domestic violence and the police are not being trained in how complex it is."

The Guardian (London), June 2007

KALPANA SHARMA
The Hindu Newspaper

Young Indian women reject sex-selective abortions

"I know women who have been persuaded to have multiple abortions and who feel absolutely rotten, but they have no choice — either abortion or divorce. But I sense things are changing with a younger generation of very well educated women who are not prepared to put up with this."

Daily Mail (London), July 2006

HILDA MORALES
Network of Non-Violence Against Women

Abuse goes unpunished in Guatemala

"Unfortunately, in Guatemala, killing a woman is like killing a fly; no importance is assigned to it . . . . the perpetrators are encouraged to continue beating, abusing and killing because they know that nothing will happen, that they won't be punished."

IPS (Latin America), November 2007

DATUK SERI ABDULLAH AHMAD BADAWI
Prime Minister of Malaysia

Women are an asset

"We have a woman who is the governor of Bank Negara, and she is one of the finest in the world. We have two women vice-chancellors in our universities, and we are in the midst of appointing a third. . . . This is a natural progression . . . as more men realize their female counterparts are playing an equally important role."

New Straits Times (Malaysia), September 2007

PUNIT BEDI
New Delhi gynecologist

Medical professionals partly responsible for sex-selective abortion

"Just as throughout history euphemisms have been used to mask mass killings, terms like 'female foeticide,'* 'son preference' and 'sex selection' are now being used to cover up what amount to illegal contract killings on a massive scale, with the contracts being between parents and doctors somehow justified as a form of consumer choice."

Sunday Times (London), August 2007

* Feticide, or foeticide, is the killing of a fetus.

JOLLY KAMUNTU
Lawyer, based in Bukavu, Dem. Republic of Congo

Congolese activists urge the prosecution of war criminals

"The ICC [International Criminal Court] defines rape as a crime of war and a crime against humanity. . . . It has the jurisdiction to arrest the big fish . . . who are in power today. If they are punished, this would intimidate the militias on the ground and give relief to the whole community living through this trauma."

Agence France-Presse, December 2007

MICHELLE BACHELET
President of Chile

Chilean leader criticizes sexism in Latin America

"In my whole political life I have never seen a male candidate whose clothes and hair are discussed. There is a machismo, and a sexism, and it is not just in Latin America. . . . If a woman talks hard then she is [described as] authoritarian, or else she's soft. [Female politicians] are often asked how they manage the children. They would never ask that of a man."

The Independent (London), April 2008

Dario La Crisis/Dario Castillejos

www.cgalecartoons.com

AIDING REFUGEES

BY JOHN FELTON

Excerpted from the CQ Global Researcher. John Felton. (March 2009). "Aiding Refugees." *CQ Global Researcher*, 59-90.

Aiding Refugees

BY JOHN FELTON

THE ISSUES

For more than two decades, the guerrilla group known as the Lord's Resistance Army (LRA) has been terrorizing villagers in Uganda — forcibly recruiting child soldiers and brutally attacking civilians. In recent years, the dreaded group has crossed the border into the Democratic Republic of Congo.

Last October, LRA marauders attacked Tambohe's village in northeastern Congo. They shot and killed her brother-in-law and two others, then torched the houses, even those with people inside.

Tambohe and her surviving family members — five adults and 10 children — fled into the forest, briefly returning five days later to bury the bodies after the raiders had left. The family then walked north for three days until they found safety in a village just across the border in southern Sudan, living with several hundred other Congolese displaced by the LRA.

"We have built a hut, and we live there," the 38-year-old Tambohe later told the medical aid group Doctors Without Borders. "The children sleep badly due to the mosquitoes and because we sleep on the ground. I sleep badly because I dream of the stench of burnt flesh. I dream they [the LRA] come and . . . take us to their camp." [1]

LRA violence is only one aspect of ongoing conflict in Congo that has killed 5 million people in the past decade and forced millions from their homes — including more than 400,000 last year, according to Human Rights Watch. [2]

Residents struggle to maintain normalcy in Kenya's Eldoret camp, home to 14,000 Kenyans who fled their homes during post-election rioting in December 2007. But they are the lucky ones. Many of the world's 26 million internally displaced people (IDPs) receive no aid at all or live in crude huts made of sticks and plastic sheeting, without reliable access to food or clean water. The U.N. High Commissioner for Refugees provided aid to some 13.7 million IDPs in 2007.

IRIN/Manoocher Deghati

Many, like Tambohe, fled their homes and crossed into another country, making them legally refugees. Under international law, she and her family should be able to remain in Sudan and receive humanitarian aid, shelter and protection because they have a "well-founded fear" of persecution if they return home. [3]

If Tambohe had fled her home but remained in Congo, she would have been considered an "internally displaced person" (IDP), and the Congolese government would be legally responsible for aiding and protecting her. But in the Democratic Republic of the Congo and many other countries, international law is little more than a theory. The Kinshasa government is weak, and the army itself has been accused of abusing civilians. [4] So helping the Tambohes of the world falls primarily to the United Nations (U.N.) and non-governmental aid agencies.

Today, there are more than 90 million refugees, displaced persons and disaster victims around the world. More than 40 million have fled conflict or violence, according to Antonio Guterres, U.N. High Commissioner for Refugees (UNHCR), who leads international efforts to aid the displaced. [5] Of those, about 16 million are refugees (including 4.6 million Palestinians) and 26 million are IDPs. (See map, p. 62.) Up to 50 million more people are victims of natural disaster, according to the U.N.'s Office for the Coordination of Humanitarian Affairs. In China's Sichuan Province, for example, many of the 5 million people who lost their homes last May in an earthquake remain homeless, and thousands of Americans are still displaced from Hurricane Katrina, which struck New Orleans in 2005. [6]

Millions of displaced people overseas live in sprawling camps or settlements established by governments or the United Nations, often in harsh desert or jungle environments. A large but unknown number of others, like Tambohe, find their own temporary shelter — sometimes living with friends or relatives but more often building makeshift tents and huts or moving into crowded rental housing in urban slums.

Food insecurity — or even starvation — rank among the most serious consequences of displacement. In Kenya, for example, last year's post-

Continued on p. 63

Most Displaced People Are in Africa and the Middle East

The U.N. High Commissioner for Refugees (UNHCR) monitors nearly 32 million people around the world who have been uprooted for a variety of reasons, including 25 million who fled their homes to escape war or conflict, mostly in Africa and the Middle East. Among those are 11 million refugees — those who have crossed borders and thus are protected by international law — and nearly 14 million internally displaced people (IDPs) who remain in their home countries. Some critics want the UNHCR to monitor and assist the world's other 12.3 million IDPs now being aided by other agencies.

Displaced Populations Monitored by the UNHCR

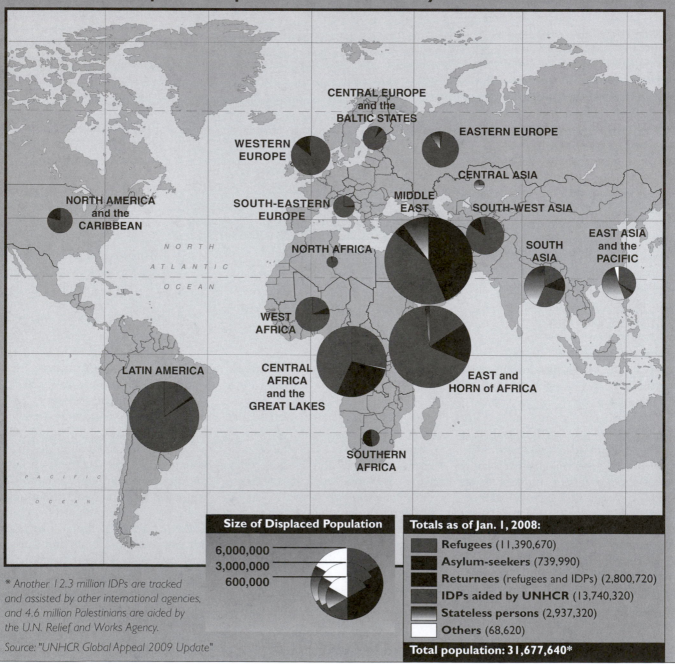

* Another 12.3 million IDPs are tracked and assisted by other international agencies, and 4.6 million Palestinians are aided by the U.N. Relief and Works Agency.

Source: "UNHCR Global Appeal 2009 Update"

Size of Displaced Population

6,000,000
3,000,000
600,000

Totals as of Jan. 1, 2008:

Refugees (11,390,670)
Asylum-seekers (739,990)
Returnees (refugees and IDPs) (2,800,720)
IDPs aided by UNHCR (13,740,320)
Stateless persons (2,937,320)
Others (68,620)

Total population: 31,677,640*

Continued from p. 61

election bloodshed caused so many farmers from key food-producing areas to flee their homes — leaving crops unplanted or unharvested — that an estimated 10 million Kenyans now face starvation. [7]

Some experts predict the world increasingly will be forced to deal with massive displacements — potentially involving hundreds of millions of people — caused by natural disasters intensified by climate change. Elisabeth Rasmusson, secretary general of the Norwegian Refugee Council, which aids and advocates for the displaced, warned last December that the world faces a potential vicious cycle: As climate change degrades the environment, it triggers more civil conflicts as people fight for access to water and other resources, further damaging the environment — displacing more people at each stage. [8]

Long before concern about climate change, however, international agencies were overwhelmed by the magnitude of conflict-caused displacements, which have been rising dramatically over the past decade. [9] And while the UNHCR's budget has nearly doubled since 2000 — from under $1 billion to $1.8 billion this year — the agency struggles to protect and care for refugees and IDPs in 116 countries around the world. As of Jan. 1, 2008, the agency was aiding 4.5 million of the world's 11.4 million refugees and 13.7 million of the world's 26 million IDPs. (*See graph at right.*) Because the UNHCR and other aid agencies often operate in or near conflict zones, the delivery of humanitarian relief can be dangerous and, at times, impossible. In the Darfur region of western Sudan, for example, aid groups repeatedly have been forced to halt aid shipments because of attacks on relief convoys. [10]

But the lack of security is only one of a daunting litany of challenges faced by the UNHCR and its dozens of partner agencies, including chronic shortages of funds and reliance on "emergency" appeals to wealthy countries, the hostility of local governments, bureaucratic turf battles and indifference among world leaders.

And, despite promises to the contrary, the U.N. Security Council often has been unable or unwilling to take effective action — such as in Rwanda in 1994 and in Darfur since 2003 — to halt horrific death and displacement tolls. In both situations, ill-equipped and undermanned U.N. peacekeepers were unable to prevent what some have called the genocidal slaughter of hundreds of thousands of people. Yet some critics question whether the U.N. is trying to do either too much or too little, and others say international refugee law needs to be updated to take into account recent trends, such as the rapid increase in IDPs.

Those living in refugee and IDP camps have more immediate concerns, including overcrowded conditions; inadequate housing, food and medical care; and the refusal of local governments to allow them to work (or even to leave

U.N. Serves About Half the World's Displaced

The U.N. High Commissioner for Refugees (UNHCR) has provided aid to an average of about 5.7 million of the globe's 11 million refugees each year — mostly in developing countries — over the past decade (blue lines). Meanwhile, the world's population of internally displaced persons (IDPs) has risen from 19 million in 1998 to 26 million in 2007. Individual governments are responsible for IDPs. But since 2005 the UNHCR has more than doubled the number of IDPs it serves each year — from 6.6 million in 2005 to 13.7 million in 2007 (orange lines).

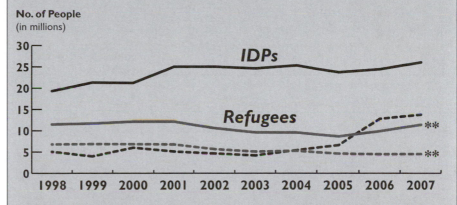

Total Refugees and IDPs vs. Those Receiving UNHCR Aid
(1998-2007)

* Does not include 4.6 million Palestinians assisted by the U.N. Relief and Works Agency in 2007.

** 2007 figures include people "in refugee-like situations" who were not included in previous years and excludes some 822,000 resettled refugees previously included in refugee statistics. Thus the 2007 data is not comparable with previous years.

Sources: 2007 U.N. High Commissioner for Refugees, Statistical Yearbook; "Global IDP Estimates (1990-2007)," Internal Displacement Monitoring Centre

Sudan Hosts Most Displaced People

Of the millions of refugees and internally displaced persons (IDPs) monitored by the U.N. High Commissioner for Refugees, Sudan houses nearly 4 million — more than any other country. Four of the top 10 host countries are in Africa. Most refugees and IDPs come from Iraq, Afghanistan, Colombia and five African countries.

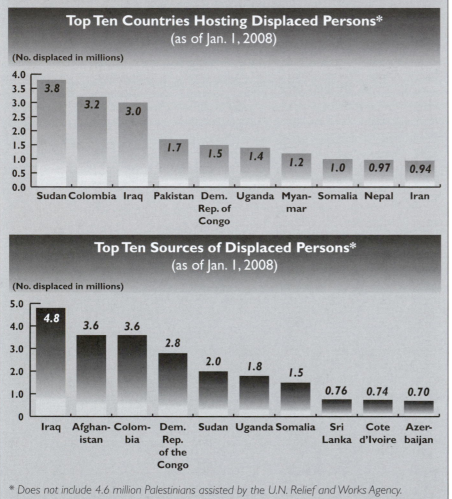

Top Ten Countries Hosting Displaced Persons*
(as of Jan. 1, 2008)

(No. displaced in millions)

Sudan 3.8, Colombia 3.2, Iraq 3.0, Pakistan 1.7, Dem. Rep. of Congo 1.5, Uganda 1.4, Myanmar 1.2, Somalia 1.0, Nepal 0.97, Iran 0.94

Top Ten Sources of Displaced Persons*
(as of Jan. 1, 2008)

(No. displaced in millions)

Iraq 4.8, Afghanistan 3.6, Colombia 3.6, Dem. Rep. of the Congo 2.8, Sudan 2.0, Uganda 1.8, Somalia 1.5, Sri Lanka 0.76, Cote d'Ivoire 0.74, Azerbaijan 0.70

* Does not include 4.6 million Palestinians assisted by the U.N. Relief and Works Agency.

Source: "UNHCR Global Appeal, 2009 Update," U.N. High Commissioner for Refugees, January 2009

the camps). Negash, an Ethiopian who has lived in Kenya's sprawling Kakuma refugee camp for nearly four years, says aid officials often don't understand how their decisions affect the camp's 50,000 residents every day. "There are people who work for agencies here that don't know what is happening in the camp," he says. "They live in their own compounds and don't really communicate with the refugees to find out what is happening to them."

The United Nations began reforming its humanitarian system in 2005, partly to address concerns about its inability to deliver timely and effective aid to internally displaced people. Jeff Crisp, director of policy and evaluations for UNHCR, says the U.N.'s reforms are having "a solid and positive impact" on the lives of displaced people even though revamping such a large-scale system of delivering aid "clearly is a work in progress."

The rise in refugees and IDPs is the direct result of dozens of small wars between rebels and government soldiers during the last 50 years, particularly in Africa and Asia. Some have dragged on for decades, creating generations of displaced families. For instance, Sudan's 20-year-long civil war displaced 400,000 people, but at least 130,000 remain in neighboring countries, according to the U.N. [11] Colombia's ongoing civil conflict has displaced nearly 10 percent of the country's population. [12]

Even when the wars end, civilians often remain displaced because they fear returning home, their homes have been destroyed or they have become settled elsewhere. In Afghanistan, for example, more than 5 million Afghan refugees have returned home since the United States ousted the Taliban regime seven years ago, but some 3 million remain in neighboring Pakistan and Iran — a large number of whom probably never will go back. [13]

The Afghan refugees represent what experts call a "protracted situation," which is defined as when at least 25,000 people are displaced from their homes for five years or more. (*See sidebar, p. 74.*) More than 30 protracted situations exist around the world, according to Elizabeth Ferris, director of the Brookings-Bern Project on Internal Displacement, run by the Brookings Institution in Washington, D.C., and the University of Bern (Switzerland) School of Law.

As governments, international agencies and specialists in the field seek better ways to protect and aid refugees and internally displaced people, here are some of the questions being debated:

Is the U.N. meeting refugees' needs?

Since its founding in 1951, the UNHCR has been the world's frontline

Refugees Fall into Eight Categories

When people flee their homes and seek aid, they can be assigned to one of eight classifications, each of which conveys unique legal rights or restrictions. For instance, some are entitled under international law to receive humanitarian aid, shelter and protection because they have a "well-founded fear" of persecution if they return home. Here are the key definitions under international law and commonly accepted practice of the various categories of people who are seeking, or in need of, assistance:

Asylum-seeker: A person who has applied (either individually or as part of a group) for legal refugee status under national and international laws. If refugee status is denied, the asylum-seeker must leave the country (and could face expulsion) unless he or she is given permission to stay on humanitarian grounds.

Internally displaced person (IDP): Someone who has been forced to flee his home due to armed conflict, generalized violence, human-rights violations or natural or man-made disasters but has not crossed an international border.

Migrants: In the absence of a universally accepted definition of a migrant, the International Organization on Migration says the term is "usually understood" to cover all cases in which "the decision to migrate is taken freely by the individual concerned for reasons of 'personal convenience' and without intervention of an external compelling factor. An "economic migrant" is someone who leaves his home country in search of better economic opportunities elsewhere.

Persons in "IDP-like" situations: This relatively new term developed by the U.N. High Commissioner for Refugees (UNHCR) describes "groups of persons who are inside their country of nationality or habitual residence and who face protection risks similar to those of IDPs, but who, for practical or other reasons, could not be reported as such." For example, the UNHCR has used the term to describe displaced people in Georgia (including former residents of the breakaway provinces of Abkhazia and South Ossetia) and Russia.

Persons in "refugee-like" situations: Another relatively recent term used by the UNHCR to describe people who are outside their country or territory of origin "who face protection risks similar to those of refugees, but for whom refugee status has, for practical or other reasons, not been ascertained." In many cases, these are refugees who have settled more or less permanently in another country on an informal basis. The largest single population in this group is the estimated 1.1 million Afghans living outside formal refugee camps in Pakistan.

Refugee: Under the 1951 Refugee Convention (as amended in 1967), a refugee is someone who, due to a "well-founded fear of being persecuted for reasons of race, religion, nationality, membership of a particular social group or political opinions," has left his home country and is unable or, owing to fear, "unwilling to avail himself of the protection of that country." A person becomes a refugee by meeting the standards of the Refugee Convention, even before being granted asylum (*see above*), which legally confirms his or her refugee status.

Returnee: A refugee or IDP who has returned to his home — or home country or region.

Stateless person: Anyone who is not recognized as a citizen of any country. Stateless persons lack national or international legal protections and cannot legally cross international borders because they don't have and cannot obtain a valid passport or other identity papers. Between 3 million and 12 million people worldwide are stateless; the wide range results from a lack of information in some countries and conflicting assessments about which groups actually are stateless.

Sources: "Glossary on Migration," International Migration Law, International Organization for Migration, Geneva, Switzerland, www.iom.int/jahia/webdav/site/myjahiasite/shared/shared/mainsite/published_docs/serial_publications/Glossary_eng.pdf; and "Glossary," U.N. High Commissioner for Refugees, Geneva, Switzerland, www.unhcr.org/publ/PUBL/4922d4390.pdf

---

agency for aiding and protecting refugees. Working with other U.N. agencies and nongovernmental agencies — such as CARE and the International Federation of Red Cross and Red Crescent Societies — the Geneva, Switzerland-based agency is spending $1.8 billion this year to provide housing, food, medical care and protection for millions of refugees and displaced persons in 116 countries. [14] The agency also decides the legal status of refugees in 75 countries that can't, or won't, make those determinations themselves. In 2007, the UNHCR determined the status of 48,745 people. [15]

Both critics and its defenders, however, say the agency often falls short of its official mandate to safeguard "the rights and well-being of refugees." [16] Barbara Harrell-Bond, the founder and former director of the Refugee Studies Center at Oxford University and a harsh critic of the UNHCR, says one of her biggest concerns is how aid programs are funded.

"The funds . . . always come from emergency budgets and are allocated to UNHCR by governments at their discretion," she says. As a result, agency programs are "at the mercy of the whims of international politics."

If world leaders become fixated on a particular crisis that is making headlines in Western countries — such as the situation in Sudan's Darfur region — refugees elsewhere suffer, Harrell-Bond says. In addition, education and

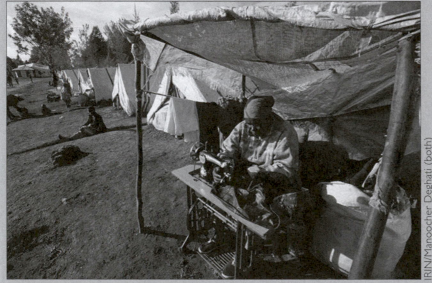

IRIN/Manoocher Deghati (both)

Camp Life

Tents patched together from scraps of cloth house Afghans living in a camp near Kabul, Afghanistan (top). The government helps Afghans uprooted by decades of war, but many face overcrowded conditions and inadequate housing, food and medical care. Typically, internally displaced persons cannot work for wages in order to preserve jobs for local residents, so some set up their own small businesses inside the camps, such as a Kenyan seamstress at the Eldoret camp in Kenya (bottom).

years. Furthermore, she adds, the UNHCR and its partner agencies routinely deny refugees' basic rights, including the right to leave the camps. Most host governments want refugees to be contained in camps, and the U.N. complies "by putting them in what amounts to gigantic cages," Harrell-Bond says.

In her 2005 book, *Rights in Exile: Janus Faced Humanitarianism,* Harrell-Bond and a co-author argue that "the rights of refugees cannot be protected in camps and settlements." They harshly criticize the UNHCR for not protecting refugees' rights, based on extensive research into the treatment of Kenyan and Ugandan refugees during the late 1990s — treatment the authors say continues today in many refugee camps.

For instance, refugees usually are not allowed to leave the camps and are not allowed to work. Harrell-Bond says the UNCHR should push governments harder to accept refugees into the local community. "Refugees can contribute to the societies where they have taken refuge and not simply live on handouts from the U.N.," she says, citing examples in Uganda and Zambia where so-called "local integration" has worked.

UNHCR Policy Director Crisp acknowledges the agency sometimes fails to meet refugees' needs but says decisions to "warehouse" refugees are made by the host countries. "In many cases, refugees are admitted to countries on strict condition that they be accommodated in camps and provided with their basic needs by UNHCR and other agencies," he says. UNHCR tries to get governments to improve refugees' situations, "but this is not always possible."

Despite such constraints, Crisp says the UNHCR is trying new approaches, particularly for those trapped in protracted situations. For instance, in 2008 the high commissioner set deadlines for getting people out of five specific protracted situations:

• Afghan refugees in Iran and Pakistan;

job training programs designed to help refugees lead dignified lives once they leave the camps are considered "development" programs, she says, which "come from a completely different budget . . . and never the twain shall meet."

Moreover, local governments rarely receive international aid for hosting refugees and usually are anxious for refugees to go home, she says, so they have little incentive to improve camp conditions. As a consequence, refugees are "just warehoused" in camps for years and

- Bosnian and Croatian refugees in Serbia;
- Eritrean refugees in eastern Sudan;
- Burundians in Tanzania; and
- Members of Myanmar's Rohingya minority who fled to Bangladesh. [17]

More broadly, as part of its 2005 reform program, the U.N. established clear guidelines for which U.N. agency should provide services in specific situations. [18] The so-called cluster approach made the UNHCR responsible for managing camps for IDPs displaced by natural disasters and providing emergency shelter and protection for IDPs displaced by conflict. [19]

A 2007 evaluation found the new approach had improved humanitarian responses in Chad, the Democratic Republic of the Congo, Somalia and Uganda. [20] Ramesh Rajasingham, head of the Displacement and Protection Support Section for the U.N.'s humanitarian affairs office, says giving UNHCR a "clear leadership" role in managing displacement camps and emergency shelters has fostered "an improved IDP response."

But some non-U.N. experts say the bureaucratic changes have produced only modest benefits. Implementation has been "half-hearted," especially in protecting IDPs, says Roberta Cohen, a senior fellow at the Brookings Institution and prominent IDP advocate. The UNHCR is not "playing the robust leadership role" she had hoped for in protecting IDPs.

Likewise, Joel Charny, vice president for policy at Refugees International, says the UNHCR's protection of IDPs remains "problematic." Ferris, Cohen's successor at the Brookings-Bern Project on Displacement, recommends a rewards structure that would give agencies and individuals an incentive to better aid and protect displaced persons.

"Agencies need to internalize their work with IDPs and not see it as something separate from their missions or a burden they have to carry," she says.

Most Refugees Flee to Neighboring Countries

Contrary to the perception that refugees are flooding into developed countries in Europe and other regions, most find asylum in neighboring countries and remain there. Only between 10 percent and 17 percent leave the countries where they were granted asylum.

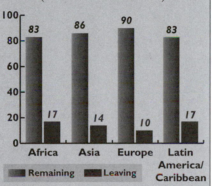

Refugees Remaining in or Leaving Their Asylum Regions
(As of December 2007)

Source: "2007 Global Trends: Refugees, Asylum-seekers, Returnees, Internally Displaced and Stateless Persons," U.N. High Commissioner for Refugees, June 2008

James Milner, a refugee policy analyst at Carleton University in Ottawa, Ontario, Canada, and former UNHCR consultant, says the agency "does a good job in some places and a bad job in some places." While it has saved millions of lives during civil wars, the agency also ends up "warehousing" refugees for long periods, he says, causing them to abandon hope for better lives and become totally dependent on aid.

Like Harrell-Bond, Milner — who coauthored a 2008 book sympathetic to the agency's successes and failures — traces most of UNHCR's problems to its funding procedures. In effect, he says, industrialized countries that provide the bulk of UNHCR's money "earmark" where they want the money to go. [21]

"The United States, for example, gives funding to emergencies it considers important" but gives less to other situations, Milner says. "When I worked in Cameroon, each October we simply ran out of funding to provide health care for nursing mothers, because that was not a priority for the people in Washington. You can criticize UNHCR for not being more aggressive in some of these situations, but when you recognize the constraints placed on UNHCR, it places the challenges in a broader context."

Should the Refugee Convention be updated?

The 1951 Convention Relating to the Status of Refugees — known as the Refugee Convention — is the basic underpinning of refugee law. Created to protect European refugees during and after World War II, the treaty was amended in 1967 to apply worldwide.

The treaty grants "asylum" to refugees, or groups of them, who can demonstrate a "well-founded fear of being persecuted" because of race, nationality, religion or political beliefs. Those who flee their country because of such a fear are considered refugees. The process of demonstrating that fear and seeking permission to stay in the country of refuge is called seeking asylum. However, in many places — including the United States — asylum seekers may be imprisoned for months or even years while their cases are reviewed. Once asylum is granted, refugees can stay in the host country until it is safe to return home. Refugees who are denied asylum often are deported, usually back to their home countries.

Even with the 1967 amendment, the convention does not apply to the vast majority of people who flee from their homes. For example, IDPs do not have legal protection because they do not cross international borders, nor do those who flee across borders to escape natural disasters. [22] Being covered by the treaty might have little significance for people forced from their homes by violent groups like the Lord's Resistance Army. Even so, some advocates say applying the treaty to IDPs might, in some cases, pressure the governments involved to take better care of their citizens.

The treaty has critics across the ideological spectrum. Some refugee advocates, including Harrell-Bond, complain that it lacks universal standards for granting asylum, so Western countries, in particular, "are free to turn away asylum-seekers on no basis whatsoever."

Some Western officials say the treaty is being misused by "economic migrants" — would-be immigrants from poor countries simply seeking a better life — who claim to be refugees but do not qualify for asylum on the basis of a fear of persecution.

The treaty "is no longer working as its framers intended," then British Home Secretary Jack Straw said in 2001, citing the large increase in displaced people worldwide. "Too much effort and resources are being expended on dealing with unfounded claims for asylum, and not enough on helping those in need of protection." [23] He called for "radical thinking" on a better way to determine who is a refugee and who is not.

Despite such concerns, many experts say the convention will not be amended or updated any time soon. The U.N. treaty-making process is cumbersome and

Chaos in Somalia Puts Nation at Risk

Humanitarian aid feeds nearly half the population.

Mohamed Abdi, his wife, and five children fled the never-ending violence in Somalia's capital city of Mogadishu last October, finding safety — but not much more — in the breakaway region of Somaliland to the north. The trip took nine days, and all along the way they feared being attacked by the opposing sides in the most recent round of conflict in Somalia.

Once they reached Somaliland, Abdi and his family found very little in the way of services, but the local government welcomed them as refugees. "We don't have much, and we depend on the kindness of these people; some days we eat, some we don't," he told the United Nations' IRIN news service in October. "But at least we have peace and security. That is what we want and the chance to make a living for our families without being afraid of being killed." [1]

Displaced people like Abdi never have it easy, often living in crude shelters and on starvation rations. But the situation is especially grave in Somalia — the only country in the world that for nearly two decades has been without even a functioning government — where a fatal combination of internal conflict and natural disaster has generated hundreds of thousands of refugees, migrants and internally displaced people (IDPs).

Ever since the last real government — a harsh dictatorship — was overthrown in 1991, hundreds of thousands of refugees settled in Kenya and other neighboring countries. Thousands of others have crossed the dangerous Gulf of Aden to equally impoverished Yemen.

Meanwhile, an estimated 1.3 million Somalis have become IDPs — displaced but living within their own country. [2] Most had fled Mogadishu, decimated by years of fighting among warlords, rebel groups, failed temporary governments and the Ethiopian army, which invaded in late 2006 and withdrew in January.

But IDPs escaping violence are not the only Somalis suffering. The U.N. Food and Agriculture Organization reported in October 2008 that 3.2 million people — 43 percent of the population — regularly need humanitarian assistance to survive. [3] While armed conflict has created most of the dislocations among Somalis, frequent droughts and floods have also caused recurrent famines that sent rural families fleeing to urban areas, often to be displaced by fighting.

Waves of conflict and displacement have swept over Somalia ever since the military dictatorship of Major General Mohamed Siad Barre was pushed from power in 1991. The most severe recent displacement occurred in August 2007, just eight months after Ethiopia invaded Somalia to oust a short-lived Islamist regime. Some 400,000 people were displaced by fighting in Mogadishu; most of them ended up in one of 200 camps that cropped up along a nine-mile stretch of the main road outside of the capital — "the most congested IDP nexus in the world," according to a refugee official. [4]

The U.N. High Commissioner for Refugees (UNHCR) and other aid groups provide limited food and medical aid to the camps, but little in the way of shelter. Patrick Duplat, an advocate for Refugees International who visited the camps twice in 2008, describes them as "mostly a sprawl of makeshift shelters — twigs and cloth, and sometimes plastic sheeting, whatever people are able to find."

Since Ethiopia withdrew its army in January, some 40,000 IDPs have returned to several Mogadishu neighborhoods, apparently with the intention of staying, according to the UNHCR. [5] Even so, continued fighting in the city has displaced an unknown number of others. The UNHCR said on Feb. 27 it is still discouraging IDPs from returning to what would be "ruined homes and livelihoods." [6]

In recent years nearly 500,000 people have fled Somalia to neighboring countries, but they have encountered daunting hazards along the way, including bandits, security forces demanding bribes and even possible death on the high seas. [7] Those who avoid violence and persecution may be eligible for refugee status and entitled to return home someday; others probably would be considered migrants because they are searching for economic opportunities overseas.

Thousands of Somalis have risked crossing the Gulf of Aden or the Red Sea by boat to reach Yemen. On Feb. 28, 45 Somalis drowned when their boat capsized as they were crossing the gulf. Those who arrive safely generally are given *de jure* refugee status, even though many might be considered migrants because they never plan to return to their homes. About 82,000 Somalis were registered as refugees in Yemen in late 2008, but the UNHCR said the total could be closer to 150,000. [8]

Most Somali refugees, however, have fled into neighboring Kenya, even though it closed its borders to Somalis in 2007. According to the U.N., some 250,000 Somali refugees are in Kenya, including at least 45,000 who entered in 2008. [9]

At the border, would-be refugees often set out on foot to the U.N.'s official transit camps at Dadaab, 50 miles inside Kenya, frequently traveling at night to evade Kenyan police. As of late January the camps held 244,127 people — nearly triple their capacity. "Trying to squeeze 200,000-plus people into an area intended for 90,000 is inviting trouble," said Craig Johnstone, deputy U.N. high commissioner for refugees, after visiting on Feb. 5. [10] The UNHCR has been trying to raise $92 million from international donors to build two new camps for 60,000 more refugees. [11]

Human Rights Watch researcher Gerry Simpson, who visited the camps in late 2008, said many people told him they had tried to register as refugees but had given up because of the lack of space in the camps. "After risking their lives to flee appalling violence in Somalia and make it to the relative safety of Kenya, they end up with nothing: no food, no shelter, and incredibly difficult access to water and health care," Simpson said. [12]

An estimated 1.3 million people have been uprooted by the ongoing conflict in Somalia but are still living inside the country. Persistent violence, drought and flooding have created one of the world's longest ongoing humanitarian crises.

AFP/Getty Images/Radu Sigheti

[1] "Fleeing from the frying pan into the fire," IRIN news service, Oct. 29, 2008, www.irinnews.org/Report.aspx?ReportId=81164.

[2] "Displaced Populations Report," U.N. Office for the Coordination of Humanitarian Affairs, Regional Office for Central and East Africa, July-December 2008, p. 5.

[3] "Poor rains intensify human suffering and deprivation — report," IRIN news service, Oct. 17, 2008, www.irinnews.org/Report.aspx?ReportId=80971.

[4] "Somalia: To Move Beyond the Failed State," International Crisis Group, Dec. 23, 2008, pp. 12, 18.

[5] "Thousands of Somalis Return to Mogadishu Despite Renewed Fighting," U.N. High Commissioner for Refugees, Feb. 27, 2009, www.unhcr.org/news/NEWS/49a7d8bb2.html.

[6] *Ibid.*

[7] "Somalia Complex Emergency: Situation Report," Jan. 15, 2009, U.S. Agency for International Development, www.usaid.gov/our_work/humanitarian_assistance/disaster_assistance/countries/somalia/template/fs_sr/fy2009/somalia_ce_sr04_01-15-2009.pdf.

[8] "2009 Global Update for Yemen," U.N. High Commissioner for Refugees, p. 1, www.unhcr.org/publ/PUBL/4922d4240.pdf.

[9] "Displaced Populations Report," *op. cit.*, p. 6.

[10] "Camp resources stretched by influx of Somali refugees," IRIN news service, Feb. 6, 2009, www.irinnews.org/Report.aspx?ReportId=82792.

[11] "Somali refugees suffer as Dadaab camp populations swell to 230,000," UNHCR, www.unhcr.org/news/NEWS/4950ef401.html.

[12] "Kenya: Protect Somali Refugees. Government and Donors Should Urgently Address Refugee Crisis," Human Rights Watch, Nov. 13, 2008, www.hrw.org/en/news/2008/11/13/kenya-protect-somali-refugees.

takes years to complete. Moreover, global interest in new treaties has dwindled in recent years, and even IDP advocates aren't willing to risk having the treaty watered down instead of strengthened.

Carleton University's Milner notes the current treaty was negotiated shortly after World War II, "when notions of human justice were quite powerful because of what happened during the war, particularly in Nazi Germany." Nearly six decades later, Western countries — the desired destination for many refugees — are increasingly reluctant to open their borders. "If we reopened the Refugee Convention, we likely would see a race to the lowest common denominator — protecting borders — rather than refugees," Milner says. "That's a risk I'm not willing to take."

Khalid Koser, an analyst specializing in refugee affairs at the Geneva Center for Security Policy, agrees. "At least the current convention has 150-odd signatories, most of whom abide by it," Koser says.

The UNHCR has expressed similar concerns. In a recent paper exploring whether those fleeing natural disasters should be given legal status under the treaty, the agency warned that any attempt to modify the convention could lower refugee-protection standards "and even undermine the international refugee-protection regime altogether." [24]

Meanwhile, Europe is engaged in a spirited debate over implementation of the treaty; since 2001 the European Union (EU) has been developing a common system for granting asylum among its 27 member countries. The European Pact on Immigration and Asylum,

Most Funds Go to Africa, Come From U.S.

More than one-third of U.N. refugee aid in 2009 will go to programs in Africa, more than any other region. In 2007, the United States contributed nearly one-third of the funds for the Office of the U.N. High Commissioner for Refugees (UNHCR) — four times more than No. 2-donor Japan.

UNHCR Budget by Region, 2009

- Africa 36%
- Middle East and North Africa 19%
- Asia and the Pacific 10%
- Europe 8%
- Americas 3%
- Global programs 6%
- Headquarters 8%
- Reserves 10%

UNHCR Donors, 2007

- United States 28.9%
- Japan 7.1%
- Sweden 6.7%
- European Commission 5.7%
- Netherlands 5.8%
- Denmark 4.6%
- United Kingdom 4.4%
- Norway 4.4%
- Canada 2.8%
- Spain 2.6%
- Other 25.9%

* Figures may not total 100 due to rounding.

Source: U.N. High Commissioner for Refugees Global Appeal 2009 Update

European Council on Refugees and Exiles, a coalition of 69 nongovernmental organizations. [26] By contrast, some other European countries, particularly in Scandinavia, accept upwards of 90 percent of asylum-seekers, Frelick notes.

"There has been an utter failure to share the refugee burdens," Frelick says. "The richer countries have done an effective job of deflecting the burden off onto the poor countries, which are responding by turning people away, even those who are legitimate refugees."

Should the United States admit more Iraqi refugees?

Fearing that some could be terrorists, the United States has been slow to accept Iraqis who have fled to neighboring countries — notably Syria and Jordan — since the U.S. invasion in 2003.

Through the middle of 2008, the Bush administration accepted only about 10,000 Iraqi refugees out of the 1-2 million who have fled, according to Refugees International and other nongovernmental organizations. [27] But under pressure from Congress and advocacy groups, it stepped up Iraqi admissions last year and admitted more than 13,800 Iraqis as permanent residents — slightly more than the administration's 12,000 annual goal for fiscal 2008, which ended on Oct. 1. The administration's 2009 goal is 17,000 Iraqi admissions. [28]

Several major refugee and human-rights groups want the U.S. quota raised to 105,000 Iraqis in 2009. Among the Iraqi refugees in Syria and Jordan are thousands who worked directly with the U.S. military and other government agencies, American contractors and the news media. Some served as translators or even intelligence operatives, while others filled jobs such as drivers and cooks.

"Their stay in neighboring states remains extremely precarious, and many live in fear of being forcibly returned

adopted by EU leaders on Oct. 16, 2008, promises that EU countries will speed up asylum determinations, eliminating delays that often stretch into months or years. [25] Refugee rights advocates, however, worry the EU is trying to close its doors to legitimate refugees, not just economic migrants who are not entitled to asylum under the treaty.

At Human Rights Watch, refugee policy Director Bill Frelick says the

new European pact also does little to relieve unequal burden-sharing. Most migrants and refugees from Africa and the Middle East enter Europe through the poorest countries in southeastern Europe, which have been rejecting refugees at very high rates. For instance, since 2004 Greece has granted asylum to fewer than 1 percent of the refugees from Iraq, Afghanistan and other countries, according to the

to Iraq, where they face death threats and further persecution," said a joint statement by Refugees International and a dozen other organizations on July 31, 2008. Helping these Iraqis re-settle in the United States "will demon-strate America's dedication to protect-ing the most vulnerable and our commitment to peace and security in the region." [29]

The U.S. Department of Homeland Security said in September it was "com-mitted to streamlining the process for ad-mitting Iraqi refugees to the U.S. while ensuring the highest level of security." [30] However, the Obama administration has not announced plans for a dramatic in-crease in admissions. A State Department spokesman said in early February a de-cision was pending.

A report released in January by the Center for American Progress, a liberal think tank in Washington, D.C., said 30,000 to 100,000 Iraqis have been "affiliated" with the Unit-ed States in one way or another dur-ing the war, and many would be "in imminent danger" of assassination if they returned home. [31]

The group advocates bringing up to 25,000 of those Iraqis and their families to the United States over the next five years. Natalie Ondiak, lead author of the proposal, says the Unit-ed States "has a moral obligation to the Iraqis who have worked for the government, were loyal to us and now fear for their lives because of the stigma of having been associated with the United States."

However, Ann Corcoran — a Mary-land blogger who runs the Refugee Resettlement Watch blog — is a vocal critic of such proposals. She cites cases in which church groups and other agencies bring refugees to the United States but fail to help them adjust to their new lives.

"These organizations are not taking very good care of the refugees who are already here, and they say they don't have the resources to do the job," she says. "So, if we are talking about another 25,000 or 100,000 refugees, where do they think these people will be cared for? Who is going to make sure they have housing and jobs and education for their children? It's just insane." [32]

A better alternative, she says "is to keep them in the region, to keep them comfortable and proceeding with their lives in the Middle East until the sit-uation in Iraq is safe enough for them to return."

Congress in 2006 created a pro-gram to speed up admissions for up to 500 Iraqi and Afghan translators per year. In 2008 Congress added an-other program allowing up to 5,000 Iraqis who worked in various capac-ities for the U.S. government or con-tractors to enter the United States in each of the five fiscal years, begin-ning in 2008. However, Ondiak says only about 600 translators gained ad-mission in 2008. ∎

More than 250,000 Sri Lankans have been forced from their homes, often repeatedly, in the latest — and possibly final — round of the 26-year war between government forces and separatist Tamil Tiger guerrillas. Above, internally displaced Tamil civilians wait to enter a government shelter near Colombo.

AP Photo/Eranga Jayawardena

BACKGROUND

Refugee Rights and Needs

Although the forced displacement of people from their homes is as old as human history, the idea that society has a moral obligation to come to their aid is relatively new.

After World War I, the newly formed League of Nations created the post of High Commissioner for Refugees but gave the office little authority and few resources. The league (the forerunner of the U.N.) also adopted two treaties in the 1930s offering limited legal protection to refugees, but only a handful of countries ratified them. [33]

The displacement of millions of peo-ple during World War II finally brought significant action on refugees. As the war was winding down, the United States and its allies created the United Nations Relief and Rehabilitation Agency, which gave emergency aid to 7 million displaced people. After the war, a successor organization, the International Refugee Organization, helped some 1 million dislocated Europeans find new homes. [34]

The modern era of international aid to refugees began in 1950-51, when the United Nations created the office of the U.N. High Commissioner for Refugees and held a special conference in Geneva to draft the treaty that became known as the Refugee Convention. Both the UNHCR and the treaty were aimed at aiding European war refugees or those who fled Eastern Europe after the Soviet Union imposed communist rule across the region. In fact, the treaty applied only to those who had become refugees before Jan. 1, 1951, and the text made clear the drafters had Europeans in mind. Moreover, the U.N. General Assembly gave the UNHCR only a three-year mandate, assuming the refugee problem would be quickly solved. [35]

In 1949, before the UNHCR started work, the U.N. Relief and Works Agency for Palestine Refugees in the Near East (known as UNRWA) was created to assist the 700,000 Palestinians who fled or were driven from their homes in what is now Israel during the 1948 Arab-Israeli war. [36] The UNRWA also was considered short-lived. But nearly 60 years later the ultimate status of the Palestinians remains unresolved, and the UNRWA is still providing food, medical care and other aid to a Palestinian population that has grown to 4.6 million. About 1.4 million Palestinians live in UNRWA camps in Jordan, Lebanon, Syria, the West Bank and Gaza Strip; the rest live on their own. [37]

Conflicts continued across the globe after World War II, some of them widely seen as proxy wars among governments and rebel groups backed by the two Cold War superpowers, the Soviet Union and the United States. In each case, dislocated civilians crossed international borders and created a new generation of refugees.

The U.N. General Assembly officially recognized the new refugee trend in 1967, adopting an amendment, or protocol, to the refugee convention. The Protocol Relating to the Status of Refugees dropped the pre-1951 limitation, giving legal protection to refugees worldwide, not just in Europe. [38] The convention and its protocol are now among the most widely adopted U.N. treaties; each has been ratified by 144 countries. [39]

The collapse of the Soviet Union in 1991 brought new hope for peace. But bloody sectarian conflicts in the Balkans and Africa's Great Lakes region shattered such dreams. Some conflicts dislocated enormous populations, but many people, for one reason or another, stayed in their own countries, where as IDPs they were not covered by the international refugee treaties.

In the 1990s international agencies and human-rights advocates began demanding aid and legal protections for these large groups. In 1992, U.N. Secretary-General Boutros Boutros-Ghali appointed Francis Deng, a former Sudanese diplomat, as the U.N.'s first special representative on internally displaced people.

Deng, who held the post until 2004, was largely responsible for drafting the Guiding Principles on Internal Displacement. [40] Although the document has never been put into international law, U.N. agencies and a dozen countries have incorporated its principles into their laws and policies. (See box, p. 82.)

However, says refugee specialist Koser at the Geneva Center for Security Policy, "there is very little political will to formalize [the principles] into a binding convention, and few states would ratify it."

Rising Displacements

U.N. officials and policy experts count more than four dozen countries — most in Africa and Asia — with significant populations displaced by civil wars or other violence. When the consequences of natural disasters are considered, however, the displacement problem becomes nearly universal. Thousands of Gulf Coast residents in the United States remain displaced by Hurricane Katrina in 2006, and millions in China's Sichuan Province are homeless nearly a year after a major earthquake.

Colombia has one of the world's largest IDP populations, and hundreds of thousands of people are still displaced in Chechnya and Georgia in the Caucuses and in Bosnia, Croatia, Kosovo and Serbia as a result of the Balkan wars. Thousands more have been displaced by ongoing conflict and instability in Somalia. (See sidebar, p. 68.)

Here are some of the displacements that are high on the international agenda:

Afghanistan — At least 6 million Afghans fled — mostly to Pakistan and Iran — between the Soviet Union's December 1979 invasion and the U.S. ousting of the Taliban government in late 2001. During periods of relative calm in the 1980s and '90s, hundreds of thousands of Afghan refugees returned home, but many fled again when fighting resumed. [41]

Shortly after a new Western-backed government took office in Kabul at the end of 2001, refugees began returning home in large numbers. Between 2002 and late 2008, about 5.6 million refugees returned, of whom nearly 4.4 million received UNHCR aid (the rest returned on their own). [42] Since 2007, thousands of refugees have returned because Pakistan closed some refugee camps, and Iran deported thousands of mostly undocumented Afghan men seeking work. [43]

Continued on p. 76

Chronology

1940s-1950s
Newly created United Nations (U.N.) aids refugees after World War II ends.

1949
U.N. Relief and Works Agency is established to aid Palestinians pushed from their homes during the 1949 Arab-Israeli war.

1950
Office of U.N. High Commissioner for Refugees (UNHCR) is created.

1951
Special U.N. conference adopts Convention Relating to the Status of Refugees (the Refugee Convention) to protect those who fled their countries before Jan. 1, 1951, to escape persecution due to "race, religion, nationality or membership of a particular social group." Generally viewed as applying only to Europeans, the treaty goes into effect in 1954.

1960s-1980s
Cold War conflicts and upheavals create waves of new refugees.

1967
U.N expands Refugee Convention to cover all refugees fleeing persecution as described in the treaty, not just Europeans who left their home countries before 1951.

1969
Organization of African Unity broadly defines a refugee in Africa as anyone who flees his country because of "external aggression, occupation, foreign domination or events seriously disturbing public order in either part or the whole of his country of origin."

1984
The Colloquium on the International Protection of Refugees in Central America, Mexico and Panama adopts the Cartagena Declaration, defining refugees as anyone fleeing their country because their "lives, safety or freedom" are threatened by "generalized violence, foreign aggression, internal conflicts, massive violation of human rights or other circumstances." Although not official policy, many regional governments adopt the declaration.

1990s-2000s
New wave of civil conflicts forces policy makers to pay more attention to the needs of people displaced within their own borders.

1992-1995
Civil conflicts in the former Yugoslavia displace several hundred thousand people.

1994
Genocidal rampage in Rwanda kills 800,000 Hutus and Tutsis; hundreds of thousands of others flee their homes, many into neighboring countries.

1997
Government-backed rebels oust longtime dictator Mobutu Sese Seko of Zaire (later the Democratic Republic of the Congo), triggering years of civil war in Africa's Great Lakes region; an estimated 5 million people die, and thousands are displaced during fighting that continues today.

1998
The Guiding Principles on Internal Displacement establish rules for aiding and protecting internally displaced persons (IDPs); the guidelines eventually are incorporated into U.N procedures but are not legally binding.

2002
About 2 million Afghan refugees return home (mostly from Pakistan and Iran) after a U.S.-led invasion topples the Taliban government. Some 6 million had fled during three decades of war — the largest number of refugees generated by any conflict since World War II.

2004
In a landmark decision, Colombia's Constitutional Court orders the government to increase aid to about 2 million people displaced by conflict.

2005
U.N. adopts "responsibility to protect" doctrine, which holds every government responsible for protecting the rights of its citizens and says the international community has a responsibility to intervene if a government abuses its own citizens. . . . U.N. gives UNHCR more responsibility for helping IDPs.

2008
U.N. launches a year-long publicity campaign to focus international attention on the needs of IDPs. . . . UNHCR starts a campaign to help end long-term displacements of those forced from their homes in Afghanistan, the Balkans, Burundi, Eritrea and Myanmar.

2009
African Union is scheduled in April to adopt a treaty recognizing the rights of internally displaced people, based on the 1998 Guiding Principles.

Millions Remain in Exile for Decades

"Whole generations of kids grow up in refugee camps."

Miljo and Milica Miljic grabbed their two children and fled Tuzla, Bosnia, in 1992, at the beginning of a nearly four-year civil war that tore their country apart. "We didn't take anything with us because we didn't have time," Miljo told a representative of the U.N. High Commissioner on Refugees (UNHCR) this past January. "We had to run for our lives. The only thing that comes to mind in such a situation is to save your children and your own life. You don't think about the photographs, about personal documents, clothes, whatever." [1]

The Miljacs are among nearly 97,000 refugees from Bosnia and Croatia who have not returned to their homes, even though the war ended in late 1995. They are still in Serbia, where the refugee population has slowly dwindled down from more than 500,000 in 1996. [2]

The words "refugees" and "displaced persons" conjure up images of short-term emergencies: people fleeing their homes temporarily because of wars, hurricanes or earthquakes, only to return home a few weeks, or at most a few months, later. While many do return home once a crisis has passed, most refugees and internally displaced persons (IDPs) remain displaced long after the emergency is over.

In fact, refugees fleeing conflict end up staying away from their homes an average of 18 years, and many IDPs are displaced for comparable periods. James Milner, a refugee expert at Carleton University in Ottawa, Canada, says some situations last even longer: The Palestinians who fled Israel during the 1948-49 Arab-Israeli war have been in exile ever since.

In recent years experts have begun focusing on "protracted situations" involving refugees and IDPs displaced for at least five years, and numerous conferences have been held to discuss the problem of long-term displacements. U.N. High Commissioner Antonio Guterres said more than 30 situations around the world involve a total of about 6 million refugees who have been living in long-term exile.

"Many are effectively trapped in the camps and communities where they are accommodated," Guterres said. "Their home countries are caught in endless conflict or afflicted by political stalemate or human-rights violations, and most are not allowed to hold jobs, work the land where they live or integrate into the local communities." [3]

Most of the long-term displaced are children and youth, says Elizabeth Ferris, director of the Brookings-Bern Project on Internal Displacement. "You have whole generations of kids who grow up and live in refugee camps, where typically you have a breakdown of normal social institutions," she says.

From 11 million to 17 million people have been displaced for at least five years but are still living inside their own countries, Ferris says. "Unfortunately, the world has paid very little attention to these situations, which are allowed to fester for years and years," she says.

Aside from the Palestinians, perhaps the best-known protracted refugee situation involves the estimated 6 million people who have fled their homes during three decades of warfare in Afghanistan, which began with the Soviet Union's invasion in 1979. Most went to neighboring Iran or Pakistan, where they settled in formal camps or moved into cities. Millions of Afghan refugees returned home after the U.S. invasion in 2001, but nearly 3 million are still refugees. [4]

Many scholars and aid officials worry that another long-term refugee situation is developing among the 2 million or more Iraqis who have fled their homeland. Although the Baghdad government has encouraged some to return, the U.N. and private aid groups say it is still too unsafe, especially for Sunni Muslims or members of other minority groups. [5]

Other protracted refugee situations prioritized by the UNHCR include:

- **Myanmar/Bangladesh.** Some 200,000 Rohingya, a Muslim ethnic group in North Rakhine state in Myanmar, fled to neighboring Bangladesh in 1991 to escape persecution by the military junta in Myanmar. Thousands have since returned to Myanmar, but the majority remain in Bangladesh and are classified by the U.N. as "stateless" persons because Myanmar no longer considers them as citizens. [6]

- **Eritrea/Sudan.** Some 90,000 Eritreans are long-term refugees in eastern Sudan, many since the late 1960s when Eritrean rebels launched a 30-year-long war against Ethiopia. (Eritrea gained its independence in 1993, but the two countries fought another bloody war from 1998 until 2000.) Additional Eritrean refugees continue to arrive in Sudan, joined by refugees from Ethiopia and Somalia. Most live in camps and lack any rights or protections but have increasingly begun to move into Khartoum and other Sudanese cities, over the government's objection. [7]

- **The Balkans.** Like the Miljics, hundreds of thousands of people dislocated by war in the former Yugoslavia during the 1990s have not returned to their home regions. Some 200,000 refugees, mostly ethnic Serbs, became naturalized citizens in Serbia rather than return to Bosnia or Croatia, where Serbs are in the minority. [8]

- **Burundi/Tanzania.** Violent civil conflict in Burundi in 1972 forced thousands to flee into neighboring Tanzania, where the government created three settlements in central and western Tanzania and provided land and other services for them. In 2007, about 218,000 refugees were still in the settlements. Under an agreement that many experts consider historic, Burundi and Tanzania decided in 2008 to resolve the status of these so-called "old settlement" refugees from 1972. Tanzania agreed to grant citizenship to, and fully integrate into local communities, some 176,000 of the remaining refugees. Those wanting to return to Burundi were to be allowed to do so by September 2009. [9]

Protracted IDP Situations

Globally, about half of the estimated 26 million IDPs displaced by violence are stuck in protracted situations, according to Neill Wright, the UNHCR's senior coordinator for IDPs. And some who were forced from their homes by natural disasters also remain displaced after five years.

Both types of protracted situations exist in Kenya, where about 350,000 people have been displaced long-term by conflict, unresolved land disputes and natural disasters. [10] Post-election violence displaced another 500,000 Kenyans in late 2007 and early 2008, but about half of those had returned home by late 2008. [11]

Ferris, of the Brookings-Bern project, says at least three-dozen countries have long-term displacement situations, and people are still being displaced in about a dozen others, such as Colombia, the Democratic Republic of the Congo and Somalia. In most other countries, the fighting has ended, but thousands remain displaced because peace agreements were never negotiated or the IDPs there are afraid, or unwilling, to return to their homes for other reasons.

Experts say no single solution will solve the protracted-displacement problem. Even negotiating peace agreements does not guarantee that displaced people can or will return home.

But policy makers have identified several essential elements that would help create "durable solutions" for protracted situations. One element, they say, is recognizing that forcing or encouraging people to return to their original homes may not always be the best solution, particularly when people have been displaced for many years, and they no longer have reasons for returning home.

An alternative to repatriation is "local integration" — allowing displaced people to become part of the local communities where they have taken refuge. This route is often politically difficult because local communities usually don't want to absorb large numbers of outsiders. Milner says he hopes Tanzania's willingness to accept Burundians displaced for nearly four decades as citizens will become a model for other countries.

"This creates a significant strategic opportunity for the international community to demonstrate that local integration can work," he says. "Now, the next step is for the donor community to meet its responsibilities to help countries, like Tanzania, that might be willing to resolve these situations."

The UNHCR also acknowledged in November 2008 that its policy of providing only short-term humanitarian aid to refugees

The U.N. Relief and Works Agency, which for 60 years has aided Palestinian refugees, was stretched thin during prolonged Israeli military strikes earlier this year. More than 1,000 Palestinians were killed and many homes were destroyed, such as this woman's house in the Jabalia refugee camp in northern Gaza.

in camps had failed to help them develop personal independence and job skills that would allow them to live on their own. Too often, a UNHCR report said, "refugees were left to live in camps indefinitely, often with restrictions placed on their rights, as well as their ability to support themselves by means of agriculture, trade or employment." [12]

Under the U.N.'s "humanitarian reform" program adopted in late 2005, the agency is changing its approach, says Jeff Crisp, director of UNHCR's policy and evaluation service.

[1] "The continuing struggle of Europe's forgotten refugees," U.N. High Commissioner for Refugees, Jan. 12, 2009, www.unhcr.org/news/NEWS/496b6ad12.html..

[2] *Ibid.*

[3] "Protracted Refugee Situations: High Commissioner's Initiative," U.N. High Commissioner for Refugees, December 2008, p. 2, www.unhcr.org/protect/PROTECTION/4937de6f2.pdf.

[4] "Protracted Refugee Situations: Revisiting The Problem," U.N. High Commissioner for Refugees, June 2, 2008, pp. 5-6, www.unhcr.org/excom/EXCOM/484514c12.pdf.

[5] "NGOs warn against encouraging large-scale refugee returns," IRIN news service, Nov. 3, 2008, www.irinnews.org/Report.aspx?ReportId=81258.

[6] "Protracted Refugee Situations: The High Commissioner's Initiative," *op. cit.,* pp. 9-11.

[7] *Ibid.,* p. 14.

[8] *Ibid.,* p. 32.

[9] *Ibid.,* pp. 25-29.

[10] "Frequently Asked Questions on IDPs," U.N. Office for the Coordination of Humanitarian Affairs, Dec. 4, 2008, p. 4.

[11] *Ibid.,* p. 2.

[12] "Protracted Refugee Situations: A discussion paper prepared for the High Commissioner's Dialogue on Protection Challenges," Nov. 20, 2008, p. 13, www.unhcr.org/protect/PROTECTION/492ad3782.pdf.

Continued from p. 72

By late 2008, the UNHCR estimated that about 2 million Afghan refugees were still in Pakistan and nearly 1 million in Iran. [44] Worried about its inability to provide housing, jobs and other services for returning refugees, the Afghan government in 2008 began discouraging large-scale returns. "We don't have the means to provide an encouraging environment for refugees

Council. "I wish we hadn't left Pakistan," said elderly returnee Golam Shah. "Life was much better there." [46]

A similar complaint came from 18-year-old Wali, who grew up in Pakistan's Jalozai refugee village. Forced out last May, he now lives in a tent in Balkh Province in northern Afghanistan. "I didn't expect to face such problems or to end up in such a place," he said. "There is nothing here — no shelter, not

Revolutionary Armed Forces of Colombia (FARC) and the National Liberation Army (ELN). Right-wing paramilitary armies formed by major landowners and elements of the military aided the anti-insurgency campaign.

Both the guerrillas and paramilitaries eventually became deeply involved in the drug trade, turning an ideological war over land reform and other social issues into a battle for control of illegal cocaine production. The government's war against cocaine — most of which is consumed in the United States — has been funded largely by Washington.

Colombia is now the hemisphere's major source of refugees, most of whom have fled to Ecuador and Venezuela; others sought refuge in Brazil, Panama and Costa Rica. [49] About 460,000 Colombians are in "refugee-like situations" — they've fled Colombia but are not officially considered refugees and receive little if any official aid. [50] The flow of refugees has worsened Colombia's relations with left-leaning Ecuador and Venezuela.

Colombia estimates it has 2.8 million registered IDPs — among the world's highest for an individual country. [51] But nongovernmental agencies say the real number is much higher. The Catholic Church-affiliated Consultancy for Human Rights and Displacement puts the number at more than 4.3 million. [52] Many displaced people do not register for fear of retaliation or being forced to return to unsafe areas. The displacement rate has escalated in recent years, according to both the government and private agencies: About 300,000 people were displaced in 2007, but 270,000 were displaced in just the first six months of 2008. [53]

Colombia's IDPs have received serious attention since the country's Constitutional Court in 2004 ordered the government to provide aid — one of the few instances where an activist court has significantly helped IDPs.

Andrea Lari, a senior advocate at

AFP/Getty Images/Alejandra Vega

Colombia's long-running rebel insurgency and the government's aggressive, U.S.-backed war against narcotics cartels have created the worst humanitarian crisis in the Western Hemisphere, according to the U.N. This family living in a tent in a Bogotá park is among at least 2.8 million displaced Colombians.

to repatriate," Shir Mohammad Etibari, minister of refugees and returnees, said in September. The U.N. and other international agencies "only make promises but do little." [45]

Another 235,000 Afghans are displaced but still in Afghanistan. Some were forced to return to Afghanistan against their will, only to find that they had no place to live and could find no jobs. Among the most vulnerable are several thousand returnees who were forced out of Pakistan and now live at a camp in the Chemtala desert, about 15 miles west of Jalalabad. Last winter they struggled to survive in mud huts and tents provided by the UNHCR and the Norwegian Refugee

enough water, no trees for firewood, no electricity and no work." [47]

Colombia — A long-running rebel insurgency and the government's aggressive, U.S.-backed war against narcotics cartels have created what the U.N. calls the worst humanitarian crisis in the Western Hemisphere. Up to half a million Colombians have fled to neighboring countries, and thousands have emigrated to the United States. At least 2.8 million mostly rural people are internally displaced in the nation of 45 million. [48]

Since the 1960s the military has brutally suppressed two leftist guerrilla groups claiming to be fighting for land reform and other social causes — the

Online Newspaper Fights for Refugees in Kenya

'We need to be able to help ourselves.'

Problems with the water supply, inadequate health inspections of food suppliers, indifferent officials. Such issues would be the meat-and-potatoes of any local newspaper. But who draws attention to such concerns in a refugee camp as big as a mid-size city?

Most refugee camps have community organizations that present residents' concerns to camp officials, but they rarely receive wide attention locally. Since last December, however, the problems faced by the 50,000 refugees at the Kakuma camp in northwest Kenya have been exposed not only to local resident but to people around the world via the camp's Internet newspaper, *Kanere* (KAkuma NEws REflector).

The paper (http://kakuma.wordpress.com) is run by staff of volunteer journalists aided by Bethany Ojalehto, a 2008 Cornell University graduate who is studying the rights of refugees at the camp on a Fulbright research scholarship. She says several refugees interested in starting a newspaper approached her for help when she arrived at the camp last October, and she agreed because their interests and her research "blended seamlessly and have now been channeled into this project."

So far *Kanere* is published only in English, which is a common language for many of the camp's residents, who can read it at computer stations in several locations. The paper's editors say they hope to expand into other languages once they get more help.

Twenty-four-year-old Qabaata, one of the paper's editors, says he fled Ethiopia in 2003 after being targeted by government security forces for writing an article supporting a student strike. A journalism student at the time, he went with other students to Kakuma after being arrested and released by authorities in Addis Ababa, Ethiopia's capital. He is seeking asylum status from the UNHCR because he says he cannot return to Ethiopia. "It is not safe for me there," he says. He hopes to win a scholarship to finish his journalism studies but has no immediate prospects for attaining that goal.

Kakuma has one of the most diverse camp populations in Africa. Opened in 1992 to aid refugees from the long civil war in southern Sudan, Kakuma now houses about 25,000 Sudanese, 18,000 Somalis, 4,500 Ethiopians and 1,800 other Africans. [1] Since mid-2008 the U.N. High Commissioner for Refugees (UNHCR) has transferred thousands of Somali refugees to Kakuma from three overcrowded camps at Dadaab, Kenya, about 700 miles to the east. (*See Somalia box, p. 68.*)

Qabaata says *Kanere* provides a unique opportunity to share concerns across the camp's different ethnic and national communities and to voice grievances to camp officials. "The refugees here don't have access to the people who are governing them," he says. "They only have access through their community leaders, but even their leaders do not always have access."

Negash, another Ethiopian refugee who works on *Kanere*, notes that one crucial issue is water. All water for the camp comes from underground aquifers and is rationed at about 20 liters per refugee per day. And some refugees have to walk long distances to get it. The paper's first issue, in December 2008, pointed out that refugees in one section of the camp had recently gone without adequate water for three days while a broken pump was being fixed. Why is water rationed for refugees, the paper asked, while U.N. and other aid agencies' staff members living nearby "are given unlimited water?"

Kanere also deals with UNHCR budget cutbacks, long food-distribution lines, the lack of job opportunities, low pay for refugees compared to local Kenyans and the "poor performance" of the camp's 14 primary and two secondary schools.

Above all, say Qabaata and Negash, *Kanere* advocates on behalf of refugees' basic human rights. "As refugees, we are told we have rights, but in reality we have no rights here in the camp," Negash says. "We hope *Kanere* will empower the refugee community, help it to be self-reliant. As it is, the humanitarian community is just making us dependent, reliant on them. We need to be able to help ourselves."

[1] "Kenya: Population of Concern to UNHCR," November 2008, p. 6, www.unhcr.org/partners/PARTNERS/4951ef9d2.pdf.

Refugees International, says the government helps IDPs survive on a daily basis but does virtually nothing to enable them to escape from urban shantytowns. The government provides "too much social welfare and not enough . . . job training or education beyond primary schools — the help needed to sustain themselves where they now live," he says. Going home "is not a serious option" for most because they have lost their land and are afraid to return.

Democratic Republic of the Congo — Hundreds of thousands of civilians continue to suffer from fighting in the eastern provinces of Africa's second-largest country — a war that officially ended more than five years ago. At least 400,000 Congolese were displaced in 2008 and early this year by continuing violence, bringing the total displaced to about 1.25 million. [54]

Two major wars — involving five other African countries at one point — raged in Congo from 1997 until peace agreements hammered out in 2002-03 ended most of the fighting and led to elections in 2006. More than 5 million people may have died during the wars — the largest toll by far of any post-World War II conflict, according to the International Rescue Committee. [55]

Lingering conflicts still plague several areas, including North Kivu Province on the borders with Rwanda and Uganda. There, remnants of the Hutu extremist forces responsible for Rwanda's genocide in 1994 have battled a rebel force claiming to support the Congolese Tutsis, members of the same ethnic group targeted by the Hutus in the Rwandan genocide. Until recently, the Congolese army had not curbed either faction.

In January, however, the Congolese and Rwandan armies launched an unusual joint military operation targeting both the Hutu and Tutsi forces in North Kivu. And in a potential step toward peace, the Rwandan army on Jan. 22 arrested the self-styled Tutsi general Laurent Nkunda, whose rebels had wreaked havoc in the region. [56] The arrest — coming on the heels of a related international campaign against the Lord's Resistance Army — offered the first tangible hope in many years that the region's troubles might some day come to an end. [57]

Iraq — The 1991 Persian Gulf War and sectarian violence following the 2003 U.S. invasion of Iraq have swelled the ranks of displaced Iraqis to between 3 million and 5 million — out of a total population of around 28 million. Most have remained in the country but fled their home regions, usually to escape sectarian violence. [58]

Many of the Iraqi IDPs live with friends or relatives and receive government food rations. For those who cannot get rations, the World Food Program on Jan. 3 announced a one-year program to aid about 750,000 Iraqis inside Iraq and 360,000 in Syria. [59]

Many IDPs live in informal camps inside Iraq. The Iraqi government early in 2008 had announced an ambitious plan to build IDP housing, but falling oil prices have forced budget cuts that endanger the effort. [60] Then in late 2008 the government moved to close some of the camps by giving families one-time $4,250 stipends to return to their homes or find new places to live. [61] The UNHCR plans to help about 400,000 Iraqi IDPs this year. [62]

Some 300,000 displaced Iraqis have returned home, and nearly two-thirds of those still displaced want to return to their original home regions, according to a survey released on Feb. 22 by the International Organization for Migration. [63]

Since 2003 at least 2 million Iraqis have fled to several neighboring countries: Syria (1.2 million), Jordan (450,000),

Permanent Solutions Sought for the Displaced

Aid agencies turning away from short-term solutions.

In the past, the U.N. High Commissioner for Refugees (UNHCR) and other aid agencies have focused primarily on short-term fixes — such as providing emergency food, medical care and other aid — for those displaced by war, conflict or natural disaster. They also generally assumed that displaced people wanted to return to their homes, and encouraging them to do so was easier than resettling them elsewhere.

But in recent years aid agencies have begun paying more attention to moving displaced people out of camps and makeshift shelters and back into normal lives.

Three so-called durable solutions have been proposed for refugees as well as internally displaced persons (IDPs), or those still living in their own countries:

- **Return or repatriation** — Returning either to their past residence or to their home neighborhood or region;
- **Local integration** — Settling permanently in the locality or country where the person has sought temporary refuge.
- **Resettlement elsewhere** — For refugees, moving to a willing third country; for IDPs, moving to a different part or region of their home countries.

In the absence of universally accepted standards for deciding when an IDP is no longer displaced, the Brookings-Bern Project on Internal Displacement in 2007 created a "Framework for Durable Solutions" for IDPs, which has been officially "welcomed" by the U.N. [1] It says IDPs' displacement should be considered ended when one of the three durable solutions occurs, and they "no longer have needs specifically related to their dis-

placement." Although former IDPs may still have humanitarian needs, at this point "their needs are basically the same as other people in the local population, and it's the government's responsibility to help them," says project director Elizabeth Ferris.

In 2007, about 2 million IDPs and 731,000 refugees returned to their home countries, their actual homes or to their home regions, according to the UNHCR. [2] About half were in the Democratic Republic of the Congo, although conflict displaced another 500,000 Congolese that same year. [3] More than half of the returning refugees — some 374,000 — were Afghans. [4]

Barbara Harrell-Bond, a veteran advocate for refugees and leading critic of the UNHCR, faults the agency for continuing to focus on repatriation for refugees, because she says integration in asylum countries "often is the only solution." UNHCR officials, however, say local integration and resettlement are difficult because host countries are not inclined to accept refugees and displaced people on a permanent basis.

But resettlement efforts are occurring, albeit on a small scale, say the UNHCR and refugee advocacy groups. In 2007, the UNHCR recommended 99,000 refugees for resettlement in third countries, nearly double the previous year, but only 70,000 were able to resettle — less than 1 percent of the total refugees. [5] Historically, the United States has accepted more refugees than any other country; in 2006, the last year for which comparative figures are available, the United States accepted 41,300 refugees — more than half of the 71,700 resettlements that occurred that year. [6]

Local integration sometimes occurs informally, particularly when displaced people are not confined to official camps or settlements. For instance, in Pakistan, many of the estimated 1.8 million remaining Afghan refugees have established new lives in Peshawar, Quetta and other cities. Many had been refugees for more than 20 years, and more than half were born outside Afghanistan; a substantial number were ethnic Pashtuns, which also is the dominant ethnic group in the border areas of Pakistan. As a result, remaining in Pakistan has been a natural solution for them. [7]

In contrast, official agreements allowing large numbers of refugees or IDPs to move permanently from camps into local communities are rare. An exception is Tanzania, where more than 200,000 Burundians have been refugees since 1972. Seeking to resolve a situation that had dragged on so long, and with U.N. help that included limited financial aid, Burundi and Tanzania agreed in 2007 that 172,000 refugees could remain in Tanzania as citizens, while 46,000 would return to Burundi. The agreement is expected to be implemented by late 2009. [8]

James Milner, of Canada's Carleton University, says Tanzania's willingness to accept long-term refugees as permanent refugees "creates a strategic opportunity for the international community to show that there are alternatives to warehousing refugees forever in camps."

The only missing element, he says, is a willingness by the major donor nations to put their money and diplomatic leverage to work to encourage other countries to follow Tanzania's example. "The United States is the hegemon in the global refugee regime," he says. "If the United States were to support more of this kind of action, eventually we could see real solutions for refugees."

Afghan refugees who have just returned from Pakistan wait to register at a transition center in Kabul in June 2008. Aid agencies have begun focusing on moving displaced people out of camps and back into normal lives, often by returning them to their home countries.

[1] "When Displacement Ends: A Framework for Durable Solutions," Brookings-Bern Project on Internal Displacement, June 2007, www.brookings.edu/reports/2007/09displacementends.aspx.

[2] "Note on International Protection," U.N. High Commissioner for Refugees, June 2008, p. 2, www.unhcr.org/publ/PUBL/484807202.pdf.

[3] *Ibid.*, p. 15.

[4] *Ibid.*

[5] *Ibid.*, p. 17.

[6] "Global Trends for 2006: Refugees, Asylum-seekers, Returnees, Internally Displaced and Stateless Persons," U.N. High Commissioner for Refugees, June 2007, p. 8, www.unhcr.org/statistics/STATISTICS/4676a71d4.pdf.

[7] "Afghanistan — The Challenges of Sustaining Returns," U.N. High Commissioner for Refugees, www.unhcr.org/cgi-bin/texis/vtx/afghan?page=intro.

[8] "Protracted Refugee Situations: The High Commissioner's Initiative," U.N. High Commissioner for Refugees, December 2008, pp. 25-29, www.unhcr.org/protect/PROTECTION/4937de6f2.pdf.

the Gulf states (150,000), Iran (58,000), Lebanon (50,000) and Egypt (40,000). [64]

Some experts question the government estimates. Amelia Templeton, an analyst at Human Rights First, suggests only about 1 million Iraqi refugees are living in neighboring countries, based on school registrations and the number of refugees receiving UNHCR aid.

In contrast to many other refugee situations, nearly all of the Iraqi refugees live in or near major cities, such as Damascus, Syria, and Amman, Jordan, because Iraq's neighbors don't permit refugee camps. A high proportion of Iraqi refugees are lawyers, doctors, professors and other well-educated professionals.

National Public Radio journalist Deborah Amos tells the stories of Iraqi refugees in Syria and Lebanon in a soon-to-be-published book. She says many of the professionals belonged to the Sunni elite or Christian minority groups (such as Chaldeans), who for centuries were tolerated in Iraq but suddenly were targeted with violence. Many have spent their life savings during the years in exile and now rely on U.N. handouts. As in much of the world, local governments will not allow the refugees to work, forcing some female refugees in Damascus to turn to prostitution to support their families, Amos writes.

Myanmar — Cyclone Nargis struck on May 2, 2008, killing 140,000 people — mostly by drowning — and forcing up to 800,000 from their homes. [65] Humanitarian agencies pressed the government to allow international aid workers into the vast Irrawaddy Delta, but the secretive generals who run Myanmar resisted the appeals for several weeks until U.N. Secretary-General Ban Ki-moon finally persuaded the top general, Thwan Shwe, to accept outside aid.

Aid agencies and foreign governments donated emergency relief supplies and began helping rebuild homes and communities. But about 500,000 people remained displaced at year's end. [66] Many of those displaced by cyclone-caused floods have faced severe water shortages in recent months due to the recent onset of the dry season and water contamination caused by the cyclone. [67] Full recovery from the cyclone could take three to four years, a senior U.N. aid official said in January. [68]

Meanwhile, members of the Muslim Rohingya minority, from the northern state of Rakhine, are officially stateless. According to Amnesty International, thousands of Rohingyas flee Myanmar each year because of land confiscation, arbitrary taxation, forced eviction and denial of citizenship. [69] Since 1991, more than 250,000 have fled, mostly to neighboring Bangladesh, where the UNHCR runs two camps housing 28,000 refugees; another 200,000 unregistered Rohingyas live outside the camps. [70]

In early 2009, the Thai navy reportedly intercepted boats carrying hundreds of Rohingya trying to cross the Andaman Sea. The action generated international outrage after CNN published a photo purportedly showing armed forces towing refugee boats out to sea and leaving the occupants to die, but the Thai government denied the reports. Some were later rescued off the coasts of India and Indonesia, but many went missing. [71]

In early February actress and U.N. goodwill ambassador Angelina Jolie visited refugee camps in Thailand housing 110,000 Karen and Kareni ethnic refugees from Myanmar. She called on the Thai government to lift its ban on refugees working outside the camps and asked the government to extend hospitality to the Rohingyas. [72]

Prime Minister Abhisit Vejjajiva had said earlier that Thailand would not build a camp for the Rohingyas and will continue to expel them. "They are not refugees," he said. "Our policy is to push them out of the country because they are illegal migrants." [73]

Leaders of the Association of Southeast Asian Nations agreed on March 2 to discuss the status of the Rohingyas at a mid-April summit in Bali. Malaysian Prime Minister, Abdullah Ahmad Badawi said the Ronhingya problem "is a regional issue that needs to be resolved regionally." [74]

Sudan — Two major internal conflicts plus other conflicts in central and eastern Africa have displaced millions

of Sudanese in the past three decades. At the beginning of 2009, more than 3.5 million were still displaced, including about 130,000 in neighboring countries. Sudan hosts more than 250,000 refugees from nearby countries. [75]

Sudan's two-decade civil war between the government in Khartoum and a separatist army in south Sudan ended with an uneasy peace in January 2005. More than 300,000 refugees who had fled the violence have returned to their home regions, but UNHCR has estimated that about 130,000 remain in Egypt, Ethiopia, Kenya and Uganda. [76] And more conflict could erupt if, as expected, the southerners vote in 2011 for full independence.

Elsewhere in Sudan, a series of interrelated conflicts between the Khartoum government and rebel groups in western Darfur have displaced about 2.7 million people and killed an estimated 300,000. [77] Although Darfur has generally faded from world headlines, the conflict continues, with about 1,000 people fleeing their homes every day. [78] Complicating the refugee crisis, 243,000 Darfuris have fled into Chad, while some 45,000 Chadians have crossed into Darfur to escape a related conflict. [79]

More than 200,000 other refugees also are in Sudan, mostly from Eritrea, having fled the long war between Eritrea and Ethiopia. [80] ∎

CURRENT SITUATION

'Responsibility to Protect'

Since last fall, 26-year-old Kandiah and his family have moved eight times to avoid the long-running civil war between the Sri Lankan army and rebels known as the Tamil Tigers. By late February they had joined several

dozen people sleeping on a classroom floor in Vavuniya, in northern Sri Lanka.

At one point, Kandiah (not his real name) and his family stayed in an area that was supposed to be safe for civilians. For more than a week, he said, "We stayed in the open air with scores of other families . . . but the shelling was intense. There was shelling every day. We barely escaped with our lives." [81]

Kandiah and his family are among more than 250,000 people forced from their homes, often repeatedly, in the latest — and possibly final — round of the 26-year war. Claiming to represent the ethnic Tamil minority, the Tigers have been fighting for independence in the eastern and northern portions of the island.

Although the conflict has been among the world's most violent, international pressure to end it has been modest, at best. The U.N. Security Council, for example, considered it an "internal" affair to be resolved by Sri Lankans themselves, not by the international community and has never even adopted a resolution about it. Norway took the most significant action, mediating a ceasefire in 2002 that lasted nearly three years.

The plight of people like Kandiah illustrates the international community's failure to follow through on promises world leaders made in September 2005. At a summit marking the U.N.'s 60th anniversary, world leaders adopted the "responsibility to protect" philosophy, which holds every government responsible for protecting its own citizens. [82] Moreover, if a government fails to protect its citizens, it cannot prevent the international community from intervening on their behalf. World leaders at the summit declared the U.N.'s right to take "collective action, in a decisive and timely manner," when governments failed to protect their own citizens. [83]

The U.N. has not followed through on that ringing declaration, however, usually because of dissension within the Security Council — the only U.N.

Continued on p. 82

At Issue:

Should the U.N. High Commissioner for Refugees help more displaced people?

JOEL R. CHARNY
VICE PRESIDENT FOR POLICY
REFUGEES INTERNATIONAL

WRITTEN FOR *CQ GLOBAL RESEARCHER*, FEBRUARY 2009

current efforts to help displaced populations do not reflect the fact that twice as many people displaced by conflict remain inside their own borders rather than crossing an international one, thus failing to become refugees protected under international law. With the U.N. High Commissioner for Refugees (UNHCR) focusing primarily on legal protection for refugees, the current system is outmoded. A bold solution is needed to prevent further unnecessary suffering.

Internally displaced people (IDPs) suffer when their governments don't aid and protect their own citizens. They also suffer from the lack of a dedicated international agency mandated to respond to their needs when their states fail. With IDP numbers growing, expanding the UNHCR's mandate to include IDPs is the best option available to fill this gap.

A dedicated agency would be more effective than the current system, characterized by the "cluster leadership" approach, under which international agencies provide help by sectors, such as health, water and sanitation and shelter. For example, in the 1990s the U.N. secretary-general mandated that UNHCR respond to the needs of IDPs displaced by the civil war in Sri Lanka. Over the years, the agency effectively fulfilled this responsibility with donor support, and the entire U.N. country team — as well as the Sri Lankan government — benefited from the clarity of knowing that the agency was in charge. Moreover, carrying out this exceptional mandate did not undermine either the UNHCR's work with refugees in the region or the right of Tamil Sri Lankans to seek asylum in southern India.

Giving one agency responsibility for an especially vulnerable population is more effective than patching together a response system with multiple independent agencies. Because the circumstances and needs of IDPs are so similar to those of refugees, and because UNHCR has a proven capacity to respond holistically to displacement, it is best suited to take on this responsibility.

Having a formal mandate for IDPs would triple UNHCR's caseload and pose an immense challenge. The agency already has difficulty fulfilling its current mandate and perpetually lacks sufficient funds. Taking the lead on internal displacement would require new thinking, more advocacy work with governments and flexible approaches to programming outside of camp settings. But the alternative is worse: Maintain the status quo and perpetuate the gap in protection and assistance for some of the world's most vulnerable people.

GUGLIELMO VERDIRAME
PROFESSOR, INTERNATIONAL HUMAN RIGHTS AND REFUGEE LAW CAMBRIDGE UNIVERSITY

CO-AUTHOR, *RIGHTS IN EXILE: JANUS-FACED HUMANITARIANISM*

WRITTEN FOR *CQ GLOBAL RESEARCHER*, FEBRUARY 2009

forced displacement is a human tragedy even when it occurs within the boundaries of a state. But the test for deciding whether it would be appropriate for the U.N. High Commissioner for Refugees (UNHCR) to add internally displaced people (IDPs) to its current mandate on a permanent basis is not one of comparability of suffering. Rather, the proper test is whether UNHCR is the right institution for dealing with this problem. I think it is not, for several reasons.

First, crossing an international boundary continues to make a difference in today's world. By virtue of being outside their country of nationality, refugees are in a different position than the internally displaced.

Second, the international legal regime for refugees was established as an exception to the sovereign prerogatives enjoyed by states over admission and expulsion of aliens in their territory. While most refugees were the victims of a human-rights violation in their home country, the focus of the refugee legal regime is not on the responsibility of the country of nationality but on the obligations of the country where they take refuge. Because internally displaced persons are still inside their home countries, protecting their rights will require different strategies and methods.

Third, human-rights bodies, including the office of the U.N. High Commissioner for Refugees, are better-placed to deal with what are, in essence, violations of human rights against citizens.

Finally, the rationale for getting the UNHCR involved with IDPs is premised on a distinctly problematic view of the organization as a provider of humanitarian relief rather than as the international protector of refugees. UNHCR's work with refugees has already greatly suffered from the sidelining of the agency's role as legal protector: The warehousing of refugees in camps is just one example. It would not help the internally displaced if the UNHCR's involvement resulted in their being warehoused in camps, as refugees already are.

In a world where asylum is under serious threat, the real challenge for UNHCR is to rediscover its protection mandate, to act as the advocate of refugees and as the institutional overseer of the obligations of states under the 1951 Refugee Convention. It is a difficult enough task as it is.

Legal Protections for Displaced Populations

A 1951 treaty gives refugees the most protection.

International law protects some — but not all — refugees who cross international borders, while the nonbinding Guiding Principles on Internal Displacement cover internally displaced people (IDPs), or those forcibly displaced within their home countries.

Here are the main laws protecting refugees and IDPs:

1951 Refugee Convention

The Convention Relating to the Status of Refugees — the basic international treaty concerning refugees — was adopted by a United Nations conference on July 28, 1951, and became effective on April 22, 1954. It defines a refugee as someone who, "owing to well-founded fear of being persecuted for reasons of race, religion, nationality, membership of a particular social group or political opinion, is outside the country of his nationality and is unable or, owing to such fear, is unwilling to avail himself of the protection of that country; or who, not having a nationality and being outside the country of his former habitual residence as a result of such events, is unable or, owing to such fear, is unwilling to return to it."

Excluded are those who flee their countries because of generalized violence (such as a civil war) in which they are not specifically targeted, or those who flee because of natural disasters or for economic reasons, such as a collapsing economy. The convention also prohibits a host country from expelling or returning refugees against their will to a territory where they have a "well-founded" fear of persecution.

The 1967 Protocol

Because the 1951 convention applied only to people who became refugees before Jan. 1, 1951, it was widely considered to apply only to European refugees from World War II. To aid those displaced by subsequent events, the United Nations adopted a new treaty, known as a Protocol, which eliminated the pre-1951 limitation. It took effect on Oct. 4, 1967. [1]

As of October 2008, 144 countries were parties to both the convention and the Protocol, though the two groups are not identical. [2]

Regional Treaties

Two regional documents expanded refugee protections of the convention and Protocol to Africa, Mexico and Central America. The 1969 Convention Governing the Specific Aspects of Refugee Problems in Africa — adopted by what is now the African Union — defined refugees in Africa, while the 1984 Cartagena Declaration on Refugees is an informal statement of principles drafted by legal experts from Mexico and Central America. [3]

Guiding Principles on Internal Displacement

The U.N. has never adopted a treaty specifically aimed at establishing legal rights for IDPs. However, in 1998 the organization endorsed a set of 30 nonbinding guidelines intended to heighten international awareness of the internally displaced and offer them more legal protection. Known as the Guiding Principles on Internal Displacement, they have been presented to the various U.N. bodies but never formally adopted.

Based on the Universal Declaration of Human Rights and other treaties and agreements, the principles provide legal and practical standards for aiding and protecting displaced people. For example, the first principle states that displaced persons should enjoy "the same rights and freedoms under international and domestic law as do other persons in their country. They shall not be discriminated against . . . on the ground that they are internally displaced."

Regional bodies (including the European Union and the Organization of American States) and numerous nongovernmental organizations have endorsed the principles, and the UNHCR has treated them as official policy since world leaders — meeting at the U.N. in September 2005 — endorsed them. Nearly a dozen countries also have incorporated all or some of the principles into national legislation. In one case, the Colombian Constitutional Court in 2001 placed them into the country's "constitutional block," effectively making them a binding part of national law. Other countries that have adopted the principles into national laws or policies include the Maldives, Mozambique, Turkey and Uganda.

IDP advocates say the most significant potential use of the Guiding Principles is in Africa, where the African Union since 2006 has been working on a plan to incorporate a version of them into a binding regional treaty. This treaty — to be called the Convention for the Prevention of Internal Displacement and the Protection of and Assistance to Internally Displaced Persons in Africa — is expected to be adopted by African leaders at a summit meeting in Kampala, Uganda, in April. [4]

---

[1] Text of the Convention and Protocol is at www.unhcr.org/protect/PROTECTION/3b66c2aa10.pdf.

[2] "States Parties to the Refugee Convention," U.N. High Commissioner for Refugees, www.unhcr.org/protect/PROTECTION/3b73b0d63.pdf.

[3] Text of Refugee Convention in Africa is at www.unhcr.org/basics/BASICS/45dc1a682.pdf; Text of the Cartegena Declaration is at www.unhcr.org/basics/BASICS/45dc19084.pdf.

[4] Text of the Guiding Principles is at www3.brookings.edu/fp/projects/idp/resources/GPEnglish.pdf.

Continued from p. 80

body authorized to take forceful action. In addition, major countries with large, well-equipped armies — notably the United States and many European countries — have been unwilling to contribute sufficient troops to U.N. peacekeeping forces. The U.N.'s inability to protect displaced people has been most evident in eastern Congo and Darfur, where peacekeeping forces, mainly from African

Union countries, are ill-equipped and undermanned. [84]

Early in February, for example, Doctors Without Borders bitterly denounced the U.N. peacekeeping mission in Congo for its "inaction" in response to the recent LRA attacks. Laurence Gaubert, head of mission in Congo for the group, said the U.N. peacekeepers "are just based in their camp, they don't go out of their camp, they don't know what is happening in the area." [85] Gaubert noted that the Security Council last Dec. 22 adopted Resolution 1856 demanding protection for civilians in Congo. [86] "This is something they have signed," she said, "but is not something you can see in the field that they have put in place." [87]

U.N. Under-Secretary-General for Humanitarian Affairs John Holmes acknowledged that the peacekeepers could do more to protect civilians but said the harsh criticism of them was "unreasonable and unjustified." Only 250-300 troops were in the area at the time, he said, and most were engineers, not combat forces. [88]

The U.N. has faced similar hurdles in trying to protect the millions of civilians displaced in Darfur since 2003. African Union peacekeepers began limited operations in Sudan in 2004 but lacked either the mandate or the resources to prevent government-backed militias or rebel groups from attacking civilians in camps and settlements. The Sudanese government agreed in 2006 and 2007 to allow beefed up U.N. peacekeeping missions, but — as in Congo — the U.N. has been unable to deploy adequate forces over such an enormous area. In Sudan, the government dragged its feet in following through on its agreement, and other countries have failed to provide the necessary money and manpower. The UNHCR operates in seven displaced-persons camps in Darfur (and in six camps in eastern Chad) but must rely on the peacekeeping mission for security. [89]

U.N. officials have repeatedly called for more forceful action to protect Darfuri civilians, only to be stymied by the

Serb refugees stage a demonstration along the Kosovo border in April 2007 to urge the U.N. to return them to their home provinces. Hundreds of thousands of people dislocated by war in the former Yugoslavia during the 1990s have not yet returned to their home regions.

AFP/Getty Images/Sasa Maricic

Security Council — largely because of resistance from China, which has economic interests in Sudan — and delaying tactics by Sudan. The Khartoum government on Feb. 17 signed an agreement with the largest Darfur rebel group, the Justice and Equality Movement, calling for negotiation of a formal peace accord within three months. [90] The hurdles to such an accord were evident the very next day, when government forces reportedly bombed some of the rebel group's positions. The future of the peace agreement was further complicated by the International Criminal Court's (ICC) landmark decision on March 4 to issue an arrest warrant for Sudanese President Omar al-Bashir, charging him with directing the mass murder of tens of thousands of Darfuri civilians and "forcibly transferring large numbers of civilians, and pillaging their property." It was the first time the Hague-based court has accused a sitting head of state of war crimes. Unless he leaves Sudan, there is no international mechanism for arresting Bashir, who denies the accusations and

does not recognize the court's jurisdiction. Some aid organizations fear the ICC ruling could trigger more violence — and thus more displacements. [91]

Focusing on IDPs

The number of people displaced by violence who remain within their own countries has been averaging more than 20 million per year, according to the Internal Displacement Monitoring Center, an arm of the Norwegian Refugee Council. More than a third of them are in just three countries: Colombia (up to 4.3 million), Sudan (3.5 million) and Iraq (up to 2.8 million). [92] Tens of millions more have been driven from their homes by natural disasters.

In December 2008, to give IDPs more international attention, the U.N.'s Office for the Coordination of Humanitarian Affairs launched a series of events focusing on IDPs, including workshops, panel discussions, a Web site and high-level conferences.

The agency is particularly concerned about displaced people who languish for years without help from their governments. "For millions of IDPs around the world, an end to their years of displacement, discrimination and poverty seems to be of little concern for those in power," said the U.N.'s Holmes. The U.N. also is encouraging governments to adopt the Guiding Principles on Internal Displacement for dealing with IDPs. And, it is pressing for "more predictable, timely and principled funding" for programs that help IDPs return home or find new homes, he said. [93]

In recent years, displaced people, usually from rural areas, have tended to head for cities. Experts say it is difficult to calculate the number of urban IDPs, but the monitoring center put the 2007 figure at 4 million, and the UNHCR estimated in 2008 that about half of the 11.4 million refugees were in cities. [94]

Urban IDPs and refugees pose logistical problems for local and international agencies charged with helping them. "In a camp, you have all these tents lined up in a row, and so it's easy to know how many people are there, and how much food and medicine you need every day," says Patrick Duplat, an advocate for Refugees International. "In an urban setting, it's much more complicated to reach people. Who is a refugee, who is an IDP and how are they different from the local population?"

U.N. High Commissioner Guterres acknowledged in a speech last October that global efforts to aid and protect urban refugees and IDPs have been "weak." [95] The approximately 2 million Iraqi refugees living in Damascus and Amman represent "a completely new and different challenge in relation to our usual activities in encampment situations," he told a conference in Norway. [96]

Last year the UNHCR tried handing out cash coupons and ATM cards to several thousand Iraqi refugees in Damascus, enabling them to buy food and other goods at local markets. The UNHCR

and the World Food Program also gave food baskets or rice, vegetable oil and lentils to Iraqi refugees considered most in need, aiding about 177,000 Iraqis in 2008. [97] But some refugees reportedly were selling their rations to pay for housing and other needs. [98]

A major step toward legally protecting African IDPs could come in April at a planned special African Union (AU) summit meeting in Uganda. Experts have been working for nearly three years on a Convention for the Protection and Assistance of Internally Displaced Persons in Africa. This treaty would incorporate some, but not all, of the 1998 Guiding Principles on Internal Displacement, which sets nonbinding standards for protecting IDPs. [99]

If a treaty is produced, ratified and implemented, it could be an important step in protecting IDPs, because so many are in Africa, says Cohen from Brookings. But she is concerned that the final treaty, which already has been revised several times, might not be as strong in protecting human rights as the voluntary Guiding Principles. "We'll have to wait and see what the leaders agree to, and even if they adopt it," she says.

Guterres strongly endorses the AU's plan for a binding treaty. He also says that because the treaty has been developed by Africans, not imposed by outsiders, it "will not be subject to questions about the legitimacy of its objectives." [100] ∎

OUTLOOK

Environmental Refugees

Environmental deterioration caused by climate change could force up to 1 billion people from their homes in coming decades, according to a paper presented to a high-level U.N. meeting last October. [101] Small island

nations, notably the Maldives in the Indian Ocean and Kiribati and Tuvalu in the Pacific, could be inundated — causing mass evacuations — if sea levels rise to the extent predicted by many scientists. [102]

Rising seas also endanger several hundred million people in low-lying coastal regions. Many of these areas are in developing countries — such as Bangladesh and the Philippines — that already are prone to cyclones, floods, earthquakes or volcanic eruptions. [103] Many scientists believe that climate change will increase the severity and frequency of weather-linked disasters, particularly cyclones and floods, thus displacing even more people in the future.

L. Craig Johnstone, deputy U.N. High Commissioner for Refugees, said "conservative" estimates predict that up to 250 million people could be displaced by the middle of the 21st century due to climate change. The minority of scientists who doubt the impact of climate change dismiss such estimates as overblown. [104] But aid officials at the U.N. and other international agencies say they have no choice but to prepare for the worst.

Regardless of the impact of climate change on displacements, experts across the spectrum say it is becoming increasingly important for the international community to decide how long to provide humanitarian aid for displaced people. Decades-long displacements are difficult for both the IDPs and refugees as well as the aid groups and host countries involved. (*See sidebar, p. 178.*)

"When can they stop being vulnerable as a result of their displacement and simply be compared to any other poor person in their country?" asks Koser, at the Geneva Center for Security Policy. He cites the 4.6 million Palestinians still being aided by the United Nations six decades after their original displacement.

UNHCR officials acknowledge that

international aid programs are not always equitable but say addressing the vulnerability of the world's poor and ending the causes of displacement depend on the political will of global leaders. In his annual remarks to the Security Council on Jan. 8, High Commissioner Guterres said global displacement issues won't be solved until the conflicts that force people from their homes are ended.

"While it is absolutely vital that the victims of armed conflict be provided with essential protection and assistance, we must also acknowledge the limitations of humanitarian action and its inability to resolve deep-rooted conflicts within and between states," he said. "The solution, as always, can only be political." [105] ∎

Notes

[1] "Only after five days we dared to bury the bodies," Doctors Without Borders, Jan. 19, 2009, www.condition-critical.org/.

[2] "Congo Crisis" fact sheet, International Rescue Committee, p. 1, www.theirc.org/resources/2007/congo_onesheet.pdf; also see "World Report 2009," Human Rights Watch, www.hrw.org/en/world-report/2009/democratic-republic-congo-drc.

[3] "Convention and Protocol Relating to the Status of Refugees," U.N. High Commissioner for Refugees, www.unhcr.org/protect/PROTECTION/3b66c2aa10.pdf.

[4] "World Report 2009," op. cit.

[5] "Statement by Mr. Antonio Guterres, United Nations High Commissioner for Refugees, to the Security Council, New York," U.N. High Commissioner for Refugees, Jan. 8, 2009, www.unhcr.org/admin/ADMIN/496625484.html.

[6] "Internally Displaced People: Exiled in their Homeland," U.N. Office for the Coordination of Humanitarian Affairs, http://ochaonline.un.org/News/InFocus/InternallyDisplacedPeopleIDPs/tabid/5132/language/en-US/Default.aspx; also see "China Earthquake: Facts and Figures," International Federation of Red Cross and Red Crescent Societies, Oct. 31, 2008, www.ifrc.org/Docs/pubs/disasters/sichuan-earthquake/ff311008.pdf.

[7] Jeffrey Gettleman, "Starvation And Strife Menace Torn Kenya," The New York Times, March 1, 2009, p. 6.

[8] "Top UNHCR official warns about displacement from climate change," U.N. High Commissioner for Refugees, Dec. 9, 2008, www.unhcr.org/news/NEWS/493e9bd94.html.

[9] "2007 Statistical Yearbook," U.N. High Commissioner for Refugees, p. 23, www.unhcr.org/cgi-bin/texis/vtx/home/opendoc.pdf?id=4981c3252&tbl=STATISTICS; "Statement by Mr. Antonio Guterres," op. cit.

[10] For background, see Karen Foerstel, "Crisis in Darfur," CQ Global Researcher, September 2008, pp. 243-270.

[11] "2009 Global Update: Sudan," U.N. High Commissioner for Refugees, pp. 1-3, www.unhcr.org/publ/PUBL/4922d4130.pdf.

[12] "Millions of Hectares of Land Secured for Internally Displaced," International Organization for Migration, Jan. 9, 2009, www.iom.int/jahia/Jahia/pbnAM/cache/offonce;jsessionid=29AD6E92A35FDE971CDAB26007A67DB2.worker01?entryId=21044.

[13] "Afghanistan — The Challenges of Sustaining Returns," U.N. High Commissioner for Refugees, www.unhcr.org/cgi-bin/texis/vtx/afghan?page=home.

[14] See "UNHCR Global Appeal, 2009"; "2009 Global Update, Mission Statement," U.N. High Commissioner for Refugees, www.unhcr.org/publ/PUBL/4922d43f11.pdf; "Statement by Mr. Antonio Guterres," op. cit.; "2009 Global Update, Working with the Internally Displaced," U.N. High Commissioner for Refugees, www.unhcr.org/publ/PUBL/4922d44c0.pdf.

[15] The Refugee Status Determination (RSD) Unit, U.N. High Commissioner for Refugees, www.unhcr.org/protect/3d3d26004.html.

[16] "2009 Global Update, Mission Statement," op. cit.

[17] "Protracted Refugee Situations: High Commissioner's Initiative," U.N. High Commissioner for Refugees, December 2008, www.unhcr.org/protect/PROTECTION/4937de6f2.pdf.

[18] "Humanitarian Reform," United Nations, www.humanitarianreform.org.

[19] "The Global Cluster Leads," U.N. Office for the Coordination of Humanitarian Affairs, http://ocha.unog.ch/humanitarianreform/Default.aspx?tabid=217.

[20] "Cluster Approach Evaluation 2007," United Nations, www.humanitarianreform.org/Default.aspx?tabid=457.

[21] The book Milner co-authored is The United Nation's High Commissioner for Refugees (UNHCR): The Politics and Practice of Refugee Protection into the 21st Century (2008).

[22] "Convention and Protocol Relating to the Status of Refugees," op. cit.

[23] "Full Text of Jack Straw's Speech," The Guardian, Feb. 6, 2001, www.guardian.co.uk/uk/2001/feb/06/immigration.immigrationandpublicservices3.

[24] "Climate change, natural disasters and human displacement: a UNHCR perspective," www.unhcr.org/protect/PROTECTION/4901e81a4.pdf.

[25] "European Pact on Immigration and Asylum," www.immigration.gouv.fr/IMG/pdf/Plaquette_EN.pdf.

[26] "ECRE calls for suspension of Dublin transfers to Greece," European Council on Refugees and Exiles, April 3, 2008, www.ecre.org/resources/Press_releases/1065.

[27] "NGO Statement Addressing the Iraqi Humanitarian Challenge," July 31, 2008, www.refugeesinternational.org/policy/letter/ngo-statement-addressing-iraqi-humanitarian-challenge.

[28] "Fact Sheet: USCIS Makes Major Strides During 2008," U.S. Citizenship and Immigration Services, Nov. 6, 2008, www.uscis.gov/portal/site/uscis/menuitem.5af9bb95919f35e66f614176543f6d1a/?vgnextoid=2526ad6f16d6d110VgnVCM1000004718190aRCRD&vgnextchannel=68439c7755cb9010VgnVCM10000045f3d6a1RCRD.

[29] "NGO Statement: Addressing the Iraqi Humanitarian Challenge," op. cit.

[30] "Fact Sheet: Iraqi Refugee Processing," U.S. Citizenship and Immigration Services, Sept. 12, 2008, www.dhs.gov/xnews/releases/pr_1221249274808.shtm.

[31] "Operation Safe Haven Iraq 2009," Center for American Progress, www.americanprogress.org/issues/2009/01/iraqi_airlift.html.

[32] Her blog site is http://refugeeresettlementwatch.wordpress.com/.

[33] "The 1951 Refugee Convention," U.N. High Commissioner for Refugees, www.unhcr.org/1951convention/dev-protect.html.

[34] Ibid.

[35] Ibid.

[36] "Establishment of UNRWA," www.un.org/unrwa/overview/index.html.

[37] "UNRWA Statistics," www.un.org/unrwa/publications/index.html.

[38] "A 'Timeless' Treaty Under Attack: A New Phase," U.N. High Commissioner for Refugees, www.unhcr.org/1951convention/new-phase.html.

[39] "States Parties to the Convention and the Protocol," U.N. High Commissioner for Refugees, www.unhcr.org/protect/PROTEC-

TION/3b73b0d63.pdf.

[40] "Guiding Principles on Internal Displacement," www3.brookings.edu/fp/projects/idp/resources/GPEnglish.pdf.

[41] "FMO Research Guide: Afghanistan," Teresa Poppelwell, July 2007, pp. 17-19, www.forcedmigration.org/guides/fmo006/.

[42] "Afghanistan — The Challenges of Sustaining Returns," U.N. High Commissioner for Refugees, www.unhcr.org/cgi-bin/texis/vtx/afghan?page=home.

[43] "Jalozai camp closed, returnees face difficulties at home," IRIN news service, June 2, 2008, www.irinnews.org/Report.aspx?ReportId=78506; also see "Iran called upon to halt winter deportations," IRIN news service, Dec. 18, 2008, www.irinnews.org/PrintReport.aspx?ReportId=82007.

[44] "Afghanistan — The Challenges of Sustaining Returns," op. cit.

[45] "Minister disputes call to boost refugee returns," IRIN news service, Sept. 10, 2008, www.irinnews.org/Report.aspx?ReportId=80218.

[46] "Cold tents for returnees in east," IRIN news service, Jan. 15, 2009, www.irinnews.org/Report.aspx?ReportId=82373.

[47] "Afghanistan at the crossroads: Young Afghans return to a homeland they never knew," U.N. High Commissioner for Refugees, Nov. 14, 2008, www.unhcr.org/cgi-bin/texis/vtx/afghan?page=news&id=491d84c64.

[48] "2009 Global Update, Colombia situation," U.N. High Commissioner for Refugees, www.unhcr.org/publ/PUBL/4922d43411.pdf.

[49] "Colombia Situation," U.N. High Commissioner for Refugees 2008-09 Global Appeal for Colombia, p. 2, www.unhcr.org/home/PUBL/474ac8e814.pdf.

[50] Ibid.

[51] "Millions of Hectares of Land Secured for Internally Displaced," International Organization for Migration, Jan. 9, 2009, www.iom.

[52] Ibid.

[53] Ibid.

[54] "2009 Global Update," Democratic Republic of the Congo, U.N. High Commissioner for Refugees, www.unhcr.org/publ/PUBL/4922d4100.pdf.

[55] "Congo Crisis" fact sheet, op. cit.

[56] "A Congolese Rebel Leader Who Once Seemed Untouchable Is Caught," The New York Times, Jan. 24, 2009, www.nytimes.com/2009/01/24/world/africa/24congo.html?_r=1.

[57] "An arresting and hopeful surprise," The Economist, Jan. 29, 2009, www.economist.com/displayStory.cfm?story_id=13022113. For background, see David Masci, "Aiding Africa," CQ Researcher, Aug. 29, 2003, pp. 697-720; John Felton, "Child Soldiers," CQ Global Researcher, July 2008.

[58] "2009 Global Update: Iraq," U.N. High Commissioner for Refugees, p. 2, www.unhcr.org/publ/PUBL/4922d4230.pdf.

[59] "WFP to help feed one million displaced Iraqis," World Food Program, Jan. 3, 2009, www.wfp.org/English/?ModuleID=137&Key=2732.

[60] "Budget cuts threaten IDP housing projects," IRIN news service, Jan. 6, 2009, www.irinnews.org/Report.aspx?ReportId=82209.

[61] "IDPs enticed to vacate southern camp," IRIN news service, Dec. 15, 2008, www.irinnews.org/Report.aspx?ReportId=81963.

[62] "2009 Global Update: Iraq," op. cit., p. 2.

[63] "Three Years of Post-Samarra Displacement in Iraq," International Organization for Migration, Feb. 22, 2009, p. 1, www.iom.int/jahia/webdav/shared/shared/mainsite/published_docs/studies_and_reports/iom_displacement_report_post_samarra.pdf.

[64] Ibid.

[65] "Post-Nargis Periodic Review I," Tripartite Core Group, December 2008, p. 4, www.aseansec.org/22119.pdf.

[66] "2009 Global Update: Myanmar," U.N. High Commissioner for Refugees, p. 2, www.unhcr.org/publ/PUBL/4922d42b0.pdf.

[67] "Cyclone survivors face water shortages," IRIN news service, Dec. 29, 2008, www.irinnews.org/Report.aspx?ReportId=82129.

[68] "Cyclone recovery 'will take up to four years,' " IRIN news service, Jan. 15, 2009, www.IRINnews.org/Report.aspx?ReportId=82383.

[69] Michael Heath, "Angelina Jolie, U.N. Envoy, Asks Thailand to Aid Myanmar Refugees," Bloomberg News, www.bloomberg.com/apps/news?pid=20601080&sid=aL5VlfM46aAc&refer=asia#.

[70] "2009 Global Update: Bangladesh," U.N. High Commissioner for Refugees, p. 1, www.unhcr.org/publ/PUBL/4922d42818.pdf.

[71] "Myanmar Refugees Rescued at Sea," The New York Times, Feb. 3, 2009, www.nytimes.com/2009/02/04/world/asia/04indo.html?ref=world.

[72] "Angelina Jolie voices support for Myanmar refugees in northern Thailand camps," U.N. High Commissioner for Refugees, Feb. 5, 2009, www.unhcr.org/news/NEWS/498ab65c2.html.

[73] Ibid.

[74] "ASIA: Regional approach to Rohingya boat people," IRIN news service, March 2, 2009, www.irinnews.org/Report.aspx?ReportId=83232.

[75] "2009 Global Update: Sudan," U.N. High Commissioner for Refugees, pp. 1-3, www.unhcr.org/publ/PUBL/4922d4130.pdf.

[76] "Number of returnees to South Sudan passes the 300,000 mark," U.N. High Commissioner for Refugees, Feb. 10, 2009, www.unhcr.org/news/NEWS/4991a8de2.html; "2009 Global Update," op. cit., p. 1.

[77] "Darfur remains tense after recent eruption of fighting, U.N. reports," IRIN news service, Jan. 28, 2009, www.un.org/apps/news/story.asp?NewsID=29699&Cr=darfur&Cr1=.

[78] "Report of the Secretary-General on the deployment of the African Union-United Nations Hybrid Operation in Darfur," United Nations, Oct. 17, 2008, p. 11, http://daccess-dds.un.org/doc/UNDOC/GEN/N08/553/95/PDF/N0855395.pdf?OpenElement.

[79] "2009 Global Update: Sudan," op. cit.; "2009 Global Update: Chad," U.N. High Commissioner for Refugees, www.unhcr.org/publ/PUBL/4922d41214.pdf.

[80] "2009 Global Update: Sudan," op. cit., p. 3; "World Refugee Survey, 2008," Sudan chapter, U.S. Committee for Refugees and Immigrants, www.refugees.org/countryreports.aspx?id=2171.

[81] "Kandiah: 'There was shelling every day. We barely escaped with our lives,' " IRIN news service, Feb. 19, 2009, www.IRINnews.org/Report.aspx?ReportId=83015.

About the Author

John Felton is a freelance journalist who has written about international affairs and U.S. foreign policy for nearly 30 years. He covered foreign affairs for the *Congressional Quarterly Weekly Report* during the 1980s, was deputy foreign editor for National Public Radio in the early 1990s and has been a freelance writer specializing in international topics for the past 15 years. His most recent book, published by CQ Press, is *The Contemporary Middle East: A Documentary History*. He lives in Stockbridge, Mass.

[82] For background, see Lee Michael Katz, "World Peacekeeping," *CQ Global Researcher*, April 2007, pp. 75-100.

[83] "World Summit Outcome 2005," U.N. General Assembly, Resolution A/RES/60/1, paragraphs 138-139, September 2005, www.un.org/summit2005/documents.html.

[84] See Foerstel, *op. cit.*

[85] "DRC: MSF denounces the lack of protection for victims of LRA violence in Haut-Uélé," Doctors Without Borders, Feb. 4, 2009, www.msf.org.

[86] Security Council Resolution 1856, Dec. 22, 2006, http://daccessdds.un.org/doc/UNDOC/GEN/N08/666/94/PDF/N0866694.pdf?OpenElement.

[87] *Ibid.*

[88] "Press Conference by Humanitarian Affairs Head on Recent Trip to Democratic Republic of Congo," U.N. Department of Public Information, Feb. 13, 2009, www.un.org/News/briefings/docs/2009/090213_DRC.doc.htm.

[89] "2009 Global Update: Sudan," *op. cit.*

[90] "Sudan and Darfur Rebel Group Agree to Peace Talks," *The New York Times*, Feb. 18, 2009, www.nytimes.com/2009/02/18/world/africa/18sudan.html?_r=1&ref=todayspaper.

[91] "Sudan bombs rebels day after Darfur deal: rebels," Agence France-Presse, Feb. 18, 2009. See Mike Corder, "International court issues warrant for Sudan president on charges of war crimes in Darfur," The Associated Press, March 4, 2009.

[92] "2009 Global Update," *op. cit.*; "Global Overview of Trends and Developments: 2007," Internal Displacement Monitoring Centre, Norwegian Refugee Council, p. 12, April 2008, www.internal-displacement.org/idmc/website/resources.nsf/(httpPublications)/0F926CFAF1EADE5EC125742E003B7067?OpenDocument.

[93] "UN launches year-long campaign to highlight, and solve, plight of displaced," IRIN news service, Dec. 18, 2009, www.un.org/apps/news/story.asp?NewsID=29358&Cr=IDPs&Cr1.

[94] "Addressing Urban Displacement: A Project Description," Internal Displacement Monitoring Centre, Norwegian Refugee Council, 2007, p. 2; also see "2007 Global Trends," U.N. High Commissioner for Refugees, June 2008, p. 2, www.unhcr.org/statistics/STATISTICS/4852366f2.pdf.

[95] "Ten years of Guiding Principles on Internal Displacement: Achievements and Future Challenges," statement by Antonio Guterres, Oslo, Oct. 16, 2008, www.unhcr.org/admin/ADMIN/48ff45e12.html.

FOR MORE INFORMATION

Brookings-Bern Project on Internal Displacement, The Brookings Institution, 1775 Massachusetts Avenue, N.W., Washington, DC, 20036; (202) 797-6168; www.brookings.edu/projects/idp.aspx. A joint project of the Brookings Institution and the University of Bern (Switzerland) School of Law; conducts research and issues reports on policy questions related to internally displaced people (IDPs).

Institute for the Study of International Migration, Georgetown University, Harris Building, Third Floor, 3300 Whitehaven St. N.W., Washington, DC, 20007; (202) 687-2258; www12.georgetown.edu/sfs/isim/index.html. An academic research center focusing on all aspects of international migration, including refugees.

Internal Displacement Monitoring Centre, Chemin de Balexert, 7-9 1219 Chatelaine Geneva, Switzerland; 41-22-799-07 00; www.internal-displacement.org. Provides regular reports on IDPs globally; the major source of information about the numbers of people displaced by conflict.

International Organization for Migration, 17 Route des Morillons, CH-1211, Geneva 19, Switzerland; 41-22-717-9111; www.iom.int. A U.N. partner (not officially within the U.N. system) that aids refugees and migrants and studies migration trends.

Norwegian Refugee Council, P.O. Box 6758, St. Olavs Plass, 0130 Oslo, Norway; 47-23-10 9800; www.nrc.no. A prominent nongovernmental organization that provides aid programs for displaced persons and advocates on their behalf.

Refugee Studies Centre, Queen Elizabeth House, University of Oxford, Mansfield Road, Oxford OX1 3TB, United Kingdom; 44-1865-270-722; www.rsc.ox.ac.uk/index.html?main. A prominent research center on refugees and the displaced. Publishes the *Forced Migration Review*, a quarterly journal written by experts in the field.

Refugees International, 2001 S St., N.W., Suite 700, Washington, DC, 20009; (202) 828-0110; www.refugeesinternational.org. Advocates on behalf of refugees and IDPs and publishes regular reports based on site visits to key countries.

U.N. High Commissioner for Refugees, Case Postale 2500, CH-1211, Geneva 2 Depot, Switzerland; 41-22-739-8111; www.unhcr.org/home.html. The U.N. agency with prime responsibility for aiding and protecting refugees; increasingly has taken on a similar role in regard to IDPs.

U.S. Committee for Refugees and Immigrants, 2231 Crystal Dr., Suite 350, Arlington VA 22202-3711; (703) 310-1130; www.refugees.org. An advocacy group that publishes reports focusing on human-rights abuses and other problems encountered by refugees and immigrants.

[96] *Ibid.*

[97] "WFP to help feed one million displaced Iraqis," World Food Program, Jan. 3, 2008, www.wfp.org/English/?ModuleID=137&Key=2732.

[98] "Iraqi refugees selling some of their food rations," IRIN news service, Jan. 28, 2009, http://one.wfp.org/english/?ModuleID=137&Key=2732.

[99] "From Voluntary Principles to Binding Standards," *IDP Action*, Jan. 9, 2009, www.id-paction.org/index.php/en/news/16-principles2standards.

[100] "Ten Years of Guiding Principles on Internal Displacement," *op. cit.*

[101] "Climate Change, Migration and Displacement: Who will be affected?" Working paper submitted by the informal group on Migration/Displacement and Climate Change of the U.N. Inter-Agency Standing Committee, Oct. 31, 2008, http://unfccc.int/resource/docs/2008/smsn/igo/022.pdf.

[102] "Climate Change and Displacement," *Forced Migration Review*, p. 20, October 2008, www.fmreview.org/climatechange.htm; for background see Colin Woodard, "Curbing Climate Change," *CQ Global Researcher*, February 2007, pp. 27-50, and Marcia Clemmitt, "Climate Change," *CQ Researcher*, Jan. 27, 2006, pp. 73-96.

[103] "Climate Resilient Cities: A Primer on Reducing Vulnerabilities to Disasters," World Bank, 2009, pp. 5-6.

[104] "Top UNHCR official warns about displacement from climate change," *op. cit.*

[105] "Statement by Mr. Antonio Guterres," *op. cit.*

Bibliography

Selected Sources

Books

Evans, Gareth, *The Responsibility to Protect: Ending Mass Atrocity Crimes Once and For All*, Brookings Institution Press, 2008.

A former Australian foreign minister and current head of the International Crisis Group offers an impassioned plea for world leaders to follow through on their promises to protect civilians, even those abused by their own governments.

Loescher, Gil, Alexander Betts and James Milner, *The United Nations High Commissioner for Refugees (UNHCR): The Politics and Practice of Refugee Protection Into the 21st Century*, Routledge, 2008.

Academic experts on refugee issues offer a generally sympathetic but often critical assessment of the UNHCR's performance as the world's main protector of refugees.

Verdirame, Guglielmo, and Barbara Harrell-Bond, with Zachary Lomo and Hannah Garry, *Rights in Exile: Janus-Faced Humanitarianism*, Berghahn Books, 2005.

A former director of the Refugee Studies Center at Oxford University (Harrell-Bond) and an expert on refugee rights at Cambridge University offer a blistering critique of the U.N. and nongovernment agencies that protect refugees.

Articles

"Managing the Right of Return," *The Economist*, Aug. 4, 2008.

The practical implications of refugees' legal right to return to their home countries are examined.

Cohen, Roberta, and Francis Deng, "The Genesis and the Challenges," *Forced Migration Review*, December 2008.

This is the keystone article in an issue devoted to the Guiding Principles on Internal Displacement 10 years after their creation. Cohen and Deng were prime movers of the document.

Feyissa, Abebe, with Rebecca Horn, "Traveling Souls: Life in a Refugee Camp, Where Hearts Wander as Minds Deteriorate," *Utne Reader*, September-October 2008, www.utne.com/2008-09-01/GreatWriting/Traveling-Souls.aspx.

An Ethiopian who has lived in northwestern Kenya's Kakuma refugee camp for 16 years writes about life in the camp.

Guterres, Antonio, "Millions Uprooted: Saving Refugees and the Displaced," *Foreign Affairs*, September/October 2008.

The U.N. High Commissioner for Refugees lays out an ambitious agenda of action to aid and protect the displaced.

Harr, Jonathan, "Lives of the Saints: International Hardship Duty in Chad," *The New Yorker*, Jan. 5, 2009, www.newyorker.com/reporting/2009/01/05/090105fa_fact_harr.

A frequent *New Yorker* contributor offers a sympathetic portrait of idealistic aid workers at refugee camps in Chad.

Stevens, Jacob, "Prison of the Stateless: The Derelictions of UNHCR," *New Left Review*, November-December 2006, www.newleftreview.org/?page=article&view=2644.

A review of the memoirs of former High Commissioner Sadako Ogata becomes a strongly worded critique of the U.N. refugee agency. A rebuttal by former UNHCR special envoy Nicholas Morris is at www.unhcr.org/research/RESEARCH/460d131d2.pdf.

Reports and Studies

"2009 Global Update," U.N. High Commissioner for Refugees, November 2008, www.unhcr.org/ga09/index.html.

Published in November, this is the most recent summary from the UNHCR of its operations, plans and budget for 2009.

"Future Floods of Refugees: A comment on climate change, conflict and forced migration," Norwegian Refugee Council, April 2008, www.nrc.no/arch/_img/9268480.pdf.

The refugee council surveys the debate over whether climate change will worsen natural disasters and force untold millions of people from their homes.

"Protracted Refugee Situations: High Commissioner's Initiative," U.N. High Commissioner for Refugees, December 2008, www.unhcr.org/protect/PROTECTION/4937de6f2.pdf.

The UNHCR offers a plan of action for resolving several long-term situations in which refugees have been trapped in camps or settlements for decades.

"When Displacement Ends: A Framework for Durable Solutions," Brookings-Bern Project on Internal Displacement, June 2007, www.brookings.edu/reports/2007/09displacementends.aspx.

This detailed blueprint for how international agencies can help IDPs find "durable solutions" to their displacements is the product of conferences and other studies.

Cohen, Roberta, "Listening to the Voices of the Displaced: Lessons Learned," Brookings-Bern Project on Internal Displacement, September 2008, www.brookings.edu/reports/2008/09_internal_displacement_cohen.aspx.

The author recommends better ways to aid and protect displaced people around the world, based on interviews with dozens of IDPs.

The Next Step:

Additional Articles from Current Periodicals

Internally Displaced Persons (IDPs)

"Colombia Trails Only Sudan in Number of Internally Displaced," EFE News Service (Spain), April 17, 2007.

A decades-old internal conflict has forced 3.8 million Colombians from their homes.

Husarska, Anna, "Iraq's Forgotten Population," *The Boston Globe*, Dec. 24, 2007, p. A11.

International law protects refugees, but internally displaced persons' problems are usually addressed by their own countries.

Namata, Berna, "AU to Hold African Convention on Displaced Persons," *The New Times* (Rwanda), Nov. 22, 2008.

The African Union is planning a continental convention regarding the protection and assistance of African IDPs.

Iraqi Refugees

"As Iraqi Death Toll Escalates, 50,000 Flee Homes Each Month," *Irish Times*, April 21, 2007.

The United Nations estimates that 2 million Iraqis have fled to neighboring countries, while another 2 million have sought safer areas inside Iraq.

Gaouette, Nicole, "U.S. Defends the Way it Deals With Iraqi Refugees," *Los Angeles Times*, Sept. 22, 2007, p. A7.

The Department of Homeland Security has received a great deal of criticism for not processing Iraqi visas quickly enough.

Safty, Adel, "Displaced and Impoverished," *Gulf News* (United Arab Emirates), March 12, 2007.

The movement of Iraqi refugees and internally displaced persons has been compared to the Palestinian exodus during Israel's establishment in 1948.

Urek, Markus, "The Drama of Iraqi Refugee Women and Children in Syria," *Turkish Daily News*, April 1, 2008.

Many Iraqi women and children seeking refuge in neighboring Syria are turning to prostitution and child labor in order to survive.

Somalia

"Yemen Receives 2,300 Refugees During the First Half of September Due to the Unstable Security Situation in Somalia," *Sanaa* (Yemen), Sept. 22, 2008.

More than 2,200 refugees from the Horn of Africa — mostly from Somalia — arrived in Yemen during the first two weeks of September 2008 fleeing violence at home.

Hill, Ginny, "Somali Refugees Brave Sea Passage to Escape Insurgency," *The Christian Science Monitor*, April 23, 2007, p. 4.

Yemen's guarantee of automatic refugee status for Somalis has led to 84,000 refugees entering the country, but many more have arrived who haven't registered.

Ochami, David, "Claims of Somali Refugees Coming to Kenya Unnoticed," *Kenya Times*, April 14, 2007.

An anti-refugee sweep of Somalis in neighboring Kenya has netted more than 500 refugees in two months.

United Nations

"Kenya and UNHCR to Open Refugee Camp in Fafi," *The Standard* (Kenya), Feb. 4, 2009.

The U.N. High Commissioner for Refugees (UNHCR) has agreed to open a new refugee camp in Kenya targeting about 55,000 refugees, most of whom are fleeing violence in Somalia.

Babakarkhel, Zubair, "Kabul Demands More Int'l Support to Repatriate Refugees," Pajhwok Afghan News, Nov. 19, 2008.

Afghanistan is asking the United Nations for long-term support for 3 million refugees who have yet to return home.

Jalloh, Bhoyy, "UNHCR Declares End of Refugee Status for Salone," *Concord Times* (Sierra Leone), June 10, 2008.

The UNHCR is ending refugee status for Sierra Leoneans who fled during the civil war, citing positive changes in the country.

CITING CQ GLOBAL RESEARCHER

Sample formats for citing these reports in a bibliography include the ones listed below. Preferred styles and formats vary, so please check with your instructor or professor.

MLA STYLE

Flamini, Roland. "Nuclear Proliferation." CQ Global Researcher 1 Apr. 2007: 1-24.

APA STYLE

Flamini, R. (2007, April 1). Nuclear proliferation. *CQ Global Researcher*, 1, 1-24.

CHICAGO STYLE

Flamini, Roland. "Nuclear Proliferation." *CQ Global Researcher*, April 1, 2007, 1-24.

Voices From Abroad:

FAYSAL MIQDAD
Assistant Foreign Minister
Syria

The U.S. occupation is to blame

"We see that Iraqi citizens have been forced to immigrate because of the difficult circumstances in Iraq in the wake of the occupation. . . . Iraqi refugees in Syria are at home and among their kinsfolk. However, we tell the international community that the reasons behind this are this occupation and the long wrongdoing which the Iraqi people were subjected to."

Al-Sharqiyah (United Arab Emirates), April 2007

NDUNG'U WAINAINA
Director, International Center for Policy and Conflict, Nairobi, Kenya

The international community must help

"The government has a responsibility to prevent internal displacement and protect IDPs when they arise. But when resettling IDPs, the state must follow UN guidelines on displacement. . . . UN rules require that IDPs be provided with material assistance to start off in life. . . . And since only developing countries are prone to this kind of calamity, resettlement of IDPs always needs huge material and financial contributions from the international community."

East African Standard (Kenya), April 2008

RAFAEL CORREA
President, Ecuador

Liberalism trumps people

"We have advocated for the free flow of people, but we've run up against the routine, immoral and inconsistent decision of neoliberalism which is interested in the free flow of capital and free-trade treaties, leaving the human being in last place on the social scale."

EFE News Service (Spain), April 2007

SAJID HUSSAIN CHATTHA
Secretary, Ministry of States and Frontier Regions, Pakistan

Pakistan: Afghans can't stay forever

"After 27 years, we don't favour the unlimited right to stay of Afghan refugees in Pakistan. The pace of returns depends on the absorption capacity, thus we advocate for the government of Afghanistan and the international community to intensify rehabilitation and reconstruction in Afghanistan."

Pajhwok Afghan News, June 2007

JOVAN KRKOBABIC
Deputy Prime Minister
Serbia

Croatia must do better

"The delegates from Croatia [said] the problem of refugees in their country had been resolved, and that it boiled down to a few sporadic cases, and the two countries could resolve this issue without international mediation. This was a false and contentious address, to say the least, especially considering that Croatia has done little to enable the Serbs to return safely to their homes."

Vecernje Novosti (Serbia), December 2008

MUKHAYMAR AL-MUKHAYMAR
Secretary-General
Jordanian Interior Ministry

Iraq must be restored

"We believe that all the efforts that seek to alleviate the suffering of the Iraqis outside Iraq are not an alternative to Iraq restoring its stability and achieving full national reconciliation between the components of its people. Such reconciliation would preserve the unity of Iraq, land and people, and prevent any segments or components of the Iraqi people from leaving their country."

Speech before UNHCR International Conference on Iraqi Refugees, April 2007

HUSSEIN HAJI AHMED
Somalian Consul-General
Yemen

More than peace alone is necessary

"They're in desperate need of shelter. . . . Peace alone is not enough for a person seeking a better life. That is why some Somalis risk their lives by agreeing to be smuggled to Gulf countries where they face as many problems as they had at sea."

U.N. Integrated Regional Information Network, October 2007

MAKA TASHUYEVA
Chechen refugee, Georgia

Impossible to live in Chechnya

"I returned to Chechnya once. It was impossible to live there and I returned to Georgia for a second time. In the future, my plan is to go to a third country. I am interested in receiving a travel document and leaving this place as soon as possible."

Rustavi (Georgia), June 2007

Christo Komarnitski, Bulgaria

RESCUING CHILDREN

BY ROBERT KIENER

Excerpted from the CQ Global Researcher. Robert Kiener. (October 2009). "Rescuing Children." *CQ Global Researcher*, 257-284.

Rescuing Children

BY ROBERT KIENER

THE ISSUES

As she sits on a swing in a children's shelter outside Phnom Penh, the dark-eyed 7-year-old Cambodian girl rarely smiles. Her wounds are still too raw.

A year earlier, Srey Tok (not her real name) was rescued from a brothel where she had been raped by men who believed sex with a virgin could cure them of AIDS. When she fought back, she was locked in a small cage for days at a time. If Srey still resisted, her captors would cut her arms and put salt into the wounds, or pull her hair out. Several times they hit her in the head with a nail-studded board. As she parts her hair to show a visitor the scars, she whimpers.

"Those men were monsters," says shelter founder Somaly Mam, a former child prostitute herself, as she wraps her arms around Srey. "It will take years for her to heal. Perhaps she never will."

Still, Mam says, Srey is "one of the lucky ones" — she was rescued. "Thousands of other little girls in Southeast Asia have been sold into prostitution" — as Srey was by her mother — "but they have disappeared," explains the 36-year-old Mam. "They have been raped, beaten, tortured and simply thrown away." Estimates range from 10,000 to 20,000 child prostitutes under age 16 in Cambodia alone, according to Mam.

Children's-rights activists say millions of children around the world are in crisis situations of one kind or another, including a staggering 1 million youngsters who are forced into prostitution every year. Some activists say

A young boy works at a balloon factory in Dhaka, Bangladesh, one of the world's poorest countries. Worldwide, about 158 million children under age 14 were working in 2006, according to the most recent U.N. statistics.

AFP/Getty Images/Munir Uz Zaman

10 million children at any one time are working as prostitutes. [1] Children routinely are trafficked across international borders, enslaved, kidnapped and forced to become soldiers or are otherwise caught in war's cross-fire.

"An estimated 300 million children are subjected to violence, exploitation and abuse," according to UNICEF (the United Nations Children's Fund). [2]

Every day, 25,000 children under age 5 — the equivalent of 125 jetliners full of youngsters, or one every 3.5 seconds — die from hunger, easily preventable diseases and other poverty-related causes. [3]

"It is a tragedy that the world needs to know more about and help solve,"

says Charles MacCormack, director of Save the Children. The Connecticut-based organization, dedicated to helping needy children around the world, recently launched its "Survive to Five" campaign to reduce the death toll among young children. [4]

But as horrific as today's under-5 death toll is, it's a vast improvement over the rate in 1990. The death rate for children under 5 in developing countries has fallen 27 percent since 1990, with some regions — Latin America and Central and Eastern Europe — seeing even more dramatic declines. (*See graph, p. 260.*) And children's lives have improved in other respects as well. Until the worsening global economy resulted in more food shortages, some developing nations, such as Malawi, were reducing malnutrition. [5] The world is close to eradicating polio, and from 1999 to 2005 child deaths from measles fell 60 percent worldwide and 75 percent in Africa. Insecticide-treated mosquito nets are helping to combat malaria, and zinc pills promise to cut diarrhea deaths. (*See story, p. 267.*) Many countries are close to enrolling all young children in primary school — both boys and girls. [6] Meanwhile, celebrities, nongovernmental organizations (NGOs), wealthy governments and foundations — including the Bill & Melinda Gates Foundation, rock star Bono and the U.S. government — have raised or committed billions of dollars in recent years to eradicate malaria and HIV-AIDS.

And just last month, on Sept. 23, British Prime Minister Gordon Brown announced a $5.3 billion financing package that will help provide free

Africa Has Highest Child Death Rates

Of the 25,000 children under age 5 who die every day in developing countries — most from preventable causes such as malaria and diarrhea — nearly half are in sub-Saharan Africa (map). While under-5 mortality rates overall in developing countries have dropped 27 percent since 1990, some regions have made more progress than others. Latin America and Central and Eastern Europe, for instance, have seen their rates decline by 55 percent, compared to a 22 percent drop in sub-Saharan Africa (bottom graph).

Under-5 Mortality Rates, 2007

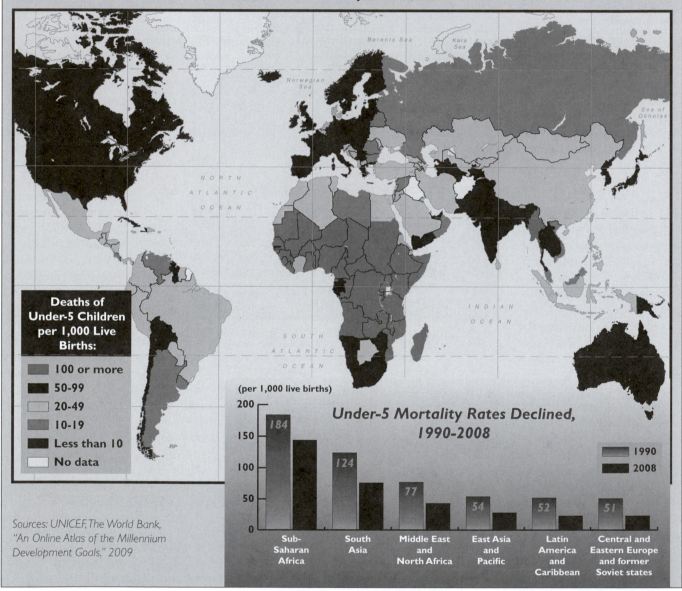

Deaths of Under-5 Children per 1,000 Live Births:
- 100 or more
- 50-99
- 20-49
- 10-19
- Less than 10
- No data

Under-5 Mortality Rates Declined, 1990-2008
(per 1,000 live births)

- Sub-Saharan Africa: 184
- South Asia: 124
- Middle East and North Africa: 77
- East Asia and Pacific: 54
- Latin America and Caribbean: 52
- Central and Eastern Europe and former Soviet states: 51

Legend: 1990, 2008

Sources: UNICEF, The World Bank, "An Online Atlas of the Millennium Development Goals," 2009

healthcare to some 10 million people — mostly women and children — in Africa and Asia. [7]

But horrific troubles still confront the world's children, including:

- An estimated 100-150 million children live on the streets — many of them runaways or abandoned — and their numbers are rising, partly due to the global economic crisis. [8]

- About 112 million children are malnourished; 9 million die before age 5. [9]
- Some 158 million children ages 5 to 14 were working in 2006,

30 percent of them in the world's poorest countries. [10]

- About 250,000 children are involved in armed conflicts, serving either as combatants, messengers, spies, porters, cooks or sex slaves. [11]

Although malaria, tuberculosis, AIDS and other diseases have claimed young lives for decades, the global economic downturn has compounded their precarious situations. Rich countries are cutting foreign aid and reducing money for children's food and medicines.

The recession "has taken a wrecking ball to the growth and development gains of the world's poorest countries," according to a recent World Bank report, which notes that the world's gross domestic product (GDP) — or total economic output — is expected to shrink 1.7 percent this year after rising for eight years. [12]

Prices for food, fuel and commodity are soaring, and poor countries — which generally escaped the subprime meltdown and the fallout from collapsing investment banks — are now facing recession. As another World Bank report noted: "Poor countries are facing a slump in their exports, [and] government budgets are badly stretched." [13]

As governments struggle, so do children who have no government programs to rely on. A drop in recycling prices means that child scavengers' daily earnings at huge garbage dumps in Phnom Penh, Cambodia, have fallen by half (to about 60 cents). "We cannot survive with these prices," says a 9-year-old girl who has lived at the dump since her parents abandoned her.

With food prices rising, the number of chronically hungry people will exceed 1 billion in 2009. [14] In Cambodia alone, the WFP already has stopped a school feeding program for some 450,000 children because of high food prices. [15]

During past economic collapses, infant mortality in sub-Saharan Africa increased by 3 percent. [16] According to Margaret Chan, director-general of the World Health Organization (WHO),

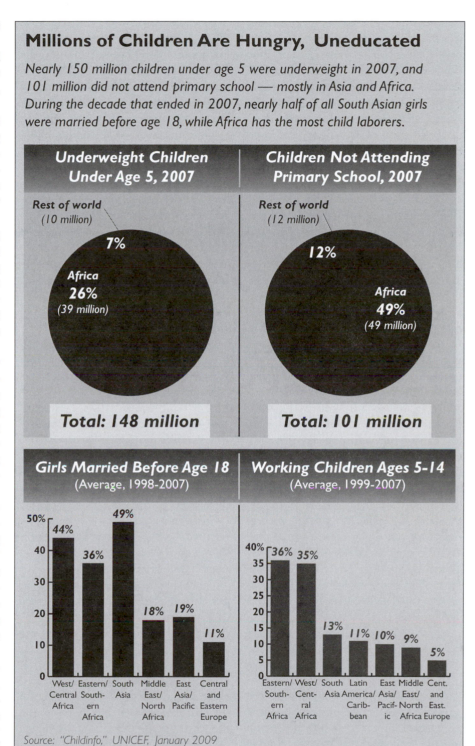

Millions of Children Are Hungry, Uneducated

Nearly 150 million children under age 5 were underweight in 2007, and 101 million did not attend primary school — mostly in Asia and Africa. During the decade that ended in 2007, nearly half of all South Asian girls were married before age 18, while Africa has the most child laborers.

Underweight Children Under Age 5, 2007

Rest of world (10 million)
7%
Africa 26% (39 million)

Total: 148 million

Children Not Attending Primary School, 2007

Rest of world (12 million)
12%
Africa 49% (49 million)

Total: 101 million

Girls Married Before Age 18 (Average, 1998-2007)

- West/Central Africa: 44%
- Eastern/Southern Africa: 36%
- South Asia: 49%
- Middle East/North Africa: 18%
- East Asia/Pacific: 19%
- Central and Eastern Europe: 11%

Working Children Ages 5-14 (Average, 1999-2007)

- Eastern/Southern Africa: 36%
- West/Central Africa: 35%
- South Asia: 13%
- Latin America/Caribbean: 11%
- East Asia/Pacific: 10%
- Middle East/North Africa: 9%
- Cent. and East. Europe: 5%

Source: "Childinfo," UNICEF, January 2009

the global downturn could cause the deaths of between 200,000 to 400,000 children each year, or up to 2.8 million additional child deaths by 2015. [17] "There is no reason [to] doubt that this will happen if we fail to act," she told the *London Times*. "More children will die because of lack of food or immunization or poor water or sanitation." [18]

And the recession is plunging more children into prostitution and child labor. "The recent economic downturn is set to drive more vulnerable children and young people to be exploited by the global sex trade," said Carmen Madriñán, executive director of the Bangkok-based End Child Prostitution, Child Pornography and Trafficking of Children for Sexual Purposes. [19]

The worldwide economic crisis has also decimated foreign-aid coffers. Donors, both governmental and private, have cut back on funding to charities, nongovernmental organizations and philanthropic humanitarian programs. For example, Catholic Relief Services, which serves more than 100 million people in more than 100 countries, is planning to reduce child-aid programs in various regions after a 13 percent drop in private donations in the first half of 2009.

Other NGOs are similarly affected. Oxfam, the London-based international charity, is planning layoffs, and CARE is trimming its budgets. [20] "There's no question these are challenging times, and we have to do more with less," says Save the Children's MacCormack.

Some aid officials criticize governments for not doing more to fund children's programs or keep aid promises. Many also fault the United States for failing to ratify the Convention on the Rights of the Child (CRC), adopted 20 years ago by the U.N. General Assembly to promote child well-being. Since then 193 countries have ratified the treaty; the United States and Somalia remain the only hold-outs.

According to the Paris-based Organisation for Economic Co-operation and Development (OECD), representing the industrialized nations, foreign aid from Europe in 2007 fell from 0.41 percent of gross national income to 0.38 percent. [21] "European governments' failure to meet aid pledges is nothing short of disgraceful," said Olivier Consolo, director of the European

Confederation of Relief and Development NGOs (CONCORD), representing more than 1,600 NGOs. "Europe likes to see itself as a world leader in development assistance, but these figures show that governments are taking a step backward." [22]

Graça Machel — Nelson Mandela's wife and founder of the Mozambique-based Foundation for Community Development — said human lives should get precedence over bank bailouts and military spending. "I don't believe the issue is money," she told a recent AIDS conference in Cape Town, South Africa. "The issue is the consciences of the people we elect. Human life is priceless; you should never bargain when it comes to saving lives." [23]

As children's-rights advocates face the daunting prospect of doing more with less, here are some of the questions they are asking:

Are rich nations giving enough aid to help children in poor countries?

How much aid is enough? In 1970 the United Nations recommended that developed nations donate 0.7 percent — less than 1 percent — of their gross national incomes to poor nations. Since then, only a handful of countries — notably Denmark, Norway and Sweden — regularly meet the 0.7 percent target. Others have fallen woefully behind. (See graphs, p. 264.)

Although total donations have regularly increased, the 0.7 percent target is a distant goal for most. For example, the United States usually gives more total dollars than any other country, but it has habitually been among the lowest when the amount is viewed as a percentage of gross income.

Although the world's 23 major donor countries gave a record $19.8 billion in 2008 — a 10.2 percent jump — it represented only 0.3 percent of GNI, a whopping $260 billion less than if all rich countries gave 0.7 percent. [24]

"Rich countries can come up with the money when they want to," said Max Lawson, head of development finance at Oxfam, citing the U.S. government's recent bailout of giant insurance company AIG, which then gave out huge executive bonuses. "AIG's executive bonuses alone could have paid for enough teachers for 7 million children in Africa. We need to . . . rescue babies not just bankers." [25]

But few believe that economically battered donor nations will donate more anytime soon. Not surprisingly, as money has become tight, debates over foreign aid's effectiveness have intensified, often centering on Africa.

Dambisa Moyo, a Zambia-born former Goldman Sachs economist who wrote Dead Aid: Why Aid Is Not Working and How There Is a Better Way for Africa, calls aid to Africa a "Band-Aid solution" at best. The more than $1 trillion in development-related aid that rich countries have sent to Africa has "made the poor poorer, and the growth slower," she wrote. "The insidious aid culture has left African countries more debt-laden, more inflation prone, more vulnerable to the vagaries of the currency market and more unattractive to higher-quality investment." [26]

William Easterly, an American economist at New York University and author of White Man's Burden: Why the West's efforts to aid the rest has done so much ill and so little good, is even harsher. "The West already spent $2.3 trillion on foreign aid over the last five decades and still had not managed to get 12-cent medicines to children to prevent half of all malaria deaths," he told the Senate Foreign Relations committee." [27]

James Shikwati, a Kenyan, who is director of the Nairobi-based Inter Region Economic Network, says aid often does more harm than good, especially when countries are flooded with emergency food aid that causes local crop prices to plummet, discouraging farmers from planting.

"In the 1990s, drought aid actually killed local production in parts of Africa and increased dependency," he says. "It's a model we see time and time again."

Corruption and poor governance also block Africa's progress, he says. "Aid money is subsidizing these corrupt, ineffective governments and keeping Africans poor," he says. The governments feel more accountable to their aid donors than to their own citizens, he adds.

Other foreign-aid critics agree. "Aid . . . makes [African] politicians much more oriented toward what will get them more money from the West than it does to making them meet the ends of their own people, which is really a scandal," said Easterly. [28]

For foreign aid to produce results, countries must develop stable governments with solid infrastructures and end official corruption. "The most obvious criticism of aid is its links to rampant corruption," wrote Moyo. "Aid flows destined to help the average African end up supporting bloated bureaucracies in . . . poor-country governments and donor-funded non-governmental organizations." [29]

But proponents of increased aid, like U.S. economist Jeffrey Sachs — director of the Earth Institute at Columbia University and special advisor to U.N. Secretary-General Ban Ki-moon — cite examples in which aid has helped millions survive. For instance, foreign aid helped to bring Rwanda back from the brink of collapse, he says. "The government's own development efforts have been very important, of course," he wrote, "but without the aid backing them, none of the recovery to date would have been possible." [30]

Others point to measles vaccination and antimalarial campaigns as proof that outside aid can accomplish goals that local governments cannot. "If outside governments and NGOs had not addressed, and funded, health issues such as maternal health, child nutrition and HIV treatment, very, very few

Children of the Streets

A homeless Indian girl sleeps in New Delhi on June 16, 2009 (top). Iraqi orphans in Baghdad smoke cigarettes and "huff" glue, a common and deadly practice of street children worldwide (bottom). An estimated 100-150 million children live on the streets — many of them runaways or abandoned by their families — and their numbers are rising, partly as a result of the global economic downturn.

governments of poor nations would have done it on their own," says Laurie Garrett, senior fellow for global health at the Council on Foreign Relations, a New York-based think tank. "For decades, money went to defense budgets, and little ended up at ministries of health."

Save the Children's MacCormack says governments can only do so much, while "charities and NGOs have a real duty to engage the public, provide the citizen commitment and help in the field from the ground up."

Continued on p. 265

Aid Hits Record But Fails to Meet Target

The world's wealthiest countries gave a record $119.8 billion in overseas development assistance (ODA) in 2008. But that represented an average of only 0.3 percent of the countries' gross national income (GNI), or less than half of the U.N.'s 0.7 percent target set in 1970. Only Denmark, Luxembourg, the Netherlands, Norway and Sweden met the 0.7 percent target (bottom graph). Aid to Africa, the world's poorest continent, declined as a proportion of total assistance.

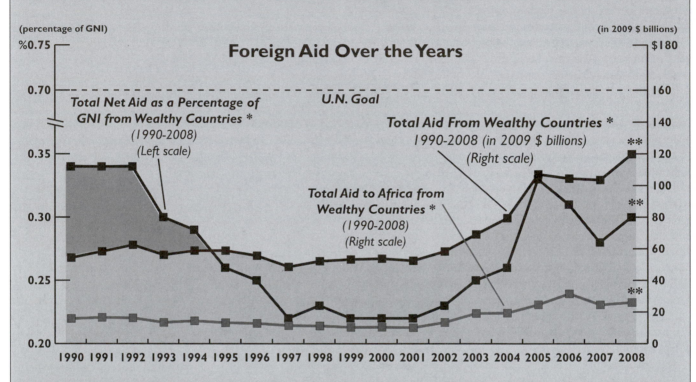

Foreign Aid Over the Years

(percentage of GNI) (Left scale) — (in 2009 $ billions) (Right scale)

Total Net Aid as a Percentage of GNI from Wealthy Countries *
(1990-2008)
(Left scale)

U.N. Goal

Total Aid From Wealthy Countries *
1990-2008 (in 2009 $ billions)
(Right scale)

Total Aid to Africa from Wealthy Countries *
(1990-2008)
(Right scale)

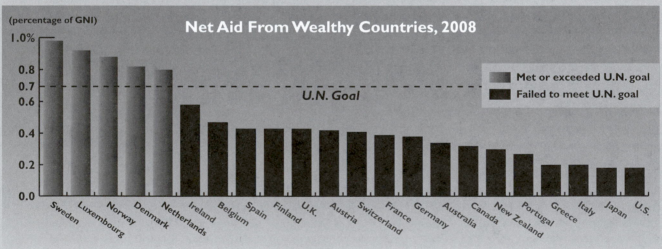

Net Aid From Wealthy Countries, 2008

(percentage of GNI)

U.N. Goal

■ Met or exceeded U.N. goal
■ Failed to meet U.N. goal

Sweden, Luxembourg, Norway, Denmark, Netherlands, Ireland, Belgium, Spain, Finland, U.K., Austria, Switzerland, France, Germany, Australia, Canada, New Zealand, Portugal, Greece, Italy, Japan, U.S.

* The 22 countries and the European Commission that are members of the Organisation for Economic Co-operation and Development's Development Assistance Committee

** Preliminary data

Source: Organisation for Economic Co-operation and Development, March 30, 2009

Continued from p. 263

Sachs, whose 2006 book *The End of Poverty* suggests how to end extreme poverty by 2025, believes developed nations must do more for Africa, especially when preventable diseases like malaria and diarrhea take so many lives. "How can we go another day when 20,000 children are going to be dying of these stupid reasons that are utterly preventable?" Sachs asked. He'd like Western governments to double their aid to Africa to $50 billion. [31]

Should the United States ratify the U.N. Convention on the Rights of the Child?

November 20 is the 20th anniversary of the adoption of the U.N. Convention on the Rights of the Child (CRC) — the most widely and rapidly ratified human-rights treaty in history. It spells out children's rights to survival and protection from abuse and exploitation, as well as their right to develop to the fullest and to participate in family, cultural and social life.

"The convention protects children's rights by setting standards in health care, education and legal, civil and social services," UNICEF says. [32]

Only the United States and Somalia, which has no functioning national government, have not ratified the treaty. Although U.S. representative to the U.N. Madeleine Albright signed the treaty on Feb. 16, 1995, the Clinton administration, under pressure from treaty opponents in the GOP-controlled Senate, never submitted it to the Senate for approval.

The United States did ratify two optional supplemental protocols, however — one banning child prostitution, pornography and trafficking and the other prohibiting the compulsory military recruitment of children under 18. The United States included a caveat, however, explaining that it permits voluntary recruitment of 17-year-olds.

Many believe America's failure to adopt the CRC undermines its inter-national leadership role in protecting children. During his presidential campaign Barack Obama confessed he found it "embarrassing" that the United States had not ratified the treaty.

During Susan Rice's confirmation hearings to become ambassador to the United Nations, CRC proponent Sen. Barbara Boxer, D-Calif., asked, "How can we be proud of our country when we haven't ratified it? In this case, the only other country, as I understand it, that hasn't ratified is Somalia. . . . We're standing with Somalia. . . . What has happened?"

Replied Rice: "The president-elect, Secretary [of State Hillary] Clinton and I share a commitment to the objectives of this treaty and will take it up as an early question." [33]

Kul Chandra Gautam, former assistant secretary-general of the United Nations and deputy executive director of UNICEF, said the U.S. handling of the treaty "baffles" many non-Americans and Americans alike. Ratification, according to Nepal-born Gautam, would be tantamount to "sticking up for the rights of the underdog." Protecting children's rights in democratic societies, he says, is urgent. "Most other problems can wait — children cannot." [34]

Meanwhile, alarmed that the CRC may again be placed on the Senate's table, opponents are reviving the same arguments espoused in 1995 to block the treaty. For instance, they say, the CRC's Geneva-based Committee on the Rights of the Child, which reviews children's rights in nations that have ratified the treaty, would usurp Americans' parental rights.

The treaty "clearly undermines parental rights in the United States," U.S. Rep. Pete Hoekstra, R-Mich., has said. He has moved to block any approval of the treaty by introducing a bill to amend the U.S. Constitution codifying a set of parents' rights. [35]

Other opponents agree. Famously, the late Sen. Jesse Helms, R-N.C., described the treaty as "a bag of worms" and a threat to the U.S. Constitution. Other critics say it would enable children to sue their parents or participate in a religion of their choosing.

Michael Smith, president of the Home School Legal Defense Association (HSLDA), in Purcellville, Va., said the CRC "would drastically weaken the United States' sovereignty over family life, which would have a substantial impact on every American family." [36]

Stephen Groves, a fellow at the Heritage Foundation, said the CRC would erode American sovereignty by giving "a group of unaccountable so-called experts in Switzerland . . . a say over how children in America should be raised, educated or disciplined." [37]

Some CRC critics have gone so far as to claim the treaty could bar U.S. parents from spanking their children or could allow children to get abortions without parental consent. "If the American public is informed on this, there's no chance it will be ratified," said the HSLDA's founder, Michael Farris. [38]

Nonsense, say the treaty's proponents. "This treaty can never usurp the national sovereignty of the United States," says Martin Scherr, vice chair of the Campaign for U.S. Ratification of the Convention on the Rights of the Child. "No treaty the United States has signed ever has. If we object to anything in it we can simply exclude those parts. And there is nothing in the treaty that would give children rights over [their] parents. Indeed, quite the contrary is true; Article Five of the treaty reinforces the right of the parent to nurture his or her child."

"Name me one country that has seen a diminution in parents' rights," says Marjorie Newman-Williams, chief operating officer at the Washington, D.C.-based Children's Defense Fund. "The rest of the world seems to be very pleased with the treaty." Nowhere in the treaty, for example, are children given the right to sue their parents.

Says Caryl M. Stern, president and CEO of the U.S. Fund for UNICEF: "In all my travels I have never heard a single person complain that the CRC has caused any such problems. On the other hand, I get asked all the time why the U.S. is one of only two nations in the world *not* to ratify the CRC."

Thomas Miller, former U.S. ambassador to Greece and now president of the United Nations Association of the USA, points out that there are no enforcement mechanisms or penalties associated with the CRC. "Critics scare people by claiming we would be invaded by United Nations' 'blue beret nannies,' " adds, Scherr, "but that's ridiculous." The treaty provides for an 18-member committee that simply "monitors" children's rights.

Although the Obama administration appears interested in getting the CRC ratified, few believe that will happen anytime soon. The administration has too much on its plate now to risk another fight, especially one that has the potential for becoming a drawn-out, polarizing "family values" debate.

As the world examines America's reluctance to ratify the bill, many wonder how U.S.-based treaty opponents can overlook how the CRC has strengthened national children's rights institutions around the world. Numerous countries — such as Italy and Sweden, where the CRC has given birth to children's ombudsmen — have strengthened children's rights while preserving the rights of parents.

"It is in the USA's interest that we ratify the CRC. It would win us support from those whose support we need in the world," says Save the Children's MacCormack. "By not ratifying it we have everything to lose and nothing to gain. The rest of the world is wondering why a nation that calls itself a world leader has not ratified it."

Should AIDS prevention be emphasized more than treatment?

The first sentence of a recent report on the effects of AIDS on children pulls no punches: "Today's youth is today's AIDS generation."

The chilling report points out that today's children have never known a world without the devastating disease and now "bear the greatest burden of the disease." [39]

Indeed, the numbers are terrifying:

- More than 33 million people live with HIV/AIDS; 2.5 million of them children under 15.
- Every day about 1,150 children become infected with HIV, mostly due to mother-to-child transmission.
- Eight children die of AIDS-related illness every 15 minutes.
- More than 13 million children have lost a parent to AIDS, a figure expected to exceed 25 million for 2010 alone.
- Nearly 90 percent of all HIV-positive children live in sub-Saharan Africa. [40]

When AIDS strikes, it destabilizes families and entire societies. "There's a knock-on effect when AIDS takes a parent," says Save the Children's MacCormack. "Children are left to take on the burdens of the family. Millions also become orphans," less than 10 percent of whom receive any public support.

AIDS is powerfully linked to poverty. "AIDS can intensify poverty, forcing families to make difficult choices between short-term necessities and long-term investments in children," notes UNICEF. A Cambodia study showed that families affected by AIDS were more likely to sell off assets and ration medical care than their unaffected neighbors. In Nigeria, families with AIDS lost about 56 percent of their income compared with healthy families. [41]

The developed world has not neglected the global AIDS epidemic. Indeed, in 2003 President George W. Bush pledged to spend $15 billion over five years to fight AIDS abroad, and Congress recently reauthorized the President's Emergency Plan for AIDS Relief (PEPFAR) to the tune of $48 billion. Other countries also have poured billions into AIDS programs, and wealthy individuals like American billionaire and CNN founder Ted Turner have earmarked millions of dollars to combat AIDS.

Thanks to all that effort and generosity — plus the 1996 invention of a combination antiretroviral drug "cocktail" that successfully treats HIV — millions of people with HIV/AIDS around the world are still alive.

But, as the disease continues to spread, many are asking if too much is being spent on AIDS treatment and not enough on prevention. "There is a dangerous trend in the AIDS establishment that wants to shift — or eliminate — funding for HIV vaccine research and prevention programs in favor of HIV treatment," says Garrett, of the Council on Foreign Relations. "Treatment should be seen as a stop-gap measure, until we can completely stop the spread of HIV. We need both treatment and prevention."

For many, the treatment/prevention question comes down to simple economics. Expensive treatments cannot be sustained, they point out, given the global economic crisis. In Africa, for example, a year of treatment typically costs $1,000 per patient. Because of the high cost of antiretroviral treatment, programs for 61 percent of the world's AIDS sufferers are now at risk, according to the World Bank. [42]

Helen Jackson, a South Africa-based HIV adviser at UNAIDS, told a recent AIDS conference in Nairobi, Kenya, "If each person who has HIV progresses to AIDS, the financial burden of sustaining treatment becomes enormous, and the only way to make sure it is sustainable is to turn off the tap of new infections. Otherwise, down the line, no countries are going to be able to afford treatment." [43]

Meanwhile, Botswana and Mozambique are among the many nations cutting back or canceling treatment programs due to lack of funding. [44]

Even in Uganda, long hailed as a model in the AIDS battle for reducing its HIV rate from double digits to 5 percent in 2001, many patients are no longer receiving free antiretroviral drugs due to cutbacks from donors. [45]

Diarrhea: Deadly No More?

A cheap, new pill helps cure a disease that kills 5,000 children a day.

In a village in sub-Saharan Africa, a mother is wailing. Her toddler, who came down with a fever and stopped eating days ago, is losing weight quickly. His belly is distended, he is dehydrated and listless. His life is literally slipping away. In days the child will die from an easily preventable disease that kills more children than either malaria or AIDS — diarrhea.

Diarrhea is the second-leading cause of death of children under 5, killing nearly 2 million children a year — or 5,000 a day.[1] Only pneumonia kills more children.

"In villages across Asia and Africa, diarrhea is still a feared killer," explains Save the Children CEO Charles MacCormack. "For centuries, those villagers have become resigned to the fact that they may lose loved ones to diarrhea."

Without proper sanitation facilities, food and water easily become infected with E. coli, rotavirus, salmonella or other intestinal bugs. If left untreated, diarrhea can cause the intestines to stop absorbing water and nutrients, quickly stealing a small child's life.

In the 1980s and '90s, however, an inexpensive mixture of sugar, salts and water — oral-rehydration therapy (ORT) — helped to slash the disease's mortality rate by half. But the disease then was largely ignored because many believed the problem had been solved. In addition, some victims saw ORT as only a stop-gap measure and stopped using it. Funding was cut, and other diseases, such as AIDS and malaria, garnered the world's attention.

"The top killer of children ended up at the end of the agenda," said vaccine specialist John Wecker.[2]

Recently, another promising cure has come to light. Several aid organizations, including Save the Children and the Bill & Melinda Gates Foundation, have been distributing zinc tablets to treat diarrhea. The results have been dramatic. The tablets have reduced diarrheal deaths in children by 13 to 21 percent.[3] The pills, which cost as little as 38 cents for a 10-14 day supply, not only stop diarrhea but also reduce the chance it will recur in the next two to three months, apparently by building up the body's immune system.[4]

"It's incredible that we can cure this disease by just pennies a day," says MacCormack. "It's a no-brainer."

The word is spreading fast. Pilot programs have begun in several African nations, and more firms are manufacturing the tablets. Mali's Ministry of Health recently added zinc supple-

ments to its list of essential medications.[5] With a new vaccine for rotavirus, another cause of diarrhea, being tested, many are optimistic that the killer illness can be eradicated.

For many around the world there's no time to lose. A mother in Mali told *Time* magazine that after she lost one son to diarrhea she was terrified when another son developed the same symptoms. However, after giving the 2-year-old zinc tablets, he "came back to life."[6]

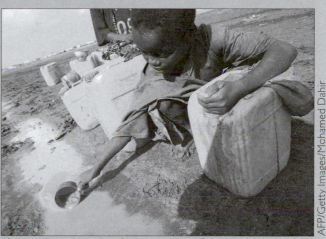

A boy collects rainwater from a puddle in Somalia in March 2009. The lack of clean water is a major cause of diarrhea — the second-leading cause of child deaths — but cheap, new zinc tablets are helping to cure the disease.

---

[1] "Save the Children Targets the Second Leading Cause of Death for Children Under 5," *Save the Children*, August 2009, www.savethechildren.org/programs/health/child-survival/survive-to-5/survive-zinc.html.

[2] Martha Dodge, "Experts: Diarrhea Neglect Killing Millions of Children," *One World US*, May 14, 2009, http://us.oneworld.net/article/362901-experts-diarrhea-neglect-killing-millions-children.

[3] "First Zinc Treatment Produced in Africa Aims to Reduce Child Deaths from Diarrhea," Academy for Educational Development, June 21, 2007, www.pshi.aed.org/news_pouznprtz.htm.

[4] "Save the Children Targets. . . ," *op. cit.*

[5] *Ibid.*

[6] Vivienne Walt, "Can One Pill Tame the Illness No One Wants to Talk About?" *Time*, Aug. 17, 2009, www.time.com/time/magazine/article/0,9171,1914655,00.html.

And such changes are only the tip of the iceberg, some observers warn.

Some donors are demanding that aid recipients establish effective prevention programs. "Donors want to be assured that rates of new infections are declining," says Garrett.

Others agree that prevention should get more attention. In a letter to *The Washington Post*, the Rev. Sam L. Ruteikara, co-chair of the Uganda National AIDS Prevention Committee, wrote, "In Uganda, we have a proverb: 'You cannot continue mopping the floor while the bro-

ken tap is still running.' Every $1 spent on treatment is $1 unspent on effective prevention."[46]

Huge disagreements exist, however, over what constitutes effective prevention. In many societies the use of condoms is taboo, and some groups reject the "ABC" ("Abstain, Be Faithful, Use a Condom") prevention message promoted by the Bush administration over sex education and condom distribution. Also, sex education does not always produce the anticipated results. In Nairobi teenagers say they were becoming "overloaded" with sex education that "makes us want to know what sex is, we want to experience it." [47]

MacCormack agrees that prevention programs must be "ramped up" before treatment costs become prohibitive, but adds, "Treatment is saving lives, and we cannot lessen our emphasis on that aspect of the issue."

Other experts say the call for more prevention is symptomatic of a "two-tiered" strategy, or an "economic caste system" regarding HIV/AIDS. It is fine for developed nations to call for more prevention programs while millions of people are dying around the world, they say. "A strategy that emphasizes prevention to the exclusion of treatment offers no hope to these tens of millions of human beings. In fact, it passes a death sentence on them," write Harvard researchers Alexander Irwin, Joyce Millen and Dorothy Fallows. [48]

While prevention is more cost effective, lives are more important than dollars, say treatment proponents. "It's relatively simple to say that dollar for dollar prevention is more cost-effective," said Chris Collins, director of the AIDS Vaccine Advocacy Coalition. "The more complex point is: What happens in societies where one in five or one in three people in the professional class are wiped out?" [49] ■

BACKGROUND

Industrial Revolution

For years, the West owed its searing image of child laborers to 19th-century British novelist Charles Dick-

ens, whose harrowing descriptions of sweatshops, foul-tempered bosses and horrific conditions reflected first-hand knowledge. When he was just 12, Dickens worked 10 hours a day in a shoe-polish factory and later used that experience to alert the world to the horrors of child labor in such books as *David Copperfield* and *Oliver Twist*.

But children had been forced into labor long before Dickens' powerful novel shined a light on the problem. More and more workers shifted from farm and home-based jobs to factory work in burgeoning cities as the Industrial Revolution created booming industries in Britain and then later in the United States. [50] Children — some as young as 4 — worked long hours operating dangerous machines in factories and underground coal mines. Children were preferred because they were cheaper, easier to manage than adults and were less apt to strike. [51] In 1788, children comprised more than 60 percent of the workforce in British and Scottish textile mills. [52]

By the early 1800s thousands of children were working for pittance wages in both Great Britain and the United States. Britain's Factory Act of 1833 set a minimum age of 9 for factory workers, but employers regularly ignored it. Indeed, very young British boys and girls, small enough to climb up and down chimneys, were often employed as chimney-sweep apprentices under horrific conditions:

"Some were forced to sleep in cellars on bags of soot, and washing facilities rarely existed. Cancer of the testicles was a common illness amongst the boys and was contracted from the accumulated soot. There was no safety clothing or safety regulation to protect the boys, and there are instances recorded where they were choked and suffocated to death by dust inhalation whilst trying to clean the chimneys. They often became trapped in the narrower flues or fell from the rotten stack to their death." [53]

In British coal mines children were enlisted to work as "trappers," stationed in damp, dark mines to open the trap doors for coal-filled carts. Mining would not be regulated until 1842, when Britain's *First Report on Children in Mines* exposed the horrible conditions. The report led to girls being banned from the mines, along with boys younger than 10. [54]

But other children were forced into factory work by their parents, who obtained falsified permits showing their children were older than they really were. Others were sold or indentured to factory owners. The government aided and abetted the owners by turning over thousands of young orphans to work in the factories and live in crowded, often-drafty barracks.

Beatings, for working too slowly or being late, were common. In 1832 a worker testified to a British Parliamentary committee: "When I was 7 years old, I went to work at Mr. Marshall's factory at Shrewsbury. If a child was drowsy, the overlooker touches the child on the shoulder and says, 'Come here.' In a corner of the room there is an iron cistern filled with water. He takes the boy by the legs and dips him in the cistern, and sends him back to work." [55]

The United States imported the concept of child labor from across the Atlantic. By 1820 nearly a quarter of the workers in the Northeast were under 16. In some cotton mills half the workers were children. [56] By the 1900s, according to historian Roger Butterfield, more than 1.7 million American children under 16 were working 13-hour days in the nation's cotton mills — 25 percent of them under 12. [57]

As in Great Britain, owners flouted minimum-age laws. When inspectors arrived, children were hidden or sent away, or investigators were told that the children were there to visit their mothers. Child-protection laws often did not

Continued on p. 270

Chronology

1800s Child labor abuses in Great Britain and the United States during the Industrial Revolution spark reform movements.

1802
Britain's factory acts limit work by women and children.

1833
Britain prohibits working in textile mills for children under 9.

1842
Massachusetts limits children's workday to 10 hours; several states follow.

1870
U.S. Census reports 250,000 children ages 10-15 are non-farm workers.

1880
Britain's Elementary Education Act makes school mandatory until the age of 10.

1900s Number of U.S. child laborers tops 2 million; reform efforts intensify.

1900
About 12 percent of Mexican textile workers are children.

1904
Britain's Prevention of Cruelty to Children Act authorizes interventions to protect children from abuse. . . . U.S. group forms to ban child labor in United States.

1916
Congress bans interstate commerce in products made by children; law is declared unconstitutional two years later.

1937
India bans children under 14 from factory or mining work.

1938
U.S. Fair Labor Standards Act prohibits child labor in products sold in interstate commerce.

1940s-1950s United Nations embraces aid to children.

1946
UNICEF is created to aid Europe's refugee children after World War II.

1950
UNICEF, other groups begin aiding children in the developing world.

1959
U.N. General Assembly adopts Declaration on the Rights of the Child.

1960s-1980s Children face new challenges as urbanization, industrialization spread through developing world.

1972
Children Act of 1972 requires British children to stay in school until 16.

1977
Geneva Conventions establish 15 as minimum age for combat soldiers.

Late 1970s
HIV/AIDS begins to spread throughout sub-Saharan Africa.

1989
U.N. General Assembly adopts Convention on the Rights of the Child (CRC); U.S., Somalia haven't ratified it.

1990s-Present Despite progress in many areas, child prostitution, trafficking and other problems abound.

1990
World Summit for Children sets 10-year goals for children's health, nutrition and education.

1995
U.S. ambassador to the U.N. Madeleine Albright signs CRC, but President Bill Clinton does not send it to the Senate.

1998
Coalition to Stop the Use of Child Soldiers is formed in London.

1999
More than 25 million people in sub-Saharan Africa have HIV/AIDS, many of them children.

2000
U.N.'s Millennium Declaration is signed by 189 countries, establishing goals for ending poverty by 2015.

2002
International Labour Organization estimates that 19 percent of children 5-14 in Asia and the Pacific are engaged in child labor.

2008
A total of 193 nations have ratified the CRC.

2009
U.N. prepares to celebrate 20th anniversary of the Convention on the Rights of the Child on Nov. 20. . . . Number of under-5 children dying annually falls below 9 million for the first time. . . . Experts fear global recession could cause 200,000 to 400,000 more under-5 deaths each year — or up to 2.8 million additional deaths by 2015.

Continued from p. 268

apply to immigrants, and dozens of immigrant girls, some as young as 12, died in the infamous Triangle Waist Factory fire (commonly called the Triangle Shirtwaist Factory fire) in New York City in 1911, which killed 146 workers. [58]

Because Canada industrialized later than the United States, child labor abuses were not as prevalent there until the early 1900s. Demand for child labor in Europe reached its peak during the pre-industrial and industrialized periods of those economies.

"The belief that idle children are immoral children who will adopt deviant behavior and commit crimes was widespread in Europe," a book reviewer noted. "This led to a social

policy of putting orphaned and pauper children to work in French hopitaux, in English Hospitals or Workhouses, Danish Bornehus, Swedish barnhus, and Russian state-sponsored hospitals. . . . This paved the way for poor and working-class families to send their children to work in the new factories, mills and mines." [59]

Child Labor Reforms

In the early 19th century, reformers sought to end some of the most egregious child labor practices. In 1802 England passed its first child labor legislation, but the measure applied only to "pauper apprentices" and was

not widely enforced. From 1819 to 1878 various "Factory Acts" raised minimum work ages and shortened working hours. In 1836 children were prohibited from working in textile mills, and in 1840 no one under 21 could work as a chimney sweep. Both laws, however, were abused for decades. Indeed, the minimum working age in the United Kingdom was not raised to 14 until 1933.

The United States was even slower to reform. Although organizations like the National Consumer's League and the National Child Labor Committee worked to ban child labor and end sweatshops, the Fair Labor Standards Act wasn't passed until 1938. It instituted firm restrictions on child labor, raising the minimum

The Unspeakable Horror: Child Rape

Some blame the "virgin cure" myth for rise in attacks.

Growing numbers of children — some just tiny infants — are being raped every day across the globe. In Zimbabwe sexual violence against children increased by more than 40 percent between 2005 and 2008. [1] In the northern Nigerian city of Kano child rape cases soared 50 percent between 2007 and 2008. [2] It's also reportedly on the rise in Afghanistan's northern provinces. [3]

But South Africa is the epicenter of child rape, with the world's largest number of recorded child sexual assaults — some 60 a day — and children's advocates believe thousands more go unreported. [4]

Reports of men raping infants outraged South Africans since an infamous 2001 case involving a 9-month-old girl. The country was also shocked when a study by the Red Cross Children's Hospital in Cape Town showed that the average age of children brought in for reconstructive surgery following a rape was 3 years old. In a recent horrific case, a 16-month-old toddler who was raped in Delft had to undergo extensive reconstruction surgery. [5]

Many blame the rise in child rapes on the mistaken belief that sex with a virgin protects a man from HIV-AIDS or can actually cure the deadly disease — the so-called "virgin cure." Mamelato Leopeng, an AIDS counselor in Johannesburg, says about a third of the HIV-infected men she meets at her clinic believe sex with a virgin will cure them, and that using a condom will void the cure. [6] Africa's traditional healers reportedly perpetuate the myth, often explaining that the blood of a virgin will "wash away" the HIV virus.

As South African rape survivor, journalist and activist Charlene Smith explained, "I was working with a 9-year-old child whose mother took her to the mother's boyfriend who was HIV-positive, and the mother watched while he raped the child. The rapist admitted this because he believed he could save himself." [7]

The belief in the healing powers of virgins' blood is not a new idea. In 19th-century England some men believed having sex with a virgin could cure venereal disease.

While experts differ on how much belief in the "virgin cure" leads to child rape, there is an undeniable link. "It is hard to find a virgin of 16 nowadays, so men are turning to babies under 10," said Leopeng, "They are looking for clean blood. It is all based on ignorance and a lack of education." [8]

The "virgin cure" myth is also perpetuated in other developing regions as well, including India and Southeast Asia. In Cambodia, for instance, a man will spend a year's wages or more to buy — and rape — a virgin.

"They are animals," says Cambodian children's-rights activist Somaly Mam. "They are ruining so many young lives."

Mam has rescued scores of girls — some as young as 5 — who have been raped in an effort to cure AIDS. The belief is so widespread in Cambodia, she says, that brothel owners and pimps will have girls who have been raped surgically sewn up repeatedly — an extremely painful procedure — so they can be sold and violated again.

Besides being traumatized by the rape itself, the young rape victims will likely contract AIDS, thus spreading the disease to a group of otherwise sexually inactive girls. [9]

Education is considered the best weapon against the practice, and some countries are launching public health education campaigns. In Zambia, for example, roadside billboards feature a picture of a young girl with the message, "Sex with me doesn't cure AIDS!" [10] And traditional healers in Zimbabwe also are being educated. But surveys show that from 18-30 percent of African men still believe the myth. [11]

Some governments are strengthening child-abuse laws. Zimbabwe, Swaziland, South Africa and Zambia have all begun to establish child-friendly courts for abused children. South Africa's Sexual Offences Act imposes harsher jail sentences for rape and allows victims to demand rapists take HIV tests. In 2000 Namibia passed the Combating of Rape Act, which ensures that victims and survivors will be informed of trial dates and any bail applications of the accused rapist.

But much more has to be done to wipe out the unspeakable crime, says Mam. "Part of the problem is that too many people are still embarrassed to talk about sex matters," she says. "Meanwhile, children are being raped and given a death sentence. The world has to wake up."

Patricia Lincoln, 16, comforts her daughter, known as "Baby Thsepang." The child was raped when she was 9 months old by her mother's HIV-positive boyfriend, triggering outrage across South Africa.

[1] "Trying to understand the unspeakable crime," IRIN, March 12, 2008, www.aegis.com/news/IRIN/2008/IR080312.html.

[2] "Child Rape on the Rise in North Nigerian City: Officials," *The Body*, Jan. 4, 2008, www.thebody.com/content/whatis/art44632.html.

[3] Aryn Baker, "Afghanistan's Epidemic of Child Rape," *Time*, Aug. 17, 2008, www.time.com/time/world/article/0,8599,1833517,00.html.

[4] "South Africa: child raped every three minutes," News24.com, Sept. 6, 2009, www.news24.com/Content/SouthAfrica/News/1059/f3fc05773cf6402cad1cfba0d a4b5428/03-06-2009%2009-06/Child_raped_every_3_min_-_report.

[5] Sibongile Mashaba, "Shocking child abuse statistics," *Sowetan*, Sept. 17, 2009, www.sowetan.co.za/News/Article.aspx?id=1066487.

[6] Adriana Stuijt, "Child rapes soared in South Africa this month," *Digital Journal*, Dec. 21, 2008, www.digitaljournal.com/article/264259.

[7] Carolyn Dempster, "South African trial brings rape into public view," news fromafrica.org, May 2, 2006, www.newsfromafrica.org/newsfromafrica/articles/ art_10669.html.

[8] *Ibid*.

[9] "Child rape survivor saves 'virgin myth' victims," CNN, June 5, 2009, www. edition.cnn.com/2009/LIVING/06/04/cnnheroes.betty.makoni/index.html.

[10] "Myths and Misconceptions about HIV/AIDS," The AIDS Pandemic, April 7, 2008, www.the-aids-pandemic.blogspot.com/2008/04/myths-and-misconceptions-about-hivaids.html.

[11] Dempster, *op. cit.*

hourly wage to 40 cents and banned children under 16 from hazardous industries. It also prohibited children from working during school hours.

Concern about children's rights grew throughout the world in the first half of the 20th century. During its first session in 1946, the U.N. General Assembly voted to establish the U.N. International Children's Emergency Fund (UNICEF) to provide short-term relief to children in war-ravaged Europe. Between 1947 and 1950, UNICEF distributed approximately $87.6 million in aid to 13 European countries. [60]

The needs were so great, however, that UNICEF's brief was broadened in 1950 to include children in developing countries. In 1953 that mandate became a permanent part of the U.N.

One of its first global campaigns was against yaws, a disease affecting millions that is easily cured with penicillin. Campaigns against tuberculosis, trachoma and malaria followed.

UNICEF continued to expand, eventually becoming a model for bringing humanitarian and economic aid to the developing world. By the mid-1950s, UNICEF was active in 100 countries, but the United Nations had not established guidelines or recommended minimum ages for child workers. [61]

21st-Century Problems

By the mid-20th century, developing countries were shaking off their colonial yokes and beginning to transform their economies. As the world's population began shifting from the countryside to huge, industrialized cities, familiar children's problems arose, including labor abuses, poverty and exploitation. Children throughout the developing world were often forced to work in dangerous, low-paid jobs to supplement their families' incomes.

The developed world took notice, determining that the key to saving the world's children was lifting their countries out of poverty. "For this they needed aid from their richer neighbors in the form of funds and technical expertise to help them industrialize," notes a UNICEF historian. [62]

Organizations, institutions and citizens in the developed world also took

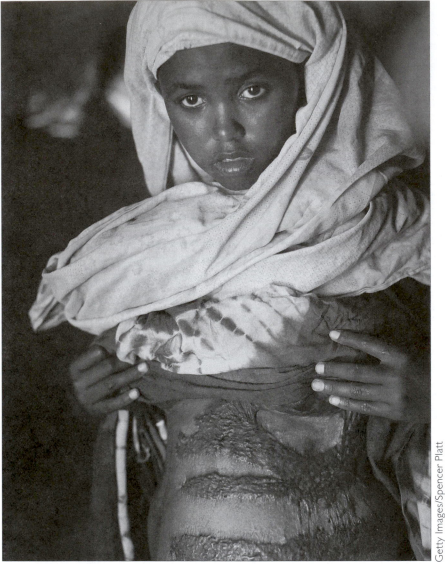

Getty Images/Spencer Platt

Naib Naema Abde Mohamed shows the scars from wounds she suffered when a shell hit her home in Mogadishu, Somalia. Having lost her two brothers and her father to the decade-long conflict in her home country, the 14-year-old now lives with her mother in the world's largest refugee complex, in Dadaab, Kenya. Besides injuries, armed conflict causes increased poverty, illiteracy, homelessness, early mortality and malnutrition among children.

zations like UNICEF launched massive immunization and "child survival" nutrition programs.

NGOs began to lobby for officially recognizing children's rights. With rapid industrialization in the developing world putting increasing stress on families, more and more children were living on city streets, being exploited, abused and deprived of their futures. [64]

In 1989 the U.N. General Assembly adopted the Convention on the Rights of the Child, the first legally binding international instrument to incorporate the full range of human rights — civil, cultural, economic, political and social. It says the world's children have the right to survive, develop to their fullest potential, be protected from harmful influences, abuse and exploitation and to participate fully in family, cultural and social life.

Article 32 says children have the right to be protected from economic exploitation and from performing work that is hazardous or will interfere with the child's education or that will harm the child's health or physical, mental, spiritual, moral or social development. The convention became law on Sept. 2, 1990 — faster than any other human rights convention — and by 2009 had been ratified by 193 countries.

'Brilliant Purpose'

Children's rights were again center stage in 1990 at the U.N. Millennium Summit, the largest gathering of world leaders in history. In the summit's final declaration the international community pledged to end global poverty and spelled out eight Millennium Development Goals (MDG), six of which relate directly to children and all of them still used to measure progress in the global war on poverty. (*See box, p. 273.*)

Progress in meeting the MDGs has been uneven. More than half of the goals are progressing too slowly and

notice. Images of underage children working in American or British textile mills have been replaced by scenes of young children working long hours at looms in Pakistan, Bangladesh and elsewhere. Underage cotton pickers may have vanished from the American South, but they still work in the cotton fields of Africa and India.

"In our country we think of these as 19th-century problems, but these are 21st-century problems," said San-

dra Polaski, deputy undersecretary for international affairs in the U.S. Department of Labor. [63]

In 1979 the world focused on children's issues by celebrating The International Year of the Child. Studies spotlighted issues ranging from poor nutrition to polio and homelessness. In the 1980s, alarmed that after decades of humanitarian work millions of children under 5 were still dying each year from preventable causes, organi-

have been further stalled by the global recession, says a 2009 U.N. report. Some countries like China are on track, but many sub-Saharan nations are woefully behind. Meeting the goals would lift 300 million children out of abject poverty, the report says, but that goal is still a long way off. [65]

While some critics bemoan the lack of progress, others praise the goals for publicizing the plight of children. "Thanks to these goals, not only U.N. agencies but the world at large knows the key measures of poverty, hunger, health and education," billionaire philanthropist Bill Gates, co-chair of the Bill & Melinda Gates Foundation, told the U.N. last year. "Some of the numbers are good and some are not. But the fact that the world is focusing on the numbers is excellent. It means people see where things are going well, and understand how we can spread those successes. They see where we're falling short, and they see the need to apply more effort and do things differently. That is the purpose of these goals, and it's a brilliant purpose." [66] ∎

CURRENT SITUATION

Deadly Birthdays

Although many developing countries are making dramatic progress at reducing child mortality, in sub-Saharan Africa 1,500 babies die each day within the first 24 hours after they are born — most from birthing complications, neonatal tetanus, malaria and other conditions.

Infant death is so common in the region that many parents "postpone naming their baby for at least a month, until they are certain they will

---

U.N. Goals Could Aid 300 Million Children

Three hundred million children would be lifted out of abject poverty if the world were to meet the U.N.'s eight Millennium Development Goals (MDGs) — adopted in 1990. But according to a 2009 U.N. report, progress is slow on more than half of the goals, which have been further stalled by the global recession.

The eight MDGs are to:

- ***Eradicate extreme poverty and hunger*** — To halve, by 2015, the proportion of people whose income is less than $1 a day and the proportion of people suffering from hunger.

- ***Achieve universal primary education*** — Ensure that by 2015 children everywhere — girls as well as boys — will be able to complete primary schooling.

- ***Promote gender equality and empower women*** — Eliminate gender disparity in primary and secondary education by 2005 and at all education levels by 2015.

- ***Reduce child mortality*** — Reduce the 1990 under-5 mortality rate by two-thirds by 2015.

- ***Improve maternal health*** — Reduce the maternal mortality ratio by three-quarters between 1990 and 2015.

- ***Combat HIV/AIDS, malaria and other diseases*** — Halt and start reversing the spread or incidence of HIV/AIDS, malaria and other major diseases by 2015.

- ***Ensure environmental sustainability*** — Integrate sustainable development principles into country policies and programs and reverse the losses of environmental resources. Cut in half by 2015 the proportion of people without sustainable access to safe drinking water. Achieve a significant improvement in the lives of at least 100 million slum dwellers by 2020.

- ***Develop a global partnership for development*** — Help developing countries achieve the other seven MDGs through additional development assistance, improved access to markets and debt relief.

---

survive infancy," says Save the Children's MacCormack.

"Throughout the developing world, the most dangerous day in a child's life is the day the child is born," he adds. Twenty-five percent of all child deaths in sub-Saharan Africa — more than 1 million annually — occur during the first month of life. [67]

Most of the deaths are preventable and would rarely claim the life of a child in a wealthy country. For example, neonatal tetanus, one of the major killers of newborns, can be prevented by a 50-cent vaccine. Pneumonia, a disease that kills nearly 1 million people a year, can be treated with antibiotics that cost less than one dollar a patient. [68] Diarrhea, another lethal killer, can be cured for pennies a day. (*See sidebar, p. 267.*)

While the under-5 mortality rate in northern Africa — Algeria, Egypt, Morocco, Libya and Tunisia — has plummeted by up to 56 percent since 1990, child survival trends in sub-Saharan Africa are still grim. In 2007 roughly one in every seven sub-Saharan children failed to reach their fifth birthday — the world's highest under-5 mortality rate. [69]

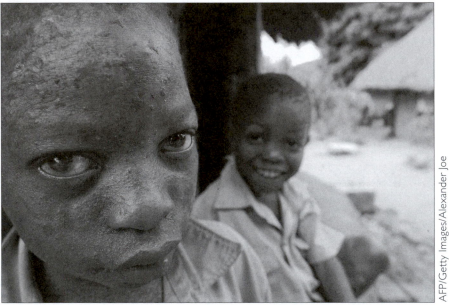

AIDS-infected orphans Evans Mahlangu (left), 13, and his brother Edmond, 8, walked across a mountain range in Zimbabwe and jumped the border to obtain free antiretroviral drugs at a hospital in neighboring Mozambique. They are among the 2.5 million children under age 15 suffering from AIDS, 90 percent of them in sub-Saharan Africa.

AFP/Getty Images/Alexander Joe

But there are some bright spots. Malaria, which kills 800,000 people annually, is being fought with insecticide-dipped nets, with dramatic results in countries like Ethiopia, Niger, Mali and Zambia. [70] Malawi has reduced its under-5 mortality rate from 210 per 1,000 live births in 1990 to 111 per 1,000 in 2007. [71]

One of the Millennium Development Goals aims to reduce by two-thirds the under-5 mortality rate by 2015. While some countries have come close to being on track, most are still falling short. To meet that goal, em-phasis must be placed on the poorest, most marginalized countries and regions, such as sub-Saharan Africa. "Business as usual will be grossly insufficient to meet these Millennium Development goals," notes a UNICEF spokesperson. "We have to redouble our efforts."

At the United Nations, the fate of child mortality once again earned worldwide attention in late September. The world must help children in crisis, President Obama said: "What happens to the hopes of a single child — anywhere — can enrich our world, or impoverish it."

But words must be backed up by actions. As Obama spoke, thousands of children across the Horn of Africa were starving to death, and millions more were facing a similar fate — victims of what Save the Children calls "East Africa's worst food crisis in decades."

How severe is the global child mortality crisis? In the time it took to read the last paragraph 10 children died from mostly preventable causes.

Child Slavery

Human-rights advocates say millions of children around the world are being enslaved today in a variety of ways — and some are tortured into submission.

"If I refused to sleep with a client, the brothel owners would take me to the dungeon in the basement and tie me to a bed. Then they would shock me with a live electric cord," says Sina, a former child prostitute in Phnom Penh, Cambodia. Kidnapped from Vietnam at 13, Sina endured years of rape and, like many others who refused to submit, was tortured.

Cambodian children's rights activist Mam remembers her own experience: "We were enslaved. If I disobeyed I was tortured in just such a dungeon. Brothel owners would tie me to a chair and throw live snakes on me."

According to UNICEF 1.2 million children are trafficked every year, and 100 million girls are involved in child labor worldwide, says the International Labour Organization. An estimated 120 million children live on the streets, and 8.4 million children work as slave laborers, sex slaves or soldiers. [72]

In the Balkans, for instance, girls as young as 8 are kidnapped, forced to beg on the streets and become prostitutes. In Afghanistan, young boys are forced to work in dangerous coal mines for just $3 a day. In India, as exemplified in the Oscar-winning movie "Slumdog Millionaire," children are deliberately maimed and forced to beg on the streets. [73]

In nearly every big city throughout the developing world children live on the streets. From New Delhi to Lagos to Bogotá, these "street kids" scratch out a living with no hope of being rescued by the social safety net that rescues children in more prosperous countries. In Eastern Europe, a "lost generation" of vulnerable children have

Continued on p. 276

At Issue:

Is more aid the best way to help the world's children?

ANN M. VENEMAN
EXECUTIVE DIRECTOR, UNITED NATIONS CHILDREN'S FUND (UNICEF)

WRITTEN FOR *CQ GLOBAL RESEARCHER*,
OCTOBER 2009

*a*id effectiveness can — and must — be measured in positive and sustainable results. While experts debate the impact aid has on development, wide consensus exists about the importance of investing in children.

Where strategic, targeted and effective interventions have increased, positive results have followed. Recent UNICEF figures show a 28 percent decline in the rate at which children die before their fifth birthday — from 90 deaths per 1,000 live births in 1990 to 65 deaths per 1,000 in 2008. Thus, compared to 1990, 10,000 fewer children are dying every day.

Key health interventions — such as immunizations, anti-malarial bed nets and Vitamin A supplementation — all have contributed. Increased measles vaccinations in sub-Saharan Africa have achieved a 91 percent reduction in measles mortality in just six years. The distribution of insecticide-treated bed nets to prevent malaria has increased more than threefold since 2000.

Early childhood lays the foundation for a lifetime. If a child suffers from malnutrition, particularly under the age of two, the child is likely to have difficulty learning in school and earning as an adult — contributing to the intergenerational cycle of poverty.

Research shows that every $1 spent on vitamin A and zinc supplementation creates more than $17 worth of benefits. Each $1 invested in girls education returns $12 in productivity. For instance, when a girl in the developing world receives seven or more years of education, she marries four years later, on average, and has 2.2 fewer children. And for every year a girl spends in secondary school, her earnings increase by an estimated 15 to 20 percent.

But to have the maximum impact on our collective future, some things must change about foreign aid. Ineffective governance and even corruption undermine aid utilization and effectiveness. Good data about where to invest and about what delivers the best results are essential to improving aid efficiency and results. Although data collection, analysis and availability have improved, more needs to be done.

Aid can be used to leverage improved national investment decisions. One UNICEF study, costing only around $12,000, so effectively identified the causes of adolescent school dropouts that the national government invested an additional $40 million in secondary education.

Properly targeted and employed, aid can help build the foundation for poverty alleviation, enhanced national capacity and sustainable growth. It also helps save countless lives.

JAMES SHIKWATI
FOUNDER AND DIRECTOR, INTER REGION ECONOMIC NETWORK
CEO, THE AFRICAN EXECUTIVE MAGAZINE

WRITTEN FOR *CQ GLOBAL RESEARCHER*,
OCTOBER 2009

*i*n Africa, conventional economic statistics are used to depict an otherwise resource-rich continent as poor. This not only drives inhabitants to lose confidence in their abilities and opportunities but also promotes a culture of dependence on external assistance. Consequently, African children are born into a cycle of artificial dependency.

The global market system that denies parents from poor countries a chance to be productive and participate in the marketplace is as dangerous to children as disease, malnutrition and the effects of war. A skewed market system that dangles money as a solution assaults parents' noble role by turning them into procreators who surrender their children's upbringing to outsiders loaded with money.

Tackling the reasons why individuals and institutions fail to provide a good environment for raising children should be a priority for everyone. Children looking into the eyes of their mothers or fathers should draw inspiration. Parents, on the other hand, should demand that institutions they built and paid for deliver better services to their children.

Aid money can never replace an environment that promotes the adoption of scientific and rational ideas. The world needs to reward parents and innovators who provide solutions to diseases, malnutrition, poor shelter, insecurity and poor education and a multitude of other problems that hamper children's optimum development.

With people in poor countries trapped in a global market system that denies them an opportunity to be industrious, some well-intentioned projects use mosquito bed-nets as a lure to encourage parents to have their children vaccinated. As an unintended consequence, some children have died from vaccine overdoses because their poor parents had them vaccinated repeatedly in order to get extra bed-nets. The quest to be industrious is exemplified by poor people's readiness to convert anti-mosquito bed-nets into fishing nets and wedding dresses.

It is tempting to push for money as a solution to save an estimated 3 million children who die annually of preventable diseases; to educate the 75 million who miss school and to rescue millions of children affected by war. However, this does not explain why parents in these scenarios are incapable economically to address the challenges their children encounter.

More aid money won't help the world's children. The freedom to exercise individuals' ingenuity and, within acceptable standards, share the fruits of their energy with society will help them more.

Continued from p. 274

been abandoned by their parents — many of whom have sought work abroad — including 350,000 such children in Romania who eke out a living by working for minimal wages, begging, stealing or prostituting themselves. [74]

Much of the slavery involves virgin girls and is exacerbated by tough economic times. For example, an Iraq-based human-rights activist recently told *Time*

which said, "Vulnerable workers — particularly migrants, including young women and even children — are more exposed to forced labor, because under conditions of hardship they will be taking more risks than before." [76]

Child slavery and trafficking occurs in rich countries as well. The State Department recently decided to include data about its investigations of such practices in the United States in its an-

of the Cambodian Children's Fund, an NGO that has rescued more than 400 children from child labor and poverty in Phnom Penh. "They need security, lodging and education."

There is hope. After announcing a crackdown on child trafficking in April, China investigated more than 700 cases in a little over a month, rescuing 1,000 children and women. [78] Thirty-six children between the ages of 5 and 15 were recently rescued in Ghana after being sold into slavery by their parents. They received no pay or schooling while "enslaved" in the local fishing industry.

Although similar rescue stories occur regularly around the world, the problem of child trafficking is growing every day. Cambodian children's rights activist Mam, who was sold into prostitution while still a child, says, "Although this is a fight we may never win, we have no choice but to keep battling. Children's lives are hanging in the balance."

The global recession is driving food prices up while forcing reductions in the amount of food aid being offered. In Cambodia, for instance, U.N. World Food Programme school meals — like these offered near Phnom Penh in 2008 — have been discontinued for 450,000 children this year. The number of chronically hungry people worldwide is projected to exceed 1 billion this year.

AP Photo/Heng Sinith

Children and Conflict

Kon Kelei, a former child solider from Sudan, is not sure how old he was when he was kidnapped by rebels and taken to a rebel military camp, where he was trained to fight. He just knows he was too little to carry a rifle.

"I was four or five," he told the Inter Press Service news agency. "An AK-47 is not made for a kid." [79]

Kelei is one of the lucky ones; he has been rehabilitated and is helping to establish the Global Network of Young People Formerly Affected by War (NYPAW), which promotes the rehabilitation and empowerment of former child soldiers. [80]

According to some estimates, 250,000 children are serving in armed conflicts around the world as soldiers, suicide bombers, sex slaves or spies. [81] As soldiers, children are considered cheap, easily controllable and expendable.

magazine that Iraqi virgins as young as 11 and 12 can be sold for anything from $2,000 to $30,000. She explained, "The buying and selling of girls in Iraq, it's like the trade in cattle. . . . I've seen mothers haggle with agents over the price of their daughters." [75]

Global recession inevitably leads to an increase in forced child labor and trafficking. "Growing poverty is making people more vulnerable to both labor and sex trafficking, boosting the supply side of human trafficking all over the world," says the U.S. State Department's 2009 "Trafficking in Persons Report." It quoted an International Labour Organisation report,

nual human trafficking report. According to the New York-based Foundation for Child Development, American children's quality of life is expected to decline through 2010 due to the financial crisis. Soon one in five American children will be "living in poverty," according to the foundation. [77]

For many children trapped in slavery around the world, there is little hope. But NGOs, government agencies and others are working to rescue children. As more and more nations and organizations like the United Nations expose child labor and trafficking abuses, countries are forced to act. "These kids have been traumatized," explains Scott Neeson, founder

And increasingly, children are being used as suicide bombers. A recent CNN report detailed how the late Baitullah Mehsud, a top Taliban leader in Pakistan, had been "buying and selling children" — some as young as 11 — to train as suicide bombers. "He has been admitting he holds a training center for young boys, for preparing them for suicide bombing," said a Pakistani army spokesman. Once trained, the children are sold to other Taliban officials for $6,000 to $12,000. [82]

Wars also have indirect consequences on children, such as the loss of sanitation services, interruption of their education and an uptick in poverty and malnutrition. "Armed conflict perpetuates poverty, illiteracy and early mortality," explains UNICEF Executive Director Ann M. Veneman.

Children's scars from armed conflict are not always as evident as a bullet wound or a lost limb, she points out. In war-torn Madagascar, for instance, a child recalls, "Every time I hear shooting, my heart beats out of control and I start to shake. My thoughts go to what might happen, and what I would do if members of my family died." [83]

Researchers studying Madagascar's conflict noted, "One long-term consequence of this crisis is the difficulty for young people to distinguish what is 'correct' and what is 'incorrect;' what is 'true' and what is 'false,' as traditional grounding values have been radically altered by recent events." [84]

Girls are especially vulnerable in armed conflicts. Some have referred to their plight as a "double tragedy," explaining that even after a war ends they still suffer from sexual harassment, physical attacks and even forced marriages to armed forces commanders. And in recent years, rape — often coupled with the maiming of young girls so they can never conceive — has increasingly been used as a weapon of war. [85]

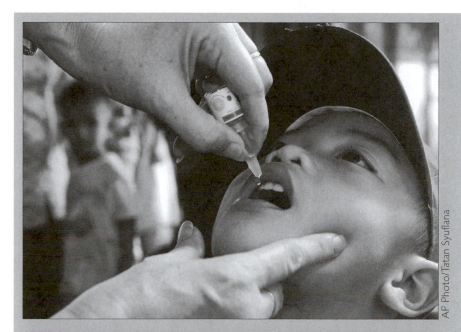

AP Photo/Tatan Syuflana

Robert Kiener

Getting Help

A girl receives polio vaccine drops in Jakarta, Indonesia (top). Global immunization programs have nearly eradicated the crippling disease. But children still face horrific man-made dangers, such as forced child labor and sex trafficking — which are on the increase due to the global recession. Two of these three Cambodian girls rescued from a Phnom Penh brothel were sold to pimps when they were just 6 years old (bottom). They are now living in a shelter run by former child prostitute Somaly Mam. An estimated 10,000 to 20,000 child prostitutes under 16 are in Cambodia. Children's-rights activists say 1 million youngsters around the world are forced into prostitution every year.

A ruined hut is all that remains of a girl's home after authorities bulldozed her shantytown near São Paulo, Brazil, on Aug. 26, 2009. World leaders pledged at a 1990 U.N. summit to meet eight Millennium Development Goals, which would help lift 300 million children out of abject poverty. But achieving that aim is still a long way off, say experts, partly because of lack of funds and political will.

AFP/Getty Images/Mauricio Lima

Even though enlisting children under 15 is now officially a war crime (due to a 1977 amendment to the Geneva Conventions and the International Convention on the Rights of the Child), the practice continues to flourish, especially among nongovernmental forces. While the United Nations has been publicizing the plight of child soldiers, armed groups continue to use children, especially in Asian, African and Middle Eastern battle zones. Last year Iraqi insurgents strapped explosives to a young girl and remotely detonated the bomb at an army command post in Yousifiyah. A 13-year-old girl blew herself up at a checkpoint in Ba'qubah, Iraq. Last May, 85 children were among the 212 suspected rebels rounded up in Chad. [86]

A recent U.N. report blames "non state actors" in Afghanistan, Burundi, Chad, Burma, Nepal, the Philippines, Somalia, Uganda and elsewhere for recruiting and using child soldiers. [87] In Chad, despite promises from both rebel groups and the government to stop recruiting child warriors, rebel groups have reportedly stepped up the recruitment of children in recent months. UNICEF says Chad currently has up to 10,000 child soldiers. [88]

Until such practices are banished, the words of one Madagascar child scarred by war will haunt everyone who hears them: "Who cares if I die? I am not alive anyway." [89] ∎

OUTLOOK

Half-Full Glass

A list of problems confronting the world's children reads like way stations on a journey through hell: infant mortality, HIV/AIDS, homelessness, child soldiers, trafficking, prostitution. And given the added impact of the global economic crisis, climate change and armed conflicts, experts say children are in greater danger than ever.

But veteran activist MacCormack of Save the Children takes a longer view. "On the whole, things are getting better," he says. "I started in this business in the 1950s, when children in South Korea and Taiwan couldn't get enough to eat. Look at them today. The pattern has repeated itself in other regions. Sure, many children are in peril, but things are constantly improving. I am an optimist."

The world will be a different place in 20 years, MacCormack says, noting that about half of the children in crisis today live in China and India, where they will inevitably benefit from the robust economic growth those countries are experiencing.

"In 20 years their lot will have improved dramatically," he says. "That will allow us to put even more of our resources into places like sub-Saharan Africa."

Thanks to the efforts of countless child advocates, the state of the world's children is improving. Since 1990 deaths of children under 5 have decreased steadily worldwide. [90] The absolute number of child deaths has declined from 12.5 million in 1990 to 8.8 million in 2008. [91] In Egypt, for instance, child mortality fell by a whopping 68 percent during that period. By promoting basic procedures such as vaccinations, oral rehydration therapies and improving health services, Egypt now leads the developing world in efforts to save the lives of its children. [92]

"Compared to 1990," said UNICEF Executive Director Veneman, "10,000 fewer children are dying every day" around the world. But, she quickly adds, "While progress is being made, it is unacceptable that each year 8.8 million children die before their fifth birthday." [93]

Much work remains to be done to attain the U.N. Millennium Development Goals, which have produced mixed results so far. At least 980 million children under 18 still lack access to improved sanitation, millions of children are victims of violence and one-fourth of children in developing countries are underweight. [94]

To solve such problems, UNICEF plans to expand its Accelerated Child Survival and Development Initiative (ACSD) to other countries in Africa and Asia. The initiative has proven how a set of well-designed interventions can transform the fate of a nation's children. Custom designed for each community's needs, a typical ACSD package contains vitamin A tablets to strengthen children's immune systems, antimalaria mosquito nets, oral rehydration therapy kits, antibiotics, antiretroviral drugs for HIV-infected mothers and more. In pilot programs in West Africa, the packages have helped to slash child mortality rates by an average of 20 percent — at a cost of only $500 to $1,000 per life saved. [95]

Although a weakening economy may tempt richer countries to cut their aid budgets, development experts say it is more important than ever to invest in the world's children. "It is important to recognize the moral imperative to act," said the London-based Overseas Development Institute. "A major share of the cost of the financial and economic crisis will be borne by hundreds of million of people who have not shared in the benefits of recent growth." [96]

Melinda Gates, co-chair of the Gates Foundation, has overseen the distribution of billions of dollars of aid money and visited scores of developing countries. "On my side of the mat," she wrote, "when my kids are sick, they get antibiotics. On the other side of the mat, when their children get sick, they may be receiving a death sentence. Those of us in the wealthy countries must try to put ourselves on the other side of the mat." [97] ■

Notes

[1] "Child Prostitution a Global Problem," *The Body*, April 22, 2002, www.thebody.com/content/whatis/art22944.html.

[2] "Child Protection From Violence, Exploitation and Abuse," UNICEF, May 2009, www.unicef.org/media/media_45451.html.

[3] "The State of the World's Children 2009," UNICEF, December 2008, www.unicef.org/sowc09/docs/SOWC09-FullReport-EN.pdf.

[4] "Survive to Five," Save the Children, www.savethechildren.org/programs/health/child-survival/survive-to-5.

[5] "The State of Food Insecurity in the World, 2008: High food prices and food security — threats and opportunities," Food and Agriculture Organization, 2008, www.fao.org/docrep/011/i0291e/i0291e00.htm.

[6] Alula Berhe Kidani, "Children and the MDGs, Progress Towards A World Fit for Children," *Sudan Vision*, April 8, 2009, www.sudanvisiondaily.com/modules.php?name=News&file=print&sid=33567.

[7] "Great leap forward on free healthcare," IRIN, Sept. 24, 2009, www.irinnews.org/report.aspx?ReportId=86280.

[8] "Children and Human Rights," Amnesty International, www.amnesty.org/en/children.

[9] "Global: WHO Snapshot of Global Health," IRIN, July 10, 2009, www.irinnews.org/Report.aspx?ReportId=85235.

[10] "Child Protection From Violence, Exploitation and Abuse," *op. cit.*

[11] *Ibid.* For background, see John Felton, "Child Soldiers," *CQ Global Researcher*, July 2008, pp. 183-211.

[12] "Averting a Human Crisis During the Global Downturn," World Bank 2009, foreword, http://siteresources.worldbank.org/NEWS/Resources/AvertingTheHumanCrisis.pdf.

[13] "The Economic Crisis and the Millennium Development Goals," The World Bank, April 24, 2009, http://web.worldbank.org/WBSITE/EXTERNAL/NEWS/0,,contentMDK:22154703~pagePK:64257043~piPK:437376~theSitePK:4607,00.html.

[14] *Ibid.* For background on the 2008 food crisis, see Marcia Clemmitt, "Global Food Crisis," *CQ Researcher*, June 27, 2008, pp. 553-576.

[15] Rosalind Ryan, "Call for global action to tackle food crisis," *Guardian*, April 22, 2008, www.guardian.co.uk/politics/2008/apr/22/development.internationalaidanddevelopment.

[16] "Africa: Mortgages and mortality," IRIN, March 6, 2009, www.irinnews.org/Report.aspx?ReportId=83344.

[17] "The Economic Crisis and the Millennium Development Goals," *op. cit.*

[18] Sam Lister, "Downturn could kill 400,000 children, warns Margaret Chan," *Times* (London), March 14, 2009, www.timesonline.co.uk/tol/life_and_style/health/article5904637.ece.

[19] Quoted in "Global recession boosts child prostitution and trafficking," IRIN, Sept. 29, 2009, www.irinnews.org/report.aspx?Reportid=86335. Also see "Financial Crisis and Human Trafficking," U.S. Department of State, 2009, www.state.gov/g/tip/rls/tiprpt/2009/124798.htm.

[20] "Less money for more work — the NGO double whammy," IRIN, April 21, 2009, www.irinnews.org/Report.aspx?ReportId=84023.

[21] The gross national income is the total net value of the goods and services produced by a country, including wages, profits, rents, interest and pensions.

[22] "Scandalous lack of progress in EU development aid," Global Movement for Children, April 10, 2008, www.gmfc.org/index.php/gmc6/content/view/full/815.

[23] "Save lives not banks, says Machel," IRIN, July 23, 2009, www.plusnews.org/Report.aspx?ReportId=85410.

[24] "Development aid at its highest level ever in 2008," Organisation for Economic Co-operation and Development, March 3, 2009, www.oecd.org/document/35/0,3343,en_2649_34487_42458595_1_1_1_1,00.html. Also see www.globalissues.org/article/35/us-and-foreign-aid-assistance.

[25] "Aid still at 1993 level despite increase," OXFAM, March 30, 2009, www.oxfam.org/en/pressroom/pressrelease/2009-03-30/aid-still-1993-level-despite-increase.

[26] Dambisa Moyo, "Why Foreign Aid Is Hurting Africa," *The Wall Street Journal*, March 21, 2009, www.online.wsj.com/article/SB123758895999200083.html.

[27] William Easterly, "Multilateral Development Banks: Promoting Effectiveness and Fighting Corruption," testimony before the Senate Committee on Foreign Relations, March 28, 2006, www.nyu.edu/fas/institute/dri/Easterly/File/oral_testimony_senate_foreign_relations_committee.pdf.

[28] John Stossel and Patrick McMenamin, "Will More Foreign Aid End Global Poverty?" ABC News, May 12, 2006, www.abcnews.go.com/2020/Story?id=1955664&page=1.

[29] Moyo, *op. cit.*

[30] William Wallis, "Is aid working?" *Financial Times Blog*, June 1, 2009, www.blogs.ft.com/arena/2009/06/01/is-aid-working/.

[31] Stossel and McMenamin, *op. cit.*

[32] "Convention on the Rights of the Child," UNICEF, August 2008, www.unicef.org/crc/.

33 Andie Coller, "Parental rights: The new wedge issue," *Politico*, April 8, 2009, www.politico.com/news/stories/0409/21041.html.

34 Sakun Akhtar, "Gautam, 72, examines child health," *The Dartmouth.com*, Feb. 3, 2009, www.thedartmouth.com/2009/02/03/news/gautam.

35 *Ibid.*

36 Michael Smith, "Home schooling: U.N. treaty might weaken families," *The Washington Times*, Jan. 11, 2009, www.washingtontimes.com/news/2009/jan/11/un-treaty-might-weaken-families/.

37 Joseph Abrams, "Boxer seeks to ratify UN treaty that may erode US rights," Fox News, Feb. 25, 2009, www.foxnews.com/politics/2009/02/25/boxer-seeks-ratify-treaty-erode-rights/.

38 David Crary, "Children's rights treaty stirs debate," The Associated Press, May 2, 2009, www.ajc.com/news/content/printedition/2009/05/02/currents0502.html.

39 "Youth In Crisis," IRIN In-depth, February 2007, p. 23, www.irinnews.org/InDepthMain.aspx?InDepthId=28&ReportId=69981.

40 "What is child survival and why does it matter?" Global Action for Children, www.globalactionforchildren.org/issues/child_survival1/.

41 "Children, AIDS and the economic crisis," UNICEF, April 2009, www.uniteforchildren.org/files/AIDSandFinancialCrisis_June_5_2009.pdf.

42 "Averting a human crisis during the global downturn," *op. cit.*

43 Daniel Ooko, "Health forum calls to avert new HIV/AIDS infections," *China View*, Feb. 24, 2009, http://english.peopledaily.com.cn/90001/90777/90855/6600165.html.

44 Vidya Krishnan, "Now, meltdown hits HIV/AIDS treatment, prevention," *Indian Express*, July 22, 2009, www.indianexpress.com/news/now-meltdown-hits-hiv-aids-treatment-preve/492360/.

45 Elvis Basudde, "Uganda: HIV/AIDS: no more free drugs," *The New Vision*, Aug. 30, 2009, www.allafrica.com/stories/200908310829.html.

46 Sam Rutekiara, "Africa's Real AIDS Priority: Prevention," *The Washington Post*, April 16, 2008, www.washingtonpost.com/wp-dyn/content/article/2008/04/15/AR2008041502738.html.

47 "Youth In Crisis," *op. cit.*, p. 24.

48 Alexander Irwin, Joyce Millen and Dorothy Fallows, "Myth Four: Prevention vs. Treatment?" *The Body*, April 2003, www.thebody.com/content/art13662.html.

49 Rachel Zimmerman and Mark Schoofs, "World AIDS Experts Debate Treatment vs. Prevention," *The Wall Street Journal*, July 2, 2002, www.aegis.com/news/wsj/2002/WJ020702.html.

50 For more details see Charles S. Clark, "Child Labor and Sweatshops," *CQ Researcher*, Aug. 16, 1996, pp. 721-744.

51 "Child Labor in U.S. History," Child Labor Public Education Project, www.continuetolearn.uiowa.edu/laborctr/child_labor/about/us_history.html.

52 "History of Child Labor," www.buzzle.com/articles/history-of-child-labor.html.

53 "A Brief History of Chimney Sweeping," www.a1specialistservices.co.uk/history.htm.

54 "Library — Children's Employment Commission Part II," The Origins Network, www.originsnetwork.com/help/popup-aboutbo-gallery employ.htm.

55 "Punishment in Factories," www.spartacus.schoolnet.co.uk/IRpunishments.htm.

56 Robert Whaples, "Child Labor in the United States," www.eh.net/encyclopedia/article/whaples.childlabor.

57 Quoted in "Children," The World Affairs Blog Network, www.children.foreignpolicyblogs.com/.

58 "The Triangle Factory Fire," www.ilr.cornell.edu/trianglefire/.

59 Carolyn Tuttle, "Centuries of Child Labour: European Experiences from the Seventeenth to the Twentieth Century; Book Reviews," Eh.net, November 2005, www.eh.net/bookreviews/library/1008.

60 See Brian Hansen, "Children in Crisis," *CQ Researcher*, Aug. 31, 2001, pp. 657-688.

61 David Koch, "About UNICEF: Who we are," www.unicef.org/about/who/index_37404.html.

62 "1946-2006: Sixty Years for Children," UNICEF, p. 11, www.unicef.org/publications/files/1946-2006_Sixty_Years_for_Children.pdf.

63 Marcy Nicholson, "Child, forced labor behind many products: study," Reuters, Sept. 10, 2009, www.reuters.com/article/domesticNews/idUSTRE5896QD20090910.

64 "1946-2006: Sixty Years for Children," *op. cit.*, p. 21.

65 "The Millenium Development Goals Report, 2009," United Nations, www.un.org/millenniumgoals/pdf/MDG_Report_2009_ENG.pdf.

66 "Bill Gates Addresses the UN General Assembly," Sept. 25, 2008, www.gatesfoundation.org/speeches-commentary/Pages/bill-gates-united-nations-2008.aspx.

67 "28 Days to save a life," IRIN, June 16, 2009, www.irinnews.org/report.aspx?ReportId=84869.

68 *Ibid.*

69 "Briefing for the day of the African Child," Save the Children, June 16, 2009, www.savethechildren.org/countries/africa/Briefing-Day-of-the-African-Child2.pdf.

70 For background, see Jason McClure, "Ethiopia Takes on Malaria," in "The Troubled Horn of Africa," *CQ Global Researcher*, June 2009, pp. 149-176.

71 "Briefing for the day of the African Child," *op. cit.*

72 "Trafficked children and child slaves," Global Angels Foundation, www.globalangels.org/pages/4686/Trafficked_Kids_&_Child_Slaves.htm.

73 See Andrew Malone, "The real Slumdog Millionaires: Behind the cinema fantasy, mafia gangs are deliberately crippling children for profit," *The Mail Online*, Jan. 24, 2009, www.dailymail.co.uk/news/worldnews/article-1127056/The-real-Slumdog-Millionaires-Behind-cinema-fantasy-mafia-gangs-deliberately-crippling-children-profit.html#ixzz0SRUGLsTY.

About the Author

Robert Kiener is an award-winning writer whose work has appeared in the *London Sunday Times*, *The Christian Science Monitor*, *The Washington Post*, *Reader's Digest*, Time Life Books, *Asia Inc.*, and other publications. For more than two decades he lived and worked as an editor and correspondent in Guam, Hong Kong and England and is now based in the United States. He frequently travels to Asia and Europe to report on international issues. He holds an M.A. in Asian Studies from Hong Kong University and an M.Phil. in International Relations from Cambridge University.

[74] "Orphans, child slaves, street kids and trafficked children," Global Angels Foundation, www.globalangels.org/pages/3660/Orphans,_Child_Slaves,_Street_Kids_and_Trafficked_Children.htm.

[75] Rania Abouzeid, "Iraq's unspeakable crime: mothers pimping daughters," *Time*, March 7, 2009, www.time.com/time/world/article/0,8599,1883696,00.html.

[76] "Financial Crisis and Human Trafficking," U.S. Department of State, www.state.gov/g/tip/rls/tiprpt/2009/124798.htm.

[77] "Child Well-Being Index (CWI) 2009, Annual Release and Special Focus Report on Anticipating the Impacts of a 2008-2010 Recession," Foundation for Child Development, May 2009, www.fcd-us.org/resources/resources_show.htm?doc_id=906348.

[78] Wang Qian, "Cops crack 700 trafficking cases," *China Daily*, June, 2009, www.chinadaily.com.cn/cndy/2009-06/02/content_7961144.htm.

[79] See "War Child," NYPAW, www.warchildholland.org/nieuws/1561/nypaw.html.

[80] Mirela Xanthaki, "Rights: Former Child Soldiers Work to Save Those Left Behind," IPS, Nov. 26, 2008, www.ipsnews.net/news.asp?idnews=44865.

[81] *Ibid*.

[82] Nic Robertson, "Pakistan: Taliban buying children for suicide attacks," CNN, July 7, 2009, www.edition.cnn.com/2009/WORLD/asiapcf/07/07/pakistan.child.bombers/index.html.

[83] "Madagascar: A shell-shocked youth," IRIN, June 24, 2009, www.irinnews.org/report.aspx?ReportId=84988.

[84] *Ibid*.

[85] Natassia Hoffet, "Rights: Girl Soldiers Used Up, Then Thrown Away," IPS, March 12, 2009, www.ipsnews.net/news.asp?idnews=46085.

[86] "Chad: Scores of children among rebels rounded up in east," IRIN, May 27, 2009, www.irinnews.org/Report.aspx?ReportId=84581.

[87] Thalif Deen, "Rights: Recruiters of Child Soldiers Defy U.N. Pressure," April 29, 2009, www.ipsnews.net/news.asp?idnews=46669.

[88] "Chad: Instability Threatens Demobilisation of Child Soldiers," IRIN, April 16, 2009, www.allafrica.com/stories/200904160862.html.

[89] "Madagascar: A shell-shocked youth," *op. cit.*

[90] Celia W. Dugger, "Child Mortality Rate Declines Globally," *The New York Times*, Sept. 10, 2009, www.nytimes.com/2009/09/10/world/10child.html.

FOR MORE INFORMATION

CARE, 151 Ellis St., N.E., Atlanta, GA 30303; (800) 521-CARE; www.care.org. Global antipoverty organization.

Catholic Relief Services, 228 W. Lexington St., Baltimore, MD 21201-3413; (888) 277-7575; www.crs.org. Aids people in more than 100 countries.

Christian Children's Fund, 2821 Emerywood Pkwy., Richmond, VA 23294; (800) 776-6767; www.christianchildrensfund.org. Works in 28 countries on critical children's issues.

Coalition to Stop the Use of Child Soldiers, P.O. Box 22696, London, U.K. N4 3ZJ; (44 20) 726-0606; www.child-soldiers.org. Works to prevent governments and insurgency groups from using children as soldiers.

Defence for Children International, P.O. Box 88, CH 1211, Geneva 20, Switzerland; (41 22) 734-0558; www.defence-for-children.org. Investigates sexual exploitation of children and other abuses.

Human Rights Watch; 350 Fifth Ave., New York, NY 10118; (212) 290-4700; www.hrw.org. Largest U.S. human-rights organization; investigates abuses around the world, including those against children.

International Labour Organization, 4, route des Morillons, CH-1211, Geneva 22, Switzerland; (41 22) 799-6111; www.ilo.org. Sets and enforces worldwide labor standards.

Save the Children, 54 Wilton Rd., Westport, CT 06880; (203) 221-4000; www.savethechildren.com. Helps children and families in 47 developing countries improve health, education and economic opportunities.

Somaly Mam Foundation, P.O. Box 4569, New York, NY 10163; (917)-388-9623; www.somaly.org. Cambodia-based foundation that rescues and rehabilitates child prostitutes in Southeast Asia.

United Nations Children's Fund (UNICEF), 3 United Nations Plaza, New York, NY 10017; (212) 326-7000; www.unicef.org. Helps poor children in 160 countries.

World Vision International, 800 West Chestnut Ave., Monrovia, Calif. 91016; (626) 303-8811; www.wvi.org. Christian relief and development organization working to promote the well-being of all people — especially children.

[91] "UNICEF: Global child mortality continues to drop," Sept. 10, 2009, www.unicef.org/media/media_51087.html.

[92] Amny Radwain, "Egypt leads in cutting infant deaths," *Time*, May 16, 2007, www.time.com/time/world/article/0,8599,1621812,00.html.

[93] *Ibid*.

[94] "What is child survival and why does it matter?" *op. cit.*

[95] "What Is the Accelerated Child Survival and Development Initiative (ACSD)?" UNICEF, www.unicefusa.org/about/faq/what-is-acsd.html.

[96] Caroline Harper, Nicola Jones, Andy McKay and Jessica Espey, "Children in times of economic crisis," Overseas Development Institute, March 2009, www.odi.org.uk/resources/download/2865.pdf.

[97] Melinda French Gates, "The other side of the mat: uniting for maternal, newborn and child survival and health," UNICEF, www.unicef.org/sowc08/docs/sowc08_panel_5_2.pdf.

Bibliography
Selected Sources

Books

Aronowitz, Alexis, *Human Trafficking, Human Misery: The Global Trade in Human Beings*, Praeger, 2009.

A criminologist in the Netherlands provides a scholarly examination of the worldwide problem of human trafficking.

Mam, Somaly, *The Road of Lost Innocence*, Spiegel & Grau, 2008.

A noted Cambodian children's advocate recounts how she went from being sold into prostitution as a child to founding and running a world-famous foundation that rescues children from a similar fate.

Moyo, Dambisa, *Dead Aid: Why Aid is Not Working and How there is a Better Way for Africa*, Farrar, Straus and Giroux, 2009.

A Zambia-born former Goldman Sachs economist argues that aid to Africa is largely ineffective and has fostered dependency, corruption and poverty.

Sachs, Jeffrey, *The End of Poverty: Economic Possibilities for our Time*, Penguin, 2006.

The celebrated Columbia University economist defends aid to developing nations and explains his plan to eliminate extreme poverty around the world by 2025.

Articles

Garrett, Laurie, "The Wrong Way to Fight Aids," *International Herald Tribune*, July 30, 2008, www.cfr.org/publication/16875/wrong_way_to_fight_aids.html.

A noted health researcher examines the HIV/AIDS "prevention versus treatment" debate.

Heilprin, John, "Obama seeks to join Global Rights of Child pact," Associated Press, June 23, 2009, www.cnsnews.com/news/article/49953.

Controversy is likely to accompany proposed U.S. ratification of the Convention on the Rights of the Child.

Shikwati, James, "Divorce Africa from the World Bank and IMF," Inter Region Economic Network, March 31, 2009, www.africanexecutive.com/modules/magazine/articles.php?article=4267.

A Kenyan economist argues that much aid to Africa benefits donors more than the recipients.

Walt, Vivienne," Diarrhea: The Great Zinc Breakthrough," *Time*, Aug. 17, 2009, www.time.com/time/magazine/article/0,9171,1914655,00.html.

Reporter Walt describes how inexpensive zinc tablets are helping to eradicate the scourge of diarrhea in Mali.

Reports and Studies

"2009 Trafficking in Persons Report," U.S. Department of State, June 2009, www.state.gov/g/tip/rls/tiprpt/2009/.

The State Department's annual report details how 12.3 million adults and children worldwide are victims of human trafficking.

"Averting a Human Crisis During the Global Downturn," The World Bank, 2009, www.siteresources.worldbank.org/NEWS/Resources/AvertingTheHumanCrisis.pdf.

The international development institution examines how the global economic crisis is affecting foreign aid.

"Children and Conflict in a Changing World," UNICEF, April 2009, www.unicef.org/publications/files/Machel_Study_10_Year_Strategic_Review_EN_030909.pdf.

A follow-up to a groundbreaking 1996 report on how armed conflict impacts children describes how millions still suffer due to war every year.

"Home Truths: Facing the Facts on Children, AIDS and Poverty," Joint Learning Initiative on Children and HIV/AIDS, February 2009, www.jlica.org/protected/pdf-feb09/Final%20JLICA%20Report-final.pdf.

An international network of AIDS experts provides a thorough, wide-ranging investigation into the world's response to children affected by HIV/AIDS.

"In-Depth: Youth in Crisis: Coming of Age in the 21st century," IRIN, July 2009, www.irinnews.org/IndepthMain.aspx?IndepthId=28&ReportId=70140.

The U.N.'s independent news agency reports on how children are being affected by issues ranging from illegal forced marriage to deteriorating education systems.

"The State of the World's Children 2009," UNICEF, January 2009, www.unicef.org/sowc09/docs/SOWC09-FullReport-EN.pdf.

The aid agency's annual report examines maternal and neonatal health and identifies actions and interventions needed to save lives.

Harper, Caroline, *et al.*, "Children in Times of Economic Crisis: Past lessons, future policies," Overseas Development Institute, March 2009, www.odi.org.uk/resources/download/2865.pdf.

A London-based think tank examines how the global economic downturn is affecting children around the world.

The Next Step:

Additional Articles from Current Periodicals

AIDS

"Australia Helps Children With HIV/AIDS," Vietnam News Agency, June 1, 2009.

The Australian embassy in Vietnam has co-organized activities for 80 children with HIV/AIDS in a northern Vietnamese province for International Children's Day.

Fointuna, Yemris, "Malnutrition Worsens in Children With HIV/AIDS," Jakarta Post, June 9, 2009.

Malnourished children have low immune systems that make them more susceptible to the effects of HIV and AIDS.

Ocowun, Chris, "NGO Takes AIDS Fight to Schools," New Vision (Uganda), Nov. 27, 2008.

Save the Children Uganda has constructed five model centers for HIV/AIDS counseling and testing.

Child Labor

"Adoption of Child Labor Policy Urged," United News of Bangladesh, March 19, 2009.

Participants at a seminar on child labor have determined that Bangladesh needs to urgently adopt a national child labor policy.

"Can Education Stop Child Labour?" Times of India, Dec. 16, 2008.

Ministers and bureaucrats across India are gathering to determine if education is a viable solution to the country's increasing rate of child labor.

"Political Will Lacking to Put an End to Child Labour, Says Brinda Karat," The Hindu (India), Dec. 13, 2008.

The Communist Party of India believes there is a lack of political will in India to stand up for the rights of children.

Koroma, Pel, "50M Euro to Tackle Child Labour," Concord Times (Sierra Leone), Sept. 29, 2008.

The government of Sierra Leone, the European Union and the International Labour Organization have signed a four-year project to combat child labor in the country through education.

Development Aid

Dilanian, Ken, "Report: U.S. Foreign Aid Needs Major Overhaul," Miami Times, April 29, 2009, p. 6A.

Programs funded by U.S. foreign aid remain disconnected from larger strategies, according to a report by the Government Accountability Office.

Je-hae, Do, "Korea to Play Greater Role in Int'l Society," Korea Times, May 1, 2009.

South Korea is planning to spend nearly $1 billion on aid to developing countries around the world in 2009, a 16-percent increase from 2008.

Kelley, Kevin J., "Critics Blast US Aid Efforts as 'Chaotic,'" The East African (Kenya), Oct. 19, 2008.

Three former U.S. Agency for International Development chiefs say agency programs are uncoordinated.

Mathiot, Cedric, "African Development Assistance Sacrificed on the Altar of the Budget," Liberation (France), Oct. 25, 2008.

France will cut official development assistance to Africa in 2009 due to a larger-than-expected budget shortfall.

U.N. Convention on the Rights of the Child

"Government Fails to Bring Laws in Conformity With UN Convention," Business Recorder (Pakistan), May 9, 2009.

Children are not protected under the current provisions of penal laws in Pakistan, going against the U.N. Convention on the Rights of the Child, which the country ratified in 1990.

"U.N. Committee to Examine Human Rights of Children in N Korea," Yonhap (South Korea), Jan. 24, 2009.

The U.N. committee that oversees the Rights of the Child treaty is set to question North Korean officials about the communist country's policies on protecting children's rights.

Stahl, Philip, "United Nations Treaty Would Protect Children's Rights," Arizona Republic, July 1, 2009, p. 34.

The U.N. Convention on the Rights of the Child recognizes that children are humans who deserve rights, while also protecting them because they hold a special place in society.

CITING CQ GLOBAL RESEARCHER

Sample formats for citing these reports in a bibliography include the ones listed below. Preferred styles and formats vary, so please check with your instructor or professor.

MLA STYLE

Flamini, Roland. "Nuclear Proliferation." CQ Global Researcher 1 Apr. 2007: 1-24.

APA STYLE

Flamini, R. (2007, April 1). Nuclear proliferation. CQ Global Researcher, 1, 1-24.

CHICAGO STYLE

Flamini, Roland. "Nuclear Proliferation." CQ Global Researcher, April 1, 2007, 1-24.

Voices From Abroad:

EMILIA CASELLA
World Food Programme
Spokeswoman, Switzerland

Economic crisis affects Guatemalan children

"Nearly 50 percent of children under five years old in Guatemala suffer from chronic under-nutrition, which can cause stunting or severe weight loss."

Thai Press Reports, September 2009

NIGEL FISHER
President and CEO
UNICEF Canada

Importance of raising AIDS awareness

"UNICEF is committed to transforming the lives of children affected by AIDS. We are enabling young children, made extremely vulnerable to abuse and exploitation by the loss of their parents, to receive an education. And, . . . we are supporting young people in some of the most impassioned and dynamic activities I have ever witnessed in educating their peers about [how] to stay strong and healthy in the face of this scourge that is ravaging their generation."

CCNMatthews (Canadian newswire), November 2006

MARLENE MUNGUNDA
Minister of Gender
Equality and Child Welfare
Namibia

Namibia needs more AIDS treatment centers

"These children need special support and care and secure access to treatment and medical facilities."

The Namibian, August 2009

TSITSI SINGIZI
Communications Officer
U.N. Children's Fund
Zimbabwe

Imprisoning children violates U.N. treaty

"UNICEF is worried by the growing number of children being incarcerated for purported crimes. The U.N. Convention on the Rights of the Child clearly states that a child shall be incarcerated only as a last resort and only for the shortest time possible."

The Herald (Harare, Zimbabwe), August 2009

RICHARD HARRISON
Civil Servant
U.N. International Civil
Service Commission
United Kingdom

U.S. failure to sign U.N. treaty is appalling

"[Having] worked for the United Nations in Geneva for 40 years, I am notably shocked that the USA and Somalia are the only two member states that have not ratified the UN Convention on the Rights of the Child."

US Newswire, June 2009

DAVID CAMERON
Leader, Conservative
Party, United Kingdom

Rich countries' aid to poor countries is vital

"I understand why people might say that . . . in economic circumstances like these . . . increasing foreign aid is the last thing we should do. But economic difficulties at home should be the time for us to reaffirm our moral responsibilities, not reduce them."

The Herald (U.K.), July 2009

KOFI ANNAN
Former U.N.
Secretary-General

More aid needed for AIDS in Africa

"Nearly 25 years into the pandemic, help is reaching less than 10 percent of the children affected by HIV/AIDS, leaving too many children to grow up alone, grow up too fast or not grow up at all."

Public Agenda (Accra, Ghana), October 2005

P. BANUMATHI
Childline Coordinator
Chennai, India

Consequences of child sex trafficking

"We have rescued innumerable children who have been trafficked, abandoned or are in conflict with the law. They come to us after suffering physical and sexual abuse, with HIV and forgotten dreams."

The Hindu, September 2009

caglecartoons.com

©Taylor Jones • Hoover Digest

Hoover Digest/Taylor Jones

CHAPTER

6

HUMAN TRAFFICKING AND SLAVERY

BY DAVID MASCI

Excerpted from the CQ Researcher. David Masci. (March 26, 2004). "Human Trafficking and Slavery." *CQ Researcher*, 273-296.

Human Trafficking and Slavery

BY DAVID MASCI

THE ISSUES

One morning in May, 7-year-old Francis Bok walked to the market in Nymlal, Sudan, to sell some eggs and peanuts. The farmer's son had made the same trip many times before.

"I was living a very good life with my family," he recalls today. "I was a happy child."

But his happy life ended that day in 1986. Arab raiders from northern Sudan swept into the village, sowing death and destruction. "They came on horses and camels and running on foot, firing machine guns and killing people everywhere," he says. His entire family — mother, father and two sisters — died in the attack.

The raiders grabbed Francis and several other children, lashed them to donkeys and carried them north for two days. Then the children were parceled out to their captors. Francis went to a man named Giema Abdullah.

For the next 10 years, the boy tended his "owner's" goats and cattle. He slept with the animals, never had a day off and was rarely fed properly.

"He treated me like an animal, he even called me an animal, and he beat me," Francis says. "There was no joy. Even when I remembered my happy life before, it only made me sad."

In 1996, Francis escaped to Sudan's capital, Khartoum; then he made his way to Cairo, Egypt, and eventually in 2000 to the United States, which admitted him as a refugee.

As all American students learn, the Civil War ended slavery in the United States in 1865. Internationally, the practice was banned by several agreements and treaties, beginning in 1926 with

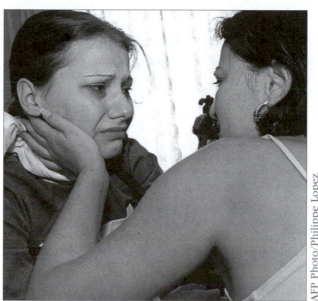

Tearful Eastern European women comfort each other after being freed in 2000 from an American-owned hotel in Phnom Penh, Cambodia, where they were forced to have sex with businessmen and government officials. Traffickers in Eastern Europe often lure young women into bondage by advertising phony jobs abroad for nannies, models or actresses.

AFP Photo/Philippe Lopez

the Slavery Convention of the League of Nations. But for tens of millions of people around the world, including millions of children like Francis, slavery never ended. An estimated 27 million people currently are held in some form of bondage, according to anti-slavery groups like Free the Slaves. [1] From the villages of Sudan and Mauritania in Africa to the factories, sweatshops and brothels of South Asia, slavery in its rawest, cruelest form is very much alive in the 21st century.

Many of those in bondage were kidnapped, like Francis. Others go voluntarily to different countries, thinking they are heading for a better life, only to be forced into a nightmare of prostitution or hard labor. Many more work as bonded laborers, tied to lifetime servitude because their father or grandfather borrowed money they couldn't repay.

Trafficking people across international borders has become a $12-billion-a-year global industry that touches virtually

every country. The U.S. government estimates that between 800,000 and 900,000 people are trafficked internationally every year, many of them women and children, transported as sex workers. [2] The total includes up to 20,000 people forcibly trafficked into the United States annually, according to the Central Intelligence Agency. [3] (*See sidebar, p. 284.*)

Lyudmilla's story is typical. Like many desperately poor young women, the single mother of three from the former Soviet republic of Moldova responded to an advertisement promising work in Italy. Instead she was taken to a brothel in Macedonia, where she spent two horrific years in sexual slavery before escaping in 2002. [4]

Venecija, a Bulgarian, also ended up in a Macedonian brothel. "We were so tired we couldn't get out of bed," she recalled. "But [we had to] put on makeup and meet customers," she said after escaping. Those who refused were beaten until they "changed their minds." [5]

Traffickers control their victims through a variety of coercive means. In addition to rape and beatings, they keep their passports, leaving them with few options if they do manage to escape.

And the violence can follow those who do get away. Mercy, a young West African woman trafficked to Italy, escaped her tormentors only to see her sister killed in retribution after Mercy told human rights groups about her experience. [6]

The vast majority of slaves and victims of human trafficking come from the poorest parts of Africa, Asia, Latin America and Eastern Europe, where, smooth-talking traffickers often easily

Where Human Trafficking Occurs

Human trafficking and slavery take place in virtually every country in the world, but the U.N. and other reliable sources say the most extensive trafficking occurs in the countries below (listed at right).

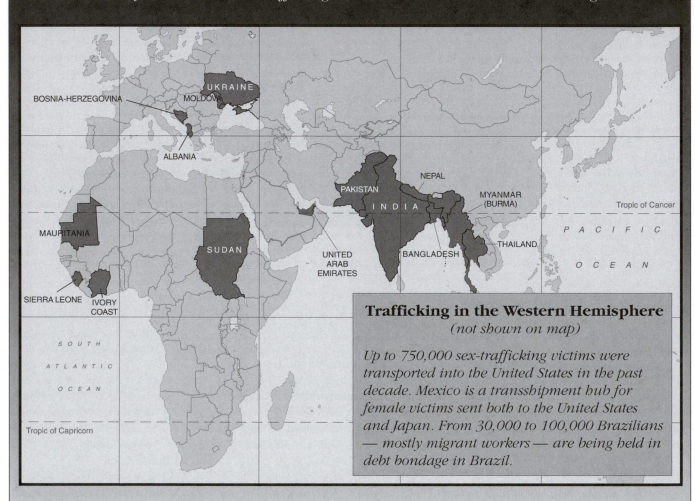

Trafficking in the Western Hemisphere
(not shown on map)

Up to 750,000 sex-trafficking victims were transported into the United States in the past decade. Mexico is a transshipment hub for female victims sent both to the United States and Japan. From 30,000 to 100,000 Brazilians — mostly migrant workers — are being held in debt bondage in Brazil.

Sources: Protection Project at Johns Hopkins University, U.S. State Department, Human Rights Watch, International Labour Organization, American Anti-Slavery Group

deceive desperate victims or their parents into believing that they are being offered a "better life."

"Being poor doesn't make you a slave, but it does make you vulnerable to being a slave," says Peggy Callahan, a spokeswoman for Free the Slaves, based in Washington, D.C.

Some Christian groups and nongovernmental organizations (NGOs) have tried to buy slaves out of bondage, particularly in Sudan, where two decades of civil war have stoked the slave trade. But many humanitarian groups argue that so-called slave redemption merely increases the demand for slaves.

International efforts to fight slavery and trafficking have increased dramatically over the last 10 years, with the United States playing a leading role. President Bush dramatized Amer-

ica's commitment in an address to the U.N. General Assembly on Sept. 23, 2003. The president had been expected to focus on security issues in the Middle East, but he devoted a substantial portion of his remarks to urging the international community to do more to fight trafficking.

"There is a special evil in the abuse and exploitation of the most innocent and vulnerable," Bush said.

Europe	
Albania	Up to 90 percent of the girls in rural areas don't go to school for fear of being abducted and sold into sexual servitude.
Bosnia and Herzegovina	A quarter of the women working in nightclubs claim they were forced into prostitution. The U.N. police task force is suspected of covering up its involvement in the sex trade.
Moldova	Up to 80 percent of the women trafficked as prostitutes in Western Europe may be Moldovans.
Ukraine	Up to 400,000 Ukrainian women have been trafficked for sexual exploitation in the past decade, Ukraine says. Ukrainian sex slaves can fetch up to $25,000 in Israel.
Africa	
Ivory Coast	A girl can allegedly be bought as a slave in Abidjan for about $7; a shipment of 10 children from Mali for work on the cocoa plantations costs about $420.
Mauritania	Light-skinned Arab Berbers today are thought to exploit hundreds of thousands of black African slaves. Slave raids in the 13th century began systemic slavery in Mauritania.
Sudan	Muslim tribesmen from northern Sudan still stage slave raids on non-Muslim Dinka peoples in the south, taking thousands of women and children.
Asia	
Bangladesh	An estimated 25,000 women and children are trafficked annually from Bangladesh.
India	Parents have sold an estimated 15 million children into bonded labor in return for meager loans from moneylenders.
Myanmar	The ruling military junta coerces minorities into forced labor in factories that benefit the regime and foreign corporations.
Nepal	A major source of women trafficked into Indian brothels; in addition, an estimated 75,000 people are trapped as bonded laborers in Nepal.
Pakistan	Millions of Pakistanis, often members of religious minorities, are forced to work as brick makers or in the fields of feudal landowners.
Thailand	Children sold by their parents make up a significant percentage of prostitutes in Thailand, which is a prime destination for pedophile sex tourists.
United Arab Emirates	Many women trafficked from the former Soviet Union end up in the UAE.

"Nearly two centuries after the abolition of the transatlantic slave trade, and more than a century after slavery was officially ended in its last strongholds, the trade in human beings for any purpose must not be allowed to thrive." [7]

The cornerstone of recent American anti-trafficking efforts is the 2000 Trafficking Victims Protection Act, which mandates the cutoff of most non-humanitarian U.S. aid for any nation deemed not trying hard enough to address the problem.

"The act breaks new ground because it actually tries to bring about changes in other countries," says Wendy Young, director of external relations for the Women's Commission for Refugee Women and Children in New York City.

"It's making a difference in countries all over the world," agrees Rep. Christopher H. Smith, R-N.J., one of the law's authors.

But critics contend the act is too weak to force real behavior changes. "It's very easy for countries to avoid sanctions just by taking a few largely meaningless actions," says Katherine Chon, co-director of the Polaris Project, an anti-trafficking advocacy group in Washington. She also accuses the administration of giving a pass to important allies, like Saudi Arabia, regardless of what they do to ameliorate their forced-labor practices.

All sides agree that many countries where trafficking occurs have a long way to go before they attain the level of economic, legal and political maturity needed to entirely eliminate the practice. "I don't think people realize just how desperately poor and chaotic many countries are today," says Linda Beher, a spokeswoman for the New York City-based United Methodist Committee On Relief, which assists trafficking victims.

A tragic consequence of this poverty is child labor, which many experts see as a cousin to slavery. In the developing world today, nearly 200 million children ages 5-14 are put to work to help support their families, according to the International Labour Organization (ILO). Almost half are under age 12, and more than 20 million are engaged in highly hazardous work, such as tanning leather or weaving rugs, exposing them to unhealthy chemicals or airborne pollutants. [8]

Some humanitarian aid workers describe much child labor as inherently coercive, because young children often have no choice.

The ILO argues that eliminating child labor and sending children to school would ultimately benefit nations with child laborers by raising income levels. (*See graph, p. 280.*) But some economists counter that putting even a fraction of the working children in school would be prohibitively expensive.

As experts debate resolving what has been called one of the greatest

John Eibner of Christian Solidarity International pays an Arab trader to free 132 slaves in Madhol, northern Sudan, in 1997. Critics of slave-redemption say it only encourages more slave-taking, but supporters say that not trying to free slaves would be unconscionable.

humanitarian problems of the 21st century, here are some of the questions they are asking:

Does buying slaves in order to free them solve the problem?

In recent years, would-be Samaritans — from Christian missionaries to famous rock musicians — have worked to free slaves in Africa. Although slave trading occurs in many countries, the rescue efforts largely have focused on war-torn Sudan, where Muslim raiders from the north have enslaved hundreds of thousands of Christian and animist tribesmen in the south.

The Sudanese government has done virtually nothing to stop the practice and has even encouraged it as a means of prosecuting the war against the rebellious south, according to the U.S. State Department's 2003 "Trafficking in Persons Report."

Since 1995, Christian Solidarity International (CSI) and other slave-redemption groups operating in Sudan say they have purchased the freedom of more than 60,000 people by providing money for local Sudanese to buy slaves and then free them. [9]

"Women and children are freed from the terrible abuse, the rape, the beatings, the forcible conversions [to Islam] — all of the horrors that are an inherent part of slavery in Sudan," said John Eibner, director of CSI's redemption program. [10]

Halfway around the world, *New York Times* columnist Nicholas D. Kristof had his own brush with slave redemption when he traveled to Cambodia and freed two female sex slaves. "I woke up her brothel's owner at dawn," he wrote of his efforts to purchase one of the prostitutes, "handed over $150, brushed off demands for interest on the debt and got a receipt for $150 for buying a girl's freedom. Then Srey Neth and I fled before the brothel's owner was even out of bed." [11]

While experts concede that slave redeemers are well-intentioned, many contend the practice actually does more harm than good. "When you have people running around buying up slaves, you help create market demand for more slaves," says Jim Jacobson, president of Christian Freedom International, a relief group in Front Royal, Va., that stopped its slave-repatriation efforts five years ago. "It's really just simple economics."

Kevin Bales, author of *Disposable People: New Slavery in the Global Economy* and president of Free the Slaves, agrees. "This is like paying a burglar to redeem the television set he just stole," says Bales, a noted expert on contemporary slavery. "It's better to find other ways to free people, like going to the police or taking them out of bondage by force."

Indeed, Jacobson says, redemption only puts more money in the pockets of unscrupulous and often violent slave traders. "These people end up taking the money and buying more guns and hiring more thugs to go out and take more slaves," he says.

In addition, the critics say, many "slaves" pretend to be in bondage to defraud Westerners. "If you talk to aid workers in these places, you'll find that [bogus slave traders] are literally picking up [already free] people from across town and 'selling' them an hour later," Free the Slaves' Callahan says.

"So much of it is a huge scam operation," agrees Jacobson. "A lot of these people aren't really slaves."

But supporters of redemption say it would be unconscionable not to attempt to free slaves, even if slavers will go out searching for new victims. "Slaves are treated so badly, especially the women and children, who have been beaten and raped," says William Saunders, human rights counsel for the Family Research Council, a conservative social-policy group, and co-founder of the Bishop Gassis Sudan Relief Fund, both in Washington. "How can you not try to free these people?"

Saunders and others also contend that slave buyers take steps to avoid creating a bigger market for slaves. "In the Sudan, they use the local currency, because a dollar or a [British] pound is the sort of powerful magnet that might give people incentives to take more slaves or present non-slaves," he says.

In addition, redemption supporters

Fighting the Traffickers

The 2000 Trafficking Victims Protection Act requires the State Department to report each year on global efforts to end human trafficking. Last year, 15 countries were placed in Tier 3, for those deemed to be doing little or nothing against trafficking. Countries in Tier 3 for three years in a row can lose all U.S. non-humanitarian aid. Tier 1 countries are considered to be actively fighting trafficking. Seventy-five countries are in Tier 2, indicating they are making some efforts against trafficking.

State Department Anti-Trafficking Ratings

Tier 1 — Actively Fighting Trafficking		
Austria	Hong Kong	Poland
Belgium	Italy	Portugal
Benin	South Korea	Spain
Colombia	Lithuania	Sweden
Czech Republic	Macedonia	Switzerland
Denmark	Mauritius	Taiwan
France	Morocco	United Arab Emirates
Germany	The Netherlands	United Kingdom
Ghana		

Tier 3 — Doing Little or Nothing		
Belize	Georgia	North Korea
Bosnia and Herzegovina	Greece	Sudan
Myanmar	Haiti	Suriname
Cuba	Kazakhstan	Turkey
Dominican Republic	Liberia	Uzbekistan

Source: "2003 Trafficking in Persons Report," Office to Monitor and Combat Trafficking in Persons, Department of State, June 2003

say, they usually cap what they will pay per person — typically $50. "There's a real effort to ensure that we don't inflate the value of slaves," says Tommy Ray Calvert, chief of external operations for the Boston-based American Anti-Slavery Group (AASG).

Calvert contends that the redemptions have helped decrease slave raids in Sudan. The redemptions "brought world attention to the issue and forced our government and others to start pressuring the Sudanese to stop this evil practice," he says.

Moreover, Saunders refutes the charge that redeemers simply set people free without trying to ensure that they are true slaves. "They try to repatriate these people directly to their villages," Saunders says. "They don't just buy their freedom and let them go."

But the critics remain dubious. "It's so hard to get anywhere in Sudan that there is no way that they could

Economic Benefits Cited for Ending Child Labor

Banning child labor and educating all children would raise the world's total income by 22 percent, or $4.3 trillion, over 20 years, according to the International Labour Organization (ILO). The principal benefit would be the economic boost that most countries would experience if all children were educated through lower secondary school, plus substantial but less dramatic health benefits. The ILO analysis assumes countries that banned child labor would pay poor parents for their children's lost wages, something critics say is unrealistically expensive.

Net Economic Benefits of Eliminating Child Labor
(as a percentage of annual gross national income)

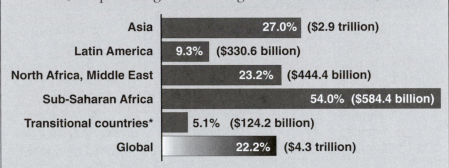

Asia	27.0%	($2.9 trillion)
Latin America	9.3%	($330.6 billion)
North Africa, Middle East	23.2%	($444.4 billion)
Sub-Saharan Africa	54.0%	($584.4 billion)
Transitional countries*	5.1%	($124.2 billion)
Global	22.2%	($4.3 trillion)

* Transitional countries — such as Taiwan, Singapore and Malaysia — are no longer considered "developing" but not yet classified as fully industrialized.

Source: "Investing in Every Child," International Programme on the Elimination of Child Labour, International Labour Office, December 2003

actually follow all of these people back to their home villages," Jacobson says. "It would take weeks or months."

Moreover, he says, "they don't have any idea whether the people they've freed have been coached or whether the village they're going to is really their village. It's simply impossible to know."

Is the Trafficking Victims Protection Act tough enough?

The $12 billion human-trafficking industry is now the world's third-largest illegal business, surpassing every other criminal enterprise except the drug and arms trades, according to the United Nations. [12]

In October 2000, the U.S. government zeroed in on the problem, enacting the Trafficking Victims Protection Act (TVPA), which targets the illegal trade both at home and abroad. [13] The law established the State Department's Office to Monitor and Combat Trafficking in Persons, which issues an annual report on what countries are doing to end trafficking.

The report uses a three-tiered system to rank countries — from states that actively fight trafficking (Tier 1) to those doing little (Tier 3). Countries classified as Tier 3 for three years in a row are subject to a cut-off of non-humanitarian U.S. aid. (*See sidebar, p. 284.*)

On the domestic side, the law allows U.S. authorities to charge alleged traffickers in the United States under the tough federal anti-racketeering law (RICO). According to the State Depart-

ment, 111 persons have been charged with trafficking in the first three years since the law was enacted, a threefold increase over the three-year period before the TVPA went into effect. [14]

The law also makes it easier for trafficked victims to acquire refugee status in the United States and allows them to sue their victimizers for damages in civil court.

President Bill Clinton signed the bill into law on Oct. 28, 2000, saying it would provide "important new tools and resources to combat the worldwide scourge of trafficking."

Today, however, critics argue that while the act is "a step in the right direction," it is ultimately not tough enough to shake up the industry, especially internationally. "Of course, it's good that we have it, but frankly we have an awfully long way to go," says the Polaris Project's Chon.

She especially criticizes provisions requiring countries to fight trafficking or face American penalties. "It's just not strong enough because it allows countries to avoid sanctions with just superficial acts," she says.

For example, she says, Japan responded to U.S. pressure to curtail sex trafficking by "giving Cambodia a few million dollars in anti-trafficking aid and holding a symposium on trafficking." But the Japanese did "not really do anything to substantially crack down on their own widespread problem."

Yet, she adds, the United States has said Japan has been tackling trafficking enough to avoid a Tier 3 classification and the prospect of sanctions. "Japan is an important ally," she says. "Need I say more?"

Other critics allege that certain countries are treated with "kid gloves" for political reasons. "States like Saudi Arabia and countries from the former Soviet Union, which are important American allies, have been pushed up to Tier 2 because stopping slavery isn't the priority [in U.S. foreign relations] it should be," says Calvert of the AASG.

Calvert is especially incensed that the government failed to classify Mauritania, on Africa's northwestern coast, in Tier 3, calling it instead a "special case" because of insufficient information to make an accurate determination. "This is a country with literally hundreds of thousands of people in chattel slavery and everyone knows it, and yet it gets a pass," he says. "That is just unbelievable to me."

But supporters contend that the TVPA, while not perfect, helps move problem countries in the right direction. "It's important to have a tool we can use to push foreign governments to act against this terrible abuse of human dignity, and this law does that," says Beher, of the United Methodist Committee On Relief.

In Japan, for instance, the law has helped make the fight against trafficking more effective, raising public awareness of the problem dramatically as a result of the debate over its ranking in the TVPA, supporters add.

"When Japan was dropped from Tier 1 to Tier 2, it was very embarrassing for them, and all of a sudden you saw this real public debate about the trafficking issue — which is a huge problem there," says Diana Pinata, a spokeswoman for Vital Voices, a global woman's advocacy group in Washington. "If nothing else, the [annual State Department trafficking] report and the threat of sanctions keeps the issue in the spotlight in these countries, and that's very positive."

Besides Japan, several other countries, including Russia, Saudi Arabia and Indonesia, have dramatically improved their anti-trafficking efforts as a result

Rescuers return 14 children to their native Bangladesh after they were abducted to India. Children in poor countries sometimes are sold by their parents or kidnapped by traffickers and forced to work without pay, frequently in hazardous conditions.

AFP Photo

of pressure brought to bear by the TVPA, says John Miller, director of the Office to Combat Trafficking. "We've seen real efforts all over the world," he says. "Some have been more substantial than others, but there already has been a lot of progress."

Moreover, Miller rejects the charge of political favoritism. "Look at the Tier 3 list, and you'll see that there are U.S. allies like Greece and Turkey there," he says. "These decisions aren't being made on the basis of politics."

Pinata agrees. "When we speak to NGO workers and others in the field working on this issue, we get the sense that the trafficking report's assessment of these countries is essentially correct," she says.

Should most forms of child labor be eliminated?

Zara Cigay, 12, and her two younger brothers don't go to school. Instead, they help their parents and extended family, migrant farm workers who pick cotton and other crops in southern Turkey.

"Wherever there is a job, we do it," said Huseyin Cigay, Zara's great-uncle. "The children work with us everywhere." [15]

More than 250 million children around the world between the ages of 5 and 17 are working, according to the ILO. Most are in developing countries in Africa and Asia, and nearly half work full time like Zara and her brothers. [16]

Many do strenuous farm labor. In cities, they do everything from retailing and domestic service to manufacturing and construction. In nations beset by civil wars, thousands of children have been forced to fight in rebel armies. [17]

A large portion of child labor is coerced, according to child-welfare experts. Children are often sold by their parents or kidnapped and forced to work virtually as slaves for no pay. In India, children are literally tied to weaving looms so that they cannot run away.

Labor experts uniformly condemn forced and bonded labor. But on the question of child labor in general, the experts are split over whether the practice should be condoned under certain circumstances.

Human rights advocates and others point to the ILO's 1999 Worst Forms of Child Labor Convention, which prohibits all full-time work and any work by children under 12 but sanctions part-time, non-hazardous labor for teenagers that does not interfere with their social development. [18]

"Under international law, children have a right to a basic education," says Karin Landgren, chief of child protection at the United Nations Children's Fund (UNICEF). "Work should never interfere with this."

In addition, Landgren says, "They need to have time to play and participate freely in their country's cultural and social life. This is vitally important if they are to develop into healthy adults."

A recent ILO report says that child labor negatively impacts all levels of society. "Child labor perpetuates poverty, because when children don't have an education and a real chance to develop to their fullest potential, they are mortgaging their future," says Frans Roselaers, director of the organization's international program on the elimination of child labor and author of the report.

Child labor also costs societies economically by producing uneducated adult workers, Roselaers says. "Countries with a lot of child workers are stunting their economic growth," he says, "because they will only end up producing an army of weak and tired workers with no skills."

But some economists counter that child labor, even full-time work, is often a necessity in developing countries. "In an ideal world, children would spend all of their time at school and at play, but poor people in poor countries don't have the kind of options that we in rich countries do," says Ian Vasquez, director of the Project on Global Economic Liberty at the Cato Institute, a libertarian think tank. "When you begin to restrict children's options for work, you can end up hurting children and their families."

Indeed, child labor often is the only thing that stands between survival and starvation, some experts say. "No parents want their child to work, but child labor helps families get by," says Deepak Lal, a professor of international-development studies at the University of California, Los Angeles. "When a country's per capita income rises to about $3,000 or $4,000, child labor usually fades away."

In addition, Lal says, working children often end up with a better education than those who don't work. "The public education system is a fail-

ure in many parts of the developing world and really doesn't offer much to the children who attend school," he says. "But if a child works and his family earns enough to send him or his siblings to private school, that can really pay off."

Finally, Vasquez argues that outlawing child labor would only drive the problem underground, where there is no government oversight, and abuses would increase. "In Bangladesh, girls were prevented from continuing to work in textile plants, so many ended up as prostitutes," he says. "People need to make money, and if you deny them one route, they'll take another."

But Roselaers counters that child workers would not be driven to more dangerous and demeaning jobs if the international community eased the transition from work to school. In the case of Bangladesh, he says, the threat of a consumer boycott by Western countries prompted textile factory owners to fire their child employees.

"The factory owners panicked and fired the kids, and so, yes, there were problems," he says. "But when groups like the ILO and UNICEF came in, we started offering the parents stipends to make up for the lost income and easing the children's transition from work to school."

Some 1 million children are now being helped to make the transition from work to school, according to a recent ILO report. [19] In India, for instance, the ILO and the U.S. Department of Labor are spending $40 million this year to target 80,000 children working in hazardous jobs. [20]

Nonetheless, Lal says, such a program could only make a small dent in the problem. "You can't give a stipend to each of the many millions of families that send their children to work," he says. "There isn't enough money to do this, so it's not a realistic solution, just a palliative that make Westerners feel good about themselves." ∎

BACKGROUND

Ancient Practice

Slavery is as old as human civilization. All of the world's great founding cultures, including those in Mesopotamia, China, Egypt and India, accepted slavery as a fact of life. [21] The practice also was common in sub-Saharan Africa and the Americas.

Neither the Bible nor the great thinkers of Greece and Rome took firm positions against slavery. Some, like the Greek philosopher Aristotle, vigorously defended it.

It was not until Enlightenment philosophers like John Locke and Voltaire established new definitions of human freedom and dignity in the 17th and 18th centuries, that large numbers of people started questioning the morality of keeping another person in bondage.

Ancient societies typically acquired slaves from outside their borders, usually through war or territorial conquest. Captives and conquered people often served as agricultural workers or domestic servants.

Slavery probably reached its zenith in ancient Greece and then Rome, where human trafficking became a huge and profitable industry. In many Greek cities, including powerful Athens and Sparta, as many as half the residents were slaves. In Rome, slavery was so widespread that even common people could afford to have one or two. [22]

Slaves in the ancient world often did more than just menial tasks. Some, especially in the Roman Empire, became physicians and poets. Others achieved great influence, managing estates or assisting powerful generals or politicians.

Continued on p. 284

Chronology

19th Century
After thousands of years, slavery is abolished in much of the world.

1821
Congress enacts the Missouri Compromise, specifying which new U.S. states will allow slavery.

1833
England outlaws slavery throughout its empire.

1839
The world's first international abolitionist group, Anti-slavery International, is founded in England.

1848
Slavery abolished in French colonies.

1863
President Abraham Lincoln issues Emancipation Proclamation.

December 1865
The 13th Amendment abolishes slavery.

1873
Spain ends slavery in Puerto Rico.

1888
Brazil outlaws slavery.

1900-1990
International treaties to halt slavery are adopted.

1919
International Labour Organization (ILO) is founded.

1926
League of Nations outlaws slavery.

1945
United Nations is founded.

1946
U.N. Children's Fund is established.

1948
U.N.'s Universal Declaration of Human Rights prohibits slavery.

1951
International Organization for Migration is founded to help migrants.

1956
Supplementary Convention on the Abolition of Slavery, the Slave Trade, and Institutions and Practices Similar to Slavery outlaws debt bondage, serfdom and other forced-labor practices.

1978
Human Rights Watch is founded.

1983
Sudan's civil war begins, pitting the Muslim north against the Christian and animist south, leading to slave raids in the south.

1990s
The end of the Cold War and other geopolitical changes allow trafficking and slavery to expand.

1991
Collapse of the Soviet Union leads to a dramatic rise in trafficking in Eastern Europe.

1994
American Anti-Slavery Group is founded.

1995
Christian and non-governmental organizations begin redeeming slaves in Sudan.

June 1, 1999
ILO adopts the Worst Forms of Child Labor Convention.

2000-Present
United States and other countries renew efforts to fight slavery and trafficking.

March 2000
Free the Slaves is founded.

Oct. 28, 2000
President Bill Clinton signs the Trafficking Victims Protection Act.

Nov. 15, 2000
United Nations approves the Protocol to Prevent, Suppress and Punish the Trafficking in Persons.

Feb. 14, 2002
Polaris Project is founded to fight trafficking.

June 10, 2002
State Department's Office to Monitor and Combat Trafficking releases its first "Trafficking in Persons Report."

March 11, 2003
Brazilian President Luiz Inacio Lula da Silva unveils anti-slavery initiative.

Sept. 19, 2003
President Bush signs Trafficking Victims Protection Act Reauthorization.

Sept. 23, 2003
President Bush delivers a major anti-trafficking address at the U.N. General Assembly.

January 2004
U.N. launches year-long commemoration of anti-slavery movement.

Summer 2004
State Department's Fourth Annual "Trafficking in Persons Report" to be released.

Fighting Trafficking in the United States

Seven men were sent to prison on Jan. 29, 2004, for holding several Latin American women against their will in South Texas, forcing them to work without pay and raping them repeatedly.

The case was the latest in a series of sex-trafficking cases prosecuted under the Trafficking Victims Protection Act (TVPA) of 2000, which established stiff penalties for human trafficking and provided mandatory restitution to victims. [1] In the last three years, the Justice Department has prosecuted 132 traffickers — three times the number charged in the three years before the law was enacted. [2]

Last year, Congress updated the law to make trafficking a racketeering offense and allow victims to sue their captors in U.S. courts.

"While we have made much progress in combating human trafficking . . . we have not yet eradicated modern-day slavery," reauthorization sponsor Rep. Christopher H. Smith, R-N.J., said during consideration of the bill by the House International Relations Committee on July 23, 2003.

The Central Intelligence Agency estimates that between 18,000 and 20,000 people are trafficked into the United States each year. [3] Many are women — kidnapped or lured here with promises of marriage or work as nannies, models, waitresses, factory workers and exotic dancers. Once they arrive, they are stripped of their passports and forced to work as sex slaves, laborers or domestic servants until their smuggling or travel "debts" are repaid. The average victim is 20 years old. [4]

"They tell them they'll make a lot of money, they'll be free, they'll have a beautiful life," says Marisa B. Ugarte, executive director of the Bilateral Safety Corridor Coalition, a San Diego organization that assists trafficking victims in Mexico and the United States. "But once they are here, everything changes."

Prior to passage of the TVPA, many of the victims were treated as criminals and subject to deportation. Today, they can apply to the Bureau of Citizen and Immigration Services for one of 5,000 "T" nonimmigrant visas available each year. The visas allow them to remain in the United States if they are assisting in the investigation or prosecution of traffickers. They may then apply for permanent residency if their removal would cause severe hardship. [5]

The Department of Homeland Security had received 721 T-status applications as of June 30, 2003: 301 were granted, 30 were denied and 390 are pending. [6]

Mohamed Mattar, co-director of the Protection Project, a human-rights research institute at Johns Hopkins University, said the visa program has been stymied by victims' reluctance to go to law enforcement authorities for help.

This fear is fed by the fact that many police officers remain unaware of the TVPA and are more likely to arrest the victims than the perpetrators, says Donna M. Hughes, an authority on sex trafficking at the University of Rhode Island.

"We need to start treating [Johns] like the perpetrators they are, and not like lonely guys," Hughes adds. "We need a renewal of ideas at the state and local level."

Under the TVPA, alien trafficking victims who do come forward can receive federal benefits normally available to refugees.

Historically, most trafficked victims have come from Latin America and Southeast Asia, smuggled across the porous Mexican border by "coyotes" or escorted by "jockeys" pretending to be a boyfriend or cousin. [7] Since the early 1990s, however, there has been an influx of women from the former Soviet Union and Central and Eastern Europe, where trafficking rings recruit women with newspaper ads and billboards beckoning them to prosperous futures in the United States.

Undocumented migrant workers are also vulnerable to traffickers. On March 2, 2004, a federal district judge sentenced Flori-

---

Continued from p. 282

Great Roman thinkers like Pliny the Younger and Cicero urged masters to treat their slaves with kindness and even to let them "share your conversations, your deliberations and your company," Cicero wrote. [23] Perhaps as a result, manumission, or the freeing of slaves by their masters, was commonplace, usually after many years of service.

Ultimately, however, Roman slavery was maintained by cruelty and violence, including the use of severe flogging and even crucifixion. Slave revolts, common in the first and second centuries B.C., were brutally suppressed.

The collapse of the western half of the Roman Empire in the 5th-century A.D. led to a new, more fragmented, power structure in Western Europe often centered around local warlords (knights) and the Catholic Church. The new order did not eliminate slavery, but in many areas slaves became serfs, or peasants tied to the local lord's land and could not leave without his permission. [24]

In the East, meanwhile, a new force — Islam — was on the rise. For the Arabs who swept into the Mediterranean basin and the Near East beginning in the 7th century, traditional slavery was a way of life, just as it

had been for the Romans. In the ensuing centuries, the Arabs brought millions of sub-Saharan Africans, Asians and Europeans to the slave markets for sale throughout the Middle East.

Meanwhile, slavery remained commonplace elsewhere. In North America, Indians along the Eastern seaboard and in the Pacific Northwest often enslaved members of other tribes taken in war. The more advanced indigenous civilizations to the south, like the Aztec and Mayans in what is now Mexico, and the Inca of Peru, also relied upon slaves. And on the Indian subcontinent, the strict Hindu caste system held tens of millions in virtual bondage.

da labor contractor Ramiro Ramos to 15 years in prison for holding migrant workers in servitude and forcing them to work in citrus groves until they had paid off their transportation debts. [8]

In some instances, diplomats and international civil servants bring domestic workers — often illiterate women from Africa, Asia and Latin America — into the United States legally, but then force them to work long hours for almost no pay. In one case, an Ethiopian maid for an International Monetary Fund staffer says she worked eight years for seven days a week, 15 hours a day for less than 3 cents an hour. [9]

Although the employer claimed the maid was his guest, he disappeared before a lawsuit filed by the maid, Yeshehareg Teferra, could be prosecuted. "I was not their guest," Teferra told a reporter. "I was their slave." [10]

Foreign diplomats bring 3,800 domestic servants into the United States each year under special temporary work visas, which allow them only to work for the employer who sponsored them. The employer promises to abide by U.S. labor laws, but there is almost no oversight of the program, so the abuse of servants remains under law enforcement's radar screen, human rights advocates say. [11]

But foreign nationals are not the only victims of domestic trafficking. Homeless and runaway American children also are preyed upon by pimps, who troll malls and clubs in search of teenagers they can "turn." Typically, the pimps befriend the girls, ply them with drugs and then use their addiction to turn them into prostitutes. [12]

There are between 100,000 and 300,000 such citizen victims in the United States, though they're more often overlooked by police, says Derek Ellerman, co-founder of the Polaris Project, a grass-roots anti-trafficking organization. "There is a glaring bias in enforcement" of the Mann Act, which bans the transport of children and adults across state lines for prostitution, Ellerman says. "U.S. kids who are being targeted [by traffickers] just are not being protected."

For the traffickers — many of them members of gangs or loosely linked criminal networks — trafficking is much more lucrative than smuggling contraband items, because human slaves can provide a source of long-term income through prostitution and forced labor. "There's a market for cheap labor, and there's a market for cheap sex, and traffickers know they can make money in it," Michele Clark, co-director of the Protection Project, says.

— Kelly Field

[1] Department of Justice press release, Jan. 29, 2004.

[2] Department of Justice press release, March 2, 2004.

[3] Department of Justice, "Assessment of U.S. Activities to Combat Trafficking in Persons," August 2003, p. 3.

[4] Amy O'Neill Richard, "International Trafficking in Women to the United States: A Contemporary Manifestation of Slavery and Organized Crime," DCI Exceptional Intelligence Analyst Program, pp. 3-5.

[5] John R. Miller, "The United States' Effort to Combat Trafficking in Persons," *International Information Program Electronic Journal*, U.S. State Department, June 2003.

[6] Department of Justice, *op. cit.*, August 2003, p. 9.

[7] Peter Landesman, "The Girls Next Door," *The New York Times Magazine*, Jan. 25, 2004.

[8] Justice Department, *op. cit.*, March 2, 2004.

[9] William Branigin, "A Life of Exhaustion, Beatings, and Isolation," *The Washington Post*, Jan. 5, 1999, p. A6.

[10] Quoted in *ibid*.

[11] Richard, *op. cit.*, p. 28,

[12] Janice G. Raymond and Donna M. Hughes, "Sex Trafficking of Women in the United States, International and Domestic Trends," Coalition Against Trafficking in Women, March 2001, p. 52.

Slavery Goes Global

In the 15th century, European explorers and adventurers sailing to new territories in Asia, Africa and the Americas began a new chapter in the history of slavery.

By 1650, the Dutch, Spanish, Portuguese, French and English had established colonies throughout the world. The new territories, especially in the Americas, produced new crops such as sugar and tobacco, as well as gold and other minerals. Initially, enslaved indigenous peoples did the harvesting and mining in South America. But ill treatment and disease quickly decimated native populations, prompting the importation of slaves from Africa.

From the mid-1500s to the mid-1800s, almost 9 million Africans were shipped mostly to Latin America — particularly to today's Brazil, Haiti and Cuba — under the most inhumane conditions. About 5 percent — about 400,000 — of all the African slaves ended up in the United States. [25]

On the sugar plantations of the West Indies and South America, crushing work and brutal punishment were the norm. Although Spain and Portugal had relatively liberal laws concerning the treatment of slaves — they could marry, sue a cruel owner and even buy their freedom — they were rarely enforced.

In the British colonies and later in the United States, slaves enjoyed somewhat better working conditions and medical care. Nonetheless, life was harsh and in some ways more difficult. Since slaves in Latin America and the Caribbean usually outnumbered Europeans, they were able to retain more of their African customs. In British America, where by 1750 whites outnumbered slaves by more than four to one, Africans quickly lost many of their cultural underpinnings.

Most American slavery was tied to the great Southern plantations that grew

Nearly 200 Million Young Kids Must Work

Nearly a fifth of the world's young children have to work, including 110 million in Asia and fully a quarter of all the children in sub-Saharan Africa.

Working Children, Ages 5 to 14, By Region
(in millions)

Region	Total Working	Percentage of children in region
Asia	110.4	18.7%
Latin America	16.5	17.0
North Africa, Middle East	9.0	10.2
Sub-Saharan Africa	37.9	25.3
Transitional countries*	8.3	14.6
Total	182.1	18.5%

* Transitional countries — such as Taiwan, Singapore and Malaysia — are no longer considered "developing" but not yet classified as fully industrialized.

Source: "Investing in Every Child," International Programme on the Elimination of Child Labour, International Labour Office, December 2003

tobacco, rice and other cash crops. Although slavery also was practiced in Northern states, it was never as widespread and had been largely abolished by 1800.

By the late 18th century, Southern slavery also appeared headed for extinction, as industrialization and other trends took hold, rendering the plantation system increasingly economically unfeasible. But Eli Whitney's invention of the cotton gin in 1793 gave American slavery a new lease on life. The gin made the labor-intensive process of separating the seeds from the cotton easy, enabling slaves to dramatically increase their output. [26]

Meanwhile, the rise of textile mills in England and elsewhere was creating a new demand for the fluffy, white fiber. By the early 19th century, many Southern plantations that had been unprofitably growing other crops were now making plenty of money using slaves to pick and process cotton.

Around the same time, however, a movement to abolish slavery began to gather steam in the Northern states. For decades, Americans had debated the morality of slavery. During deliberations over independence in 1776, many delegates to the Second Continental Congress — including John Adams, Benjamin Franklin and Virginia slaveholder Thomas Jefferson — had pushed to make the elimination of slavery part of the movement for America's independence. But resistance from the South and the need for colonial unity against the British doomed the proposal.

The debate over slavery, however, did not go away. The issue complicated the new country's efforts to form its governing institutions and to expand westward, forcing increasingly abolitionist Northerners and slaveholding Southerners to craft tortured compromises to keep the nation together.

In 1789, delegates to the Constitutional Convention hammered out the infamous Three-fifths Compromise, permitting each slave to be counted as three-fifths of a person for purposes of apportioning the number of representatives each state had in the new Congress. [27] And in 1821, Congress passed the Missouri Compromise, drawing a line westward along the 36.30 parallel. The new Western states above the line would be admitted to the Union as "free" states, while those below the boundary would be so-called slave states.

Outlawing Slavery

Much of the rest of the world, however, was abolishing slavery. In the early 1800s, many of the newly independent nations of Spanish America won their independence and immediately outlawed human bondage. Simón Bolívar, who liberated much of Latin America, was a staunch abolitionist, calling slavery "the daughter of darkness." [28]

In Europe, the tide also was turning. Largely due to the efforts of abolitionist William Wilberforce, the British Empire outlawed the practice in 1833, although de facto slavery continued in India and some other colonies. In 1848, France also freed the slaves in its colonies.

However, in the United States, peaceful efforts at compromise over slavery failed, and the issue finally helped trigger the Civil War in 1861. In 1863, during the height of the conflict, President Abraham Lincoln issued the "Emancipation Proclamation," freeing all slaves in the Southern, or Confederate, states. Soon after the war ended with Union victory in 1865, the 13th Amendment to the Constitution abolished slavery altogether. [29]

After the Civil War, the worldwide abolition of slavery continued. Spain outlawed the practice in Puerto Rico in 1873 and in Cuba in 1886. More important, Brazil began dismantling its huge slave infrastructure in 1888.

Today, slavery is illegal in every country in the world and is outlawed by several treaties. "In international law, the outlawing of slavery has become what is called *jus cogens*, which means that it's completely accepted and doesn't need to be written into new treaties and conventions," says Bales of Free the Slaves.

The foundation of this complete acceptance rests on several groundbreaking international agreements, beginning with the 1926 Slavery Convention of the League of Nations, which required signatory countries to work to abolish every aspect of the practice. [30]

Slavery also is banned by the 1948 Universal Declaration of Human Rights, which holds that "no one shall be held in slavery or servitude; slavery and the slave trade shall be prohibited in all their forms." [31]

Other conventions prohibiting the practice include the 1930 ILO Convention on Forced Labor and a 1956 Supplementary Convention on the Abolition of Slavery, the Slave Trade, and Institutions and Practices Similar to Slavery.

More recently, the United Nations in 2001 approved a Protocol to Prevent, Suppress and Punish the Trafficking in Persons as part of a major convention on fighting organized crime. The protocol requires signatories to take action to fight trafficking and protect its victims. It has been signed by 117 countries and ratified by 45. [32] While the United States has not yet ratified the document, it has the support of the White House and is expected to win Senate approval in the near future. ■

Six-year-old Ratan Das breaks rocks at a construction site in Agartala, India, where he earns about 40 cents a day to supplement his widowed mother's 60-cents-per-day income. India has more child laborers than any other country — about 120 million — followed by Pakistan, Bangladesh, Indonesia and Brazil.

AFP Photo

CURRENT SITUATION

Human Trafficking

The poorest and most chaotic parts of the developing world supply most trafficking victims — often women and children destined for the sex trade.

In South Asia, young women and children routinely are abducted or lured from Nepal, Pakistan, India, Bangladesh, Cambodia and Myanmar (Burma) to work in brothels in India's large cities, notably Bombay, and the Persian Gulf states. Thousands also end up in Bangkok, Thailand's capital and an infamous sex-tourism mecca.

In Asia, the victims' own families often sell them to traffickers. "In Nepal, entire villages have been emptied of girls,"

says Pinata of Vital Voices. "Obviously, this could not have happened without the complicity between traffickers and the victims' families."

Parents sell their children for a variety of reasons — virtually all linked to poverty, Pinata says. "Some think the child will have a better life or that their daughter will be able to send money home," she says. "For some, it's just one less mouth to feed."

"Even when they have a sense of what their children will be doing, many parents feel they don't have a choice," adds UNICEF's Landgren. "They feel that literally anything is better than what they have now."

In Eastern Europe, traffickers often lure women into bondage by advertising in local newspapers for nanny positions in the United States or Western Europe. For instance, Tetiana, a Ukrainian woman, was offered 10 times her salary to be an au pair in Italy. Instead she was forced into prostitution in Istanbul, Turkey. [33]

Others are promised work as models or actresses. In some cases, the victims even put up their own money for their travel expenses, only to find themselves prisoners in a European brothel or in Mexico, awaiting transport across the border to the United States. [34]

Even those who understand at the outset that they are going to be prostitutes are not prepared for the brutality they face. "They're unaware of how much abuse, rape, psychological manipulation and coercion is involved," says the Polaris Project's Chon.

Eastern Europe is particularly fertile ground for sex traffickers, she says. The collapse of communism more than a decade ago has left many parts of the region, especially Ukraine, Moldova and Belarus, economically and politically stunted. "These countries are just full of desperate people who will do anything for a chance at a better life," she says.

To make matters worse, brothel owners prize the region's many light-skinned, blonde women. "Lighter women are very popular in places like the United States, Europe and Asia," Chon says. "So these women are in demand."

In Africa, more people are trafficked for forced labor than as sex slaves. "In Africa, you have a lot of people being taken and sent to pick cotton and cocoa and other forms of agricultural labor," says Vital Voices' Pinata.

Regardless of their origin, once victims are lured into a trafficking ring, they quickly lose control over their destiny. "If they have a passport, it's usually taken from them and they're abused, physically and psychologically, in order to make them easier to control," says the United Methodist Committee On Relief's Beher.

When victims of trafficking reach their final destination, they rarely have freedom of any kind. "A 16-year-old girl who had been trafficked into Kosovo to be a prostitute told me that when she wasn't working in the bar, she was literally locked into her room and not allowed out," Beher says. "That's the sort of thing we see all the time."

Organized crime plays a key role in most human trafficking. "Most of what you are dealing with here is criminal networks," says Miller of the Office to Combat Trafficking. "You can't

take someone out of the Czech Republic and drive her to the Netherlands and hand her over to another trafficker and then to a brothel without real cooperation."

Indeed, smuggling rings often team up with criminal groups in other countries or maintain "branch offices" there. And most traffickers are involved in other criminal activities, such as drugs and weapons smuggling. "Many drug gangs in Southeast Asia are spin-

A 16-year-old Cambodian girl rescued from a brothel peers from her hiding place in Phnom Penh. An estimated 300,000 women are trapped in slave-like conditions in the Southeast Asian sex trade. Cambodia recently agreed to join the first U.N. program aimed at halting the trafficking of women in the region.

ning off into trafficking because it's very low risk and very lucrative," says the Women's Commission's Young, who adds that unlike a shipment of drugs, human cargo can earn traffickers money for years.

These crime networks, especially in Eastern Europe and Asia, operate freely, in large part because they have corrupted many local officials. "So many people are being moved across borders that it's impossible to believe that government officials aren't cooperating," Young says. "Like drugs and

other illegal activities, this is very corrupting, especially in poor countries where the police are poorly paid."

In addition to stepping up law enforcement, countries can do many things to fight trafficking, UNICEF's Landgren says. "For example, the United Kingdom has a new system that keeps tabs on children entering the country," she says. "By keeping track of children that come in from abroad, we can better protect them."

And in Brazil, where landowners often lure peasants to their farms with promises of work only to put them in debt bondage, President Luiz Ignacio Lula da Silva has stepped up efforts to free forced laborers. Lula, as the president is called, also has called for a change in the constitution to allow the confiscation of land for those convicted of enslaving workers.

Even countries that have long allowed trafficking are beginning to address the issue. Moldova, for instance, has begun prosecuting traffickers and has created a database of employment agencies that help people find legitimate work abroad. [35]

NGOs have also taken steps to help. For instance, some groups run safe houses where trafficking victims who escape can find shelter and security. "We provide them with medical and psychological care," says Beher, whose group operates a house in Kosovo's capital, Pristina. "We allow them to stay until they recover and then help them to get home, which is usually somewhere else in Eastern Europe, like Romania or Moldova."

Continued on p. 290

At Issue:

Is the Trafficking Victims Protection Act tough enough?

REP. CHRISTOPHER H. SMITH, R-N.J.
CHAIRMAN, U.S. HELSINKI COMMISSION

WRITTEN FOR *THE CQ RESEARCHER*, MARCH 15, 2004

*e*ach year, nearly a million people worldwide are bought and sold into the commercial sex industry, sweatshops, domestic servitude and other dehumanizing situations.

In October 2000, President Clinton signed into law the Trafficking Victims Protection Act (TVPA), which I authored. It provided a multifaceted approach to halting human trafficking through law enforcement, prevention and aid to victims. It also represented two major policy changes: up to life in prison for those who traffic in humans and treatment of the people trafficked — largely women, children, and teenagers — as victims rather than as criminals. In 2003, the law was expanded and strengthened.

As President Bush noted in his historic speech at the United Nations in September 2003, the global community must do more to eradicate human slavery. But significant progress has been made in just a few years, thanks largely to the law's three-tier system and annual "Trafficking in Persons Report" mandated by the law.

When the first report came out, the State Department listed 23 nations in Tier 3 as the worst offenders. It pulled no punches and did not hesitate to name offending nations, including our allies, if they were not making "serious and sustained" efforts to fight trafficking. Naming names was a measure I fought hard to include in the law, even though it was initially opposed by the previous administration.

Thanks to the report and the threat of sanctions, most nations have improved their record on trafficking. Only 15 countries were in Tier 3 during the most recent 2003 report, and most of them made enough progress in the ensuing months to avoid economic sanctions. The State Department is continually improving the scope of the report so it will present the most accurate and thorough picture of the worldwide trafficking problem.

The message from the United States is loud and clear: If you are committed to the fight against human slavery, we welcome you as an ally. But if you continue to look askance when it comes to this horrible crime and pretend you don't have a trafficking problem, we're going to aggressively push you to make reforms, and we'll use economic sanctions as a means to that end.

TOMMY CALVERT, JR.
CHIEF OF EXTERNAL OPERATIONS,
AMERICAN ANTI-SLAVERY GROUP

WRITTEN FOR *THE CQ RESEARCHER*, MARCH 15, 2004

*m*ost anti-slavery experts would agree the TVPA is a good law, but that slavery can be defeated in our lifetime only if we give the law priority in attention and funding — and apply it equally to friends and foes alike.

The "Trafficking in Person's Report" (TIPS) required by the law does not reveal the full story on global slavery, but only a snapshot. The criteria used to determine progress in the fight against slavery — by focusing on government action rather than on total slavery within a nation's borders — skew our view of realities on the ground.

South Korea, for example, has a serious problem with trafficking — an estimated 15,000 people trafficked per year — but it is ranked in Tier 1, the best ranking a government can receive. Nations can create many seemingly tough laws and programs to fight slavery. However, organized crime may still run thriving trafficking operations in the face of such policies, which may in reality be weak or ineffectual.

Last year marked the first time that countries designated by the "Trafficking In Persons Report" as the worst offenders — Tier 3 — would automatically be subject to U.S. sanctions, which can only be waived by the president.

The State Department gave wide latitude to the standards for Tier 2, perhaps to keep strategic allies from being hit with sanctions. Both Brazil and Saudi Arabia, for instance, received Tier 2 designations. But Brazil's president has launched one of the world's most ambitious plans to end slavery, while Saudi Arabia has no laws outlawing human trafficking and has prosecuted no offenders. Thus, the report's rankings equate a major national initiative to end slavery with royal lip service.

Some Middle Eastern and North African countries may have advanced in the rankings because they are being courted by the administration to support the war on terror and our plans for change in the region. But there is evidence these countries have not really progressed in the fight against human bondage.

The long-term effect of such discrepancies is to reduce the credibility of the report and lengthen the time it takes to eradicate slavery.

Continued from p. 288

The Polaris Project maintains three 24-hour hotlines (in English, Thai and Korean) in the United States to allow both victims and third parties to report trafficking activity. Polaris also has a trafficking database to help law enforcement and other officials gather information about potential cases.

But international organizations and NGOs can only do so much, says Beher, because impoverished, poorly governed countries will always be breeding grounds for trafficking. "Until the causes disappear, all we in the international aid community can do is fight the symptoms," she says.

"In order to really get rid of this problem," Beher continues, "you need political stability and a strong civil society, which in turn leads to the rule of law and stronger law enforcement. You know, there's a reason why there aren't a lot of Finnish people being trafficked."

But Calvert of the American Anti-Slavery Group says governments and international organizations could virtually shut down the trade in human beings if they wanted to. "The international community is in a state of denial and lacks the commitment to fight this," he says. "Look at Britain: They had whole fleets of ships devoted to stopping the slave trade on the high seas, and it worked."

Calvert says the United Nations and other international groups should be more aggressive and uncompromising in combating slavery. "They had weapons inspectors didn't they?" he asks. "Well that's what we need to fight this. We need that kind of action."

Pakistani Minister for Education Zobaida Jalal and Deputy Labor Under Secretary for International Labor Affairs Thomas Moorhead sign an agreement in Islamabad on Jan. 23, 2002, calling for the U.S. to provide $5 million to help educate working children in Pakistan.

Slavery and Forced Labor

Slavery today bears little resemblance to earlier forms of bondage. For instance, 150 years ago in the American South, a healthy slave was a valuable piece of property, worth up to $40,000 in today's dollars, according to Free the Slaves. [36] By contrast, slaves today are often worth less than $100, giving slaveholders little incentive to care for them.

Although slavery exists nearly everywhere, it is most prevalent in the poorer parts of South Asia, where an estimated 15 million to 20 million people are in bonded labor in India, Pakistan, Bangladesh and Nepal.

Bonded labor usually begins when someone borrows money from someone else and agrees to work for that person until the debt is paid. In most cases, the debt is never paid and the borrower and his immediate family become virtual slaves, working in exchange for basic amenities like food and shelter.

"Often you see a whole family in bondage for three or four generations because once someone borrows a small amount of money you're trapped," says Callahan of Free the Slaves. "You don't pay off the principal of the loan, you just keep paying off the interest."

Bonded laborers work at jobs ranging from making bricks in Pakistan to farming, cigarette rolling and carpet making in India. In the western Indian state of Gujarat, some 30,000 bonded families harvest salt in the marshes. The glare from the salt makes them color-blind. When they die, the laborers cannot even be cremated, according to Hindu custom, because their bodies have absorbed too much salt to burn properly. [37]

Slavery is also widespread in sub-Saharan Africa, where the Anti-Slavery Group estimates that at least 200,000 people are in bondage. Besides Sudan, the largest concentration of African slaves is in Mauritania. For hundreds of years, Mauritania's lighter-skinned ruling elite kept their darker compatriots in a system of chattel slavery, with generations being born into servitude. Although the country formally outlawed slavery in 1980, the practice is thought to still be widespread.

"For the thousands of slaves who were legally freed in 1980, life did not change at all," Bales writes. "No one bothered to tell the slaves about it. Some have never learned of their legal freedom, some did so years later, and for most legal freedom was never translated into actual freedom." Today, slaves are still "everywhere" in Mauritania "doing every job that is hard, onerous and dirty." [38]

Slaves also pick cotton in Egypt and Benin, harvest cocoa and other crops in Ivory Coast and mine diamonds in Sierra Leone.

In addition, hundreds of youngsters are abducted each year and forced to become soldiers for rebel fighters in war zones like Uganda and Congo.

Child soldiers often are made to do horrible things. A girl in Uganda who was kidnapped at 13 was forced to kill and abduct other children during her five years in captivity. [39]

But slavery also flourishes beyond the developing world. Although the problem is not as widespread, forced labor and servitude also occur in Europe and the United States — in brothels, farms and sweatshops. "It's amazing, but there are slaves in the United States doing all kinds of things," says Miller of the Office to Combat Trafficking. "Recently authorities found a group of Mexican [agricultural workers] who had been trafficked to work for no pay in Florida. It's unbelievable."

Moreover, slavery is not confined to just seedy brothels or plantations. In upscale American neighborhoods too, people, usually from other countries, have been enslaved, often as domestics. Last year, for instance, a suburban Maryland couple was convicted of forced labor for coercing an illegal alien from Ghana to work seven days a week as a domestic servant without pay. And from time to time, foreign diplomats are found to be harboring unpaid domestic workers from their home countries who cannot leave to work for someone else because the diplomats hold their visas. [40] ∎

OUTLOOK

Impact of Globalization

The increasing ease of travel and communication brought about by globalization has helped many industries, including illegal ones like trafficking and slavery.

"Globalization has certainly made trafficking and slavery easier, but it is a double-edged sword," says Jacobson of Christian Freedom International. "It has also helped us to more quickly and ef-

fectively shine a spotlight on the evil thugs who are doing these bad things."

Moreover, Jacobson says, as globalization improves the general standard of living in the developing world, it becomes harder for traffickers to prey on innocents. "When the boats are rising for everyone, poverty and despair are alleviated," he says. "When someone gets a job and education and health care, they are much less susceptible to being abused."

The Polaris Project's Chon is also optimistic, although for different reasons. "I'm very upbeat about all of this, because tackling these problems is a matter of political will, and I think the world is slowly beginning to pay more attention to these issues," she says. "I feel as though we're at the same point as the [American] abolitionist movement at the beginning of the 19th century, in that things are slowly beginning to move in the right direction."

Rep. Smith agrees. "There's a fever all over the world to enact new, tough policies to deal with this," he says. "Because the U.S. is out front on this, a lot of countries are beginning to follow suit."

Moreover, the optimists note, victims themselves are increasingly fighting for their rights. "There is a silent revolution going on right now, in places like India, where people are literally freeing themselves from slavery," says Callahan of Free the Slaves, referring to thousands of quarry slaves in northern India who recently have left their bondage and begun new lives. "If this kind of thing keeps up, in a few decades these problems will be blips on the radar screen compared to what they are today."

But Beher of the United Methodist Committee on Relief sees little change ahead because of continuing poverty and societal dysfunction. "The problems that lead to trafficking and slavery are very complicated, and there are no easy fixes," she says. "We need to build up the economies and the civil society of the places where these things happen in order to get rid of this once and for all. And I'm afraid that that is going to take many decades."

Indeed, "Things could get a lot worse before they get better," warns Young of the Women's Commission for Refugee Women and Children, comparing trafficking to the drug trade.

"It's so profitable, and there is so little risk in getting caught that it seems like there will be plenty of this kind of thing going on for the foreseeable future." ∎

Notes

[1] See www.freetheslaves.net/slavery_today/index.html.

[2] Figure cited in "2003 Trafficking in Persons Report," U.S. Department of State, p. 7.

[3] Frank Trejo, "Event Underscores Scope, Toll of Human Trafficking," *Dallas Morning News*, March 4, 2003, p. 3B.

[4] Richard Mertens, "Smuggler's Prey: Poor Women of Eastern Europe," *The Christian Science Monitor*, Sept. 22, 2002, p. A7.

[5] Quoted in *ibid*.

[6] "Trafficking in Persons Report," *op. cit.*, p. 6.

[7] The entire text of President Bush's speech can be found at www.whitehouse.gov/news/releases/2003/09/20030923-4.html.

About the Author

David Masci specializes in science, religion and foreign-policy issues. Before joining *The CQ Researcher* in 1996, he was a reporter at Congressional Quarterly's *Daily Monitor* and *CQ Weekly*. He holds a law degree from The George Washington University and a B.A. in medieval history from Syracuse University. His recent reports include "Rebuilding Iraq" and "Torture."

8 "IPEC Action Against Child Labour: 2002-2003," International Labour Organization, January 2004, p. 15; see also ILO, "Investing in Every Child," December 2003, p. 32.

9 Figure cited in Davan Maharaj, "Panel Frowns on Efforts to Buy Sudan Slaves' Freedom," *Los Angeles Times*, May 28, 2002, p. A3.

10 Quoted from "60 Minutes II," May 15, 2002.

11 Nicholas D. Kristof, "Bargaining For Freedom," *The New York Times*, Jan 21, 2004, p. A27.

12 Figure cited at "UNICEF Oral Report on the Global Challenge of Child Trafficking," January 2004, at: www.unicef.org/about/TraffickingOralreport.pdf.

13 Full text of the law is at: www.state.gov/documents/organization/10492.pdf. The law was reauthorized in December 2003.

14 Figures cited at www.state.gov/g/tip/rls/fs/28548.htm.

15 Richard Mertens, "In Turkey, Childhoods Vanish in Weary Harvests," *The Christian Science Monitor*, May 8, 2003, p. 7.

16 ILO, *op. cit.*

17 See Brian Hansen, "Children in Crisis," *The CQ Researcher*, Aug. 31, 2001, p. 657.

18 See: www.ilo.org/public/english/standards/ipec/ratify_govern.pdf.

19 ILO, *op. cit.*, January 2004, p. 37.

20 "With a Little U.S. Help, ILO Targets Child Labour," *Indian Express*, March 3, 2004.

21 Hugh Thomas, *World History: The Story of Mankind from Prehistory to the Present* (1996), pp. 54-55.

22 *Ibid.*, pp. 105-107.

23 Quoted in Michael Grant, *The World of Rome* (1960), p. 116.

24 Thomas, *op. cit.*, pp. 107-110.

25 Figures cited in *ibid.*, p. 279.

26 John Hope Franklin and Alfred A Moss, Jr., *From Slavery to Freedom: A History of African-Americans* (2000), p. 100.

27 *Ibid.*, p. 94.

28 From a speech before the Congress of Angostura in 1819. See http://www.fordham.edu/halsall/mod/1819bolivar.html.

29 Franklin and Moss, *op. cit.*, p. 244.

30 The full text of the convention can be found at www.unicri.it/1926%20slavery%20convention.pdf.

31 Quoted at www.un.org/Overview/rights.html.

32 A complete list of those countries that have signed and ratified the protocol are at www.unodc.org/unodc/en/crime_cicp_signatures_trafficking.html.

33 Sylvie Briand, "Sold into Slavery: Ukrainian Girls Tricked into Sex Trade," Agence

FOR MORE INFORMATION

American Anti-Slavery Group, 198 Tremont St., Suite 421, Boston, MA 02116; (800) 884-0719; www.iabolish.com.

Casa Alianza, 346 West 17th St., New York, N.Y.10011; (212) 727-4000; www.casa-alianza.org. A San Jose, Costa Rica, group that aids street children in Latin America.

Christian Children's Fund, 2821 Emerywood Parkway, Richmond, VA 23294; (800) 776-6767; www.christianchildrensfund.org. CCF works in 28 countries on critical children's issues.

Christian Freedom International, P.O. Box 535, Front Royal, VA 22630; (800) 323-CARE (2273); (540) 636-8907; www.christianfreedom.org. An interdenominational human rights organization that combines advocacy with humanitarian assistance for persecuted Christians.

Christian Solidarity International, Zelglistrasse 64, CH-8122 Binz, Zurich, Switzerland; www.csi-int.ch/index.html. Works to redeem slaves in Sudan.

Defence for Children International, P.O. Box 88, CH 1211, Geneva 20, Switzerland; (+41 22) 734-0558; www.defence-for-children.org. Investigates sexual exploitation of children and other abuses.

Free the Children, 1750 Steeles Ave. West, Suite 218, Concord, Ontario, Canada L4K 2L7; (905) 760-9382; www.freethechildren.org. This group encourages youth to help exploited children.

Free the Slaves, 1326 14th St., N.W., Washington, DC 20005; (202) 588-1865; www.freetheslaves.net.

Human Rights Watch, 350 Fifth Ave., New York, NY 10118; (212) 290-4700; www.hrw.org. Investigates abuses worldwide.

International Labour Organization, 4, route des Morillons, CH-1211, Geneva 22, Switzerland; www.ilo.org. Sets and enforces worldwide labor standards.

Polaris Project, P.O. Box 77892, Washington, DC 20013; (202) 547-7990; www.polarisproject.org. Grass-roots organization fighting trafficking.

United Methodist Committee On Relief, 475 Riverside Dr., New York, NY 10115; (800) 554-8583; gbgm-umc.org. Worldwide humanitarian group.

United Nations Children's Fund (UNICEF), 3 United Nations Plaza, New York, NY 10017; (212) 326-7000; www.unicef.org. Helps poor children in 160 countries.

Women's Commission on Refugee Women and Children, 122 East 42nd St., 12th Floor, New York, NY 10168-1289; (212) 551-3088; www.womenscommission.org. Aids trafficking victims in the developing world.

World Vision International, 800 West Chestnut Ave., Monrovia, Calif. 91016; (626) 303-8811; www.wvi.org. A Christian relief and development organization established in 1950.

France Presse, Jan. 28, 2004.

34 Peter Landesman, "The Girls Next Door, *The New York Times Magazine*, Jan. 25, 2004, p. 30.

35 "Trafficking in Person's Report," *op. cit.*, p. 107.

36 See www.freetheslaves.net/slavery_today/index.html.

37 Christopher Kremmer, "With a Handful of Salt," *The Boston Globe*, Nov. 28, 1999.

38 Kevin Bales, *Disposable People: The New Slavery in the Global Economy* (1999), p. 81.

39 Thomas Wagner, "Study Documents Trauma of Child Soldiers," Associated Press Online, March 11, 2004.

40 Ruben Castaneda, "Couple Enslaved Woman," *The Washington Post*, June 10, 2003, p. B1.

Bibliography
Selected Sources

Books

Bales, Kevin, *Disposable People: New Slavery in the Global Economy*, University of California Press, 1999.
  The president of Free the Slaves and a leading expert on slavery offers strategies to end the practice.

Bok, Francis, *Escape From Slavery: The True Story of My Ten Years In Captivity and My Journey to Freedom in America*, St. Martin's Press, 2003.
  A former slave in Sudan tells the gripping story of his ordeal and eventual journey to the United States.

Franklin, John Hope, and, Alfred Moss Jr., *From Slavery to Freedom: A History of African Americans*, McGraw-Hill, 2000.
  Franklin, a renowned professor emeritus of history at Duke University and Moss, an associate professor at the University of Maryland, discuss the slave trade and slavery in the United States up to the Civil War.

Articles

"A Cargo of Exploitable Souls," *The Economist*, June 1, 2002.
  The article examines human trafficking of prostitutes and forced laborers into the United States.

Bales, Kevin, "The Social Psychology of Modern Slavery," *Scientific American*, April 2002, p. 68.
  A leading expert on slavery examines the psychological underpinnings that may drive both traffickers and slaveholders as well as their victims.

Cockburn, Andrew, "Hidden in Plain Sight: The World's 27 Million Slaves," *National Geographic*, Sept. 2003, p. 2.
  A correspondent for London's *Independent* takes a hard look at slavery; includes chilling photographs of victims.

Hansen, Brian, "Children in Crisis," *The CQ Researcher*, Aug. 31, 2001, pp. 657-688.
  Hansen examines the exploitation of children around the world, including sexual slaves and forced laborers.

Kristof, Nicolas D., "Bargaining For Freedom," *The New York Times*, Jan. 21, 2004, p. A27.
  The veteran columnist describes how he "bought" and freed two sex slaves in Cambodia. The article is part of Kristof's series on his experiences in Southeast Asia.

Landesman, Peter, "The Girls Next Door," *The New York Times Magazine*, Jan. 25, 2004, p. 30.

Landesman's detailed exposé of trafficking focuses on the importation of young girls into the U.S. for prostitution.

Maharaj, Davan, "Panel Frowns on Efforts to Buy Sudan Slaves Freedom," *Los Angeles Times*, May 28, 2002, p. 3.
  The article details the controversy surrounding the practice of slave redemption in Sudan.

Mertens, Richard, "Smugglers' Prey: Poor Women of Eastern Europe," *The Christian Science Monitor*, Sept. 25, 2002, p. 7.
  The article examines the plight of Eastern European women trafficked into sexual slavery who manage to escape.

Miller, John, R., "Slavery in 2004," *The Washington Post*, Jan. 1, 2004, p. A25.
  The director of the State Department's Office to Monitor and Combat Trafficking in Persons argues that the Trafficking Victims Protection Act has prodded other countries to act.

Power, Carla, *et al.*, "Preying on Children," *Newsweek*, Nov. 17, 2003, p. 34.
  The number of children being trafficked into Western Europe is rising, helped by more porous borders and the demand for young prostitutes.

Vaknin, Sam, "The Morality of Child Labor," United Press International, Oct. 4, 2002.
  UPI's senior business correspondent argues that organizations opposed to most forms of child labor impose unrealistic, rich-world standards on the poorest countries.

Reports

"Investing in Every Child: An Economic Study of the Costs and Benefits of Eliminating Child Labor," International Labour Organization, December 2003.
  The ILO contends that ending child labor would improve economic growth in the developing world.

"IPEC Action Against Child Labor: 2002-2003," International Labour Organization, January 2004.
  The report charts the progress made by the ILO's International Program on the Elimination of Child Labor (IPEC), which funds anti-child labor initiatives around the world.

"Trafficking in Persons Report," U.S. Department of State, June 2003.
  The annual report required by the Trafficking Victims Protection Act assesses global anti-trafficking efforts.

The Next Step:

Additional Articles from Current Periodicals

Children

Byrne, Eileen, "Morocco Wants Children Out of Workshops and Into School," *Los Angeles Times*, Dec. 29, 2002, p. A18.

Children as young as seven earn a dollar a day working a six-day week; intense poverty means laws against child labor go unenforced.

Iritani, Evelyn, "Child Labor Rules Don't Ease Burden in Bangladesh," *Los Angeles Times*, May 4, 2003, p. C1.

Critics of an agreement with Bangladesh to eliminate child labor in garment factories say many children end up in more dangerous jobs.

Kirk, Danica, "Albania Told to Halt Trade of Children," *The Washington Post*, Dec. 7, 2003, p. A27.

In a country so poor government aid sometimes arrives by horse-drawn cart, child trafficking is a low priority for the Albanian government.

McKelvey, Tara, "The Youngest Soldiers," *Chicago Tribune*, May 26, 2003, Tempo Section, p. 1.

A surplus of small arms and a shortage of adults in populations ravaged by war resulted in a surge in the number of child soldiers, up to 300,000 globally.

Power, Carla, "Preying on Children," *Newsweek*, Nov. 17, 2003, p. 34.

Poor economic conditions in Eastern Europe and Africa combine with fractured and sometimes hurtful laws to fuel an increase in European child trafficking.

Sengupta, Somini, "Child Traffickers Prey on Bangladesh," *The New York Times*, April 29, 2002, p. A6.

Thousands of Bangladeshi children are trafficked abroad each year; many boys serve as camel jockeys in the Persian Gulf.

Government Policies

Allen, Mike, "Bush Warns U.N. Assembly About Dangers of Trade in Sex Slaves," *The Washington Post*, Sept. 24, 2003, p. A23.

President Bush for the first time mentioned the fight against human trafficking when he addressed the General Assembly.

Branigin, William, "Va. Aid Group Helps Victims of Human Trade," *The Washington Post*, March 6, 2003, p. B8.

Boat People SOS aids people like Quang Thi Vo, a Vietnamese woman who worked as a virtual slave in a Korean-owned factory in American Samoa.

Continetti, Matthew, "On Human Bondage," *The Weekly Standard*, Oct. 6, 2003.

President Bush's comments to the U.N. urging the fight against human trafficking are mirrored by more aggressive U.S. prosecution of traffickers.

Finley, Bruce, "Human Rights Color Trade Debate," *The Denver Post*, April 22, 2002, p. A1.

A proposal to grant President Bush increased authority to reach trade agreements is influenced by slave-labor concerns in Myanmar and elsewhere.

Haugen, Gary, "State's Blind Eye on Sexual Slavery," *The Washington Post*, June 15, 2002, p. A23.

The author argues that the annual "Trafficking in Persons Report" by the Department of State gives a passing grade to many countries where sex trafficking is unpunished.

McKenzie, Glenn, "Nigeria Targets Traffickers Who Exploit Children," *Chicago Tribune*, Oct. 26, 2003, News Section, p. 4.

Operations in Nigeria aim to free children and teens who labor in granite quarries for 20 cents a day.

Miller, John, "Slavery in 2004," *The Washington Post*, Jan. 1, 2004, p. A25.

The director of the State Department's anti-trafficking section describes how the threat of economic penalties can motivate countries to fight slavery and forced labor.

Sex Trade

Binder, David, "In Europe, Sex Slavery Is Thriving Despite Raids," *The New York Times*, Oct. 20, 2002, p. A8.

A U.S.-funded, multinational anti-trafficking operation in Europe had mixed results.

Faiola, Anthony, "N. Korean Women Find Life of Abuse Waiting in China," *The Washington Post*, March 3, 2004, p. A20.

Female North Korean refugees are regularly forced into sexual servitude in China; their captors threaten them with deportation back to North Korea, where a worse fate awaits.

Macintyre, Donald, "Base Instincts," *Time Asia*, Aug. 12, 2002, p. 18.

Members of Congress demand action to address concerns U.S. troops frequent Korean bars and clubs staffed by women trafficked from the Philippines and Russia.

Mertens, Richard, "Smugglers' Prey: Poor Women of E. Europe," *The Christian Science Monitor*, Sept. 25, 2002, p. 7.

Peacekeepers and international police forces in Bosnia and Kosovo formed the core customers of traffickers who bought and sold women like cattle.

Montlake, Simon, "In Thailand, a Struggle to Halt Human Trafficking," *The Christian Science Monitor*, Aug. 29, 2003, p. 9.

Poverty and exploitation are more common elements in Thai prostitution than outright coercion; some Burmese women return to the brothels voluntarily.

Sulavik, Christopher, "Facing Down Traffickers," *Newsweek*, Aug. 25, 2003, p. 27.

The poverty accompanying the collapse of the Soviet Union made it relatively easy to exploit desperate, young women from impoverished former Soviet satellites.

Situation in America

"A Cargo of Exploitable Souls," *The Economist*, June 1, 2002.

The State Department estimates that every year approximately 50,000 people are forcibly trafficked into the United States.

Lochhead, Carolyn, "Sex Trade Uses Bay Area to Bring in Women, Kids," *San Francisco Chronicle*, Feb. 26, 2003, p. A3.

Trafficking is a bigger problem on the West Coast because of better access from Asia and Mexico.

O'Connor, Anne-Marie, "Gathering Fights Those Who Deal in Human Lives," *Los Angeles Times*, Aug. 25, 2002, p. B10.

Police, human rights activists and social workers from the U.S. and Mexico discussed ways to fight the international sex trade.

Roche, Walter, and Willoughby Mariano, "Trapped in Servitude Far From Their Homes," *The Baltimore Sun*, Sept. 15, 2002, p. 1A.

Micronesians and Marshall Islanders are brought to the United States on false pretenses and forced to labor in virtual servitude for minimal pay.

Wallace, Bill, and Jim Herron Zamora, "Sex Trafficking Ruthless, Lucrative," *San Francisco Chronicle*, Jan. 24, 2004, p. A1.

Raids on San Francisco brothels highlight the nation's $9 billion-a-year trade in human flesh; lured by profit, new operators spring up overnight.

Sudan

"A Modern Tale of Slavery, Survival, and Escape," *The Christian Science Monitor*, Dec. 19, 2003, p. 11.

Excerpts are presented from a book by a young Sudanese boy who was captured by northern militiamen and spent 10 years as a slave.

Kristof, Nicholas, "A Slave's Journey in Sudan," *The New York Times*, April 23, 2002, p. A23.

Applying pressure on the Sudanese government and engaging them rather than applying sanctions is the most effective means to fight slavery.

Lacey, Marc, "Panel Led by U.S. Criticizes Sudan's Government Over Slavery," *The New York Times*, May 23, 2002, p. A17.

A multinational commission formed by the United States condemned Sudan for allowing slavery to flourish.

Maharaj, Davan, "Panel Frowns on Efforts to Buy Sudan Slaves' Freedom," *Los Angeles Times*, May 28, 2002, p. A3.

A U.S.-led commission on slavery in Sudan discourages the buying back of slaves because the money provides an incentive for taking more slaves.

Martin, Randolph, "Sudan's Perfect War," *Foreign Affairs*, March/April 2002, p. 111.

The story of Sudan's endless war is a confluence of tribal enmities, religious fanaticism, political opportunism and access to oil.

CITING THE CQ RESEARCHER

Sample formats for citing these reports in a bibliography include the ones listed below. Preferred styles and formats vary, so please check with your instructor or professor.

MLA STYLE

Jost, Kenneth. "Rethinking the Death Penalty." The CQ Researcher 16 Nov. 2001: 945-68.

APA STYLE

Jost, K. (2001, November 16). Rethinking the death penalty. *The CQ Researcher, 11*, 945-968.

CHICAGO STYLE

Jost, Kenneth. "Rethinking the Death Penalty." *CQ Researcher*, November 16, 2001, 945-968.

CLOSING GUANTÁNAMO

BY KENNETH JOST

Excerpted from the CQ Researcher. Kenneth Jost. (February 27, 2009). "Closing Guantánamo." *CQ Researcher*, 177-200.

Closing Guantánamo

BY KENNETH JOST

THE ISSUES

Mohammed Jawad has spent more than a quarter of his young life in the prison at Guantánamo Bay, Cuba, for an offense he says he didn't commit.

The government says the Afghani teenager threw a grenade at a U.S. military jeep in Kabul in 2002, wounding two American soldiers and their Afghan interpreter.

Jawad, who was 16 or 17 at the time, claims he was working to clear land mines when the attack occurred and that another youth was responsible. Jawad says he confessed under coercion while in custody in Afghanistan and again at the U.S. detention camp at Guantánamo Bay, Cuba, only after more than a year of abusive interrogation.

Then, in a pair of rulings in October and November, an Army judge threw out the confessions that the prosecution had said were central to the case. Col. Stephen Henley ruled that Jawad had confessed the first time only after Afghan soldiers threatened to kill him and his family. The statements made in Guantánamo, Henley said, were also coerced. [1]

With a case so badly handled, Jawad would seem to be an obvious candidate for release from the controversial prison camp that President George W. Bush ordered to be established in 2002 for "enemy combatants" captured in the Afghanistan war or elsewhere. In its final week in office, however, the Bush administration on Jan. 13 urged the review panel that acts as an appeals court for the military commission system at Guantánamo to reverse the rulings in Jawad's case and allow the prosecution to go forward.

President Barack Obama signs an executive order on Jan. 22 — his second full day in office — to close the U.S. prison at Guantánamo Bay within a year. Human-rights advocates and lawmakers on both sides of the political aisle agree the controversial facility should be closed. But finding countries willing to take the 241 detainees remains a problem, and Republicans are warning they will oppose efforts to house prisoners in the United States.

After taking office only a week later, President Obama signed an executive order for a review of all pending Guantánamo cases and the closure of the facility — which now houses 241 prisoners — within one year. In Jawad's case, however, the new administration returned to the military review panel to ask for a 120-day delay before it rules on Jawad's case. The panel granted the request, over the objections of Jawad's lawyers.

Obama's action — on his second full day in office — moved toward fulfilling his repeated campaign pledge to close Guantánamo, known as "Gitmo." Human rights advocates, who have strongly criticized Guantánamo and the legal rules the Bush administration established for enemy combatant cases,

are applauding Obama's move.

"Today is the beginning of the end of this sorry chapter in our nation's history," Elisa Massimino, executive director and CEO of Human Rights First, said after Obama signed the order. "The message this sends to the world could not be clearer: The United States is ready to reclaim its role as a nation committed to human rights and the rule of law."

Even some former Bush administration officials agree the time has come to close the facility. John Bellinger, who was legal adviser at the State Department and National Security Council during the Bush administration, says he has "very strongly" supported closing this "albatross around our necks."

"The benefits of Guantánamo have been outweighed by the legacy costs of Guantánamo, and that has been true for some time," says Charles "Cully" Stimson, former assistant secretary of Defense for detainee affairs and now a senior legal fellow at the conservative Heritage Foundation. The facility has taken "a moral toll" on the U.S. image at home and abroad, he says.

Robert Chesney, a respected national security expert now a visiting professor at the University of Texas Law School in Austin, says Guantánamo reflects a broader failure of policy on how to deal with suspected terrorists captured both within and outside the United States since the Sept. 11, 2001, attacks on the World Trade Center and Pentagon by the Islamic terrorist group al Qaeda.

"For more than seven years, we've struggled to define a counterterrorism policy that is effective, that is politically sustainable and simultaneously reflects our core values as Americans," Chesney

America's Controversial Prison in the Caribbean

The U.S. Naval Station at Guantánamo Bay has come a long way since its days as a coaling station. The U.S. acquired the 45-mile-square base on Cuba's southeastern tip in 1903 after helping the island, a former Spanish colony, gain its independence during the Spanish-American war. Today the base houses about 8,400 U.S. personnel — including about 2,200 military and civilian personnel at the detention facilities — and 241 prisoners.

remarked as he opened a panel discussion at the school on Feb. 3. "We have not yet succeeded in doing this." [2]

Despite indications of editorial and public support for Obama's action, Republicans are raising questions and apparently setting the stage to criticize the closure if suspected terrorists are transferred to facilities within the United States. ""Most families neither want nor need hundreds of terrorists seeking to kill Americans in their communities," House GOP Whip Eric Cantor of Virginia said in a statement issued the same day.

Another critic, however, notes that Obama's executive order did nothing other than promise a review of case files

and set a goal of closing the facility. "He hasn't really done much," says Andrew McCarthy, legal editor of *National Review* and chairman of the Center for Law and Counterterrorism at the Foundation for the Defense of Democracies.

McCarthy has backhanded praise for the interim nature of Obama's move, which he says contrasts with candidate Obama's "demagogic, overheated rhetoric" during the campaign. "What he has obviously found is that there are very difficult issues, very complex issues that have to be worked through with respect to the detainees," McCarthy says.

"It was unfortunate that he and people who are like-minded were crit-

ical of Guantánamo," McCarthy adds, "when in point of fact if you didn't have Guantánamo, you would need to have something like it, whether it was inside the United States or outside." (*See sidebar, p. 188.*)

In establishing Guantánamo, President Bush said the camp would be used to house "the worst of the worst" suspected terrorists. But the national security and human-rights camps diverge on how to regard the 779 prisoners who have been held at Guantánamo over its seven-year history, some 540 of whom have been released. Among the detainees still being held, Bellinger predicts the Obama administration will find "a lot of bad people left, or at least many in the gray area."

"We've known all along that not everyone held at Guantánamo had any business being held there at all," counters Sharon Bradford Franklin, senior counsel with the Constitution Project, an advocacy group that seeks to find consensus on constitutional issues.

Outside government, the most extensive study of the Guantánamo detainees appears to have been conducted by Benjamin Wittes, a senior fellow at the Brookings Institution think tank and author of a highly regarded new book on counterterrorism policies, *Law and the Long War*. Wittes writes that his examination of the information publicly available on the detainees indicated many of them had incriminating ties to al Qaeda. An updated compilation by Wittes available on the Brookings Web site, however, shows that only a small fraction of the prisoners still being held are considered major al Qaeda leaders. [3] (*See chart, p. 184.*)

Paradoxically, Obama's pledge to close Guantánamo appears to be contributing to an increase in tensions in the prison camp. A special Defense Department review team that spent almost two weeks at Guantánamo concluded in February that detainees are being treated humanely in compliance with the provisions of the Geneva Conventions regarding wartime captives. But the report noted a nearly sixfold increase in disciplinary incidents by detainees since September 2008 and tied the increase in part to detainees' "uncertainty and anxiety about the future." [4]

Along with Guantánamo, the Obama administration inherits an array of legal proceedings. Obama's order froze proceedings in the military tribunal system, which thus far has secured three convictions: Ali Hamza Ahmad Suliman al-Bahlul, Osama bin Laden's alleged media secretary, was found guilty of 35 counts relating to support of terrorism and sentenced to life in prison; Salim Ahmed Hamdan, bin Laden's former driver, was convicted on reduced charges; and David Hicks, the so-called Australian Taliban, pleaded guilty to one count of providing material support of terrorism. He and Hamdan were essentially sentenced to time served and have since been released. But pending cases in federal courts up to and including the Supreme Court are continuing.

The high court is scheduled to hear a case on April 22 testing whether the government can hold without trial a Qatari native — Ali Saleh Kahlah al-Marri — as an enemy combatant after he was arrested while lawfully residing in the United States on a student visa. In a closely divided ruling, the federal appeals court in Richmond, Va., said yes — but with more judicial scrutiny than proposed by the Bush administration. In one of its first moves, the Obama administration asked for and was granted an extension of time to file the government's brief with the high court.

In a separate case, the federal appeals court for the District of Columbia is reconsidering whether former Guantánamo detainees can sue government officials for alleged torture and religious discrimination. The Supreme Court sent the case back to the appeals court in December to consider the impact of the justices' decision in June that Guantánamo detainees can use federal habeas corpus to challenge their confinement. [5]

Former detainee Said Ali al-Shihri's return to terrorist activity in Yemen underscores the complications in carrying out Obama's decision to close down Guantánamo, The New York Times *said.*

The pending cases are forcing the Obama administration to make policy decisions sooner than the one-year timetable outlined for closing Guantánamo, according to Chesney. "There will not be as much new time as the administration would like," Chesney said at the panel discussion. "The litigation calendar will force them to take positions much faster than that."

As the administration's review continues, here are some of the major questions being debated:

Should the government continue repatriating Guantánamo detainees to other countries?

The day after President Obama signed the executive order on closing Guantánamo, a front-page *New York Times* story stated that one of the detainees already released from the camp, Said

Ali al-Shihri, had returned to terrorist activity as the head of al Qaeda's Yemeni branch. The newspaper said that Al Shihri's role — allegedly announced in an Internet statement and confirmed by U.S. counterintelligence officials — "underscores the complications" in carrying out Obama's decision. [6]

In the seven years it has taken to complete legal proceedings against three Guantánamo detainees, the Bush administration released nearly 540 other prisoners, most of them to their home countries after what former State Department legal adviser Bellinger describes as "arduous negotiations." In the administration's last week in office, the Defense Department claimed that 18 of those released have been confirmed as "returning to the fight," and another 43 are suspected of having done so. [7]

The Defense Intelligence Agency report has no specifics and — like earlier DIA compilations on the subject — widely questioned. "I don't want to deride that as an urban myth, but I don't have a very high level of confidence in the claims," says Eugene Fidell, president of the National Institute of Military Justice, who teaches military law at Yale Law School. Nevertheless, the total figure of 61 — representing 11 percent of those released — is cited by national security hawks as evidence that the emphasis on reducing the Guantánamo population has been and still is mistaken.

"Thus far, it's shown itself to be a terrible idea," says McCarthy, a former federal prosecutor. "To the extent that we're trying to shovel people into other countries, all that does is to empty out Gitmo, but it doesn't make the problem any better. It makes the problem in many ways worse."

Sending Guantánamo detainees to third countries, however, is the first — and principal — step in the blueprint for closing the facility that human-rights advocates issued while the presidential campaign was under way. Under the plans outlined by Human Rights First and the Center for Strategic and International Studies (CSIS), detainees who could not be tried in the United States might be transferred to their home countries or third countries for prosecution. Those not suspected of criminal activity should be repatriated or — if they faced the likelihood of torture — sent to third countries. [8]

The report by a CSIS working group, questions the claimed number of detainees who have returned to terrorist activities, but acknowledges the "security risks" in the policies. "There are risks associated with keeping Guantánamo open and there are risks with closing Guantánamo," says report author Sarah Mendelson, director of the center's human-rights and security initiative. "We came to the conclusion that the cost of keeping Guantánamo open is far greater than the cost of closing it."

The blueprint for closing the camp may rest, in part, on unrealistic premises, however. Prosecution, repatriation and resettlement have all proved to be elusive goals. "Virtually no country has been able to detain or prosecute the people we've returned to them," Bellinger says. As one example, he says there are no domestic laws making it a crime to travel to Afghanistan, where many of the detainees were taken into custody.

As for repatriation, the Saudi government is credited with operating a model rehabilitation program, but in early February it listed as terrorism suspects 11 former Guantánamo prisoners who went through the program. Yemen, the home country of the largest number of remaining detainees, has no rehabilitation program whatsoever. [9]

In any event, McCarthy mocks the whole concept of rehabilitation. "You can't really seriously think that you're going to send these people to Saudi Arabia, which is the cradle of Wahhabism, and through re-education camp and then they're not going to be a jihadist any more," he says. "It's just a silly idea."

Resettlement presents its own difficulties, Bellinger says. "Most of these countries don't want these people back," he says. "They view them as troublemakers." And third countries — notably, in Europe — are reluctant to admit detainees that the U.S. government has publicly labeled as dangerous terrorists. Matthew Waxman, a Columbia Law School professor who served in the Bush administration in the then new position of assistant secretary of Defense for detainee affairs, says the Obama administration will face "a very difficult road" in persuading third countries to admit released detainees unless the United States itself is willing to resettle some of them.

Mendelson predicts that European governments will be more willing to work with the Obama administration — given its commitment to closing Guantánamo — than they were while Bush was in office. The CSIS report also outlines steps to strengthen law enforcement, detention facilities and reintegration programs in other countries where detainees are sent after release. Still, Mendelson writes, "We cannot guarantee nor will we pretend that the risk of releasing or transferring detainees is zero."

Waxman agrees. "All options to close Guantánamo carry some risks," he says.

Should Guantánamo detainees be prosecuted in civilian courts?

FBI agents arrested Jose Padilla as he arrived at Chicago's O'Hare International Airport on May 8, 2002, on suspicion of planning to plant so-called dirty bombs at sites in the United States. The Bush administration held the Brooklyn-born Padilla as an enemy combatant for more than three years. But because of his U.S. citizenship, Padilla was held not in Guantánamo but at the U.S. Naval Brig in Charleston, S.C.

Fearing an adverse ruling in Padilla's habeas corpus challenge to his confinement, the government decided early in 2006 to indict Padilla and try him in a civilian criminal court. The strategy paid off on Aug. 16, 2007, when a federal jury in Miami convicted Padilla of conspiracy and material support of terrorism — charges that led to the 17-year prison sentence he is now serving. [10]

Critics of Guantánamo — and its military tribunals — point to the Padilla trial and scores of others since 2001 as evidence that civilian courts are up to the task of prosecuting suspected terrorists. The U.S. criminal justice system "has proven an effective venue for prosecuting terrorist suspects," Mendelson writes in the CSIS report, "especially when compared with the military commissions." The report counts 107 jihadist terrorist cases — some with multiple defendants — tried in civilian courts since 2001 with 145 convictions. [11]

"We recommend very firmly that prosecutions should be handled by Article III courts," says the Constitution Project's Franklin, referring to the constitutional provisions establishing the federal judiciary. Military law may be applicable for "actual combatants captured on the battlefield," she acknowledges, but all others "can be and should be prosecuted in civilian courts."

National security hawks like McCarthy and a range of other experts, including some Guantánamo critics, counter by pointing to a host of practical difficulties in prosecuting enemy combatants in civilian courts. Speaking at the Texas law school panel, Wittes, a former editorial writer on legal issues for *The Washington Post*, outlined several reasons why such prosecutions "might not be viable" for many Guantánamo detainees. Evidence against some may be tainted by coercion or torture, unavailable because classified as secret or inadmissible because of mundane courtroom issues, such as proving chain of custody or the like. And in many cases the quantity and quality of the evidence may simply be insufficient, Wittes says, to meet the beyond-a-reasonable-doubt standard applicable in criminal trials.

McCarthy, one of the prosecutors in the 1995 conspiracy conviction of Omar Abdel-Rahman, the so-called blind sheik implicated in the 1993 World Trade Center bombing, says terrorism defendants' rights to discover prosecution evidence present a problem even in a successful case. "The discovery rules and the trial process itself [are] an intelligence gold mine for the terrorist organization at large," he says. "And there is no real way to prevent that from happening if you're going to have a trial that deserves the name of a trial."

McCarthy and Wittes both favor creation of what is being called a national security court to handle terrorism cases. In general, proponents of such courts envision a specialized federal civilian court applying the substantive and procedural law of military tribunals. A national security court would be "a better fit," McCarthy says, than either the regular civilian justice system or the military commissions operating at Guantánamo. (See "At Issue," p. 193.)

The military tribunals, in fact, appear not to have performed to anyone's satisfaction. CSIS's Mendelson calls them "ineffective and inefficient." From a somewhat different perspective, ex-Pentagon official Stimson says he pronounced the system "dead" more than a year ago. Despite his service in the Defense Department, Stimson favors federal court trials for the more complex Guantánamo cases because federal prosecutors are likely to be more experienced than most military lawyers.

Human-rights advocates generally minimize the difficulties claimed by the critics of civilian trials. The CSIS report notes, for example, that the federal statute against material support of terrorism does not require "heavy evi-

Most Americans Now Favor Closing Base

More than half of all Americans said in January they favor closing the U.S. military prison at Guantánamo Bay, Cuba, up from one-third two years earlier.

Do you think the United States should close the prison at Guantánamo Bay?

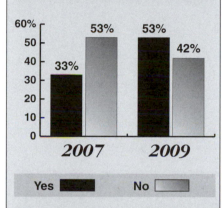

2007   *2009*

Yes ▆   No ▢

Note: Percentages not shown of those with no opinion.

Sources: Gallup Poll; Washington Post/ABC News Poll

dentiary burdens" and permits long prison sentences. In any event, the report adds, the use of civilian trials "denies terrorist suspects the symbolic value of special, extrajudicial treatment."

Columbia Law School's Waxman expects the Obama administration to look at criminal prosecutions as "the preferred option" for detainees who are not released to other countries, and he supports that stance. "One of the lessons of the Bush years is that legitimacy is not only important from a rule of law perspective but also from a strategic perspective," he says. "The United States has a strategic interest in promoting certain rule-of-law principles and in demonstrating the legal durability and legitimacy of its counterterrorism policies to garner additional international cooperation."

Should some Guantánamo detainees be held indefinitely without military or civilian trial?

Four times, the Bush administration went before the Supreme Court to claim the power to hold suspected enemy combatants for indefinite periods with no more than a limited right to challenge their detentions and no more than the most limited judicial review. And four times the Supreme Court said no.

In the first of the rulings, the court in 2004 said U.S. citizens held as enemy combatants were entitled to some hearing before "a neutral decisionmaker." On the same day, the court issued the first of a series of three decisions on the foreigners held at Guantánamo. The series culminated in the 2008 ruling that guaranteed the detainees the right to challenge their incarceration through federal habeas corpus proceedings. [12]

The expansive claim to hold wartime captives indefinitely was one of the primary criticisms that human-rights advocates made against the Bush administration's Guantánamo policies. "The sheer fact of using the geographic location of Guantánamo is not . . . the source of the problem," explains Franklin of the Constitution Project. "The source of the problem was the notion of the prior administration that this created a law-free zone, a legal black hole, and that they could be exempt from any of the principles of the U.S. Constitution, international law or the Geneva Conventions" dealing with wartime captives.

Now, two of President Obama's principal appointees on detention and interrogation policies are signaling that this administration, too, will claim some power to hold suspected terrorists captured in war-like circumstances for indefinite periods. "There's going to be a group of prisoners that, very frankly, are going to have to be held in detainment for a long time," CIA Director-designate Leon Panetta told the Senate Intelligence Committee during his confirmation hearing on Feb. 5.

Few Leaders Among Guantánamo Detainees

The 241 prisoners being held at the U.S. Naval Station at Guantánamo Bay include 36 alleged al Qaeda or Taliban leaders and 199 fighters or operatives, according to an independent examination of the records (top). Among the detainees who have responded to the military's allegations against them, nearly two-thirds have admitted some affiliation with terrorist organizations; the remainder deny any association with al Qaeda or the Taliban (bottom)

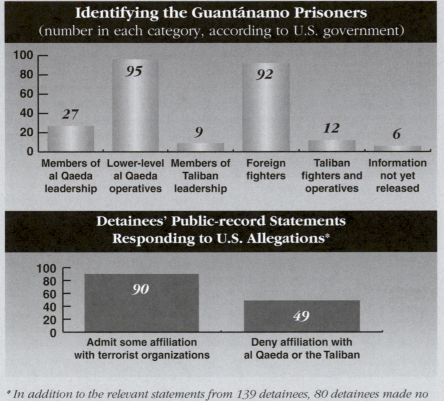

Identifying the Guantánamo Prisoners
(number in each category, according to U.S. government)

Members of al Qaeda leadership	27
Lower-level al Qaeda operatives	95
Members of Taliban leadership	9
Foreign fighters	92
Taliban fighters and operatives	12
Information not yet released	6

Detainees' Public-record Statements Responding to U.S. Allegations*

Admit some affiliation with terrorist organizations	90
Deny affiliation with al Qaeda or the Taliban	49

* In addition to the relevant statements from 139 detainees, 80 detainees made no statements or made statements that do not materially bear on the military's allegations against them.

Source: Benjamin Wittes and Zaahira Wyne, The Current Detainee Population of Guantánamo: An Empirical Study, *Brookings Institution, January 2009, www.brookings.edu/reports/2008/1216_detainees_wittes.aspx*

In his confirmation hearing earlier, Attorney General-designate Eric Holder had endorsed the power to hold an enemy combatant "for the duration of the conflict," but only with judicial review at least once a year to determine whether the prisoner is dangerous. "That kind of review has to be a part of what we do," Holder told the Senate Judiciary Committee on Jan. 16.

Human-rights advocates are concerned. "If we go down the road of a detention-without-charge regime, we will ultimately be moving Guantánamo to the United States rather than closing it," says Mendelson at CSIS.

"The Obama administration made great gains when it announced the plan to close Guantánamo," Jennifer Daskal, senior counterterrorism counsel for Human Rights Watch, told the *Los Angeles Times*. "Many of those gains will be undercut if the administration is perceived as merely transferring the system of indefinite detention to U.S. soil." [13]

Security-minded experts, however, say the power to hold enemy combatants without trial is both well established and essential. "In our wars, we have held millions of prisoners of war, and they've never had legal proceedings," says McCarthy. He labels as "preposterous" the human-rights groups' stance that the government cannot hold enemy combatants indefinitely.

Unlike the Bush administration, however, defenders of the detention power are calling for Congress and the courts to be involved in establishing rules for holding enemy combatants and reviewing their confinement. "There are some number of people that we're going to have to continue to detain outside the criminal justice system," the Brookings Institution's Wittes said during the Texas law school panel. He calls for Congress to authorize detention and for any detentions to be reviewed by federal courts.

Former Bush administration officials Bellinger and Stimson also say the other branches of government need to be involved. Bellinger wants Congress to authorize detentions for specified periods of time after a given date. Stimson says detentions should be "subjected to periodic review — a very robust review — with heavy lawyer and court involvement."

Military-law expert Fidell, however, opposes any legislation authorizing preventive detention. "I don't think it can be done consistent with our legal system," he says. The Constitution Project's Franklin agrees. "We should be taking people into custody only if we can make a probable-cause showing that they have committed a terrorism offense," she says.

Stimson believes only a "very few" detainees may be too dangerous to release but impossible to try. Over time, he says, there will be a growing presumption against continued detention.

He even predicts that the Obama administration might decide that it is not worthwhile to continue to hold this small category of detainees and will find a way to transfer them.

University of Texas law Professor Chesney, however, is not surprised the administration is defending the detention power for now. "The Obama administration is not going to completely forswear the power to hold clandestine, non-state actors," he says. Like others, however, he calls for judicial review to ensure proper treatment and adequate basis for continued detention.

"The executive order leaves open a range of options of how [the administration] is going to detain terrorism suspects in the future, and that's a good thing," says Columbia law Professor Waxman. "It would be an error to close off options." ∎

BACKGROUND

'The Least Worst Place'

With the nation still reeling from the 9/11 terrorist attacks, President Bush made the fateful decision in fall 2001 that suspected enemy combatants captured in Afghanistan and suspected terrorists apprehended elsewhere would be held at the U.S. Naval Station at Guantánamo Bay, Cuba. The decision came to be criticized on two related grounds. The detainees were held out of sight and largely incommunicado, and the administration argued against any judicial review over the detainees. More than two years after the first detainees arrived at Gitmo, the Supreme Court dealt the administration's legal strategy a setback by ruling in June 2004 that federal courts had jurisdiction to hear habeas corpus challenges by the detainees.

Congress set the stage for the detentions by passing, at Bush's request, a resolution authorizing the use of force against "those nations, organizations and persons" responsible for the 9/11 attacks. Bush used the resolution to launch a war against Afghanistan's Taliban government, which he said had harbored the al Qaeda terrorist organization. He then signed an executive order on Nov. 13 authorizing the Defense Department to detain al Qaeda members or anyone else responsible for terrorist activity against the United States and to try the detainees, if at all, before military tribunals.

After consulting with the Justice Department, Defense Secretary Donald Rumsfeld decided to hold the detainees at Guantánamo, which he described on Dec. 27 as "the least worst place" for confinement. The Justice Department's Office of Legal Counsel supported the decision, predicting that federal courts likely would rule detainees at Guantánamo had no access to federal courts to challenge their confinement.

Initially, the decision appeared to be drawing tentative acceptance, with Guantánamo viewed as a logical place to hold suspected terrorists — a secure facility removed from areas of conflict. Military authorities welcomed reporters to the base to tout the speed in constructing the jail cells of the so-called Camp X-Ray.

Criticism began, however, within days of the first prisoners' arrival on Jan. 11, 2002. The International Red Cross faulted the administration for permitting release of pictures of the detainees as they arrived. Amnesty International criticized holding the detainees incommunicado. Criticism increased as Bush announced — and reconfirmed over opposition from Secretary of State Colin Powell — that the detainees would not be regarded as covered by the provisions of the Geneva Conventions. Several European governments said the detainees should be granted prisoner-of-war status.

The controversy moved into the courts on Feb. 19, when lawyers from the Center for Constitutional Rights filed a habeas corpus petition challenging the detentions on behalf of two Britons, Shafiq Rasul and Javaid Iqbal, and David Hicks, an Australian. The petition claimed the prisoners were being held in "indefinite" and "unreviewable" detention in violation of international law and the U.S. Constitution. "The government has just gone too far here," said the center's president, Michael Ratner.

Legal experts questioned that day cast doubt on the prisoners' chances. "The case has a gut appeal," George Washington University law professor Mary Cheh remarked. "But not everything that is deeply troubling is unconstitutional." [14] The experts' doubts appeared to be well-founded when U.S. District Judge Colleen Kollar-Kotelly rejected the challenge in July, ruling that the detainees had no constitutional rights because Guantánamo was not formally part of the United States.

Meanwhile, the administration was making the momentous decision behind the scenes to authorize "enhanced interrogation" techniques against some of the Guantánamo detainees as well as some of the suspected terrorists being held at then-secret CIA prisons in Europe. In a critical step, the Justice Department's Office of Legal Counsel issued an advisory memorandum on Aug. 1, 2002, advising the CIA that a specific list of interrogation techniques would not constitute torture because they were not "specifically intended to inflict severe pain and physical suffering."

Armed with that opinion, military intelligence agents sought and obtained permission to use techniques such as sleep deprivation against some Guantánamo detainees. FBI agents disagreed on the legality and the effectiveness of the techniques, but Rumsfeld signed off on some of the methods in a memo dated Dec. 2. He rescinded the approval for some of the techniques in April 2003. Rasul and Iqbal contend in pending lawsuits that they continued to be mistreated up until their eventual release in March 2004.

In the habeas corpus case, the Guantánamo detainees lost a second round with a ruling in March 2003 by the U.S. Court of Appeals for the District of Columbia Circuit. The appellate judges upheld the lower court's ruling that the Guantánamo detainees could not use habeas corpus to challenge their confinement. In November the Supreme Court agreed to rule on the issue in a pair of consolidated cases — *Rasul v. Bush* and a second case on behalf of a dozen Kuwaitis.

The move set up the first definitive test of the administration's legal strategy and ended seven months later with a limited but decisive setback. By a 6-3 vote, the court ruled on June 28, 2004, that federal courts had jurisdiction to hear the habeas corpus cases. The ruling left all other issues for future cases. Dissenting justices said the ruling was bad law and bad policy. But Ratner hailed the decision. "This is a major victory for the rule of law," he said.

'A Law-Free Zone?'

The Bush administration dug in its heels after the Supreme Court's habeas corpus decision by twice persuading Congress to approve legislation to keep the Guantánamo detainees out of federal court. Instead, the administration planned to try the detainees before specially created military "commissions" with limited substantive and procedural rights. Legal challenges slowed the commissions, however, and eventually led to two additional Supreme Court rulings rejecting the administration's strategy. At the same time, the administration worked to transfer Guantánamo detainees to their home countries but encountered reluctance and resistance as other countries came to view the facility as emblematic of a policy of lawless mistreatment of wartime captives.

The administration fashioned its Guantánamo policies against the backdrop of a worldwide controversy over mistreatment of enemy combatants symbolized by the documented abuse of Iraqi pris-

oners at the U.S.-run jail at Abu Ghraib, outside Baghdad. Images broadcast around the world beginning in May 2004 touched off demands at home and abroad for stronger rules to require humane treatment of all U.S.-held prisoners, including the Guantánamo detainees. But the administration also wanted to cut off habeas corpus petitions.

The result was the Detainee Treatment Act, passed in December 2005, which prohibited inhumane treatment of prisoners and limited interrogation techniques used by military intelligence agents to those approved in the *U.S. Army Field Manual*. But the act also sought to bar federal courts from hearing habeas corpus petitions by Guantánamo detainees, including cases already pending.

Meanwhile, the military commission proceedings were being challenged by one of the Guantánamo prisoners, Salim Ahmed Hamdan, a Yemeni-born Muslim accused of being the driver for the al Qaeda leader, Osama bin Laden. Hamdan had been captured in Afghanistan, brought to Guantánamo in January 2002 and designated as eligible for trial in July 2003. He then filed a habeas corpus petition challenging the military commissions as inconsistent with the Uniform Code of Military Justice (UCMJ) and the procedural provisions of the Geneva Conventions.

After conflicting rulings from lower courts, the Supreme Court ruled, 5-3, in Hamdan's favor in June 2006. Preliminarily, the court held that the Detainee Treatment Act did not eliminate habeas corpus cases filed before the law was enacted. The court went on to hold that President Bush had failed to show any need to depart from the UCMJ's regular procedures for military trial. The majority also said the military commissions did not comply with the Geneva Conventions.

The administration pushed Congress to respond quickly by passing a new law, the Military Commissions Act, which revised procedures for the military tribunals and explicitly barred all habeas

corpus petitions from Guantánamo. To help move the bill, Bush announced on Sept. 6, 2006, that he was transferring 14 "high-value" terror suspects to Guantánamo from the secret CIA prisons. The transferred prisoners included Khalid Shaikh Mohammed, accused of masterminding the 9/11 attacks and eventually identified as one of three prisoners subjected to waterboarding during interrogation. With midterm congressional election campaigns under way, Bush's decision to move high-profile al Qaeda suspects to Guantánamo spurred Congress to act on a supposed Guantánamo fix before the elections. Congress completed action on the bill at the end of the month; Bush signed it into law on Oct. 17.

The revamped military commissions finally produced the system's first conviction in March 2007, when the Australian Hicks pleaded guilty to a newly codified charge of providing material support to terrorism. Hicks, a convert to Islam, had been turned over to U.S. forces by the U.S.-backed Northern Alliance in Afghanistan in November 2001. A military panel sentenced Hicks to seven years' imprisonment on the charge, but under the plea deal he was returned to Australia to serve only an additional nine months. After his release, Hicks acknowledged that he trained at al Qaeda camps and fought for the Taliban, but he denied any hostile actions against the United States.

Hicks' guilty plea came not long after the D.C. Circuit in February had given the Bush administration a legal victory by upholding the Military Commissions Act, including its bar to habeas corpus petitions by the Guantánamo prisoners. In June, however, the Supreme Court agreed to hear the appeals by the detainees. The lead case, *Boumediene v. Bush*, was brought on behalf of six Algerians arrested in Bosnia on suspicion of plotting to bomb the U.S. Embassy in Sarajevo. In dramatic arguments in December, Solicitor General Paul Clement

Continued on p. 188

Chronology

2001-Present

U.S. Naval Station at Guantánamo Bay, Cuba, is used to hold enemy combatants after 9/11; Bush administration loses effort to block federal court challenges; Obama administration promises to close prison camp by Jan. 22, 2010

2001

Terrorists attack the United States (Sept. 11). . . . Congress authorizes use of military force against countries, organizations or individuals responsible for attacks (Sept. 18). . . . U.S. forces capture hundreds of suspected "enemy combatants" in Afghanistan war; President George W. Bush signs executive order authorizing military detention (Nov. 13). . . . Guantánamo Bay is chosen for detention facility; Justice Department predicts detainees cannot use habeas corpus to challenge their confinement (Dec. 28).

2002

First detainees brought to Guantánamo (Jan. 11); detentions prompt immediate controversy and legal challenges (January-February); challenges rejected in several courts. . . . Justice Department memo narrows definition of "torture," approves some "enhanced" interrogation techniques (Aug. 1). . . . Pentagon officials sign off on enhanced interrogation (November/December).

2003

Federal appeals court bars habeas corpus by Guantánamo detainees (March 11). . . . Defense Secretary Donald Rumsfeld approves new interrogation rules, including 24 of 35 recommended enhanced techniques (April 16). . . . Supreme Court agrees to rule on habeas corpus issue (Nov. 10).

2004

Four Britons released to United Kingdom, with no charges; later file civil suits for damages (March 9). . . . Images of inmate-abuse at Abu Ghraib prison in Iraq broadcast worldwide (May). . . . Supreme Court upholds federal court jurisdiction over detainees' habeas corpus petitions (June 28).

2005

Detainee Treatment Act (DTA) limits interrogation techniques, bars habeas corpus for detainees (December).

2006

Supreme Court allows pending habeas corpus cases despite DTA; rules military commissions violate U.S. military law, Geneva Conventions (June 29). . . . President Bush announces transfer of 14 "high-value" prisoners to Guantánamo (Sept. 6). . . . Congress passes, Bush signs Military Commissions Act; law prohibits all pending, future habeas corpus actions by detainees, allows limited review of military commissions by appeals court (October).

2007

Military Commissions Act upheld by D.C. Circuit court in *Boumediene* case (Feb. 20) . . . Australian David Hicks pleads guilty to supporting terrorism; sent to Australia to finish serving sentence (March). . . . Supreme Court decides to review *Boumediene* decision; hears arguments (Dec. 5).

2008

Democrat Barack Obama, Republican John McCain cinch nominations for president, promise to close Guantánamo (spring). . . . Supreme Court rules, 5-4, Military Commissions Act unconstitutional; ruling guarantees habeas corpus rights for detainees (June 12). . . . Salim Ahmed Hamdan, driver for al Qaeda leader Osama bin Laden, convicted on reduced charges, given 5-1/2-year sentence (Aug. 6-7); released to Yemen (Nov. 25). . . . Federal judge orders 17 Chinese Muslims held at Guantánamo brought to U.S. for release (Oct. 7). . . . Obama elected, begins transition (November-December). . . . Five of six detainees in *Boumediene* case ordered released by federal judge for lack of evidence (Nov. 21).

2009

Military judge says would-be hijacker Mohammed al Qahtani was "tortured" while at Guantánamo (Jan. 14). . . . Obama sworn in; denies "false choice" between liberty, security (Jan. 20). . . . Obama signs executive order to close Guantánamo within one year; orders review of detainee cases; limits use of enhanced interrogation techniques (Jan. 22). . . . Military judge says would-be hijacker Mohammed al Qahtani was "tortured" while at Guantánamo (Jan. 14). . . . Obama sworn in; denies "false choice" between liberty, security (Jan. 20). . . . Obama signs executive order to close Guantánamo within one year; orders review of detainee cases; limits use of "enhanced interrogation" techniques (Jan. 22). . . . Administration reaffirms opposition to habeas corpus for prisoners held at Bagram Air Force Base in Afghanistan (Feb. 20). . . . First Guantánamo detainee released under Obama administration; upon arrival in Britain, Binyam Mohamed describes "medieval" torture during detention in Morocco (Feb. 22-23). . . . Pentagon review team says Guantánamo meets Geneva Conventions standards; human rights groups disagree (Feb. 23). . . . Defense Department review team says Guantánamo conditions comply with Geneva Conventions; rights groups disagree (Feb. 23).

From Imperial Outpost to Post-9/11 'Gulag'

Inside the prison at Guantánamo Bay.

The prison camp that became a reviled symbol of the Bush administration's "war on terror" welcomes visitors — in person or online — to witness what is officially described as "safe, humane, legal and transparent care and custody of detained enemy combatants."

The online tour of the detention camp at the U.S. Naval Station, Guantánamo Bay, Cuba (www.jtfgtmo.southcom.mil) depicts a state-of-the-art correctional facility with a 12,000-volume library, exercise equipment and recreational areas.

The pictures contrast sharply with the indelible images first shown to the world after suspected terrorists from Afghanistan and elsewhere began arriving in January 2002: prisoners in orange jumpsuits forced to crouch near chain-link fences or being led around in shackles by burly guards.

The 320 open-air, steel-mesh cages of Camp X-Ray were in use only until April 2002, but a federal judge has ordered them preserved as evidence in litigation challenging the conditions of confinement. Today, most of the 241 detainees are housed in three facilities built later as Guantánamo — widely known as "Gitmo" — was transformed from short-term expedient to long-term policy.

There are three main camps, according to an online primer provided by *The Miami Herald* (www.miamiherald.com/Guantánamo). Camp 4 resembles a traditional prisoner-of-war camp with 10-cot bunkhouses and common eating area, communal showers and athletic facilities. Camp 5 is a maximum-security facility with single-prisoner cells controlled by a centralized locking system and closed-circuit surveillance. Camp 6 was converted from minimum to maximum security after a fight between guards and detainees in Camp 4 in May 2006. The facility has single-occupancy cells where prisoners are locked up 22 hours a day.

In addition, about 15 men are believed to be housed in super-secret Camp 7, which was built for the "high-level" former CIA captives that Bush ordered transferred to Guantánamo in September 2006. The existence of the camp was not confirmed until December 2007, and its exact location remains shrouded. Among the prisoners believed to be there is Khalid Sheikh Mohammed, charged along with four others with masterminding the Sept. 11, 2001, terrorist attacks on the United States.

A separate facility, dubbed Camp Justice, was built during the Bush administration to hold trials of detainees before the specially created military commissions. President Obama suspended those proceedings for 120 days pending an interagency review of detainees' case files by Attorney General Eric Holder. [1]

The naval base itself houses about 8,400 U.S. military and civilian personnel — including 2,200 at the detention facilities. It occupies a 45-square-mile tract — about three-fourths the size of the District of Columbia — near the southeastern tip of Cuba. The United States acquired the base under a lease with Cuba in 1903 after helping the former Spanish colony gain its independence as part of the Spanish-American War. [2]

U.S. rights to the base — then used as a coaling station — were reaffirmed in a 1934 treaty that calls for the United States to pay Cuba about $4,000 per year. Termination of the lease requires consent of both governments. The United States has continued to pay the lease amount, but since the Cuban Revolution of the late 1950s the government of Fidel Castro has refused to cash the checks.

The base made news in 1958, when 29 sailors and Marines were kidnapped by Cuban rebels and held for 22 days. During the Cuban Missile Crisis four years later, civilian and military personnel and families were evacuated. Two years later, Castro's government cut off water and supply routes to the base. Since then, the base has had its own power and water sources.

Guantánamo faded from the news and receded in strategic significance until the 1980s and '90s, when it became a holding facility for Cuban and Haitian refugees fleeing to the United States. Under Presidents George H. W. Bush and Bill Clinton, the Coast Guard picked up the refugees on rafts on the high seas and held them in ramshackle facilities on the base to avoid bringing them to U.S. soil.

The Clinton administration lost a legal battle over the refugee issue in June 1993, when a federal judge ordered that 150 HIV-positive Haitian refugees who qualified for political asylum could not be excluded from the United States because of their health status. Later that month, however, the Supreme Court ruled the government could return Haitian refugees captured at sea to their home country without giving them the chance to apply for asylum.

Guantánamo receded from the news for the rest of the decade but emerged in fall 2001 when the Defense and Justice departments decided it was the best place to bring enemy combatants captured in the Afghanistan war and suspected terrorists rounded

Continued from p. 186

contended that the act gave the detainees sufficient judicial review to substitute for habeas corpus.

Representing the detainees, former Solicitor General Seth Waxman insisted the government's argument amounted to treating Guantánamo as a "law-

free zone." In June 2008, the court sided narrowly but decisively with the detainees against the government. Writing for a five-vote majority, Justice Anthony M. Kennedy said the detainees were entitled to habeas corpus because the United States exercised "de facto sovereignty" over Guantánamo.

'An Enormous Failure'

Political and legal events combined in 2008 to create broader support for closing Guantánamo. The Bush administration resisted the conclusion, however, even as both major-party

up elsewhere. A legal opinion by John Yoo, then a deputy in the Justice Department's Office of Legal Counsel and now a law professor in California, forecast — wrongly — that the Supreme Court would not allow Guantánamo prisoners to challenge their detention in court because the base was not on U.S. soil.

In a new book detailing the initial history of the detention camp, Karen Greenberg, executive director of the Center on Law and Security at New York University School of Law, says the first commander, Marine Brig. Gen. Michael Lehnert, welcomed visits by the International Committee of the Red Cross (ICRC) and sought to comply with the Geneva Conventions even though President Bush had said they did not apply. Lehnert was eased out within a few months, however, after Defense Secretary Donald Rumsfeld ordered more stringent treatment of the prisoners to aid interrogation. [3]

For more than a year, official policy approved by Rumsfeld sanctioned "enhanced interrogation" techniques at the camp such as sleep deprivation, "stress positions" and forced nakedness. Rumsfeld withdrew approval for many of the challenged techniques in a memorandum signed in April 2003. Criticism of the camp continued, however. In November 2004 a leaked ICRC report described some discipline for prisoners as "tantamount to torture." In May 2005, the human-rights group Amnesty International labeled Guantánamo "the gulag of our time."

Through the years, some international visitors have dissented from this image of the camp. After visiting in 2007, Brookings scholar Wittes described the camp as "coolly professional." [4] Charles "Cully" Stimson, an assistant secretary of Defense who helped oversee the facility from January 2006 to February 2007, says interrogation complied with the *U.S. Army Field Manual*. "During my tenure and going forward, we were not engaged in any practices that would be considered cruel, inhuman or degrading at all," he says.

A guard talks to a Guantánamo detainee inside the open yard at Camp 4, the medium-security detention center that resembles a military prisoner of war camp.

AFP/Getty Images/Brennan Linsley

prayer beads and cap. The Muslim prisoners are aided in their religious observances by arrows in each cell pointing to Mecca and by prison schedules that take account of the observance of daily prayers.

As part of the Obama administration's decision to close Guantánamo within one year, Defense Secretary Robert Gates ordered a review to determine whether the camp complies with all provisions of the Geneva Conventions on humane treatment of wartime captives. The report, released on Feb. 23, found no violations but recommended some changes to improve conditions. Human-rights groups faulted the report and called for broader changes.

Meanwhile, White House Counsel Gregory Craig and Attorney General Holder visited the prison in separate day visits on Feb. 19 and 23, respectively. No reporters accompanied either official, and neither had immediate comments after returning to Washington.

Stimson and others note the many stresses for the young guards at the camp, ranging from periodic hunger strikes to urine- and feces-filled baggies thrown in a guard's face. The Guantánamo Web site notes without comment the different conditions of confinement for "compliant" and "noncompliant" prisoners. But the site also says that all prisoners "regardless of compliancy" are furnished a Koran, prayer mat,

[1] For a description, see Jeffrey Toobin, "Camp Justice," *The New Yorker*, April 14, 2008, pp. 32-38.

[2] Some background drawn from U.S. Navy, "History of Guantánamo Bay," undated (www.cnic.navy.mil/Guantánamo/index.htm). For a detailed history, the site recommends M.E. Murphy, *The History of Guantánamo Bay 1494-1964*, published in two volumes in 1953 and 1964.

[3] Karen Greenberg, *The Least Worst Place: Guantánamo's First 100 Days* (2009). For a summary, see Karen Greenberg, "When Gitmo Was (Relatively) Good," *The Washington Post*, Jan. 25, 2009, p. B1.

[4] Benjamin Wittes, *Law and the Long War: The Future of Justice in the Age of Terror* (2008), p. 73.

presidential candidates endorsed the step, and the government's stance in Guantánamo cases met a host of legal difficulties in court. Obama's election — after he had strongly criticized Bush policies in a range of areas — seemed to portend quick action on Guantánamo. But the executive order that

Obama signed on his second full day in the White House only started a process and gave the administration a full year to complete the closure of the camp.

By the time of the Supreme Court decision recognizing habeas corpus rights for Guantánamo prisoners,

Obama and McCain had cinched their respective nominations. Both had already endorsed closing Guantánamo, but they differed on the court ruling. Obama hailed the decision as a victory for the rule of law, while McCain called it "one of the worst decisions" in the country's history. President Bush said he agreed with the dissenters in the case, but promised to comply. Behind the scenes, Bush's advisers considered closing the camp but rejected the idea — despite Bush's professed desire to do so — because of what the advisers concluded were unacceptable political and legal risks. [15]

Meanwhile, the administration was heading toward a serious embarrassment in the first-ever military commission trial: the prosecution of Salim Hamdan, the detainee most closely identified with challenging the Guantánamo regime. When Hamdan's trial opened on July 22, the prosecution depicted his role as bin Laden's former driver as vital to al Qaeda's war against the United States. Defense lawyers instead painted him as a poor Muslim in need of a job. After a two-week trial, the military jury sided mostly with the defense. The panel acquitted Hamdan of the most serious charges and convicted him on Aug. 6 only of material support of terrorism. The next day, the jury sentenced Hamdan to an unexpectedly short 5-1/2 years; the judge said he would credit Hamdan with the 61 months he had already served.

With economic issues dominating the presidential campaign, Obama and McCain devoted scant attention to Guantánamo during their parties' national conventions in late August and early September, respectively. Obama had laid out his position earlier, on June 18, where he called Guantánamo "an enormous failure" and "legal black hole" that had weakened support abroad for U.S. anti-terrorism policies. In his acceptance speech, Obama made only a less specific promise to "restore our moral standing." Accepting the GOP nomination a week later, McCain thanked Bush for keeping the country safe after 9/11 and left any criticism of Bush policies unspoken.

In the fall, the administration sustained two more blows to its Guantánamo policies when two federal judges in Washington — for the first time — ordered the release of detainees. On Oct. 7, Judge Ricardo Urbina directed the government to free 17 Chinese Muslims, known as Uighurs, who had been held at Guantánamo since they were rounded up in Afghanistan in fall 2001. The Uighurs, ethnic Turkic Muslim separatists from western China, contended they had been seeking refuge from the Chinese government. The administration initially described them as terrorists, but by 2008 acknowledged they were not enemy combatants. The dissident Uighurs remained at Guantánamo, however, because they could not be sent back to China, which classifies Uighurs as terrorists, and no other country would take them. The government won an appeals court stay of Urbina's ruling quickly, and later — after Obama took office — a reversal of the decision. (*See sidebar, p. 191.*)

The next month, Judge Richard Leon ruled the government had no legal basis for holding five of the six detainees from the *Boumediene* case. Speaking from the bench — with the prisoners listening by teleconference from Guantánamo — Leon noted that the government had dropped charges relating to the alleged bombing plot but still contended the group planned to go to Afghanistan to fight against U.S. forces. Leon said the government's case relied "exclusively" on classified evidence from one unnamed source whose reliability and credibility could not be adequately evaluated. He called the evidence "too thin a reed" to justify continued imprisonment and ordered five of the six released "forthwith." Leon found sufficient evidence, however, to justify the charge that Bensayah Belkacem had aided transportation logistics for al Qaeda members.

With Obama preparing to take office, the government suffered one more setback: On Jan. 14 Leon ordered the release of a Chadian-born detainee, Mohammed al Gharani, who had been captured at age 14 and accused by other detainees of having lived in al Qaeda guest houses. The evidence was inconsistent and unverified, Leon said.

Eight days later, Obama signed the executive order promising a new review of all the Guantánamo case files and closure of the facility within a year. McCain was among those who endorsed the president's decision. [16] ∎

CURRENT SITUATION

Detainee Cases Reviewed

A Justice Department task force is beginning close review of case files on the 241 remaining Guantánamo detainees following visits to the prison camp by two top Obama administration officials and the first release of a detainee since Obama took office.

White House Counsel Gregory Craig and Attorney General Holder made separate day trips to Guantánamo in late February, the first visits to the facility for each. No reporters accompanied Craig or Holder on the trips. Craig was accompanied on his Feb. 18 trip by Jeh C. Johnson, the Defense Department's general counsel. Holder took half a dozen close aides with him for a similar trip on Feb. 23. A Justice Department spokesman told reporters in Washington that Holder was to discuss case histories of specific detainees and tour detention facilities and Camp Justice, the courtroom complex built for the military commissions.

Among those accompanying Holder was Matthew Olsen, a veteran Justice Department official whom Holder named on Feb. 20 to head an interagency task force charged with assembling information on each of the remaining detainees and recommending proper dispositions of their cases. Olsen had been a Justice Department prosecutor for nearly 10 years before being named in September 2006

Continued on p. 192

What Can Be Done With the Uighurs?

Even the U.S. wants to release 17 Chinese Muslims.

Seventeen Chinese Muslims held at the Guantánamo prison camp since 2002 deny that they are "enemy combatants" against the United States. The government agrees and wants to release the men, members of the Uighur Muslim community in western China.

When a federal judge last fall ordered that the Uighurs be brought to the United States to be released, however, the Bush administration appealed the decision. And last week the federal appeals court for the District of Columbia Circuit agreed that federal courts cannot order a foreigner admitted into the United States — a ruling that leaves the puzzle for the Obama administration to try to solve. [1]

The Uighurs are members of a Turkic ethnic group considered by the Chinese government to be separatist terrorists. Before the Sept. 11, 2001, terrorist attacks on the United States, the dissident Uighurs had been receiving firearms training at a camp run by the Eastern Turkistan Islamic Group near Tora Bora, Afghanistan — the same area where al Qaeda training camps are found. They fled to Pakistan after U.S. air strikes destroyed their camp but were captured, turned over to U.S. forces and brought to Guantánamo.

Initially, the government depicted the Uighurs as enemy combatants because of alleged connections between the Turkistan group and al Qaeda or Afghanistan's Taliban government. But the U.S. Court of Appeals for the District of Columbia, ruling on a habeas corpus case brought by one of the Uighurs, said the government had not produced enough evidence to support the accusation. [2]

The Bush administration bowed to the ruling and stepped up efforts to release the men to third countries. The Uighurs cannot be returned to their home country because they contend — and the U.S. government does not dispute — that they could face arrest, torture or execution in China. But the government's six-year-long depiction of the Uighurs as dangerous terrorists has left other countries reluctant to accept them.

In October, U.S. District Judge Ricardo Urbina moved to resolve the dilemma by ordering the Uighurs to be released into the United States. After questioning the government's claim that the Uighurs could be dangerous if admitted into the country, Urbina ruled on Oct. 7 that their continued detention was unlawful. "Separation of powers concerns do not trump . . . the unalienable right of liberty," he said. [3]

The government immediately asked for and obtained a stay to Urbina's ruling pending an appeal. The three-judge panel's Feb. 18 ruling on the appeal backed the government's position that Urbina had exceeded his authority.

"It is not within the province of any court, unless expressly authorized by law, to review the determination of the political branch of the government to exclude a given alien," Senior Circuit Judge A. Raymond Randolph wrote for a two-judge majority. The third judge, Judith Rogers, disagreed with the legal ruling but said Urbina had acted prematurely because the Uighurs had never sought admission to the United States.

The case was argued before the appellate panel on Nov. 24, while the Bush administration was still in office. With the case pending, lawyers for the Uighurs wrote to Obama administration officials on Jan. 23 — the day after President Obama signed an executive order promising to close Guantánamo within one year — urging that the men be immediately released.

A Washington, D.C.-based association of Uighurs offered to help the prisoners establish residences in the United States. "We have people offering them places to stay, English training, employment," said Nury Turkel, a past president of the Uyghur American Association. "We don't want anyone to think they will be a burden on society." [4]

Lawyers for the Uighurs said they would continue their efforts to free the men, but one said the appeals court decision limits the impact of the Supreme Court's decision in June 2008 guaranteeing Guantánamo detainees the right to habeas corpus. "You win and still can't get out," Susan Baker Manning told *The Washington Post*. The administration had no immediate comment on the decision. [5]

Seventeen Chinese Muslims, or Uighurs, held since 2002 have been ordered released from Guantánamo. Five other Uighurs, including the four above, were recently released to Albania.

Center for Human Rights in the Americas

---

[1] The decision is *Kiyemba v. Obama*, 08-5424, U.S. Court of Appeals for the District of Columbia Circuit, Feb. 18, 2009, http://pacer.cadc.uscourts.gov/common/opinions/200902/08-5424-1165428.pdf. For coverage, see Lyle Denniston, "Uighurs Barred From U.S.," SCOTUSBlog, Feb. 18, 2009, www.scotusblog.com/wp/uighurs-barred-from-us/#more-8725. Background drawn from court opinion and ongoing coverage on SCOTUSBlog.

[2] The case is *Parhart v. Gates*, 532 F.3d 834 (D.C. Cir. 2008). For coverage, see William Glaberson, "Evidence Faulted in Detainee Case," *The New York Times*, July 1, 2008, p. A1.

[3] For coverage, see Ben Winograd, "Judge Orders Uighurs to U.S.; Government Appeals," SCOTUSBlog, Oct. 7, 2008. The story links to a transcript of the Oct. 7 hearing before Urbina.

[4] Quoted in Steve Hendrix, "D.C. Area Families Are Ready to Receive Uighur Detainees," *The Washington Post*, Oct. 8, 2008, p. A8. The association uses a different spelling of Uighur.

[5] Quoted in Del Quentin Wilber and Carrie Johnson, "Court Blocks Release of 17 Uighurs Into U.S.," *The Washington Post*, Feb. 19, 2009, p. A4.

Continued from p. 190

as deputy assistant attorney general for the then newly established National Security Division.

Olsen's task force will be dealing with case files that one former military prosecutor has described as being in "a state of disarray." Darrel Vandeveld, a former lieutenant colonel in the Army Reserve, made the critical statement in January, four months after he had resigned as a prosecutor in Guantánamo for what he said were reasons of conscience. [17]

Vandeveld, a senior deputy attorney general in Pennsylvania in civilian life, told *The Washington Post* that case files were disorganized, information scattered between different databases and physical evidence stored in unknown locations or in some instances missing. Military officials denied Vandeveld's accusations, *The Post* said. The newspaper quoted Col. Lawrence Morris, chief military prosecutor, as saying that Vandeveld had not raised concerns with him and also suggesting that Vandeveld had resigned after being passed over for a promotion.

In a second story, however, *The Post* quoted ex-Defense official Stimson as saying that while at the Pentagon he had persistent problems compiling information on individual detainees. The newspaper also noted references in Justice Department filings in habeas corpus cases to the unexpected difficulties the government faced in assembling case files on individual detainees.

The officials' trips came as the administration was completing preparations for the release of one of the highest-profile Guantánamo detainees: Binyam Mohamed, an Ethiopian-born British citizen who had been accused of planning to detonate "dirty bombs" in the United States. Mohamed claimed that after being held in Afghanistan and Pakistan, he was transferred to Morocco for 18 months and tortured there before being brought to Guantánamo.

Mohamed was flown from Guantánamo on Feb. 22 and arrived in England the next day. As part of the release, Mohamed reportedly agreed to a lifetime prohibition against travel to the United States. *The New York Times* reported that the British government told U.S. officials that, under British and European human-rights laws, it could not impose other travel or surveillance restrictions on Mohamed. [18]

The Justice Department announced Mohamed's departure in a press release instead of the Defense Department, as had been the practice under the Bush administration. The Justice Department has said that an additional 57 detainees have been approved for transfer or release, but are awaiting agreements with third countries. That number includes the 17 Chinese Muslims and three others who have won habeas corpus cases but are not yet released.

Obama administration officials are counting on increased cooperation between other countries, including U.S. allies in Europe, to help empty Guantánamo before Obama's one-year deadline for closing the facility. At least three countries — Spain, Estonia and Latvia — have signaled a willingness to accept released detainees, but Italy says it won't because no Italians are being held there. "I can absolutely rule out that the closing of Guantánamo will have any consequences for Italy," Gianfranco Fini, the speaker of Italy's Chamber of Deputies and a close ally of Prime Minister Silvo Berlusconi, was quoted as telling House Speaker Nancy Pelosi, D-Calif., on Feb. 16 during a visit by the U.S. lawmaker. [19]

The Guantánamo developments come against a backdrop of concern among some human-rights and civil liberties advocates about the direction of Obama administration policies on national security issues. The American Civil Liberties Union, for example, criticized the administration after Justice Department lawyers in February reaffirmed before a federal appeals court the invocation of the state secrets privilege to try to block the trial of a suit by former prisoners attacking the practice of "rendition" of detainees to other countries. [20]

Meanwhile, the administration is giving no encouragement to proposals on Capitol Hill for an in-depth investigation of Bush administration detention and interrogation policies. Senate Judiciary Committee Chairman Patrick J. Leahy, D-Vt., is proposing a "truth commission" to look at interrogation and detention, among other topics. But Obama gave the proposal no support when questioned at his first prime-time news conference. "Generally speaking, I'm more interested in looking forward than I am in looking back," Obama said on Feb. 9.

Torture Suits Stymied

A civil suit by four Britons released from Guantánamo in 2004 after two years' confinement could result in the first detailed courtroom airing of allegations of torture and abusive treatment of detainees at the U.S. prison camp. But — barring an unlikely shift by the Obama administration — the case will come to trial only if a federal appeals court decision dismissing the suit is reversed either by that court or by the Supreme Court.

The suit is one of several cases seeking to air former detainees' allegations of torture that have been stymied because of legal or diplomatic hurdles. The roadblocks are persisting even after the Pentagon's top judge in the Guantánamo detainee cases in January confirmed allegations of torture used against a Saudi national identified as a would-be 9/11 hijacker. And so far the Obama administration has shown no signs of easing barriers to former detainees seeking compensation in civil courts for mistreatment while prisoners at Guantánamo or elsewhere during the Bush administration.

The four British Muslims all claim they were rounded up by mistake during the Afghanistan war in fall 2001 and subjected to abusive interrogation

Continued on p. 194

At Issue:

Should Congress create a national security court for enemy combatant cases?

ANDREW C. MCCARTHY
LEGAL-AFFAIRS EDITOR,
NATIONAL REVIEW

WRITTEN FOR *CQ RESEARCHER*, FEB. 20, 2009

EDWARD L. DOWD JR. (left)
FORMER U.S. ATTORNEY, EASTERN DISTRICT OF MISSOURI;
EARL SILBERT, *FORMER U.S. ATTORNEY, DISTRICT OF COLUMBIA*

WRITTEN FOR *CQ RESEARCHER*, FEB. 20, 2009

*i*t has been a relief to see President Obama retreat from the irresponsible rhetoric of his campaign regarding various security measures that have protected the nation from a reprise of the Sept. 11 attacks. The president now explicitly recognizes that there are numerous terrorists who threaten the United States but cannot be tried in the civilian courts — his preferred forum. The answer is a special national security court.

As we learned in the 1990s, the federal courts are more than adequate in providing due process for jihadists hell-bent on killing Americans. All of the terrorists indicted were convicted. Nevertheless, due process for our enemies, while not unimportant, can never be our primary aim, not if government is to tend to its first responsibility — the security of the governed.

Between the 1993 bombing of the World Trade Center and its destruction on 9/11, radical Islam became bigger and bolder. American targets were repeatedly attacked — including Khobar Towers (19 U.S. Air Force members killed), the U.S. embassies in eastern Africa (over 200 killed) and the *USS Cole* (17 U.S. sailors killed). Yet, because of the high burdens and elaborate protections of the criminal justice system — a system designed to protect Americans — only 29 terrorists were successfully prosecuted in the eight-year period when prosecution in federal court was our nation's principal counterterrorism strategy.

The effect of this weak response was to encourage more attacks. Indeed, Osama bin Laden himself has been under charges by the Justice Department since June 1998 but has killed thousands of Americans in the ensuing decade — adding counts to the indictment does not seem to deter him much. Ditto Khalid Shaikh Mohammed, who had also been under indictment for years while he planned the 9/11 atrocities. It told our enemies that we could be attacked with virtual impunity.

We have not suffered another attack since 9/11 primarily because we moved in late 2001 to a law-of-war paradigm, which permits terrorists — enemies in war, not just defendants in a case — to be detained without trial, until the conclusion of hostilities. That philosophy, coupled with a comprehensive counterterrorism strategy that does not unduly rely on criminal prosecutions, has helped us prevent terrorist attacks from happening, rather than contenting ourselves with prosecuting a handful of jihadists after innocents have been slaughtered.

If we don't want 9/11 results, we can't go back to a 9/10 mentality.

*a*s former federal prosecutors, we have a deep understanding and appreciation for the enormity of the crimes that terrorists commit. We strongly support the severe punishment of convicted terrorists. However, we should not create national security courts to handle these prosecutions.

For over 230 years, federal courts have protected our fundamental constitutional rights while overseeing the prosecution and punishment of criminals, including terrorists. Indeed, over the past 20 years, more than 120 terrorism-related cases were prosecuted without jeopardizing our national security. This well-tested system is responsible for the convictions of Timothy McVeigh and Terry Nichols (Oklahoma City bombers), Ramzi Yousef and Sheikh Abdel Rahman (1993 World Trade Center bombers), Zacarias Moussaoui (member of al Qaeda who was involved in 9/11), and many others.

National security court proposals, by lessening due-process standards, threaten to undermine the constitutional rights safeguarded by our existing criminal justice system. Moreover, by depriving suspects of basic constitutional rights, any convictions by national security courts would be subject to challenge.

The argument that terrorist suspects require a special "terrorist court" with fewer rights undermines the presumption of innocence at the heart of the American judicial system. We do not yet know who among the detainees are guilty of acts of terrorism and who might be innocent. While we share the goal of convicting those who commit terrorist crimes, we cannot support a separate and unequal criminal justice system that does not protect basic constitutional rights. Nor should we adopt national security courts to oversee a legalized system of indefinite preventive detention without trial for terrorist suspects. Detaining individuals indefinitely without charge simply because we "believe" they are dangerous would violate both our Constitution and fundamental American values.

We join with the Constitution Project's bipartisan Liberty and Security committee in urging that our traditional federal courts continue to be the venue for prosecutions for terrorism offenses.

To do otherwise would allow our ideals and rights to be destroyed by the very terrorists we are seeking to convict. As we undertake the critical task of closing detention facilities and prosecuting detainees for crimes of international terrorism, we should reject this dangerous proposal.

Administration Backs Bagram Detentions

Conditions called more severe than at Guantánamo

As the detainee population at Guantánamo Bay, Cuba, has fallen, the number of alleged enemy combatants being held at Bagram Air Force base in Afghanistan, outside the capital city of Kabul, has soared to more than 600 prisoners. Conditions at their makeshift prison are described as more severe than those at Guantánamo.

Under President George W. Bush, the government claimed the power to hold the Bagram prisoners indefinitely without charge — the same legal position that the Supreme Court ultimately rejected in regard to the Guantánamo detainees. Now a federal judge in Washington is considering habeas corpus petitions challenging their detentions filed by four prisoners who were captured outside Afghanistan and brought to Bagram. [1]

The four prisoners — two Yemenis, an Afghan and a Tunisian — deny any affiliation with al Qaeda or the Taliban or hostile conduct or activities directed against the United States. The government is claiming that the prisoners have no right to challenge their detentions because they are being held outside U.S. territory.

Lawyers from the Stanford International Human Rights Clinic, the International Justice Network and the Yale International Human Rights Clinic represent the four men. In a Jan. 7 hearing, Barbara Olshansky, a visiting professor at Stanford University, told Judge John Bates that the case showed that the government "has not learned the lessons of Guantánamo."

Bates, who was appointed to the bench by Bush in 2001, signaled doubts about the government's position in the hearing, according to The Associated Press. [2] "These individuals are no different than those detained at Guantánamo except where they're housed," Bates said during the three-hour hearing.

Bates also challenged arguments by Justice Department lawyer John O'Quinn that the prisoners could not be released because they might return to the battlefield. "They were not on the battlefield to begin with," Bates said. O'Quinn disagreed. "Post-9/11, the battle is not limited to the traditional battlefield," he said.

In the hearing, Bates questioned whether the government's stance would change once President Obama took office. O'Quinn said he could not answer. Two weeks later, Bates on Jan. 22 issued an order asking the new administration whether it wanted to "refine its views" in the case. In a two-sentence reply filed on Feb. 20, the administration said, "the Government adheres to its previously articulated position."

---

[1] The case is *Makaleh v. Gates*, U.S. District Court for the District of Columbia Circuit, 06-1669. Background drawn from Eric Schmitt, "Two Prisons, Similar Issues for President," *The New York Times*, Jan. 27, 2009, p. A1; Lyle Denniston, "Obama asked for views on Bagram detainees," SCOTUS-Blog, Jan. 23, 2009, www.scotusblog.com/wp/obama-asked-for-views-on-bagram-detainees.

[2] Lara Jakes, "Detainees in Afghanistan seeking right for release," The Associated Press, Jan. 7, 2009.

Continued from p. 192

amounting to torture at Guantánamo before essentially being cleared and released after diplomatic pressure from the British government. Three of the men — Shafiq Rasul, Asif Iqbal and Rhuhel Ahmed — say they were aiding humanitarian relief efforts in Afghanistan when they were captured by forces aligned with the notorious Uzbek warlord Rashim Dotsum and turned over to U.S. forces for a bounty. The fourth, Jamal al-Harith, was taken into custody when U.S. forces took over a Taliban jail where he was being held on suspicion of being a British spy.

In their civil suit filed in federal court in Washington in 2004 after their release, the men claim that they were subjected at Guantánamo to beatings, solitary confinement, exposure to extreme heat and cold, threats of attack from unmuzzled dogs, nudity and sleep deprivation. In addition to those claimed constitutional violations, the suit claims that alleged interference with their religious beliefs violated the federal Religious Freedom Restoration Act.

Without addressing the allegations, the government won a ruling from the U.S. Court of Appeals for the District of Columbia Circuit in January 2008 dismissing the suit on legal grounds. The three-judge panel rejected the constitutional claims because the plaintiffs were held outside U.S. territory. As an alternative basis for dismissal, the court said the military officials named as defendants were entitled to qualified immunity from suit. [21]

The Supreme Court in December ordered the appeals court to reconsider the decision in light of its June 12 ruling permitting Guantánamo detainees to bring habeas corpus actions. The appeals court has ordered a new round of briefs to be filed in March, but Eric Lewis, the private lawyer representing the men, is pessimistic about getting a ruling from a panel that he describes as "not sympathetic." He says he will appeal an unfavorable ruling to the Supreme Court.

"Civil accountability is the one mechanism of accountability that's out there," says Lewis, a Washington attorney handling the case on a pro bono basis. "There's been a fair amount of confirmation [of mistreatment] that's come in, essentially through statements made, books written, but no judicial accountability."

In another high-profile Guantánamo-related case, the Obama administration in February followed the Bush administration's stance in invoking a "state secrets" privilege to block a civil suit by five current or former detainees over the Bush administration's practice of "extraordinary rendition," or sending suspected terrorists to other countries, where they allege they were tortured. The plaintiffs are seeking civil damages from a private airline for its alleged role in transporting them in cooperation with the CIA.

The Bush administration won a lower court ruling to dismiss the case on the ground that a trial would inevitably disclose state secrets. When the case was argued on Feb. 9 before the federal appeals court in San Francisco, Justice Department lawyers reaffirmed that position and said under questioning the stance had been "thoroughly vetted with appropriate officials" in the new administration.

Two of the five plaintiffs were eventually taken to Guantánamo. One was released in 2008; the other — Binyham Mohamed — was released on Feb. 22. The British government says it has evidence Mohamed was tortured while in Moroccan custody, but blocked its release after the Bush administration threatened to review intelligence sharing arrangements with Britain if the material was disclosed. After a British court reluctantly bowed to that decision, the White House issued a statement thanking the British government "for its continued commitment to protect sensitive national security information." [22]

Allegations of torture at Guantánamo gained new currency after the Defense Department judge overseeing the military commissions system confirmed that she blocked the prosecution of Mohammed al-Qahtani in May 2008 because she was convinced he had been tortured. Susan Crawford, who has the title of convening authority of the military commissions, made the statement in an interview with *The Washington Post's* Bob Woodward published in January. [23]

Qahtani is alleged to have planned to join the 9/11 hijackings but was denied entry into the United States. He was captured in Afghanistan, transported to Guantánamo and interrogated over 50 days from November 2002 to January 2003.

In the interview, Crawford details "abusive" techniques that included prolonged interrogation and forced nudity that had "a medical impact" on him. "His treatment met the legal definition of torture," Crawford is quoted as saying. Military prosecutors attempted to file new charges without using statements made during the interrogation, but Crawford said in the interview that she would not allow the case to proceed. ∎

OUTLOOK

Looking for Closure

With the Guantánamo prison camp now slated to be closed, the Pentagon is making available on its Web site the most complete picture of conditions at the facility the government has ever published. The 85-page report by the review team appointed by Defense Secretary Gates in January details everything from the detainees' bedding, clothing and food and water to religious practices, health care and access to lawyers and others.

Despite finding the facility in compliance with humane-treatment requirements of the Geneva Conventions, the report recommends a number of steps "consistent with the approach of Chain of Command to continually enhance conditions of detainment." As examples, the team — headed by Adm. Patrick Walsh, vice chief of naval operations — recommends increasing detainees' opportunities for socialization, improving trust between health providers and detainees and video recording all interrogations.

At some length, the report describes the procedures for force-feeding hunger strikers and concludes the practices comply with international law standards. But the report fails to note — except in a letter from the American Civil Liberties

Union attached as an appendix — that some 30 detainees, more than 10 percent of the population, are now on hunger strikes to protest conditions at the camp. Two prisoners, the ACLU says, have been force-fed through their noses since August 2005.

Human-rights groups and lawyers for the detainees rejected the report's conclusions. Susan Havens, a New York City lawyer who has been visiting Guantánamo since 2004, told *The New York Times* that conditions "are worse than they have ever been." The ACLU pronounced the conditions in violation of domestic and international law, and along with Amnesty International and Human Rights First called for a host of specific changes plus monitoring by independent human-rights groups. [24]

As the dispute illustrates, the Obama administration is not yet satisfying the groups that waged seven years of legal and political warfare against the Bush administration's policies on detention and interrogation. Whether or not President Obama succeeds in closing the Guantánamo prison camp by Jan. 22, 2010, the Guantánamo story — in all its ramifications — seems likely to continue, perhaps for years to come.

The administration's increased transparency regarding Guantánamo is apt to result in increased news coverage as detainees are transferred or released to other countries or brought to the United States for trial or detention. Many of the detainees will themselves seek out coverage. When he arrived in Britain this week, ex-detainee Binyam Mohamed issued a statement through the human-rights group Reprieve: "I am not asking for vengeance, only that the truth should be made known, so that nobody in the future should have to endure what I have endured." [25]

Other detainees are less likely to seek attention, but critics of the administration probably will scrutinize the background and biographies of prisoners as they are released and watch for any evidence that any of them turn to anti-U.S. activities. "The Republican Party or at least parts of it are ready, willing and able to jump if some person who is released creates some havoc," says military-law expert Fidell.

Court cases are certain to drag on, repeatedly giving the administration hard choices to adopt or repudiate legal stances the government took under President Bush. The administration may be able to skirt one high-profile case: the habeas corpus appeal by Ali Saleh Kahlah al-Marri, the Qatari arrested as an al Qaeda sleeper agent while in the United States on a student visa. Chesney, the Texas law professor, and other observers speculate that the government could avert the April 27 arguments at the Supreme Court by indicting him and prosecuting him in a civilian criminal court. Civil cases seeking damages for past conduct, however, are less susceptible to being sidestepped.

The possible transfer of any of the prisoners to U.S. facilities is already stirring opposition from lawmakers or other officials in communities that might be affected. Possible detention facilities in the United States include the U.S. Disciplinary Barracks at Fort Leavenworth, Kansas, the military's only maximum-security prison; Camp Pendleton in California; the Charleston Naval Brig in South Carolina, and the federal Supermax prison in Florence, Colo.

Lawmakers from all four states are raising objections. Both Kansas senators — Republicans Sam Brownback and Pat Roberts — have introduced legislation along with Missouri Republican. Sen. Christopher "Kit" Bond to require a 90-day study before any transfer. Rep. Henry Brown, R-S.C., has a similar bill for his state. Rep. Duncan Hunter, R-Calif., wants to prohibit use of federal funds to transfer detainees to Camp Pendleton, which is near his San Diego-area district. And members of Colorado's congressional delegation had earlier argued that a civilian prison is unsuitable for military purposes. [26]

Meanwhile, the war in Afghanistan could further increase the number of prisoners at Bagram Air Base — and the number of legal challenges. "Afghanistan is still a physical location of actual counter-insurgency where the war is heating up not cooling down," Chesney says.

Any congressional moves to investigate Bush administration policies will also serve to prolong the story and help spotlight Obama policies as well. In addition, legislative proposals to regulate terrorism-related detention, interrogation and surveillance — including preventive detention — could force the administration's hands on some policy areas. But, says Brookings scholar Wittes, "Congress since the war on terror has never been the lead actor and it will not be."

In a somewhat surprising comment, White House counsel Craig left open the possibility of administration support for preventive detention. "It's possible but hard to imagine Barack Obama as the first president of the United States to introduce a preventive-detention law," Craig told the *New Yorker's* Jane Mayer. [27]

Facing innumerable economic issues, Congress is showing no interest so far in revisiting the detention and interrogation issues that sharply divided Democrats and Republicans over the past seven years. But Craig is making clear that the White House understands the administration's actions will be closely watched.

"We don't own the problem — it was created by the previous administration," Craig said in the interview. "But we'll be held accountable for how we handle this."

Notes

[1] For coverage, see Lyle Denniston, "Jawad Torture Case Put on Hold," SCOTUSBlog, Feb. 4, 2009, www.scotusblog.com/wp/?s=jawad.

[2] A Webcast of the panel discussion, "The Post-Guantánamo Era: A Dialogue on the Law and Policy of Detention and Counterterrorism," is available at www.utexas.edu/law/news/2009/020309_webcast_post_Guantánamo.html. Other speakers included Bellinger; Stephen Vladeck, a professor at American University College of Law in Washington; and Benjamin Wittes of the Brookings Institution. Quotes in this report from Bellinger and Wittes are from the panel discussion. For background on counterterrorism policies since 9/11, see these *CQ Researcher* reports: Peter Katel, "Homeland Security," Feb. 13, 2009, pp. 129-152; Peter Katel and Kenneth Jost, "Treatment of Detainees," Aug. 25, 2006, pp. 673-696; Peter Katel, "Global Jihad," Oct. 14, 2005, pp. 857-880; Kenneth Jost, "Re-examining 9/11," June 4, 2004, pp. 493-516; Mary H. Cooper, "Hating America," Nov. 23, 2001, pp. 969-992; and David Masci and Kenneth Jost, "War on Terrorism," Oct. 12, 2001, pp. 817-848. See also these *CQ Global Researcher* reports: Robert Kiener, "Crisis in Pakistan," December 2008, pp. 321-348; Sarah Glazer, "Radical Islam in Europe," November 2007, pp. 265-294, and Seth Stern, "Torture Debate," September 2007, pp. 211-236.

[3] Benjamin Wittes, *Law and the Long War: The Future of Justice in the Age of Terror* (2008), pp. 72-102; Benjamin Wittes and Zaahira Wyne, "The Current Detainee Population of Guantánamo," Brookings Institution, Dec. 16, 2008 (periodically updated), www.brookings.edu/reports/2008/1216_detainees_wittes.aspx.

[4] Department of Defense, "Review Of Department Compliance With President's Executive

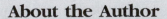

About the Author

Associate Editor **Kenneth Jost** graduated from Harvard College and Georgetown University Law Center. He is the author of the *Supreme Court Yearbook* and editor of *The Supreme Court from A to Z* (both *CQ Press*). He was a member of the *CQ Researcher* team that won the American Bar Association's 2002 Silver Gavel Award. His previous reports include "Treatment of Detainees" and "War on Terrorism."

Order On Detainee Conditions Of Confinement," February 2009, p. 5, App. 18, www.defenselink.mil/pubs/pdfs/REVIEW_OF_DEPART-MENT_COMPLIANCE_WITH_PRESIDENTS_EXECUTIVE_ORDER_ON_DETAINEE_CONDI-TIONS_OF_CONFINEMENTa.pdf.

[5] The case is *Boumediene v. Bush*, 553 U.S. — (June 12, 2008). For an account, see Kenneth Jost, "Guantánamo Detainees Entitled to Habeas Corpus," *Supreme Court Yearbook 2007-2008.*

[6] Robert F. Worth, "Freed by U.S., Saudi Becomes a Qaeda Chief," *The New York Times*, Jan. 23, 2009, p. A1.

[7] For coverage, see David Morgan, "Pentagon: 61 ex-Guantánamo detainees return to terrorism," Reuters, Jan. 13, 2009.

[8] Human Rights First, "How to Close Guantánamo: Blueprint for the Next Administration," August 2008 (updated November 2008), www.humanrightsfirst.org/pdf/080818-USLS-gitmo-blueprint.pdf; Center for Strategic and International Studies, "Closing Guantánamo: From Bumper Sticker to Blueprint," September 2008, www.csis.org/hrs/gtmoreport. See also Human Rights Watch, "Fighting Terrorism Fairly and Effectively," Nov. 16, 2008, www.hrw.org/en/reports/2008/11/16/fighting-terrorism-fairly-and-effectively.

[9] Robert F. Worth, "Saudis Issue List of 85 Terrorism Suspects," *The New York Times*, Feb. 4, 2009, p. A5.

[10] For coverage, see Abby Goodnough and Scott Shane, "Padilla Is Guilty on All Charges in Terror Trial," *The New York Times*, Aug. 17, 2007, p. A1; Adam Liptak, "A New Model of Terror Trial," *The New York Times*, Aug. 18, 2007, p. A1.

[11] CSIS Report, *op. cit.*, pp. 15-16.

[12] The cases are *Hamdi v. Rumsfeld*, 542 U.S. 507 (2004); *Rasul v. Bush*, 542 U.S. 466 (2004); *Hamdan v. Rumsfeld*, 548 U.S. 557 (2006); and Boumediene, *op. cit.* For accounts, see respective editions of Kenneth Jost, *Supreme Court Yearbook*, CQ Press.

[13] Quoted in Julian E. Barnes, "Review of Guantánamo Detainees Begins," *Los Angeles Times*, Feb. 14, 2009, p. A11.

[14] Ratner quoted in Philip Shenon, "Suit to Be Filed on Behalf of 3 Captives," *The New York Times*, Feb. 19, 2002, p. A5; Cheh quoted in Naftali Bendavid, "U.S. illegally holding 3 detainees in Cuba, suit claims; Legal experts say families' lawyers face uphill battles," *Chicago Tribune*, Feb. 20, 2002, p. 3.

[15] See Steven Lee Myers, "Bush Decides to Keep Guantánamo Open," *The New York Times*, Oct. 21, 2008, p. A16.

[16] Executive Order: Review and Disposition of Individuals Detained at the Guantánamo Bay Naval Base and Closure of Detention Facilities, www.whitehouse.gov/the_press_office/Closure_Of_Guantanamo_Detention_Facilities/, Jan. 22, 2009.

[17] See Peter Finn, "Evidence in Terror Cases Said to Be in Chaos," *The Washington Post*, Jan. 14, 2009, p. A8. Additional quotes and background from a follow-up story by Karen De Young and Peter Finn, "Guantánamo Case Files in Disarray," *ibid.*, Jan. 25, 2009, p. A5.

[18] See Raymond Bonner, "Detainee to Return to Britain, as Efforts to Prove Torture Claims Continue," *The New York Times*, Feb. 23, 2009, p. A5.

[19] "Officials says Italy will not take Gitmo inmates," The Associated Press, Feb. 16, 2009.

[20] The U.S. case pending before the Ninth Circuit is *Mohamed v. Jeppesen Dataplan*, Inc., 08-5693. For coverage, see Maura Dolan and Carol J. Williams, "Court urged to deny rendition trial," *Los Angeles Times*, Feb. 10, 2009, p. A10. See also Glenn Greenwald, "Binyam Mohamed, war crimes investigations, and American exceptionalism," *Salon.com*, Feb. 19, 2009.

[21] The decision is *Rasul v. Myers*, 06-5209, D.C. Circuit, Jan. 11, 2008, http://pacer.cadc.us-courts.gov/docs/common/opinions/200801/06-5209a.pdf.

[22] For a critical account before Mohamed's release, see Glenn Greenwald, "Binyam Mohamed, war crimes investigations, and American exceptionalism," *Salon.com*, Feb. 19, 2009.

[23] Bob Woodward, "Detainee Tortured, Says U.S. Official," *The Washington Post*, Jan. 14, 2009, p. A1.

[24] Havens quoted in William Glaberson, "Administration Draws Fire for Report on Guantánamo," *The New York Times*, Feb. 24, 2009, p. A13. The ACLU, Amnesty International and Human Rights First letters are included as appendices to the Pentagon report, *op. cit.*

[25] Reprieve-UK represents about 30 Guantánamo detainees; Mohamed's statement is available on its Web site: www.reprieve.org.uk/Press_Statement_of_Binyam_Mohamed.htm.

[26] Suzanne Gamboa, "Lawmakers: Guantánamo detainees should 'Keep Out,'" The Associated Press, Feb. 2, 2009.

[27] Jane Mayer, "The Hard Cases," *The New Yorker*, Feb. 23, 2009, p. 41.

Bibliography

Selected Sources

Books

Cole, David, *Justice at War: The Men and Ideas That Shaped America's War on Terror*, New York Review Books, 2008.

A professor at Georgetown University Law Center critically examines the roles played by, among others, Vice President Dick Cheney, attorneys general John Ashcroft and Alberto Gonzales and Justice Department lawyer John Yoo in the formation of the Bush administration's legal policies in the war on terror. Includes chapter notes.

Greenberg, Karen, *The Least Worst Place: Guantánamo's First 100 Days*, Oxford University Press, 2009.

This early history of the prison camp at Guantánamo Bay depicts the supplanting of a military commander's liberal policies by more stringent conditions and treatment as ordered by Defense Secretary Donald Rumsfeld. Greenberg is executive director of the Center on Law and Security, New York University School of Law. Includes notes, six-page bibliography.

Marguiles, Joseph, *Guantánamo and the Abuse of Presidential Power*, Simon & Schuster, 2006.

This critical account is by one of the lawyers in the Supreme Court case that opened the door to habeas corpus challenges by Guantánamo detainees. Includes notes.

Mayer, Jane, *The Dark Side: The Inside Story of How the War on Terror Turned into a War on American Ideals*, Doubleday, 2008.

A writer for *The New Yorker* provides a detailed, critical account of the Bush administration's policies on detention, interrogation and surveillance. Includes notes, nine-page bibliography.

Wittes, Benjamin, *Law and the Long War: The Future of Justice in the Age of Terror*, Penguin, 2008.

A legal scholar at the Brookings Institution argues in this influential, ideology-crossing book for new bodies of law — to be crafted by Congress and the executive — dealing with detention, interrogation, trial and surveillance in the new national security environment in "the age of terror."

Worthington, Andy, *The Guantánamo Files: The Stories of the 774 Detainees in America's Illegal Prison*, Pluto Press, 2007, www.andyworthington.co.uk/.

An avowedly leftist British journalist gives detailed accounts of the experiences of prisoners held at Guantánamo and at Bagram Air Base in Afghanistan, relating disturbing allegations of mistreatment and intimidation. Includes detailed notes. Worthington updates his coverage on his Web site: www.andyworthington.co.uk/. For first-person accounts by former detainees, see Moazzam Begg with Victoria Brittain, *Enemy Combatant: My Imprisonment at Guantánamo, Bagram, and Kandahar* (New Press, 2006) and Murat Kurnaz with Helmut Kuhn, *Five Years of My Life: An Innocent Man at Guantánamo* (Palgrave/Macmillan, 2008).

Articles

Chandrasekaran, Rajiv, "From Captive to Suicide Bomber," *The Washington Post*, Feb. 22, 2009, p. A1; "A 'Ticking Time Bomb' Goes Off," *ibid.*, Feb. 23, 2009, p. A1.

The two-part story traces the story of Abdallah al-Ajmi from his capture in Afghanistan and nearly four-year imprisonment at Guantánamo through his release to his native Kuwait and his death as a "suicide bomber" in Iraq in an attack on an Iraqi outpost that killed 13 Iraqi soldiers.

Toobin, Jeffrey, "Camp Justice," *The New Yorker*, April 14, 2008, p. 32.

The CNN legal affairs correspondent provides a close look at the court facilities at Guantánamo — built for military commission proceedings that President Obama suspended as part of his review of detainees' cases and his plan to close the prison camp by 2010.

Reports and Studies

Garcia, Michael John, *et al.*, "Closing the Guantánamo Detention Center: Legal Issues," Congressional Research Service, Jan. 22, 2009, http://assets.opencrs.com/rpts/R40139_20090122.pdf.

The 37-page, carefully annotated report thoroughly covers the legal background and current legal issues relating to the closing of the Guantánamo detention center.

Prieto, Daniel B., "War About Terror: Civil Liberties and National Security After 9/11," Council on Foreign Relations, February 2009, www.cfr.org/publication/18373/.

The 116-page "working paper" by an adjunct fellow at the Council on Foreign Relations comprehensively examines civil liberties issues in regard to post-9/11 national security policies. The working paper is based on work by a task force composed of more than two dozen members that — according to the council's president — "was unable to agree on a set of meaningful conclusions" on the issues discussed.

Wittes, Benjamin, and Zaahira Wyne, "The Current Detainee Population of Guantánamo," Brookings Institute, Dec. 16, 2008 (periodically updated), www.brookings.edu/reports/2008/1216_detainees_wittes.aspx.

The site provides the most up-to-date information on the Guantánamo detainees.

On the Web

The Miami Herald has provided comprehensive coverage of Guantánamo and compiled much of that coverage on a continuously updated section of its Web site: www.miami-herald.com/Guantánamo/.

The Next Step:

Additional Articles from Current Periodicals

Bagram Air Base Prisoners

Lasseter, Tom, "Abuse Plagued Afghan Camps, Too," *Seattle Times*, June 16, 2008, p. A3.

Former guards and detainees say Bagram Air Base was a center of systematic brutality for nearly two years.

Schmitt, Eric, "Two Prisons, Similar Issues for President," *The New York Times*, Jan. 27, 2009, p. A1.

The fate of hundreds of prisoners at Bagram Air Base — with few privileges and virtually no access to lawyers — presents an early challenge to the Obama administration.

Wilber, Del Quentin, "In Courts, Afghanistan Air Base May Become Next Guantánamo," *The Washington Post*, June 29, 2008, p. A14.

The Justice Department says Bagram prisoners shouldn't have the same rights as those in Guantánamo.

Civilian Trials

Conery, Ben, "Rules for Trials Seen As Lacking," *The Washington Times*, July 22, 2008, p. A3.

The Supreme Court has given Guantánamo detainees the right to use civilian courts to challenge detention but offers little guidance on how such hearings should be conducted.

Issenberg, Sasha, and Farah Stockman, "McCain Blasts Ruling on Guantánamo," *The Boston Globe*, June 14, 2008, p. A6.

Sen. John McCain, R-Ariz., has criticized a Supreme Court ruling giving Guantánamo prisoners the right to challenge their detention in civilian courts.

Rosenberg, Carol, "Senator: Give Detainees Rights," *The Miami Herald*, March 24, 2007, p. A3.

Sen. Arlen Specter, R-Pa., favors restoring civilian court review of Guantánamo detention cases to ensure the availability of habeas corpus rights for detainees.

White, Josh, "Guantánamo Detainee Rejects Court Procedure," *The Washington Post*, April 30, 2008, p. A4.

Military hearings for Guantánamo detainees have been criticized for their departures from established procedures.

Releasing Detainees

Barnes, Julian E., "Justice Begins Review of Guantánamo Detainees," *Los Angeles Times*, Feb. 14, 2009, p. A11.

The Obama administration has begun reviewing which detainees at Guantánamo can be prosecuted and which can be transferred to other countries.

Clancy, Paddy, "Ireland Wants Gitmo Prisoners," *Irish Voice*, Jan. 28, 2009, p. 6.

Ireland is prepared to resettle detainees from the U.S. military facility in Guantánamo Bay, Cuba, so long as there is a common European Union approach.

Mazzetti, Mark, and Scott Shane, "Where Will Guantánamo Detainees Go?" *The New York Times*, Jan. 24, 2009, p. A13.

Republican lawmakers argue that closing Guantánamo could allow terrorists to get off on legal technicalities and be released across the United States.

Sell, Julie, "Europe Weighs Helping U.S. Close Guantánamo," *Myrtle Beach Sun-News* (South Carolina), Jan. 20, 2009, p. A11.

European politicians are debating whether to help President Obama closed Guantánamo by accepting some of the detainees.

Uighurs

Gillies, Rob, "3 Uighurs at Guantánamo Ask Canada for Asylum," The Associated Press, Feb. 4, 2009.

Three Uighurs cleared for release from Guantánamo have applied for political asylum in Canada amid fears of prosecution if they were turned over to China.

Spiegel, Peter, and Barbara Demick, "Poised for Release — But to Where?" *Los Angeles Times*, Feb. 18, 2009, p. A5.

China is insisting that Uighurs held at Guantánamo by the United States be sent back to China to face trial for separatist activities.

Yen, Hope, "Conservatives Call on Bush to Free Muslim Uighurs," *The Miami Herald*, Nov. 20, 2008.

A group of Republicans has called on President Bush to release 17 Uighurs at Guantánamo, claiming their continued detention undermines U.S. standing in the world.

CITING CQ RESEARCHER

Sample formats for citing these reports in a bibliography include the ones listed below. Preferred styles and formats vary, so please check with your instructor or professor.

MLA STYLE

Jost, Kenneth. "Rethinking the Death Penalty." CQ Researcher 16 Nov. 2001: 945-68.

APA STYLE

Jost, K. (2001, November 16). Rethinking the death penalty. *CQ Researcher, 11*, 945-968.

CHICAGO STYLE

Jost, Kenneth. "Rethinking the Death Penalty." *CQ Researcher*, November 16, 2001, 945-968.

CHAPTER

8

TORTURE DEBATE

BY SETH STERN

Excerpted from the CQ Global Researcher. Seth Stern. (September 2007). "Torture Debate." *CQ Global Researcher*, 211-236.

Torture Debate

BY SETH STERN

THE ISSUES

It is called, simply, waterboarding. A prisoner is strapped to a board with his feet above his head, his mouth and nose covered, usually with cloth or cellophane. Water is then poured over his face, inducing gagging and a terrifying sense of drowning.

The U.S. government — which has been accused of using waterboarding on detainees it suspects are terrorists — denies that it practices torture or cruel, inhuman or degrading treatment. The Central Intelligence Agency (CIA) says it must use what it calls "enhanced interrogation techniques" — to obtain critical information from "enemy combatants" in the war on terrorism. [1] But human rights advocates say waterboarding and other abusive interrogation tactics are prohibited by international law.

To be sure, the United States is far from the worst offender when it comes to mistreating prisoners. Even human rights advocates who complain the most bitterly about the tactics used in America's war on terror say they don't compare to those utilized by the world's worst human rights abusers.

"Nothing the administration has done can compare in its scale to what happens every day to victims of cruel dictatorships around the world," Tom Malinowski, Human Rights Watch's Washington advocacy director, told the U.S. Senate Foreign Relations Committee on July 26. "The United States is not Sudan or Cuba or North Korea." [2]

Indeed, about 160 countries practice torture today, according to human rights groups and the U.S. State Department. [3] In July, for example, six

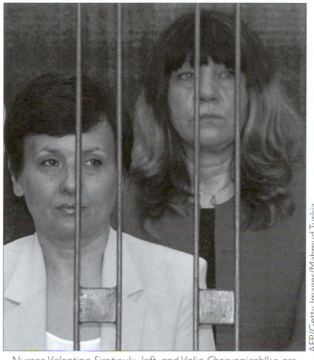

Nurses Valentina Siropoulu, left, and Valia Cherveniashlka are among six Bulgarian medical workers who were tortured while imprisoned for eight years in Libya on charges they infected hundreds of Libyan children with HIV-AIDS. They were released in August. About 160 countries torture prisoners, despite six international treaties banning the practice.

Bulgarian medical workers freed after eight years in a Libyan prison said they had been tortured. "We were treated like animals," said Ashraf al-Hazouz, one of the prisoners, who had been accused of deliberately infecting Libyan children with the HIV-AIDS virus. Hazouz said the Libyans attached electrodes to his genitals and feet, unleashed attack dogs on him and tied his hands and legs to a metal bar, spinning him "like a chicken on a rotisserie." [4]

While other countries' abuse methods may seem more abhorrent, human rights advocates worldwide complain angrily that America's detention and interrogation practices in the post-9/11 war on terror have lowered the bar for torturers worldwide, giving habitual abusers a new justification for their behavior.

America's detention policies since Sept. 11, 2001, "are a gift to dictators everywhere" who "use America's poor example to shield themselves from international criticism and pressure," Malinowski said. Abusive governments now routinely "justify their own, longstanding practices of systematically violating basic human rights norms" by arguing that they — like the United States — must use torture to deal with the threat of international terrorism. [5]

U.S. counterterrorism policies that anger allies and human rights activists include the indefinite detentions — without a guaranteed trial or right to counsel — of hundreds of alleged terrorists at Guantánamo Bay, Cuba, beginning shortly after 9/11. Then in April 2004 CBS' "60 Minutes II" televised explosive photographs that circulated around the world portraying harsh interrogation methods that reportedly had migrated from Guantánamo to the U.S.-run Abu Ghraib military prison near Baghdad. A year later *The Washington Post* revealed that the CIA was operating so-called "black sites" — secret prisons in Eastern Europe and Southeast Asia where detainees were subjected to extreme interrogation methods, allegedly including waterboarding. [6] Finally, news that the United States was kidnapping terror suspects from foreign locations and transporting them to interrogation sites in third countries with reputations for practicing torture — a tactic known as extraordinary rendition — triggered further global outrage. [7]

By adopting such measures, the United States has lost its moral authority to condemn torture and human rights abuses in other countries, say critics. "It's a very bad precedent for people to be able

Torture Still in Use Throughout the World

Some 160 countries practice torture, according to a 2005 survey of incidents reported by the U.S. Department of State and Amnesty International. Besides using torture to solicit information, some countries use it to punish or intimidate dissidents, separatists, insurgents and religious minorities. The Council of Europe accuses the U.S. Central Intelligence Agency (CIA) of using its rendition program to send kidnapped terror suspects to be interrogated in 11 cities — all in countries that practice torture.

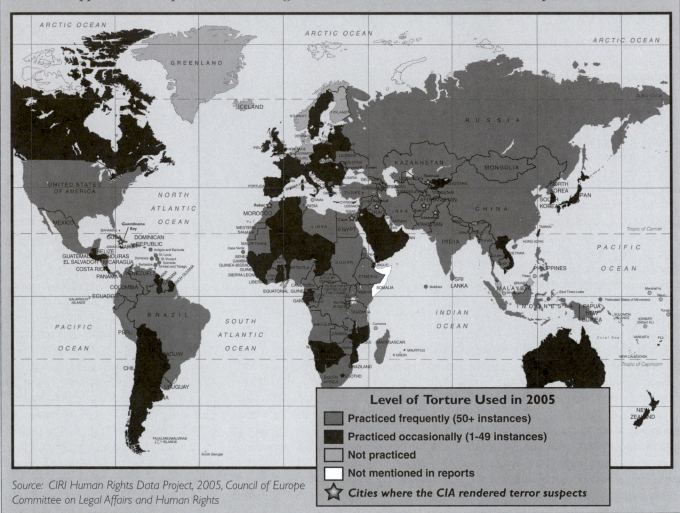

Level of Torture Used in 2005

- Practiced frequently (50+ instances)
- Practiced occasionally (1-49 instances)
- Not practiced
- Not mentioned in reports
- ☆ Cities where the CIA rendered terror suspects

Source: CIRI Human Rights Data Project, 2005, Council of Europe Committee on Legal Affairs and Human Rights

to say 'the U.S. — the biggest democracy promoter in the world — has to use it, why can't we?' " says physician Bhogendra Sharma, president of the Center for Victims of Torture in Nepal, which treats victims tortured by both the Nepalese government and Maoist guerrillas.

Few American ambassadors today "dare to protest another government's harsh interrogations, detentions without trial, or even 'disappearances,' knowing how easily an interlocutor could turn the tables and cite U.S. misconduct as an excuse for his government's own abuses," said a 2007 Human Rights Watch (HRW) report. [8]

Sarah Leah Whitson, HRW's director for the Middle East and North Africa, says when she visits officials in those regions to discuss their use of torture, their first reply now is often, "What about the United States? Go talk to the U.S. government."

The worldwide anger triggered by America's post-9/11 detention and interrogation policies stems not only from the perception that notorious governments now feel free to continue torturing prisoners. It also stems from widespread perceptions that:

- The United States' overwhelming military and technological superiority have made it arrogant, immune from having to abide by international norms.

- America's pervasive cultural influence has, since 9/11, "normalized" torture by spreading the concept across the globe that torture works and can be legally or morally justified.
- The United States has squandered its historic position as the world's leader in the fight against human rights abuses, opening itself to charges of being a hypocrite.

When the U.S. State Department released its annual report on human rights violators in 2005, both China and Russia said the United States has its own abuses to explain. "Unfortunately, [the report] once again gives us reason to say that double standards are a characteristic of the American approach to such an important theme," said a statement issued by the Russian foreign ministry. "Characteristically off-screen is the ambiguous record of the United States itself." [9]

Disappointment over U.S. tactics has been widespread. *El Tiempo*, a leading newspaper in Bogotá, Colombia, editorialized in 2005: "It seems incredible that these kind of un-civilizing backward steps are coming from a country which declares itself a defender of Western values and which has been so on more than one occasion." [10]

A 2006 survey of 26,000 people in 25 countries found that 67 percent disapproved of U.S. treatment of detainees in Guantánamo and other prisons. Some of the highest disapproval rates were among America's closest allies in Europe — which have suffered their own terrorist attacks since 9/11 — and Middle Eastern allies such as Lebanon and Egypt, who fear the growing influence of Islamic extremists. [11]

But the 9/11 attacks did more than raise the profile of the torture debate in the United States. An Australian law professor has become one of the world's most vocal advocates for "life-saving compassionate torture," which he says is justified if it elicits crucial

Severe Torture Still Used by Many Nations

According to the U.S. State Department and Human Rights Watch, the following nations are among those condoning widespread and particularly severe forms of torture:

 **China:** Prison guards are forbidden from using torture, but former detainees report the use of electric shock, beatings and shackles. Among those targeted for abuse are adherents of the outlawed Falun Gong spiritual movement, Tibetans and Muslim Uighur prisoners.

 **Egypt:** Government interrogators from the State Security Investigations arm of the Ministry of the Interior regularly torture suspected Islamic militants, including prisoners transferred to Egypt by the United States. Victims were kicked, burned with cigarettes, shackled, forcibly stripped, beaten with water hoses and dragged on the floor.

 Indonesia: Security officers in Aceh Province systematically torture suspected supporters of the armed Free Aceh movement, using beatings, cigarette burning and electric shock.

 **Iran:** Political prisoners are subjected to sensory deprivation known as "white torture" — they are held in all-white cells with no windows, with prison clothes and even meals all in white.

 Morocco: Terrorism suspects detained after a May 2003 attack in Casablanca were subjected to torture and mistreatment, including severe beatings.

 Nepal: Both government security personnel and Maoist rebels employ torture, including beating the soles of victims' feet, submersion in water and sexual humiliation.

 Nigeria: Armed robbery and murder suspects are subjected to beatings with batons, horse whips, iron bars and cables.

 North Korea: Captors routinely tortured and mistreated prisoners using electric shock, prolonged periods of exposure, humiliations such as public nakedness, being hung by the wrists and forcing mothers recently repatriated from China to watch the infanticide of their newborn infants.

 Russia: Russian security forces conducting so-called anti-terror operations in Chechnya mutilate victims and dump their bodies on the sides of roads.

 Uganda: Government security forces in unregistered detention facilities torture prisoners with caning and severe beatings and by inflicting pain to the genitals.

 Uzbekistan: Police, prison guards and members of the National Security Service routinely employ suffocation, electric shock, deprivation of food and water and sexual abuse. Prison regulations in 2005 permitted beatings under medical supervision.

Sources: "Human Rights Watch's 2007 World Report;" U.S. State Department "2006 Country Reports on Human Rights Practices"

Views Differ on U.S. Interrogation Tactics

A wide gulf exists between Americans' and Europeans' views of how the United States treats terrorism suspects. Americans are almost evenly split on whether the United States uses torture, but three-quarters of Germans and nearly two-thirds of Britons believe it does. And while just over half of Americans think U.S. detention policies are legal, 85 percent of Germans and 65 percent of Britons think they are illegal.

Is it your impression that the U.S. government is . . .

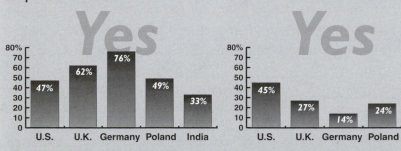

. . . currently allowing interrogators to use torture to get information from suspected terrorists?

Yes

U.S.	47%
U.K.	62%
Germany	76%
Poland	49%
India	33%

. . . making every effort to make sure that interrogators never use torture?

Yes

U.S.	45%
U.K.	27%
Germany	14%
Poland	24%
India	23%

Is it your impression that current U.S. policies for detaining people it has captured and is holding in Guantánamo Bay are or are not legal, according to international treaties on the treatment of detainees?

Are legal

U.S.	52%
U.K.	22%
Germany	8%
Poland	18%
India	28%

Are not legal

U.S.	38%
U.K.	65%
Germany	85%
Poland	50%
India	34%

Source: "American and International Opinion on the Rights of Terrorism Suspects, International Questionnaire," WorldPublicOpinion.org, June 2006

information needed to prevent future terrorist attacks and save innocent lives. (*See "At Issue," p. 229.*)

But critics of that argument point out that torture is not only used to extract life-saving information from terrorists but also to punish political dissidents, suspected criminals — who sometimes are innocent — and religious minorities. China, for instance, tortures members of the Falun Gong spiritual movement, Tibetan dissidents and Muslims from the Uighur region, according to Human Rights Watch.

In Iraq — where former leader Saddam Hussein was notorious for torturing political enemies — the U.S. occupation has not curbed the prevalence of torture by government agents or insurgents. In fact, say human rights advocates, the level of torture perpetrated by the Shiite-dominated Iraqi government and affiliated militias reportedly has escalated as the country has descended into civil strife. (*See sidebar, p. 218.*)

Despite the damage done to America's reputation by its counterterrorism tactics, President Bush in July said he was authorizing the CIA to reopen its overseas black sites. Bush had announced last September that the use of secret prisons had been suspended and that the prisoners were being transferred to Guantánamo. That decision was prompted by the U.S. Supreme Court's ruling that all U.S. detainees, including those held by the CIA, were covered by the Geneva Conventions' guidelines for the treatment of wartime detainees.

The administration said in July 2007 the CIA would comply with the conventions in its treatment of prisoners at the sites. But Bush's new order did not ban waterboarding or any other controversial interrogation techniques and gave interrogators wide latitude if their purpose is to gather intelligence needed to prevent terrorist attacks. [12]

The Bush administration and its supporters argue the United States is operating within the confines of U.S. and international law and that aggressive interrogation methods are needed to protect against future terrorist attacks. "These are dangerous men with unparalleled knowledge about terrorist networks and their plans for new attacks," President Bush said in 2006. "The security of our nation and the lives of our citizens depend on our ability to learn what these terrorists know." [13]

With America seen as abandoning its role as the world's ethical standard-bearer, human rights groups complain that the European Union (EU) has not stepped up to fill the void. The EU has dragged its feet in questioning U.S. interrogation policies, say critics, and some EU countries have secretly allowed U.S. aircraft to use their airports for rendition flights. Some renditions involved innocent citizens who were tortured in countries long known to abuse prisoners, such as Egypt and Syria. Besides generating outrage among close U.S. allies such as Canada, the incidents have led to prosecutions in Germany and Italy of Americans allegedly involved in the renditions.

As the Bush administration continues to defend itself against global criticism of its counterterrorism policies, these are some of the questions being asked:

Is torture effective?

Advocates and opponents of torture and other coercive techniques can look at the same evidence about their effectiveness and come to very different conclusions.

Take the case of Khalid Shaikh Mohammed, a senior al Qaeda operative and the alleged principal architect of the 9/11 attacks. He was captured in Pakistan in 2003 and interrogated by U.S. intelligence agents — reportedly using waterboarding — before being transferred to military custody at Guantánamo. [14] In a military hearing in March 2007 the Defense Department released a transcript of his confession in which he took credit for 31 different terrorist operations, including planning the 9/11 attacks in the United States and the beheading of *Wall Street Journal* reporter Daniel Pearl.

CIA Director Michael Hayden cited coercive interrogation techniques employed against detainees such as Mohammed (dubbed K.S.M. by intelligence agents) as an "irreplaceable" tool that helped yield information that has helped disrupt several terrorist plots since 9/11. "K.S.M. is the poster boy for using tough but

Vann Nath, one of only seven people to survive the Khmer Rouge's infamous Tuol Sleng prison, looks at a photo of Kaing Guek Eav, who ran the murderous regime's security service. Eav was recently found living in Cambodia as a born-again Christian. He was indicted by a U.N.-backed tribunal in July for his role in the torture and deaths of 14,000 men, women and children at the facility. His trial is expected to begin in 2008.

legal tactics," said Michael Sheehan, a former State Department counterterrorism official. "He's the reason these techniques exist." [15]

But opponents of aggressive interrogation techniques, like Col. Dwight Sullivan, head defense lawyer at the Office of Military Commissions, cite Mohammed's serial confessions as "a textbook example of why we shouldn't allow coercive methods." [16]

Some intelligence experts doubt the veracity of portions of Mohammed's information. For one thing they don't think a single operative — even one as high ranking as he — could have been involved in 31 separate terrorist plots. And those intimately associated

with the Pearl case are highly skeptical that Mohammed himself murdered Pearl, as he claimed.

"My old colleagues say with 100-percent certainty that it was not K.S.M. who killed Pearl," former CIA officer Robert Baer told *New Yorker* writer Jane Mayer. And Special Agent Randall Bennett, who oversaw security at the U.S. consulate in Karachi when Pearl was killed, said "K.S.M.'s name never came up" during his interviews with those convicted in 2002 of the murder. [17]

Skeptics of torture's effectiveness say most people — to end their suffering — will provide false information. For instance, a torture victim deprived of his clothes will feel so "ashamed and humiliated and cold," said retired FBI counterterrorism agent Dan Coleman, "he'll tell you anything you want to hear to get his clothing back. There's no value in it." [18]

Others say torture doesn't work against zealots. "People who are committed to their ideology or religion . . . would rather die than speak up," says Sharma at the Center for Victims of Torture in Nepal.

Both opponents and supporters of coercive interrogation methods, however, agree torture is useful for other purposes. Many countries use torture to punish dissidents, separatists or guerrillas and to intimidate others from joining such groups. "The real purpose of torture is oppression of one or the other kind, to send a signal to anyone who is an opponent that there is a very, very grave risk," says Sune Segal, head of communications for the Copenhagen-based International Rehabilitation Council for Torture Vic-

tims, which collaborates with 131 treatment centers around the world. "It's not about soliciting information."

Underlying the debate is the fact that little scientific evidence exists about whether torture works. A recent Intelligence Science Board study concluded that "virtually none" of the limited number of techniques used by U.S. personnel in recent decades "are based on scientific research or have even been subjected to scientific or systematic inquiry or evaluation." [19]

Darius Rejali, a political science professor at Reed College in Portland, Ore., says regimes that employ torture aren't likely to divulge their findings, and torturers themselves have very little incentive to boast about their work, which is punishable under international law. "Torture travels by back routes," Rejali says. "There's rarely training, so there is no particular mechanism for determining whether it works."

Experienced interrogators who have talked about their work say pain and coercion are often counterproductive. John Rothrock, who as a U.S. Air Force captain in Vietnam headed a combat interrogation team, said he didn't know "any professional intelligence officers of my generation who would think this is a good idea." [20]

Experts say the most effective interrogations require a trained interrogator. Coleman says he learned to build a rapport with even the worst suspects rather than trying to intimidate them. He would patiently work to build a relationship in which the target of his interrogation would begin to trust him and ultimately share information.

You try to "get them to the point, in the intelligence world, where they commit treason," he said. [21]

Is torture ever justified?

Australian law Professor Mirko Bagaric at Deakin University in Melbourne

Torture Has Escalated in Iraq

Saddam's brutal legacy survives.

The fall of Saddam Hussein and more than four years of U.S. occupation have done little to curb torture in Iraq. In fact, the level of torture perpetrated by government personnel and militias reportedly has escalated as the country has descended into what many consider a civil war.

The use of torture in Iraq is "totally out of hand," said Manfred Nowak, a U.N. official appointed to study torture around the world, and "many people say it is worse than it had been in the times of Saddam Hussein." [1]

Bodies brought to the Baghdad morgue often bear signs of acid-induced injuries, broken limbs and wounds caused by power drills and nails, said U.N. investigators. [2] The torture is mostly being perpetrated by the largely Shiite ministries of the Interior and Defense as well as by private Shiite militias, according to Sarah Leah Whitson, Human Rights Watch's program director for the Middle East and North Africa.

"The torture committed in the Ministry of Interior facilities we documented is certainly comparable to torture and abuse that's been recorded in the Baath prisons prior to the war," says Whitson.

In 2006 U.S. and Iraqi troops discovered a secret Baghdad

prison run by the Interior Ministry, known as Site 4, where some of the more than 1,400 prisoners were found to have been subjected to systematic abuse.

Human rights advocates say the widespread use of torture is being fueled by the breakdown of law and order and the continued employment of officials who previously used torture during Saddam's regime. The weakened Iraqi central government has been unable to rein in the abuse of prisoners in these facilities, despite promises to do so. There has been less documented evidence of torture by Sunni insurgents, Whitson points out. Sunnis usually execute their victims, often by beheading.

A January 2005 report by Human Rights Watch found that police, jailers and intelligence agents — many of whom had similar jobs under Saddam — were "committing systematic torture and other abuses." Despite being "in the throes of a significant insurgency" in which thousands of police officers and civilians are being killed, the report said, "no government — not Saddam Hussein's, not the occupying powers and not the Iraqi interim government — can justify ill-treatment of persons in custody in the name of security." [3]

The government of Iraqi Prime Minister Nuri Kamal al-Maliki has been slow to respond to reports of torture by governmental personnel, say human rights advocates. The Iraqi government "made all kinds of promises and commitments to investigate and review" allegations of torture in 2005, Whitson says, but since then the Interior Ministry "has only gone further outside control of the government," as war and sectarian violence have escalated. "There's not a commitment to making this issue a priority."

When British and Iraqi special forces raided the office of an Iraqi government intelligence agency in the southern city of Basra in March 2007, they found prisoners exhibiting signs of torture. Al-Maliki condemned the raid, but not the abuse it uncovered. [4]

Torture has continued since the start of the U.S. military occupation in Iraq. A 2004 report by the International Committee of the Red Cross found that after Saddam's fall Iraqi authorities beat detainees with cables, kicked them in the genitals and hung them by handcuffs from iron bars of cell windows for several hours at a time. [5]

Torture is also being employed in Kurdistan, a semi-autonomous region in northern Iraq that is the most stable part of the country. Human Rights Watch reported in July 2007 that detainees accused of anti-government activities were subjected to torture and other mistreatment. [6]

The torturers are security forces and personnel at detention facilities operated by the two major Kurdish political parties — the Kurdistan Democratic Party and the Patriotic Union of Kurdistan — which operate outside control of the region's government, the report said. Detainees have been beaten, put in stress positions and handcuffed for several days at a time.

Nonetheless, the abuses in Kurdistan do not equal those occurring elsewhere in Iraq. "Certainly the situation in mainland Iraq is much worse," says Whitson.

[1] BBC News, "Iraq Torture 'worse than Saddam,' " Sept. 21, 2006.

[2] *Ibid*.

[3] Doug Struck, "Torture in Iraq Still Routine, Report Says," *The Washington Post*, Jan. 25, 2005, p. A10.

[4] Kirk Semple, "Basra Raid Finds Dozens Detained by Iraqi Unit," *The New York Times*, March 5, 2007.

[5] "Report of the International Committee of the Red Cross on the Treatment by the Coalition Forces of Prisoners of War and Other Protected Persons by the Geneva Conventions in Iraq During Arrest, Internment and Interrogation," February 2004, www.globalsecurity.org/military/library/report/2004/icrc_report_iraq_feb2004.pdf.

[6] "Caught in the Whirlwind: Torture and Denial of Due Process by the Kurdistan Security Forces," Human Rights Watch, July 3, 2007, http://hrw.org/reports/2007/kurdistan0707/.

prompted a vigorous public debate in May 2005 when he suggested that torture is sometimes morally justified.

"Given the choice between inflicting a relatively small level of harm on a wrongdoer and saving an innocent person, it is verging on moral indecency to prefer the interests of the wrongdoer," Bagaric wrote in *The Age*, a leading daily paper in Melbourne. Such cases are analogous to a situation in which a wrongdoer threatens to kill a hostage unless his demands are met, he said. "In such a case, it is not only permissible but desirable for police to shoot (and kill) the wrongdoer if they get a 'clear shot.' " [22]

In the United States, Harvard Law Professor Alan Dershowitz has argued that the legal system should adjust to the reality that if it could prevent a catastrophic terrorist attack that could kill millions, interrogators will probably torture a suspect whether or not it's legal. In emergencies, he contends,

courts should issue "torture warrants" to interrogators trying to prevent such attacks.

"A formal, visible, accountable and centralized system is somewhat easier to control than an ad hoc, off-the-books and under-the-radar-screen non-system," Dershowitz wrote. [23]

Those who justify torture in certain situations usually invoke a hypothetical "ticking time bomb" scenario in which interrogators torture a suspect to obtain information that can help prevent an imminent attack. Twenty-five years ago, long before the rise of Islamist terrorists, philosophy Professor Michael Levin of the City University of New York hypothesized a similar scenario in *Newsweek*.

"Suppose a terrorist has hidden a bomb on Manhattan Island, which will detonate at noon on 4 July. . . . Suppose, further, that he is caught at 10 a.m. that fateful day, but — preferring death to failure — won't disclose where

the bomb is. . . . If the only way to save those lives is to subject the terrorist to the most excruciating possible pain, what grounds can there be for not doing so?" [24]

But opponents of torture say such perfect "ticking time bomb" scenarios occur in the movies, but rarely in real life. Interrogators usually aren't positive they have captured the one person with knowledge of a real plot. And even if they torture such a suspect, it usually won't prevent the attack because his accomplices will proceed without him, critics say.

"I was in the Army for 25 years, and I talked to lots of military people who had been in lots of wars. I talked to lots of people in law enforcement," says James Jay Carafano, a fellow at the conservative Heritage Foundation. "I've never yet ever found anyone that's ever confronted the ticking time bomb scenario. That's not the moral dilemma that people normally face." [25]

"The United States is a nation of laws," says Sen. Patrick J. Leahy, a Vermont Democrat who chairs the Senate Judiciary Committee, "and I categorically reject the view that torture, even in such compelling circumstances, can be justified." Even if harsh interrogation techniques do not rise to the level of torture, he said, they are probably illegal under international laws that prohibit cruel, inhumane or degrading treatment of prisoners.

Law professors and philosophers widely agree that torture is always immoral and should not be legalized. Once torture is allowed in extreme circumstances, they point out, it quickly spreads to less urgent situations. "It has a tendency to just proliferate," says Raimond Gaita, a professor of moral philosophy at King's College in London.

He cites the experience of Israel, which authorized coercive interrogation techniques in 1987 in limited circumstances. But interrogators in the field used more aggressive techniques with more suspects than intended.

Eitan Felner, former director of the Israeli Information Center for Human Rights in the Occupied Territories, writes the lesson of Israel's experience is "the fallacy of believing — as some influential American opinion-makers do today — that it is possible to legitimize the use of torture to thwart terrorist attacks and at the same time restrict its use to exceptional cases." [26]

Instead, torture should remain illegal and interrogators faced with the time-bomb scenario should be in the same legal position as someone who commits civil disobedience, say opponents. "Anyone who thinks an act of torture is justified should have . . . to convince a group of peers in a public trial that all necessary conditions for a morally permissible act were indeed satisfied," writes Henry Shue, a professor of politics and international relations at the University of Oxford. [27]

Human Rights advocates say that — while not explicitly endorsing torture

— U.S. policies have changed the dialogue about torture around world. "It used to be these things were automatically bad," says Jumana Musa, advocacy director for Amnesty USA. "Now, there's a cost-benefit analysis and the notion that this isn't really that bad."

Have U.S. attitudes toward torture changed?

Some prominent American politicians and some soldiers, albeit anonymously, have recently endorsed torture as a way to prevent terrorist attacks or save lives.

At a May 2007 GOP presidential debate, Rudolph W. Giuliani, the mayor of New York during the Sept. 11 terror attacks, said if elected president he would advise interrogators "to use every method they could think of" to prevent an imminent catastrophic terror attack. Other candidates were even more explicit, embracing torture with an openness that would have been unheard of before 9/11. California Rep. Duncan Hunter said he would tell the Defense secretary: "Get the information," while Colorado Rep. Tom Tancredo endorsed waterboarding. [28]

Some U.S. military personnel who have served in Iraq express similar attitudes. More than a third of the 1,700 American soldiers and Marines who responded to a 2006 survey said torture would be acceptable if it helped save the life of a fellow soldier or helped get information, and 10 percent admitted to using force against Iraqi civilians or damaging their property when it wasn't necessary. [29]

But many top U.S. military leaders, interrogators and veterans denounce torture as ineffective and say it will only make it more likely that American captives will be tortured in the future. Sen. John McCain, R-Ariz., who was tortured while a prisoner of war in Vietnam, has spoken out forcefully against torture and led the 2005 effort in Congress to limit the kinds

of interrogation methods U.S. military personnel can use.

"We've sent a message to the world that the United States is not like the terrorists. [W]e are a nation that upholds values and standards of behavior and treatment of all people, no matter how evil or bad they are," McCain said. Furthermore, he added, disavowing torture will "help us enormously in winning the war for the hearts and minds of people throughout the world in the war on terror." [30]

A 2006 public opinion survey by the University of Maryland's Program on International Policy Attitudes (PIPA) suggests that most Americans reject the use of torture. The PIPA poll found that 75 percent of Americans agreed that terror detainees had "the right not to be tortured." Fifty-seven percent said the United States should not be permitted to send terror suspects to countries known to torture, and 73 percent said government officials who engage in or order torture should be punished. Fifty-eight percent of Americans said torture was impermissible under any circumstances — about the same percentage as those in countries like Ukraine, Turkey and Kenya — but lower than the percentages in Australia, Canada and France. [31]

Some critics fear that since 9/11 U.S. television shows and movies have changed the way torture is portrayed, making torture more palatable to Americans and the rest of the world.

"It used to be the bad guys who used these techniques," says David Danzig of Human Rights First, a New York-based advocacy group that works to combat genocide, torture and human rights abuses. "You saw it infrequently — an average of four or five times a year — and when you did see it, it was space aliens or Nazis doing it, and it almost never worked. Now it's often the heroes who are using these techniques."

The number of instances of torture portrayed on television jumped from almost none in 1996 to 228 in 2003, according to the Parents Television Council. [32]

Fox Television's "24" has come to symbolize that almost tectonic shift in TV's treatment of torture. The hero of the show — which debuted two months after 9/11 — is Jack Bauer, a member of a unit charged with preventing catastrophic terrorist attacks, including nuclear and poison gas attacks on American cities such as Los Angeles. Bauer and his comrades have been shown using electrical wires, heart defibrillators, physical assaults and chemical injections to obtain information vital to preventing the attacks. [33]

The show's creator has insisted he is not trying to present a realistic — or glamorized — view of torture and that Bauer is portrayed as paying a high psychological price for using torture. [34]

But critics say the show — enormously popular in the United States and throughout the world — is changing how American citizens and soldiers view torture. "The biggest lie that has gained currency through television is that torture is an acceptable weapon for the 'good guys' to use if the stakes are high enough. . . . It is a lie," wrote John McCarthy, a journalist who was held hostage in Lebanon in the late 1980s. He accused the entertainment industry of "minimizing the true horrors of torture by failing to show the very profound impact it has on victims' lives." [35]

The show "leaves a message with junior soldiers that it's OK to cross the line in order to gather intelligence and save lives," said Danzig.

Senior American military officials were so worried about the show's impact that Brig. Gen. Patrick Finnegan, dean of the United States Military Academy, and top FBI and military interrogators visited the set in 2006. Finnegan told the show's creators it gives U.S. military personnel the wrong idea and has hurt America's image abroad by suggesting the United States condones torture. [36]

An American soldier threatens an Iraqi detainee with an attack dog in one of the graphic Abu Ghraib prison abuse photos that shocked the world in 2004. Human rights advocates worldwide say America's harsh post-9/11 detention and interrogation practices lowered the bar for torturers worldwide. Twelve low-level U.S. military personnel have since been convicted for their roles in the abuse, which an Army investigation described as "sadistic, blatant and wanton criminal" abuse.

Getty Images/The Washington Post

The show's impact on world opinion of Americans has been the subject of numerous debates — both in the United States and abroad — including a 2006 panel discussion at the Heritage Foundation. The show reinforces a world view of Americans as people who succeed by "breaking the law, by torturing people, by circumventing the chain of command," said David Heyman, director of Homeland Security at the nonpartisan Center for Strategic and International Studies, which focuses on security issues. [37]

Carafano, the Heritage fellow, said the program "just sort of confirms [the] prejudice" of those "who think ill of us" already. [38]

The show was also debated in June at a conference of North American and European judges in Ottawa, Canada. U.S. Supreme Court Justice Antonin Scalia argued that government agents should have more latitude in times of crisis. "Jack Bauer saved Los Angeles," said Scalia. "He saved hundreds of thousands of lives." [39]

Scalia's comments sparked heated retorts from the other judges and a subsequent *Globe and Mail* editorial. "Jack Bauer is a creation of wishful thinking. . . . He personifies the wish to be free of moral and legal constraints. . . . That's why constitutions exist; it's so tempting when fighting perceived evil to call for Jack Bauer." But, left unchecked, the commentary concluded, "Jack Bauer will poison liberty's fount." [40]

The popular TV program, however, doesn't seem to have clouded the vision of a group of American high school students invited to the White House in June to receive the prestigious Presidential Scholar award. They handed President Bush a handwritten letter urging him to halt "violations of the human rights" of terror suspects. "We do not want America to represent torture," said the letter. [41] ∎

BACKGROUND

Ancient Practice

Torture has been embraced by some of the world's most enlightened civilizations. Egyptian wall paintings and friezes depict scenes of horrific treatment of enemies. [42]

THE RACK.

Cuthbert Simpson, a Protestant martyr, suffers on the rack in the Tower of London in 1563. Torture has been used over the centuries to solicit information and to punish political and religious dissenters.

AFP/Getty Images/Hulton Archive

In ancient Greece, slaves and foreigners could be tortured lawfully but free citizens could not. The same held true in ancient Rome, where free citizens could only be tortured in cases of treason. Slaves could be beaten, whipped, stretched on the rack or burned with hot irons — as long they were not permanently injured or killed. [43]

The use of torture in Europe expanded in the 13th century after Italian city-states began to require stricter proof of guilt in criminal trials. Before that, guilt or innocence was proven by combat or endurance trials in which God was expected to favor the innocent. [44] Under the reforms, defendants could only be found guilty if two witnesses testified against them or the accused confessed to the crime. When there were no witnesses, torture was used to produce confessions, a practice that would persist for the next 500 years in Europe.

Torture was also used to punish prisoners in public spectacles, often attended by cheering crowds. In the technique known as "pressing to plead" weights were piled on the prisoner's body, crushing him until he confessed — or died. Victims were also stretched on a device called the rack — sometimes until their bones were pulled out of their sockets. Britain's King Henry VIII used torture against those who challenged his position as head of the Church of England. Queen Elizabeth I employed torture against those suspected of treason.

Particularly brutal torture methods gained religious sanction during the inquisitions conducted by the Roman Catholic Church to stamp out heresy. In 1252, Pope Innocent IV formally authorized the use of torture against heretics. In Spain for instance, victims were bound to a turning wheel as various body parts — the soles of their feet or the eyes — were brought closer and closer to a fire. In Italy, victims were suspended by their arms — tied behind their backs — from a pulley attached to a beam. The "strappado," as it was called, was then repeatedly jerked to increase the pain. Weights sometimes were attached to the victim's feet to increase the agony, often fracturing bones and tearing limbs from the body. [45]

In the early 17th century, some Europeans tried to regulate torture. Dutch legal scholar Johannes Voet, for instance, argued that torture should only be used when there are "grave presumptions" against the accused. He also suggested that the youngest member of any group of defendants be tortured first, because the youngest was thought most likely to talk. [46]

In 1754 Prussia became the first modern European state to abolish torture. Ten years later, in his seminal book *On Crimes and Punishments*, Italian philosopher and penal reformer Cesare Beccaria denounced torture as "a sure route for the acquittal of robust ruffians and the conviction of weak innocents." The book reflected emerging Enlightenment-era ideals about individual rights and the proper limits on punishment. [47] Within a century, most of Europe had banned torture, in part because convictions without eyewitness testimony or confessions were increasingly

Continued on p. 224

Chronology

1700s Torture is banned in Europe.

1754
Prussia becomes first European state to abolish torture; other European countries soon follow suit.

1900-1950
Torture re-emerges, then is prohibited.

1917
Russian Revolution gives birth to communism, which will foster totalitarian regimes that will torture perceived enemies of the state.

1933
Nazis take over Germany and soon begin torturing civilian prisoners.

1948
U.N. adopts Universal Declaration of Human Rights banning torture.

1949
Geneva Conventions ban all use of "mutilation, cruel treatment and torture" of prisoners of war.

1950s-1960s
Torture continues, despite international ban.

1954
France tortures thousands of Algerians during Algeria's war for independence.

1961
Amnesty International is founded after two Portuguese students are jailed for seven years for toasting freedom.

1970s-1990s
Democracies — as well as authoritarian regimes — continue to torture.

1971
British interrogators use the "five techniques" against Irish Republican Army suspects. European Court of Human Rights calls the methods illegal.

1975
Khmer Rouge takes over Cambodia and soon begins torturing and murdering thousands of detainees.

1978
Human Rights Watch is founded.

1987
Israel authorizes use of aggressive interrogation techniques during widespread Palestinian unrest.

1999
Israel's Supreme Court bans torture and abusive interrogation methods.

2000s-Present
Rise of Islamic terrorist attacks sparks increasing use of torture.

2001
Muslim terrorists kill 3,000 in Sept. 11 attacks. . . . Hundreds of Muslims are detained in the United States and Afghanistan. . . . Fox Television's "24" begins showing U.S. agents using torture.

2002
First "enemy combatants" captured in Afghanistan arrive at Guantánamo naval base in Cuba. President Bush says they will be treated humanely, but that they are not protected by Geneva Conventions. . . . In September Syrian-born Canadian Maher Arar is detained during a stopover in New York and is sent to Syria for interrogation, where he is tortured.

March 30, 2004
U.S. Supreme Court rules Alien Tort Claims Act can be used to sue human rights abusers.

April 27, 2004
CBS News' "60 Minutes II" airs photographs of U.S. troops abusing prisoners at Abu Ghraib prison in Iraq.

November 2005
Washington Post reports the CIA detains terror suspects in secret prisons where detainees allegedly are subjected to coercive interrogation techniques. . . . U.S. government insists it does not torture. Congress passes Detainee Treatment Act, prohibiting torture and mistreatment of prisoners but limiting detainees' rights to challenge their detentions.

2006
On June 29, Supreme Court rules U.S. detainees are subject to the Geneva Conventions. . . . Military Commissions Act authorizes new courtroom procedures for enemy combatants but allows greater flexibility for CIA interrogations.

2007
A German court orders 13 U.S. intelligence agents arrested for their alleged role in rendering a German citizen to Afghanistan. . . . Canada apologizes to Arar for allowing him to be taken to Syria. . . . In July, President Bush authorizes the CIA to reopen secret overseas prisons. . . . International war crimes tribunal in Cambodia indicts former Khmer Rouge leader Kaing Geuk Eav for the torture and murder of thousands of prisoners. . . . Libya admits it tortured Bulgarian medical personnel imprisoned for eight years.

Careful Training Creates Soldiers Who Torture

Most defy sadistic stereotype.

Torturers are made, not born. That was the finding of a Greek psychology professor who studied the military regime that came to power in Greece after a 1967 coup. Until it fell in 1974, the dictatorship carefully trained soldiers to gather information and squelch dissent through torture. That's when Professor Mika Haritos-Fatouros tried to understand how the soldiers had been turned into torturers. In one of the most in-depth studies of torturers ever conducted, she interviewed 16 former soldiers and reviewed the testimony of 21 others and their victims. [1]

Many of her interviewees defy the stereotype of sadistic men who take pleasure in abuse. Haritos-Fatouros found that the torturers were simply plucked from the ranks of ordinary soldiers and trained. One, from a farm family, was a 33-year-old high school teacher married with two children by the time Haritos-Fatouros interviewed him. But for 18 months he had tortured prisoners and ordered others to do so.

The army sought young recruits from rural, conservative families who were physically healthy, of normal intelligence, conformist in nature and compliant. They underwent three months of intensive "training," during which they were broken down physically and mentally — a process that began almost before they arrived at the training facility. The abuse of the torturers-in-training intensified during the subsequent weeks as they were allowed little sleep and ordered to run or hop everywhere they went.

The aim "was to minimize all resistance by instilling in the cadets the habit of obeying without question an order without logic," Haritos-Fatouros wrote. [2] In short, they were programmed to blindly obey authority and dehumanize their victims.

Gradually, they were desensitized to torture. First, they participated in group beatings. One of the torturers said the first time he participated in a group beating he went to his cousin's house and cried. But it got easier each time, he said. Later, they ratcheted up to inflicting electric shocks and other serious abuse.

The underlying goal, Haritos-Fatouros concluded, was making the torturers believe they were "not, in fact, inflicting a savage and horrifying violation upon another human being."

"They brainwashed us," one torturer said. "It was only later we realized that what we did was inhuman. It was only after I finished my military service that it occurred to me that most of us beat up prisoners because we'd been beaten up ourselves." [3]

Another torturer told her, "When I tortured, basically, I felt it was my duty. A lot of the time I found myself repeating the phrases I'd heard in the lessons, like 'bloody communists' and so on. I think I became worse as time went on. I became more a part of the system. I believed in the whole system." [4]

Haritos-Fatouros' chilling conclusion: "We are all, under the right conditions, capable of becoming torturers." [5]

---

[1] Mika Haritos-Fatouros, *The Psychological Origins of Institutionalized Torture* (2003).

[2] *Ibid.*, p. 46.

[3] *Ibid.*, p. 95.

[4] *Ibid.*, p. 82.

[5] *Ibid.*, p. 229.

Continued from p. 222

allowed, reducing the need for torture. But torture continued to thrive in Africa, Asia and the Middle East. In 1852, for example, leaders of an outlawed religious group in Persia — modern-day Iran — were "made into candlesticks" — with holes dug into their flesh into which lighted candles were inserted. [48]

By 1874, French author Victor Hugo naively declared "torture has ceased to exist." But torture continued to be used against insurgents in Austria and Italy and against opponents of the Tsarist government in Russia.

Changing Norms

By the 20th century, social norms about punishment had changed; the upper classes no longer wanted to watch gruesome public spectacles. Torture sessions became secretive affairs, conducted in prison basements and detention centers. [49]

In the first half of the 20th century, torture was employed by totalitarian governments in countries such as Germany, Russia, Italy and Japan. [50] The Nazis tortured prisoners of war to get information and conducted horrific medical experiments on Jewish and Gypsy civilians in concentration camps. Japanese soldiers severely abused and tortured Allied prisoners.

After the horrors of World War II, torture and lesser forms of abuse known as cruel, inhumane and degrading treatment were outlawed by a series of treaties: the 1948 Universal Declaration of Human Rights, the Geneva Conventions of 1949 and the 1984 Convention Against Torture. (*See box, p. 226.*)

Torture persisted during the second half of the century, however, particularly in authoritarian countries. For instance, Soviet and Chinese communist regimes tortured political and religious dissidents. Cambodia's murderous Khmer

Rouge military regime had a 42-page interrogation manual for use at its Tuol Sleng torture center during the 1970s.

Many repressive regimes were supported by the United States, which was fighting a proxy Cold War with the Soviet Union in developing countries like Vietnam, El Salvador and Guatemala. Because such governments were resisting socialist or communist insurgencies, the United States often provided them with guns, military aid and training, even though they were known to use torture.

In the 1970s, President Jimmy Carter broke with the past by announcing that the nation's foreign policy henceforth would be based on advancing human rights. Congress passed a law requiring the State Department to issue annual reports on the human rights records of any country that received U.S. economic or military aid. [51] Although the law remains on the books and the State Department continues to issue its annual human rights "country reports," the foreign policy focus on human rights faded under Carter's successor, Ronald Reagan, who placed fighting communism above protecting human rights.

Since the 1970s, however, greater scrutiny by Western governments, the U.N., the EU and human rights groups has prompted changes in how countries torture. Increasingly, methods were adopted that don't leave visible scars, such as beating the soles of feet, sleep deprivation, sexual humiliation and electric shock.

Democracies' Experience

It wasn't only communists and dictators who tortured captives after World War II. Democratic countries — including Great Britain, France and Israel — all used torture or other forms of abuse during the last half of the century, usually in response to what they viewed as imminent threats from religious or political dissidents.

But the democracies ended up alien-ating their own citizens as well as the occupied populations, according to Christopher Einolf, a University of Richmond sociologist who has studied the history of torture. Torture also proved difficult to control once it was authorized.

For instance, France initiated an intensive counterinsurgency strategy — which included torture — in Algeria after the Algerian National Liberation Front began a terrorist bombing campaign in 1956 to force France to cede control of the colony. France's strategy sometimes is cited as evidence that torture works. [52]

But Rejali at Reed College says France succeeded in gathering information because informants voluntarily cooperated — not as a result of torture. And tortured suspects often gave their interrogators the names of rival insurgents, dead militants or old hiding places rather than good information, he says.

Lou DiMarco, a retired U.S. Army lieutenant colonel who teaches at the Command and General Staff College, Fort Leavenworth, Kan., contends the French experience in Algeria also proves the difficulty of controlling torture. "In Algeria, officially condoned torture quickly escalated to prolonged abuse, which resulted in permanent physical and psychological damage as well as death," he wrote. [53]

Similarly, the British, facing a spike in Irish Republican Army (IRA) violence in Northern Ireland in 1971, turned to aggressive interrogation techniques, including the "five techniques" — a combination of hooding, noise bombardment, food and sleep deprivation and forced standing. Individually, any one of these techniques could be painful, but taken together, "they induced a state of psychosis, a temporary madness with long-lasting after-effects," wrote John Conroy in his book, *Unspeakable Acts, Ordinary People: The Dynamics of Torture.* [54]

Tom Parker, a former British counterterrorism agent, says extreme interrogation methods had "huge" adverse consequences for Britain: They alienated Ireland — not a natural ally of the IRA — and enabled Ireland to successfully challenge British interrogation methods in the European Court of Human Rights.

Israel approved similar methods in 1987 after its security services were found to be using illegal interrogation techniques on Palestinian detainees in the occupied territories. Officials felt it would be better to allow a few psychological methods and "moderate physical pressure." But coercive methods proved hard to regulate and keep under control. [55]

In 1999, Israel's Supreme Court outlawed such techniques as cruel and inhuman treatment.

Post-9/11 Crackdown

After the 9/11 attacks, aggressive interrogation of suspects became a key — and highly controversial — part of U.S. antiterrorism strategy. On Nov. 13, 2001, President Bush signed an executive order allowing the military to detain and try "enemy combatants" outside the United States.

Defense Secretary Donald H. Rumsfeld announced the next month that enemy combatants detained in Afghanistan would be transferred to Guantánamo. In February 2002 Bush said the United States would treat the detainees humanely but did not consider them legitimate prisoners of war protected by the Geneva Conventions, which ban torture and "cruel, inhuman and degrading treatment."

U.S. interrogators used the same harsh methods designed to train American personnel to resist torture if captured. The so-called "Survival, Evasion, Resistance and Escape" (SERE) techniques included physical and mental pressure ("stress and duress") and sleep deprivation.

Rumsfeld formally approved many of these techniques in December 2002, including prolonged standing, use of dogs and the removal of clothing; he later rescinded approval for some of the methods. [56] Mohammed al-Qhatani

— the alleged 20th 9/11 hijacker who had been captured along the Pakistani-Afghan border — says he was interrogated for 20-hour stretches, forced to stand naked while being menaced by dogs and barred from praying during Ramadan unless he drank water, which Islam forbids during Ramadan's fasting periods. The Pentagon said such techniques were designed to "prevent future attacks on America." [57]

But some within the administration disapproved. In July 2004 Alberto J. Mora, the Navy's general counsel, warned in a 22-page memo that circumventing the Geneva Conventions was an invitation for U.S. interrogators to abuse prisoners. [58]

His prediction was prescient. SERE techniques apparently migrated to U.S. facilities in Afghanistan and Iraq, where they were reportedly employed by inadequately trained and unsupervised personnel. What began as "a set of special treatments" had

become routine, wrote Tony Lagouranis, a former Army interrogator in Iraq. [59]

In late 2003 American military personnel at Abu Ghraib prison committed the abuses that generated the most public outrage, thanks to graphic photographs taken by the soldiers involved that eventually were circulated by news media around the world. An Army investigation later detailed "sadistic, blatant and wanton criminal" abuse that included beating detainees with a broom handle, threatening male detainees with rape, sodomizing another with a chemical light stick and frightening them with dogs. [60] Twelve U.S. military personnel have since been convicted for their roles in the abuse.

Mistreatment of Iraqi detainees was not just limited to Abu Ghraib. A military jury convicted Chief Warrant Officer Lewis Welshofer of negligent homicide after an interrogation in a facility in western Iraq in which he put a

sleeping bag over the head of Iraqi Gen. Abed Hamed Mowhoush, sat on his chest and covered the general's mouth while asking him questions. American civilian contractors working alongside CIA and military interrogators in Iraq have also been accused of mistreating detainees.

Ever since the 9/11 attacks, a furious legal debate, both inside and outside the Bush administration, has examined the kinds of coercive interrogation methods the military and CIA can employ and the extent to which the United States must abide by international law. In 2005 Congress sought to limit the use by U.S. personnel of cruel, inhumane and degrading treatment in the Detainee Treatment Act. [61]

Then in 2006 the Supreme Court ruled that all prisoners held by the United States — including those in CIA custody — were subject to Common Article 3 of the Geneva Conventions,

Five International Treaties Ban Torture

Torture has been banned by international treaties since 1948. Key provisions include:

Universal Declaration of Human Rights (1948)

"No one shall be subjected to torture or to cruel, inhuman or degrading treatment or punishment."

Adopted by U.N. General Assembly on Dec. 10, 1948, **www.un.org/Overview/rights.html**.

Third Geneva Convention, Common Article 3 (1949)

Regarding the treatment of civilians and prisoners of war, "the following acts are and shall remain prohibited at any time:

   (a) violence to life and person, in particular murder of all kinds, mutilation, cruel treatment and torture;

   (b) taking of hostages;

   (c) outrages upon personal dignity, in particular humiliating and degrading treatment . . ."

Adopted on Aug. 12, 1949, by the Diplomatic Conference for the Establishment of International Conventions for the Protection of Victims of War, held in Geneva, Switzerland; effective Oct. 21, 1950, **www.icrc.org/ihl.nsf/0/e160550475c4b133c12563cd0051aa66?OpenDocument**.

International Covenant on Civil and Political Rights (1966)

Article 7

No one shall be subjected to torture or to cruel, inhuman or degrading treatment or punishment. In particular, no one shall be subjected without his free consent to medical or scientific experimentation.

Article 10

All persons deprived of their liberty shall be treated with humanity and with respect for the inherent dignity of the human person.

Adopted the U.N. General Assembly on Dec. 16, 1966, and opened for signature and ratification; became effective on March 23, 1976, **www.unhchr.ch/html/menu3/b/a_ccpr.htm**.

Protocol Additional to the Geneva Conventions of Aug. 12, 1949, relating to the Protection of Victims of International Armed Conflicts (1977)

Article 75: Fundamental guarantees

1. ". . . persons who are in the power of a Party to the conflict . . . shall be treated humanely in all circumstances and shall enjoy, as a minimum, the protection provided by this Article without any adverse distinction based upon race, colour, sex, language, religion or belief, political or other opinion, national or social origin, wealth, birth or other status, or on any other similar criteria. Each Party shall respect the person, honour, convictions and religious practices of all such persons.

2. The following acts are and shall remain prohibited at any time and in any place whatsoever, whether committed by civilian or by military agents:

   (a) Violence to the life, health, or physical or mental well-being of persons, in particular:
   - (i) Murder;
   - (ii) Torture of all kinds, whether physical or mental;
   - (iii) Corporal punishment; and
   - (iv) Mutilation;

   (b) Outrages upon personal dignity, in particular humiliating and degrading treatment, enforced prostitution and any form of indecent assault;

   (c) The taking of hostages;

   (d) Collective punishments; and

   (e) Threats to commit any of the foregoing acts.

Adopted by the Diplomatic Conference on the Reaffirmation and Development of International Humanitarian Law applicable in Armed Conflicts on June 8, 1977; became effective on Dec. 7, 1979, www.unhchr.ch/html/menu3/b/93.htm.

Convention Against Torture and Other Cruel, Inhuman or Degrading Treatment or Punishment (1984)

Article 1

". . . the term 'torture' means any act by which severe pain or suffering, whether physical or mental, is intentionally inflicted on a person for such purposes as obtaining from him or a third person information or a confession, punishing him for an act he or a third person has committed or is suspected of having committed, or intimidating or coercing him or a third person, or for any reason based on discrimination of any kind, . . .

Article 2

1. Each State Party shall take effective legislative, administrative, judicial or other measures to prevent acts of torture in any territory under its jurisdiction.

2. No exceptional circumstances whatsoever, whether a state of war or a threat of war, internal political instability or any other public emergency, may be invoked as a justification of torture.

3. An order from a superior officer or a public authority may not be invoked as a justification of torture.

Article 3

1. No State Party shall expel, return ("refouler") or extradite a person to another State where there are substantial grounds for believing that he would be in danger of being subjected to torture.

2. For the purpose of determining whether there are such grounds, the competent authorities shall take into account all relevant considerations including, where applicable, the existence in the State concerned of a consistent pattern of gross, flagrant or mass violations of human rights."

Adopted by the U.N. General Assembly on Dec. 10, 1984, and opened for signature and ratification; became effective on June 26, 1987, www.unhchr.ch/html/menu3/b/h_cat39.htm.

which outlaws torture or cruel and inhuman treatment of wartime detainees. (*See box, p. 226.*) [62] Later that year Congress passed another bill, the Military Commissions Act, endorsed by the Bush administration. It limited military interrogators to techniques that would be detailed in an updated *Army Field Manual.* The law did not specify, however, which interrogation methods CIA personnel can use — an omission designed to provide flexibility for interrogators at secret CIA facilities where "high value" prisoners are interrogated.

When *The Washington Post* revealed in 2005 that the CIA was operating secret prisons in eight countries in Eastern Europe, Thailand and Afghanistan, the administration had at first refused to confirm the story. [63] In 2006 Bush finally acknowledged the facilities existed, pointing out that, "Questioning the detainees in this program has given us information that has saved innocent lives by helping us stop new attacks — here in the United States and across the world." [64]

In 2007, Human Rights Watch and *The Post* detailed the experience of one former CIA detainee — Marwan Jabour, a Palestinian accused of being an al-Qaeda paymaster — who spent two years in a CIA-operated prison.

Jabour says he was kept naked for the first three months of his detention in Afghanistan. The lights were kept on 24 hours a day, and when loud music wasn't blasted through speakers into his cell, white noise buzzed in the background. And while he was frequently threatened with physical abuse, he says he was never beaten during 45 interrogations. He was also deprived of sleep and left for hours in painful positions. He was ultimately transferred to Jordanian and then Israeli custody, where a judge ordered his release in September 2006. [65]

CIA detainees also reportedly have been subjected to waterboarding and had their food spiked with drugs to loosen their inhibitions about speaking. [66]

The United States did not allow the International Committee of the Red Cross (ICRC) to visit the CIA's detainees until 2006. A subsequent ICRC report based on interviews with 15 former CIA detainees concluded that the detention and interrogation methods used at the "black sites" were tantamount to torture, according to confidential sources quoted in *The New Yorker*. [67]

The United States has strongly denied the ICRC's conclusions and claims the program is closely monitored by agency lawyers. "The CIA's interrogations were nothing like Abu Ghraib or Guantánamo," said Robert Grenier, a former head of the CIA's Counterterrorism Center. "They were very, very regimented. Very meticulous." The program is "completely legal." [68]

Unlike the CIA's secret prisons, the agency's use of so-called "extraordinary renditions" predated the 9/11 attacks. The first terror suspects were rendered to Egypt in the mid-1990s. [69] But the practice expanded greatly after 9/11, with up to 150 people sent to countries such as Morocco, Syria and Egypt between

Syrian-born Canadian citizen Maher Arar was picked up by the CIA in 2002 at John F. Kennedy International Airport in New York and taken to Syria, where he was imprisoned for a year and tortured with electric cables. He was later cleared of any links to terrorism. Human rights advocates say the CIA's so-called extraordinary rendition program "outsources" torture to countries known to abuse prisoners. The U.S. Justice Department said Syria had assured the United States it would not torture Arar.

2001 and 2005. Many, like Abu Omar — an imam with alleged links to terrorist groups — were snatched off the street. Omar, an Egyptian refugee, was kidnapped from Milan in February 2003 and sent to Egypt where he says he was tortured for four years before being released in 2007. [70]

U.S. officials have repeatedly insisted the United States does not send detainees to countries where they believe or know they'll be tortured. [71] But such declarations ring hollow for human rights advocates like Malinowski. "The administration says that it does not render people to torture," he told the Senate Foreign Relations Committee. "But the only safeguard it appears to have obtained in these cases was a promise from the receiving state that it would not mistreat the rendered prisoners. Such promises, coming from countries like Egypt and Syria and Uzbekistan where torture is routine, are unverifiable and utterly untrustworthy. I seriously doubt that anyone in the administration actually believed them." [72]

Renditions usually require the complicity of the countries where the suspects are grabbed. A 2006 report by the Council of Europe's Parliamentary Assembly tried to identify all the member countries that have allowed rendition flights to cross their airspace or land at their airports. [73]

One was the Czech Republic, which reportedly allowed three different jets to land at Prague's Ruzyně Airport during at least 20 different rendition flights, triggering anger from some Czechs. "No 'law enforcement,' 'intelligence,' or 'security' argument in support of torture can ever be anything but inhumane," wrote Gwendolyn Albert, director of the Czech League of Human Rights, in 2006 in *The Prague Post*. [74]

Former CIA operative Melissa Boyle Mahle condemns torture but has defended renditions and the need for absolute secrecy. "Renditions should be conducted in the shadows for optimal impact and should not, I must add, leave elephant-sized footprints so as to not embarrass our allies in Europe," she wrote in a 2005 blog entry. "During my career at the CIA, I was involved in these types of operations and know firsthand that they can save American lives." [75] ■

CURRENT SITUATION

Rendition Fallout

Kidnapping and shipping off allies' citizens to be harshly interrogated in foreign countries has strained relations with America's friends. Prosecutors in Germany and Italy are attempting to prosecute U.S. personnel for their role in renditions, and the rendition of Canadian citizen Maher Arar to Syria has chilled relations between Canada and the United States.

Continued on p. 230

At Issue:

Is torture ever justified?

MIRKO BAGARIC
PROFESSOR OF LAW, DEAKIN UNIVERSITY
MELBOURNE, AUSTRALIA

WRITTEN FOR *CQ GLOBAL RESEARCHER*, AUGUST 2007

despite its pejorative overtone, we should never say never to torture. Torture is bad. Killing innocent people is worse. Some people are so depraved they combine these evils and torture innocent people to death. Khalid Shaikh Mohammed, who is still gloating about personally beheading American journalist Daniel Pearl with his "blessed right hand," is but just one exhibit.

Torture opponents must take responsibility for the murder of innocent people if they reject torture if it is the only way to save innocent lives. We are responsible not only for what we do but also for the things we can, but fail, to prevent.

Life-saving torture is not cruel. It is morally justifiable because the right to life of innocent people trumps the physical integrity of wrongdoers. Thus, torture has the same moral justification as other practices in which we sacrifice the interests of one person for the greater good. A close analogy is life-saving organ and tissue transplants. Kidney and bone marrow transplants inflict high levels of pain and discomfort on donors, but their pain is normally outweighed by the benefit to the recipient.

Such is the case with life-saving compassionate torture. The pain inflicted on the wrongdoer is manifestly outweighed by the benefit from the lives saved. The fact that wrongdoers don't consent to their mistreatment is irrelevant. Prisoners and enemy soldiers don't consent to being incarcerated or shot at, yet we're not about to empty our prisons or stop trying to kill enemy soldiers.

Most proponents of banning torture say it does not produce reliable information. Yet there are countless counter-examples. Israeli authorities claim to have foiled 90 terrorist attacks by using coercive interrogation. In more mundane situations, courts across the world routinely throw out confessions that are corroborated by objective evidence because they were only made because the criminals were beaten up.

It is also contended that life-saving torture will lead down the slippery slope of other cruel practices. This is an intellectually defeatist argument. It tries to move the debate from what is on the table (life-saving torture) to situations where torture is used for reasons of domination and punishment — which is never justifiable.

Fanatics who oppose torture in all cases are adopting their own form of extremism. It is well-intentioned, but extremism in all its manifestations can lead to catastrophic consequences. Cruelty that is motivated by misguided kindness hurts no less.

SUNE SEGAL
HEAD OF COMMUNICATIONS UNIT
INTERNATIONAL REHABILITATION COUNCIL
FOR TORTURE VICTIMS
COPENHAGEN, DENMARK

WRITTEN FOR *CQ GLOBAL RESEARCHER*, AUGUST 2007

taking a utilitarian "greater good" approach in the wake of 9/11/2001, some scholars argue that torture is justified if used to prevent large-scale terror attacks. That argument rests on several flawed assumptions.

The claim that torture — or what is now euphemistically referred to as "enhanced interrogation techniques" — extracts reliable information is unfounded. The 2006 *U.S. Army Field Manual* states that "the use of force . . . yields unreliable results [and] may damage subsequent collection efforts." As laid out in a recent *Vanity Fair* article, it was humane treatment — not torture — of a detainee that led to the arrest of alleged 9/11 mastermind Khalid Shaikh Mohammed. In the same article, a U.S. Air Force Reserve colonel and expert in human-intelligence operations, drives home the point: "When [CIA psychologists argue that coercive interrogation] can make people talk, I have one question: 'About what?' "

But even if torture did "work," is it justified when a suspect is in custody and presumed to possess information about an imminent attack likely to kill thousands of people?

No, for several reasons. First, the above scenario assumes the person in custody has the pertinent information — a presumption that is never foolproof. Thus, by allowing torture there would be cases in which innocent detainees would be at risk of prolonged torture because they would not possess the desired information.

Second, it might be argued that mere circumstantial evidence suggesting the detainee is the right suspect is enough to justify torture or that torturing a relative into revealing the suspect's whereabouts is acceptable.

Third, if one form of torture — such as "waterboarding" — is allowed to preserve the "greater good," where do we go if it doesn't work? To breaking bones? Ripping out nails? Torturing the suspect's 5-year-old daughter?

Fourth, torture is not a momentary infliction of pain. In most cases the victim — innocent or guilty — is marked for life, as is the torturer. As a former CIA officer and friend of one of Mohammed's interrogators told *The New Yorker* in an Aug. 13, 2007, article: "[My friend] has horrible nightmares. . . . When you cross over that line, it's hard to come back. You lose your soul."

That's why we refrain from torture: to keep our souls intact. Torture is the hallmark of history's most abhorrent regimes and a violation of civilized values. Taking the "greater good" approach to torture is intellectually and morally bankrupt.

Continued from p. 228

In Italy, the former chief of Italy's intelligence service is on trial for Omar's 2003 abduction in a case that threatens to ensnare top officials of the current and past Italian governments. A U.S. Air Force colonel and 25 CIA operatives also were indicted but are being tried in absentia because the United States has blocked their extradition. [76]

Similarly, a court in Munich ordered the arrest of 13 American intelligence operatives in January 2007 for their role in the kidnapping of a German citizen interrogated for five months at a secret prison in Afghanistan. But Germany, unlike Italy, does not allow trials in absentia, so an actual trial is unlikely because the United States will not extradite the defendants. [77]

Other European governments may be called to task for their role in U.S. renditions. Investigations have been initiated by Spain, and the Most Rev. John Neill — archbishop of Dublin — said the Irish government compromised itself by allowing rendition flights to land at Shannon Airport.

Meanwhile, on this side of the Atlantic, Canadian-U.S. relations are strained by the case of Syrian-born Canadian citizen Maher Arar. The McGill University graduate was returning to Canada from Tunisia in September 2002 when he landed at John F. Kennedy International Airport in New York during a stopover. U.S. immigration authorities detained him after seeing his name on a terrorist "watch" list.

After two weeks of questioning, he was flown to Jordan and then driven to Syria. During a yearlong detention by Syrian military intelligence, Arar says he was beaten with two-inch-thick electric cables. "Not even animals could withstand it," he said later. [78]

He was released in October 2003. A Canadian inquiry cleared Arar of any links to terrorism and said the Royal Canadian Mounted Police had given U.S. authorities erroneous information about him. Canada's prime minister apol-

ogized to Arar in January 2007 and announced an $8.9 million compensation package. Canada has also demanded an apology from the U.S. government and asked that Arar's name be removed from terrorist watch lists. [79]

U.S. federal courts have dismissed a lawsuit by Arar, and Attorney General Alberto R. Gonzales said Syria had assured the United States it would not torture Arar before he was sent there.

But Paul Cavalluzzo, a Toronto lawyer who led the government investigation of Arar's case, calls Gonzales' claim "graphic hypocrisy," pointing out that the U.S. State Department's own Web site lists Syria as one of the "worst offenders of torture."

"At one time, the United States was a beacon for the protection of human rights, whether internationally or domestically. Certainly, the Arar case was one example that lessened [that] view [among] Canadians."

Suing Torturers

Criminal prosecutions and civil lawsuits are pending against alleged torturers in several courts around the world.

In the United States, Iraqis claiming they were mistreated by American military personnel and private contractors are seeking redress under a little-used 18th-century law. The Alien Tort Claims Act, which originally targeted piracy, allows federal courts to hear claims by foreigners injured "in violation of the law of nations or a treaty of the United States."

In May 2007, the American Civil Liberties Union used the law to sue Jeppesen Dataplan Inc., a subsidiary of the Boeing Co., on behalf of three plaintiffs subjected to renditions. The company is accused of providing rendition flight services to the CIA. Two additional plaintiffs joined the suit in August. [80]

The law also was used in a class-action suit against Titan Corp. and CACI International Inc., military contractors that provided translators and interrogation ser-

vices at Abu Ghraib. The suit asserts the two companies participated in a "scheme to torture, rape and in some instances, summarily execute plaintiffs." CACI called it a "malicious recitation of false statements and intentional distortions." [81]

The law was rarely used until the late 1970s, when human rights groups began suing abusive foreign officials. Since then it has been used to sue a Paraguayan police chief living in Brooklyn accused of torturing and killing a young man in Paraguay, an Ethiopian official, a Guatemalan defense minister and the self-proclaimed president of the Bosnian Serbs.

Advocates of such suits say they are important tools in holding abusers accountable. "It is truly a mechanism that provides for policing international human rights abuses where a criminal prosecution may not necessarily be feasible," says John M. Eubanks, a South Carolina lawyer involved in a suit that relies on the statute. The home countries of human rights abusers often lack legal systems that enable perpetrators to be held accountable.

"America is the only venue where they're going to be able to get their case heard," says Rachel Chambers, a British lawyer who has studied the statute.

Although the U.S. Supreme Court affirmed the use of the statute in 2004, legal experts disagree about just how much leeway the court left for future plaintiffs. [82]

Moreover, the statute can't provide redress in lawsuits against the U.S. government for the mistreatment of prisoners. The United States has successfully challenged such lawsuits by claiming sovereign immunity, a doctrine that protects governments against suits. The same defense has protected individuals sued in their official government capacity, according to Beth Stephens, a professor at Rutgers School of Law, in Camden, N.J. It is unclear how much protection private contractors such as CACI can claim for providing support services for interrogations.

Meanwhile, in Cambodia a U.N.-backed tribunal in July accused former Khmer

Rouge leader Kaing Guek Eav of crimes against humanity for his role in the torture and deaths of 14,000 prisoners at Tuol Sleng. Only seven people who entered the prison emerged alive. The trial is expected to begin in 2008. [83]

And in Sierra Leone former Liberian President Charles Taylor is facing a U.N.-backed war-crimes tribunal for his role in financing and encouraging atrocities — including torture — committed during the civil war in neighboring Sierra Leone. The trial has been delayed until January 2008. [84]

The 'Black Sites'

In July, when President Bush authorized the CIA's secret prisons to be reopened, the executive order laid out the administration's position on how the "enhanced interrogation" program will fully comply "with the obligations of the United States under Common Article 3" of the Geneva Conventions, which bans "outrages upon personal dignity, in particular humiliating and degrading treatment."

The president's order said the United States would satisfy the conventions if the CIA's interrogation methods don't violate federal law or constitute "willful and outrageous acts of personal abuse done for the purpose of humiliating the individual in a manner so serious that any reasonable person, considering the circumstances would deem the acts to be beyond the bounds of human decency."

The language appears to allow abusive techniques if the purpose is to gather intelligence or prevent attacks, say critics. "The president has given the CIA carte blanche to engage in 'willful and outrageous acts of personal abuse,' " wrote former Marine Corps Commandant P. X. Kelley and Robert Turner, a former Reagan administration lawyer. [85]

Human rights advocates are troubled by the executive order's lack of an explicit ban on coercive interrogation techniques such as stress positions or extreme sleep deprivation, which military interrogators are explicitly barred from using in the latest *Army Field Manual*, issued in 2006.

Media reports suggested the Bush administration also has sought to maintain other methods, such as inducing hypothermia, forced standing and manipulating sound and light. [86]

"What we're left with is a history of these kinds of techniques having been authorized, no explicit prohibition and we don't know what the CIA is authorized to do," says Devon Chaffee, an attorney with Human Rights First. "This creates a real problematic precedent."

Human rights advocates worry that foreign governments may cite Bush's executive order to justify their own coercive interrogations. "What they did is lower the bar for anybody," says Musa, the advocacy director for Amnesty USA.

In August, the American Bar Association passed a resolution urging Congress to override the executive order. [87] Also that month, Democratic Sen. Ron Wyden of Oregon vowed to block President Bush's nominee to become the CIA's top lawyer. Wyden said he was concerned that the agency's senior deputy general counsel, John Rizzo, had not objected to a 2002 CIA memo authorizing interrogation techniques that stopped just short of inflicting enough pain to cause organ failure or death.

"I'm going to keep the hold [on Rizzo] until the detention and interrogation program is on firm footing, both in terms of effectiveness and legality," Wyden said. [88] ∎

OUTLOOK

No Panaceas

Human rights advocates worry countries that have tortured in the past will feel more emboldened to do so in the future as a result of U.S. government policies.

"This is just empowering the dictators and torturing governments around the world," said Whitson of Human Rights Watch.

They also worry that China, a rising superpower, is an abuser itself and has proven willing to do business with countries with histories of abuse in Central Asia and Africa.

HRW Executive Director Kenneth Roth also complains that — as its membership swells and the difficulty of reaching consensus grows — the European Union appears unable or unwilling to act. "Its efforts to achieve consensus among its diverse membership have become so laborious that it yields a faint shadow of its potential," he says.

The future direction of U.S. interrogation policies could depend heavily on the outcome of the 2008 American presidential election, which will likely determine the fate of what has become the most important symbol of U.S. detention policies: the prison for enemy combatants at Guantánamo. All the Democratic presidential candidates say they would close the facility, according to a study of candidate positions by the Council on Foreign Relations. [89]

On the Republican side, only two candidates — Rep. Ron Paul, R-Texas, and Sen. McCain — have advocated, shutting the facility, and neither has been among the leaders in the polls. Mitt Romney, the former Massachusetts governor who has been among the front-runners this summer, suggested doubling the size of Guantánamo if he became president.

But regardless of who wins the election, human rights advocates do not look to a new occupant of the White House as a panacea. Amnesty USA's Musa says new administrations are often skittish about radically changing course from predecessors' foreign policies.

"It's not the absolute cure for all ills," she says. ∎

Notes

1 See Jonathan S. Landay, "VP confirms use of waterboarding," *Chicago Tribune*, Oct. 27, 2006, p. C5; and "Interview of the Vice President by Scott Hennen, WDAY at Radio Day at the White House," www.whitehouse.gov/news/releases/2006/10/20061024-7.html. Also see John Crewdson, "Spilling Al Qaeda's secrets; 'Waterboarding' used on 9/11 mastermind, who eventually talked," *Chicago Tribune*, Dec. 28, 2005, p. C15. Also see Brian Ross and Richard Esposito, "CIA's Harsh Interrogation Techniques Described," ABC News, Nov. 18, 2005, www.abcnews.com.

2 Testimony by Tom Malinowski before Senate Committee on Foreign Relations, July 26, 2007.

3 David Cingranelli and David L. Richards, CIRI Human Rights Data Project, 2005, http://ciri.binghamton.edu/about.asp.

4 Quoted in Molly Moore, "Gaddafi's Son: Bulgarians Were Tortured," *The Washington Post*, Aug. 10, 2007, p. A8.

5 "In the Name of Security: Counterterrorism and Human Rights Abuses Under Malaysia's Internal Security Act," Human Rights Watch, http://hrw.org/reports/2004/malaysia0504/.

6 Dana Priest, "CIA Holds Terror Suspects in Secret Prisons," *The Washington Post*, Nov. 2, 2005, p. A1; also see Rosa Brooks, "The GOP's Torture Enthusiasts," *Los Angeles Times*, May 18, 2007, www.latimes.com/news/opinion/commentary/la-oe-brooks18may18,0,732795.column?coll=la-news-comment-opinions.

7 For background see Peter Katel and Kenneth Jost, "Treatment of Detainees," *CQ Researcher*, Aug. 25, 2006, pp. 673-696.

8 Kenneth Roth, "Filling the Leadership Void: Where is the European Union?" *World Report 2007*, Human Rights Watch.

9 Edward Cody, "China, Others Criticize U.S. Report on Rights: Double Standard at State

Department Alleged" *The Washington Post*, March 4, 2005, p A14.

10 Lisa Haugaard, "Tarnished Image: Latin America Perceives the United States," Latin American Working Group, March 2006.

11 "World View of U.S. Role Goes from Bad to Worse," Program on International Policy Attitudes, January 2007, www.worldpublicopinion.org/pipa/pdf/jan07/BBC_USRole_Jan07_quaire.pdf.

12 See Karen DeYoung, "Bush Approves New CIA Methods," *The Washington Post*, July 21, 2007, p. A1.

13 See "President Discusses Creation of Military Commissions to Try Suspected Terrorists," Sept. 6, 2006, www.whitehouse.gov/news/releases/2006/09/20060906-3.html.

14 Crewdson, *op. cit.*

15 Jane Mayer, "The Black Sites," *The New Yorker*, Aug. 13, 2007, pp. 46-57.

16 *Ibid.*

17 *Ibid.*

18 Jane Mayer, "Outsourcing Torture," *The New Yorker*, Feb. 14, 2005, p. 106.

19 Intelligence Science Board, "Educing Information, Interrogation: Science and Art," Center for Strategic Intelligence Research, National Defense Intelligence College, December 2006, www.fas.org/irp/dni/educing.pdf.

20 Anne Applebaum, "The Torture Myth," *The Washington Post*, Jan. 12, 2005, p. A21.

21 Henry Schuster, "The Al Qaeda Hunter," CNN, http://edition.cnn.com/2005/US/03/02/schuster.column/index.html.

22 Mirko Bagaric, "A Case for Torture," *The Age*, May 17, 2005, www.theage.com.au/news/Opinion/A-case-for-torture/2005/05/16/1116095904947.html.

23 Alan Dershowitz, *Why Terrorism Works: Understanding the Threat, Responding to the Challenge*, Yale University Press, 2003, pp. 158-159.

24 Michael Levin, "The Case for Torture," *Newsweek*, June 7, 1982.

25 " '24' and America's Image in Fighting Terrorism," Heritage Foundation Symposium, June 30, 2006.

26 Eitan Felner, "Torture and Terrorism: Painful Lessons from Israel," in Kenneth Roth, *et al.*, eds., *Torture: Does it Make Us Safer? Is It Ever OK? A Human Rights Perspective* (2005).

27 Henry Shue, "Torture," in Sanford Levinson, ed., *Torture: A Collection* (2006), p. 58.

28 See Brooks, *op. cit.*

29 Humphrey Hawksley, "US Iraq Troops 'condone torture,' " BBC News, May 4, 2007, http://news.bbc.co.uk/2/hi/middle_east/6627055.stm.

30 "Bush, McCain Agree on Torture Ban," CNN, Dec. 15, 2005, www.cnn.com/2005/POLITICS/12/15/torture.bill/index.html.

31 "American and International Opinion on the Rights of Terrorism Suspects," Program on International Policy Attitudes, July 17, 2006, www.worldpublicopinion.org/pipa/pdf/jul06/TerrSuspect_Jul06_rpt.pdf.

32 Allison Hanes, "Prime time torture: A U.S. Brigadier-General voices concern about the message the show '24' might be sending to the public and impressionable recruits," *National Post*, March 19, 2007.

33 Evan Thomas, " '24' Versus the Real World," *Newsweek Online*, Sept. 22, 2006, www.msnbc.msn.com/id/14924664/site/newsweek/.

34 Jane Mayer, "Whatever It Takes," *The New Yorker*, Feb. 19, 2007, www.newyorker.com/reporting/2007/02/19/070219fa-fact_mayer?printable=true.

35 John McCarthy, "Television is making torture acceptable," *The Independent*, May 24, 2007, http://comment.independent.co.uk/commentators/article2578453.ece.

36 Mayer, Feb. 19, 2007, *ibid*.

37 Heritage symposium, *op. cit.*

38 *Ibid.*

39 Colin Freeze, "What would Jack Bauer do?," *Globe and Mail*, June 16, 2007, www.theglobeandmail.com/servlet/story/LAC.20070616.BAUER16/TPStory/TPNational/Television/.

40 "Don't Go to Bat for Jack Bauer," *Globe and Mail*, July 9, 2007, www.theglobeandmail.com/servlet/story/RTGAM.20070709.wxetorture09/BNStory/specialComment/home.

41 The Associated Press, "Scholars Urge Bush to Ban Use of Torture," *The Washington Post*, June 25, 2007, www.washingtonpost.com/wp-dyn/content/article/2007/06/25/AR2007062501437.html.

42 See David Masci, "Torture," *CQ Researcher*, April 18, 2003, pp. 345-368.

43 James Ross, "A History of Torture," in Roth, *op. cit.*

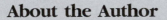

About the Author

Seth Stern is a legal-affairs reporter at the *CQ Weekly Report*. He has worked as a journalist since graduating from Harvard Law School in 2001, including as a reporter for the *Christian Science Monitor* in Boston. He received his undergraduate degree at Cornell University's School of Industrial and Labor Relations and a master's degree in public administration from Harvard's Kennedy School of Government. He is co-authoring a biography of Supreme Court Justice William J. Brennan Jr.

[44] John Langbein, "The Legal History of Torture," in Levinson, *op. cit.*

[45] Brian Innes, *The History of Torture* (1998), pp. 13, 43.

[46] Roth, p. 8.

[47] Ross, p. 12.

[48] Darius M. Rejali, *Torture & Modernity: Self, Society, and State in Modern Iran* (1994), p. 11.

[49] *Ibid.*, p. 13.

[50] Christopher J. Einolf, "The Fall and Rise of Torture: A Comparative and Historical Analysis," *Sociological Theory 25:2*, June 2007.

[51] For background, see R. C. Schroeder, "Human Rights Policy," in *Editorial Research Reports 1979* (Vol. I), available in *CQ Researcher Plus Archive*, http://library.cqpress.com. Also see "Foreign Aid: Human Rights Compromise," in *CQ Almanac*, 1977.

[52] Darius Rejali, "Does Torture Work?" *Salon*, June 21, 2004, http://archive.salon.com/opinion/feature/2004/06/21/torture_algiers/index_np.html.

[53] Lou DiMarco, "Losing the Moral Compass: Torture & Guerre Revolutionnaire in the Algerian War," *Parameters*, Summer 2006.

[54] John Conroy, *Unspeakable Acts, Ordinary People: The Dynamics of Torture* (2001).

[55] Miriam Gur-Arye, "Can the War against Terror Justify the Use of Force in Interrogations? Reflections in Light of the Israeli Experience," in Levinson, *op. cit.*, p. 185.

[56] Jess Bravin and Greg Jaffe, "Rumsfeld Approved Methods for Guantánamo Interrogation," *The Wall Street Journal*, June 10, 2004.

[57] Department of Defense press release, June 12, 2005, www.defenselink.mil/Releases/Release.aspx?ReleaseID=8583.

[58] Jane Mayer, "The Memo," *The New Yorker*, Feb. 27, 2006, pp. 32-41.

[59] Tony Lagouranis, *Fear Up Harsh: An Army Interrogator's Dark Journey Through Iraq* (2007), p. 93.

[60] A summary of the Taguba report can be found at www.fas.org/irp/agency/dod/taguba.pdf.

[61] "Bush Signs Defense Authorization Measure With Detainee Provision," *CQ Almanac 2005 Online Edition*, available at http://library.cqpress.com.

[62] The case is *Hamdan v. Rumsfeld*, 126 S. Ct. 2749 (2006).

[63] Priest, *op. cit.*

[64] "President Discusses Creation of Military Commissions to Try Suspected Terrorists," *op. cit.*

[65] Dafna Linzer and Julie Tate, "New Light Shed on CIA's 'Black Site' Prisons," *The Washington Post*, Feb. 28, 2007, p. A1.

[66] Mark Bowden, "The Dark Art of Interrogation," *The Atlantic*, October 2003.

FOR MORE INFORMATION

Amnesty International USA, 5 Penn Plaza, New York, NY 10001; (212) 807-8400; www.amnestyusa.org. U.S.-affiliate of London-based international human rights organization.

Center for Victims of Torture, 717 East River Rd., Minneapolis, MN 55455; (612) 627-4231; www.cvt.org. Operates healing centers in Minneapolis-St. Paul and Liberia and Sierra Leone. Also trains religious leaders, teachers, caregivers and staff from other NGOs about the effects of torture and trauma.

Human Rights First, 333 Seventh Ave., 13th Floor, New York, NY 10001-5108; (212) 845-5200; www.humanrightsfirst.org. A New York-based advocacy group that combats genocide, torture and other human rights abuses; founded in 1978 as the Lawyers Committee for Human Rights.

Human Rights Watch, 350 Fifth Ave., 34th floor, New York, NY 10118-3299; (212) 290-4700; www.hrw.org. Advocates for human rights around the world.

International Rehabilitation Council for Torture Victims, Borgergade 13, P.O. Box 9049 DK-1022; Copenhagen K, Denmark; +45 33 76 06 00; www.irct.org. Umbrella organization for worldwide network of centers that treat torture victims.

Medical Foundation for the Care of Victims of Torture, 96-98 Grafton Rd., Kentish Town, London NW5 3EJ; (020) 7813 9999; www.torturecare.org.uk. Trains and provides medical personnel to aid victims of torture.

Office of the High Commissioner for Human Rights, 8-14 Ave. de la Paix, 1211 Geneva 10, Switzerland; (41-22) 917-9000; www.unhchr.ch. United Nations agency that opposes human rights violations.

[67] Mayer, Aug. 13, 2007, *op. cit.*

[68] *Ibid.*

[69] Mayer, Feb. 14, 2005, *op. cit.*

[70] Ian Fisher and Elisabetta Povoledo, "Italy Braces for Legal Fight Over Secret CIA Program," *The New York Times*, June 8, 2007.

[71] Jeffrey R. Smith, "Gonzales Defends Transfer of Detainees," *The Washington Post*, March 8, 2005, p. A3.

[72] Malinowski testimony, *op. cit.*

[73] Council of Europe Parliamentary Assembly, "Alleged secret detentions in Council of Europe member states, 2006," http://assembly.coe.int/CommitteeDocs/2006/20060606_Ejdoc162006PartII-FINAL.pdf.

[74] Gwendolyn Albert, "With Impunity," *Prague Post*, April 12, 2006, www.praguepost.com/articles/2006/04/12/with-impunity.php.

[75] http://melissamahlecommentary.blogspot.com/2005/12/cia-and-torture.html.

[76] Elisabetta Povoledo, "Trial of CIA Operatives is delayed in Italy," *The International Herald Tribune*, June 18, 2007.

[77] Jeffrey Fleishman, "Germany Orders Arrest of 13 CIA Operatives in Kidnapping of Khaled el-Masri" *Los Angeles Times*, Jan. 31, 2007.

[78] Mayer, Feb. 14, 2005, *op. cit.*

[79] "Arar Case Timeline," Canadian Broadcasting Company, www.cbc.ca/news/background/arar.

[80] Christine Kearney, "Iraqi, Yemeni men join lawsuit over CIA flights," Reuters, Aug. 1, 2007.

[81] Marie Beaudette, "Standing at the Floodgates," *Legal Times*, June 28, 2004.

[82] The case is *Sosa v. Alvarez-Machain*, 2004, 542 U.S. 692 (2004).

[83] Ian MacKinnon, "War crimes panel charges Khmer Rouge chief," *The Guardian*, Aug. 1, 2007.

[84] "Taylor Trial Delayed until 2008," BBC News, Aug. 20, 2007, http://news.bbc.co.uk/2/hi/africa/6954627.stm.

[85] P. X. Kelley and Robert F. Turner, "War Crimes and the White House," *The Washington Post*, July 26, 2007.

[86] Thomas, *op. cit.*

[87] Henry Weinstein, "ABA targets CIA methods, secret law," *Los Angeles Times*, Aug. 14, 2007.

[88] The Associated Press, "Dem blocking Bush pick for CIA lawyer," MSNBC, Aug. 16, 2007, www.msnbc.msn.com/id/20294826.

[89] "The Candidates on Military Tribunals and Guantánamo Bay," Council on Foreign Relations, July 17, 2007, www.cfr.org/publication/13816/.

Bibliography

Selected Sources

Books

Bagaric, Mirko, and Julie Clarke, *Torture: When the Unthinkable Is Morally Permissible*, State University of New York Press, 2007.
Bagaric, an Australian law professor, argues torture is sometimes morally justified and should be legally excusable.

Conroy, John, *Unspeakable Acts, Ordinary People: The Dynamics of Torture*, Random House, 2000.
A reporter examines the history of torture.

Dershowitz, Alan M., *Why Torture Works: Understanding the Threat, Responding to the Challenge*, Yale University Press, 2003.
A Harvard law professor argues that torture will be employed by interrogators, so courts should issue "torture warrants" to bring some legal oversight to the process.

Haritos-Fatouros, Mika, *The Psychological Origins of Institutionalized Torture*, Routledge, 2003.
A sociologist explores the indoctrination of Greek torturers during military rule of the country during the 1970s.

Lagouranis, Tony, *Fear Up Harsh: An Army Interrogator's Dark Journey Through Iraq*, NAL Hardcover, 2007.
A former U.S. Army interrogator describes the use of coercive techniques by American soldiers.

Levinson, Sanford, ed., *Torture: A Collection*, Oxford University Press, 2004.
Essays by academics and human rights advocates examine the historical, moral and political implications of torture.

Rejali, Darius, *Torture and Democracy*, Princeton University Press, 2007.
A Reed College professor and expert on torture traces its history from the 19th century through the U.S. occupation of Iraq.

Articles

"Torture in the Name of Freedom," *Der Spiegel*, Feb. 20, 2006, www.spiegel.de/international/spiegel/0,1518, 401899,00.html.
The German news magazine concludes the United States is ceding its moral authority on the issue of torture.

Bowden, Mark, "The Dark Art of Interrogation," *The Atlantic Monthly*, October 2003, www.theatlantic.com/doc/200310/bowden.
An American journalist examines interrogation methods employed by U.S. personnel since the 9/11 terrorist attacks.

Einolf, Christopher J., "The Fall and Rise of Torture: A Comparative and Historical Analysis," *Sociological Theory*, June 2007, www.asanet.org/galleries/default-file/June07STFeature.pdf.
A University of Richmond sociology professor explains the continued prevalence of torture during the 20th century.

Mayer, Jane, "The Black Sites," *The New Yorker*, Aug. 13, 2007, p. 46, www.newyorker.com/reporting/2007/08/13/070813fa_fact_mayer.
A journalist examines the history of the CIA's secret "black site" prisons for high-value terror suspects.

Mayer, Jane, "Outsourcing Torture," *The New Yorker*, Feb. 14, 2005, www.newyorker.com/archive/2005/02/14/050214fa_fact6.
The reporter traces the history of the U.S.'s "extraordinary rendition" policy.

Mayer, Jane, "Whatever It Takes," *The New Yorker*, Feb. 19, 2007, www.newyorker.com/reporting/2007/02/19/070219fa_fact_mayer.
The article examines the popular television show "24" and its role in "normalizing" perceptions of torture.

Ozdemir, Cem, "Beyond the Valley of the Wolves," *Der Spiegel*, Feb. 22, 2006, www.spiegel.de/international/0,1518,401565,00.html.
A Turkish member of parliament discusses a popular Turkish movie that depicts American soldiers mistreating Iraqi civilians.

Reports and Studies

"Alleged secret detentions and unlawful inter-state transfers involving Council of Europe member states," Committee on Legal Affairs and Human Rights Council of Europe Parliamentary Assembly, June 7, 2006, http://assembly.coe.int/CommitteeDocs/2006/20060606_Ejdoc162006PartII-FINAL.pdf.
An organization of European lawmakers examines the role of European governments in U.S. renditions.

"Educing Information, Interrogation: Science and Art," Foundations for the Future Phase 1 Report, Intelligence Science Board, December 2006, www.fas.org/irp/dni/educing.pdf.
Too little is known about which interrogation methods are effective.

"Tarnished Image: Latin America Perceives the United States," Latin American Working Group, www.lawg.org/docs/tarnishedimage.pdf.
A nonprofit group examines Latin American press coverage of U.S. policies, including its interrogation of detainees.

The Next Step:

Additional Articles from Current Periodicals

CIA Secret Prisons

"Secret CIA Prisons Confirmed By Polish and Romanian Officials," *Guardian Unlimited* **(United Kingdom), June 8, 2007.**

Polish and Romanian security officials told European Council investigators that they secretly held some of America's most important prisoners after the Sept. 11 attacks.

Gélie, Philippe, "Test of Strength Between CIA and White House Escalates," *LeFigaro.fr* **(France), Nov. 10, 2005.**

The CIA asked the Justice Department to investigae who leaked information regarding the existence of its secret prisons to reporters.

Shane, Scott, "Rights Groups Call for End to Secret Detentions," *The New York Times*, **June 7, 2007, p. A18.**

Human rights groups have identified 39 individuals they believe to have been secretly imprisoned by the United States.

Shrader, Katherine, "CIA Fires Employee for Alleged Leak on Prisons Story," The Associated Press Worldstream, April 22, 2006.

The CIA has terminated a top intelligence analyst who admitted leaking classified information that led to the exposure of a network of secret prisons.

Prosecuting and Suing Torturers

Emslie, Katie, "CIA to Be Sued By Civil Rights Group Over 'Torture Flights,' " *Evening News* **(Scotland), Dec. 3, 2005, p. 2.**

The American Civil Liberties Union plans to sue the CIA to prevent suspected terrorists from being flown to other countries.

Eunjung, Ariana, and Sam Diaz, "Advocates Sue Yahoo In Chinese Torture Case," *The Washington Post*, **April 19, 2007, p. D1.**

A human rights group is accusing Yahoo! of abetting the torture of pro-democracy writers by releasing data that allowed China's government to identify them.

Harnden, Toby, "CIA Spies Fear Prosecution Over Secret Prisoners," *Sunday Telegraph* **(United Kingdom), Sept. 10, 2006.**

CIA officers involved in the Bush administration's secret prisons may face prosecution for illegally detaining and interrogating terrorism suspects.

Renditions

"CIA Accused of Using Firms to Transfer Terror Suspects," *Turkish Daily News*, **April 6, 2006.**

Amnesty International has alleged that the CIA has been hiring private aircraft firms to transfer terror suspects to foreign countries to be interrogated.

"Report Rendered," *The Economist*, **June 10, 2006, p. 49.**

A European Council report charges that at least seven European governments have been complicit in the unlawful rendition of terror suspects.

Fleishman, Jeffrey, "Germany Orders Arrest of 13 CIA Operatives in Kidnapping of Khaled el-Masri," *Los Angeles Times*, **Jan. 31, 2007, p. A1.**

German investigators recommend that prosecutors issue arrest warrants for U.S. intelligence operatives who allegedly kidnapped, beat and detained a German terror suspect.

Harbeson, John W., "America's Renditions Are a Mockery of Human Rights," *The Nation* **(Kenya), April 29, 2007.**

Extraordinary rendition undermines the integrity of nations claiming to uphold human rights.

Torture Debate

Evangelista, Patricia, "Art of Fear," *Philippine Daily Inquirer*, **June 10, 2007.**

The U.N. Convention Against Torture declares that freedom from torture is a right that cannot be curtailed by national interests or even clear and present danger.

Hirsh, Michael, and Mark Hosenball, "The White House: The Politics of Torture," *Newsweek*, **Sept. 25, 2006, p. 32.**

Despite calls from Republican senators to ban torture, the Bush administration wants to maintain several CIA-approved harsh interrogation techniques for use against suspected terrorists.

Rauch, Jonathan, "The Right Approach to Rough Treatment," *National Journal*, **Sept. 23, 2006.**

If torture could prevent a major terrorist attack, it would seem immoral to make it off-limits.

CITING *CQ GLOBAL RESEARCHER*

Sample formats for citing these reports in a bibliography include the ones listed below. Preferred styles and formats vary, so please check with your instructor or professor.

MLA STYLE

Flamini, Roland. "Nuclear Proliferation." CQ Global Researcher 1 Apr. 2007: 1-24.

APA STYLE

Flamini, R. (2007, April 1). Nuclear proliferation. *CQ Global Researcher, 1*, 1-24.

CHICAGO STYLE

Flamini, Roland. "Nuclear Proliferation." *CQ Global Researcher*, April 1, 2007, 1-24.

Voices From Abroad:

TONY BLAIR
Then-Prime Minister, United Kingdom

What's the actual threat?

"People devote the most extraordinary amount of time in trying to say that the Americans, on rendition, are basically deporting people . . . and people spend very little time in actually looking at what the threat is that we face and America faces, from terrorism and how we have to deal with it."

The Independent (United Kingdom), February 2006

MICHAEL IGNATIEFF
Member of Parliament, Canada

Taking the high ground

"The moral imperative, 'Do not torture, any time, anywhere, in any circumstances,' is mandated by the United Nations convention against torture and other cruel, inhuman or degrading treatment or punishment. The fact that terrorists torture does not change these imperatives. Compliance does not depend on reciprocity."

Business Day (South Africa), April 2006

BASIL FERNANDO
Executive Director, Asian Human Rights Council

A benefit to the elite

"There is still reluctance on the part of Thai elite to eliminate torture. . . . [Those in power fear] police will no longer be an instrument in

their hand. They have to accept that police can investigate everyone and that the police will become a friend of the ordinary man."

Bangkok Post, July 2006

EDITORIAL
The Indian Express

We are all capable of torture

"Living in a country where torture has become banal, we know it is just as likely to emanate from disgruntled and disaffected fellow citizens as it is from the institutions mandated to protect us — the army, the police, the paramilitary. When authoritarianism and violence become common currency across classes . . . then nobody has qualms disrespecting the basic tenets of civilised political discourse, behaviour, and transaction."

November 2005

MANFRED NOWAK
Anti-Torture Investigator, United Nations

Torturers should pay the costs

"Countries where torture is widespread or even systematic should be held accountable to pay. . . . If individual torturers would have to pay all the long-term rehabilitation costs, this would have a much stronger deterrent effect on torture than some kind of disciplinary or lenient criminal punishment."

Address before U.N. Human Rights Council, Geneva, April 2007

NARMIN UTHMAN
Minister of Human Rights, Iraq

No torture in Abu Ghraib

"Abu Ghraib prison is currently under the supervision of the Human Rights Ministry, and our [inspection] committees have not found evidence of any use of torture. . . . The change in the treatment of [prisoners by] the jail guards in Abu Ghraib prison has had a great impact on changing the Americans' policy towards Iraqi prisoners in general."

Al-Arabiya TV (Dubai), February 2006

LARRY COX
Executive Director, Amnesty International

EU needs better policies

"By the EU adopting anemic rules for the commerce of torture instruments, it essentially allows the practice to continue, now with an official wink and nod. These directives fail to provide broad and tough policies to guarantee that businesses do not profit by the sale of these repulsive tools."

U.S. Newswire, February 2007

KOFI ANNAN
Then-Secretary-General, United Nations

Torture is torture, by any name

"Fifty-seven years after the Universal Declaration of Human Rights prohibited all forms of torture and cruel, inhuman or degrading treatment or punishment, torture remains an unacceptable vice. . . . Nor is torture permissible when it is called something else. . . . Humanity faces grave challenges today. The threat of terror is real and immediate. Fear of terrorists can never justify adopting their methods."

Speech during International Human Rights Day, December 2005

HUMAN RIGHTS LESSON 1

ARES. caglecartoons.com/espanol

Caglecartoons.com/Ares

CHILD SOLDIERS

BY JOHN FELTON

Excerpted from the CQ Global Researcher. John Felton. (July 2008). "Child Soldiers." *CQ Global Researcher*, 183-211.

Child Soldiers

BY JOHN FELTON

THE ISSUES

Ishmael Beah kept on the move in the bush for months with some of his friends to escape the chaos of war-torn Sierra Leone in the early 1990s. Their greatest fear was ending up in the clutches of rebel groups who abducted young boys to join them in fighting against the government and raping, murdering and mutilating civilians. Instead, they wound up in the hands of government soldiers, which wasn't much better.

"We were told that our responsibilities as boys were to fight in this war or we would be killed," he told a U.S. Senate committee last year. "I was 13 years old." [1]

Then, recalling his first day in battle, Beah told the panel that after less than a week of training in how to use AK 47s, M16s, machine guns and rocket-propelled grenades, the adult soldiers led him and his friends into the forest to ambush rebels. "My squad had boys who were as young as 7 . . . dragging guns that were taller than them as we walked to the frontlines."

At first, "I couldn't shoot my gun," he remembered. "But as I lay there watching my friends getting killed . . . I began shooting. Something inside me shifted and I lost compassion for anyone. After that day, killing became as easy as drinking water." For the next two years, Beah said, "all I did was take drugs, fight and kill or be killed."

Children always have been among the first victims of warfare, usually as innocent bystanders. Indeed, in most conflicts, more women and children die — from a combination of disease, starvation or violence — than soldiers. Children also have been pressed into service occasionally as fighters, often as the last, desperate resort of losing armies. [2]

But in recent times tens of thousands of children like Beah have been actively and regularly used in warfare. Since the closing decades of the 20th century, rebel groups and even government armies routinely have used children in combat or supporting roles throughout Africa, Asia, Europe and Latin America.

Many of these children were forced to participate in or witness acts almost beyond comprehension, including:

Former child soldier Ishmael Beah addresses a 2007 international conference on child soldiers. His best-selling autobiography about his horrific experiences in Sierra Leone has raised public awareness of the use of children in armed conflicts.

AFP/Getty Images/Jack Guez

- The 1994 genocide in Rwanda during which at least 800,000 people were slaughtered within a few weeks, many hacked to death with machetes;
- Sierra Leone's civil war in which children were forced to kill their parents and cut off the hands and feet of civilians;
- Indiscriminate guerrilla attacks on noncombatants in Colombia and Sri Lanka;
- The forced murders of their own family members and neighbors, perpetrated at the direction of the Lord's Resistance Army (LRA), a rebel group led by fanatical recluse Joseph Kony in northern Uganda and neighboring countries.
- The use of children, in some cases preteens, as suicide bombers by several groups, including the Tamil Tigers in Sri Lanka, the Taliban in Afghanistan and the Palestinian groups Hamas and Islamic Jihad.

Thousands of other children raided and burned villages, shouldered automatic weapons in combat or served as porters, spies or decoys. The girls were often forced to satisfy the sexual appetites of the guerrillas.

The U.N.'s Special Representative for Children and Armed Conflict, Radhika Coomaraswamy, says there are at least 250,000 child soldiers worldwide. [3] But other experts say the nature of civil conflicts makes it difficult to compile accurate records.

"It's absolutely impossible to determine the number of child soldiers with any accuracy," says Victoria Forbes Adam, executive director of the London-based Coalition to Stop the Use of Child Soldiers. "We think it is in the many tens of thousands, but that is a

Continued on p. 187

Dozens of Countries Use Child Soldiers

Tens of thousands of children under age 18 — some as young as 5 — serve as soldiers or spies for rebel groups, government-linked paramilitary militias or government armed forces. Most are recruited or conscripted in Africa and Asia. Government armed forces in several industrialized countries induct under-18-year-olds but don't use them in combat.

Countries That Use Child Soldiers
(Between April 2004-October 2007)

How child soldiers are used:

- Recruited by government forces; used as government spies and in combat by government forces, rebel groups and paramilitaries
- Recruited by government forces; used in combat by government forces, rebel groups and paramilitaries
- Recruited by government forces; used in combat by government forces
- Recruited by government forces; used in combat by government forces and rebel groups
- Used as soldiers by rebel groups and government-linked paramilitaries
- Used in combat by government forces and rebel groups and as government spies
- Used in combat by rebel groups and government-linked paramilitaries and as government spies
- Used in combat by rebel groups and as government spies
- Used in combat by government-linked paramilitaries and armed groups
- Recruited by government forces
- Used in combat by rebel groups

* Deployed children under 18 to Iraq, where they were exposed to risk of hostilities.

Source: "Child Soldiers: Global Report 2008," Coalition to Stop the Use of Child Soldiers

Laws and Resolutions Dealing with Child Soldiers

Several United Nations treaties make it illegal under international law for governments or rebel groups to recruit and use children in warfare, including:

- **Additional Protocols to the Geneva Conventions (1977)** — Establishes age 15 as the minimum for participation in armed combat by government forces or nongovernmental groups; applies both to international and domestic conflicts.

- **Convention on the Rights of the Child (1989)** — Prohibits the recruitment and use of children under 15 by armed groups; a compromise is reached after objection by the United States, Britain and the Netherlands to an 18-year-old standard. The United States and Somalia are the only countries that have not ratified it. [1]

- **Rome Statute (1998)** — Creates the International Criminal Court and defines as a war crime the recruitment or use in combat of children under 15.

- **Worst Forms of Child Labour Convention (1999)** — Adopted by member states of the International Labor Organization; defines a child as anyone under 18 and says child labor includes "forced or compulsory recruitment of children for use in armed conflict."

- **Optional Protocol to the Convention on the Rights of the Child (2000)** — Raises to 18 the minimum age for using children in conflicts, prohibites compulsory recruitment by governments or non-state groups of anyone under 18; allows governments to recruit 16- and 17-year-olds for military service if the recruitment is voluntary and approved by the parents or legal guardians. The United States ratified it in 2002. [2]

Since 1999, the U.N. Security Council has adopted six resolutions pertaining to children in armed conflict:

- **Resolutions 1261 (1999) and 1314 (2000)** — Calls on all parties to respect international law concerning the protection of children, including girls, in armed conflict.

- **Resolution 1379 (2001)** — Asks the U.N. secretary-general to create a blacklist of those who recruit child soldiers.

- **Resolutions 1460 (2003) and 1539 (2004)** — Calls for children to be included in programs designed to help former soldiers disarm, demobilize and reintegrate into society; suggests implementation of country-specific, targeted measures.

- **Resolution 1612 (2005)** — Creates a mechanism for monitoring and disseminating information on six types of child-rights violations; creates a Security Council Working Group to recommend measures on a per-situation basis; urges those using children in conflict to establish action plans for their release and reintegration.

[1] Available at www.unhchr.ch/html/menu2/6/crc/treaties/crc.htm.
[2] Available at www.unhchr.ch/html/menu2/6/crc/treaties/opac.htm.

Continued from p. 185

complete guesstimate." Leaders of armed groups, particularly rebels fighting in the bush, generally refuse to open their rosters to international inspection, she explains, and "children come in and out of conflicts, they die of illness, they die of injuries, or they may simply be missing from their communities."

However, many more children are recruited by official national armies than by rebel groups, according to some studies. About 500,000 under-18-year-olds serve at any given time in government armies and paramilitary groups in about 50 countries, according to P.W. Singer, a senior fellow at the Brookings Institution think tank in Washington, D.C., who has written widely on the problem. (*See map, p. 186.*) Most serve in reserve units until they are called into combat, Singer writes. [4]

The United Nations and human rights groups have accused some countries of forcibly recruiting children for their armies. The military government of Myanmar, for example, allegedly rewards recruiters with money and bags of rice for luring children into the army, according to Human Rights Watch (HRW). [5]

The presence of children in combat can make conflicts more persistent because conflicts involving children "are easier to start, more difficult to end, and more likely to resume," says Singer. Children are so readily available, cheap and expendable — from the viewpoint of leaders of armed groups — that using them can be an incentive to start conflicts and keep fighting even if success seems futile, he says.

Defining a "child soldier" is a complex issue. Who is a child? And who is a soldier? As set out in several U.N.

treaties since World War II, a child is anyone under 18. The most recent legal definition is contained in the 2000 Optional Protocol to the Convention on the Rights of the Child on the Involvement of Children in Armed Conflict — known as the "Optional Protocol." It allows governments to recruit 16- and 17-year-olds but prohibits them from serving in combat. The United States and 25 other countries recruit under-18-year-olds into their armed services, according to the Coalition to Stop the Use of Child Soldiers. [6] Under the Optional Protocol, "non-state actors" such as rebel groups, may not recruit anyone under 18.

But many rebel leaders around the world either ignore the prohibition or claim not to know the ages of their recruits. "They say, 'The children come to us without any birth certificates, so how are we to know how old they are?' "

Continued on p. 189

---

19 African Commanders Charged with Using Child Soldiers

A total of 19 former and current commanders — all from Africa — have been charged with enlisting children under age 15 as soldiers. Four are serving time in prison after being convicted. Six are on trial, while six have been charged but never captured. Most were accused of other war crimes as well, including murder, rape, abductions, forced labor and looting. No commanders from other countries have been charged for using child soldiers.

Country Commander	Military Group*	Status
Democratic Republic of the Congo		
Thomas Lubanga Dyilo *Lubanga*	Union of Congolese Patriots	International Criminal Court trial indefinitely suspended 6/2008; his release is pending appeal
Germain Katanga	Patriotic Forces of Resistance	ICC pre-trial hearings began 5/27/2008
Mathieu Ngudjolo Chui	Front for National Integration	ICC pre-trial hearings began 5/27/2008
Kyungu Mutanga *Katanga*	Mai-Mai	In Congolese custody
Jean-Pierre Biyoyo	Mudundu 40	Sentenced to 5 years by Congolese military tribunal 3/2006; escaped
Bosco Ntaganda	Union of Congolese Patriots	ICC warrants issued 8/22/2006
Liberia		
Charles Taylor *Taylor*	Former president, Liberia	Trial continues at Special Court of Sierra Leone
Sierra Leone		
Alex Tamba Brima	Armed Forces Revolutionary Council	Convicted, serving 50 years
Brima Bazzy Kamara	Armed Forces Revolutionary Council	Convicted, serving 45 years
Santigie Borbor Kanu	Armed Forces Revolutionary Council	Convicted, Serving 50 years
Allieu Kondewa	Civil Defense Forces	Convicted, 8-year sentence increased to 20 years, 5/2008
Issa Hassan Sesay	Revolutionary United Front	Joint trial in Special Court of
Morris Kallon	Revolutionary United Front	Sierra Leone expected to
Augustine Gbao	Revolutionary United Front	conclude in August
Uganda		
Joseph Kony *Kony*	Lord's Resistance Army	ICC warrant issued 7/8/2005
Vincent Otti	Lord's Resistance Army	Reportedly killed in 2007
Raska Lukwiya	Lord's Resistance Army	Killed, 2006
Okot Odiambo	Lord's Resistance Army	ICC warrant issued 7/8/2005
Dominic Ongwen *Otti*	Lord's Resistance Army	ICC warrant issued 7/8/2005

* The accused were serving with these groups at the time of their alleged crimes. Some are in other groups now.

Sources: United Nations; Human Rights Watch; Special Court of Sierra Leone, www.sc-sl.org/RUF-Casesummary.html

Continued from p. 187

says U.N. Special Representative Coomaraswamy, who has negotiated with many rebel leaders in Africa and Asia.

Perhaps the most precise definition of a child soldier was produced at a conference of scholars and representatives of various child-protection agencies, organized in 1997 by the United Nations Children's Fund (UNICEF). Convening in Cape Town, South Africa, the group developed the so-called Cape Town Principles, which define a child soldier as anyone under 18 "who is part of any kind of regular or irregular armed force" in any capacity, including cooks, porters, messengers and non-family members accompanying such groups. Also included were girls recruited for sexual purposes and those forced into marriage. [7]

However, David M. Rosen, a professor of anthropology and law at Fairleigh Dickinson University in Madison, New Jersey, argues that the age "when the young are fit to be warriors" varies from culture to culture. [8] In some societies, he wrote in a provocative 2005 book, "young people are deliberately socialized into highly aggressive behavior, and both individual and collective violence are highly esteemed." Other societies, he added, put more emphasis "on peaceful resolution of disputes." Rosen contends the United Nations and international humanitarian organizations have used the subject of child soldiers to advance their own agendas, including, in his view, protecting post-colonial governments in Africa and Asia against internal rebellion and denouncing Israel for its attacks on Palestinians while ignoring terrorist attacks perpetrated by Palestinian child soldiers.

Children end up in armies and rebel groups for a variety of reasons, depending on the circumstances. All too often, children are abducted from their villages or displaced-person camps or — like Beah — are swept up by government armies. Leaders of armed groups

AFP/Getty Images/Guido Benschop

Former Liberian President Charles Taylor, in handcuffs, arrives in the Netherlands in 2006 for his war crimes trial before the Special Court of Sierra Leone in The Hague. Taylor is accused of sponsoring and aiding rebels who carried out murders, sexual slavery, mutilations and the conscription of child soldiers during the civil war in Sierra Leone. The trial continues.

often use narcotics to dull the fears of their child soldiers or to stimulate them for combat. Beah's experiences were similar to those of Albert, a former child soldier who told Amnesty International he was forced to join a rebel group in the Democratic Republic of the Congo when he was 15.

"[T]hey would give us 'chanvre' [cannabis] and force us to kill people to toughen us up," he recalled. "Sometimes they brought us women and girls to rape. . . . They would beat us if we refused." [9]

Many young children join armed groups voluntarily because their families can't support them, or they're lured by the prospect of carrying a gun and

wearing a snazzy uniform. Others are enticed by recruiters who make extravagant promises to the children and their families that they have no intention of keeping.

The child soldier problem has captured the world's attention intermittently over the past two decades — most often when children are found to engage in atrocities. Conflicts in the West African nations of Liberia and Sierra Leone during the 1990s seemed to represent the quintessential use of child soldiers in brutal circumstances.

In Liberia, Charles Taylor rose to power at the head of a rebel army composed substantially of young fighters

Continued on p. 191

Former Girl Soldiers Get Little Aid

Many programs often ignore their needs.

When she was 12 years old, Lucy Aol was abducted by the Lord's Resistance Army (LRA), a rebel group in northern Uganda. They made her walk several hundred miles to a hideout in southern Sudan.

"We were used like slaves," she recently recalled. "We used to work in the fields or collect firewood from 7 in the morning until 5 in the evening, and we were given no food. If you made a mistake or refused, they would beat us," she said. "The three girls who were taken from my village with me were beaten to death."

A year after she was abducted, Aol was forced to become the "wife" of a rebel commander. She and her "husband" later fled the rebel group together, but he was killed, and she discovered she was pregnant, and at age 16 she gave birth to a daughter. Now 21, Aol is studying environmental health at a college in Uganda. [1]

Similar stories could be told by thousands of girls in recent decades. Up to 40 percent of the children serving in some armed groups are girls. [2] A 2004 study found that girls served in 38 regional conflicts between 1990 and 2003 and were fighters in all but four. [3] Yet, the plight of young girls forced to join armed groups still isn't on the radar screens of many governments and world leaders — or even those working to reintegrate former male child soldiers into society.

Only in the last few years have aid programs taken girls' needs into consideration, and they still are not being given as much attention or help as the boys. Many girls also avoid official postwar reintegration programs for fear of being stigmatized.

"Boys might be called rebels, but girls are not just rebels. They may have been raped, they may feel spiritually polluted or unclean, and if they are mothers they may be called the mothers of rebel children, and so they are isolated," says Michael Wessells, a professor of psychology at Randolph-Macon College in Virginia who has aided former child soldiers in Africa and Asia for three decades. "But all they want is to be like other children."

"In many parts of the world, if you are female and you're not a virgin, you are not marriageable," says Neil Boothy, a professor at Columbia University who has developed and studied aid programs for former child soldiers for two decades. "And marriage remains the economic pathway for most women in most societies."

Only a few postwar integration programs, however, provide vocational training for both girls and boys. One exception is a program in northern Uganda run by local organizations supported by the Anglican Church. It allows both girls and boys who had been in armed groups to attend a technical school where they learn basic business skills and agricultural trades, such as beekeeping.

A recent study of former LRA girl soldiers focused on several thousand girls and young women who had been forced to "marry" rebel commanders. [4] The study said the presence of forced wives in rebel units "served to bolster fighter morale and

support the systems which perpetuate cycles of raiding, looting, killing, and abduction." Thus, says study co-author Dyan Mazurana, forcing girls to become commanders' wives is an integral part of how many armed groups conduct their business — not an incidental factor that can be ignored by governments and aid groups in their postwar negotiations with rebels.

A Palestinian policeman teaches a girl how to use an AK-47 assault rifle in a Gaza refugee camp in southern Gaza Strip. Palestinian extremist groups reportedly have used children as suicide bombers.

Reuters/Ahmed Jadallah

The leaders of local communities often argue that the best way to deal with the forced wives of rebels after a war "is for them to stay with their captors," she continues. But the young women overwhelmingly reject that idea.

Grace Akallo — abducted by the LRA in 1996 but who escaped after seven months — says she "can't imagine" any girl wanting to stay with her captors. "We were all so anxious to get away from them, we would do anything to get away from them," says Akallo, now a college student in the United States.

Complicating the situation, says Wessells, are girls who joined armed groups voluntarily to avoid abusive parents, to escape arranged marriages or in hopes of finding a better life. These girls are often more reluctant than abducted girls to return to their communities after the war, so they are unlikely to seek help from official aid programs, Wessells says.

[1] "In the Tragedy of Child-soldiering in Africa, a Girl's Story Finds a Happy Ending," The Associated Press, Aug. 25, 2007.

[2] Hilde F. Johnson, deputy executive director, UNICEF, address to the Ministerial Meeting on Children and Armed Conflict, Oct. 1, 2007, a follow-up to the Paris Principles and Paris Commitments, formulated in February 2007, www.unicef.org/protection/files/Final-Paris-Principles-1Oct07-HFJ-speech.pdf.

[3] Susan McKay and Dyan Mazurana, "Where are the Girls? Girls in Fighting Forces in Northern Uganda, Sierra Leone, and Mozambique. Their Lives During and After War," International Centre for Human Rights and Democracy, Montreal, 2004, pp. 22, 25.

[4] Kristopher Carlson and Dyan Mazurana, "Forced Marriage within the Lord's Resistance Army, Uganda," Feinstein International Center, Tufts University, May 2008.

Continued from p. 189

whom he sent out to rape, pillage and murder. In neighboring Sierra Leone, the Revolutionary United Front (RUF) — a rebel group armed and supported by Taylor — forced its child soldiers to mutilate victims in one of the most depraved civil conflicts in modern times. These wars spawned other conflicts in the region, notably in Guinea and the Côte d'Ivoire, sometimes involving child soldiers who crossed borders to keep fighting because it was the only life they knew.

Beah, who was fortunate enough to be removed from the Sierra Leone conflict by UNICEF, recounted his story in the gripping 2007 bestseller, *A Long Way Gone: Memoirs of a Boy Soldier*. [10] The book, and Beah's engaging media appearances, quickly drew more public attention to the child soldier issue than stacks of U.N. reports and resolutions had done.

Besides being an appealing advocate for child soldiers, Beah, now in his late-20s, shows that child soldiers can return to a normal life once they're removed from conflict and receive appropriate assistance from groups specializing in protecting children. Admittedly, as a ward of the U.N. system for several years, Beah had opportunities few other former soldiers enjoy. Even so, child-protection experts emphasize that even after committing heinous acts or suffering deep psychological or physical injuries, former child soldiers can be rehabilitated.

As governments and international organizations around the globe wrestle with the problem of child soldiers, here are some of the questions being addressed:

Does "naming and shaming" help prevent the use of child soldiers?

In his most recent report on children and armed conflict, released in January, United Nations Secretary-General Ban Ki-moon identified 40 governments or rebel groups, in 13

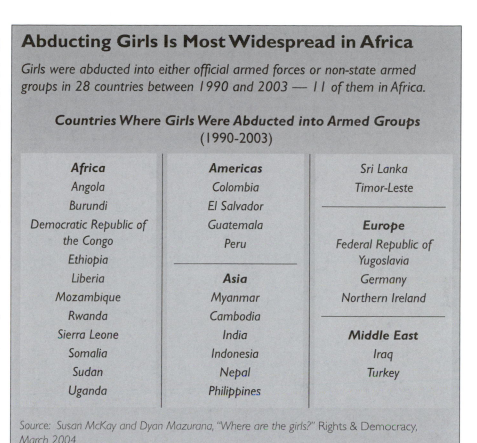

Abducting Girls Is Most Widespread in Africa

Girls were abducted into either official armed forces or non-state armed groups in 28 countries between 1990 and 2003 — 11 of them in Africa.

Countries Where Girls Were Abducted into Armed Groups (1990-2003)

Africa	Americas	Sri Lanka
Angola	Colombia	Timor-Leste
Burundi	El Salvador	
Democratic Republic of the Congo	Guatemala	**Europe**
Ethiopia	Peru	Federal Republic of Yugoslavia
Liberia	**Asia**	Germany
Mozambique	Myanmar	Northern Ireland
Rwanda	Cambodia	
Sierra Leone	India	**Middle East**
Somalia	Indonesia	Iraq
Sudan	Nepal	Turkey
Uganda	Philippines	

Source: Susan McKay and Dyan Mazurana, "Where are the girls?" Rights & Democracy, March 2004

conflicts, that recruited and used child soldiers. [11] This report was a key component of the U.N.'s policy of publicly identifying those who recruit and use child soldiers — and condemning them for it. The U.N. has been in the "naming and shaming" business since November 2001, when the Security Council adopted Resolution 1379, asking the secretary-general to identify governments and groups that engaged in the practice. [12]

Secretary-General Kofi Annan submitted his first such report in 2002, and subsequent reports have been filed each year.

Human-rights advocacy groups, such as Amnesty International and HRW, also have made naming and shaming an important part of their campaigns to draw attention to the use and abuse of child soldiers. These groups issue their own reports on specific conflicts, and a collaboration of such groups, the Coali-

tion to Stop the Use of Child soldiers, periodically publishes a comprehensive assessment of the use of child soldiers worldwide. The coalition's most recent report, "Child Soldiers Global Report 2008," was published in May. [13]

In his 2007 report, Secretary-General Ban said naming offending parties "has proven to have a deterrent effect" and has allowed the U.N. and other agencies to maintain political pressure and take action against those who are "persistent violators of child rights." [14]

U.N. Special Representative Coomaraswamy says it's also significant that the child soldier problem is the only "thematic issue" regularly addressed by the Security Council — as opposed to specific crises in individual countries. The council has established a "working group" that meets every two months to discuss the secretary-general's reports. On behalf of the Security Council, the working group condemns those who continue using child soldiers and praises those who agree to stop the practice.

"People do listen to the Security Council," Coomaraswamy says. "They may not always act in ways we wish they would, but they do listen, and this should not be dismissed."

Girl soldiers serve with Maoist rebels near Kathmandu. According to a recent U.N. report, the group refuses to release its child soldiers on a regular basis despite signing an historic peace pact with the Nepalese government.

Jo Becker, child rights advocacy director of HRW, agrees naming and shaming has had some impact, but mostly on governments. For example, she notes, governments in Chad, the Democratic Republic of the Congo and Myanmar have pledged to stop using child soldiers due to international pressure. And while these and other governments haven't always kept their promises, at least they have taken the first step of forswearing their use, she says.

Some rebels have responded to international pressure, such as the Tamil Tigers of Sri Lanka, who "promote themselves as a reputable group and rely very heavily on contributions from the international diaspora of Tamils," Becker points out. According to the U.N., the group has released

some child soldiers — but certainly not all of them — and continued recruiting children well into 2007, although in lower numbers than in previous years. [15]

However, leaders of many other groups — such as Kony, of the Lord's Resistance Army — appear to have little or no regard for how they are seen internationally and are not swayed by having their names published in U.N. reports. "Kony's name was already mud and could hardly get any worse," says Christopher Blattman, an assistant professor of political science and economics at Yale University who has done extensive research on Kony.

An even more skeptical view comes from Singer at Brookings, who says most of those who use child soldiers see it as a purely pragmatic rather than a moral issue. "You can't shame the shameless," Singer says, "but you can create some sense of accountability by figuring out what their interests are, what drives their calculations and how you can alter their calculations." Prosecuting and im-

posing sanctions are more effective parts of a "cost structure" that can be imposed on those who use child soldiers, Singer says.

Some experts argue that naming and shaming can be useful in some cases but counterproductive in others. "If you are . . . trying to use communication and negotiations channels [with rebels] to get the release of child soldiers, it can be undermined by strident or hostile criticism of the group," says Michael Wessells, a professor of psychology at Randolph-Macon College in Virginia, who has worked with programs to aid child soldiers for nearly three decades. "The door closes, and the lives of children are damaged even further."

For instance, Blattman says pending International Criminal Court (ICC) indictments of Kony and four of his commanders may have helped persuade Kony to authorize aides to enter into peace negotiations with the Ugandan government in hopes the indictments would be lifted. But the court's insistence on maintaining the indictments "could now be an impediment to peace because it doesn't offer them [Kony and his commanders] much of an option," Blattman says. If Kony faces a choice of prison or lifetime exile, he probably will choose exile and continued conflict, Blattman adds, prolonging his two-decade-long war well into the future.

Nevertheless, Wessells says, it is "profoundly important to make clear that it is not OK for leaders of armed groups to say they can do whatever they want." Reflecting concerns about the potential negative consequences of naming and shaming, an international forum of experts on child soldiers, meeting in Switzerland in 2006, called for more research on the effectiveness of naming and shaming. [16]

Should the United States prosecute alleged child soldiers detained at Guantánamo Bay?

An alleged terrorist captured in Afghanistan when he was 15 could be the first person tried for war crimes committed as a child. Omar Ahmed Khadr, now 21, is facing trial by a military commission after spending nearly six years in prison at the U.S. military base at Guantánamo Bay, Cuba.

The son of a financier for the al Qaeda Islamic terrorist group, Khadr is charged with murder, spying against the United States and other crimes. He allegedly threw a grenade that killed a U.S. soldier and injured others in Afghanistan on July 27, 2002. [17] Khadr was seriously wounded during the fighting and was transferred to Guantánamo in November 2002, where he was placed under the jurisdiction of the U.S. military commission created after the Sept. 11, 2001, terrorist attacks.

The commission in late 2007 and early 2008 rejected several motions filed by Khadr's attorneys challenging the proceedings, including one contending Khadr had been illegally recruited by his father into working as a translator at al Qaeda training camps in Afghanistan. Col. Peter Brownback, the commission's judge, dismissed that motion on April 30 on the grounds that Congress did not set a minimum age for defendants when it authorized the military commissions in 2006. [18] Khadr's trial is scheduled to begin in October.

HRW and other groups have denounced the government's handling of Khadr, noting that he was treated as an adult despite his age when he allegedly committed the crimes and has been held in "prolonged" periods of solitary confinement for more than five years. [19] In an *amicus curiae* brief submitted to the commission on Jan. 18 on behalf of 23 members of Canada's parliament and 55 legal scholars from Canada, Sarah H. Paoletti, clinical supervisor and lecturer at the Transnational Legal Clinic at the University of Pennsylvania School of Law, argued that Khadr's prosecution "is in stark opposition to longstanding and well-established precedent under in-

ternational law protecting the rights of children unlawfully recruited into armed conflict." [20]

Paoletti's brief said recent treaties and agreements suggest that former child soldiers should be offered rehabilitation and reintegration back into their communities rather than prosecution. For instance, the 1998 Rome Statute, which created the ICC, denied the court jurisdiction over anyone younger than 18 at the time of the alleged crime. This ban does not apply to courts or tribunals established by national governments. [21]

Similarly, a set of "principles" negotiated by representatives of countries and nongovernmental organizations in Paris last year suggested that former child soldiers should not be prosecuted but rather treated as "victims of offences against international law, not only as perpetrators. They must be treated in accordance with international law in a framework of restorative justice and social rehabilitation, consistent with international law, which offers children special protection through numerous agreements and principles." [22]

David M. Crane, former chief prosecutor at the U.N.-backed Special Tribunal for Sierra Leone, is one of the most prominent opponents of Khadr's prosecution. He says he decided not to prosecute child soldiers — even those who had committed "horrendous crimes" — because adults were the responsible parties. "Even if a child willingly goes along, he really has no choice in the matter, and this certainly appears to be true in the case of Khadr," who was under the influence of his father, Crane says.

The U.N.'s Coomaraswamy has appealed to the United States to halt the prosecution, saying "children should not be prosecuted for war crimes." She is pleased that Khadr's military lawyers are fighting the prosecution "tooth and nail."

The Pentagon has defended its prosecution on the grounds that none of

the international treaties dealing with children and armed conflict expressly forbid a national government from prosecuting alleged child soldiers. In fact, a prosecution motion in the case argued that the Optional Protocol obligated the government to take legal action against Khadr. Al Qaeda itself violated that treaty by recruiting Khadr, the prosecution said, so dismissing the charges against him — as his defense lawyers argued — "would effectively condone that alleged violation by allowing Khadr to escape all liability for his actions and would further incentivize such actions." [23]

In another government defense of the Khadr case, the Pentagon official in charge of detention policy, Sandra L. Hodgkinson, told a U.N. committee on May 22 that the U.S. detention of Khadr and other juveniles in Afghanistan and Iraq reduces the threat that they will be used to carry out suicide bombings and other attacks. "If there is a sense that juveniles cannot be removed from the battlefield, there is a valid concern that the tactic of recruiting children will be further utilized against coalition forces and innocent civilians in Iraq and Afghanistan," she said. [24]

Although Khadr is a Canadian citizen by birth, Canada has refused to intervene on the grounds that he has been charged with a serious crime. Even so, the Canadian Supreme Court on May 23 denounced the early stages of the U.S. handling of his case. In a unanimous opinion, the court said U.S. legal processes at Guantánamo in 2002-03 "constituted a clear violation of fundamental human rights protected by international law." Moreover, the court said the Canadian government erred in turning over to U.S. authorities information about interviews with Khadr conducted by the Canadian intelligence service in 2003; Khadr's defense lawyers were entitled to see some of these documents, the court said. [25]

In a follow-up to that decision, a lower-court judge in Canada ruled on June 25 that Khadr's lawyers could be given a document and recordings describing alleged mistreatment of him by U.S. officials at the Guantánamo prison in 2004.

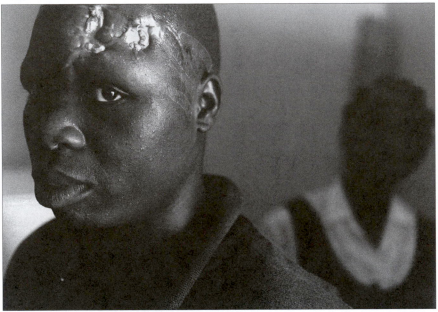

Simon, now 19, spent eight years as a child soldier with the Lord's Resistance Army (LRA) after being abducted from his home in northern Uganda. During that time he saw hundreds of people killed, including some who were hacked to death in front of him, and he was forced to kill other child abductees who tried to escape. Besides his psychological wounds, he is struggling to recover form a head wound received during combat. The LRA is led by Joseph Kony, a notorious, self-styled prophet who was indicted by the International Criminal Court in 2005 but remains at large.

Getty Images/Andy Sewell

Another alleged child soldier held at Guantánamo, Mohammed Jawad, was captured in Afghanistan in December 2002 when he was either 16 or 17 and charged last January with attempted murder and intentionally causing bodily harm. The military alleges he threw a hand grenade into a vehicle carrying two U.S. soldiers and their Afghan interpreter. [26] Jawad's case is still in the early stages of consideration by a military commission at Guantánamo.

Hearings on both the Khadr and Jawad cases continued in mid-June despite a major Supreme Court ruling on June 12 that Guantánamo prisoners could challenge their detentions in U.S. federal court. The decision didn't directly go to the actions of the military commissions, but defense lawyers already have said they will use it to challenge a broad range of government actions concerning the detainees.

Should Congress pass legislation to combat the use of child soldiers overseas?

The child soldier issue has reached the U.S. Congress, which is considering two bills intended to put some force behind American criticisms of the use of child soldiers. The House-passed Child Soldier Prevention Act would bar U.S. military aid or arms sales to governments that recruit or use child soldiers (defined as children under 16 voluntarily recruited into an official army or under 18 forced to join an army). The U.S. president could waive the ban by declaring that it is in America's national interest to provide aid or sell weapons to governments that use child soldiers.

The Senate, meanwhile, passed the Child Soldiers Accountability Act, which would make it a crime under U.S. law for anyone, anywhere, to recruit a child under 15 into an armed group or use a child in combat. The measure also prohibits entry into the United States of anyone who recruits or uses child soldiers under 15.

Sen. Richard L. Durbin, D-Ill., one of the bill's sponsors, said it would help "ensure that the war criminals who recruit or use children as soldiers will not find safe haven in our country and will allow the U.S. government to hold these individuals accountable for their actions." [27] Senate aides say there has been no active opposition so far to either measure.

The House-passed measure potentially could prove controversial, however, because the national police force in Afghanistan — a key U.S. ally — has been accused of forcibly recruiting children under 18. The State Department cited the allegations in its 2007 human rights report on the country. [28]

Afghanistan was scheduled to receive about $8 million in military aid in fiscal 2008, according to the Center for Defense Information, a liberal think tank in Washington. The center said the bill could affect military aid to six other countries unless the president waived the provisions. The center compared the State Department's 2007 human rights reports — which dealt with child soldiers for the first time — and the administration's allocations of military aid as well as its arms sales to foreign countries. The six other countries that used child soldiers in some official capacity while receiving U.S. military aid were Chad, the Democratic Republic of the Congo, Somalia, Sri Lanka, Sudan and Uganda. Most of the aid programs were small and included only military training — generally considered the stepping stone to a broader relationship between the U.S. and foreign militaries. [29]

Sen. Durbin said the bill "would ensure that U.S. taxpayer dollars are not used to support this abhorrent practice by government or government-sanctioned military and paramilitary organizations." The United States could continue military aid if the president chose to do so, Durbin added, "but it would be used only to remedy the problem by helping countries successfully demobilize their child soldiers and professionalize their forces." [30]

Neither of the two measures has encountered any formal opposition in either chamber of Congress. Although the Bush administration has taken no formal position on either bill, congressional aides and lobbyists favoring the proposals say they expect the White House to oppose them as a matter of course because legislation limiting a president's flexibility in foreign policy is generally resisted. ■

BACKGROUND

Child Armies Proliferate

An explosion of civil conflicts around the globe during the last half of the 20th century was accompanied by several developments that ensured children would bear much of the burden of war. Chief among them was the invention of simple-to-use, lightweight weapons — especially automatic rifles and rocket launchers. Even a 10-year-old can carry and use the world's most ubiquitous weapon: the Kalashnikov assault rifle, or AK-47.

After the collapse of communism in Eastern Europe and the Soviet Union between 1989-91, millions of Kalashnikovs and other Soviet weapons fell into the hands of unscrupulous arms dealers, who sold them to rebel leaders and warlords around the world. They often paid with narcotics, dia-

monds or other resources plundered from their own countries.

Rebels claiming to be fighting for social justice or a host of other causes found they could easily fill their ranks with children. An official of the Chadian military explained their advantages: "Child soldiers are ideal because they don't complain, they don't expect to be paid and if you tell them to kill, they kill." [31]

Children also are easy to abduct or force into military service, especially if they live in unprotected villages or communal facilities, such as refugee camps, where they are often protected only by mothers and unarmed humanitarian workers. "All the boys in the village were asked to join the army," a former child soldier told author Singer. "There was no way out. If I left the village I would get killed by the rebels who would think that I was a spy. On the other hand, if I stayed in the village and refused to join the army, I wouldn't be given any food and would eventually be thrown out, which was as good as being dead." [32]

Social and economic conditions in many poor countries, such as poverty and lack of educational and job opportunities, make children susceptible to the call of combat. "Demagogues, warlords, criminals and others find it easier to recruit when a large population of angry, listless young men fill the street," Singer said. [33]

Impressionable children also can find military life alluring. When a recruiter from the army or a rebel group shows up and offers an impoverished child the opportunity to wear a uniform and make himself feel powerful by carrying a gun, the sales pitch is often difficult to resist.

U.N. Roles

The task of curtailing the use of under-age fighters has fallen largely to the United Nations, which has had only limited success. The U.N. has

taken a two-pronged approach: getting a treaty enacted making it illegal for governments and armed groups to use children under 18 in combat and establishing a system for identifying armed groups that recruit and use child soldiers. The Security Council has threatened to sanction more than a dozen persistent violators of the law but has taken that step only once, in Côte d'Ivoire in West Africa.

Several treaties and regulations adopted by the U.N. after World War II created a legal structure offering theoretical protection to children and discouraging their use in warfare, including the 1948 Universal Declaration of Human Rights, the Geneva Conventions of 1949 and Additional Protocols to those conventions adopted in 1977 and the 1989 Convention on the Rights of the Child. These treaties were strengthened substantially in 2000 with adoption of the Optional Protocol, which specifically barred non-state armed groups from recruiting or using any children under 18 but allowed governments to recruit children 16 or 17 as long as they weren't used in combat until they turned 18. In essence, the treaty made it illegal under international law for anyone to use a child under 18 in combat. In addition, the 1998 Rome Statute — which went into effect in 2002 and created the International Criminal Court — defined as a "war crime" the conscription or use in war of any child under 15.

Since 1996 the Security Council also has adopted six resolutions dealing specifically with children and armed conflict. The last four of these (Resolution 1379 adopted in 2001, Resolution 1460 adopted in 2003, Resolution 1539 adopted in 2004, and Resolution 1612 adopted in 2005) created a system under which U.N. officials monitor the impact of armed conflicts on children and publicly identify countries and groups that illegally recruit and use children in combat.

In some cases, when confronted by the U.N. with solid evidence about their use of child soldiers, warlords have promised to release them. Some have kept their promises, notably the leaders of three groups in Côte d'Ivoire who were subjected to Security Council sanctions in 2006. [34] Most others broke their promises. In Somalia, for example, the Union of Islamic Courts, which briefly held power in 2006, told U.N. officials they would stop using child soldiers, but didn't. [35]

Children at War

The United Nations, nongovernmental groups and academic experts have identified nearly 50 civil conflicts since World War II that have involved children, mostly in sub-Saharan Africa. The following examples are representative of recent or ongoing conflicts involving heavy use of child soldiers:

Colombia — The long-running, multifaceted civil conflict in Colombia has featured the most extensive use of child soldiers in the Americas. According to various estimates, 11,000 to 14,000 Colombians under 18 have been recruited into the country's armed groups. [36] Most are members of the two leftist guerrilla factions, the Revolutionary Armed Forces of Colombia (FARC) and the National Liberation Army (ELN). Several thousand underage fighters also have been associated with right-wing paramilitary groups aligned with the government, the military and major landowners; the largest paramilitary force is the United Self-Defense Forces of Colombia (AUC). [37]

The Colombian army also used under-18-year-olds as fighters until 2000, when it reportedly halted the practice after domestic and international protests. But there have been reports about the army's continued use of children. American journalist Jimmie Briggs said the army still recruits soldiers under 18

but assigns them to non-combat duty until they turn 18. [38] In its "2008 Global Report," the Coalition to Stop the Use of Child Soldiers cited the army for using captured children for intelligence-gathering. [39]

Significantly, since 1999 more than 3,300 former child soldiers (mostly from the FARC) have gone through the government-sponsored demobilization, disarmament and reintegration process — one of the few major demobilization efforts ever conducted during an ongoing conflict. [40]

Democratic Republic of the Congo — The Congolese war — the biggest and deadliest since World War II — took place in the former Zaire from about 1998 until 2003. It involved more than a dozen guerrilla groups and, at various points, the armies or paramilitary groups from Angola, Burundi, Rwanda, Uganda and Zimbabwe. The International Rescue Committee has estimated that up to 5.5 million people — about one-tenth of the Congo's population — may have died as a result of the conflict. [41]

Many of the armed groups used children as fighters or in support roles. In 2002, as part of the war was ending, UNICEF estimated that about 33,000 children were involved in the fighting — or 20 percent of active combatants. [42] In June 2007, U.N. Secretary-General Ban told the U.N. Security Council that 29,291 children had been released by armed groups during the previous three years under a U.N.-sponsored demobilization program. However, due to alleged mismanagement of the program and a failure by donor nations to fulfill their funding pledges, only about half of the former child soldiers had received aid to reintegrate into their communities, the report found. [43]

Although peace agreements were signed in 2002 and 2003, fighting has continued in parts of eastern Congo, where renegade Tutsi commander Laurent Nkunda leads a militia in fight-

ing the Congolese army. Nkunda claims his group is protecting Congo's minority Tutsi population — an ethnic group that was slaughtered by the hundreds of thousands during the 1994 genocide in Rwanda.

The U.N. has accused Nkunda of forcibly recruiting hundreds, and possibly several thousand, children. [44] Nkunda, along with other rebels, signed a cease-fire agreement on Jan. 23, 2008, pledging to end the fighting. [45] Reports since then have suggested the cease-fire merely reduced the level of fighting rather than stopping it. [46] Government security forces also used child soldiers, at least through 2007, according to the U.S. State Department. [47]

Liberia — From the early 1990s until President Charles Taylor was ousted from power in 2003, Liberia was a focal point for several civil conflicts in West Africa, all involving child soldiers. During the early 1990s, Taylor led a rebel army, composed in large part of children, which controlled much of Liberia. After he became president in 1997, he also backed rebel groups in neighboring Côte d'Ivoire, Guinea and Sierra Leone.

Taylor's support for the notorious Revolutionary United Front in Sierra Leone — in exchange for access to diamonds and other natural resources in rebel-controlled areas — was the basis for his indictment on 11 war-crimes charges by a U.N.-sponsored tribunal. His trial, which began in July 2007, is still under way. The regional impact of the war in Liberia and Taylor's sponsorship of neighboring rebel armies continued at least until 2005. According to the Coalition to Stop the Use of Child Soldiers, rebel groups in Guinea and Côte d'Ivoire were still recruiting child soldiers (and former child soldiers who had reached age 18) from Liberia. [48]

Myanmar — The U.N., HRW and other organizations say the secretive military government of Myanmar (formerly Burma) makes widespread use

Continued on p. 198

Chronology

1980s *Civil conflicts in Africa and Asia begin to use children in combat.*

1983
Tamil Tiger insurgency erupts in Sri Lanka. The group later gains notoriety for its use of suicide bombers and thousands of child soldiers.

1987
Joseph Kony's Lord's Resistance Army in Uganda begins abducting children for use as soldiers.

1989
U.N. General Assembly adopts Convention on the Rights of the Child, which establishes 15 as the minimum age for recruiting children into armed forces. Eventually, 190 countries ratify the treaty; the United States refuses to ratify it.

1990s *Genocide in Rwanda focuses global attention on child soldiers.*

1994
Thousands of children take part in Rwandan genocide.

1996
UNICEF's Landmark "Impact of Armed Conflict on Children" report focuses international attention on child soldiers.

1997
Zaire's dictator Mobutu Sese Seko is ousted by Laurent Kabila's rebel group, which uses several thousand child soldiers. Kabila's backers in Rwanda and Uganda later turn against him, setting off a war using tens of thousands of child soldiers. . . . Ugandan diplomat Olara Otunu becomes the U.N.'s first Special

Representative for Children and Armed Conflict.

1998
Human-rights organizations form Coalition to Stop the Use of Child Soldiers.

1999
First U.N. resolution on child soldiers, Resolution 1261, condemns abduction and recruitment of children for combat.

2000s *U.N. steps up efforts to combat use of child soldiers.*

2000
U.N. "Optional Protocol" sets 18 as the minimum age for children in combat and bars non-state armed groups from recruiting or using children under 18.

2001
U.N. Security Council asks secretary-general to identify parties recruiting or using children in armed conflicts.

2002
U.S. Senate ratifies Optional Protocol.

2003
U.N. Secretary-General Kofi Annan submits first report listing groups recruiting and using children in armed conflicts. Security Council asks secretary-general to report on actions being taken by armed groups cited in his report to stop the use of children.

2004
Security Council calls for "action plans" to stop use of child soldiers.

2005
Security Council establishes monitor-

ing and reporting mechanism on children and armed conflict. . . . International Criminal Court (ICC) issues war crimes arrest warrants for Lord's Resistance Army leader Kony and four commanders for forced recruitment and use of child soldiers in Uganda.

2006
ICC charges Thomas Lubanga Dyilo, leader of the rebel Union of Congolese Patriots, with using child soldiers.

2007
UNICEF and the French government sponsor a conference in Paris on preventing the use of child soldiers and aiding children in post-conflict situations. . . . *A Long Way Gone: Memoirs of a Boy Soldier*, by Ishmael Beah, becomes worldwide bestseller and focuses new attention on child soldiers. . . . Four former militia leaders are convicted by a U.N.-backed special tribunal on charges that they recruited and used child soldiers during the war in Sierra Leone — the first time an international court has addressed the use of child soldiers. . . . Former Liberian President Charles Taylor goes on trial at the Special Court of Sierra Leone (at The Hague) on 11 charges of war crimes and crimes against humanity, including conscripting children into the armed forces and using them in combat.

2008
Cease-fire agreement signed in January offers a potential end to fighting in eastern Congo, where the use of child soldiers is common. . . . ICC temporarily halts its first-ever case, against Congolese rebel leader Lubanga because of a dispute over the handling of confidential evidence.

Continued from p. 196

of children in its army even though the minimum recruitment age is 18. [49] According to HRW, government recruiters force boys under 18 to lie about their ages or falsify induction forms to meet quotas. [50] The government began recruiting children extensively in the 1990s, when it more than doubled the size of the army — from 200,000 to 500,000 — to combat an upsurge in a decades-old separatist insurgency in Karen state in southeastern Myanmar, the group said. [51]

Responding partly to pressure from the U.N., the government in 2004 created a committee to prevent the military recruitment of under-18-year-olds. Since then, government representatives have insisted the army has no under-age soldiers. However, Secretary-General Ban wrote in a November 2007 report that recruitment continued unabated, with recruiters still rewarded with cash and a bag of rice for each new solider they produced, regardless of his age. [52]

U.N. and HRW officials do not know how many children now serve in the Myanmar military because the government severely restricts international access to the country. However, the HRW report quoted several former soldiers as estimating that 20 to 50 percent of the soldiers in their units had been underage. [53]

Former Child Soldiers Can Become Good Citizens

But reintegration must be handled carefully by aid agencies.

"*My parents ran away when they saw me. I had to follow them; they thought I would abduct them.*"
— Former girl child soldier, 15 [1]

"*We feel different because of the way other children look at us; it seems as if we are not children born from this land. They view us as though we come from a different place.*"
— Former boy child soldier, 17 [2]

For many child soldiers, the end of a war can be nearly as traumatic as the conflict itself. Some cannot remember anything but warfare and have little concept of what normal civilian life is like. Others suffered serious physical wounds, and most endure at least short-term psychological problems, and sometimes drug addiction.

Returning child soldiers often find that one or both parents have been killed or may have moved elsewhere. Parents also are sometimes reluctant to accept a returning child whom they no longer know or understand, especially if the child was forced to commit atrocities — sometimes even against his own family.

Because their schooling has been interrupted, most former child soldiers have few job skills appropriate to civilian society. Governments and international aid agencies often include provisions for child soldiers in official programs to disarm, demobilize and reintegrate rebel fighters. But several experts in the field say many of these so-called DDR programs are underfunded, badly managed or lack appropriate resources to meet the special needs of children.

Many researchers consider economic opportunity as the greatest need faced by former child soldiers. "When they go home, their struggles are going to be largely economic — as much, if not more so, than mental health or some other concerns," says Neil Boothby, director of the Program on Forced Migration and Health at Columbia University. "They need to learn how to make a living in a peaceful and useful way. Their fights will be against poverty as much as to maintain mental health."

Boothby and other experts say research also refutes public perceptions — fostered by some news accounts — that former child soldiers are so deranged they cannot adapt to civilian life. At least two studies have found that former child soldiers tend to be good citizens once they are integrated back into their home communities. A long-term study of nearly 40 former child soldiers in Mozambique — all of them demobilized in 1988 — showed they have "turned out quite well," co-author Boothby says. [3] "They are perceived by their communities to be good neighbors, a high percentage are active in the equivalent of the PTA and many are leaders in their communities. It dispels the notion that there are lost generations" of former child soldiers. "The only time you lose generations is when you don't help them after a crisis."

Another study — of young Ugandans abducted by the notorious Lord's Resistance Army (LRA) — also found "a greater propensity toward engaged citizenry, including voting at higher rates and being more involved with community leadership" than their counterparts. [4] Christopher Blattman, a co-author of that study and an assistant professor from Yale University, says only a small minority of youth abducted by the LRA were so traumatized they could no longer function in society.

Grace Akallo, who was abducted at 15, says her personal experience demonstrates that children can overcome their past so long as they get help. "I suffered a lot in the LRA, but I went back to school and my family, and I am fine now. So long as a child gets an opportunity for a future, that child can be OK."

Experts who have assisted or studied former child soldiers say several important lessons have been learned during recent post-conflict experiences, including:

- Governments and aid agencies administering post-war reintegration programs should be cautious about making cash payments to former child soldiers. Giving returnees clothing, food, job training, medical aid and psychological counseling is appropriate, experts say, but in many circumstances giving them cash is not. "We know from many different contexts that when young people in these situations are given cash, bad things happen," says Michael

Wessells, a psychology professor from Randolph-Macon College in Virginia, who has helped and studied child soldiers in Africa and Asia. "Commanders sometimes grab the cash and use it to recruit other children, so it runs counter to the intended purpose." A cash payment also can be seen as a reward for serving in an armed group, which is counterproductive, he says. On the other hand, Boothby says cash payments can help in some circumstances if they are carefully monitored to ensure the money benefits the children.

- Girls who have served with armed groups have different needs from boys, particularly if they return from the bush with children. Child soldier aid programs recently have begun to consider girls' special needs, such as child care, assistance with reproductive health matters and psychological aid to deal with the potential stigmatization in their home communities, where the girls are considered "unclean" because of their forced sexual relationships with rebel commanders.

- Reintegration programs should consider the needs of local communities, and community members should be involved in the process. Programs designed by officials in aid agencies or even by government officials in the conflict country often fail because they ignore local situations.

- Donor countries and aid agencies that fund reintegration programs should commit for the long haul. In several recent cases, money ran out before the bulk of former fighters returned from the bush, leaving thousands of youths feeling angry and betrayed. U.N. officials say that after the long war in the Democratic Republic of the Congo, for example, only about half of former child and adult fighters received assistance. [5]

- Targeting aid exclusively or primarily to former members of armed groups risks stigmatizing them and fostering jealousy among their neighbors. Thus, aid programs should be directed at entire communities, not just individuals, Wessells says. Moreover, all children who have served with armed groups — whether as porters, spies or as "wives" of commanders — should be eligible for reintegration aid, not just the fighters, experts say.

AFP/Getty Images/Sena Vidanagama

Former Sri Lankan Tamil Tiger fighters Velayutham Chuti, 18, (left) and 14-year-old Pulidha Logini (right) celebrate with their families after being released by a rival rebel group. The Hindu Tamil Tigers reportedly have used thousands of children in their long battle against the predominantly Buddhist government, making the Tigers one of the world's most persistent users of child soldiers.

[1] "Returning Home: Children's Perspectives on Reintegration: A Case Study of Children Abducted by the Lord's Resistance Army in Teso, Eastern Uganda," Coalition to Stop the Use of Child Soldiers, February 2008, p. 14.

[2] *Ibid.*, p. 16.

[3] N. Boothby, J. Crawford and J. Halperin, "Mozambique Child Soldier Life Outcome Study: Lessons Learned in Rehabilitation and Reintegration," *Global Public Health*, February 2006.

[4] "Making Reintegration Work for Youth in Northern Uganda," The Survey of War Affected Youth, www.sway-uganda.org.

[5] "Report of the Secretary General on Children and Armed Conflict in the Democratic Republic of the Congo," June 28, 2007, pp. 14-15.

Many of the country's non-state military groups also use underage soldiers, but the extent is unknown, according to both the U.N. and HRW. [54]

Sri Lanka — The Liberation Tigers of Tamil Eelam (LTTE), better known as the Tamil Tigers, reportedly has used thousands of children in the Hindu group's long battle against the majority Sinhalese (mostly Buddhist) government, making it one of the world's most persistent

users of child soldiers. A breakaway rebel faction, known as the Karuna group, which in recent years has been aligned with the government, also reportedly has used child soldiers. [55] A cease-fire negotiated by Norwegian diplomats in February 2002 helped reduce violence for more than three years, but several incidents in 2005 and 2006 led to an escalation of fighting, particularly in the north, which continues today.

The cease-fire essentially collapsed in 2006, and the government formally withdrew from it in mid-January 2008. The U.N. had estimated a year earlier that at least 67,000 people had died in the quarter-century of conflict. [56]

The total number of children caught up in the conflict is unknown. However, a UNICEF database showed that between 2002 and 2007 the Tigers recruited 6,248 children, and up to 453

Congo Reintegrates the Most Child Soldiers

More than 104,000 child soldiers have been demobilized and reintegrated into society worldwide, including 27,000 in the Democratic Republic of the Congo — more than any other country. UNICEF estimates up to 33,000 children were involved in the long-running Congolese war — the biggest and deadliest since World War II. Uganda, where the Lord's Resistance Army notoriously relied on abducting children, has reintegrated 20,000 former child soldiers into their communities. Outside Africa, Sri Lanka has reintegrated more child soldiers than any other country.

Number of Child Soldiers Reintegrated Into Society
(since 1998)

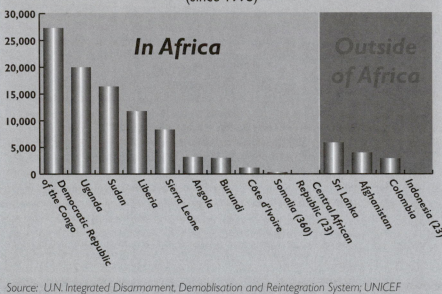

Source: U.N. Integrated Disarmament, Demoblisation and Reintegration System; UNICEF

children were recruited by the Karuna group during the last three years of that period. UNICEF said these figures most likely understate the actual use of child soldiers, because the agency relies on voluntary reporting by parents and community leaders, who often withhold information because they fear retaliation. [57] Whatever the actual total, the Tamil Tigers have used children actively in fighting, including as suicide bombers — a technique the group introduced to the world in the 1980s.

U.N. officials and human rights groups have accused the government of complicity in the Karuna group's use of child soldiers and even allowing the group to recruit or abduct children in government-controlled areas.

In some cases army units allegedly have participated actively in forcibly recruiting children. [58] The government has denied these accusations.

The Tamil Tigers pledged in 2007 to stop recruiting child soldiers and release all of those in its custody by the end of that year. As of January 2008, however, UNICEF listed 1,429 cases in which a recruited child soldier had not been released, including at least 168 children who were still under 18. [59]

Sudan — Africa's largest country has experienced two major conflicts and several smaller ones in recent years — all involving child soldiers. Secretary-General Ban reported in 2007 that more than 30 armed groups operated in Sudan. [60]

Ban's report and independent human rights groups have found that children have been recruited and used as soldiers by the government's Sudan Armed Forces, by the pro-government militias known as the Janjaweed (which operate in the western region of Darfur), by the main Darfur rebel groups — the Justice and Equality Movement (JEM) and the Sudan Liberation Army (SLA), which have both splintered into factions — and by armed groups in southern Sudan, including the region's main rebel group, the Sudan People's Liberation Army (SPLA). [61]

The Security Council's Working Group on Children and Armed Conflict has repeatedly — most recently in February 2008 — condemned the "continuous recruitment and use of children" by the government and armed groups in Sudan and demanded that the children be released so they could be reintegrated into their families and communities. [62]

In southern Sudan, the government and the SPLA signed a peace agreement in January 2005 ending a 20-year conflict. The agreement called for creation of a "government of national unity," but real unity has been elusive, as the Khartoum government and the former rebels continue to bicker about many of the same issues that fueled the war, including control over oil production in the region. [63]

Between 2001 and early 2006 the SPLA demobilized about 20,000 former child soldiers, but the Coalition to Stop the Use of Child Soldiers reported that as of late 2007 about 2,000 children remained under the militia's control. [64] Secretary-General Ban reported in August 2007 that the SPLA had made "significant progress" by releasing at least 47 children in one of its units, but two armed groups associated with the government's army had not fulfilled their promises to release children. [65]

In Darfur, the fighting remains well below the peak of the conflict in

2002-03, but serious violence continues despite the presence of a U.N. peacekeeping mission. Ban's report found that nearly all armed groups in Darfur, including the Sudanese army and its related militias, continued to recruit and use children as fighters. [66]

The conflict in Darfur also has spilled into neighboring conflicts in Chad and the Central African Republic, where government armies and rebel groups (some supported by the Sudanese government) have recruited and used child soldiers. The Chadian government, in turn, reportedly participated in the forced recruitment in 2006 of nearly 5,000 Sudanese refugees, including several hundred children, by one of the Darfur rebel groups. [67]

Uganda — As in Sierra Leone, the use and abuse of child soldiers has reached a depraved level in Uganda, largely due to the fanatical Kony's Lord's Resistance Army. The United Nations has estimated that Kony, a violent, self-styled prophet, abducted or forced nearly 25,000 children into his army between 1986 and 2005. [68] However, independent experts have said the U.N. estimate counts only former LRA members who later turned themselves into Ugandan government reception centers. Researchers at Tufts University in Boston estimate that the LRA abducted at least 60,000 boys and girls, and that 15-20 percent of the boys and 5 percent of the girls died during the war, said Yale's Blattman, one of the researchers.

Human rights groups say the LRA continues to abduct children, although in lower numbers than earlier. [69] Blattman says his team believes the LRA now has fewer than 1,000 people — adults or children — in its ranks. The International Criminal Court in July 2005 issued arrest warrants for Kony and four of his aides, charging them with war crimes, including the use of child soldiers; at least one of the aides reportedly has since died. [70]

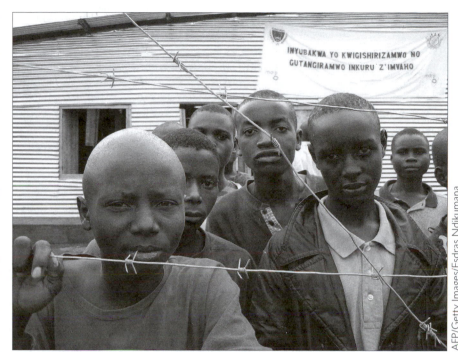

Former child soldiers at a demobilization camp in Burundi wait to be reintegrated back into society. About 104,000 children worldwide have been reintegrated into their communities after serving in various rebel or government armed forces.

The LRA was one of several Ugandan groups that took up arms in 1986 against the new government of Yoweri Museveni, himself a former rebel leader who had used large numbers of child soldiers during a five-year war against President Milton Obote. Kony claimed to be fighting on behalf of his own ethnic group in northern Uganda, the Acholi people, but ultimately the Acholi became the principal victims in the two-decade-long war between the LRA and the government. [71] Kony reportedly claims his fight is ordained by God. At a 2006 meeting with Ugandan officials, Kony denied that his forces had committed atrocities and insisted "the tragedy that was taking place in Uganda was done by the Uganda government." [72]

The war developed a critical international dimension in the mid-1990s, when Sudan armed Kony's forces to help in its own war against the SPLA in southern Sudan. Kony used southern Sudan as a base from which to launch attacks against both the SPLA and the Ugandan army. He later established bases in the Democratic Republic of the Congo and the Central African Republic. [73]

The conflict in northern Uganda peaked after March 2002, when the Ugandan government launched an offensive against the LRA, which responded by targeting civilians as well as government forces. Over the next two years Kony increased the pace of abductions of children, forcing many of them to endure beatings and to carry out atrocities against each other and against civilians, sometimes even members of their own families. Girls were forced into virtual slavery, the youngest ones as servants and the older ones as "wives' of LRA commanders, says Grace Akallo, who was abducted at 15 and held for seven months until she escaped. Fearing such abductions, thousands of children living in rural villages trudged long distances every evening to sleep in larger towns considered safe. Known as "night commuters," the children became the most visible symbols to the outside world of the horrors in northern Uganda. [74] Despite denials, the

Ugandan government also recruited children into its army and local pro-government militias called the UPDF, according to U.N. officials and human rights groups. [75]

The fighting slowed significantly in 2005, when Sudan signed a peace accord with the rebels in southern Sudan and, reportedly, ended much of its support for Kony — a development that

February 2008, but Kony himself failed to show up for much-publicized signing ceremonies in April and May, reportedly fearing he might be arrested to face war crimes charges. [78] Uganda has offered to request that the charges against Kony be dropped so he could be tried in a local tribunal, but so far this has not been enough incentive for him to turn himself in. ∎

cruiting and using child soldiers.

In its last two resolutions on child soldiers — Resolution 1539 in 2004 and Resolution 1612 in 2005 — the Security Council threatened to impose "targeted measures" (primarily sanctions) against armed groups that defy international demands to stop using children in combat, but so far it has not taken any action. The council "needs to show that the threats they make are not empty threats," says Becker, of Human Rights Watch.

Top U.N. officials in recent months also have called on the council to follow through on its threats to punish those who use child soldiers. In his annual report on children and armed conflict, published in January, Secretary-General Ban suggested the council impose various measures, including banning the export or supplying of weapons, banning military assistance, imposing travel restrictions on government officials or leaders of armed groups, preventing armed groups and their leaders from accessing the international financial system and referring violators to the ICC for possible war-crimes punishment. [79]

And on Feb. 12, Special Representative Coomaraswamy confronted the council directly on the issue, pointing out that U.N. reports over the past five years had identified 16 "persistent violators" of international law, some of whom were "making efforts" to comply with the law, while others "remain in contempt of the council and its resolutions." [80]

She doubts the council will impose sanctions anytime soon, however, which she finds frustrating. "You have to realize that [imposing sanctions] is the most extreme action the Security Council can take in any context," she says. "And this is the Security Council, where there are always strong political considerations, and they are very cautious, so I think it will be some time down the road before they agree on sanctions."

Her comments reflect the fact that all actions by the Security Council require

The use of child soldiers, like these, by the Chadian military was officially prohibited in May 2007, but as a government official explained, using children is "ideal" because "they don't complain, they don't expect to be paid and if you tell them to kill, they kill."

AFP/Getty Images/Sonia Rolley

led to efforts to end the war in northern Uganda. Peace talks between Uganda and LRA representatives began in Juba, southern Sudan, in 2006. A cease-fire signed in August that year generally has held, resulting in the longest sustained period of peace in northern Uganda in more than two decades. [76] Although the LRA is no longer operating in northern Uganda, it is still present in the Central African Republic, Congo and Sudan and reportedly has continued abducting children well into 2008, according to a June 23 report by Secretary-General Ban. [77]

A diplomat negotiating on Kony's behalf initialed a peace agreement in

CURRENT SITUATION

"Empty Threats"

United Nations officials and independent human rights groups say the U.N. Security Council risks losing credibility because of its failure to follow through on repeated threats to impose sanctions against governments and armed groups that persist in re-

extensive compromise among countries with often-conflicting viewpoints, and the council cannot act unless there is unanimous agreement among all five of its permanent, veto-wielding members (Britain, China, France, Russia and the United States). In recent years China and Russia have been the most reluctant of the so-called "permanent five" to intervene in what they consider the domestic affairs of member states.

On the same day Coomaraswamy called for Security Council action, the council said it was "gravely concerned by the persistent disregard of its resolutions on children and armed conflict by parties to armed conflict." The council also said it "reaffirms its intention to make use of all the tools" provided in its previous resolutions. However, it did not mention sanctions nor did it take any specific action — either then or in subsequent months. [81]

As Becker's comments suggest, independent human-rights groups are equally frustrated with the Security Council's lack of action. In two reports last January, the Watchlist on Children and Armed Conflict (a coalition of human rights groups) detailed several cases in which the council suggested it would act against violators but did not. [82] Becker says the council's reluctance to act means that "as long as governments and commanders of these groups know they can recruit and use child soldiers without serious consequences, in particular to them personally, they will do it. But if their visas are denied or their assets are frozen or they suffer some real penalties, they will at least think twice about it."

U.N. officials say they repeatedly have confronted government officials and leaders of armed groups with evidence of their use of child soldiers, often to be greeted with outright denials or with vague pledges to stop the practice. "Their justification is, 'We don't go out and recruit,' which of course is not true," says Coomaraswamy, who

often meets with leaders of armed groups using child soldiers. "They say, 'The children are hanging out at the gates, they want to join, many of them are orphans, how can I send them away?' This is usually the line, along with, 'We give them food, they are so happy,' that kind of thing."

Prosecuting Violators

The international community has another, stronger weapon against government leaders and military commanders who use child soldiers: Prosecution for war crimes. So far 19 commanders — all from Africa — have faced charges or prosecution either at the International Criminal Court or in special war crimes tribunals. Five have been convicted; the others are either on trial, awaiting trial, still at large or have reportedly died.

Four of the five convictions were handed down by the U.N.-supported special tribunal on war crimes committed during the brutal civil war in Sierra Leone, which raged from 1991 to 2002. The Hague-based Special Court for Sierra Leone in June 2007 convicted and sentenced three members of the Armed Forces Revolutionary Council — Alex Tamba Brima, Brima Bazzy Kamara and Santigie Borbor Kanu — on charges the rebel group committed war crimes and recruited and used child soldiers. It was the first time an international tribunal had ruled on the recruitment of child soldiers. "These convictions are a groundbreaking step toward ending impunity for commanders who exploit hundreds of thousands of children as soldiers in conflicts worldwide," Human Rights Watch said at the time. [83] The three men were sentenced to prison terms ranging from 45 to 50 years, and those sentences were affirmed in February by the court's appellate division.

A fourth man, Allieu Kondewa, a member of the Civil Defense Forces militia, was convicted in August 2007 on

several charges, including recruitment of child soldiers. [84] He was sentenced to eight years in prison, which has since been increased to 20 years. [85]

Crane, the Syracuse University law professor who was the first prosecutor at the Sierra Leone court, says those convictions established important precedents. "This tells the leaders of these kinds of groups all over the world, 'If you are committing international crimes like abducting children and making them kill people, you can be convicted and sent to prison for the rest of your life.' "

A tribunal in the Democratic Republic of the Congo in March 2006 convicted Jean-Pierre Biyoyo, former commander of the Mudundu 40 armed group, on charges of recruiting and using child soldiers. Although he was sentenced to death, the sentence was reduced to five years' imprisonment. [86] Three months later he escaped from prison and eventually joined rebel leader Nkunda in North Kivu province, according to the U.S. State Department. [87]

Among the dozen other officials and warlords charged with war crimes for using child soldiers, the most prominent defendant is Taylor of Liberia, who currently is on trial before the Special Court for Sierra Leone on 11 charges of war crimes and crimes against humanity, including the use child soldiers. [88]

The International Criminal Court has charged three former Congolese guerrilla leaders with various war crimes, including the use of child soldiers. Thomas Lubanga Dyilo, leader of the Union of Congolese Patriots, had been scheduled to be the first person ever tried by the court. He was charged in 2006 with enlisting, recruiting and using child soldiers during the long and bloody fighting in Ituri region in eastern Democratic Republic of the Congo. [89]

However, the case appeared on the verge of collapse in early July as the result of a dispute between the U.N. and the ICC judges over U.N. documents that the prosecution had used to develop its charges. The U.N. had given the documents to the prosecution on a confidential basis. The court's judges indefinitely halted the Lubanga case on June 13 because the documents contain "exculpatory material" that should have been made available to the defense. An initial attempt to work out a compromise failed, and the trial judges on July 2 ordered Lubanga's eventual release as the "logical consequence" of the earlier decision. The prosecution appealed the decision to halt the case, and the ICC's appellate chamber said on July 7 that Lubanga should remain in prison until it had ruled on that appeal. News reports said ICC officials were still hoping for a compromise on the documents issue.

Human Rights Watch expressed disappointment over the legal wrangling, saying the failure of the case would deny justice to the alleged victims of Lubanga's actions. "The victims are the ones who suffer as a result of these embarrassing legal difficulties at the ICC," HRW counsel Param-Preet Singh says. Even so, she adds, denying Lubanga a fair trial "would also be an injustice, and the ICC cannot afford that, either." [90]

The possible collapse of the Lubanga case also came as a disappointment to the U.N., which had expected the case to establish legal doctrines on punishing those who recruit and use child soldiers. In a statement after the June 13 decision to halt the trial, U.N. Special Representative Coomaraswamy urged that the trial "not be compromised for technical reasons" and noted that the case "is considered a major milestone in international attempts" to eradicate the practice of using child soldiers."

U.S. Legislation

Both of the U.S. bills concerning child soldiers have made some progress but are still pending, with time running out for action during an elec-

A young Congolese Patriotic Union soldier totes his rifle in the Democratic Republic of the Congo. In addition to rebel groups, Congo's government also uses child soldiers. Congo is one of seven countries — including Afghanistan, Chad, Somalia, Sri Lanka, Sudan and Uganda — that have used child soldiers while receiving U.S. military aid. Legislation pending before Congress would bar military aid to any country that uses child soldiers.

AFP/Getty Images/Simon Maina

tion year. The House approved the Child Soldier Prevention Act — which would bar military aid and arms sales to countries using child soldiers — on Dec. 4, 2007. It was included in a measure to reauthorize a 2000 anti-human-trafficking law. [91] The vote on the underlying bill was 405-2, with no opposition to the child soldier provisions. The Senate, by contrast, has passed the Child Soldiers Accountability Act, which criminalizes the use of child soldiers and bars entry into the United States by anyone using child soldiers. The measure was approved by unanimous consent on Dec. 18, 2007.

Senate sponsors combined both bills into one measure, the Child Soldier Accountability and Prevention Act of 2008 (S 3061), introduced on May 22 by

Joseph R. Biden, D-Del., and Sam Brownback, R-Kan. The measure is pending before the Senate Judiciary Committee, after markup was delayed on June 26 by an unnamed Republican senator who put a hold on the bill. ∎

OUTLOOK

Child Terrorists?

Some of the recent conflicts that have involved the most widespread and notorious use of child soldiers have ended with formal peace agreements or dwindled into low-level, sporadic fighting. Among them were the interrelated conflicts in West Africa; the huge, pan-African war in the Democratic Republic of the Congo; and civil wars in the Balkans, El Salvador and Indonesia. The latest global survey by the Coalition to Stop the Use of Child Soldiers said the number of countries where children were directly involved in conflicts declined from 27 in 2004 (when the group issued its previous report) to 17 by the end of 2007. [92]

Becker, of Human Rights Watch, says the decline is good news but does not mean the child-soldier problem has disappeared. "Some conflicts are ending, but that does not mean that children are no longer being used in war," she says. "When armed conflicts occur, children are almost inevitably involved." As examples, Becker cites new, or newly revived conflicts in the past two years in the Central African Republic, Chad and Somalia — all involving extensive use of children.

Moreover, new conflicts can be expected because the underlying conditions that led to most of the world's civil conflicts remain unresolved. "It's not like we have fewer poor kids today,

Continued on p. 206

At issue:

Should the U.S. prosecute alleged child soldiers at Guantánamo?

DAVID B. RIVKIN, JR.
PARTNER, BAKER HOSTETLER LLP, WASHINGTON, D.C.
FORMER JUSTICE DEPARTMENT OFFICIAL AND ASSOCIATE WHITE HOUSE COUNSEL DURING THE REAGAN AND GEORGE H.W. BUSH ADMINISTRATIONS

WRITTEN FOR *CQ GLOBAL RESEARCHER*, JUNE 2008

*i*n a challenge to the laws of war employed by the United States since 9/11, critics claim the military commission prosecution of Omar Ahmed Khadr is illegitimate. A Canadian national, Khadr is accused of committing war crimes while fighting with al Qaeda in Afghanistan when he was 15. His lawyers argue he is a "child soldier" and thus immune from liability. These claims have no legal or policy merit.

Although the Optional Protocol to the Convention on the Rights of the Child bars recruitment and use of juveniles for combat, terrorist groups are not likely to comply with the protocol or worry about potential liability for their non-compliance. But this is irrelevant to Khadr's liability.

As presiding Judge Peter Brownback has properly ruled, the Military Commissions Act of 2006 gave the commission jurisdiction to try war-related offenses committed by juveniles, and nothing in U.S. law or the Constitution contradicts that. He also has properly concluded that no international treaty, convention or customary law norm establishes age as a bar to war-crimes prosecutions. Indeed, Khadr's lawyers have not cited any international law supporting their extraordinary claim of legal immunity.

This leaves the United States with a choice of whether to continue with Khadr's prosecution or exercise prosecutorial discretion and dismiss all charges against him — even if his prosecution is legally permissible. But first one must ask whether prosecuting him makes policy sense or is fair and just. Would we not be better served by sending Khadr home to be reunited with his family?

The answer is no. The gravity of the alleged offenses and the fact that he chose to join al Qaeda, an unlawful enemy entity, strongly mitigate against granting him immunity. Plus, he performed these actions at 15 — an age old enough to assess the moral and legal implications of his behavior.

Moreover, proponents of immunity fail to see that it would only further incentivize the continued recruitment of child soldiers and the use of children in the commission of war crimes. This result would neither benefit juveniles involved nor help their victims, who usually are civilians.

More broadly, granting him immunity would further debase international laws against war crimes — laws that have taken centuries to develop and are absolutely necessary if 21st-century warfare is not to descend into unbridled barbarism and carnage, to the detriment of the civilized world.

JO BECKER
ADVOCACY DIRECTOR, CHILDREN'S RIGHTS DIVISION, HUMAN RIGHTS WATCH; FOUNDING CHAIRMAN, COALITION TO STOP THE USE OF CHILD SOLDIERS

WRITTEN FOR *CQ GLOBAL RESEARCHER*, JUNE 2008

*S*ince 2002 the United States has held at least 23 detainees who were under 18 at the U.S. military base at Guantánamo Bay, Cuba. Two of them, Omar Khadr and Mohammad Jawad, are being prosecuted before U.S. military commissions for allegedly throwing grenades at American soldiers in Afghanistan. Khadr was 15 when he reportedly killed U.S. Army Sgt. First Class Christopher Speer and injured other soldiers in a July 2002 firefight. Jawad was 16 or 17 in December 2002 when he allegedly tossed a grenade into a military vehicle and injured two U.S. soldiers and an Afghan translator.

During the more than five years that Khadr and Jawad have been detained at Guantánamo, the United States has ignored their juvenile status. In violation of international juvenile-justice standards, the two have been incarcerated with adult detainees, subjected to prolonged solitary confinement, denied direct contact with their families and refused educational opportunities or rehabilitation.

Under juvenile-justice standards and international guidelines for the treatment of former child soldiers, children should be treated according to their unique vulnerability, lower degree of culpability and capacity for rehabilitation. Although international law does not preclude prosecution of child soldiers for serious crimes, their rehabilitation and reintegration into society must be paramount.

America's treatment of Jawad and Khadr cannot be construed as rehabilitative. They are confined in small cells for 22 hours a day, with little more than a mattress, the Koran and toilet paper. Their attorneys say Jawad and Khadr have been tortured. Khadr says his interrogators shackled him in painful positions, threatened him with rape and used him as a "human mop" after he urinated on the floor during one interrogation session. Jawad was moved from cell to cell and deprived of sleep. Eleven months after arriving at Guantánamo, Jawad tried to hang himself with his shirt collar. His lawyer says he suffers from severe depression and appears to have lost touch with reality.

Under juvenile-justice principles, cases involving children must be resolved quickly and their detention be as short as possible. But Khadr and Jawad were held for more than three years before even being charged. Now, five years after their apprehension, there is no foreseeable end to their ordeal.

Guantánamo, with its flawed military commissions, is no place for children. The United States should either transfer their cases to U.S. federal court and apply fundamental standards of juvenile justice, or release them for rehabilitation.

Continued from p. 204

fewer orphans who can be recruited by warlords," says Singer of the Brookings Institution. "You still have these problems on a global scale."

Specialists in the field, as well as government officials worldwide are particularly concerned about what appears to be the increasing use of children as terrorists, including as suicide bombers. The Tamil Tigers developed the tactic two decades ago, even fashioning suicide bomb vests in small sizes for children, according to some sources. [93]

Suicide bombing as a terrorist tactic has spread in recent years to other parts of South and Central Asia — including Afghanistan, India and Pakistan — to Colombia and to the Middle East, including extremist Palestinian factions, and Iraq. [94] Children in their early- and mid-teens have carried out, or attempted, suicide attacks in nearly all these places, sometimes causing large-scale fatalities. In Iraq, U.S military officials have said insurgents often use children to place the roadside bombs, known as "improvised explosive devices," that typically kill American troops.

Singer does not expect terrorism and the use of children by terrorists to diminish anytime soon, despite the efforts of the U.S. "war" against terrorism. In fact, he says, "we could see the use of children as terrorists globally, if you put yourself in the position of the planners of these attacks and how they might be looking to expand their operations."

As for combating the more conventional use of children in civil conflicts, the U.N.'s Coomaraswamy is optimistic the world is ready to act more decisively. "This is an issue on which you have a near-global consensus on the need for action, not just rhetoric," she says. "Not that we will be able to stop all recruitment and use of child solders, but I think we can lessen it quite a bit in the next decade."

She and other experts had hoped that the two most prominent cases in-volving use of child soldiers — the ongoing Taylor tribunal and the ICC case against Lubanga — would produce ground-breaking convictions demonstrating that the use of children in war will be punished.

The dismissal of the Lubanga case could give added importance to the Taylor trial, where Crane, the former special prosecutor in Sierra Leone, expects a guilty verdict. "That will have an incredible ripple effect, particularly on the dictators and warlords of the world," he says. "It says that the lives of their citizens matter. In particular, it shows Africans themselves that their lives matter." ∎

Notes

[1] Testimony of Ishmael Beah, Senate Judiciary Subcommittee on Human Rights and the Law, hearing on "Casualties of War: Child Soldiers and the Law," April 24, 2007, http://judiciary.senate.gov/testimony.cfm?id=2712&wit_id=6387.

[2] P. W. Singer, *Children at War* (2006), p. 23.

[3] "Some 250,000 children worldwide recruited to fight in wars — UN official," United Nations Department of Public Information, Jan. 30, 2008, www.un.org/apps/news/story.asp?NewsID=25450&Cr=children&Cr1=conflict#.

[4] Singer, *op. cit.*, p. 30.

[5] "Sold to be Soldiers: The Recruitment and Use of Child Soldiers in Burma," Human Rights Watch, October 2007, www.hrw.org/reports/2007/burma1007/burma1007web.pdf.

[6] "Child Soldiers Global Report 2008," Coalition to Stop the Use of Child Soldiers, p. 29, www.childsoldiersglobalreport.org/files/country_pdfs/FINAL_2008_Global_Report.pdf.

[7] "Cape Town Principles and Best Practices," April 1997, UNICEF, p. 8, www.unicef.org/emerg/files/Cape_Town_Principles(1).

[8] David M. Rosen, *Armies of the Young: Child Soldiers in War and Terrorism* (2005), p. 4.

[9] "Childhood Denied: Child Soldiers in Africa," Amnesty International, available online under the title "Democratic Republic of Congo: Children at War," on p. 7, at www.amnesty.org/en/library/asset/AFR62/034/2003/en/dom-AFR620342003en.pdf.

[10] Ishmael Beah, *A Long Way Gone: Memoirs of a Boy Soldier* (2007).

[11] "Children and Armed Conflict, Report of the Secretary General," Dec. 21, 2007, pp. 40-45.

[12] U.N. Security Council Resolution 1379, www.securitycouncilreport.org/atf/cf/{65BFCF9B-6D27-4E9C-8CD3-CF6E4FF96FF9}/CAC%20SRES%201379.pdf.

[13] "Child Soldiers Global Report 2008," *op. cit.*

[14] "Children and Armed Conflict," *op. cit.*, p. 33.

[15] "Report of the Secretary General on Children and Armed Conflict in Sri Lanka," Dec. 21, 2007, pp. 3-7.

[16] "International Forum on Armed Groups and the Involvement of Children in Armed Conflict: Summary of Themes and Discussion," Coalition to Stop the Use of Child Soldiers, August 2007, p. 16, www.child-soldiers.org/child-soldiers/Armed_groups_forum_report_August_2007_revision_0ct07.pdf.

[17] "Military Commission Charges Referred," U.S. Department of Defense news release, April 24 2007, www.defenselink.mil/releases/release.aspx?releaseid=10779. For background, see David Masci and Kenneth Jost, "War on Terrorism," *CQ Researcher*, Oct. 12, 2001, pp. 817-848; also see Peter Katel and Kenneth Jost, "Treatment of Detainees," *CQ Researcher*, Aug. 25, 2006, pp. 673-696.

[18] "Ruling on Defense Motion for Dismissal Due to Lack of Jurisdiction Under the MCA in Regard to Juvenile Crimes of a Child Soldier," *United States of America v. Omar Ahmed Khadr*, April 30, 2008, www.defenselink.mil/news/d20080430Motion.pdf.

[19] "Letter to U.S. Secretary of Defense Robert Gates on Omar Khadr," Human Rights Watch, April 2, 2008, www.hrw.org/english/docs/2008/02/01/usint17956.htm.

[20] *Amicus curiae* brief contained in the April 30 ruling, note 19 above, pp. 108-146.

[21] Rome Statute of the International Criminal Court, United Nations Doc. A/CONF.183/9, July 17, 1998.

[22] "The Paris Principles: Principles and Guidelines on Children Associated with Armed Forces or Armed Groups," February 2007, section 3.6, www.diplomatie.gouv.fr/en/IMG/pdf/Paris_Conference_Principles_English_31_January.pdf.

[23] "Government's Response to the Defense's Motion for Dismissal Due to Lack of Jurisdiction under the MCA in Regard to Juvenile Crimes of a Child Soldier," Jan. 25, 2008. p. 9, footnote 3.

[24] Deputy Assistant Secretary of Defense Sandra L. Hodgkinson, testimony to the U.N. Committee on the Rights of the Child Concerning U.S. Implementation of the Optional Protocol on Children in Armed Conflict,

May 22, 2008, p. 26, www2.ohchr.org/english/bodies/crc/docs/statements/48USAOpening_Statements.pdf.

[25] Randall Palmer, "Top Court Says Canada Complicit in Guantánamo Base," Reuters, May 23, 2008.

[26] "Military Commission Charges Referred," U.S. Department of Defense, Jan. 31, 2008, www.defenselink.mil/releases/release.aspx?releaseid=11655.

[27] *Congressional Record*, Dec. 18, 2007, p. S15941.

[28] "Country Reports on Human Rights Practices: Afghanistan," U.S. State Department, March 11, 2008. www.state.gov/g/drl/rls/hrrpt/2007/100611.htm.

[29] "U.S. Military Assistance to Governments and Government-Supported Armed Groups Using Child Soldiers, 2002-2008," Center for Defense Information, April 2, 2008, p. 1, www.cdi.org/PDFs/CS_MilAssist08.pdf.

[30] "Casualties Of War: Child Soldiers and The Law," Sen. Dick Durbin, April 24, 2007, http://durbin.senate.gov/showRelease.cfm?releaseId=280883.

[31] "Report of the Secretary General on Children and Armed Conflict in Chad," United Nations, July 3, 2007, p. 7; also see "Early to War: Child Soldiers in the Chad Conflict," Human Rights Watch, July 2007, www.hrw.org/reports/2007/chad0707/.

[32] Singer, *op. cit.*, p. 63.

[33] *Ibid.*, p. 41.

[34] "Security Council committee concerning Côte d'Ivoire issues list of individuals subject to measures imposed by Resolution 1572 (2004)," SC/8631, U.N. Department of Public Information, Feb. 7, 2006.

[35] "Report of the Secretary General on Children and Armed Conflict in Somalia," May 7, 2007, p. 13, www.unhcr.org/cgi-bin/texis/vtx/refworld/rwmain?docid=4850fe4e2.

[36] Jimmie Briggs, *Innocents Lost: When Child Soldiers Go to War* (2005), p. 41.

[37] "Child Soldiers Global Report 2008," *op. cit.*, pp. 101-103; "Overcoming Lost Childhoods: Lessons Learned from the Rehabilitation and Reintegration of Former Child Soldiers in Colombia," YCare International, 2007, p. 4; "You'll Learn Not to Cry: Child Combatants in Colombia," Human Rights Watch, September 2003, www.hrw.org/reports/2003/colombia0903/.

[38] Briggs, *op. cit.*, p. 56.

[39] "Child Soldiers Global Report 2008," *op. cit.*, p. 101.

[40] *Ibid.*, p. 102.

[41] "Mortality in the DRC: An Ongoing Crisis," International Rescue Committee, January 2008, www.theirc.org/media/www/congo-crisis-fast-facts.html.

[42] "Child soldier recruitment continues," United Nations Integrated Regional Information Network, Feb. 19, 2007.

[43] "Report of the Secretary General on Children and Armed Conflict in the Democratic Republic of the Congo," June 28, 2007, pp. 14-15, http://daccessdds.un.org/doc/UNDOC/GEN/N07/390/16/PDF/N0739016.pdf?OpenElement.

[44] *Ibid.*, pp. 3-6.

[45] "MONUC welcomes the success of the Goma conference and the signing of its acts of engagement," United Nations Mission in the Democratic Republic of the Congo, Jan. 23, 2008, www.monuc.org/News.aspx?newsId=16531.

[46] "After two key deals, what progress towards peace in North Kivu?" United Nations Integrated Regional Information Network, May 14, 2008, www.reliefweb.int/rw/rwb.nsf/db900sid/KKAA-7EN5EQ?OpenDocument&rc=1&cc=cod.

[47] "Report on Human Rights, Democratic Republic of the Congo, 2007," U.S. Department of State, www.state.gov/g/drl/rls/hrrpt/2007/100475.htm.

[48] "Child Soldiers Global Report," *op. cit.*, p. 212.

[49] "Report of the Secretary General on Children and Armed Conflict in Myanmar," Nov. 16, 2007, pp. 4-5.

[50] "Sold to be Soldiers," *op. cit.*

[51] *Ibid.*, pp. 25-26.

[52] "Report of the Secretary General on Children and Armed Conflict in Myanmar," *op. cit.*, pp. 5-6.

[53] "Sold to be Soldiers," *op. cit.*, p. 60.

[54] *Ibid.*, p. 94.

[55] "Report of the Secretary General on Children and Armed Conflict in Sri Lanka," Dec. 21, 2007.

[56] "United Nations Concerned by Civilian Deaths in Sri Lanka," U.N. Department of Public Information, Jan. 2, 2007, www.un.org/News/Press/docs/2007/iha1248.doc.htm.

[57] "No Safety, No Escape: Children and the Escalating Armed Conflict in Sri Lanka," Watchlist on Children and Armed Conflict, April 2008, p. 5.

[58] "Complicit in Crime: State Collusion in Abductions and Child Recruitment by the Karuna Group," Human Rights Watch, January 2007, www.hrw.org/reports/2007/srilanka0107/.

[59] "Press Conference on Children and Armed Conflict in Sri Lanka," U.N. Department of Public Information, April 14, 2008, www.un.org/News/briefings/docs/2008/080414_Children.doc.htm.

[60] "Report of the Secretary General on Children and Armed Conflict in the Sudan," Aug. 29, 2007, p. 4, www.cfr.org/publication/11358/report_of_the_secretarygeneral_on_children_and_armed_conflict_in_the_sudan.html.

[61] *Ibid.*, pp. 5-6.

[62] "Conclusions on Parties in the Armed Conflict in the Sudan," Working Group on Children and Armed Conflict, U.N. Security Council, Feb. 5, 2008, p. 1.

[63] "Report of the Secretary General on the Sudan," Jan. 31, 2008, p. 2.

[64] "Child Soldiers Global Report 2008," *op. cit.*, p. 319.

[65] "Report of the Secretary General on Children and Armed Conflict in the Sudan," *op. cit.*, pp. 2, 5.

[66] *Ibid.*, p. 6.

[67] "Child Soldiers Global Report 2008", *op. cit.*, pp. 89, 93.

[68] "Report of the Secretary-General on Children and Armed Conflict in Uganda," May 7, 2007, p. 3.

[69] "Child Soldiers Global Report 2008," *op. cit.*, p. 347; "Uganda: LRA Regional Atrocities Demand Action," Human Rights Watch, May 19, 2008, www.hrw.org/english/docs/2008/05/19/uganda18863.htm.

[70] "Report of the Secretary-General on Children and Armed Conflict in Uganda," *op. cit.*, p. 4.

[71] "Child Soldiers Global Report 2008," *op. cit.*, p. 347.

[72] "The Shadows of Peace: Life after the LRA," IRIN news service, Sept. 18, 2006.

[73] "Optimism prevails despite setback in peace talks," IRIN news service, April 18, 2008.

[74] "Stolen Children: Abduction and Recruitment in Northern Uganda," Human Rights Watch, March 2003, www.hrw.org/reports/2003/uganda0303/.

[75] "Report of the Secretary-General on Children and Armed Conflict in Uganda," *op. cit.*, pp. 2, 5.

[76] "Living with the LRA: The Juba Initiative," IRIN news service, May 1, 2008.

[77] "Additional report of the Secretary-General on children and armed conflict in Uganda," United Nations, p. 3, June 23, 2008, http://daccess-ods.un.org/access.nsf/Get?OpenAgent&DS=s/2008/409&Lang=E.

[78] Charles Mpagi Mwanguhya, "Peace Deal Dissolves," Institute for War and Peace Reporting, May 19, 2008, www.iwpr.net/?p=acr&s=f&o=344708&apc_state=henh.

[79] "Report of the Secretary-General on Children and Armed Conflict," Dec. 21, 2007, p. 37.

[80] "Statement in the Security Council by Special Representative of the Secretary General for Children and Armed Conflict Radhika Coomaraswamy," Feb. 12, 2008.

[81] "Statement by the President of the Security Council," Feb. 12, 2008, http://daccess-ods.un.org/access.nsf/Get?Open&DS=S/PRST/2008/6&Lang=E&Area=UNDOC.

[82] "Getting it Done and Doing It Right: A Global Study on the United Nations-led Monitoring and Reporting Mechanism on Children and Armed Conflict," Watchlist on Children and Armed Conflict, January 2008, www.watchlist.org/reports/pdf/global-v8-web.pdf; and "The Security Council and Children and Armed Conflicts: Next Steps towards Ending Violations Against Children," Watchlist on Children and Armed Conflict, January 2008.

[83] Christo Johnson, "Sierra Leone tribunal issues historic verdicts," *The Independent* (London), June 21, 2007.

[84] "Report of the Special Representative of the Secretary General for Children and Armed Conflict," Aug. 13, 2007, p. 5; Coalition to Stop the Use of Child Soldiers, www.child-soldiers.org/childsoldiers/legal-framework.

[85] See www.sc-sl.org/CDF-Timeline.html.

[86] "Report of the Secretary General on Children and Armed Conflict in the Democratic Republic of the Congo," *op. cit.*, p. 27.

[87] "Report on Human Rights, Democratic Republic of the Congo, 2007," U.S. State Department, www.state.gov/g/drl/rls/hrrpt/2007/100475.htm.

[88] "Report of the Special Representative of the Secretary General for Children and Armed Conflict," *op. cit.*

[89] "The Prosecutor v. Thomas Lubanga Dyilo," International Criminal Court, www.icc-cpi.int/cases/RDC/c0106/c0106_doc.html.

[90] "International Criminal Court's Trial of Thomas Lubanga 'Stayed,' " Human Rights Watch, http://hrw.org/english/docs/2008/06/19/congo19163.htm.

[91] For background, see David Masci, "Human Trafficking and Slavery," *CQ Researcher*, March 26, 2004, pp. 273-296.

[92] "Child Soldiers Global Report 2008," *op. cit.*, p. 12.

[93] Singer, *op. cit.*, p. 118.

[94] *Ibid.*, pp. 117-119.

FOR MORE INFORMATION

Amnesty International, 1 Easton St., London WC1X 0DW, United Kingdom; 44-20-7413-5500; http://web.amnesty.org. Actively advocates on a wide range of human rights issues, including child soldiers.

Child Rights Information Network, c/o Save the Children, 1 St. John's Lane, London EC1M 4AR, United Kingdom; 44-20-7012-6866; www.crin.org. Advocates for enforcement of international legal standards protecting children; associated with Save the Children-UK.

Coalition to Stop the Use of Child Soldiers, 4th Floor, 9 Marshalsea Road, London SE1 1EP, United Kingdom; 44-20-7367-4110/4129; www.child-soldiers.org. A coalition of international human rights groups that sponsors conferences and issues regular reports on child soldiers in armed conflicts.

Human Rights Watch, 350 Fifth Ave., 34th Floor, New York, NY 10118-3299; (212) 290-4700; http://hrw.org/campaigns/crp/index.htm. One of the most active international groups pushing governments, the United Nations and other agencies to stop using child soldiers.

International Committee of the Red Cross, 19 avenue de la Paix, CH 1202 Geneva, Switzerland; 41-22-734-6001; www.icrc.org/web/eng/siteeng0.nsf/html/children!Open. Advocates on behalf of all victims of war, including child soldiers.

United Nations Children's Fund (UNICEF), UNICEF House, 3 United Nations Plaza, New York, NY 10017; (212) 325-7000; www.unicef.org. Monitors the impact of war on children, including the recruitment and use of child soldiers.

United Nations Special Representative of the Secretary-General for Children and Armed Conflict, United Nations S-3161, New York, NY 10017; (212) 963-3178; www.un.org/children/conflict/english/home6.html. The primary U.N. official dealing with children and armed conflict; works with governments and armed groups to develop action plans for releasing child soldiers and easing the burden of children in conflict; issues regular reports on the world's most serious conflicts.

Watchlist on Children and Armed Conflict, c/o Women's Commission for Refugee Women and Children, 122 East 42nd St., 12th Floor, New York, NY 10168-1289; (212) 551-3111; www.watchlist.org. Publishes studies and advocates strong international action to aid children caught up in armed conflict.

War Child International, 401 Richmond St. West, Suite 204, Toronto, Ontario, Canada M5V3A8; (416) 971-7474; www.warchild.org/index.html. A coalition of groups advocating on behalf of children caught in armed conflicts.

About the Author

John Felton is a freelance journalist who has written about international affairs and U.S. foreign policy for nearly 30 years. He covered foreign affairs for the *Congressional Quarterly Weekly Report* during the 1980s, was deputy foreign editor for National Public Radio in the early 1990s and has been a freelance writer specializing in international topics for the past 15 years. His most recent book, published by CQ Press, is *The Contemporary Middle East: A Documentary History*. He lives in Stockbridge, Mass.

Bibliography

Selected Sources

Books

Beah, Ishmael, *A Long Way Gone: Memoirs of a Boy Soldier*, Sarah Chrichton Books, 2007.

A former child soldier tells his compelling story of being recruited into one of Sierra Leone's rebel groups at age 13.

Briggs, Jimmie, *Innocents Lost: When Child Soldiers Go to War*, Basic Books, 2005.

A New York journalist provides first-hand reports about child soldiers in Afghanistan, Colombia, Sri Lanka and Uganda.

Rosen, David M., *Armies of the Young: Child Soldiers in War and Terrorism*, Rutgers University Press, 2006.

An American anthropologist examines legal and political issues surrounding the use of child soldiers.

Singer, P. W., *Children at War*, University of California Press, 2006.

A senior fellow at the Brookings Institution provides a comprehensive overview of the use of child soldiers.

Wessells, Michael, *Child Soldiers: From Violence to Protection*, Harvard University Press, 2006.

A professor of psychology at Randolph-Macon College examines issues involving child soldiers, drawing on his own three decades of experiences reintegrating former child soldiers into their former communities.

Articles

Boustany, Nora, "Report: Brokers Supply Child Soldiers to Burma," *The Washington Post*, Oct. 31, 2007, p. A16.

Burma's military government has been forcibly recruiting child soldiers through brokers who buy and sell boys to help the army deal with personnel shortages, according to a detailed report by Human Rights Watch.

Pownall, Katy, "In the Tragedy of Child-Soldiering in Africa, a Girl's Story Finds a Happy Ending," The Associated Press, Aug. 25, 2007.

A former female child soldier in Uganda is now studying environmental health at a university.

Reports and Studies

"Child Soldiers: Global Report 2008," Coalition to Stop the Use of Child Soldiers, May 2008, www.childsoldiersglobalreport.org/.

A nongovernmental organization offers its latest report on the use of child soldiers, including assessments of how well the United Nations and others are combating the problem.

"Children in Conflict: Eradicating the Child Soldier Doctrine," The Carr Center for Human Rights Policy, Kennedy School of Government, Harvard University, www.hks.harvard.edu/cchrp/pdf/ChildSoldierReport.pdf.

The center recommends international action to combat the use of child soldiers.

"Getting it Done and Doing It Right: A Global Study on the United Nations-led Monitoring and Reporting Mechanism on Children and Armed Conflict," Watchlist on Children and Armed Conflict, January 2008, www.watchlist.org/news/reports/pdf/global-v8-web.pdf.

A watchdog group critiques the U.N. Security Council's system of monitoring the impact of armed conflict on children, including child soldiers.

"Making Reintegration Work for Youth in Northern Uganda," The Survey of War Affected Youth, November 2007, www.sway-uganda.org/SWAY.ResearchBrief.Reintegration.pdf.

This report summarizes two phases of a long-term study of the economic, educational, social and other needs of former child soldiers in the Lord's Resistance Army in northern Uganda.

"The Security Council and Children and Armed Conflicts: Next Steps towards Ending Violations Against Children," Watchlist on Children and Armed Conflict, January 2008, http://watchlist.org/docs/Next_Steps_for_Security_Council_-_Child_Soldiers_Coalition_and_Watchlist_-_January_2008.pdf.

The watchdog group recommends that the U.N. Security Council take tougher measures against those who continue to use child soldiers.

"Soldiers of Misfortune: Abusive U.S. Military Recruitment and Failure to Protect Child Soldiers," American Civil Liberties Union, May 2008, www.aclu.org/intlhumanrights/gen/35245pub20080513.html.

A civil rights organization critiques U.S. policies toward the use of child soldiers, including voluntary recruitment of teenagers under 18 and detention of under-18-year-old alleged terrorists by the military.

U.N. Reports

"Children and armed conflict: Report of the Secretary-General," U.N. Security Council, Dec. 21, 2007, http://daccessdds.un.org/doc/UNDOC/GEN/N07/656/04/PDF/N0765604.pdf?OpenElement.

In his latest annual report to the U.N. Security Council, Secretary-General Ban Ki-moon listed 40 groups in 13 countries around the world that continue to use child soldiers. A complete list of other U.N. reports on conflicts affecting children is at www.un.org/children/conflict/english/reports.html.

The Next Step:

Additional Articles from Current Periodicals

Demobilization and Reintegration

"Chad Making No Effort to Demobilise Child Soldiers: HRW," Agence France-Presse, July 16, 2007.

Chad's government has not fulfilled its promise to demobilize the country's child soldiers, according to Human Rights Watch.

"Somalia Calls for Aid to Rehabilitate Some 70,000 Child Soldiers," Ethiopian News Agency, Feb. 3, 2007.

The Somali Transitional Federal Government is seeking international aid to help demobilize and reintegrate the country's child soldiers.

Nyanzi, Peter, "World Bank to Aid LRA, ADF Ex-Rebels," _Daily Monitor_ (Uganda), Dec. 6, 2007.

The World Bank and other donors have agreed to hold a forum for policy experts on how to address the disarmament, demobilization and reintegration of former child soldiers in Uganda.

Girl Soldiers

"Girl Tagged as Guerrilla Died in Crossfire: CHR," _Philippine Daily Inquirer_, June 7, 2007.

The Philippine military has been cleared of charges of killing a 9-year-old girl suspected of being a communist rebel after it was determined she died in crossfire.

" 'I Wanted to Take Revenge,' " _The Guardian_ (England), July 7, 2006.

A new report suggests that girls' motivation for engaging in combat is much more complex than previously believed.

Brown, Jonathan, "Life After Conflict for the Girl Soldiers of Ivory Coast," _The Independent_ (England), Dec. 22, 2007.

Former girl soldiers in the Ivory Coast are often rejected by their parents and society when they try to return home from conflict.

International Trials

"Trio Found Guilty of Conscripting Boy Soldiers for War," _Aberdeen Press & Journal_ (Scotland), June 21, 2007.

In a landmark decision, a U.N.-backed court has convicted three former military leaders in Sierra Leone on multiple counts of war crimes, including the use of child soldiers.

"Verhofstadt Advocates Kony's Arrest," _De Standaard_ (Belgium), Sept. 26, 2007.

Belgium's prime minister has called for the international community to arrest one of Uganda's most notorious recruiters of child soldiers.

Naming and Shaming

"UN Agency Wants to Talk to the Taliban on the Issue of Child Soldiers," _Pajhwok Afghan News_, Feb. 1, 2008.

The United Nations has included the Taliban on its "List of Shame" in hopes of encouraging dialogue over the release of child soldiers.

Klapper, Bradley S., "European, Muslim Clash Over Darfur," _The Associated Press Worldstream_, Oct. 4, 2006.

African countries have generally opposed the "naming and shaming" of countries that commit human rights violations, except in the case of Israel.

Osike, Felix, and Henry Mukasa, "Belgium Wants Rebel Chief Arrested," _New Vision_ (Uganda), Sept. 26, 2007.

Belgium has openly called for the arrest and prosecution of leaders of the Lord's Resistance Army, saying that "naming and shaming" policies are not effective enough.

U.S. Policy

"US Legislation Aims to Stop Use of Child Soldiers," _U.S. Newswire_, April 20, 2007.

A bill introduced in the Senate would restrict American military assistance for governments that employ child soldiers.

Glaberson, William, "A Legal Debate in Guantánamo on Boy Fighters," _The New York Times_, June 3, 2007, p. A1.

Defense attorneys argue that military prosecutors are violating international law by filing charges against a suspected al Qaeda operative who was 15 when he allegedly killed an American soldier.

CITING _CQ GLOBAL RESEARCHER_

Sample formats for citing these reports in a bibliography include the ones listed below. Preferred styles and formats vary, so please check with your instructor or professor.

MLA STYLE

Flamini, Roland. "Nuclear Proliferation." CQ Global Researcher 1 Apr. 2007: 1-24.

APA STYLE

Flamini, R. (2007, April 1). Nuclear proliferation. _CQ Global Researcher_, 1, 1-24.

CHICAGO STYLE

Flamini, Roland. "Nuclear Proliferation." _CQ Global Researcher_, April 1, 2007, 1-24.

Voices From Abroad:

PERNILLE IRONSIDE
Congo Protection Officer, UNICEF

Need for survival fosters fighting

"There are not just two groups. There are scores of groups, each with its own constituency, and the central economic drive of survival attracts people to fighting, both adults and children. They are not going to school; they are not eating; and the power associated with being a member of an armed group may allow them to get something they can't get otherwise."

The Christian Science Monitor, September 2007

ALLAN ROCK
Former Canadian ambassador to United Nations

Easy victims

"Children are of great value to warlords because they're malleable . . . and can be held under the power of the leaders with the use of drugs. Once they are recruited, neither their own countries nor the international community will devote the resources needed to help them recover. This is a crime that does terrible harm not only to the victims [of child soldiers] but to the children themselves."

Toronto Star, June 2007

LISA ALFREDSON
Coalition to Stop the Use of Child Soldiers

Children are too young for battle

"In a lot of countries people under age 18 are not allowed to make important decisions such as voting or having the right to buy alcohol or cigarettes. Yet they are permitted to join the armed forces and go into battle — often in situations which must be difficult to understand."

The Guardian (England), June 2008

ISHMAEL BEAH
First Advocate for Children Affected By War, UNICEF

There's another choice

"For many observers, a child who has known nothing but war, a child for whom the Kalashnikov is the only way to make a living and for whom the bush is the most welcoming community, is a child lost forever for peace and development. I contest this view. For the sake of these children, it is essential to prove that another life is possible."

The Associated Press, November 2007

RADHIKA COOMARASWAMY
Special Representative for Children and Armed Conflict, United Nations

Soldiers are 'just children'

"When you first meet them, and they are about 13 and 14, you are actually a little apprehensive because they come in with the swagger of grown men. They have been carrying guns, they have broad shoulders, they act very masculine. But then when you begin to talk to them, and if you talk long enough, they break into being just children."

Canberra Times, December 2007

BINALAKSHMI NEPRAM
Founding Secretary, Control Arms Foundation of India

Rebels provide protection

"While the government is not giving enough support and compensation to victims, rebel groups are willing to step in to act as guardians."

Times of India, November 2007

CHARLES ACHODO
Liberia Policy Adviser, U.N. Development Programme

Reintegration is underfunded

"In the conflict phase, the [donor] money flows freely, but the environment is not yet conducive [to improving the situation]. But, when peace comes and you have the capacity to do stuff, the funds dry up."

The Christian Science Monitor, November 2006

SALIFU KAMARA
Former Child Soldier Revolutionary United Front, Sierra Leone

'God is enough'

"I was not born a boy soldier; my captives forced me to become one. I had to obey them to stay alive today. When you have nothing left but God, that is the time you realize that God is enough."

Worldpress.org, January 2008

ROMÉO DALLAIRE
Retired General, Canada

Human rights abuse goes unaddressed

"It is easier and cheaper to recruit child soldiers, and ultimately the world lets them get away with it. We go to war over money, ground, and resources like oil, but not over human-rights abuse like using children as principal weapons of war. We choose not to go to war with biological and nuclear weapons, but go to war with children."

Public Agenda (Ghana), July 2007

caglecartoons.com/espanol

Ares/caglecartoons.com

Excerpted from the CQ Researcher. Thomas J. Billitteri. (July 25, 2008). "Human Rights in China." *CQ Researcher*, 601-624.

Human Rights in China

BY THOMAS J. BILLITTERI

THE ISSUES

At a ceremony in March in flower-bedecked Tiananmen Square, Vice President Xi Jinping suggested the Beijing Olympics would lead China and people the world over to join hands in creating "a more harmonious and better future."[1]

The event underscored China's hope that 19 years after its violent suppression of protesters in Tiananmen Square, it could present a new face to the world. China's nationalistic pride in its rise as a global power is palpable, and the country is clearly anxious to showcase its hypersonic economic growth and its embrace of what communist officials call the "rule of law."

But human-rights advocates say that while some facets of Chinese society have indeed improved in recent years, repression and inequity still affect millions of people. The critics say that behind the sheen of progress and prosperity — the ubiquitous construction cranes and thousands of new factories — the Chinese Communist Party (CCP) still stifles dissent and tramples basic freedoms of speech, religion and assembly at home and abets human-rights abuses in places like Sudan's Darfur region.

"When you come to the Olympic Games in Beijing, you will see skyscrapers, spacious streets, modern stadiums and enthusiastic people," Teng Biao and Hu Jia, two of China's most prominent human-rights activists, wrote last year. "You will see the truth, but not the whole truth. . . . You may not know that the flowers, smiles, harmony and prosperity are built on a base of grievances, tears, imprisonment, torture and blood."[2]

In April Hu was sentenced to three-and-a-half years in prison. A month before his arrest, he had deplored the "human-rights disaster" in China during testimony via the Internet to the European Parliament's Subcommittee on Human Rights.[3]

In many ways, China's rigid societal control is at odds with its economic revolution and the accompanying rapidly expanding middle class, dynamic new urban architecture and thousands of new laws and regulations. By 2006 the nation boasted 11 million private entrepreneurs and 4.3 million private firms, banned until the early 1980s. China's middle class, barely evident in the early 1990s, had exploded to 80 million people by 2002, and by 2025 is expected to number an astonishing 520 million.[4]

Yet a litany of serious abuses by the Chinese government persists, according to the U.S. advocacy group Freedom House and others, including:

- Imprisoning more journalists than any other country;
- Maintaining one of the world's most sophisticated systems of blocking Web-site access and monitoring e-mail;
- Prescribing the death penalty for scores of non-violent crimes, including tax fraud and "the vague offense of 'undermining national unity.' " Amnesty International estimated 470 people were executed death last year, based on public reports, but said the true figure is thought to be far higher;
- Maintaining a one-child policy that sometimes leads to forced abortions and human trafficking; and
- Repressing religious freedom of Falun Gong adherents, Tibetan Buddhists, Christians, Muslims and others.[5]

Security threats related to the Olympics have led China to take the kind of actions that have outraged the West and sparked internal unrest. In July, an execution squad publicly shot three young men in the public square of the city of Yengishahar. They had been convicted of having ties to terrorist plots, which authorities said were part of an effort to disrupt the Games by a separatist group seeking independence on behalf of Muslim Uyghurs.[6] The executions did not quell fears of terrorism as the Olympics drew nearer, however. At least

Policemen train outside the Olympic Stadium in Beijing on July 21. Concern about terrorism during the Games has led China to take the kinds of actions that have outraged the West and sparked internal unrest, such as the recent public execution of three young men reportedly with terrorist ties. China is hoping the Olympics will showcase its economic and social gains, but critics say the Communist Party still stifles dissent and tramples basic freedoms.

AFP/Getty Images/Mark Ralston

China Gets Low Human-Rights Rating

In a survey of citizens in 24 nations, China received lower marks for respecting its citizens' rights than the United States and France but higher marks than Russia, Saudi Arabia and Iran. China's approval ratings were highest among Pakistanis, Nigerians and Tanzanians and lowest in Europe, Japan and the Americas.

Percentage in Selected Countries Who Say Governments Respect the Personal Freedoms of Their People

	United States	France	China	Russia	Saudi Arabia	Iran
United States	75%	66%	14%	23%	13%	8%
Germany	70	86	13	16	24	6
Great Britain	69	78	12	18	14	12
France	65	77	7	14	20	5
Russia	66	67	39	45	23	22
Lebanon	55	87	48	38	64	29
Egypt	44	50	34	29	60	28
Japan	80	78	6	22	24	10
China	50	58	n/a	52	34	38
Pakistan	45	34	66	33	67	56
Brazil	51	53	22	26	11	5
Mexico	50	45	33	28	10	8
Nigeria	72	60	72	40	54	39
Tanzania	67	68	65	50	35	31
Median*	**65%**	**63%**	**30%**	**28%**	**24%**	**10%**

* Median percentages are shown for all 24 countries in the survey, but not all countries surveyed are shown above.

Source: "Some Positive Signs for U.S. Image," Pew Global Attitudes Project, June 2008

two died and 14 were injured in a pair of bus bombings in the city of Kunming as authorities tightened security for the Games. [7]

Meanwhile, a scramble this summer to clear Beijing's air and regatta waters in preparation for the Olympics highlighted China's colossal environmental woes, which have sparked thousands of mass protests throughout the country over health and safety issues.

Reconciling the two faces of China — repressive yet forward-looking — is not easy. Many experts note that Beijing's overriding goal is to develop the country as a world power and push its economy into the 21st century while keeping a lid on internal dissent that could weaken the Communist Party — a difficult balancing act given the country's unprecedented speed of change.

Chinese embassy officials in Washington declined to discuss the status of human rights in their country. But in April, Luo Haocai, director of the China Society for Human Rights Studies, said that after three decades of rapid economic development, China is on a path to developing human rights with Chinese characteristics.

"China believes human rights like other rights are not 'absolute' and the rights enjoyed should conform to obligations fulfilled," he said. "The country deems human rights not only refer to civil rights and political rights but also include the economic, social and cultural rights. These rights are inter-related." [8]

The upcoming Olympics — and President George W. Bush's decision to attend the opening ceremonies despite China's human-rights record — has focused attention on the question of how far the West should go in pressing China to improve its human rights. Asked whether Bush's attendance would induce China to concede on its human-rights issues, Foreign Ministry spokesman Qin Gang suggested that any changes would not be influenced by Western pressure.

"We have been committed to improving human rights not on the premise of the will of any nation, group, organization or individual, nor because of a certain activity to be held that makes us concede to the human-rights issue," he said. Still, Qin said, a human-rights dialogue between China and the United States held in May — the first since 2002 — was "positive" and "constructive." [9]

Wu Jianmin, a professor at China Foreign Affairs University and former ambassador to France, said that in trying to modernize, China is "striking a delicate balance" among stability, development and reform. Stability is a "known condition for development," and development is "the aim," he said. "We are facing many problems. I believe that only development can provide solutions. Reform is a driving force. We can't afford to go too fast. Too fast will disturb stability." [10]

Experts caution that China's human-rights picture is highly complex and difficult to characterize without nuance and historical perspective. "Things are moving forward and backward at the same time at different paces at different places," says John Kamm, executive director of the Dui Hua Foundation, a human-rights group in San Francisco and Hong Kong.

China's human rights present a "moving target," adds Margaret Woo, a professor at Northeastern University School of Law and co-editor of the forthcoming book, *Chinese Justice: Civil Dispute Resolution in China*. "It really depends on what time you're talking about, what particular topic, whether you're looking at it in terms of its progress vs. where it is today. It's not an easy, simple yes-or-no answer."

The tension in China between progress and repression emerged in full force after the massive earthquake in Sichuan Province in May, killing nearly 70,000 Chinese. Prime Minister Wen Jiabao and President Hu Jintao both toured the disaster zone, with Wen visiting an aid station and exhorting rescue workers not to give up on saving lives, and Hu clasping hands with survivors. [11] But behind the scenes, local Chinese officials have tried to stifle complaints of parents whose children died in collapsed schools, reminding them that disturbing the social order is against the law. [12]

Despite concern over China's human-rights behavior, its rising prominence as an economic powerhouse and national-security ally has led U.S. policy makers to act in ways that satisfy neither Chinese officials nor Western human-rights advocates. In March, just as a massive pro-independence protest erupted in Tibet, leading to violent clashes with Chinese security forces, the State Department removed China from its list of the world's 10 worst human-rights violators. Activists denounced the move, and *The New York Times* opined that removing China from the list "looked like a political payoff to a government whose help America desperately needs on difficult problems." [13] Yet the State Department's annual report on global human rights called China an "authoritarian state" whose record remained "poor." [14] It cited:

- Extrajudicial killings, torture and coerced confessions of prisoners;
- Coercive birth-limitation policies sometimes resulting in forced abortions;

- Severe repression of minorities;
- Use of forced labor, and other violations;
- Judicial decision-making often influenced by bribery, abuse of power and other corruption and a criminal-justice system biased toward a presumption of guilt, especially in high-profile or politically sensitive cases.

In another report in May, the State Department charged that China "continued to deny its citizens basic democratic rights" and called for the government to bring its practices in line with international norms. [15]

Foreign Ministry spokesman Qin called the May report "unreasonable." "We remind the U.S. side to pay more attention to its own human-rights problems, stop interfering in the internal affairs of other countries with such issues as democracy and human rights, and do more things that are conducive to the advancement of Sino-U.S. mutual trust and bilateral relations." [16]

As thousands of foreigners descend upon Beijing for the Olympic Games,

here are some of the main questions surrounding human rights in China:

Is China's human-rights record improving?

China is making strides toward protecting personal rights, though experts say the gains are uneven, incomplete and driven by political pragmatism.

"It really depends on how you break it down," says Minxin Pei, a senior associate in the China Program at the Carnegie Endowment for International Peace. The government has, for example, loosened up in recent years on personal freedoms, such as the freedom to travel, while civil or political rights remain "very limited," he says.

It is now "fair game" to discuss public-policy issues such as health care, housing, the environment and education, Pei says, and even to "take government to task for not doing a good job." But, "you cannot challenge the Communist Party in a frontal way and call for democratic elections."

"On balance, human rights are improving because the pressure from

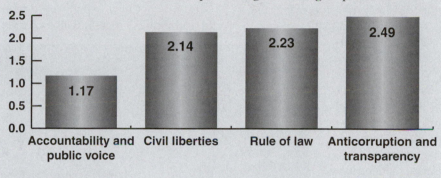

China's Human-Rights Record Is Lackluster

China performs poorly in all four human-rights categories studied by the pro-democracy group Freedom House. On a scale of 0 to 7 — with 7 representing the best performance — China scored less than 3 in all four categories and lowest (1.17) in "accountability and public voice" (free elections, media independence and freedom of expression).

China's Human Rights Report Card, 2007
(on a scale of 0 to 7, with 7 representing the strongest performance)

Accountability and public voice	Civil liberties	Rule of law	Anticorruption and transparency
1.17	2.14	2.23	2.49

Source: "Country Report — China," Freedom House, 2007

society is so enormous," Pei said. "Also, the legitimacy of repression is declining. Even the government understands there are certain things you cannot use force to deal with, and international pressure is also rising."

Cheng Li, a senior fellow at the Brookings Institution think tank in Washington who moved from Shanghai to the United States in 1985, says compared to decades past, human rights in China "are improving, there's no question about that."

Cheng, also a professor of government at Hamilton College, points out that during the Cultural Revolution in the 1960s and '70s, China was "like a prison," and human suffering was widespread. Even 20 years ago, around the time of the Tiananmen Square crackdown, Cheng says, Chinese authorities viewed discussions about human rights as "propaganda or Western hypocrisy."

But in recent years, China gradually has loosened up on some fronts, according to Cheng. He notes that dissidents have been able to give interviews to foreign media, some intellectuals have been critical of the Chinese government and significant progress has occurred toward instituting legal and economic reforms. Although "no fundamental breakthrough" has occurred on such issues as ethnic freedom, Tibet and treatment of the outlawed Falun Gong spiritual movement, "in general terms, China is more open and freer than at anytime in recent history," Cheng says.

Wang Chen, director of the Information Office of China's State Council, said human rights do not advance overnight but rather through "a gradual process."

"China is a developing country with a population of 1.3 billion, and China's human-rights development still faces many problems and difficulties," Wang said. "To respect and protect human rights and promote all-round development of human rights is a long-term arduous task for the Chinese government and Chinese people." [17]

But many China experts are doubtful significant progress will occur in the immediate future. James Mann, a former diplomatic correspondent for the *Los Angeles Times* and now author in residence at Johns Hopkins University's Paul H. Nitze School of Advanced International Studies, says that despite some gains in recent years, China still lacks the freedoms that form the bedrock of civil society in the West.

"If you define human rights to include personal freedoms such as what people can wear and what music they can listen to, then human rights have definitely expanded," says Mann, author of *The China Fantasy: How Our Leaders Explain Away Chinese Repression*. But, "if you define human rights

in the truest political sense — the right to oppose the government, the right to dissent — then they've made remarkably little progress over the last 30 years. Each time you think there's been a step forward, you see retrogression."

Kirk Donahoe, assistant director of the Washington-based Laogai Research Foundation, which monitors Chinese human-rights violations, including in the prison system, is similarly downbeat. "The political progress has just not kept pace with the economic progress," he says.

"Sure, people's living standards have improved, and a lot of times when you talk to the Chinese people they'll mention living standards and health and medication as being indicative of a better human-rights situation."

But, Donahoe says, "the basic situation has not improved" when measured in traditional Western terms: freedom of speech and religion, the right to criticize the government and dissent from official policy, free elections, and so on.

While China's constitution guarantees certain rights, such as freedom of speech and religion, Donahue says, "as long as there's a one-party system in place, these reforms don't carry much weight."

Human-rights advocates have voiced particular concern over violations in the months leading up to the Olympics. "Over the past year, we have continued to document not only chronic human-rights abuses inside China, such as restrictions on basic freedoms of speech, assembly and political participation, but also abuses that are taking place specifically as a result of China's hosting the 2008 Summer Games," said Sophie Richardson, advocacy director of Human Rights Watch's Asia Division.

AFP/Getty Images/Frederic J. Brown

Prominent human-rights activist Hu Jia, right, with his wife Zeng Jinyan in 2007, was sentenced to three-and-a-half years in prison. A month before his arrest, he had deplored the "human-rights disaster" in China.

"Those include an increasing use of house arrest and charges of 'inciting subversion' as [a] means of silencing dissent, ongoing harassment of foreign journalists despite new regulations protecting them and abuses of migrant construction workers without whose labors Beijing's gleaming new skyline would not exist." [18]

"People do have more choice in their daily lives" than in decades past, says Minky Worden, media director of Human Rights Watch and editor of *China's Great Leap: The Beijing Games and Olympian Human Rights Challenges*. "But if they try to cross one of the invisible red lines by posting something on the Internet, criticizing the government, if they fall afoul of a corrupt party official in their village, the political situation can still be very harsh."

During the one-year run-up to the Olympics, Worden says, Human Rights Watch has seen "a fairly systematic deterioration of human rights across most of the measurable areas. After a couple of decades of progress, we're seeing a retrenchment."

Will China's exploding growth lead to Western-style democracy?

Some China experts say the middle class is the key to China's future.

"If the middle class believes that its interests are being adequately tended to by the state, then there will be less pressure for democracy," says Harry Harding, university professor of international affairs at The George Washington University (GWU). "If they think the state is violating or ignoring their interest, then the desire for democracy can become extremely powerful."

For now, many analysts argue, China's expanding middle class tends to be highly nationalistic, supportive of the central government and concerned that if Western-style rights are given to the country's massive poor population, the interests of wealthier Chinese could suffer.

Johns Hopkins University's Mann says "people tend to assume that as a country becomes more prosperous it will develop an independent civil society. . . . But China seems to be developing a new political model in which the emerging middle class, which as a percentage of the overall population is still small, has much closer ties to the existing regime than we've seen elsewhere. It's not just that they may not be independent enough to push for democracy. They may be threatened by democracy because in China, where you have 500-800 million poor peasants or migrant workers either in the countryside or the edges of cities, there is fear among the emerging middle class that with democracy they will be outvoted, and that their interests will not emerge on top."

Nevertheless, democracy — at least focused on the local level and in a form shaped to Chinese political culture — has been a hot topic within the administration of President Hu. Writing before the 17th Congress of China's Communist Party last fall, Brookings scholar David Shambaugh alerted readers to "expect lots of 'democracy' initiatives."

"While these initiatives do not constitute democratic institutions and procedures as recognized in real democracies, they nonetheless represent serious efforts to broaden what the Chinese describe as 'inner-party democracy,' 'electoral democracy' and extra-party 'consultative democracy,'" he wrote. "All of these forms go under the broad rubric of 'socialist democracy' or 'democracy with Chinese characteristics.' " [19]

Scholars say that while China allows — and sometimes even encourages — criticism of corrupt local party officials, it keeps a tight lid on dissent aimed at the central government out of fear that it could lead to chaos and threaten the party's control.

"At this point in China's political development, there isn't a lively multi-party system, and there isn't an established political institution for political transition," says Northeastern University's Woo. "So imagine if your sole source of legitimacy goes out the window. What's going to happen to the country? They've never been able to figure that one out yet."

Some China scholars argue that China inevitably will move toward some kind of democracy that includes a multiparty political system. "The question for China is not whether, but when and how," says Pei, of the Carnegie Endowment for International Peace. "You can definitely say 20 years from now, China probably will be democratic and will have a multiparty system."

But others are doubtful. In *The China Fantasy*, Mann critiques scenarios often held by policy elites in the West — that capitalism will lead to democracy in China or that social or economic upheavals will undermine the current regime. He poses a third scenario: that China will continue to grow stronger economically but retain its authoritarian ways. The West should not continue to overlook China's human-rights violations at home and its support for repressive regimes elsewhere, he argues.

"[W]e should not assume China is headed for democracy or far-reaching political liberalization," Mann writes. "China will probably, instead, retain a repressive one-party political system for a long time. In fact, such an outcome may not bother the American or European business and government leaders who deal regularly with China; it may indeed be just the China they want.

"But they rarely acknowledge that they would be content with a permanently repressive and undemocratic China. . . . Instead, they foster an elaborate set of illusions about China, centered on the belief that commerce will lead inevitably to political change and democracy." [20]

China Holds More Than 700 Political Prisoners

China is detaining or imprisoning 734 political prisoners, according to the Congressional-Executive Commission on China.* Many were convicted of overstepping government speech or media regulations or inciting separatism — as occurred recently in Tibet and Xinjiang Province. Prisoners representing a range of offenses are profiled below.

Selected Political Prisoners in China

Name / Reason for detention	Ethnic group	Date of detention	Length of sentence
Adrug Lupoe	Tibetan	Aug. 21, 2007	10 years
Lupoe and other protesters climbed onto a stage where Chinese officials were speaking and called for the Dalai Lama's return to Tibet, freedom of religion and the return of exiled figure Gedun Choekyi Nyima. The Ganzi Intermediate People's Court convicted him of espionage and inciting "splittism."			
Abdulghani Memetemin	Uiyghur	July 26, 2002	9 years
Memetemin provided information to the East Turkistan Information Center, a Munich-based organization advocating independence for Xinjiang Province. The group is designated by China as a terrorist organization. He was sentenced by the Kashgar Intermediate People's Court for "supplying state secrets to an organization outside the country." On top of his prison sentence, he received three years' deprivation of political rights.			
Chi Jianwei	Han	Oct. 18, 2006	3 years
Chi was detained for participating in a sit-in and distributing materials from the Falun Gong spiritual group, which were found in his home. Shangcheng District People's Court charged him with "using a cult to undermine implementation of the law."			
Shi Tao	Han	Nov. 24, 2004	10 years
Shi was convicted of disclosing state secrets to foreigners after disobeying a government order limiting journalists' reports during the 15th anniversary of the Tiananmen democracy protests. Shi e-mailed his notes to the *Democracy Forum*, a U.S.-based online newspaper. His conviction was based in part on evidence provided by the China office of Yahoo!, which agreed to pay his legal expenses.			
Tenzin Deleg	Tibetan	April 7, 2002	20 years
Deleg was convicted of exploding bombs and scattering separatist leaflets. Deleg and an accomplice were sentenced to death, but Deleg's sentence was commuted to life imprisonment. He is reportedly being treated for heart disease in Chuandong Prison in Sichuan Province.			

* Congress created the commission in 2000 to monitor human rights and the development of the rule of law in China. It consists of nine senators, nine House members and five senior administration officials.

Source: "Political Prisoner Database," Congressional-Executive Commission on China, June 26, 2008

Should U.S. companies in China push for human-rights reforms?

In April, actress Mia Farrow, chairwoman of the humanitarian group Dream for Darfur, criticized most of the major corporate sponsors of the Beijing Olympics, including Visa and Coca-Cola, for their alleged failure to take meaningful steps to pressure China to help end human-rights abuses in war-ravaged Darfur.

"Because sponsors are desperate to win the hearts and minds of 1.3 billion potential consumers in China, they have been frozen into silence on Darfur," Farrow said. "If the Summer Games go down in history as the Genocide Olympics, it will be because of the Chinese government's support of the regime in Sudan, abetted by the moral cowardice of the sponsors who would not speak out publicly about the genocide in Darfur." [21]

China's growing thirst for oil has led it to deal with resource-rich nations that have been ostracized by the West for human-rights abuses. Sudan, for instance, where more than 200,000 people have died in fighting in the Darfur region since 2003, is one of China's biggest oil suppliers. China repeatedly has blocked efforts by the West to impose sanctions against Sudan and until recently was reluctant even to pressure the Sudanese government to curb the fighting. [22]

But some companies returned fire on Dream for Darfur. Coca-Cola's chief executive called its approach "flawed." "It judges concern by one narrow measure — the degree to which one pushes a sovereign government in public — while ignoring what we and others are doing every day to help ease the suffering in Darfur," wrote Coke CEO Neville Isdell. He added: "Our approach encompasses: immediate relief to those on the ground; investments to address water, one of the conflict's underlying causes; and efforts to bring local and international stakeholders together to develop long-term solutions." [23]

While many scholars and human-rights activists say corporations have an important role to play in pushing China toward human-rights and political reforms, some recommend a more low-key dialogue with Chinese officials while ensuring that their own corporate operations within China are clean of any taint of abuse.

"Private discussion and dialogue instead of finger pointing" is the best approach says the Brookings Institution's Cheng.

In a commentary in *Condé Nast Portfolio*, New York University business Professor Tunku Varadarajan explored the question of whether companies receiving global exposure from sponsoring the Olympics should press for human-rights improvement in China. [24] "At the very least," he wrote, the corporations "owe it to us to show that they are not wholly blind to human-rights issues." While they "cannot be asked to entirely subordinate the interest of their stockholders to those of a more amorphous group of stakeholders," he wrote, "the global practice of capitalism is not a morality-free exercise."

As a first step, advises Georges Enderle, a professor of international business ethics at the University of Notre Dame, companies "should keep their own house in order in China [and] treat their employees decently and according to American standards."

U.S. and foreign companies can help bolster the rule of law in China, he says, by following a major, new labor law in China and help explain to Chinese companies why the law is important. The law requires employers to provide workers with written contracts, restricts the use of temporary workers and makes it more difficult to lay off employees. It also strengthens the role of the Communist Party's monopoly union and allows collective bargaining for pay and benefits. [25]

The law was developed despite stiff objections from many multinational companies, who said it would significantly increase labor costs and reduce flexibility. As passed, the measure softened some controversial provisions but kept others. [26]

While it has drawn wide international attention, the law nonetheless "may fall short of improving working conditions for the tens of millions of low-wage workers who need the most help," said *The New York Times* — "unless it is enforced more rigorously than existing laws, which already offer protections that on paper are similar to those in developed economies." [27]

The *Times* pointed out that "abuses of migrant laborers have been endemic in boom-time China" and noted the labor law was passed shortly after Chinese officials and state media exposed the widespread use of slave labor in brick kilns and coal mines. [28]

Michael A. Santoro, a professor of ethics at the Rutgers University business school and author of *Profits and Principles: Global Capitalism and Human Rights in China*, says preaching to the Chinese about human rights simply engenders hostility toward Westerners. But foreign companies, he argues, should be far more aggressive in holding the Chinese government to trade and business standards that China itself committed to when it became a member of the World Trade Organization (WTO) in 2002.

By aggressively enforcing those standards and exercising the rights granted to them under the WTO, he argues, foreign companies could help promote the rule of law in China and provide moral support to citizens who are challenging China's government on political and human-rights issues.

"How many cases do you think foreign companies have brought" against China so far under the WTO rules? Santoro asks. "Try zero." Even if China retaliated, WTO provisions entitle companies to resolve their disputes with the Chinese government through a fair and independent court system in China, Santoro says. And if that fails, he adds, a dispute becomes an international trade case.

"We have this whole legal mechanism in place, and nobody's using it." Instead, business leaders continue "to work within the old paradigm of power in China," using personal connections rather than international law to resolve business disputes.

While not suggesting that multinational businesses always deal with China in the most confrontational way, Santoro says "they need to start thinking about the fact that they have economic rights — and not economic privileges that the [Chinese] government is granting to them."

As flawed as China's judicial system is, Santoro says, "we see very brave Chinese citizens pushing the envelope" on labor, environmental and economic-rights issues in the Chinese judiciary. But he says, "the foreign business community and the foreign legal community are not doing nearly enough to promote the rule of law in China." ∎

BACKGROUND

Mao's Legacy

China's human-rights practices have been under scrutiny for generations. Some scholars have painted Chairman Mao Zedong, who founded the People's Republic of China, as one of history's worst monsters. A controversial 2005 biography claims he was responsible for more than 70 million deaths in peacetime, with nearly 38 million dying of starvation and overwork during the Great Leap Forward and an accompanying famine. [29]

Whatever the true death figure, and notwithstanding that some Chinese continue to revere him, Mao's legacy is widely viewed as shameful. During his disastrous 10-year Cultural Revolution in the 1960s and '70s, even top political and military leaders were subject to arbitrary arrest, torture and extrajudicial execution. [30] Young intellectuals were forced into "reeducation" camps to work alongside peasants, Red Guards beat citizens for perceived slights to the authorities and Western music and other cultural expressions were suppressed.

In February 1972 Mao and President Richard M. Nixon met in Beijing in a spectacle that gave American television viewers a window on a China they had not seen for more than two decades. The visit, the first by a U.S. president to China, marked the first steps toward normalizing relations between the two countries and helped lay the groundwork for China's opening to the West.

Following Mao's death in 1976, hopes for democracy grew in China. In 1978 — 30 years ago this year — China adopted a "Reform and Opening" policy, which, while fostering dramatic economic and cultural changes also led to a vast chasm between rich and poor

and what critics say has been a legacy of human-rights violations, including relocations of Chinese citizens to make way for new development, government corruption and other abuses.

The push for greater freedom suffered its most notorious setback in 1989, when Chinese tanks crushed a pro-democracy movement in Tiananmen Square and the nearby Avenue of Eternal Peace.

Ma Jian, a well-known Chinese writer, described what happened: "The protests had been set off by the death of the reform-minded party leader Hu Yaobang. College students had camped out in the square — the symbolic heart of the nation — to demand freedom, democracy and an end to government corruption. There they fell in love, danced to Bob Dylan tapes and discussed Thomas Paine's 'Rights of Man.'

"The city had come out to support the protesters: workers, entrepreneurs, writers, petty thieves. After the tanks drove the students from the square in the early hours of June 4, 1989, nearby shop owners turned up with baskets of sneakers to hand out to protesters who'd lost their shoes in the confrontation. As soldiers opened fire in the streets, civilians rushed to the wounded to carry them to the hospital." [31]

According to the PBS TV program "Frontline," the Chinese Red Cross initially reported 2,600 were killed, then quickly retracted that figure under intense pressure from the government. The official Chinese government figure is 241 dead, including soldiers, and 7,000 wounded. [32]

Ma went on to say that the Communist Party in China rewrote history and "branded the peaceful democracy movement a 'counterrevolutionary riot' and maintained that the brutal crackdown was the only way of restoring order. . . .

"Realizing that their much vaunted mandate to rule had been nullified by the massacre, the party focused on economic growth to quell demands for po-

litical change. Thanks to its cheap, industrious and non-unionized labor force, China has since become a world economic power, while the Communist Party has become the world's best friend."

About 130 prisoners are still being held for their role in the Tiananmen protests, according to Human Rights Watch. [33]

The Tiananmen massacre isolated China on the global stage for years afterwards and helped defeat its bid to host the 2000 Olympics. "[W]hen the application was made in 1993, the sounds of the gunshots in Beijing were still ringing in people's ears," according to Chinese journalist Li Datong. [34]

In the nearly two decades since Tiananmen, experts say, China has changed in some significant ways, including the attitude of its youth toward the government. "In 1989," says Kamm of the Dui Hua Foundation, "young people were very critical of the government, and that was in line with international outrage over Tiananmen. Today the situation is radically different. You still have international concern over the bad human-rights record, but in China you have extreme nationalism, which basically says 'my country right or wrong' and 'how dare you criticize my government because in doing so you criticize China and by doing that you criticize me.' "

A University of Hong Kong survey this spring found that most Hong Kong residents continue to believe that Chinese students were right to protest at Tiananmen and that the government's reaction was wrong, but 85 percent said human rights in China had improved since 1989. [35]

Catalog of Abuses

China's selection to host the 2008 Games was predicated in part on promises to improve its human rights. Beijing Mayor Liu Qi told the International Olympic Committee the Games

Continued on p. 612

Chronology

1890s-1970s
Mao Zedong founds People's Republic of China.

1893
Mao is born in Hunan province.

1949
Mao leads Communists to power.

1958
Mao launches Great Leap Forward to increase industrial and agricultural production, causes deadly famine.

1959
Great Leap Forward opponent Liu Shaoqi replaces Mao as chairman of the People's Republic.

1966
To reassert his power, Mao launches Cultural Revolution; repression of human rights and religion causes political and social chaos.

1972
President Nixon visits China.

1976
Mao dies; power fight ensues.

1978
China adopts "reform and opening up" policy spurring economic growth and progress on human rights.

1980s-1990s
Economic reforms stimulate development, but pro-democracy efforts meet resistance.

1982
New Chinese constitution promises to protect freedom of speech, press, assembly, association and other rights, but crackdowns persist.

1987
China sets up China Academic Network, its first computer network.

1989
Military brutally clears pro-democracy demonstration in and around Beijing's Tiananmen Square, resulting in hundreds of deaths.

1991
China's State Council issues white paper on human-rights record.

1993
European Parliament denounces repression in Tibet and opposes China's bid to host 2000 Olympics.

1994
Advocacy groups complain about President Bill Clinton's decision to delink human rights and trade in dealing with China.

1999
Beijing bans Falun Gong spiritual movement as part of continuing repression of Christian house churches, Muslim Uyghurs and others.

* * *

2000s
Human-rights abuses continue to mar China's international image.

2001
Beijing wins bid to host 2008 Summer Olympics. . . . China receives formal approval to join World Trade Organization.

2002
Hu Jintao elected general secretary of Chinese Communist Party.

2002-2004
China suppresses media coverage of SARS outbreak.

2003
Hu Jintao becomes China's president; Wen Jiabao becomes premier.

2004
Zhao Yan, a Chinese researcher working for *The New York Times* in China, is charged with disclosing state secrets to the newspaper; charges are later dismissed.

2007
President Bush meets with President Hu in Australia and emphasizes U.S. concern about human rights. . . . Yahoo! officials defend company's role in jailing of Chinese journalist Shi Tao, sentenced in 2005 to 10 years. . . . Human-rights activist Hu Jia arrested. . . . Dozens of women in southwest China reportedly forced to have abortions.

March 2008
Foreign journalists restricted from traveling to Tibet as monks and other pro-independence demonstrators engage in deadly clashes with Chinese police. . . . State Department removes China from list of top 10 human-rights violators but says its record remains "poor."

April 2008
Olympic Torch Relay hit by anti-China protesters around the world.

May 2008
Earthquake kills nearly 70,000 in central China, opening country to scrutiny by Western reporters and leading to charges of poor building standards and government corruption.

July 2008
China scrambles to deal with environmental woes and prepare the country for start of Olympic Games.

Aug. 8-24
Olympics to be held in Beijing.

Intimidation of Press Said to Be Widespread

But private media continue to push boundaries.

With the Olympic Games approaching, media representatives and human-rights advocates have stepped up their perennial calls for greater press freedom for both Chinese reporters and foreign correspondents working in China.

Press advocates say China has violated temporary regulations it established 18 months ago that allow foreign correspondents more latitude in covering the country before and during the Games. The rules, which took effect in January 2007, expire in October. In early July China repeated its pledge to abide by the rules, with Li Changchun, a high-ranking Chinese official, encouraging foreign journalists to report "extensively" on the games. [1]

But free-press advocates say reporting efforts by foreign and domestic journalists, Chinese cyber-dissidents, bloggers and others have been anything but unfettered. Shortly before Li's statement, Human Rights Watch released a report concluding that China continued to thwart and threaten foreign journalists.

Drawing on more than 60 interviews with correspondents in China between December 2007 and this past June, the report said correspondents and their sources continued to experience intimidation and obstruction when pursuing articles that could embarrass authorities, uncover official wrongdoing or chronicle social unrest. [2]

Chris Buckley, a senior correspondent for Reuters, was beaten and detained by "plainclothes thugs" last September after interviewing rural citizens seeking redress for abuses by local authorities, Human Rights Watch said. In October, it said, a Eu-

ropean TV correspondent experienced similar treatment when trying to report on provincial unrest.

Other groups also have voiced strong complaints about China's disregard for free expression. In a report reissued this year, the New York-based Committee to Protect Journalists cited a "yawning gap between China's poor press-freedom record and promises made in 2001 when Beijing was awarded the Olympic Games." [3] As of early July, more than two dozen Chinese journalists remained in prison, the group said. [4]

Reporters Without Borders, a Paris-based press-advocacy group, said China jails more journalists, cyber-dissidents, Internet users and freedom of expression campaigners than any other country. [5]

But China's journalistic scene is not uniformly bleak. As the nation's economy has boomed, a climate of spirited competitiveness has developed among private Chinese newspapers and magazines, some with a zest for investigative reporting and the willingness and ability to push censorship boundaries. Also, the temporary rules established for the Olympics have helped open a window on China. The rules coincided with this year's massive earthquake in Sichuan Province, which was heavily covered by both Western and Chinese media.

Still, journalists have experienced harassment. They were banished from strife-torn Tibet, where riots last March generated some of the biggest international news of the year. [6] And after the earthquake, the *Wall Street Journal* reported, officials in Xianger, a coal-mining town, "prevented foreign reporters from entering areas

Continued from p. 610

"will help promote our economic and social progress and will also benefit the further development of our human-rights cause." [36] Yet, critics charge that China has not lived up to its word.

Some of the criticism stems from its crackdown this spring in Tibet and widely perceived failure to do more to stem abuses in places like Darfur. But rights advocates also express a more general concern over practices within China, despite the economic gains of some citizens in recent years.

"In some limited aspects, there has been some progress" on human rights, says Sharon Hom, executive director of Human Rights in China, an international organization founded in 1989

by Chinese students and scholars. For example, she cites "the 400 million lifted out of absolute poverty."

"However, for the vast majority — the migrants, the rural inhabitants, the urban poor, ethnic-minority groups, Tibetans, Uyghurs, Mongols — which together comprise the vast majority of the 1.3-billion population — the human-rights situation has not only not improved, it has absolutely deteriorated in the last 20 years with respect to the right of individuals to have . . . religious [freedom], cultural freedom [and] the freedom of expression and association."

What's more, Hom says most Chinese continue to lack decent housing, jobs, education and health care and that the problems are so severe the Communist Party has recognized the

need for improvement because of the social unrest they have generated.

Hom cautions that it is impossible to know the full extent of human-rights abuses in China because of the centralized control exerted under the one-party system, the state-of-the-art technology to monitor and filter information and the pervasive state-secrets system.

A detailed report last year by Human Rights in China said the state-secrets system "perpetuates a culture of secrecy that is not only harmful but deadly to Chinese society." [37] The system controls the flow of data on everything from the effects of environmental damage in urban industrial areas to forced abortions and deaths among political prisoners, Hom explains. "Anything and everything

where schools collapsed, stopped parents from speaking with reporters elsewhere and in some case have threatened parents trying to voice their anger." [7]

Chinese journalists face particular challenges in reporting on issues that government authorities deem threatening to state security or the Communist Party. The Committee to Protect Journalists noted in its report that censorship of domestic reporters in China "remains in force across all regions and types of media," with "all news outlets . . . subject to orders from the Central Propaganda Department" and provincial authorities blocking coverage of sensitive local issues.

Journalists must avoid reporting on the military, ethnic conflict, religion issues (especially the outlawed Falun Gong movement) and the internal workings of the government and Communist Party, the committee said. "Coverage directives are issued regularly on matters large and small. Authorities close publications and reassign personnel as penalties for violating censorship orders." [8]

The committee also noted that even Western Internet service providers have yielded to government pressure, pointing out that Yahoo turned over e-mail account information that led to the imprisonment of a journalist and several dissidents, Microsoft deleted a reporter's blog, and Google "launched a self-censoring Chinese search engine." [9]

In a new book on China, Philip P. Pan, former Beijing bureau chief for *The Washington Post*, describes how Cheng Yizhong, editor in chief of *The Southern Metropolis Daily*, ran an exposé on the *shourong* system, a detention-center network used to enforce a passport policy designed to keep "undesirables" out of cities. After *The Daily* reported on a detainee's death, it was announced that Premier Wen had done away with the *shourong* regulations and was going to shut the detention centers. But *The Daily* paid a high price for its success: Advertisers were directed away from the paper, its general manager was sentenced to prison and Cheng himself was arrested and held for five months. [10]

[1] "China pledges media freedom at Olympic Games," The Associated Press, July 11, 2008.

[2] See "China's Forbidden Zones: Shutting the Media out of Tibet and other 'Sensitive' Stories," Human Rights Watch, July 2008, http://hrw.org/reports/2008/china0708/.

[3] "Falling Short," Committee to Protect Journalists, updated and reissued June 2008, p. 8, http://cpj.org/Briefings/2007/Falling_Short/China/china_updated.pdf.

[4] "One month before the Olympics, media face huge hurdles," Committee to Protect Journalists, July 8, 2008.

[5] "2008 Annual report — Asia-Pacific: China," Reporters Without Borders, p. 79, www.rsf.org/IMG/pdf/rapport_en_asie.pdf.

[6] For background, see Brian Beary, "Separatist Movements," *CQ Global Researcher*, April 2008, pp. 85-114.

[7] James T. Areddy, "China Stifles Parents' Complaints About Collapsed Schools," *The Wall Street Journal*, June 18, 2008, p. 10A.

[8] "Falling Short," *op. cit.*, p. 8.

[9] *Ibid.*, p. 9.

[10] Michiko Kakutani, "Dispatches From Capitalist China," *The New York Times*, July 15, 2008. See Philip P. Pan, *Out of Mao's Shadow* (2008).

could be deemed a state secret, even retroactively," she says.

Despite the lack of reliable data, journalists and Western governments have nonetheless compiled thousands of pages of documentation in recent years on human-rights abuses in China. Amnesty International, for example, says it believes a "significant drop in executions" is likely to have occurred since the Supreme People's Court review of death sentences was restored in 2007, but that China remains the world leader in the use of the death penalty, with roughly 68 offenses punishable by death, including non-violent ones such as embezzling and certain drug-related crimes. [38]

In its 2008 report on global human rights, Amnesty estimates that at least 470 people were executed and 1,860 sentenced to death in 2007, based on public reports, "although the true figures were believed to be much higher." [39] Kamm of the Dui Hua Foundation estimates there were 5,000 executions last year, compared with perhaps 15,000 in the late 1990s.

"[D]eath penalty trials continued to be held behind closed doors, police often resorted to torture to obtain 'confessions,' and detainees were denied prompt and regular access to lawyers," the Amnesty report said.

Amnesty's catalog of abuses is far broader than the death penalty. For example, it said "torture in detention remained widespread." Also, "while space for civil society activities continued to grow, the targeting of human-rights defenders who raised issues deemed to be politically sensitive intensified." China continued to tightly control the flow of news and information, Amnesty said, noting that around 30 journalists were known to be in prison along with at least 50 individuals for posting their views on the Internet. (*See sidebar, p. 612.*)

In addition, millions of Chinese were impeded in their quest for religious freedom, with Falun Gong practitioners, Uyghur Muslims, Tibetan Buddhists and underground Christian groups "among those most harshly persecuted."

One-Child Policy

Advocates also point to threats to women's rights in China, including forced abortions, a problem long

Environmental Problems Spark Unrest, Health Woes

Protests reflect rise of citizen activism, hope for future.

In 2005, thousands rioted in a village in southeastern China, breaking windows and overturning police cars to protest factory pollution.

"The air stinks from the factories," said villager Wang Yuehe. "We can't grow our crops. The factories had promised to do a good environmental job, but they have done almost nothing."[1]

The episode marked one of numerous pollution-related protests — many peaceful but some violent — that have occurred in China in recent years as the nation's exploding economic growth has led to some of the world's worst environmental damage in history.

Experts say the problem has had massive human-rights consequences, including an alarming rate of cancer deaths, shrinking access to clean water and forced relocations of citizens to make way for new buildings and infrastructure.

Pollution has haunted the Olympics, too. In the city of Qingdao, for example, thousands of people were mobilized this summer to clean algae from the Yellow Sea, where the Olympic sailing regatta was planned. Concerns arose that the foul-smelling algae would impede sailing competitions. And marathoners have worried that they would have trouble breathing in Beijing's smog-saturated air. To counter the pollution, Beijing officials removed 300,000 high-polluting vehicles from local roads and then temporarily removed half of all vehicles as the Games drew nearer. They also were preparing contingency plans to temporarily close factories in northern China if necessary.[2]

But the problems surrounding the Olympics are only a small drop in a much bigger ocean of ecological blight in China.

Elizabeth Economy, author of *The River Runs Black: The Environmental Challenges to China's Future*, wrote recently in *Foreign Affairs* that "fully 190 million Chinese are sick from drinking contaminated water. All along China's major rivers, villages report skyrocketing rates of diarrheal diseases, cancer, tumors, leukemia and stunted growth."[3]

Economy, who is director for Asia Studies at the Council on Foreign Relations, also noted that in a survey of 30 cities and 78 counties released in 2007, China's Ministry of Public Health blamed worsening air and water pollution for drastic increases in cancer — a 19 percent rise in urban areas and 23 percent rise in rural areas since 2005.

Moreover, Economy wrote, a research institute affiliated with China's State Environmental Protection Administration estimated that 400,000 premature deaths occur each year due to air-pollution-related respiratory diseases — a number she said could be conservative. Indeed, she noted, a joint research project of the World Bank and Chinese government put the figure at 750,000, but Beijing reportedly did not want to release the figure, fearing it would incite social unrest.

China's environmental woes have led to so many stability-threatening mass protests that officials have backed away from some controversial industrial projects.

"China's greatest environmental achievement over the past decade has been the growth of environmental activism among the Chinese people," said Economy. "They have pushed the boundaries of environmental protection well beyond anything imaginable a decade ago."[4]

associated with the government's "one-child" family-planning policy, which restricts the rights of parents to choose the number of children they will have and the interval between births.[40]

The law gives married couples the right to have one birth but allows eligible couples to apply for permission to have a second child if they meet conditions in local and provincial regulations, according to the U.S. State Department's annual review of human rights in China for 2007. Enforcement varied from place to place, and was more strictly applied in cities than rural areas, the report says.[41]

Couples who have an unapproved child must pay a "social compensation fee" up to 10 times a person's

annual disposable income. "The law requires family-planning officials to obtain court approval before taking 'forcible' action, such as detaining family members or confiscating and destroying property of families who refuse to pay social compensation fees," the report said. "However, in practice this requirement was not always followed."

Hom says that while fines for having an unapproved child are legal under Chinese law, forced abortions are not, and property destruction is not a legal enforcement mechanism set forth in the one-child population policy. "It is the coercive and often illegal implementation of the policy that produces these abuses," she says."

The State Department review drew attention to the role that incentives play in enforcement of the one-child policy. "Officials at all levels remained subject to rewards or penalties based on meeting the population goals set by their administrative region," it said. "Promotions for local officials depended in part on meeting population targets."

Hom says that "of all the policies introduced by the Communist Party, the one-child population policy is the most hated and the most resisted. The vast majority of the people, meaning the rural-area people — really hate it."

She says she has visited villages where parents have more than one child and even as many as four or five. Those unable to pay the penalty may give

In her *Foreign Affairs* article, Economy wrote that China's explosive development "has become an environmental disaster."

"Clearly, something has got to give," she wrote. "The costs of inaction to China's economy, public health and international reputation are growing. And perhaps more important, social discontent is rising. The Chinese people have clearly run out of patience with the government's inability or unwillingness to turn the environmental situation around. And the government is well aware of the increasing potential for environmental protest to ignite broader social unrest." [5]

Yet, some observers — even within the ecological arena itself — see reason for hope. In a response to Economy's article entitled "China's Coming Environmental Renaissance," Yingling Liu, China program manager at the Worldwatch Institute, an environmental advocacy group, said Economy "underestimates the level of efforts now under way to address these problems, both in the Chinese government and in the growing private sector, as well as the degree to which the United States and other industrial countries are complicit in China's environmental woes.

Heavy pollution envelops Beijing during morning rush hour in June. Officials are temporarily removing half the vehicles from the city before Olympic Games begin in August.

AFP/Getty Images/Mark Ralston

"As a Chinese citizen and researcher who has followed these developments for many years, I am more optimistic that China is beginning to turn the corner on its monumental environmental challenges," she wrote. [6]

Also cautiously hopeful is James Fallows, a national correspondent for *The Atlantic Monthly* who lives in China. After visiting a cement plant in Shandong Province that recycles its heat to help generate electricity and researching other "green" projects, Fallows wrote, "China's environmental situation is disastrous. And it is improving. Everyone knows about the first part. The second part is important, too." [7]

[1] Jim Yardley, "Thousands of Chinese Villagers Protest Factory Pollution," *The New York Times*, April 13, 2005.

[2] Jim Yardley, "Chinese Algae threatens Olympic Sailing," *The New York Times*, July 1, 2008, p. A6.

[3] Elizabeth C. Economy, "The Great Leap Backward?" *Foreign Affairs*, September/October 2007.

[4] Quoted in James Fallows, "China's Silver Lining," *The Atlantic Monthly*, June 2008.

[5] Economy, *op. cit.*

[6] Yingling Liu, "China's Coming Environmental Renaissance," Worldwatch Institute, Nov. 29, 2007, www.worldwatch.org/node/5510.

[7] Fallows, *op. cit.*

birth outside the village and bring the child back later, she says.

While enforcement of China's family-planning policy can vary by place and circumstance, the State Department said that "there continued to be sporadic reports of violations of citizens' rights by local officials attempting to reduce the number of births in their region."

In southwest China, dozens of women were forced to have abortions in 2007 even as late as their ninth month of pregnancy, according to evidence uncovered and reported by National Public Radio. [42]

"I was scared," Wei Linrong told NPR, after 10 family-planning officials came to her home in Guangxi Province in April 2007 and told her and her husband,

who already have one child, that they would have to abort their 7-month-old fetus. "If you don't go [to the hospital], we'll carry you," they told her. Wei said the hospital was "full of women who'd been brought in forcibly." After the baby was aborted, she said, the nurses "wrapped it up in a black plastic bag and threw it in the trash."

In the U.S. Congress, one of the most vocal critics of China's human-rights record has been Rep. Chris Smith, R-N.J. "The one-child policy makes brothers and sisters illegal in China," he said in Beijing this summer. It "relies on forced abortion, ruinous fines and other forms of coercion to achieve its goals. . . . The one-child-per-couple policy has not only killed

tens of millions of children and wounded their mothers but has led to a serious disparity between the number of boys and girls. The missing girls [phenomenon] is not only a heartbreaking consequence of the one-child policy but is catastrophic for China." [43]

Laws and regulations in China forbid terminating pregnancies based on a fetus's gender, the State Department report said, "but because of the intersection of birth limitations with the traditional preference for male children, particularly in rural areas, many families used ultrasound technology to identify female fetuses and terminate these pregnancies."

China's male-to-female birth ratio for first births in rural areas was about

123 to 100, the report said. The national average in China was about 120 to 100. For second births, the national ratio was 152 to 100.

China's National Population and Family Planning Commission denied a direct connection between family planning and skewed gender ratios at birth, but it promoted expanded programs to raise awareness of the imbalance and improve protection of the rights of girls, the State Department reported.

Great "Walk" Forward

Despite what often appears as a depressing litany of abuses against China's vast population, especially its poor, many Western observers are guardedly optimistic. George J. Gilboy, a senior fellow at the MIT Center for International Studies, and Benjamin L. Read, an assistant professor in the politics department of the University of California-Santa Cruz, wrote recently that "in contrast to those who see a stagnant China, political and social dynamism is at work."

They point out that to preserve its power, the Chinese Communist Party "has chosen to revitalize itself and to adjust to new social realities, efforts that have intensified since the leadership team of President Hu Jintao and Premier Wen Jiabao came to power in 2002-2003." Still, the authors note that changes are "uneven and fragile" and that "political and social reform in China continues to 'walk,' not march, forward." [44]

Wu, at China Foreign Affairs University, when asked this year what the West doesn't understand about China, replied, "First, they don't like our system. They say, look, your system's not democratic, you don't respect human rights." But, Wu added, "You know why Chinese started the revolution? For human rights. Before 1949 [the] Chinese population [was] 500 million people. Four hundred million people were hungry. And they couldn't go on like that."

The former ambassador to France went on to say that China's massive modernization effort is occurring "for human rights" — "to make Chinese, every Chinese, better." People in the West see China "with Western eyes," he said. "They believe — some of them — we have to behave like them. It's impossible. You are American and I'm Chinese." The Chinese people, he said, are "used to strong central authorities. More than 2,000 years."

Noting America's own long road to women's suffrage and civil rights for blacks, he added, "You are where you are after more than two centuries of revolution. How can you expect others to do the same thing as you? It's impossible." [45]

Wu rejected the notion that people in China are afraid to speak about issues in ways that appear to challenge the country's leadership. "People are expressing themselves," he said — maybe not in the way people in the United States do, he added, "but . . . you are where you are after more than centuries of evolution." ∎

CURRENT SITUATION

Olympic Heat

As the Aug. 8 start of the Olympic Games approaches, emotions over China's human-rights record are rising with the temperature.

"Tragically, the Olympics has triggered a massive crackdown designed to silence and put beyond reach all those whose views differ from the official 'harmonious' government line," said Rep. Smith in Beijing in early July. [46]

He and Rep. Frank R. Wolf, R-Va., said they had come to meet with Chinese citizens pressing for greater polit-

ical and religious freedoms, but the Chinese authorities pressured or prevented nine activists from meeting with them, according to documents the lawmakers handed out. Wolf and Smith presented officials with a list of 734 Chinese prisoners whom they said were jailed for dissent and urged President Bush not to attend the Games unless major progress on human rights occurred quickly. [47]

But China reacted sharply, saying Smith and Wolf's attempted meetings violated the purported reason for their visit. "The two U.S. congressmen came to China as guests of the United States Embassy to engage in internal communications and consultations" and "should not engage in activities incompatible with the objective of their visit and with their status," said Foreign Ministry spokesman Liu Jianchao. Wolf later called his point "simply ridiculous." [48]

The harsh exchange underscored the degree to which the Olympics have become a major rallying point for Western critics of China's human-rights practices. Some of the sharpest barbs have been reserved for the government's handling of journalists. (See sidebar, p. 612.)

Human Rights Watch charges that despite promises to lift media restrictions leading up to the games, China continues to thwart foreign journalists. "[S]ystematic surveillance, obstruction, intimidation of sources and pressure on local assistants are hobbling foreign correspondents' efforts to pursue investigative stories," the group said in early July. [49]

Human Rights Watch added that temporary government regulations in effect until Oct. 17 allow foreign journalists to conduct interviews with consenting Chinese organizations or citizens but do not grant similar freedoms to Chinese reporters. While some correspondents say the regulations have spurred improvements, most say they "have done little to enable them to

Continued on p. 618

Should the U.S. use trade sanctions against China to promote human rights?

TIENCHI MARTIN-LIAO
DIRECTOR, LAOGAI RESEARCH
FOUNDATION

WRITTEN FOR *CQ RESEARCHER*, JULY 2008

*i*t is widely believed that U.S. trade sanctions against Cuba, Iraq, Iran and North Korea have been ineffective. Using economic means to achieve political ends usually fails. Nevertheless, sanctions have been applied repeatedly because they send a clear, disapproving message to the targeted country.

But with China, trade sanctions could be more fruitful. Unlike North Korea or Iran, China is not an isolated country harboring strong anti-American sentiment. It is an emerging superpower intent upon gaining international respect and has gone to great lengths to promote a positive image. If the United States could convince some of its European and Asian allies to support sanctions, the pressure on China would be substantial.

Moreover, communist ideology is bankrupt, and China's leadership now derives its legitimacy almost solely from the booming economy. While a disruption to the enormous U.S.-China trade would affect both countries, the U.S. economy is more flexible than the Chinese economy and probably could more quickly adapt to a sudden fluctuation in trade. Conceivably, just the threat of trade sanctions could convince the Chinese leadership to grant some concessions.

Now, with the Olympics rapidly approaching, China's human-rights situation is worsening. Because President Hu Jintao wants China to be seen as a "harmonious society," peasant workers, environmentalists, human-rights defenders, vagabonds and those with criticisms or grievances are being silenced. The 80,000 protests that occur annually are being crushed at the first sign of trouble. Earlier this year the world saw China crack down on mass demonstrations in Tibet and grieving parents protesting shoddy school construction in Sichuan after the earthquake. The Chinese Communist Party controls the army, police, courts, media, banks and all manufacturing, as well as China's only pseudo-union. It also decides who leaves the country or goes to jail and what can be said, read and heard.

If the United States had made permanent, normalized trade relations with China conditional upon China making reasonable progress on human rights, we might be witnessing the rise of a very different China today. But the Bush administration has adopted a friendly — sometimes almost embracing — China policy. Meanwhile, the suppression of so-called troublemakers and religious and ethnic groups has intensified.

Thus, China is denying freedom to a fifth of the world's population — a problem the United States will have to address at some point. When it does so, economic sanctions should not be out of the question.

JAMES A. DORN
CHINA SPECIALIST AND VICE PRESIDENT
FOR ACADEMIC AFFAIRS, CATO INSTITUTE

WRITTEN FOR *CQ RESEARCHER*, JULY 2008

*u*sing trade sanctions against China to promote human rights would do the opposite. Unlike trade, protectionism denies individuals the freedom to expand their effective alternatives, thus limiting their choices. Sanctions would fuel the flames of economic nationalism, harm U.S. consumers and embolden hard-liners in Beijing.

Before China opened to the outside world in 1978, the state dominated the economic landscape, private property was outlawed and capitalists were considered criminals. Today millions of people engage in trade, private ownership is widespread and civil society is advancing, as was evident in the spontaneous response to the Sichuan earthquake.

In 1995, Jianying Zha wrote in her book *China Pop*, "The economic reforms have created new opportunities, new dreams and to some extent a new atmosphere and new mindsets. . . . There is a growing sense of increased space for personal freedom." That is even truer today as a growing proportion of urban residents own their own homes, and more than 200 million people use the Internet — increasingly to challenge government power.

A 2005 GlobeScan poll of 20 countries found that China had the highest percentage of respondents (74 percent) who agreed that the "free-market economy is the best system on which to base the future of the world." And a 2006 Chicago Council on Global Affairs poll found that 87 percent of those surveyed in China had a favorable view of globalization. That positive attitude toward economic liberalism is good for China and good for the world.

Increasing commercial ties has helped spread the flow of information about alternative forms of government as well as improve living standards in China. Isolating China would do little to advance human rights — as we have learned from North Korea and Cuba. Instead, sanctions would be an act of economic suicide, endanger U.S.-China relations and threaten world peace.

It makes no sense to use such a blunt instrument in an attempt to "advance" human rights in China when trade itself is an important human right. Instead, the United States should continue its policy of engagement and avoid destructive protectionism.

It would be more constructive to welcome China as a normal rising power, admit it to the G-8 and continue the Strategic Economic Dialogue initiated by Presidents Bush and Hu. At the same time, we should not ignore the human rights violations that do occur and use diplomatic pressure to help move China toward a legitimate rule of law.

Continued from p. 616

report on issues government officials are determined to conceal," Human Rights Watch said. "Those include high-level corruption, ethnic conflicts, social unrest, public health crises and the workings of China's large detention system, including prisons, labor camps, mental hospitals and police stations." [50]

Wang Baodong, the Chinese Embassy's spokesman in Washington, wrote in June that the regulations had "given foreign journalists full freedom to report from China in the run-up to and during the Beijing Olympics," noting that more than 25,000 foreign correspondents were expected to cover the event. "Of course," he added, "they are expected to follow China's law, and to present to the world a real China with their pens and lenses." [51]

Johns Hopkins University's Mann doubts the Olympics — or media coverage of the Games — will move China toward greater freedom and human rights.

"I actually thought — wrongly — that in the year or so moving up to the Olympics, there might be some political opening in China," he says. "My frame of reference was a period of about four to six months before [President] Bill Clinton visited China in 1998, when there was a great relaxation in China."

But, Mann continues, the current period "isn't the same. Last fall and this spring, China really got threatened by a series of different events and decided to tighten up the climate. It became more afraid of upheaval. So the reality is, we're going to have an Olympics where the Chinese govern-

ment now sees it as something to get through," rather than an opportunity for greater opening.

The upheaval in Tibet, the controversy over China's alleged lack of action on Darfur and protests during the Olympic-torch relay are among the events over which the regime felt threatened, Mann says.

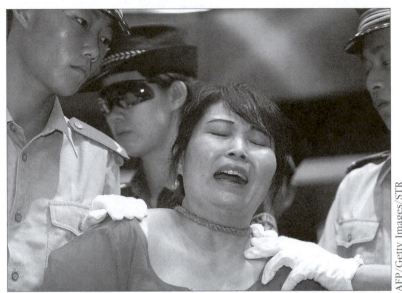

Drug peddler Wang Xiongyin cries after being sentenced to death in Guangzhou. China imposes the death penalty for many non-violent crimes, including "undermining national unity." Amnesty International estimates 470 people were sentenced to death last year but said the true figure may be far higher.

AFP/Getty Images/STR

Others point to last fall's 17th National Congress of the Communist Party, held every five years in China to praise past leaders, welcome new ones and help shape the country's future direction. In the meeting, President Hu vowed to address social, environmental and corruption problems in China and called for "intra-party democracy" that allows more party officials to participate in decision making. But Hu said the Communist Party must remain "the core that directs the overall situation and coordinates the efforts of all quarters." [52]

In the months leading up to the meeting, says Worden of Human Rights Watch, a "chill . . . went into place" as government officials sought to fore-

stall disruption and protests. For example, she said, the government emptied the "Petitioner's Village" in Beijing, where citizens living outside the capital gathered to seek help from the central government in grievances against local officials.

"At one point [the village] had as many as 10,000 petitioners in Beijing. The last several thousand were cleared out in September before the Party Congress. These are people who have the legal right to petition the government dating back centuries, and they travel from the provinces to do so, often because of egregious cases of corruption, and then the local officials with whom they have the grievances will often send thugs to beat them up and haul them back to their home provinces. That's what's happened to most of them before the Olympics."

Authorities also reportedly cracked down on the Internet, closing tens of thousands of Web sites on which visitors could post opinions. [53]

Despite what many see as China's tightening political atmosphere, many China-watchers say the Olympics inevitably will have some effect on China's internal policies.

In a piece comparing the Beijing Olympics and the 1988 Games in Seoul, South Korea, Richard Pound, a longtime member of the International Olympic Committee, wrote that "no host country of the Olympic Games has ever been the same after the Games . . . especially countries that had been closed or particularly authoritarian. China will not be unaffected. . . . Its size and present governance may mean that the change does not occur as quickly as it might in other countries. Its lack of transparency may also mean that the elements of change are not easily apparent, which will not mean that they are not occurring. Patience and firmness on the part of the international community can be effective catalysts — as can the Olympic Games." [54]

Internet's Impact

China has some 223 million Internet users, almost as many as in the United States. [55] And many think the Internet will continue discomforting Communist authorities and may ultimately bring about human-rights reforms. Despite the government's efforts to control its use, the Internet remains a powerful and pervasive force for change.

For instance, in southwest China's Guizhou Province some 30,000 rioters torched government buildings this summer to protest officials' handling of a teenage girl's death, a case chronicled by Chinese journalists and Internet bloggers. News reports said police called the death a suicide, angering people who believed she was raped and murdered, possibly by someone close to local authorities. [56]

In the ensuing days, however, authorities announced that four officials had been fired for "severe malfeasance" over an alleged cover-up in the case, *The Wall Street Journal* reported. The shift appeared to have resulted from pressure exerted by Chinese journalists and bloggers. When mainstream Web sites began to delete posts on the case, some bloggers got creative, the *Journal* noted, including by writing their postings backward to avert censorship. [57]

While tech-savvy dissidents may be fighting creatively against local corruption and other ills, it is not at all clear how much educated young Chinese will stir things up on the human-rights front, including on tinderbox issues such as Tibetan independence and China's role in the Darfur crisis.

"Educated young Chinese, far from being embarrassed or upset by their government's human-rights record, rank among the most patriotic, establishment-supporting people you'll meet," wrote Matthew Forney, a former Beijing bureau chief for *Time*. [58] He went on to say "most young, ethnic Chinese strongly support their government's suppression of the recent Tibetan uprising."

Forney said the most obvious explanation for young people's unquestioning support of the government is China's education system, "which can accurately be described as indoctrination." He also suggested that few young people experience political repression, most are too young to remember the Tiananmen Square massacre and many lack life experiences that would help them gain perspectives other than the government's viewpoint.

"Educated young Chinese are . . . the biggest beneficiaries of policies that have brought China more peace and prosperity than at any time in the past thousands years," Forney wrote. "They can't imagine why Tibetans would turn up their noses at rising incomes and the promise of a more prosperous future. The loss of a homeland just doesn't compute as a valid concern."

Unless big changes occur in China's education system or economy, Forney concluded, Westerners won't find allies among most Chinese on issues like Tibet and Darfur for some time to come. "If the debate over Tibet turns this summer's contests in Beijing into the Human Rights Games . . . ," he wrote, "Western ticket-holders expecting to find Chinese angry at their government will instead find Chinese angry at them." ■

OUTLOOK

Chinese-style Change

The West's immediate focus on China may fade once the Olympic Games end, but concern about human-rights reform is likely to persist long into the future.

While China has made "great progress in human-rights construction," said Luo of the China Society for Human Rights Studies, "China's political and economic systems are not perfect." [59]

"The democracy and the legal system are not complete," he continued, "and urban and rural development are imbalanced. There are still problems in employment, education, medical care, housing, social welfare, income distribution, production safety and environmental protection."

But China had never ignored those problems, Luo insisted. "Some Western countries have always adopted a double standard on the human-rights issue and condemned China and other developing countries, but turned a blind eye to their own human-rights problems."

Western experts are variously optimistic and pessimistic about China's human-rights picture, but many agree the Communist Party is likely to pay more attention to citizens' grievances in coming years out of a pragmatic desire to maintain supremacy and keep the country from spinning out of control.

"Over time the government will become more responsive to the demands of its people, and the judicial system will afford more protections for people who are arrested," says the Dui Hua Foundation's Kamm. "We should first be looking at those things, rather than jumping in and saying, will China fully respect human rights by a certain date or be a democracy."

Pointing to the recent Guizhou uprising over the girl's death, Kamm notes that "if that had happened in 1989, it would have been suppressed incredibly hard [and] called a counterrevolutionary riot and the perpetrators put in prison for 20 years or life. Now it's called a mass incident, and the [state-controlled press] has given it extraordinary coverage by Chinese standards."

Still, Kamm says government officials are not acting out of altruism in such cases. They are "being forced to respond more and more to the people . . . in order to stay in power," he says

Northeastern University law Professor Woo says China is trying to move not toward Western-style democracy but toward a model of "soft authoritarianism," in which officials relax some controls to build support for the governing regime.

She notes, for example, the passage in 2007 of a landmark property-rights law designed to provide citizens with a grievance process and adequate compensation when the government takes property for economic development — a huge issue in recent years given the countless Chinese who have been forced out of their homes.

Nonetheless, Woo says, economic reforms have also led China to pull back from health, welfare and labor protections, widening the gap between the rural poor and rising urban middle class and increasing social unrest.

Ultimately, she says, the outlook for human rights in China is mixed. "I don't ever think China will be the same kind of democracy you see in this country," she says. "But I think it has changed a lot." ■

Notes

[1] "Chinese president announces official start of Olympic torch relay," GOV.cn (Chinese government's official Web portal), March 31, 2008, http://english.gov.cn/2008-03/31/content_933196.htm.

[2] Teng Biao and Hu Jia, "The Real China and the Olympics," open letter, Sept. 10, 2007, accessed at Web site of Human Rights Watch, http://china.hrw.org/press/news_release/the_real_china_and_the_olympics.

[3] Minky Worden, ed., *China's Great Leap: The Beijing Games and Olympian Human Rights Challenges* (2008), pp. 36-37.

[4] All data were cited in corresponding footnotes in Cheng Li, ed., *China's Changing Political Landscape* (2008), p. 2.

[5] "Ten Things You Should Know About China," Freedom House, www.freedomhouse.org/template.cfm?page=379.

[6] Edward Cody, "Across China, Security Instead of Celebration," *The Washington Post*, July 19, 2008, p. A1.

[7] Jim Yardley, "2 Die in Blasts on Chinese Buses," *The New York Times*, July 22, 2008, p. A6.

[8] Xinhua News Agency, "China's protection of human rights differs from Western countries," April 21, 2008, http://news.xinhuanet.com/english/2008-04/21/content_8021857.htm.

[9] Xinhua News Agency, "Spokesman: China's human rights improvement self-directed," June 3, 2008, www.china-embassy.org/eng/zt/zgrq/t443623.htm.

[10] Margaret Warner, interview with former Ambassador Wu Jianmin, PBS' "The NewsHour with Jim Lehrer," May 30, 2008, www.pbs.org/newshour/bb/asia/jan-june08/jianmin_05-30.html.

[11] Mary Hennock and Melinda Liu, "China's Tears: The Sichuan earthquake could change the way Chinese see their leaders," *Newsweek*,

May 17, 2008, www.newsweek.com/id/137519.

[12] James T. Areddy, "China Stifles Parents' Complaints About Collapsed Schools," *The Wall Street Journal*, June 18, 2008, p. 10A.

[13] "China Terrorizes Tibet," editorial, *The New York Times*, March 18, 2008.

[14] "Country Reports on Human Rights Practices — 2007," U.S. Department of State, March 11, 2008.

[15] "2008 Country Reports on Advancing Freedom and Democracy," U.S. Department of State, May 23, 2008, www.state.gov/g/drl/rls/afdr/2008/104760.htm.

[16] Xinhua News Agency, "FM: U.S. report on China democracy, human rights 'unreasonable,'" http://news.xinhuanet.com/english/2008-06/02/content_8301760.htm.

[17] Xinhua News Agency, *op. cit.*, April 21, 2008.

[18] Sophie Richardson, "The Impact of the 2008 Olympic Games on Human Rights and the Rule of Law in China," statement to the Congressional-Executive Commission on China, Feb. 27, 2008, http://cecc.gov/pages/hearings/2008/20080227/richardson.php.

[19] David Shambaugh, "China: Let a Thousand Democracies Bloom," *International Herald Tribune*, July 6, 2007, accessed at www.brookings.edu/opinions/2007/0706china_shambaugh.aspx.

[20] James Mann, *The China Fantasy: How Our Leaders Explain Away Chinese Repression* (2007), p. xiii.

[21] "Olympic Corporate Sponsors Still Silent on Darfur," Dream for Darfur, press release, April 24, 2008, www.dreamfordarfur.org/index.php?option=com_content&task=view&id=183&Itemid=51. The report is "The Big Chill: Too Scared to Speak, Olympic Sponsors Still Silent on Darfur," Dream for Darfur, www.dreamfordarfur.org/storage/dreamdarfur/documents/executive_summary_jj_revised.pdf. See also Stephanie Clifford, "Companies Return Criticism From Darfur Group," *The New York Times*, April 25, 2008.

[22] For background see Karen Foerstel, "China in Africa," *CQ Global Researcher*, January 2008, pp. 1-26.

[23] Neville Isdell, "We help Darfur but do not harm the Olympics," *Financial Times*, April 17, 2008, www.ft.com/cms/s/0/bba2d544-0c88-11dd-86df-0000779fd2ac.html.

[24] Tunku Varadarajan, "No Word From Our Sponsors," *Condé Nast Portfolio*, July 2008, p. 21.

[25] Joseph Kahn and David Barboza, "China Passes a Sweeping Labor Law," *The New York Times*, June 30, 2007.

[26] *Ibid.*

[27] *Ibid.*

About the Author

Thomas J. Billitteri is a *CQ Researcher* staff writer based in Fairfield, Pa., who has more than 30 years' experience covering business, nonprofit institutions and public policy for newspapers and other publications. He has written previously for *CQ Researcher* on "Domestic Poverty," "Curbing CEO Pay" and "Mass Transit." He holds a BA in English and an MA in journalism from Indiana University.

28 *Ibid.*

29 See Jung Chang and Jon Halliday, *Mao: The Unknown Story* (2005). For a review of the book see Michiko Kakutani, "China's Monster, Second to None," *The New York Times*, Oct. 21, 2005, www.nytimes.com/2005/10/21/books/21book.html?scp=6&sq=mao+and+deaths&st=nyt.

30 Yu Keping, "Ideological Change and Incremental Democracy in Reform-Era China," in Li, *op. cit.*, p. 46. Yu, deputy director of the Bureau of Translation of the Chinese Communist Party Central Committee, also is director of the China Center for Comparative Politics and Economics and director of the Center for Chinese Government Innovations, at Beijing University.

31 Ma Jian, "China's Grief, Unearthed," op-ed, *The New York Times*, June 4, 2008, p. A23.

32 "China in the Red," "Frontline," Public Broadcasting Service, Feb. 13, 2003.

33 Christopher Bodeen, The Associated Press, "Olympic debate focuses on Tiananmen prisoners," *Columbus Dispatch*, June 4, 2008, www.dispatch.com/live/content/national_world/stories/2008/06/04/ap_tianamen_0604.ART_ART_06-04-08_A5_S5AD44G.html?sid=101.

34 Quoted in Worden, *op. cit.*, p. 26.

35 Keith Bradsher, "Vigil for Tiananmen Dead Draws Fewer in Hong Kong," *The New York Times*, June 5, 2008, p. A10, www.nytimes.com/2008/06/05/world/asia/05hong.html?scp=1&sq=%22vigil+for+tiananmen+dead&st=nyt.

36 Quoted in Official Web site of the Beijing 2008 Olympic Games, http://en.beijing2008.cn/spirit/beijing2008/candidacy/presentation/n214051410.shtml.

37 "State Secrets: China's Legal Labyrinth," Human Rights in China, http://hrichina.org/public/contents/article?revision%5fid=41506&item%5fid=41421#TOC.

38 "Stop Executions," Amnesty International, www.amnesty.org/en/human-rights-china-beijing-olympics/issues/death-penalty.

39 "Report 2008: The State of the World's Human Rights," Amnesty International, http://thereport.amnesty.org/eng/Homepage.

40 U.S. Department of State, *op. cit.* March 11.

41 *Ibid.*

42 Louisa Lim, "Cases of Forced Abortions Surface in China," National Public Radio, April 23, 2007, www.npr.org/templates/story/story.php?storyId=9766870.

43 Remarks of U.S. Rep. Chris Smith, Beijing, July 1, 2008, accessed at http://chrissmith.house.gov/UploadedFiles/080701BeijingPresser20001.pdf.

44 George J. Gilboy and Benjamin L. Read, "Political and Social reform in China: Alive and Walking," *The Washington Quarterly*, summer 2008.

45 Warner, *op. cit.*

46 Chris Buckley, Reuters, "U.S. lawmakers decry Olympics after dissidents blocked," July 1, 2008, www.washingtonpost.com/wp-dyn/content/article/2008/07/01/AR2008070100751.html.

47 *Ibid.* President Bush has said he will attend the opening ceremony.

48 *Ibid.*

49 "China: Olympics Media Freedom Commitments Violated," Human Rights Watch, press release, July 7, 2008, www.hrw.org/english/docs/2008/07/03/china19250.htm.

50 *Ibid.*

51 Wang Baodong, "Opposing view: China welcomes the world," *USA Today*, June 16, 2008, http://blogs.usatoday.com/oped/2008/06/opposing-view-2.html.

52 Joseph Kahn, "China's Leader Closes Door to Reform," *The New York Times*, Oct. 16, 2007, www.nytimes.com/2007/10/16/world/asia/16china.html?scp=3&sq=china+and+party+congress&st=nyt.

53 Peter Ford, "Why China shut down 18,401 websites," *The Christian Science Monitor*, Sept. 25, 2007, www.csmonitor.com/2007/0925/p01s06-woap.html.

54 Richard Pound, "Olympian Changes: Seoul and Beijing," in Worden, *op. cit.*, pp. 96-97.

55 Geoffrey A. Fowler and Juliet Ye, "Chinese Bloggers Score a Victory Against the Government," *The Wall Street Journal*, July 5-6, 2008, p. 7A.

56 *Ibid.* See also, Ye and. Fowler, "Chinese Bloggers Scale the 'Great Firewall' in Riot's Aftermath, *The Wall Street Journal*, July 2, 2008, p. 7A.

57 Fowler and Ye, *op. cit.*

58 Matthew Forney, "China's Loyal Youth," *The New York Times*, April 13, 2008, www.nytimes.com/2008/04/13/opinion/13forney.html?scp=1&sq=china's%20loyal%20youth&st=cse.

59 Xinhua News Agency, "Expert: China never shuns human rights problems," April 21, 2008, http://news.xinhuanet.com/english/2008-04/21/content_8021473.htm.

FOR MORE INFORMATION

Amnesty International, 5 Penn Plaza, 16th floor, New York, NY 10001; (212) 807-8400; www.amnesty.org. London-based organization that promotes human rights worldwide.

China Aid Association, P.O. Box 8513, Midland, TX 79708; (888) 889-7757; www.chinaaid.org. Monitors religious persecution in China.

Committee to Protect Journalists, 330 7th Ave., 11th Floor, New York, NY 10001; (212) 465-1004; www.cpj.org. Promotes press freedom around the world.

Dui Hua Foundation, 450 Sutter St., Suite 900, San Francisco, CA 94108; (415) 986-0536; www.duihua.org. Promotes human rights through dialogue with China.

Embassy of the People's Republic of China in the United States, 2300 Conn. Ave., N.W., Washington, DC 20008; (202) 328-2500; www.china-embassy.org/eng. Provides news and other information on China.

Human Rights in China, 350 Fifth Ave., Suite 3311, New York, NY 10118; (212) 239-4495; www.hrichina.org. Founded in 1989 by Chinese students and scholars to promote human rights in China and worldwide.

Human Rights Watch, 350 Fifth Ave., 34th floor, New York, NY 10118-3299; (212) 290-4700; www.hrw.org; Promotes human rights around the world and investigates abuses.

Laogai Research Foundation, 1109 M St., N.W., Washington, DC 20005; (202) 408-8300/8301; www.laogai.org. Documents and reports on human-rights abuses in China.

Reporters Without Borders, 1500 K St., N.W., Suite 600, Washington, DC 20005; (202) 256-5613; www.rsf.org. Paris-based group that promotes press freedom and works to protect safety of journalists.

Bibliography

Selected Sources

Books

Li, Cheng, ed., *China's Changing Political Landscape: Prospects for Democracy*, Brookings Institution Press, 2008.

A Brookings Institution scholar and professor of government at Hamilton College in Hamilton, N.Y., presents a collection of scholarly articles on the economic, political and social challenges facing China.

Mann, James, *The China Fantasy: How Our Leaders Explain Away Chinese Repression*, Viking, 2007.

The author in residence at Johns Hopkins University's Paul H. Nitze School of Advanced International Studies and former Beijing bureau chief for the *Los Angeles Times* argues that "we should not assume China is headed for democracy or far-reaching political liberalization."

Santoro, Michael A., *Profits and Principles: Global Capitalism and Human Rights in China*, Cornell University Press, 2000.

A Rutgers University business-ethics professor focuses on the human-rights responsibilities and contributions of multinational corporations operating in China.

Worden, Minky, ed., *China's Great Leap: The Beijing Games and Olympian Human Rights Challenges*, Seven Stories Press, 2008.

The media director of Human Rights Watch presents a collection of articles by experts on human rights in China.

Articles

Gilboy, George J., and Benjamin L. Read, "Political and Social Reform in China: Alive and Walking," *The Washington Quarterly*, summer 2008, www.twq.com/08summer/docs/08summer_gilboy-read.pdf.

The head of an international energy firm in China (Gilboy) who is also a senior fellow at the MIT Center for International Studies, and an assistant professor at the University of California-Santa Cruz (Read) argue that "political and social reforms are alive" in China but that the country "is moving forward at a walking pace . . . on a long, potentially tumultuous path."

Pei, Minxin, "How China Is Ruled," *The American Interest*, Vol. III, No. 4, March/April 2008, www.the-american-interest.com/ai2/article.cfm?Id=403&MId=18.

A senior associate in the China Program at the Carnegie Endowment for International Peace argues that "the cost of China's post-1989 strategy resides in its success: The [Communist] Party has been so well protected that its own lassitude has led to internal decay."

Thornton, John L., "Long Time Coming: The Prospects for Democracy in China," *Foreign Affairs*, January/February 2008, www.foreignaffairs.org/20080101faessay87101/john-l-thornton/long-time-coming.html.

A professor at Tsinghua University's School of Economics and Management in Beijing and chair of the Brookings Institution board says how far China's liberalization will go remains an open question.

Varadarajan, Tunku, "No Word From Our Sponsors," *Condé Nast Portfolio*, July 2008.

A business professor at New York University and former assistant managing editor of *The Wall Street Journal* argues that big companies receiving global exposure from the Beijing Olympics should do more to press for human-rights reforms.

Reports and Studies

"China (includes Tibet, Hong Kong, and Macau): Country Reports on Human Rights Practices — 2007," U.S. Department of State, March 11, 2008, www.state.gov/g/drl/rls/hrrpt/2007/100518.htm.

This annual assessment concludes that human rights "remained poor" last year in China.

"China: Persecution of Protestant Christians in the Approach to the Beijing 2008 Olympic Games," Christian Solidarity Worldwide, produced in association with China Aid Association, June 2008, http://chinaaid.org/pdf/Pre-Olympic_China_Persecution_Report_in_English_June2008.pdf.

The approach of the Beijing 2008 Olympic Games has been accompanied by a "significant deterioration" in religious freedom for China's Protestant Church, the report says.

"Falling Short: Olympic Promises Go Unfulfilled as China Falters on Press Freedom," Committee to Protect Journalists, June 2008, http://cpj.org/Briefings/2007/Falling_Short/China/china_updated.pdf.

An update of an August 2007 report, this lengthy document says "China jails journalists, imposes vast censorship and allows harassment, attacks and threats to occur with impunity."

"State Secrets: China's Legal Labyrinth," Human Rights in China, 2007, www.hrichina.org/public/PDFs/State-Secrets-Report/HRIC_StateSecrets-Report.pdf.

The international, nongovernmental organization says that "by guarding too much information . . . the complex and opaque state-secrets system perpetuates a culture of secrecy that is not only harmful but deadly to Chinese society."

The Next Step:

Additional Articles from Current Periodicals

Environment

Bradsher, Keith, "China Reports Declines in 3 Major Pollutants, Reversing Trend," *The New York Times*, **June 6, 2008, p. A12.**
China's Ministry of Environmental Protection announced that emissions of three important pollutants declined in 2007.

Economy, Elizabeth C., "The Great Leap Backward?" *Foreign Affairs*, **September/October 2007, p. 38.**
The risks to China's economy, public health, international reputation and social stability will increase so long as its environmental woes continue.

Ramzy, Austin, "Airing Out Beijing," *Time*, **Jan. 21, 2008, p. 1.**
Pollution in Beijing regularly hits levels two to three times what is considered safe by the World Health Organization.

Olympics

Casert, Raf, "Belgian Athletes Will Be Barred From Talking Politics at the Olympic Sites in Beijing," The Associated Press, Jan. 23, 2008.
The Belgian Olympic Committee is prohibiting its athletes from raising human-rights and other political issues in Beijing.

Economy, Elizabeth C., and Adam Segal, "China's Olympic Nightmare," *Foreign Affairs*, **July/August 2008, pp. 47-56.**
The Games have highlighted not only the "awesome achievements" of the current regime but also its "grave shortcomings."

Haddon, Katherine, "China Rights Abuses Worsening in Olympic Run-Up: Amnesty," Agence France-Presse, April 1, 2008.
China's crackdown on dissent prior to the Olympic Games has exacerbated its human-rights record.

Mooney, Paul, "Olympic Crackdown," *U.S. News & World Report*, **Feb. 25, 2008, p. 28.**
China is using the Olympics to showcase its political and economic strength to the world, not to improve its human-rights situation.

Press Freedom

Cody, Edward, "Chinese Editor Freed After 4 Years," *The Washington Post*, **Feb. 10, 2008, p. A17.**
A senior editor at a Chinese newspaper was released from prison after serving four years for corruption charges that journalists say were trumped up by officials in retaliation for aggressive reporting.

Cody, Edward, "One Year Out From Olympics, A Test of

Openness in Beijing," *The Washington Post*, **Aug. 7, 2007, p. A1.**
International human-rights groups have accused the Chinese government of reneging on promises of press freedom.

Lague, David, "China Frees a Journalist It Accused of Spying," *The New York Times*, **Feb. 6, 2008, p. A10.**
China has decided to release a Hong Kong journalist jailed on charges of spying on Taiwan after an international campaign called for his release.

Tibet

"A Lama in Sheep's Clothing?" *The Economist*, **May 10, 2008.**
China's attitude toward Tibet and its people is based on fear and distrust, according to the Dalai Lama.

Demick, Barbara, "Protests in Tibet Unnerve an Already Besieged China," *Los Angeles Times*, **March 13, 2008, p. A3.**
Pro-independence demonstrations in Tibet have rattled the Chinese government as it tries to contain growing criticism over its human-rights record.

Fimrite, Peter, "China Official Raps Western Media 'Bias' on Tibet," *The San Francisco Chronicle*, **May 1, 2008, p. B3.**
A Chinese consular official in San Francisco has lashed out at the Western media for taking the Dalai Lama's side on the Tibet issue.

Mahbubani, Kishore, "Tibet Through Chinese Eyes," *Newsweek International*, **May 5, 2008.**
Until the West starts trying to understand the Chinese perspective on Tibet, friction will continue to grow, and Tibetans themselves will be the biggest victims.

CITING *CQ RESEARCHER*

Sample formats for citing these reports in a bibliography include the ones listed below. Preferred styles and formats vary, so please check with your instructor or professor.

MLA STYLE
Jost, Kenneth. "Rethinking the Death Penalty." CQ Researcher 16 Nov. 2001: 945-68.

APA STYLE
Jost, K. (2001, November 16). Rethinking the death penalty. *CQ Researcher, 11*, 945-968.

CHICAGO STYLE
Jost, Kenneth. "Rethinking the Death Penalty." *CQ Researcher*, November 16, 2001, 945-968.

CRISIS IN DARFUR

BY KAREN FOERSTEL

Excerpted from the CQ Global Researcher. Karen Foerstel. (September 2008). "Crisis in Darfur." *CQ Global Researcher*, 243-270.

Crisis in Darfur

BY KAREN FOERSTEL

THE ISSUES

It was mid-afternoon when helicopters suddenly appeared and opened fire on the terrified residents of Sirba, in Western Darfur. Then hundreds of armed men riding horses and camels stormed the village, followed by 30 military vehicles mounted with weapons.

"The cars . . . were shooting at everyone, whether a woman, man or child," said Nada, one of the survivors. "They were shooting at us even when we were running away." [1]

Almost simultaneously, another attack was taking place a few miles away in the town of Abu Suruj. Witnesses say Sudanese soldiers and members of the notorious *janjaweed* militia shot people, set homes on fire and stole livestock. Many died in flames inside their huts. Three-quarters of the village was burned to the ground, as government planes bombed the town and surrounding hills where residents had fled for cover.

But that wasn't all. In a third nearby village, Silea, women and girls were raped and two-thirds of the town was destroyed by fire. Among the victims was Mariam, 35, who was shot as she tried to stop looters.

"They told me to leave and not to take anything, and then one of the men on a Toyota shot me, and I fell down," she said. Her father found her and took her by horse-drawn cart to a regional clinic. "I was pregnant with twins, and I lost them while we made the trip," she said. "I lost so much blood." [2]

In all, nearly 100 people were killed and 40,000 civilians driven from their homes in a single day, according to

Villages continue to be attacked and burned in Darfur by the notorious Arab janjaweed militia — aided by aerial bombing by the Sudanese government — despite a two-year-old peace agreement between the government and rebel groups. The prosecutor for the International Criminal Court recently said the government's "scorched earth" tactics amount to genocide, but others say there is insufficient evidence that civilians have been targeted because of their ethnicity.

Courtesy of Brian Steidle

Human Rights Watch (HRW), a global advocacy group. The Sudanese military said the strikes were in retaliation against the Justice and Equality Movement (JEM), an anti-government rebel group that had recently launched a military offensive in the region, attacking a police station, killing three civilians and detaining local officials.

While HRW criticized the rebels for operating around populated areas, it strongly condemned the Sudanese government for targeting civilians and using a "scorched earth" policy to clear the region and make it easier to go after JEM positions. [3]

Indeed, civilians have been targeted and terrorized throughout the long and

bloody fighting in Darfur between non-Arab rebel groups who want to overthrow the Sudanese government and government troops backed by Arabic *janjaweed* militias.* During the peak fighting between 2003 and 2005, from 200,000 to 400,000 people — mostly civilians — died from armed attacks as well as famine and disease. More than 2.4 million Sudanese — about a third of the population — have been forced to flee their homes since 2003; tens of thousands now live in refugee camps across the region. [4]

But the same-day attacks in the three villages did not occur during the period of peak fighting. They occurred on Feb. 8 of this year, nearly two years after rebels and the government signed the Darfur Peace Agreement (DPA) in May 2006.

The continuing conflict has sparked the world's largest humanitarian mission, with more than 17,000 aid workers now stationed in Darfur. [5] And the situation is deteriorating. Observers predict next year will be one of the worst ever.

Growing banditry and lawlessness have made much of Darfur — a region in western Sudan as large as France — inaccessible to aid workers. [6] Rising food prices, drought and a poor cereal harvest also are combining to form what Mike McDonagh, chief of the U.N. Office for Coordination of Humanitarian Affairs, described as a "perfect storm." [7]

---

* The word *janjaweed*, which means devil on a horse, is used to describe horsemen from the nomadic Arab tribes in Darfur that have been armed and supported by the Sudanese government.

Conflict Continues Despite Cease-Fire Accords

Darfur is an ethnically diverse area about the size of France in western Sudan — Africa's largest country. It has been wracked by decades of tension — and more recently open warfare — over land and grazing rights between the nomadic Arabs from the arid north and predominantly non-Arab Fur, Masalit and Zaghawa farmers in the more fertile south. A third of the region's 7 million people have been displaced by the conflict, which continues despite numerous cease-fire agreements. The United Nations has set up several camps inside Darfur and in neighboring Chad for those fleeing the violence.

Key:
— State boundaries
● Refugee camp
○ Camp for displaced persons

Sources: USAID satellite imagery, Aug. 13, 2007; United Nations Office for the Coordination of Humanitarian Affairs, June 2, 2008

Already, conditions are dire:

- In the first five months of this year, 180,000 Darfuris were driven from their homes. [8]
- More than 4.2 million people in Darfur now rely on humanitarian aid for food, water and medical care. [9]
- Attacks against aid workers have doubled since last year. [10] (*See chart, p. 253.*)
- The U.N. World Food Program was forced to cut its food rations in Darfur by 40 percent this year because of repeated attacks by armed gangs. [11]
- About 650,000 children — half of the region's children — do not receive any education. [12]

While attacks on civilians have decreased since the peace deal was signed, international watchdog groups say the drop has little to do with increased security. "A third of the population has been displaced, so the targets are fewer," says Selena Brewer, a researcher with Human Rights Watch. "But there are far more perpetrators."

The fighting between non-Arab rebels and the Arab-led government's forces — backed by the *janjaweed* — has morphed into all-out lawlessness. The two main rebel groups — the JEM and the Sudanese Liberation Army/Movement (SLA/M) — have splintered into more than a dozen factions that fight among themselves as much as against the government. Moreover, some disaffected *janjaweed* fighters have joined the rebels, and skirmishes between ethnic tribes are increasing. Bandits attack civilians, aid workers and international peacekeepers almost at will. [13]

"We no longer know who is attacking," says Denise Bell, a Darfur specialist with Amnesty International USA.

To make matters even more complicated, Darfur has become the staging ground for a proxy war between Sudan and its western neighbor Chad. The two governments support opposing groups in the region with the goal of launching coup attempts against one another. As arms pour into the area, civilians are the primary victims.

Many describe the conflict as Arabs vs. non-Arabs. "The *janjaweed* . . . would tell us that the black Africans were a lesser race and that they shouldn't be there . . . and that they would drive them out or kill them," said former U.S. Marine Capt. Brian Steidle, whose book about his six months as an unarmed military observer in Darfur was made into an award-winning documentary. [14]

But most observers say the situation is more complicated than that. Nearly all Darfuris speak Arabic, and nearly all are Muslims. Generations of intermarriage have resulted in little physical difference between the groups, and not all Arab tribes have joined the *janjaweed* while some Arab groups have even been targeted themselves — although most of the victims are from the non-Arab Fur, Masalit and Zaghawa ethnic groups.

But poverty, drought and the on-going conflict have led to increased tensions between Arab groups, who are mainly nomadic, and non-Arabs, who are mainly farmers, as they compete for dwindling land and water resources. [15] The Sudanese government is widely accused of doing all it can to inflame these historical tensions and grow support among its Arab political base in Darfur by arming and recruiting the *janjaweed* to clear the region of non-Arabs.

But most agree race has little to do with government motives. "It's all about divide to rule. It's just the government using one lot of poor people against another lot of poor people," says Gillian Lusk, associate editor of the London-based newsletter *Africa Confidential*. "It's not about ethnic supremacy. If the so-called Arabs don't help the government, it will kill them, too. It's just renting them."

Although Sudan says its attacks in Darfur comprise a "counterinsurgency" campaign, the prosecutor for the International Criminal Court (ICC) refuted that claim in July when he sought an indictment against Sudanese President Omar Hassan Al-Bashir for genocide and crimes against humanity. [16]

"The most efficient method to commit genocide today in front of our eyes is gang rapes, rapes against girls and rapes against 70-year old women," Chief ICC Prosecutor Luis Moreno-Ocampo said as he described the brutality of the war in Darfur. "Babies born as a result have been called

janjaweed babies, and this has led to an explosion of infanticide." In addition, he said, "Al-Bashir is executing this genocide without gas chambers, without bullets and without machetes. The desert will do it for them. . . . Hunger is the weapon of this genocide as well as rape." [17]

Many hope the prosecutor's action will pressure Sudan to halt its attacks in Darfur. But others fear an indictment would prompt Bashir to prevent

peacekeepers and Western aid organizations from working in Darfur.

"[An indictment] would have very serious consequences for peacekeeping operations, including the political process," U.N. Secretary-General Ban Ki-moon said. "I'm very worried. But nobody can evade justice." [18]

While the ICC is considering charging Bashir with genocide, many aid groups, governments and the United Nations have avoided using the "G-

Lack of Resources Hampers Peacekeepers

More than a year after the U.N. authorized the largest peacekeeping force in the world in Darfur, the joint U.N.-African Union (UNAMID) force has received only 37 percent of the nearly 32,000 military, police and civilian personnel that were authorized and 72 percent of the funds. Much of the force's equipment has been delayed by Sudanese customs, hijacked by bandits or simply not provided by international donors. For instance, by the end of May not a single military helicopter had been donated to the force.

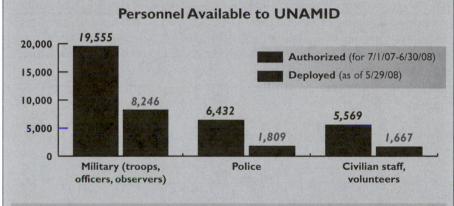

Personnel Available to UNAMID

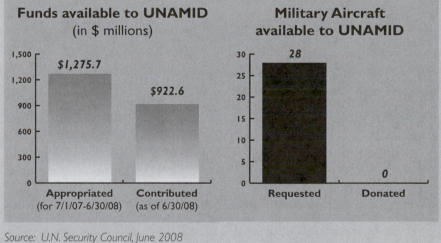

Funds available to UNAMID
(in $ millions)

Military Aircraft available to UNAMID

Source: U.N. Security Council, June 2008

word" to describe the situation in Darfur. Some say the reluctance stems from the fact that international law requires countries to take action to "prevent and punish" genocide. But others, including Amnesty International, say that despite the obvious atrocities, there is insufficient evidence civilians were targeted because of their ethnicity. [19]

The international community also disagrees on how to solve the crisis. While the United States and the United Nations have sanctioned the Bashir government, the move has largely been opposed by China, Russia, Arab nations and the African Union (AU) — a political and economic coalition of African countries.

cil, China repeatedly has used its veto threat to block action against Sudan. [20]

Over the past year, however, as the Beijing Olympics brought international attention to China's human-rights policies — its government has played a more active role in trying to solve the crisis. It appointed a special envoy to help negotiate a peace settlement and helped convince Sudan to allow a joint U.N.-African Union peacekeeping force — known as UNAMID — to enter Darfur. In July China sent 172 engineers to join the peacekeeping force, bringing China's participation in the mission to more than 300 personnel. [21]

Nearly a year into their mission, however, the force is severely un-

Darfur is "a test case for international response — or the inability of the international community to respond — to this type of situation," says Imani Countess, senior director for public affairs at TransAfrica Forum, which campaigns for human rights in Africa. "It's a damning indictment against the government of Sudan, because it refuses to end the violence. But it's also a pretty damning indictment of the international community."

And while the international community stands by, the situation in Darfur threatens to destabilize the entire region. Millions of refugees from the area are creating economic and political chaos in Sudan and neighboring countries, and the region's porous borders have turned Darfur into the headquarters for rebels from Chad and the Central African Republic.

The growing crisis also threatens to undo the precarious 2005 Comprehensive Peace Agreement (CPA) that ended the bloody 20-year civil war between North and South Sudan — Africa's longest civil war.

"A lot of attention has been diverted to Darfur," causing backsliding and insufficient funding for implementing the peace agreement, says Bell of Amnesty International. "Darfur threatens to overshadow the CPA. If the CPA falls, the country falls. The international community needs to be much more aware of that."

In June, Jan Eliasson — the U.N.'s special envoy to Darfur — resigned, blaming himself, the U.N. and the international community for not doing enough to bring peace to the region. He said attention has been too narrowly focused on Darfur alone and that a more comprehensive strategy — addressing the many tensions and conflicts across the region — must now be pursued.

"This simply cannot go on," Eliasson said. "A new generation in Sudan may be doomed to a life in conflict, despair and poverty. The international community should have learned

During a 2007 visit to Sudan, Chinese President Hu Jintao reviews Sudanese troops with President Omar Hassan al-Bashir. In the run-up to the Beijing Olympics this summer, China came under intense international pressure to use its economic clout as Sudan's biggest oil buyer and weapons supplier to convince Bashir to stop the slaughter in Darfur. Hu convinced Bashir to allow joint U.N.-African Union peacekeeping forces to enter Darfur, but critics say China could do much more.

AFP/Getty Images/Isam Al-Haj

"China is uniquely positioned to fix this," says Alex Meixner, director of government relations for the Save Darfur Coalition. "They have a fair amount of leverage over Bashir." China buys two-thirds of Sudan's petroleum — much of which comes from the south — and is its largest supplier of weapons. But as a member of the U.N.'s Security Coun-

dermanned, underequipped and under constant attack. Although authorized to have 26,000 military and police peacekeepers — the largest deployment in the world — fewer than half that number have been deployed and not a single military helicopter has been donated to the force. (See graph, p. 247.) [22]

enough lessons from other conflicts where the populations were left to stagnate and radicalize in camps." [23]

As the situation deteriorates in Darfur, these are some of the questions being asked:

Has genocide occurred in Darfur?

In July 2004, the U.S. Congress declared the violence in Darfur "genocide" and urged President George W. Bush to do the same. But for months afterward, Secretary of State Colin L. Powell studiously avoided using the word, on the advice of government lawyers.

Under the International Convention on the Prevention and Punishment of Genocide, any signatory country — including the United States — which determines that genocide is occurring must act to "prevent and punish" the genocide. However, while some believe the 1948 treaty requires military intervention to stop the killing, others believe economic sanctions alone are permitted. [24]

The Bush administration used the word to describe what is happening in Darfur only after religious groups launched a lobbying and media campaign condemning the Sudanese government for "genocide." In May 2004, the U.S. Holocaust Memorial Museum issued a "genocide alert" for Darfur, and two months later the American Jewish World Service and the Holocaust Museum founded the Save Darfur Coalition — an alliance of secular and religious groups calling for international intervention to halt the violence. [25] That August, 35 evangelical Christian leaders said genocide was occurring in Darfur and asked the administration to consider sending troops. [26]

A month later, Powell finally capitulated, telling the Senate Foreign Relations Committee, "We concluded — I concluded — that genocide has been committed in Darfur and that the government of Sudan and the *janjaweed* bear responsibility — and genocide may still be occurring." [27] Powell then called on the U.N. to take action for

Defying the Court

Surrounded by security guards, Sudanese President Omar Hassan al-Bashir (center, top), greets supporters in North Darfur just days after the chief prosecutor at the International Criminal Court accused him of masterminding genocide in the region. Bashir dismissed the accusations as lies and vowed not to cooperate with the court. Soon after the accusation, the Sudanese government convicted and sentenced to death more than three dozen rebels — including these prisoners — in connection with a daring attack last May on Khartoum, the capital, in which more than 200 people were killed.

the "prevention and suppression of acts of genocide." [28] A week later, the United States pushed a resolution through the General Assembly threatening Sudan with economic sanctions if it did not protect civilians in Darfur. [29]

But most other governments and international humanitarian groups — including Amnesty International — say genocidal intent has not been proven.

"There is a legal definition of genocide, and Darfur does not meet that

Climate Change Blamed for Darfur Conflict

Nomads and farmers battle for scarce water and arable land.

For generations, Arab nomads in Darfur enjoyed a symbiotic relationship with their farming non-Arab neighbors. As the seasons changed, the nomads would bring their livestock from the arid north to the greener lands to the south during the dry season and then lead them back north during the rainy season. The non-Arabs, who came from several different ethnic groups, would allow the nomads to graze camels, sheep and goats on their farmlands, and in exchange the livestock would provide fertilizer for the farmers' crops. [1]

That relationship, however, began to change about 75 years ago. And today, what had once been a convenient alliance between nomads and farmers has exploded into a bloody war between Darfur's Arabs and ethnic African tribes.

While many blame the bloodshed on political or ethnic divisions, others say climate change lies at the root of the devastation. "It is no accident that the violence in Darfur erupted during the drought," U.N. Secretary-General Ban Ki-moon said. "Until then, Arab nomadic herders had lived amicably with settled farmers." [2]

Most people use "a convenient military and political shorthand" to describe Darfur as an ethnic conflict between Arab militias fighting black rebels and farmers, Ban explained. And, while the conflict involves a complex set of social and political causes, it "began as an ecological crisis, arising at least in part from climate change," he said.

According to the U. N., average precipitation in Sudan has declined 40 percent since the early 1980s. [3] Signs of desertification began emerging as far back as the 1930s. A lake in El-Fashir in northern Darfur reached its lowest water level in 1938, after which wells had to be drilled to tap into underground water supplies. Villages in northern Darfur increasingly were evacuated because of disappearing water supplies. [4]

In the 1980s a severe drought and famine made the northern areas nearly impossible to cultivate, forcing nomadic tribes to migrate even further south and increasingly encroach upon their farming neighbors' more fertile lands. [5] To prevent damage from the nomad's passing herds, the farmers began to fence off their shrinking fertile plots. Violent land disputes grew more and more common.

"Interestingly, most of the Arab tribes who have their own land rights did not join the government's fight," said David Mozersky, the International Crisis Group's project director for the Horn of Africa. [6]

A new report by the European Commission predicts that increasing drought and land overuse in North Africa and the Sahel — the semi-arid swath of land stretching from the Atlantic Ocean to the Horn of Africa — could destroy 75 percent of the region's arable land. As land and water resources disappear, the report said, such violent conflicts will increase around the world. [7]

"Already today, climate change is having a major impact on the conflict in and around Darfur," the report said. [8]

Economist Jeffrey Sachs, director of the Earth Institute at Columbia University, said Darfur is an example of the conflicts that increasingly will erupt because of climate change.

"What some regard as the arc of Islamic instability, across the Sahel, the Horn of Africa, Yemen, Iraq, Pakistan and Afghanistan, is more accurately an arc of hunger, population pressures, water stress, growing food insecurity and a pervasive lack of jobs," Sachs wrote earlier this year, using Darfur as an example of a conflict sparked by climate change. [9]

But others say climate change is just an excuse used by the Sudanese government to relieve itself of responsibility. Politics is the real cause of the bloodshed in Darfur, many say, with President Omar Hassan al-Bashir's government bearing full blame for the ongoing violence.

"Jeffrey Sachs and Ban Ki-moon said it's essentially environmental. How dare they?" says Gillian Lusk, associate editor of the London-based newsletter *Africa Confidential.* "The essential issue is the Sudan government went in there and killed people." And any attempts "to turn it into a primary ethnic or environment issue are dangerous."

Still, many international leaders say Darfur is a warning sign of growing environmental degradation. "Climate change is already having a considerable impact on security," French President Nicolas Sarkozy told an international governmental conference in April. "If we keep going down this path, climate change will encourage the immigration of people with nothing towards areas where the population does have something, and the Darfur crisis will be only one crisis among dozens." [10]

[1] Stephan Faris, "The Real Roots of Darfur," *The Atlantic,* April 2007, www.theatlantic.com/doc/200704/darfur-climate.

[2] Ban Ki-moon, "A Climate Culprit in Darfur," *The Washington Post,* June 16, 2007, p. A15.

[3] *Ibid.*

[4] M. W. Daly, *Darfur's Sorrow* (2007), pp. 141-142.

[5] Gerard Prunier, *Darfur: The Ambiguous Genocide* (2005), pp. 49-50.

[6] Faris, *op. cit.*

[7] "Climate Change and International Security," The High Representative and the European Commission, March 14, 2008, p. 6, http://ec.europa.eu/external_relations/cfsp/doc/climate_change_international_security_2008_en.pdf.

[8] *Ibid.*

[9] Jeffrey Sachs, "Land, Water and Conflict," *Newsweek,* July 14, 2008.

[10] "Climate change driving Darfur crisis: Sarkozy," Agence France-Presse, April 18, 2008, http://afp.google.com/article/ALeqM5h7l_NjlMjZF-QWDOwxIbibX5AeuA.

legal standard," former President Jimmy Carter said last year. "The atrocities were horrible, but I don't think it qualifies to be called genocide. If you read the law textbooks . . . you'll see very clearly that it's not genocide, and to call it genocide falsely just to exaggerate a horrible situation — I don't think it helps." [30]

Not surprisingly, Sudan denies targeting ethnic groups in Darfur, instead blaming the massive deaths on tribal conflict, water disputes and collateral military damage. "We do not deny that atrocities have taken place," says Khalid al-Mubarak, a media counselor at the Sudanese Embassy in London. "We do deny that they have been planned or systematic. They happened in an area out of reach of the central government. The government could not have planned or controlled it."

A U.N. commission investigating the conflict also said genocidal intent has not been proven, but it did say Sudanese forces working with *janjaweed* militias had "conducted indiscriminate attacks, including killing of civilians, torture, enforced disappearances, destruction of villages, rape and other forms of sexual violence, pillaging and forced displacement." [31]

"I don't think it matters [whether you call it genocide or not]," says *Africa Confidential's* Lusk. "In terms of legitimizing intervention, it might be important. But no one wants to get involved anyway."

In a joint statement in May, the three leading American presidential candidates at the time — Sens. Barack Obama, D-Ill., Hillary Rodham Clinton, D-N.Y., and John McCain, R-Ariz., — called the situation in Darfur "genocide" and promised, if elected, to intervene. [32]

Some other U.S. politicians — including Democratic vice presidential nominee and Foreign Relations Committee Chairman Sen. Joseph R. Biden, of Delaware — have called for military intervention to halt the mass killings. [33] Susan Rice, a foreign policy adviser to Obama, has called for legislation authorizing the use of force. [34]

But experts say the international backlash against the Iraq War — including the abuse of Muslim prisoners at Abu Ghraib prison by U.S. soldiers — makes intervention in another Muslim country unlikely any-

time soon, whether the word genocide is used or not. "Sudan can say all this 'genocide' stuff is a conspiracy to steal [their] oil," says Peter Moszynski, a writer and aid worker with 25 years of experience in Sudan. "With the Iraq backlash, Bashir became bulletproof."

Sudan is Africa's fifth-largest oil producer, with proven reserves of 5 billion barrels. Experts say in the next few years Sudan's daily production could reach 700,000 barrels — enough for nearly 30 million gallons of gasoline a day — about 10 percent of U.S. daily needs. [35]

The United States is also in the awkward position of balancing its national-security interests against calls to end the genocide. Since the Sept. 11, 2001, terrorist attacks in the United States, Sudanese officials have worked closely with the CIA and other intelligence agencies to provide information on suspected terrorists. Although Sudan is on the U.S. list of "state sponsors of terrorism," a 2007 State Department report called Sudan "a strong partner in the War on Terror." [36]

"I am not happy at all about the U.S. working with Sudan," says El-Tahir El-Faki, speaker of the JEM legislative assembly. "Definitely it is genocide in Darfur. They are targeting ethnic people with the aim of eliminating people. . . . It will be contrary to American interest supporting a government that is killing people."

Regardless of what the violence is called, most agree the label is meaningless if nothing is done to stop the killing. "It's like walking down the street and you see someone being beaten up. You don't stop and think whether it's bodily harm or not. You stop and help and let the lawyers figure out the legal side later," says. James Smith, head of the Aegis Trust, a British group that works to halt genocide. "Stopping genocide is more of a political and moral question than a legal one."

"The legal framework exists to prevent or mitigate genocide if the political will is sufficient," he continues. "However, politicians and diplomats create legal ambiguity to mask their disinterest in protecting lives in certain far-away countries."

Would arresting Sudanese President Bashir do more harm than good?

In July, when he asked the International Criminal Court to charge Bashir with genocide and other war crimes, the ICC prosecutor cast aside all the debate over how to label the violence in Darfur. Bashir's motives were "largely political," ICC prosecutor Luis Moreno-Ocampo said. "His pretext was a 'counterinsurgency.' His intent was genocide. . . . He is the mastermind behind the alleged crimes. He has absolute control." [37]

The court is expected to decide this fall whether to accept the charges and issue an arrest warrant. Many heralded the prosecutor's unprecedented request — the first genocide indictment sought for a sitting head of state — as a critical first step to peace in Darfur.

"Darfur has had very little justice of any kind. They've been let down by the African Union, by the U.N. peacekeeping force, by other countries," says *Africa Confidential's* Lusk. "It's about time a small sign of justice appeared on the horizon. Impunity has reigned for 19 years. This action says this is not a respectable government."

But others fear an indictment could spark reprisal attacks against foreign peacekeepers and aid workers by the Sudanese government and could block a peace settlement. Sudan's U.N. ambassador, Abdalmahmood Abdalhaleem Mohamad, said the charges would "destroy" efforts towards a peace agreement in Darfur. "Ocampo is playing with fire," he said. "If the United Nations is serious about its engagement with Sudan, it should tell this man to suspend what he is doing with this so-called indictment. There will be grave repercussions." [38]

Sudanese officials said that while they would not retaliate with violence, they could not guarantee the safety of any individual. "The U.N. asks us to keep its people safe, but how can we guarantee their safety when they want

staff and cut back on operations that could endanger civilian staff. [41]

Meanwhile, the African Union (AU), the Arab League and others asked the U.N. to delay the ICC legal action, which some say could be used as a bargaining chip to force Bashir to end the killing. "We are asking that the ICC indictment be deferred to give peace a chance,"

Former U.S. Special Envoy for Sudan Andrew Natsios agrees an indictment could derail peace negotiations and make it impossible to hold free and fair elections, scheduled next year. "The regime will now avoid any compromise or anything that would weaken their already weakened position, because if they are forced from office they'll face trials before the ICC," Natsios wrote. "This indictment may well shut off the last remaining hope for a peaceful settlement for the country." [44]

The United States — which, like Sudan, has never ratified the treaty creating the ICC — nevertheless said Sudan must comply with the ICC. But the U.S. envoy to the United Nations has been vague on whether the United States would support a deferral. "We haven't seen anything at this point that could have the support of the United States," said U.S. Ambassador to the United Nations Zalmay Khalilzad. "We certainly do not support impunity for crimes."

But he added, "As you know also, we're not a member of the ICC. So there are various factors in play here. And as I said, I don't see any action on this in the council that would provide impunity anytime in the foreseeable future." [45]

Others point out that efforts to solve the crises diplomatically were faltering long before the ICC prosecutor's recommendations. "The process hasn't gotten anywhere," says veteran aid worker Moszynski. "If we're going to say 'never again,' we've got to do it. Someone must be held accountable.

In any case, he added, the pending ICC charges — and potential indictments — have turned Bashir into an international "pariah," making it nearly impossible for him to play any leadership role on the international stage.

After years of fighting the Sudanese government, rebels in Darfur — like these from the Sudanese Liberation Army/Movement (SLA/M) — have splintered into more than a dozen factions that fight among themselves as much as against the government. Meanwhile, bandits are attacking civilians, aid workers and international peacekeepers almost at will, contributing to rampant lawlessness in the region.

Lynsey Addario

to seize our head of state?" asked Deputy Parliament Speaker Mohammed al-Hassan al-Ameen. [39]

The Sudanese government, which refused to hand over two other officials indicted for war crimes last year by the ICC, said it would not cooperate with the ICC's latest efforts either.

The United Nations evacuated staff from the region shortly after Ocampo made his announcement. [40] Representatives from the five permanent members of the U.N. Security Council — Britain, China, France, Russia and the United States — met with U.N. officials to discuss the safety of the peacekeeping force in Darfur, which evacuated non-essential

Nigerian Foreign Affairs Minister Ojo Maduekwe said after an emergency meeting on the issue by the African Union's Peace and Security Council in July. China and Russia also support deferring ICC action. [42]

Others fear the request for delay could produce its own backlash — among the rebels. Leaders of JEM and one of the SLA's factions said they will no longer recognize AU efforts to mediate peace because of its request for a deferral. "The African Union is a biased organization and is protecting dictators and neglecting the African people," said Khalil Ibrahim, president of JEM. [43]

Is China blocking peace in Darfur?

In the year leading up to the Beijing Olympics, U.S. government leaders, human-rights activists and Hollywood's elite used the international sporting event as a platform to criticize China's policy toward Darfur.

China is Sudan's biggest trading partner, weapons supplier and oil-industry investor. It has built a 957-mile-long pipeline in Sudan — one the largest foreign oil projects in China's history. It also has constructed three arms factories in Sudan and provided small arms, anti-personnel mines, howitzers, tanks, helicopters and ammunition. China also has done more than any other country to protect Khartoum from U.N. sanctions. [46]

China "potentially has the most influence with Sudan," says Amnesty International's Bell. "People who are the main [economic] players are able to dictate the rate of progress that is made."

American actress Mia Farrow last year branded the Beijing Olympics the "Genocide Olympics," and Hollywood producer Steven Spielberg stepped down as one of the event's artistic advisers, citing the ongoing violence in Darfur. [47] Last May, a bipartisan group of 108 members of Congress warned the Chinese government that if China did not pressure Sudan to do more to help Darfur, protests and boycotts could destroy the Olympics.

"[We] urge you to protect your country's image from being irredeemably tarnished, through association with a genocidal regime, for the purpose of economic gains," the group wrote. "[U]nless China does its part to ensure that the government of Sudan accepts the best and most reasonable path to peace, history will judge your government as having bankrolled a genocide." [48]

The day after the letter was sent, China appointed a special envoy for Darfur and since then has made several moves to mitigate the crisis. [49] In addition to sending 315 engineers to join the UNAMID peacekeeping force to build roads, bridges and wells, China last May donated more than $5 million in humanitarian aid and in February handed over a $2.8 million package of financial and development aid. [50] According to

Aid Workers Face Danger

Eight humanitarian workers in Darfur were killed and 117 kidnapped within the first five months of 2008. Rising lawlessness has made parts of Darfur inaccessible to the 17,000 aid workers stationed in Darfur to help the more than 4 million people affected by the ongoing fighting between government and rebel forces, militia attacks and inter-tribal fighting.

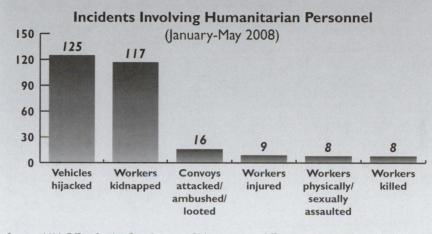

Incidents Involving Humanitarian Personnel
(January-May 2008)

Vehicles hijacked	Workers kidnapped	Convoys attacked/ ambushed/ looted	Workers injured	Workers physically/ sexually assaulted	Workers killed
125	117	16	9	8	8

Source: U.N. Office for the Coordination of Humanitarian Affairs

China's official news agency, China has given a total of $11 million in humanitarian aid to Darfur, and Chinese companies have spent about $50 million on development projects in the region, including 53 miles of water pipelines. [51]

"We have done as much as we can," said China's assistant foreign minister Zhai Jun. "China remains committed to resolving the Darfur issue and has made unremitting efforts." [52]

But many say China could do much more, and that its millions of dollars in arms sales to Sudan feed the continuing violence. "They've taken some action, but not nearly enough," says Meixner of the Save Darfur Coalition. "They sent engineers to UNAMID, but they're kind of milking that. I look at that as China's having kept these engineers in their back pocket until right before the Olympics."

More meaningful, he says, would be an immediate halt or reduction in China's arms sales to Sudan. According to Amnesty International, China sold Sudan $24 million worth of arms and am-

munition in 2005, plus $59 million worth of parts and aircraft equipment. [53]

In March 2005, the U.N. banned the sale of weapons to any combatants for use in Darfur. [54] But earlier this year the BBC reported that China had been providing trucks being used by the Sudanese military in Darfur. China admitted that 212 trucks were exported to Sudan in 2005 but said all were for civilian use and were only later equipped with guns in a defensive move by the government to stave off rebel attacks. [55]

"The Western media and in particular the activities of some nongovernmental organizations have caused China's role to be distorted," said China's Special Envoy to Darfur, Liu Guijin. [56]

China, which repeatedly has opposed or abstained from U.N. votes to sanction or condemn Sudan's actions in Darfur, says diplomacy and humanitarian support are the best path to peace. It has expressed "great concern" over the ICC prosecutor's request for an arrest warrant against Bashir and is considering supporting an effort to delay further action by the court. [57]

Some say such "subtle diplomacy" has persuaded Sudan to reduce military attacks in Darfur and improved conditions for civilians. Former U.S. Envoy Natsios told a Senate hearing last year that Beijing complemented rather than undercut Washington's sanctions-based policy and said China had convinced Sudan to accept UNAMID peacekeepers. "There has been a lot of China-bashing in the West, and I'm not sure, to be very frank with you, that . . . it's very helpful," he told the committee. [58]

Others say that while China is a powerful player in Sudanese affairs, Beijing alone cannot be blamed for the continuing violence. "The finger is pointed first at the Sudan government, and then China . . . and then many other countries," says *Africa Confidential's* Lusk.

John Prendergast, co-chair of the anti-genocide ENOUGH Project, agreed. "Unless China and the U.S. are both exerting much more pressure on Sudan, the crisis will continue to spiral out of control," he said. "China has unique economic leverage, while the U.S. retains leverage based on its ability to confer or withdraw legitimacy." [59] ■

BACKGROUND

Ostrich Feathers, Ivory and Slaves

The name Darfur comes from the Arabic word "dar," meaning home, and the name of the principal ethnic group of the region, the non-Arab Fur. For centuries, however, Darfur has been home to a wide range of people — both Arab and non-Arab. Darfur is at the crossroads of Africa and the Middle East, and Islamic traders as well as pilgrims traveling to Mecca have long traversed the province — leaving their cultural and religious imprint. [60] Today, around 90 percent of all Darfuris are Muslim. [61] After generations of intermarriage between Arabs and non-Arabs, it is nearly impossible to discern the ethnic ancestry of the people of Darfur, other than through cultural traditions: "Arabs" tend to be nomadic and "non-Arabs" tend to be farmers. Blurring the lines even further, it is not uncommon for people to call themselves Arab one day and non-Arab another. [62]

Around 1650, a Fur sultanate was established, and the region became a prosperous trading center for such goods as ostrich feathers, ivory and black slaves. [63] Over the next two centuries, the sultanate spread across 80 percent of the area known today as Darfur, encompassing 40 to 90 different ethnic groups or tribes. [64] The sultanate was considered one of the region's most powerful kingdoms, wholly separate in culture and heritage from the rest of modern-day Sudan.

In 1899, Egypt and Britain — which had occupied Egypt since 1882 — assumed joint authority over Sudan with the British taking the South and Egyptians taking the North. Even before Sudan came under joint control, Egyptian rulers had for decades occupied northern Sudan, amassing great wealth, largely from kidnapping black Africans from the South and selling them into slavery. Southern resentment against the North for the brutal slave trade remains today. [65]

Sudan's division between Britain and Egypt set the stage for the clashing cultures and religions that would later lead to the Sudanese civil war that raged for more than 20 years. The Egyptian North — with a higher concentration of Arabic population — was predominantly Islamic, while those in the South were animists or Christians. British missionaries were dispatched to spread the Christian faith in the South.

In 1916, Darfur was annexed by Sudan, merging two states with vastly different cultures and political structures. [66] "There was the problem of differential integration: Darfur is not the Sudan," says Gerard Prunier, author of the book *Darfur: The Ambiguous Genocide*. "Darfur was the easternmost sultanate in Africa, not part of the Nile Valley" as is the rest of Sudan.

And the colonial authorities did nothing to help integrate Darfur into their new state, largely ignoring the former sultanate and giving various tribes semi-autonomous rule over their individual lands. But tribal leaders were often illiterate and corrupt and did little to help Darfur. By 1935, only four government primary schools existed in all of Darfur. [67] Health care and economic development also were nonexistent under the colonial rulers, who actually boasted of keeping Darfur poor and powerless.

"We have been able to limit education to the sons of chiefs and native administration personnel," wrote Philip Ingleson, governor of Darfur from 1935 to 1944, "and we can confidently look forward to keeping the ruling classes at the top of the educational tree for many years to come." [68]

Independence and Instability

After World War II, Britain began withdrawing from Sudan and reconnecting the North and South. The British handed power over to northern Arab elites in Khartoum, which became the center of government. [69] Once again, Darfur was ignored.

"Darfur had no say whatsoever over the structure or features of an independent Sudan," Prunier says.

In fact, much of the conflict in Darfur has its roots in the post-independence history of eastern Sudan, which involved a long-running civil war between the

Continued on p. 256

Chronology

1899-1956
Colonization sows seeds of poverty and division.

1899
Britain takes control of mostly Christian southern Sudan; Egypt takes the predominantly Muslim north.

1916
Sudan annexes Darfur.

1956
Britain and Egypt turn control of Sudan over to northern Arab elites.

———— • ————

1957-Early '70s
Multiple coups switch control of Sudan between military and civilian governments; Darfur remains neglected as civil war rages in the east.

1964
Civilians overthrow Sudan's military government.

1965
Chadian fighters establish bases in Darfur after civil war breaks out in neighboring Chad.

1969
Gen. Jaafar al-Nimeiri takes control of Sudan in military coup.

1972
Sudan's civil war ends when peace agreement is signed in Addis Ababa.

———— • ————

Late '70s-'80s
Darfur serves as staging ground for Chadian rebels; Libya arms Darfuri rebels; rising Islamic extremism sparks renewed civil war in eastern Sudan; famine and drought devastate Darfur.

1976
Libyan-backed Darfuri rebels attack Khartoum, are defeated. Government tracks down and kills alleged sympathizers in Darfur.

1983
Nimeiri imposes sharia law and nullifies peace agreement, triggering new civil war in eastern Sudan.

1984
Drought devastates Darfur; Arabs and non-Arabs fight over land, water.

1985
Civilian uprising overthrows Nimeiri.

———— • ————

1989-1999
Civil war intensifies; U.S.-Sudanese tensions increase.

1989
Gen. Omar Hassan al-Bashir seizes power, embraces militant Islam and hosts al Qaeda's Osama bin Laden.

1993
U.S. lists Sudan as a state sponsor of terrorism.

1996
Sudan expels bin Laden under U.S. pressure.

1997
China agrees to build oil refinery in Khartoum, becomes Sudan's leading weapons supplier.

1998
U.S. bombs Khartoum pharmaceutical factory, claiming it produces chemical weapons, which is never proven.

2000-2005
War breaks out in Darfur. U.S. says genocide is occurring in Darfur. Civil war in eastern Sudan ends.

2001
President George W. Bush appoints former Sen. John C. Danforth, R-Mo., as special envoy to Sudan to try to settle the civil war.

2003
Darfur rebels attack North Darfur's capital, marking start of war in Darfur. A cease-fire is reached in the civil war between northern and southern Sudan.

2004
U.S. House of Representatives labels the fighting in Darfur as "genocide." . . . U.N. imposes arms embargo on Darfur and endorses deployment of African Union (AU) peacekeepers.

2005
Sudan's 20-year civil war in the east ends with signing of peace accord.

———— • ————

2006-Present
Darfuri peace deal dissolves; rebel groups splinter; peacekeepers fail to control chaos.

2006
Darfur Peace Agreement is signed by government and one rebel group.

2007
U.N. creates joint U.N.-AU peacekeeping force.

2008
During run-up to Beijing Olympics, human-rights activists accuse China of abetting genocide in Darfur. . . . International Criminal Court considers indicting Bashir for genocide and war crimes.

Continued from p. 254

Arab- and Muslim-dominated North and the oil-rich, Christian and animist South. Darfur also became a political pawn in strategic maneuverings by Sudan, Chad and Libya, with each country arming rebel groups in the region to further their parochial interests.

Within months of Sudan's independence in January 1956, the consolidation of power in the Arab North sparked rebellion in the South. Over the next 10 years, a series of political coups alternated the government in Khartoum between military and civilian power, as civil war continued between the North and the South. Yet successive administrations continued to ignore growing poverty and dissent in Darfur. In 1972 the military government of Gen. Jaafar Nimeiri signed a peace agreement in Addis Ababa, Ethiopia, providing substantial power- and wealth-sharing between the North and South but offering nothing to the Darfuris.

However, the North-South tensions remained, and growing conflict in neighboring Chad created even more instability in Sudan. Arab rebels from Chad who opposed their country's Christian government used Darfur as a home base for their own civil war. Libyan leader Muammar Qaddafi — hoping to create a powerful Arab belt stretching into central Africa — supported the Chadian rebels and proposed a unified Arab state between Libya and Sudan, but Nimeiri rejected the offer. Angered by Nimeiri's rejection and Sudan's agreement to end the civil war with the Christians in South Sudan, Qaddafi labeled Nimeiri a traitor to the Arab cause and began arming militant Arab organizations in Darfur who opposed the governments of both Chad and Sudan.

In 1976, Libyan-backed rebels attacked Nimeiri's government in Khartoum but were defeated in three days. The Sudanese military then hunted down and killed Darfuri civilians accused of sympathizing with the insurgents. [70]

Suddenly, after years of neglect,

Arabs Criticized for Silence on Atrocities

Islamic countries also lag in donations, troop support.

The thin, white-haired man living in a U.N. refugee camp in Chad was soft-spoken but fervent as he thanked Americans "and the free world" for the food, medicine and other donations sent to the victims of the conflict in Darfur.

But, he asked a visiting filmmaker intently, tears trickling down his face, "Where are the Arab people? I am Muslim. We receive nothing from Islamic people." [1]

While nations around the world have criticized the Arab-dominated Sudanese government for not halting the rapes and murders of Muslims in the beleaguered region, other Arab governments have been largely silent about the atrocities being committed against Muslims by other Muslims.

"The Islamic world's response to the daily killings and suffering of millions of Muslims in Darfur has been largely silent — from both civil society as well as the institutions and majority of Islamic governments," said the newly formed Arab Coalition for Darfur, representing human-rights groups from 12 Muslim countries. "The Islamic world must decide to end its wall of silence, before it is too late." [2] The coalition made its statement in June before the Organization of the Islamic Conference, an intergovernmental organization of 57 Muslim nations.

Moreover, among the world's Arab governments — many of them awash in petrodollars — only the United Arab Emirates (UAE) earmarked any money ($100,000) specifically for aid to Darfur this year.* The rest of the international community donated more than $100 million, according to ReliefWeb, run by the U.N. Office for the Coordination of Humanitarian Affairs, including $28 million from the European Commission and $12 million from the United States. [3]

Moreover, only 587 of the 12,000 U.N. peacekeepers in Darfur have come from nations belonging to the 22-member Arab League. Of those, 508 were from Egypt, and the rest came from Jordan, Mauritania, Yemen and Libya. [4]

Amjad Atallah, senior director for international policy and advocacy with the Save Darfur Coalition, charges that the Arab League is more worried about protecting Arab leaders than about representing ordinary Arabs. "They seem to have a more compelling need to come to the defense of Arab states than for the people suffering under the regimes," says Atallah.

For its part, the Arab League did help convince Sudan to allow peacekeepers from the joint U.N.-AU peacekeeping mission into Darfur. And in 2004, an Arab League Commission of Inquiry into Darfur publicly condemned military attacks against civilians as "massive violations of human rights." But after Sudan complained, the statement was removed from the Arab League Web site. [5]

And in July, when the International Criminal Court prosecutor sought to indict Sudanese President Omar Hassan al-Bashir for genocide and war crimes, the Arab League expressed "solidarity with the Republic of Sudan in confronting schemes that undermine its sovereignty, unity and stability." The group said the charges would undermine ongoing negotiations to stop the violence in Darfur, and that Sudan's legal system was the appropriate place to investigate abuses in Darfur. [6] The league

---

* The UAE and Saudi Arabia, however, did contribute a total of $44 million to Sudan as a whole — about 3 percent of the $1.3 billion contributed to Sudan by the international community.

turned down several requests to be interviewed for this article.

While Arab governments have been muted in their criticism of the situation in Darfur, the citizens of Arab countries are more outspoken. According to a poll last year, a vast majority of the public in Morocco, Egypt, Saudi Arabia, the UAE, Turkey and Malaysia think their countries should do more to help Darfur. And more than three-quarters of the Muslim respondents said Arabs and Muslims should be as concerned about the situation in Darfur as they are about the Arab-Israeli conflict.

"The poll shatters the myth that Arabs and Muslims don't care about Darfur," said James Zogby, president of the Arab American Institute, which commissioned the poll. "While they fault news coverage for not being extensive enough, Arabs and Muslims feel compelled by the images and stories they see coming out of Darfur. The poll clearly illustrates a great degree of concern among Muslims, even rivaling that of another longstanding issue to Arabs and Muslims, the Arab-Israel conflict." [7]

Last year, the institute launched an Arabic-language television advertising campaign calling for increased action to help the people of Darfur. The commercial, which featured first-hand accounts in Arabic from victims of the violence in Darfur, concluded by saying, "Palestine, Lebanon, Iraq — Darfur. We must pray for them all." [8]

Darfuri refugees pray at an improvised mosque in a refugee camp in Chad. Arab governments have been largely silent about the Muslim-on-Muslim violence in Darfur and have contributed little aid to the victims.

[1] Quoted from "The Devil Came on Horseback" documentary film, Break Thru Films, 2007.

[2] "Arab Panel Scolds Islamic World for Darfur Silence," Agence France-Presse, June 20, 2008, http://news.yahoo.com/s/afp/20080620/wl_mideast_afp/sudandarfurunrestrightsislamoic_080620190222. The coalition represents human rights groups from Egypt, Jordan, Bahrain, Algeria, Iraq, Yemen, Syria, Libya, Mauritania, Kuwait, Saudi Arabia and the Palestinian territories.

[3] "Sudan 2008: List of all commitments/contributions and pledges as of 18 August 2008," U.N. Office for the Coordination of Humanitarian Affairs, http://ocha.unog.ch/fts/reports/daily/ocha_R10_E15391_asof__08081816.pdf.

[4] "UN Mission's Contributions by Country," United Nations, June 2008, www.un.org/Depts/dpko/dpko/contributors/2008/jun08_5.pdf.

[5] Nadim Hasbani, "About The Arab Stance Vis-à-vis Darfur," Al-Hayat, March 21, 2007, International Crisis Group, www.crisisgroup.org/home/index.cfm?id=4722.

[6] "Arab League Backs Sudan on Genocide Charges," The Associated Press, July 19, 2008, http://www.usatoday.com/news/world/2008-07-19-Sudan_N.htm.

[7] "Majorities in six countries surveyed believe Muslims should be equally concerned about Darfur as the Arab-Israeli conflict," Arab American Institute, press release, April 30, 2007, www.aaiusa.org/press-room/2949/aaizogby-poll-muslims-across-globe-concerned-about-crisis-in-darfur.

[8] "AAI Launches Darfur Ads Aimed at Arabic-Speaking International Community," Arab American Institute, press release, Jan. 8, 2007, www.aaiusa.org/press-room/2702/aai-launches-darfur-ads-aimed-at-arabic-speaking-international-community.

Darfur was getting the attention of Sudan's political leaders — but not the kind it had wanted. The ongoing violence also catapulted Darfur's various local tribes into the broader polarized conflict between "Arabs" and "non-Arabs," depending on which regime they supported. [71]

Making matters worse, a drought and famine in the early 1980s plunged Darfur deeper into poverty and desperation. For the next two decades, the nomadic "Arabs" and the farming "non-Arabs" increasingly fought over disappearing land and water resources. (See sidebar, p. 250.) The Arab-led government in Khartoum frequently intervened, providing arms to its nomadic Arab political supporters in Darfur, who in turn killed their farming neighbors. [72]

Another Civil War

After the failed coup by Libyan-backed Arab rebels in 1976, Nimeiri tried to appease radical Islamic groups who felt he was disloyal to the dream of a united Arab front. He named leading Islamist opposition leaders to important government posts, including extremist Hassan al-Turabi as attorney general. [73]

The discovery of oil in Southern Sudan in the late 1970s added to the pressure from the increasingly Islamic government to back away from the Addis Ababa peace agreement, because the Arab authorities in the North did not want to share the profits with the Christian South, as the peace deal stipulated. In 1983, Nimeiri ordered the 11-year-old agreement null and void, began imposing strict Islamic law, or sharia, across the country and transformed Sudan into an Islamic state. [74] Southern opposition groups formed the Sudan People's Liberation Army (SPLA) and civil war broke out again.

In 1985 civilians overthrew Nimeiri, and hopes began to emerge for a new peace settlement. But in yet another coup in 1989, Bashir seized power with the help of the National Islamic Front (NIF) and its leader, former Attorney General Turabi. [75]

Then-Gen. Bashir and the NIF embraced militant Islam and welcomed foreign jihadists, including Osama bin Laden. In 1993, the United States added Sudan to its list of state sponsors of terrorism,

Throughout the war, China sold arms to Sudan, and in 1997 China — whose domestic oil-production capacity had peaked — agreed to build an oil refinery near Khartoum and a massive pipeline from southern Sudan to Port Sudan on the Red Sea in the north. [78] Bashir declared that the "era of oil production" had begun in Sudan

wanted to achieve our aims by democratic and peaceful means," said Idris Mahmoud Logma, one of authors and a member of the rebel Justice and Equality Movement. "Later, we realized the regime would only listen to guns." [80]

But international attention remained focused on peace prospects between the North and South, overshadowing the book's impact. The first peace talks began in Nairobi, Kenya, in January 2000. At about the same time, Bashir pushed his former ally, the radical Islamist Turabi, out of power — a move away from religious extremism in the view of the international community. [81]

Human-rights advocates in London call on the international community to stop the violence in Darfur. The conflict erupted in 2003, when ethnic Africans in western Sudan took up arms against the central government in Khartoum, accusing it of marginalizing them and monopolizing resources.

Getty Images/Cate Gillon

and President Bill Clinton imposed economic sanctions against Sudan in 1996 and 1997. In 1998, after U.S. embassies were bombed in Kenya and Tanzania, the United States bombed a Khartoum pharmaceutical factory claiming it was producing chemical weapons. The allegation was never proven. [76]

Meanwhile, Bashir and the NIF launched a bloody counterinsurgency against the South, which became one of the deadliest wars in modern history. An estimated 2 million people died before the fighting ended in 2003. At least one out of every five Southern Sudanese died in the fighting or from disease and famine caused by the war. Four million people — nearly 80 percent of the Southern Sudanese population — were forced to flee their homes. [77]

and that the country would soon become economically self-sufficient despite the U.S. sanctions. [79]

Darfur Erupts

Darfur, meanwhile, was suffering from economic neglect, and numerous non-Arab tribes faced repression from government-supported militias. In 2000, the non-Arabs began to fight back, especially after the so-called *Black Book* circulated across the region describing how a small group of ethnic northern tribes had dominated Sudan since independence, at the expense of the rest of the country — especially Darfur.

"When we were writing the book, we were not thinking of rebellion. We

In 2001, President Bush dispatched former Sen. John C. Danforth, R-Mo., as a special envoy to Sudan to help bring the North and South toward a peace agreement. [82] Just days after the appointment, terrorists attacked the World Trade Center and the Pentagon, prompting Sudan to cooperate with the United States to avoid retaliatory strikes. The two countries soon began sharing intelligence on terrorists, including information about al Qaeda, bin Laden's terrorist organization. [83]

For the next 18 months, as peace negotiators debated splitting wealth and power between the North and South, they never considered sharing any of the pie with Darfur. Moreover, an international community focused on ending the civil war ignored the increasing repression in Darfur and the rebel groups preparing to fight.

In April 2003, just months before a North-South ceasefire was signed in Naivasha, Kenya, Darfuri rebels attacked the airport in El-Fashir, the capital of North Darfur, killing 30 government soldiers and blowing up aircraft. Rebels killed more than 1,000 Sudanese soldiers in the following months. [84]

"The Darfuris saw they had no shot at being part of the process," says Prendergast of the ENOUGH Project. "Leaving these guys out helped reinforce their desire to go to war. Darfur was completely ignored during the first term of the Bush administration, allowing Khartoum to conclude it could do whatever it wanted to in Darfur."

Indeed, Khartoum counterattacked, enlisting the brute force of the desperately poor Arab *janjaweed* militias the government had armed years earlier to settle internal land disputes. Over the next two years, up to 400,000 people died in the conflict by some estimates, and nearly 2.4 million people were displaced. [85] Civilian populations primarily from the Fur, Zaghawa, and Masalit ethnic groups — the same ethnicities as most of the rebel SLA/M and JEM groups — were the main targets.

Through most of the early fighting, global attention remained focused on negotiations to stop the North-South civil war, which officially ended in January 2005 when the government and the SPLA signed the Comprehensive Peace Agreement.

But by then Darfur had already spun out of control. The U.N. human rights coordinator for Sudan the previous April had described the situation in Darfur as "the world's greatest humanitarian crisis," adding "the only difference between Rwanda and Darfur is the numbers involved." [86] Human rights and religious groups had launched a media and lobbying campaign demanding that the international community act. In July 2004, the U.S. House of Representatives called the violence in Darfur "genocide."

A few days later, the U.N. passed its first resolution on Darfur, imposing an arms embargo on militias in the region and threatening sanctions against the government if it did not end the *janjaweed* violence. It also endorsed the deployment of African Union peacekeeping troops. [87] The resolution, the first of a dozen the U.N. would pass regarding Darfur over the next four years, was approved by the Security Council with 13 votes and two abstentions — from China and Pakistan. [88]

"What they've done is produce a lot of pieces of paper," says Brewer, of Human Rights Watch. "But they haven't been reinforced. Khartoum has played a very clever game. They stop aggression just long enough for the international community to look away, and then they start all over again."

Over the past four years rebel groups and Sudanese officials have agreed to a variety of ceasefires and settlements, which one or all sides eventually broke. The most recent — the Darfur Peace Agreement — was reached in May 2006, but only the government and one faction of the SLA/M signed the deal; JEM and another SLA/M faction refused to participate. [89] The SLA/M soon splintered into more than a dozen smaller groups, and fighting grew even worse. [90]

The African Union peacekeepers — under constant attack from rebels and bandits — proved ineffective. So in 2006, the U.N. voted to send international troops to bolster the AU mission. Bashir initially blocked the proposal as a "violation of Sudan's sovereignty and a submission by Sudan to outside custodianship." [91]

But after extended negotiations with China, the AU and the U.N., Bashir finally agreed. In July 2007, the Security Council unanimously voted to send up to 26,000 military and police peacekeepers as part of the joint U.N.-AU force. U.N. Secretary-General Ban heralded the unanimous vote as "historic and unprecedented" and said the mission would "make a clear and positive difference." [92]

But just three months before the peacekeepers began arriving in January 2008, hundreds of rebels in 30 armed trucks attacked a peacekeeping base in the Darfur town of Haskanita, killing at least 10 soldiers, kidnapping dozens more and seizing supplies that included heavy weapons.

"It's indicative of the complete insecurity," said Alun McDonald, a

spokesman for the Oxfam aid organization in Sudan. "These groups are attacking anybody and everybody with total impunity." [93]   ∎

CURRENT SITUATION

Indicting Bashir

The summer's Olympic Games in Beijing thrust Darfur back into international headlines. Movie stars, activists and athletes have criticized China's continued cozy relationship with the Bashir government and called on the world to stop the violence. Olympic torch-carrying ceremonies in cities around the world were interrupted by protesters complaining about China's support for Sudan and its recent crackdown on dissenters in Tibet. [94]

But even bigger news in the weeks leading up to the Games was the ICC prosecutor's effort to charge Bashir with genocide and war crimes. While, the ICC is not expected to decide until later this year whether to indict and arrest Bashir, the decision could be delayed even further if the Security Council agrees with the AU and others that the indictment should be deferred. The council can defer for 12 months — and indefinitely renew the deferral — any ICC investigation or prosecution. [95]

The ICC's move was not its first against Sudanese officials. On March 31, 2005, the United Nations passed a resolution asking the ICC prosecutor to investigate allegations of crimes against humanity and war crimes in Darfur. After a 20-month investigation, the prosecutor presented his evidence to the court in February 2007 and the court agreed two months later to issue arrest warrants for Sudan's former Interior

More Than 4.2 Million Affected by Crisis

Continued violence forced nearly 180,000 Darfuris to abandon their homes in the first five months of this year, bringing to 4.2 million the number affected by the ongoing conflict. While from 200,000 to 400,000 have been killed, nearly 2.4 million have been displaced. Many now live in U.N. camps inside Sudan — set up for so-called internally displaced persons (IDPs) — or have fled to refugee camps in neighboring Chad.

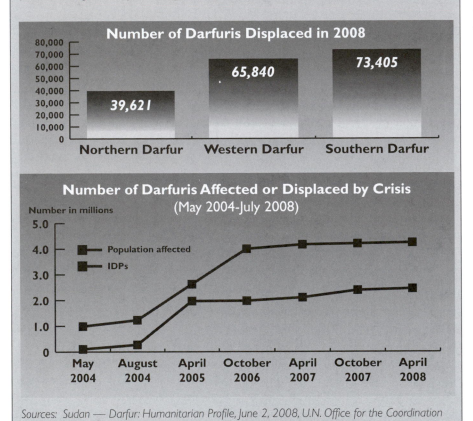

Number of Darfuris Displaced in 2008

Northern Darfur: 39,621
Western Darfur: 65,840
Southern Darfur: 73,405

Number of Darfuris Affected or Displaced by Crisis
(May 2004-July 2008)

Number in millions

— Population affected
— IDPs

May 2004, August 2004, April 2005, October 2006, April 2007, October 2007, April 2008

Sources: Sudan — Darfur: Humanitarian Profile, June 2, 2008, U.N. Office for the Coordination of Humanitarian Affairs; United Nations Sudan Information Gateway

Minister Ahmad Harun and *janjaweed* leader Ali Kushayb.[96] Bashir has refused to hand over either man, and Harun has since been named head the Ministry of Humanitarian Affairs and oversees the government's activities to aid the victims of the atrocities.[97]

This July, just days after the court's announcement about Bashir, the Sudanese president traveled to Darfur and met with 600 refugees from various tribes, including those he is accused of inflicting war crimes against. He promised to send them farming equipment and to free more than 80 rebels imprisoned last May after an attack on Khartoum's twin city Omdurman. Bashir called the prisoners "boys" and said they would be freed and pardoned — although he did not say when.[98]

Sudan also appointed its own prosecutor to investigate war crimes in Darfur and said it was sending legal teams to the region to monitor the situation. Sudan, which is not a signatory of the treaty that created the ICC, said its legal system was adequate to look into alleged abuses in Darfur and that it would pass legislation making genocide a punishable crime in Sudan.[99]

International Betrayal

Despite Secretary-General Ban's confidence in the new UNAMID peacekeeping force, deadly assaults against the mission have occurred almost non-stop. The first UNAMID peacekeeper — a civilian police inspector from Uganda — was killed in May, just four months after the new force began arriving.

On July 9, seven peacekeepers were killed and dozens more injured when their convoy was ambushed by hundreds of horsemen and 40 trucks mounted with machine guns and antiaircraft weapons. The two-hour firefight marked the first time UNAMID had to use force to protect itself, and some observers described it as being near the point of "meltdown."[100]

"The effort being achieved so far is not enough," said, Fadallah Ahmed Abdallah, a Sudanese city official in Darfur working with the peacekeepers. "Sometimes we feel UNAMID itself needs some protection, because UNAMID is not at full strength."[101]

More than a year after the UNAMID force was authorized, only a third of the 26,000 troops are on the ground, and not a single military transport or tactical helicopter among the 28 requested has been deployed to patrol the area — which is the size of France.

On July 31, the day UNAMID's mandate was to expire, the Security Council extended it for a year.[102] Meanwhile, 36 human rights groups — along with Nobel Peace Prize laureate Desmond Tutu and former President Carter — issued a report revealing that countries were not donating helicopters that are desperately needed by UNAMID to restore order.[103] The report said a handful of NATO countries and others that typically contribute aircraft to peacekeeping missions — specifically India, Ukraine, Czech Republic, Italy, Romania and

Spain — could easily provide up to 70 helicopters for the mission. (*See graphic, p. 247.*)

"Many of these helicopters are gathering dust in hangars or flying in air shows when they could be saving lives in Darfur," said the report, entitled "Grounded: the International Community's Betrayal of UNAMID." [104]

"It's really shameful," says Brewer of Human Rights Watch. "But it's not just helicopters. They need water, trucks, everything. I don't know whether it's because countries don't have faith in UNAMID, or they don't want to put their troops as risk or if it's fear of being involved in something that will fail."

Brewer also blames the Sudanese government for delaying delivery of peacekeepers' equipment and refusing to accept troops from Western countries. Aside from peacekeepers, aid workers also are being targeted by rebel factions and bandits searching for food and supplies. Eight aid workers were killed in the first five months of 2008, and four times as many aid vehicles were hijacked during the first quarter of this year compared to the same period last year. [105] Armed gangs also attacked 35 humanitarian compounds during the first quarter — more than double the number during the same period last year. [106]

"We are now in the worst situation ever" — even worse than when the government-rebel conflict was at its peak, says Hafiz Mohamed, Sudan program coordinator with Justice Africa, a London-based research and human rights organization. "At least in 2004 we only had two rebel movements. Now we have more than 12 SLA factions and more than four JEM factions. Security-wise, Darfur is worse than in 2004."

In May, SLA Unity rebels arrested a dozen Sudanese government employees in Darfur gathering census information for next year's national elec-

AFP/Getty Images/Mustafa Ozer

AFP/Getty Images/Jose Cendon

Life in the Camps

About a third of the Darfuri population has been forced to flee their homes since 2003, with many now living in refugee camps in Darfur or neighboring Chad. Conditions in the camps, like these near Nyala, are harsh. Children (bottom) attend class at a makeshift outdoor school, but about 650,000 don't attend school at all.

tions. The rebels, who believe the census will be inaccurate — depriving Darfur of political representation — vowed to try the census takers in military courts as "enemies," which carries the death penalty. [107]

Rebel attacks also are increasing outside Darfur. Last year JEM — which wants to overthrow the Sudanese government — attacked government positions and kidnapped two foreign workers at a Chinese-run oil field in neighboring Kordofan province. "This is a message to China and Chinese oil companies to stop helping the government with their war in Darfur," said JEM commander Abdel Aziz el-Nur Ashr. [108] JEM has said oil revenues are being used to continue the fighting in Darfur.

JEM rebels made their most audacious push against the government in May, when they reached suburban Khartoum before being repelled by Sudanese forces. Sudan immediately cut

Both sides remain deadlocked over some of the most contentious issues of the 2005 peace treaty, including how to draw the North-South border and how to split oil profits. The South has a large portion of the country's oil reserves while the North has most of the infrastructure. The South has repeatedly accused the North of not sharing oil revenue fairly, while the North has charged the South with mishandling their portion of the funds. [110]

Mission Impossible?

While the U.N. has been slow to send in troops and materiel, individual governments and private organizations have provided billions of dollars' worth of food, water, housing, medicine and other humanitarian aid to Darfur and the nearby refugee camps in Chad.

In 2004, when the war between rebels and government forces was at its peak, only 230 relief workers were stationed in the region. [111] Today, there are more than 17,000 national and international aid workers from some 80 NGOs, 14 U.N. agencies and the Red Cross/Red Crescent Movement. [112]

"The humanitarian response has been incredible," providing "a staggering amount of money, a staggering number of people," says Brewer. However, she says she sometimes wonders if people are substituting aid for serious "political engagement to find a solution."

And most agree that only political engagement — coming from a unified global community — can solve the ongoing conflict.

"We need more coordinated diplomacy. We can't have different messages coming from France, China, the U.N., the U.S. and African nations," says Meixner of the Save Darfur Coalition. "Bashir can thwart one or two, but if there's a united front, including China and African nations, it's not so easy."

Specifically, he says, multilateral sanctions should be adopted. "Sudan is the test case for multilateralism," he says.

But others say "regime change" is the only viable solution. "I don't think we'll find a political solution for the Darfur crisis if the current government stays in power," says Mohamed of Justice Africa. "Since 1997 we've had six agreements, the CPA, the DPA. This regime will never honor any agreement. . . . If [the international

An African Union (AU) peacekeeper offers bread to two women near the West Darfur town of Murnei. The women said they were raped, beaten and robbed by janjaweed militiamen when they left their refugee camp to gather firewood — a common occurrence in Darfur. After being criticized as ineffective, the AU force has been beefed up this year with 10,000 U.N. military and police peacekeepers. Another 16,000 have been authorized.

off diplomatic ties with Chad, which it accused of sponsoring the attack. Chadian officials denied any involvement but accused Sudan of launching a similar attack against their capital three months earlier. [109]

"The entire region is affected by what is happening in Darfur," says Mohamed of Justice Africa. "It's a proxy war. Unless we resolve the relationship between Chad and Sudan, we will not have an agreement for peace in Darfur."

Meanwhile, relations between North and South Sudan are worsening.

Under the Comprehensive Peace Agreement (CPA), a referendum is scheduled for 2011 on whether the South will secede from the North. Some wonder if tensions between the two sides will hold until then.

"There are real prospects of another North-South war," says Sudan expert Moszynski. "South Sudan is spending 40 percent of their budget on military. They're preparing for the next war with the North. There are a lot of problems in Sudan. In between all of that, they're not going to sort out Darfur."

Continued on p. 264

At Issue:

Would military intervention solve the crisis in Darfur?

HAFIZ MOHAMED
SUDAN PROGRAM COORDINATOR
JUSTICE AFRICA

WRITTEN FOR *CQ GLOBAL RESEARCHER*, **AUGUST 2008**

IMANI COUNTESS
SENIOR DIRECTOR FOR PUBLIC AFFAIRS
TRANSAFRICA FORUM

WRITTEN FOR *CQ GLOBAL RESEARCHER*, **AUGUST 2008**

*t*he current crisis in Darfur has claimed more than 200,000 lives and displaced millions — due primarily to the Sudanese government's counterinsurgency policy, which uses the *janjaweed* as proxy fighters and bombs villages with government aircraft.

Despite more than 16 U.N. Security Council resolutions and authorization of a joint U.N.-African Union peacekeeping mission in Darfur (UNAMID), the mass killing and displacement of civilians continues. The parties to the conflict have signed many cease-fire agreements since 2004, but all of them have been violated, and even the mechanisms for monitoring the cease-fires have failed. Early last month, peacekeepers were attacked in Darfur, primarily because they were outmanned and outgunned. No country has provided them even with helicopters.

Hardliners within Sudan's National Congress Party still believe in a military solution to the crisis and use any means to defeat the Darfuri armed movements. All their rhetoric about being committed to a peaceful solution is just for public opinion and not a genuine endeavor to achieve a peaceful settlement to the conflict. They will only accept peace if they are pressured to do so or feel the war is unwinable.

The regime is in its weakest position since taking power in 1989 and will only cave when it feels threatened. For example, after the International Criminal Court prosecutor initiated proceedings recently to indict the Sudanese president, the government began mobilizing the public to support the president and seek a peaceful resolution.

There is strong evidence that military intervention is needed to stop the killing of civilians and force the Sudanese government to seriously seek a peaceful solution for the crisis. This could start by imposing a no-fly zone on Darfur, which would prevent the government from using its air force to bomb villages and give air support to the *janjaweed*'s attacks; the normal sequences for the attacks on the villages is to start an attack from the air by using the government bombers or helicopter machine guns, followed by attacks by militia riding horses or camels.

A no-fly zone will stop this, and many lives will be saved. The no-fly zone can start by using the European forces based in neighbouring Chad. The UNAMID forces then can be used to monitor movement on the ground and intervene when necessary to stop the ground attacks on villages.

*f*or the sake of the 2 million displaced peoples and 200,000 killed, the international community should mount a military force that would protect and restore the dignity and livelihoods to those raped, tortured and maimed by the Sudanese government. But whatever peace comes to Sudan will be the result of those who brought the issue to the world stage: Darfurians supported by millions around the globe who are standing in the breach created by the failures and inaction of the nations of the world.

Truth be told, not one major military or economic power is willing to expend the political capital required to solve the crisis in Darfur.

For the United States, Darfur has become "collateral damage" in the global war on terror. The administration states that genocide is occurring, yet it continues to share intelligence with key Sudanese officials implicated in the tragedy in Darfur — sacrificing thousands of Darfuri lives in exchange for intelligence and extraditions of suspected terrorists.

Other Western nations provide plenty of rhetoric and limited sanctions. But they have failed miserably where it counts: providing adequate support for the joint African Union-U.N. peacekeeping force in Darfur. According to AfricaFocus, UNAMID is "understaffed, underequipped, underfunded and vulnerable to attacks." The U.N. authorized up to 19,555 military personnel for the mission, plus 6,432 police and more than 5,000 civilians. But so far fewer than 8,000 troops and 2,000 police have been deployed, along with just over 1,000 civilians. Critical equipment is lacking, and more than half of the $1.3 billion budget was unpaid as of the end of April.

For the international community as a whole — particularly China and India — continued access to Sudan's oil is the major interest.

If military intervention is not the answer, then what will work? Continued pressure from below. In the United States, the Bush administration was compelled to name the crisis "genocide" because of pressure from faith-based, human-rights and social-justice groups. Across the country, divestment activity — modeled after the anti-apartheid campaigns of the 1970s and '80s — has forced U.S. monies out of Sudan. The transnational human-rights movement will continue to pressure governments, businesses and multilateral institutions to move beyond rhetoric to effective human-centered engagement.

Continued from p. 262

community] managed to overthrow the regime, there is the possibility of a permanent solution."

But Alex de Waal, a program director at the Social Science Research Council in New York and author of *Darfur: A Short History of a Long War*, says global and Arab anger sparked by the Iraq War leaves "zero chance" that the international community will launch any military action against another Muslim country.

However, Obama foreign affairs adviser Rice — a former Clinton-era State Department official — said the U.N. should not let the experience in Iraq deter military action. "Some will reject any future U.S. military action, especially against an Islamic regime, even if purely to halt genocide against Muslim civilians," Rice told a Senate committee in April 2007. "Sudan has also threatened that al Qaeda will attack non-African forces in Darfur — a possibility, since Sudan long hosted bin Laden and his businesses. Yet, to allow another state to deter the U.S. by threatening terrorism would set a terrible precedent. It would also be cowardly and, in the face of genocide, immoral." [113]

Meanwhile, the U.N. has unsuccessfully tried to resurrect peace talks between the Bashir government and rebel groups. Talks in Libya were called off last October after rebel factions refused to participate. [114]

"The last six months have seen some very negative developments," former U.N. Special Envoy Eliasson said upon his resignation in June. If the international community's energy is not mobilized to halt the fighting, he continued, "we risk a major humanitarian disaster again. The margins of survival are so slim for the people of Darfur." [115] The U.N. could start showing its commitment, he said, by stationing his replacement full time in Sudan. Eliasson had been headquartered in Stockholm.

The new U.N. special envoy, Burkino Faso's foreign minister Djibril Bas-

sole, is hopeful. "This will be a difficult mission," he said after his first visit to Sudan in July. "But it's not mission impossible." [116] ∎

OUTLOOK

Bleak Future

As unstable and violent as the past four years have been for Darfur, the next three could be even more tumultuous — for the entire country.

Under Comprehensive Peace Agreement provisions, elections must be held next year — the first in 23 years. In preparation Sudan conducted its first census since 1993 earlier this year, but many doubt that either the census results — or the vote count — will be accurate. [117]

Displaced Darfuris in refugee camps don't trust the government to take an accurate headcount. Indeed, the huge numbers of displaced persons seem to make both an accurate census and democratic elections nearly impossible.

"It's hard to see how elections can take place in a fair and free way in Darfur," says Lusk of *Africa Confidential*. "Half the people are dead, and the other half are in camps."

"The [displaced] people are concerned that if they register to vote while living in the camps, . . . they will lose their land," says Brewer. "There is great lack of clarity in land law."

Some wonder if the Bashir government will back out of the elections altogether, but Sudanese officials insist the polling will be held. "Rebels said the census should not take place, but it did take place," says Mubarak of the Sudanese Embassy in London. "The elections will go ahead."

But elections will at best do little to help the people of Darfur and at worst prompt further violence from those who oppose the results, say some observers.

"The elections will have no impact on Darfur — if they happen," says former U.S. Rep. Howard Wolpe, D-Mich., who directs Africa programs at the Woodrow Wilson Center. "At the end of the day, elections have no impact . . . if you haven't built a sense of cohesion or a way of moving forward."

After the elections, the Sudanese people must brace themselves for another potential upheaval — caused by a planned 2011 referendum on Sudanese unity. While the South appears ready to vote for secession, many say Khartoum will never let that happen.

Others say secession could spell dark times for Darfur. "If the South secedes, [Bashir's National Congress Party] will have greater power in the North, and that is worse for Darfur," says Brewer. "If they vote for power sharing, it could be good for Darfur."

Meanwhile, all eyes are waiting to see whether the ICC will give in to pressure to defer action on Bashir's indictment and how Bashir and the rebel groups will respond to either an indictment or a delay.

The November U.S. presidential election could also bring about some changes. Both McCain and Obama have said they will pursue peace and security for Darfur with "unstinting resolve." And Obama's running mate, Foreign Relations Committee Chairman Biden, was unequivocal last year when he advocated U.S. military intervention. "I would use American force now," Biden said during hearings before his panel in April 2007. "It's time to put force on the table and use it." Biden, who had also pushed for NATO intervention to halt anti-Muslim genocide in Bosnia in the 1990s, said 2,500 U.S. troops could "radically change" the situation on the ground in Darfur. "Let's stop the bleeding. I think it's a moral imperative." [118]

Given the uncertainties of the Sudanese elections, the growing North-South acrimony, the continued fighting between Chad and Sudan and the upcoming ICC decision, most experts say it is nearly impossible to predict what will happen in Darfur in the future.

"Even five years is too far to predict what will happen," says author Prunier. "You have to take it in steps. First look at what happens in 2009, then what happens leading up to the referendum, then what happens after that."

Most agree, however, that whatever future lies ahead for Darfur, it will likely be bleak.

"Sudanese politics is like the British weather: unpredictable from day to day but with a drearily consistent medium-term outlook," de Waal of the Social Science Research Council wrote recently. "There are few happy endings in Sudan. It's a country of constant turbulence, in which I have come to expect only slow and modest improvement. Sometimes I dream of being wrong." [119] ∎

Notes

[1] "They Shot at Us as We Fled: Government Attacks on Civilians in West Darfur," Human Rights Watch, May 2008, p. 18, www.hrw.org/reports/2008/darfur0508/.

[2] *Ibid.*, p. 19.

[3] *Ibid.*, p. 2.

[4] "Darfur Crisis: Death Estimates Demonstrate Severity of Crisis, but Their Accuracy and Credibility Could Be Enhanced," Government Accountability Office, November 2006, pp. 1-2, 7. The U.S. State Department puts the death toll for the period 2003-2005 at between 98,000 and 181,000.

[5] "Sudan — Darfur: Humanitarian Profile," United Nations Office for the Coordination of Humanitarian Affairs, June 2, 2008, www.unsudanig.org/library/mapcatalogue/darfur/data/dhnp/Map%201226%20Darfur%20Humanitarian%20Profile%20June%203%202008.pdf.

[6] *Ibid.*

[7] Sarah El Deeb, "UN warns of bad year in Darfur," The Associated Press, June 22, 2008, www.newsvine.com/_news/2008/06/16/1581306-un-warns-of-bad-year-in-darfur.

[8] "Darfur faces potential food crisis unless action taken now, warn UN agencies," UN News Centre, United Nations, June 23, 2008, www.un.org/apps/news/story.asp?NewsID=27114&Cr=darfur&Cr1=.

[9] "Darfur 2007: Chaos by Design," Human Rights Watch, September 2007, p. 20.

[10] El Deeb, *op. cit.*

[11] "Darfur faces potential food crisis," *op. cit.*

[12] "Almost Half of All Darfur Children Not in School, Says NGO," BBC Monitoring International Reports, Feb. 29, 2008.

[13] Stephanie McCrummen, "A Wide-Open Battle For Power in Darfur," *The Washington Post*, June 20, 2008, p. A1, www.washingtonpost.com/wp-dyn/content/article/2008/06/19/AR2008061903552_pf.html.

[14] Quoted from "The Devil Came on Horseback" documentary, Break Thru Films, 2007.

[15] Julie Flint and Alex de Waal, *Darfur: A Short History of a Long War* (2005), p. 10.

[16] Colum Lynch and Nora Boustany, "Sudan Leader To Be Charged With Genocide," *The Washington Post*, July 11, 2008, p. A1, www.washingtonpost.com/wp-dyn/content/article/2008/07/10/AR2008071003109.html. Also see Kenneth Jost, "International Law," *CQ Researcher*, Dec. 17, 2004, pp. 1049-1072.

[17] Quoted in Hussein Solomon, "ICC pressure shows some result; An arrest warrant for Sudan's President Al-Bashir has resulted in a flurry of activity for change in Darfur," *The Star* (South Africa), Aug. 21, 2008, p. 14.

[18] "Court Seeks Arrest of Sudan's Beshir for 'genocide,'" Agence France-Presse, July 14, 2008.

[19] For background, see Sarah Glazer, "Stopping Genocide," *CQ Researcher*, Aug. 27, 2004, pp. 685-708.

[20] For background, see Karen Foerstel, "China in Africa," *CQ Global Researcher*, January 2008, pp. 1-26.

[21] Alexa Olesen, "China Appoints Special Envoy for Darfur," The Associated Press, May 11, 2007; "China paper decries Sudan's Bashir arrest move," Reuters, July 17, 2008; "China boosts peacekeepers in Darfur," Agence France-Presse, July 17, 2008, http://afp.google.com/article/ALeqM5jxVo9_9z2jJm2wxZW65dyP8CflEw.

[22] Neil MacFarquhar, "Why Darfur Still Bleeds," *The New York Times*, July 13, 2008, www.nytimes.com/2008/07/13/weekinreview/13macfarquhar.html.

[23] "Darfur's Political Process in 'Troubled State of Affairs,'" U.N. Security Council press release, June 24, 2008, www.un.org/News/Press/docs/2008/sc9370.doc.htm.

[24] Glazer, *op. cit.*, p. 687.

[25] Neela Banerjee, "Muslims' Plight in Sudan Resonates with Jews in U.S.," *The New York Times*, April 30, 2006, www.nytimes.com/2006/04/30/us/30rally.html.

[26] Alan Cooperman, "Evangelicals Urge Bush to Do More for Sudan," *The Washington Post*, Aug. 3, 2004, p. A13, www.washingtonpost.com/wp-dyn/articles/A35223-2004Aug2.html.

[27] Glenn Kessler and Colum Lynch, "U.S. Calls Killings in Sudan Genocide," *The Washington Post*, Sept. 10, 2004, p. A1, www.washingtonpost.com/wp-dyn/articles/A8364-2004Sep9.html.

[28] "The Crisis in Darfur: Secretary Colin L. Powell, Written Remarks Before the Senate Foreign Relations Committee," Secretary of State press release, Sept. 9, 2004.

[29] "Security Council Declares Intention to Consider Sanctions to Obtain Sudan's Full Compliance With Security, Disarmament Obligations in Darfur," U.N. Security Council press release, Sept. 18, 2004, www.un.org/News/Press/docs/2004/sc8191.doc.htm.

[30] Opheera McDoom, "Statesmen Say Darfur Violent and Divided," Reuters, Oct. 4, 2007, http://africa.reuters.com/wire/news/usnMCD351991.html.

[31] "UN Report: Darfur Not Genocide," CNN.com, Feb. 1, 2005, http://edition.cnn.com/2005/WORLD/africa/01/31/sudan.report/. See also Marc Lacey, "In Darfur, Appalling Atrocity, but Is That Genocide?" *The New York Times*, July 23, 2004, p. 3, http://query.nytimes.com/gst/fullpage.html?res=9B04E0DC163DF930A15754C0A9629C8B63.

[32] Hillary Rodham Clinton, John McCain and Barack Obama, "Presidential Candidates' Statement on Darfur," May 28, 2008, www.cfr.org/publication/16359/presidential_candidates_statement_on_darfur.html?breadcrumb=%2Fregion%2F197%2Fsudan.

[33] George Gedda, "Biden Calls for Military Force in Darfur," The Associated Press, April 11, 2007.

[34] Susan E. Rice, "The Escalating Crisis in Darfur," testimony before the U.S. House Committee on Foreign Affairs, Feb. 8, 2007, www.brookings.edu/testimony/2007/0208africa_rice.aspx.

[35] Opheera McDoom, "Analysis — Darfur Scares European Investors Off Sudan's Oil," Reuters, Aug. 3, 2007. One barrel of oil produces 42 gallons of gasoline. Also see Energy Information Administration database, at http://tonto.eia.doe.gov/dnav/pet/pet_cons_psup_dc_nus_mbblpd_a.htm.

[36] "US Sanctions on Sudan," U.S. Department of State fact sheet, April 23, 2008, www.state.gov/p/af/rls/fs/2008/103970.htm. Also see "Country Reports on Terrorism," U.S. Department of State, April 30, 2007, Chapter 3, www.state.gov/s/ct/rls/crt/2006/82736.htm.

37 "Situation in Darfur, The Sudan: Summary of the Case," International Criminal Court, July 14, 2008, www.icc-cpi.int/library/organs/otp/ICC-OTP-Summary-20081704-ENG.pdf.

38 Colum Lynch and Nora Boustany, "Sudan Leader To Be Charged With Genocide," *The Washington Post*, July 10, 2008.

39 *Ibid.*

40 Stephanie McCrummen and Nora Boustany, "Sudan Vows to Fight Charges of Genocide Against Its Leader," *The Washington Post*, July 14, 2008, www.washingtonpost.com/wp-dyn/content/article/2008/07/14/AR2008071400112_pf.html.

41 Mohamed Osman, "Sudan Rejects Genocide Charges Against President," The Associated Press, July 14, 2008.

42 Anita Powell, "AU to Seek Delay in al-Bashir Indictment," The Associated Press, July 21, 2008.

43 Opheera McDoom, "Darfur Rebels Condemn AU on ICC Warrant," Reuters, July 22, www.alertnet.org/thenews/newsdesk/L22832812.htm.

44 Andrew Natsios, "A Disaster in the Making," The Social Science Research Council, Making Sense of Darfur blog, July 12, 2008, www.ssrc.org/blogs/darfur/2008/07/12/a-disaster-in-the-making/.

45 "Media Stakeout with Ambassador Zalmay Khalilzad," Federal News Service, July 22, 2008.

46 Foerstel, *op. cit.*, pp. 7, 13. Also see "Sudan," *Political Handbook of the World*, CQ Press (2008).

47 Danna Harman, "Activists Press China With 'Genocide Olympics' Label," *The Christian Science Monitor*, June 26, 2007, www.csmonitor.com/2007/0626/p13s01-woaf.html.

48 "Letter to Chinese President Hu Jintao," Rep. Steven Rothman Web site, May 7, 2007, http://foreignaffairs.house.gov/press_display.asp?id=345.

49 Alexa Olesen, "China Appoints Special Envoy for Darfur," The Associated Press, May 11, 2007.

50 See Jason Qian and Anne Wu, "Playing the Blame Game in Africa," *The Boston Globe*, July 23, 2007, www.iht.com/articles/2007/07/23/opinion/edqian.php; "China boosts peacekeepers in Darfur," *op. cit.*

51 "China envoy: more humanitarian aid to Darfur," Xinhua, Feb. 26, 2008, www.chinadaily.com.cn/china/2008-02/26/content_6483392.htm.

52 Robert J. Saiget, "China says can do no more over Darfur," Agence France-Presse, June 26, 2008, http://afp.google.com/article/ALeqM5gD2S4zFfzj6CZfnluWi5Kq4eFrgw.

53 Danna Harman, "How China's Support of Sudan Shields A Regime Called 'Genocidal,' " *The Christian Science Monitor*, June 26, 2007, www.csmonitor.com/2007/0626/p01s08-woaf.html.

54 Security Council Resolution 1591, United Nations, March 29, 2005, www.un.org/Docs/sc/unsc_resolutions05.htm.

55 "China says BBC's accusation on arms sales to Sudan 'ungrounded,' " Xinhua, July 18, 2008, http://news.xinhuanet.com/english/2008-07/18/content_8570601.htm.

56 Saiget, *op. cit.*

57 Audra Ang, "China urges court to rethink Sudan arrest warrant," The Associated Press, July 15, 2008.

58 Harman, *op. cit.*

59 Lydia Polgreen, "China, in New Role, Presses Sudan on Darfur," *International Herald Tribune*, Feb. 23, 2008, www.iht.com/articles/2008/02/23/africa/23darfur.php.

60 M. W. Daly, *Darfur's Sorrows* (2007), p. 1.

61 "Crisis Shaped by Darfur's Tumultuous Past," PBS Newshour, April 7, 2006, www.pbs.org/newshour/indepth_coverage/africa/darfur/political-past.html.

62 Gerard Prunier, *Darfur: The Ambiguous Genocide* (2007), pp. 4-5.

63 Daly, *op. cit.*, p. 19.

64 Prunier, *op. cit.*, p. 10. Also see Flint and de Waal, *op. cit.*, p. 8.

65 Prunier, *op. cit*, p. 16.

66 *Ibid.*, pp. 18-19.

67 *Ibid.*, p. 30.

68 *Ibid.*

69 Don Cheadle and John Prendergast, *Not On Our Watch* (2007), p. 53.

70 Prunier, *op. cit.*, pp. 45-46.

71 *Ibid.*

72 Cheadle and Prendergast, *op. cit.*, p. 73.

73 *Ibid.*, p. 55.

74 *Ibid.*, p. 56.

75 *Ibid.*, p. 57.

76 Polgreen, *op. cit.*

77 "Sudan: Nearly 2 million dead as a result of the world's longest running civil war," The U.S. Committee for Refugees, April 2001.

78 "Sudan, Oil and Human Rights," Human Rights Watch, September 2003, www.hrw.org/reports/2003/sudan1103/index.htm; "Sudan's President Projects the Export of Oil," *Africa News*, July 13, 1998.

79 "President's Revolution Day Address," BBC Worldwide Monitoring, July 5, 1998.

80 "Crisis Shaped by Darfur's Tumultuous Past," *op. cit.*

81 Prunier, *op. cit.*, p. 88.

82 "President Appoints Danforth as Special Envoy to the Sudan," White House press release, Sept. 6, 2001, www.whitehouse.gov/news/releases/2001/09/20010906-3.html.

83 Polgreen, *op. cit.*

84 Prunier, *op. cit.*, pp. 95-96.

85 "Darfur Crisis," *op. cit.*, p. 1. Also see Sheryl Gay Stolberg, "Bush Tightens Penalties Against Sudan," *The New York Times*, May 29, 2007, www.nytimes.com/2007/05/29/world/africa/29cnd-darfur.html.

86 Gerard Prunier, "The Politics of Death in Darfur," *Current History*, May 2006, p. 196.

87 Security Council Resolution 1556, United Nations, July 30, 2004, www.un.org/Docs/sc/unsc_resolutions04.html.

88 "Security Council Demands Sudan Disarm Militias in Darfur," U.N. press release, July 30, 2004, www.un.org/News/Press/docs/2004/sc8160.doc.htm.

89 "Background Notes: Sudan," U.S. State Department press release, April 24, 2008, www.state.gov/r/pa/ei/bgn/5424.htm.

90 Scott Baldauf, "Darfur Talks Stall After Rebels Boycott," *The Christian Science Monitor*, Oct. 29, 2007, www.csmonitor.com/2007/1029/p06s01-woaf.html.

About the Author

Karen Foerstel is a freelance writer who has worked for the Congressional Quarterly *Weekly Report* and *Daily Monitor, The New York Post* and *Roll Call*, a Capitol Hill newspaper. She has published two books on women in Congress, *Climbing the Hill: Gender Conflict in Congress* and *The Biographical Dictionary of Women in Congress*. She has worked in Africa with ChildsLife International, a nonprofit that helps needy children around the world, and with Blue Ventures, a marine conservation organization that protects coral reefs in Madagascar.

[91] Lydia Polgreen, "Rebel Ambush in Darfur Kills 5 African Union Peacekeepers in Deadliest Attack on the Force," *The New York Times*, April 3, 2007.

[92] "Secretary-General Urges All Parties to Remain Engaged, As Security Council Authorizes Deployment of United Nations-African Union Mission in Sudan," U.N. Security Council press release, July 31, 2007, www.un.org/News/Press/docs/2007/sgsm11110.doc.htm.

[93] Jeffrey Gettleman, "Darfur Rebels Kill 10 in Peace Force," *The New York Times*, Oct. 1, 2005, www.nytimes.com/2007/10/01/world/africa/01darfur.html.

[94] For background, see Brian Beary, "Separatism Movements," *CQ Global Researcher*, April 2008.

[95] "Arab League Backs Recourse to UN on Sudan War Crimes," Agence France-Presse, July 21, 2008.

[96] "The Situation in Darfur, the Sudan," International Criminal Court fact sheet, www.icc-cpi.int/library/organs/otp/ICC-OTP_Fact-Sheet-Darfur-20070227_en.pdf.

[97] "Arrest Now!" Amnesty International fact sheet, July 17, 2007, http://archive.amnesty.org/library/Index/ENGAFR540272007?open&of=ENG-332.

[98] Sarah El Deeb, "Sudan's President Pays Visit to Darfur," The Associated Press, July 24, 2008.

[99] Abdelmoniem Abu Edries Ali, "Sudan Appoints Darfur Prosecutor," Agence France-Presse, Aug. 6, 2008.

[100] Stephanie McCrummen, "7 Troops Killed in Sudan Ambush," *The Washington Post*, July 10, 2008, www.washingtonpost.com/wp-dyn/content/article/2008/07/09/AR2008070900843.html.

[101] Jennie Matthew, "Darfur hopes dim six months into UN peacekeeping," Agence France-Presse, June 25, 2008.

[102] "Security Council extends mandate of UN-AU force in Darfur," Agence France-Presse, July 31, 2008.

[103] "Aid groups urge helicopters for Darfur," Agence France-Presse, July 31, 2008, http://afp.google.com/article/ALeqM5i2aYTRiEePGRmbRqVQbByF28X_RQ.

[104] "Grounded: the International Community's Betrayal of UNAMID — A Joint NGO Report," p. 4, http://darfur.3cdn.net/b5b2056f1398299ffe_x9m6bt7cu.pdf.

[105] "Sudan — Darfur: Humanitarian Profile," *op. cit.*

[106] "Darfur Humanitarian Profile No. 31," Office of U.N. Deputy Special Representative of the U.N. Secretary-General for Sudan, April 1, 2008, p. 4, www.unsudanig.org/docs/DHP%2031_1%20April%202008_narrative.pdf.

[107] Opheera McDoom, "Darfur rebels say they arrest 13 census staff," Reuters, May 4, 2008, www.reuters.com/article/homepageCrisis/idUSL04471626._CH_.2400.

[108] "Darfur rebels say they kidnap foreign oil workers," Reuters, Oct. 24, 2007, www.alert-net.org/thenews/newsdesk/MCD470571.htm.

[109] Shashank Bengali, "Darfur conflict stokes Chad-Sudan tensions," McClatchy-Tribune News Service, June 14, 2008, www.mcclatchydc.com/160/story/40518.html.

[110] Jeffrey Gettleman, "Cracks in the Peace in Oil-Rich Sudan As Old Tensions Fester," *The New York Times*, Sept. 22, 2007, www.nytimes.com/2007/09/22/world/africa/22sudan.html?fta=y.

[111] "Sudan — Darfur: Humanitarian Profile," *op. cit.*

[112] "Darfur Humanitarian Profile No. 31," *op. cit.*, p. 6.

[113] Susan E. Rice, Testimony before Senate Foreign Relations Committee, April 11, 2007.

[114] "Darfur envoys end visit without date for peace talks," Agence France-Presse, April 19, 2008.

[115] Steve Bloomfield, "Negotiators quit Darfur, saying neither side is ready for peace," *The Independent* (London), June 27, 2008, www.independent.co.uk/news/world/africa/negotiators-quit-darfur-saying-neither-side-is-ready-for-peace-855431.html.

[116] "Darfur mediator arrives for a 'difficult mission,' " *The International Herald Tribune*, July 21, 2008.

[117] Opheera McDoom, "Counting begins in disputed Sudan census," Reuters, April 22, 2008, www.reuters.com/article/homepageCrisis/idUSMCD246493._CH_.2400.

[118] Presidential Candidates' Statement on Darfur, *op. cit.* Gedda, *op. cit.*

[119] Alex de Waal, "In which a writer's work — forged in the heat of chaos — could actually save lives," *The Washington Post*, June 22, 2008, p. BW 11, www.washingtonpost.com/wp-dyn/content/article/2008/06/19/AR2008061903304_pf.html.

FOR MORE INFORMATION

Aegis Trust, The Holocaust Centre, Laxton, Newark, Nottinghamshire NG22 9ZG, UK; +44 (0)1623 836627; www.aegistrust.org. Campaigns against genocide around the world and provides humanitarian aid to genocide victims.

African Union, P.O. Box 3243, Addis Ababa, Ethiopia; +251 11 551 77 00; www.africa-union.org. Fosters economic and social cooperation among 53 African nations and other governments.

Amnesty International, 1 Easton St., London, WC1X 0DW, United Kingdom, +44-20-74135500; www.amnesty.org. Promotes human rights worldwide, with offices in 80 countries.

Council on Foreign Relations, 1779 Massachusetts Ave., N.W., Washington, DC 20036; (202) 518-3400; www.cfr.org. A nonpartisan think tank that offers extensive resources, data and experts on foreign policy issues.

Human Rights Watch, 350 Fifth Ave., 34th Floor, New York, NY 10118-3299; (212) 290-4700; www.hrw.org. Investigates human-rights violations worldwide.

Justice Africa, 1C Leroy House, 436 Essex Road, London N1 3QP, United Kingdom; +44 (0) 207 354 8400; www.justiceafrica.org. A research and advocacy organization that campaigns for human rights and social justice in Africa.

Save Darfur Coalition, Suite 335, 2120 L St., N.W., Washington, DC 20037; (800) 917-2034; www.savedarfur.org. An alliance of more than 180 faith-based, advocacy and humanitarian organizations working to stop the violence in Darfur.

Social Science Research Council, 810 Seventh Ave., New York, NY 10019; (212) 377-2700; www.ssrc.org. Studies complex social, cultural, economic and political issues.

TransAfrica Forum, 1629 K St., N.W., Suite 1100, Washington, DC 20006; (202) 223-1960; www.transafricaforum.org. Campaigns for human rights and sustainable development in Africa and other countries with residents of African descent.

Bibliography

Selected Sources

Books

Cheadle, Don, and John Prendergast, *Not On Our Watch*, Hyperion, 2007.

Cheadle, who starred in the African genocide movie "Hotel Rwanda," and human-rights activist Prendergast explore the Darfur crisis, with tips on how to impact international policy. Forward by Holocaust survivor and Nobel Peace Prize-winner Elie Wiesel, and introduction by Sens. Barack Obama, D-Ill., and Sam Brownback, R-Kan.

Daly, M. W., *Darfur's Sorrow*, Cambridge University Press, 2007.

An historian and long-time observer of Sudan traces the complex environmental, cultural and geopolitical factors that have contributed to today's ongoing conflict. Includes a timeline of events in Darfur since 1650.

Flint, Julie, and Alex de Waal, *Darfur: A Short History Of a Long War*, Zed Books, 2005.

Two longtime observers of Sudan and Darfur explore the genesis of today's bloodshed and describe the various actors in the conflict, including the region's many ethnic tribes, the *janjaweed* militia, Libyan leader Muammar Qaddafi and the current Sudanese government.

Prunier, Gerard, *Darfur: The Ambiguous Genocide*, Cornell University Press, 2007.

A French historian who has authored several books on African genocide provides a comprehensive account of the complex environmental, social and political roots of the ongoing fighting in Darfur.

Articles

"Timeline: Conflict in Darfur," *The Washington Post*, June 19, 2008, www.washingtonpost.com/wp-dyn/content/article/2008/06/19/AR2008061902905.html.

This brief narrative outlines the fighting in Darfur and various efforts to find peace over the past five years.

Faris, Stephan, "The Real Roots of Darfur," *The Atlantic Monthly*, April 2007, p. 67.

Climate change and shrinking water supplies have motivated much of the fighting between Darfur's nomadic Arabs and ethnic African farmers.

Macfarquhar, Neil, "Why Darfur Still Bleeds," *The New York Times*, July 13, 2008, p. 5.

A veteran foreign correspondent discusses the many factors fueling the fighting in Darfur and how international leaders now recommend a comprehensive solution.

McCrummen, Stephanie, "A Wide-Open Battle for Power in Darfur," *The Washington Post*, June 20, 2008, p. A1.

The rebellion in Darfur has devolved into chaos and lawlessness that threatens civilians, aid workers and peacekeepers.

Natsios, Andrew, "Sudan's Slide Toward Civil War," *Foreign Affairs*, May/June 2008, Vol. 87, Issue 3, pp. 77-93.

The former U.S. special envoy to Sudan says that while attention is focused on Darfur another bloody civil war could soon erupt between Sudan's north and south.

Prunier, Gerard, "The Politics of Death in Darfur," *Current History*, May 2006, pp. 195-202.

The French historian discusses why the international community has been unable to solve the crisis in Darfur.

Reports and Studies

"Darfur 2007: Chaos by Design," Human Rights Watch, September 2007, http://hrw.org/reports/2007/sudan0907/.

Through photographs, maps, first-hand accounts and statistics, the human-rights group summarizes the events that led to the conflict and describes Darfuris' daily struggles.

"Darfur Crisis," Government Accountability Office, November 2006, www.gao.gov/new.items/d0724.pdf.

The report analyzes the widely varying estimates on the number of deaths caused by the Darfur conflict and reviews the different methodologies used to track the casualties.

"Displaced in Darfur: A Generation of Anger," Amnesty International, January 2008, www.amnesty.org/en/library/info/AFR54/001/2008.

Using interviews and first-hand accounts, the human-rights group vividly describes the death and destruction in Darfur and recommends ways to end the fighting.

"Sudan — Darfur: Humanitarian Profile," United Nations Office for the Coordination of Humanitarian Affairs, June 2, 2008, www.unsudanig.org/.../darfur/data/dhnp/Map%201226%20Darfur%20Humanitarian%20Profile%20June%203%202008.pdf.

This frequently updated U.N. Web site provides maps and charts illustrating areas hit worst by the crisis, the number of attacks on humanitarian workers and the number of people affected by the fighting.

"They Shot at Us As We Fled," Human Rights Watch, May 2008, www.hrw.org/reports/2008/darfur0508/.

Using first-hand accounts from victims, the report describes how attacks against Darfuri villages in February 2008 violated international humanitarian law.

The Next Step:

Additional Articles from Current Periodicals

Arab League

"Darfur Rebel Group Censures Arab League, AU Position on ICC," Sudan Tribune (France), July 20, 2008.

A Darfur rebel group has criticized the Arab League for supporting Sudan in its dispute with the International Criminal Court (ICC) over charges of genocide filed against Sudanese President Omar Hassan al-Bashir.

"Muslim Groups Urge Arab League to Play Active Role in Solving Sudan's Crisis," Sudan Tribune (France), March 28, 2008.

A coalition of Muslim groups complains that the Darfur crisis, which has claimed the lives of at least 200,000 Muslims, has not captured the attention of the Muslim world.

Sirri, Mustafa, and Sawsan Abu-Hasan, "JEM Accuses the Arab League of Discriminating Among the Sudanese on the Basis of Colour and Ethnic Background," Al-Sharq al-Awsat (Saudi Arabia), May 25, 2008.

The Sudanese Justice and Equality Movement has accused the Arab League of isolating itself from the Sudanese people and the situation in Darfur, where Arab militias have been attacking residents of the mostly black farming communities.

Chinese Involvement

"China Appeals for More Cooperation Between Sudan, UN on Darfur," Suna (Sudan), Nov. 10, 2007.

China's ambassador to Sudan says working together the two countries can help bring peace to Darfur.

"China's Role in Darfur Positive," Chinadaily.com.cn, Feb. 18, 2008.

China has helped the Sudanese government, United Nations and African Union establish a joint force to address the humanitarian crisis in Darfur.

Bloomfield, Steve, "Chinese Envoy to Put Pressure on Sudan Over Darfur," The Independent (England), May 11, 2007.

China has appointed a special envoy to Darfur to help head off criticisms over its policy positions on the troubled region.

Cooper, Helene, "Darfur Collides With Olympics, And China Yields," The New York Times, April 13, 2007, p. A1.

Nongovernmental organizations and other advocacy groups have linked the killings in Darfur to the Beijing Olympics.

Environment

"Underground Lake May Ease Darfur Crisis," Belfast Telegraph (Northern Ireland), July 19, 2007.

A suspected lake under the Darfur region could help alleviate the civil war if drinking water could be pumped to the surface.

Demontesquiou, Alfred, "Climate Change Deepens Darfur's Despair," The Advertiser (Australia), June 28, 2007, p. 19.

War has left land in Darfur increasingly uninhabitable and has helped intensify tensions amid a drought with no end in sight.

Ki-moon, Ban, "A Climate Culprit in Darfur," The Washington Post, June 16, 2007, p. A15.

It is no coincidence that violence erupted in Darfur during a period of extended drought in the region.

Genocide

"Bush Launches Attack Against 'Genocide' in Darfur," Aberdeen Press & Journal (Scotland), May 30, 2007.

President Bush has called the crisis in Darfur genocide and has imposed economic sanctions against Sudan.

Bloomfield, Steve, "African Union: Suspend Sudan Genocide Charge," The Independent (England), July 15, 2008.

The African Union has asked the International Criminal Court to suspend its genocide charges against President Bashir until the problems in Darfur are sorted out.

Kolieb, Jonathan, "Darfur Horrors Aren't 'Genocide,' " Baltimore Sun, Dec. 16, 2007, p. 15A.

Referring to the Darfur situation as "genocide" is flawed in legal terms and is unhelpful in resolving the crisis.

Marquand, Robert, "Why Genocide Is Difficult to Prosecute," The Christian Science Monitor, April 30, 2007, p. 1.

An ICC prosecutor did not charge a Sudanese interior minister and a *janjaweed* leader with genocide because their actions did not fit the definition under the 1948 Geneva Convention.

CITING CQ GLOBAL RESEARCHER

Sample formats for citing these reports in a bibliography include the ones listed below. Preferred styles and formats vary, so please check with your instructor or professor.

MLA STYLE
Flamini, Roland. "Nuclear Proliferation." CQ Global Researcher 1 Apr. 2007: 1-24.

APA STYLE
Flamini, R. (2007, April 1). Nuclear proliferation. *CQ Global Researcher*, 1, 1-24.

CHICAGO STYLE
Flamini, Roland. "Nuclear Proliferation." *CQ Global Researcher*, April 1, 2007, 1-24.

Voices From Abroad:

LOUISE ARBOUR
U.N. High Commissioner for Human Rights

History will judge

"The desperate plight of the people of Darfur has for too long been neglected or addressed with what the victims should rightly regard — and history will judge — as meek offerings, broken promises and disregard."

Voice of America News, December 2006

LIU JIANCHAO
Foreign Ministry Spokesman, China

Constructive dialogue is necessary

"On this issue, putting up banners and chanting slogans alone can not help resolve the humanitarian issue in Darfur. What is most important is to promote the peace process in Darfur with realistic, constructive and practical action. . . . We also hope relevant people will objectively view China's position on the Darfur issue, and do some concrete things for the people of Darfur in a down-to-earth manner."

Xinhua news agency (China), February 2008

OMAR HASSAN AL-BASHIR
President, Sudan

ICC will not hold us back

"Every time we take a step forward, make progress and signs of peace emerge, those people [International Criminal Court] try to mess it up, return us to square one and dis-tract us with marginal issues and false allegations. . . . Ocampo's talk will not bother us or distract us from our work."

The Associated Press, July 2008

PAUL RUSESABAGINA
Celebrated former hotel manager, Rwanda

Too much concern over sovereignty

"When modern genocide has loomed, the United Nations has shown more concern for not offending the sovereignty of one of its member nations, even as monstrosities take place within its borders. Yet 'national sovereignty' is often a euphemism for the pride of dictators. Darfur is just such a case. The world cannot afford this kind of appeasement any longer."

The Wall Street Journal, April 2006

DAVID MOZERSKY
Horn of Africa Project Director, International Crisis Group

Broader talks needed on Darfur

"The only way to make progress is to give enough time for ongoing rebel unification efforts to succeed and to broaden talks to involve the full range of actors in the conflict. They must seek to identify individuals to represent the interests of these groups at the peace talks, giving specific attention to the representation of women, civil society, the internally displaced and Arabs."

allAfrica.com, December 2007

KOFI ANNAN
Then Secretary-General, United Nations

'Never again' rings hollow

"To judge by what is happening in Darfur, our performance has not improved much since the disasters of Bosnia and Rwanda. Sixty years after the liberation of the Nazi death camps and 30 years after the Cambodian killing fields, the promise of 'never again' is ringing hollow."

Speech before Human Rights Watch in New York, December 2006

MUSTAFA UTHMAN ISMA'IL
Presidential adviser, Sudan

Death tolls in Darfur are exaggerated

"The United Nations reports indicate that some 200,000 people have been killed in Darfur. However, we, in Sudan, believe that these reports are question-able. They have been prepared by Western organizations that want no good for Darfur. Anyone who follows up on the Western media finds that the situation in Darfur has been clearly exaggerated, as if the developments in Darfur were more serious than what happens in Iraq. More than one million people have been killed in Iraq."

Elaph (England), May 2008

JAMES SMITH
Chief Executive Officer, Aegis Trust

More than a civil war

"Painting the crisis in Darfur as merely a civil war encourages further delays — which could cause the loss of thousands of lives. The motives of the perpetrators in Darfur go well beyond territorial conflict. As put by one *janjaweed*: 'We have a dream. We want to kill the Africans.'"

The Guardian (England), September 2006

MOST OF THEM ARE DEAD OR GONE. SO YOU CAN COME IN.

UN

SUDAN DARFUR REGION

HACHFELD

Neues Deutschland/Germany/Rainer Hachfeld

THE TROUBLED HORN OF AFRICA

BY JASON MCLURE

Excerpted from the CQ Global Researcher. Jason McLure. (June 2009). "The Troubled Horn of Africa." *CQ Global Researcher*, 149-176.

The Troubled Horn of Africa

BY JASON MCLURE

THE ISSUES

Halima Warsame's husband and son were killed two years ago after a mortar shell landed on their shop in Mogadishu, the war-torn capital of Somalia. But the impoverished nation's long civil war wasn't finished with her yet.

After living in a camp for people who had fled the fighting, she returned home in April. But in mid-May renewed fighting forced her to return to the camp.

"I thought with the Ethiopian troops gone and the new government [in place] everything would be alright, only it got worse," she says. "I don't see any hope that our situation will ever improve." [1]

Indeed, there is little reason for optimism. During just two weeks in May, at least 67,000 people were driven from their homes in the beleaguered seaside capital by clashes between the country's U.N.-backed transitional government and Islamist extremists. But they are just the latest victims. Somalia's 18-year civil war has killed tens of thousands, forced nearly 1.3 million people from their homes and created a lawless safe haven for pirates and suspected terrorists. [2]

Once a gem of Italian colonial architecture overlooking the Indian Ocean, parts of Mogadishu have been reduced to a moonscape of gutted buildings where warring militias wielding shoulder-fired grenade launchers and AK-47s periodically wreak havoc, sending civilians fleeing to dozens of primitive camps surrounding the city.

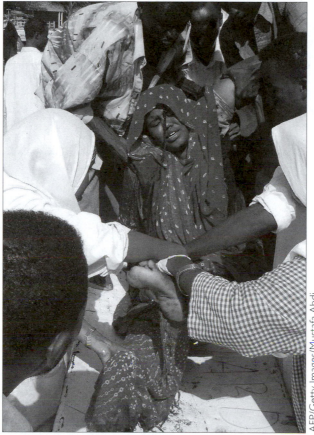

A Somali woman wounded in fighting between government soldiers and Islamist insurgents last June is among thousands of civilians killed or wounded in Somalia's 18-year civil war. The conflict has destabilized the entire region, forcing nearly 1.3 million people from their homes and creating a lawless safe haven for pirates and terrorists.

AFP/Getty Images/Mustafa Abdi

The fighting has continued despite more than a dozen attempts to establish a central government — including the latest, in January, when moderate Islamist Sheikh Sharif Sheikh Ahmed became president. In fact, Ahmed's government is said to have, at best, a tenuous hold on just a few blocks of the capital itself. The ongoing security vacuum has encouraged the clan violence and anarchy that make Somalia a global poster child for a "failed state."

But the fighting in Somalia is only part of an interrelated web of conflicts plaguing the Horn of Africa — one of the most benighted corners of the world's poorest continent. Archrivals Ethiopia and tiny Eritrea have backed factions in Somalia's civil war and continue to arm rebel groups destabilizing the region. And both nations have kept tens of thousands of troops dug in along their mutual border since the end of a 1998-2000 border war that killed 70,000.

In January, Ethiopia ended a two-year occupation of Mogadishu, where it initially succeeded in ousting an Islamist alliance that U.S. officials feared was courting links with the al Qaeda terrorist group. Western nations have showered Ethiopia with billions of dollars in aid and avoided criticizing the regime's recent clampdown on opposition parties, journalists and human rights activists.

Eritrea, once admired for its self-sufficiency and discipline, has become an isolated dictatorship facing possible international sanctions for having backed the Islamist insurgents in Somalia. Meanwhile Eritrea's effort to build a military counterweight to much-larger Ethiopia has kept more than a third of its productive population serving in the military. [3]

"Eritrea and Ethiopia are battling to determine which will be the dominant power in the region," says Dan Connell, a former adviser to the Eritrean government and author of the book *Against All Odds: A Chronicle of the Eritrean Revolution*. "The border issue is more excuse than cause."

Thus beleaguered by poor governance, conflict and poverty, Ethiopia and Eritrea rank near the bottom on the United Nations' 179-country Human Development Index, which ranks countries by life expectancy,

Grinding Poverty Afflicts Most of Africa's Horn

The four nations in the Horn of Africa cover an arid swathe about three times the size of Texas. More than 100 million people live in the war-torn region — 85.2 million of them in landlocked Ethiopia, Africa's second-most populous country. Tiny Djibouti is the smallest with half a million people. Ethiopia and Eritrea are near the bottom on the U.N.'s 179-nation Human Development Index, which ranks countries by life expectancy and other factors. Somalia doesn't even make the list, since it has no way to collect statistics. Some analysts say the area's poverty and weak or corrupt governments make it a safe haven for Islamic terrorists and pirates.

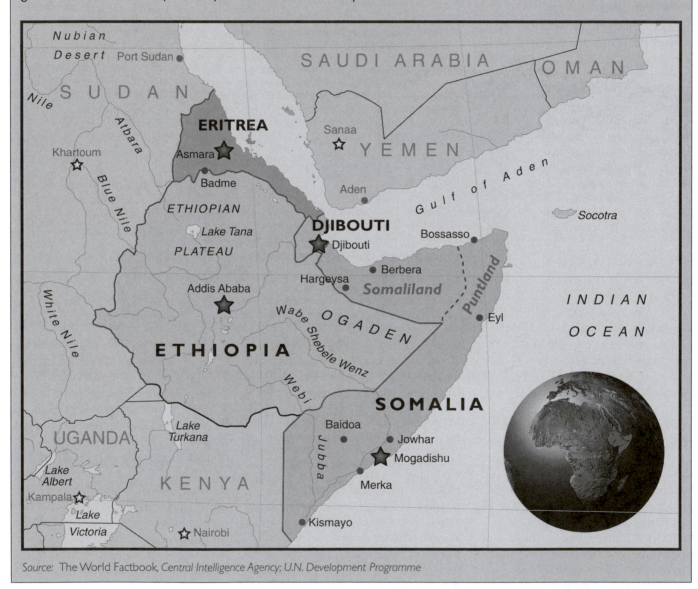

Source: The World Factbook, *Central Intelligence Agency; U.N. Development Programme*

literacy and other factors. Somalia, with no functioning central government to collect statistics, doesn't even make the list. [4] But with 40 percent of the population needing emergency aid, U.N. officials describe Somalia as the world's worst humanitarian and security crisis. [5]

"The region seems to be going backwards fast," says Ioan Lewis, a retired professor at the London School of Economics who has written several books on Somalia. "Whether it can change gear and change course, I really don't know."

The region's human rights record worries the international community as much as its dire economic conditions. The European Parliament on

Jan. 15 expressed its "great concern" for the state of "human rights, the rule of law, democracy and governance in all countries of the Horn of Africa," where there were "credible reports of arbitrary arrests, forced labour, torture and maltreatment of prisoners, as well as persecution of journalists and political repression." [6]

The chaos has provided refuge to suspected al Qaeda terrorists and allowed pirates to wreak havoc on international shipping. The conflict and poverty have sent millions of refugees fleeing to neighboring countries or to camps in Somalia for internally displaced persons (IDPs) where they depend on international aid agencies for food and shelter — aid that is often blocked by violence, theft or piracy. (*See graph, p. 157.*) [7]

Somalia's civil war has been fuelled in large part by distrust and competition between the country's Byzantine network of clans and subclans and by warlords with a vested interest in instability. A brief flicker of hope accompanied the withdrawal of Ethiopian troops in January and the accession of Sheikh Ahmed to the presidency of the country's Transitional Federal Government. But that hope was dimmed by fierce fighting in April and May and the capture of key towns by Islamist insurgents. Even veteran observers of Somalia marvel at the seeming senselessness of the fighting.

"All I can say now is that I have felt it a privilege to observe a people who shot themselves in the foot with such accuracy and tumbled into the abyss in such style," Aidan Hartley, a Kenyan-born Reuters correspondent who covered Somalia in the early 1990s, wrote in a 2003 book. [8]

Such sentiments are still echoed today. "We are all . . . shocked that Somalis keep finding reasons to kill Somalis," said Ahmedou Ould-Abdallah, a Mauritanian diplomat who is the U.N. special envoy to Somalia, during a Feb. 2 press conference.

Horn of Africa at a Glance

Somalia

Area: 246,201 sq. miles (slightly smaller than Texas)
Population: 9.8 million (July 2009 est.)
GDP per capita: $600 (2008 est.)
Unemployment rate: n/a
UN Human Development Index rank: not included
Religion: Sunni Muslim
Government: Sheikh Sharif Sheikh Ahmed was elected president in January 2009; Somaliland in the north remains autonomous, having declared its own local government in 1991 but has not been recognized internationally. Puntland, in the northeast, declared itself the Puntland State of Somalia in 1998 but has refrained from making a formal bid for independence.

Ethiopia

Area: 435,186 sq. miles (about twice the size of Texas)
Population: 85.2 million (July 2009 est.)
GDP per capita: $800 (2008 est.)
Unemployment rate: n/a
UN Human Development Index rank: 169 (out of 179)
Religion: Christian, 61%; Muslim, 33%; other 6%
Government: Federal republic, bicameral Parliament; Prime Minister Meles Zenawi was elected in 2000.

Eritrea

Area: 46,842 sq. miles (slightly larger than Pennsylvania)
Population: 5.6 million (July 2009 est.)
GDP per capita: $700 (2008 est.)
Unemployment rate: n/a
UN Human Development Index rank: 164 (out of 179)
Religion: Muslim, Coptic Christian, Roman Catholic, Protestant
Government: Provisional government since independence from Ethiopia in 1991, constitutional options presented but none yet implemented; single-party state run by the leftist People's Front for Democracy and Justice; President Isaias Afwerki elected by National Assembly in 1993 in country's only election so far.

Djibouti

Area: 8,880 sq. miles (about the size of New Jersey)
Population: 516,055 (July 2009 est.)
GDP per capita: $3,700 (2008 est.)
Unemployment rate: 59% in urban areas, 83% in rural areas (2007 est.)
UN Human Development Index rank: 151 (out of 179)
Religion: Muslim 94%, Christian 6%
Government: Republic; President Ismail Omar Guelleh has held office since 1999.

Source: The World Factbook, *Central Intelligence Agency; U.N. Development Programme*

The four nations of Africa's Horn — Somalia, Ethiopia, Eritrea and the microstate Djibouti — cover an arid swathe about three times the size of Texas. About 100 million people live in the region — 85.2 million of them in Ethiopia, Africa's second-most populous country after Nigeria. To the north, tiny Eritrea — which split away from Ethiopia in 1993 — maintains Africa's largest army in an effort to deter its southern neighbor from invading.

in Somalia and Ethiopia to seek humanitarian aid. [9]

And the long-term trends are equally worrying. About 80 percent of Ethiopians and Eritreans are subsistence farmers or herders. Agricultural production per capita has declined in Ethiopia since the 1960s, while the population has more than tripled. [10] Eritrea's government-controlled economy has eliminated nearly all private enterprise, and its farmers don't produce enough food to feed the country, a situation exacerbated by the government's decision not to demobilize tens of thousands of farmers from the military. [11] Somalia, which imports about 60 percent of the grain needed to feed its estimated 8 to 10 million people, has little prospect of feeding itself anytime soon.

"Ethiopia adds to its population between 1.5 to 2 million people a year," says David Shinn, U.S. ambassador to the country from 1996 to 1999. "That is not sustainable for a country that has been unable to feed itself for more than three decades."

While Somalia's humanitarian disaster is the region's most pressing issue, a longer-term question is whether the war-wracked country as presently configured can survive. Its northwestern region, known as Somaliland, has declared independence after building a functional administration and maintaining a comparatively peaceful, democratic existence for the last decade.

"The hard questions have not been asked as to what sort of a nation-state Somalia should look like," says Rashid Abdi, a Nairobi-based analyst for the International Crisis Group, a conflict-resolution think tank. "The focus has been on creating a national government. Unfortunately, in spite of a lot of investment in the last 15 years, we are nowhere near a functioning, credible nation-state."

Western policy in the region has been influenced largely by the perception that Somalia's lawlessness provides a safe haven for al Qaeda. Somalia's radical Islamist al-Shabaab militia, the most pow-

Death and Demonstrations

The remains of Somalis killed during Ethiopia's two-year occupation are recovered near a former Ethiopian military camp in Somalia (top). More than 10,000 people reportedly were killed during the occupation, which ended in January. Ethiopia also has come under international criticism for a recent crackdown on opposition leaders, the press and human rights organizations. Protesters demonstrate against Prime Minister Meles Zenawi during the April meeting of world leaders in London (bottom).

Conflict is not new to the Horn of Africa, where the predominately Christian highlanders of the Ethiopian plateau have been fighting with the Muslim lowlanders of eastern Ethiopia (known as the Ogaden) and Somalia for centuries. But the region is also periodically plagued by famine, due to a rapidly growing population and increasingly unpredictable rainfall. This year the warfare and drought will force about 15.5 million people

erful group battling the transitional government, has links to al Qaeda and reportedly has been recruiting jihadists in the United States. [12] And while recent reports indicate that hundreds of foreign fighters from the Middle East and Muslim communities in North America and Europe have arrived in Somalia, analysts disagree over whether Somalia's Islamic radicals pose any real threat outside of the Horn. [13] Some blame the George W. Bush administration in particular for fomenting chaos in Somalia by arming warlords whose sole virtues were their willingness to fight Islamic groups.

"Violent extremism and anti-Americanism are now rife in Somalia due in large part to the blowback from policies that focused too narrowly on counterterrorism objectives," writes Kenneth Menkhaus, an American Horn of Africa specialist from Davidson College who worked as a U.N. official in Somalia in the 1990s. [14]

If there is reason for optimism, it is that the new Obama administration in Washington has signaled its willingness to focus more on human rights and stability and less on waging war against radical Islamists and their allies. Such a move would involve both pressing Ethiopia to resolve its border dispute with Eritrea and showing a greater willingness to work with moderate Islamists in Somalia, who many believe are the only force capable of bridging the divide between the country's constantly warring clans.

As analysts and diplomats discuss the Horn of Africa's future, here are some of the questions being debated:

Is there a real threat of international terrorism from Somalia?

When 17-year-old Burhan Hassan didn't come home from school in Minneapolis last Nov. 4, his mother thought he was at a local mosque. Unfortunately he wasn't. Although his family had fled Somalia when he was a toddler, Burhan — it turned out — had embarked that day for the southern Somali port town

of Kismayo, a stronghold of al-Shabaab, the military wing of the Islamic Courts Union (ICU) that briefly controlled southern Somalia in 2006 before being ousted by Ethiopian troops.

U.S. law enforcement and counterterrorism officials fear Burhan is one of about 20 young Somali-Americans who may have left the United States since mid-2007 to join the group, which the State Department considers a terrorist organization. [15] The fear is that they may return to the United States or Europe as part of a sleeper cell, sent by a group that is increasingly vociferous about its links to international terrorism. Since 2007 some Amer-

Newly elected Somalia President Sheikh Sharif Sheikh Ahmed is regarded by many as one of the few men whose clan base and political skills might bring peace to the war-ravaged country. Somalia has had no effective central authority since former president Mohamed Siad Barre was ousted in 1991, touching off an endless cycle of war between rival factions.

ican generals have considered Somalia a "third front in the war on terror," [16] and U.S. military planes are a common sight over the nation. [17] *

---

* In 2003, the U.S. opened a military base in Djibouti, less than 30 miles from the border of Somalia. Camp Lemonier houses about 2,000 U.S. personnel who monitor suspected terrorists in the Horn of Africa and train the militaries of Ethiopia and other U.S. allies.

A spokesman for al-Shabaab said it began seeking links with al Qaeda after it was listed as a terrorist group by the Bush administration in 2008. Before that, Shabaab "had no official links with al Qaeda," Sheikh Mukhtar Robow, a spokesman for the group, said in 2008. Now, however, "we're looking to have an association with them. Al Qaeda became more powerful after it was added to the list; we hope that it will be the same with us." [18]

Experts differ on whether the links are substantive. Those who worry that Somalia has become a safe haven for terrorists point out that several Somali Islamist leaders were trained in al Qaeda camps in the Afghanistan-Pakistan border regions in the 1990s before returning to Somalia to help form al-Ittihad al-Islamiya, a forerunner of al-Shabaab.

"We face a very serious counterterrorism challenge in Somalia, with extremists affiliated with al Qaeda training and operating in substantial portions of southern Somalia," said Susan Rice, the Obama administration's U.N. ambassador, during confirmation hearings in

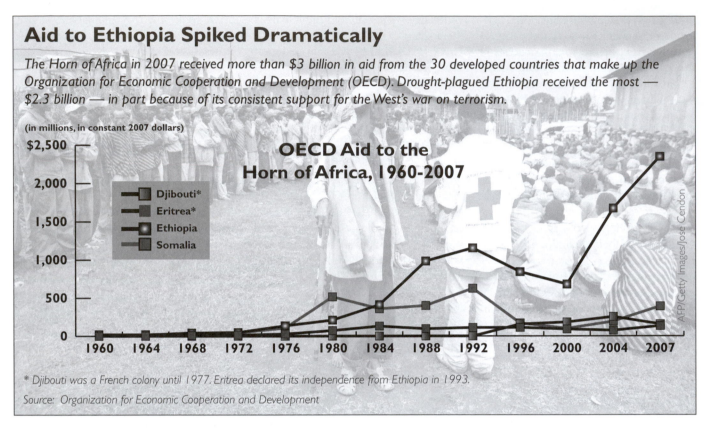

Aid to Ethiopia Spiked Dramatically

The Horn of Africa in 2007 received more than $3 billion in aid from the 30 developed countries that make up the Organization for Economic Cooperation and Development (OECD). Drought-plagued Ethiopia received the most — $2.3 billion — in part because of its consistent support for the West's war on terrorism.

OECD Aid to the Horn of Africa, 1960-2007

(in millions, in constant 2007 dollars)

Legend:
- Djibouti*
- Eritrea*
- Ethiopia
- Somalia

* Djibouti was a French colony until 1977. Eritrea declared its independence from Ethiopia in 1993.

Source: Organization for Economic Cooperation and Development

AFP/Getty Images/Jose Cendon

January. "And that has the potential to pose a serious and direct threat to our own national security."

Those concerned about the terrorism threat from Somalia often cite Gouled Hassan Dourad, a Somali national who was trained in Afghanistan, captured in Somalia in 2004 and held in the CIA's secret prison system before being transferred to Guantánamo Bay in 2006. The United States claims he supported al Qaeda's East Africa cell and was privy to plots to attack an Ethiopian airliner and the U.S. military base in Djibouti in 2003. [19] Likewise, Fazul Abdullah Mohammed — a Comoran national accused of involvement in the 1998 bombings of U.S. embassies in Kenya and Tanzania and suspected in the 2002 truck bombing of the Paradise Hotel in Mombasa that killed 15 — is also thought to have taken refuge in Somalia. [20] A third figure, Hassan al-Turki, is said to run a training camp for Islamist militants in southern Somalia, and,

like Mohammed, has been the target of an unsuccessful U.S. air strike in Somalia. [21]

"Definitely you have the al Qaeda East Africa cell that has only been able to function in Somalia with the protection of Somali Islamist movements," says Andre LeSage, an American Horn of Africa specialist at the Pentagon's National Defense University. "Previously, it had been with the protection of al-Ittihad, now it's with the protection of al-Shabaab."

But others say the international terrorism threat from Somalia has been exaggerated, both by al Qaeda and by the United States and its allies. "There is very strong documentation, using declassified al Qaeda documents, indicating that it was in and out of Somalia starting in 1992-1993," says Shinn, the former ambassador to Ethiopia. "They had relatively little success, however. They thought it was going to be relatively easy pickings until they learned Somalis could be just as obstreperous

with them as with everyone else. It was very tough sledding.

"Over time they've had increasing success. But I think there is a certain amount of hype here," he says, especially when the West compares al-Shabaab to the ultra-conservative Taliban in Afghanistan. "The idea that the Taliban is moving into Somalia is just utter nonsense."

Indeed, some argue that U.S. support for Ethiopia's 2006 invasion of Somalia and subsequent U.S. air strikes in Somalia that have often mistakenly killed civilians have been counterproductive and have helped to radicalize the population — increasing the terrorism threat. But so far, these analysts point out, no Somali-born citizens have been involved in successful acts of international terrorism.

"The Ethiopian invasion was totally negative," says Lewis, the Somali historian. "The terrorist threat is much more real now than before the interventions."

Coordinated suicide attacks last October on five separate targets in the autonomous Somali regions of Somaliland and Puntland — apparently carried out by al-Shabaab — have raised fears the group's capacity for such tactics is growing. [22]

"The suicide bombings in Puntland and Somaliland were clear evidence that these guys have the capacity to work outside their comfort zone," says Menkhaus. "They've also demonstrated their capacity to induce some young men to commit suicide, which is fairly new to Somalia.

"Where will the next threat present itself? Kenya, Ethiopia, Djibouti? Shabaab has every reason to keep this conflict internationalized," he adds.

Is Somalia a viable state?

In the 18 years since the fall of dictator Mohamed Siad Barre, Somalia's foundations have steadily crumbled, with two large northern swathes of the country declaring themselves autonomous or independent entities.

In some ways, the Somalia that existed in the three decades before 1991 — a unified Somalia with a capital in Mogadishu — was an historical anomaly. It never existed previously and has not existed since. Though some analysts express optimism about the newest U.N.-backed Transitional Federal Government (TFG) formed in February, the fact remains that its 14 predecessors since 1991 have all failed. [23]

The TFG struggles to control the port of Mogadishu, which is its main source of revenue, and has authority over just a tiny fraction of Somali territory. Though the current government has 36 cabinet ministers, most of the ministries have no employees and no budget. [24] The situation is so chaotic that businessmen print their own currency, and educated Somalis seek passports from neighboring countries to facilitate international travel.

Despite a string of U.N.-funded peace-and-reconciliation conferences in neighboring countries, a constantly shifting

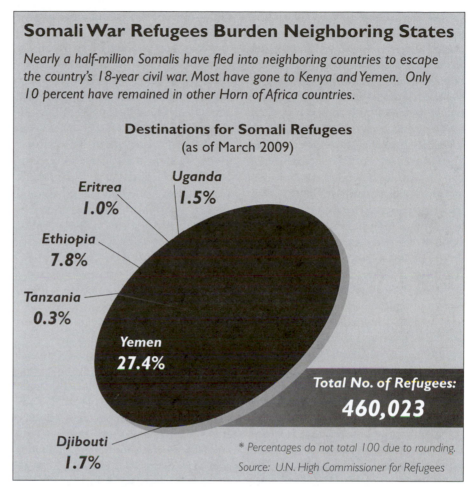

Somali War Refugees Burden Neighboring States

Nearly a half-million Somalis have fled into neighboring countries to escape the country's 18-year civil war. Most have gone to Kenya and Yemen. Only 10 percent have remained in other Horn of Africa countries.

Destinations for Somali Refugees
(as of March 2009)

Eritrea 1.0%
Uganda 1.5%
Ethiopia 7.8%
Tanzania 0.3%
Yemen 27.4%
Djibouti 1.7%

Total No. of Refugees: 460,023

* Percentages do not total 100 due to rounding.

Source: U.N. High Commissioner for Refugees

array of militia groups has defied outside attempts at reconciliation. In 2008, World Food Programme convoys bringing aid from Mogadishu to refugee camps 18 miles away needed to pass through more than a dozen checkpoints controlled by different militia groups, according to Peter Smerdon, a spokesman for the program.

"There are too many separate interests on the ground in Somalia," says LeSage, of the National Defense University. "You have so many different power centers there, and each one is being held by a different faction leader. They don't all share the same agenda for the way forward for the government. . . . You've already got 30-odd political groups just in Mogadishu."

The notable exception is Somaliland, formerly controlled by Britain. It declared independence from Somalia in

1991, ratified a national constitution in 2001 and has remained relatively peaceful since then. Its autonomous government, based in Hargeysa, prints money, operates a police force and issues passports. The region's combination of electoral democracy and clan-based power-sharing has drawn widespread praise, though so far no other government has recognized its independence.

"Somalia hasn't been functioning as a unified state at all, and Somaliland is virtually a separate state that really requires international recognition," says historian Lewis. "I don't think Somalia needs to exist in its present fashion."

Mohamed Hassan, Somaliland's ambassador to Ethiopia, says his homeland's independence was inevitable: "It was a bad marriage, and when a marriage is bad you have to separate.

"We don't know who to talk to now in Somalia," he continues. "There is no central government. They are so fragmented. They have been killing and killing and killing and oppressing. The people of Somaliland have enjoyed peace, security and democracy, and they're confident they can continue."

Because of the lack of international recognition, however, the region has not garnered needed development aid or political support. Many countries are reluctant to recognize breakaway states unless it is politically expedient to do so, and there is no coherent international policy for recognizing separatist states. [25]

"There is no way Somaliland will rejoin Somalia, not in my lifetime," says Abdi, the International Crisis Group analyst. "They are dead-set on independence. If we don't reward Somaliland with some form of recognition, they risk sliding back. I think they are the most democratic administration in the Horn of Africa."

Neighboring Puntland also has functioned largely autonomously from both the Islamist militias and the Western-backed transitional government in the south. Dominated by the Majerteyn subclan of Somalia's Darod clan, the region declared itself the Puntland State of Somalia in 1998 but has refrained from making a formal independence bid. [26] That's in part because Abdullahi Yusuf, a native of Puntland, served as president of the TFG in Mogadishu for four years until being pressured to resign in December.

Puntland also has made democratic strides. The regional president was ousted in a parliamentary election in January by Abdirahman Mohamed Farole, a former finance minister. [27] But the area's reputation has been harmed by its status as a launching point for dozens of pirate attacks in 2008 and 2009. In December a U.N. report expressed concern "about the apparent complicity in pirate networks of Puntland administration officials at all lev-

els" — a charge Puntland officials have disputed. [28] (*See sidebar, p. 162.*)

"They are somewhere between secession and union with the rest of Somalia," says Abdi. "Depending on how things evolve in the next few months, Puntland is just hedging its bets. If they think union with Somalia is a dead-end, they will go their own way."

Recognition for either autonomous region would likely have to come first from Ethiopia, the regional power and a close ally of both administrations, or from the African Union (AU). So far both have refrained from doing so. "Those areas are pretty well-secured," Jean Ping, the Gabonese chairman of the African Union Commission, told a Jan. 27 press conference. "But the AU is characterized by respect for the territorial integrity of Somalia."

The United States has said it prefers a unified Somalia. "We will stay in line with the AU; that was the Bush administration's policy," says Jendayi Frazer, the U.S. assistant secretary of state for African affairs from 2005 to 2008. And it's a policy the Obama administration is likely to continue.

Most analysts say a unified Somalia would need a decentralized administrative system in order to be effective. "Our insistence that Somalis remake themselves in our image with ministries of this and this and this isn't realistic," says Menkhaus, the former U.N. official in Somalia. "A state that could emerge in a more organic way is possible. That might include a full array of local Islamic courts, municipalities and hybrid arrangements involving professional groups and clerics."

Should the United States reconsider its policies toward Ethiopia?

Ethiopia's human rights record is among the worst on the continent. But because the predominantly Christian nation — Africa's second-most populous country — cooperates in counterterrorism efforts, the United States and its European allies rarely criticize

Prime Minister Meles Zenawi's government.

"There has been full support largely because they view the region through the counterterrorism lens, and Ethiopia has been considered the primary partner in the region," says Leslie Lefkow, a researcher at Human Rights Watch. "This has been problematic because it's ignored the very serious downward trajectory of Ethiopia's human rights record."

Indeed, the Zenawi government has become increasingly repressive in recent years:

- During an ongoing offensive against insurgents in eastern Ethiopia's Somali-speaking Ogaden region, Ethiopian troops have been accused of burning villages, raping women and summarily executing civilians suspected of supporting the separatist Ogaden National Liberation Front. [29]

- Opposition leader Birtukan Mideksa has been held in solitary confinement since December, when she was jailed for life for disputing terms of a pardon agreement that freed her and other opposition leaders from prison in 2007. [30]

- In April 2008, the ruling party and its allies swept to victory in local elections after major opposition parties withdrew, citing government intimidation.

- In January Ethiopia's parliament effectively banned foreign aid agencies from funding groups that promote democracy and human or women's rights. [31]

Lefkow also points out that U.S. support for Ethiopia's invasion of Somalia has not been rewarded by the death or capture of major terrorist suspects. "The small number of people that the U.S. was interested in have not been detained," she says. "The scores of people who were detained in 2007 were either not implicated at all in anything or were very minor people."

Ethiopia Takes On Malaria

New effort attacks a deadly foe.

When malaria swept through the green hills of his village in southwest Ethiopia three years ago, Biya Abbafogi was lucky. The 35-year-old coffee farmer and three of his children were stricken with the deadly, mosquito-borne disease, but they all survived. Thirteen neighbors and friends in Merewa didn't.

"We would take one child to the hospital and come back and another one would be sick," he says.

The treatment Abbafogi and his family received was cheap by Western standards — just $40. But that was about a third of his annual coffee earnings, and the bills from the medical clinic — located two hours away by foot — forced Abbafogi to sell one of the oxen he used to plow his small corn field.

But today things are much better for Merewa's 4,335 residents, thanks to two young women trained to treat and prevent malaria and other common ailments. They're not doctors or nurses, and they haven't been to college. But with just one year of training they've cut malaria rates during the infectious season from 15 to 20 new cases per day to one to three.

Merewa's success has been replicated all across Ethiopia, where the government has dispatched an army of up to 30,000 "health extension workers" in the past four years. With money from donors like the Geneva-based Global Fund and the Carter Center in Atlanta, the women have distributed 20 million mosquito-repelling nets and offered basic malaria testing and treatment in isolated villages dozens of miles from the nearest paved road.

Every year 4 million Ethiopians contract malaria, which is particularly deadly for children. As many as one in five youngsters under age 5 who get the disease die from it. In response, Ethiopia is at the forefront of two major public-health initiatives in poor countries. The first, known as task-shifting, trains lower-skilled health professionals — who are cheaper to pay and easier to retain — to provide basic treatments and teach prevention. The second aims to distribute anti-malarial bed nets to 600 million Africans living in mosquito-infested regions by 2011.

Ethiopia's poverty helped drive the new approach. As one of the world's poorest countries, Ethiopia has trouble keeping doctors from moving to better-paying jobs overseas, says Tedros Adhanom, Ethiopia's health minister. "Right now, 50 percent of the doctors Ethiopia trains will emigrate," he says. To compensate, he says, Ethiopia is training more doctors — medical schools admitted 1,000 students in 2008, four times more than in 2007 — and shifting as much work as possible to nurses and health extension workers.

Lower-skilled extension workers don't emigrate, and they're also willing to work for less and to serve in rural areas, Adhanom says. "To tackle our health problems, the solutions are simple," he says. "You don't need highly skilled people to tell you how to prevent malaria."

Health workers learn 16 different health-education and treatment interventions, including midwifery, malaria treatment and hygiene education. They also make sure villagers are vaccinated and organize insecticide spraying to kill malaria-transmitting mosquitoes.

The mosquito net distribution program faces many obstacles in a country where many of the 85 million citizens live miles from paved roads. But improved technology offers hope the new anti-malaria effort will succeed where earlier attempts failed.

Bed nets not only provide a physical barrier against malaria-bearing mosquitoes but also kill the pests with insecticide sprayed on the nets. In the past, bed nets had to be dipped in chemicals annually to retain their potency. But newer nets are treated with long-lasting chemicals that require re-dipping only once every three to four years.

Dipping the older nets every year posed "a huge logistical problem" in rural places, Adhanom says. "Fewer than 40 percent of villagers would show up to have their old nets dipped. That really compromised the whole program."

So far, the combined initiatives seem to be working. Malaria prevalence dropped by 67 percent in Ethiopia between 2001 and 2007, according to a World Health Organization study, while the number of deaths of children under 5 has dropped 56 percent. [1]

---

[1] "Impact of the Scale-Up of Anti-Malarial Interventions Measured Using Health Facility-Based Data in Ethiopia," World Health Organization, Feb. 1, 2008.

Western support for Ethiopia's 2006 invasion of Somalia — as well as Ethiopia's continued occupation of territory awarded to Eritrea in 2002 by the Eritrea-Ethiopia Boundary Commission — have led to growing resentment toward the West among Ethiopia's rivals.

"Sovereign Eritrean territories are still under Ethiopian occupation," Eritrean President Isaias Afwerki said in April 2008. [32] "This is basically the problem of the United States. Ethiopia doesn't have the power to occupy Eritrean territory without the support and encouragement of the U.S. administration. And this is the core of the problem."

"U.S. support for the Ethiopian invasion and pursuit of terrorist targets in Somalia in the name of the war on terrorism have further weakened Washington's credibility in the Horn of Africa and galvanised anti-American feeling among insurgents and the general populace," says a December 2008 report from the International Crisis Group. [33]

Connell, the former adviser to Eritrea, says Ethiopia has manipulated

U.S. support to its own ends. "Ethiopia is embroiled in a self-interested effort to promote its interests at the expense of its neighbors," he says. "We cannot build relations with so-called anchor states under such circumstances. Tamp down the regional confrontations, however, and the relationship again makes sense from our perspective. Let it fester and we will again and again be drawn into fights that are not of our own making and not in our interests."

Others say the United States won't offend Ethiopia because it has contributed peacekeepers to help monitor the conflicts in Sudan's Darfur region and Burundi and supports the Comprehensive Peace Agreement between north and south Sudan. And despite human rights abuses, Ethiopia's governance looks good in comparison with neighboring Eritrea, Sudan and Somalia.

"What you have is a very difficult balancing act where you try to push Ethiopia to open up on human rights . . . without jeopardizing Ethiopia's help on regional issues," says Shinn, the former ambassador to Ethiopia. "I don't take the opinion that you should just hammer them on human rights and let the other side drop off. On the other hand, I don't think their help in counterterrorism and peacekeeping is so important you ignore human rights."

While some critics of the regime say the United States and other Western countries should cut economic aid to Ethiopia over concerns about rising oppression, others say that would be naïve. (*See "At Issue," p. 169.*)

The Bush administration's top diplomat for Africa agrees. "Obviously, we have a lot of interests in Ethiopia," says Frazer. "Ethiopia has one of the largest, best-trained militaries in Africa. There are many Ethiopians in the United States, and Ethiopia is a major player within the African Union."

The Obama administration is still formulating its policy toward the region

but has suggested that democratic reforms will have a higher priority than counterterrorism cooperation.

"It is extremely important that Ethiopia . . . not close down its democratic space, that it allow its political opposition — its civil society — to participate broadly in the political life of that country," Johnnie Carson, Obama's assistant secretary of state for African affairs, told a Senate subcommittee on April 29. "We have our strongest relationships among our democratic partners where we share ideals and values together, rather than where we share common enemies together. A balanced relationship is absolutely essential." ∎

BACKGROUND

Christian Kingdoms

Christianity arrived in Ethiopia in the early 4th century A.D., about 300 years before it arrived in England. According to tradition, two shipwrecked Syrian sailors brought the religion to what the Romans called Abyssinia. [34] A series of Christian kingdoms would rise and fall in the Ethiopian highlands until the 14th century, when feudalism descended over the country.

The dark ages lasted until the 1850s, when central authority was resurrected by the emperors Tewodros II, Yohannes IV and Menelik II. By the 1890s, Italy — a latecomer to the race for colonies in Africa — had conquered much of present-day Eritrea, which had only sporadically been under Ethiopian rule. But Italy's colonial ambitions were checked when Menelik's troops resoundingly beat back an Italian invasion from its Eritrean colony in 1896, ensuring that Ethiopia would remain the lone African nation never colonized by Europeans.

After becoming emperor in 1930, Haile Selassie, a former noble from the

eastern city of Harar, barely had time to consolidate his rule before facing another challenge from Italy. In 1935 up to 100,000 Italian troops invaded northern Ethiopia. Selassie appealed to the League of Nations for help, but was rebuffed by France and the United Kingdom. Backed by bombers and tanks, the Italians had conquered most of Ethiopia's main cities by 1936, forcing Selassie into exile in Britain. [35]

But the Fascist Italians never controlled the countryside, and by 1941 a British-backed Ethiopian insurgency had ousted them. [36] Selassie reasserted the country's sovereignty in 1942 and turned to a new patron, the United States, to escape falling into Britain's colonial sphere. [37]

Compared with Ethiopia's rich history of ancient lords and kings ruling over peasant farmers in the cool highlands, Somalia's history is one of desert nomads who appeared in the Horn of Africa relatively late. Newly Islamized Somalis first began expanding south from the coastal area near the modern port of Berbera in northwestern Somalia in the 10th century. Fiercely independent camel and goat herders, Somalis have only rarely been brought under the control of a central state. A notable exception occurred during the holy wars against Ethiopia in the 13th-16th centuries, which culminated in the mid-16th century, when a predominantly Muslim army under Ahmed Gragn — "Ahmed the Left-Handed" — conquered much of the Ethiopian highlands.

The clan is the foundation and defining feature of Somali society. It is also at the root of the nation's problems, fostering factionalism and competition for resources rather than a sense of nationhood. The four major clan groups — Darod, Hawiye, Isaq and Dir — are each divided into sub-clans and sub-sub-clans, defined by shared ancestors going back hundreds of years. [38]

Continued on p. 162

Chronology

1850s-1940s
Britain, France, Italy and Ethiopia divvy up the Horn of Africa, setting the stage for later ethnic disputes.

———— • ————

1950s-1970s
Emperor Haile Selassie's grip on Ethiopia and Eritrea weakens as Somalia gains independence.

1952
U.N. panel rules Eritrea should become part of a federation with Ethiopia rather than gain independence.

1960
Somalia gains independence, uniting British Somaliland with Italian Somalia, but not Somali-speaking regions of Kenya, Ethiopia and Djibouti. . . . Eritrean exiles in Egypt found Eritrean Liberation Front to fight for independence, beginning a three-decade-long struggle.

1969
Somalia's democratically elected president is assassinated. Military seizes power under Gen. Siad Barre, who proclaims Somalia a socialist state.

1974
Coup deposes Ethiopia's Selassie. Military group called the Derg takes control under Col. Mengistu Haile Mariam, establishing communist government.

1977-1978
Somalia conquers much of southeastern Ethiopia before Soviet Union enters war on Ethiopia's side. Barre turns away from communist bloc.

1980s-1990s
Civil wars overthrow authoritarian rulers across the Horn, but Somalia fails to recover.

1983-1985
Drought triggers massive famine in Ethiopia, exacerbated by Mengistu's efforts to block food supplies to northern areas held by Eritrean and Tigray rebels. . . . Up to a million people die.

1991
As Soviet Union collapses, Ethiopia's Derg is overthrown by Eritrean and Tigrayan rebels from the North. Clan militias oust Barre regime in Somalia and then turn on one another. Somalia's civil war begins.

1992-1995
U.N. and U.S. try to help Somalia after up to 300,000 die from famine due to civil war and drought. U.S. withdraws in 1994 after U.S. troops die in "Black Hawk Down" incident.

1993
Eritreans vote for independence.

1998-2000
Ethiopia and Eritrea go to war over economic and border disputes. Ethiopia advances into Eritrea by 2000, capturing disputed town of Badme. U.N. peacekeepers begin patrolling border zone.

———— • ————

2000s *U.S. focus on anti-terrorism in the Horn leads to realigned loyalties.*

2001
Somaliland, which declared independence in 1991, ratifies constitution that endorses independence from southern Somalia, still mired in civil war. . . . Sept. 11 terrorist attacks on U.S. put focus on fighting al Qaeda threats in Somalia. Eritrean President Isaias Afwerki arrests Eritrean dissidents and closes private press.

2002
Eritrea-Ethiopian Boundary Commission awards Badme to Eritrea, but Ethiopia continues occupation.

2005
Ethiopia's first multiparty elections end badly as opposition leaders protest government claims of victory. At least 193 protesters are killed by Ethiopian security forces in Addis Ababa and thousands more injured. Government jails more than 120 opposition leaders, journalists and human rights activists.

2006
Islamic Courts Union (ICU) defeats U.S.-backed warlords in Mogadishu to take control of southern Somalia. Eritrean-armed ICU threatens jihad against Ethiopia.

December 2006
U.S.-backed Ethiopian troops invade Somalia, eventually ousting ICU. Efforts to install U.N.-backed Transitional Federal Government (TFG) amid Islamist insurgency fail due to resentment of Ethiopian occupation and intransigence of TFG President Abdullahi Yusuf.

December 2008-Present
Ethiopian troops withdraw from Somalia; Islamist militias still control much of the south. Yusuf resigns. Sheikh Sharif Sheikh Ahmed, former ICU chairman, becomes president of U.N.-backed Somali government. . . . Shabaab and hardline militias declare war on Sheikh Ahmed's new government. Islamists capture additional towns in southern Somalia.

Continued from p. 160

By the 19th century, France, Britain and Italy were competing with the rulers of Zanzibar, Egypt, Oman and Ethiopia for control of Somali lands. By the 1890s, the French had taken control of what is now Djibouti; Britain had established a protectorate in Somaliland; the Italians controlled central and southern Somalia and the Ethiopians ruled the Ogaden — now eastern Ethiopia. [39]

After World War II Italy was given "trusteeship" of its Somali territory, where it had developed banana and mango plantations using forced labor during the colonial era. But as independence movements swept the continent in the 1950s, the U.N. decided to unify British and Italian Somalia into a single independent state. [40] The move dashed nationalists' hopes for a Greater Somalia encompassing Somali-speaking populations in Djibouti, northern Kenya and the Ogaden.

Rise of Dictatorships

In the 1960s Somalia's young, democratically elected government unsuccessfully tried to expand its territory through a brief war with Ethiopia and by sponsoring Somali rebels in Kenya's Somali-speaking Northern Frontier District. [41] The assassination of President Abdirashid Ali Sharmarke in 1969 by one of his bodyguards heralded the

Somali Pirate Attacks on the Increase

Sophisticated gangs rake in millions in ransoms, thwart navy patrols.

"I will never go back to sea," 25-year-old seaman Jiang Lichun told the *China Daily* after being held hostage for seven months by Somali pirates in the Gulf of Aden. [1] During his harrowing 2007 ordeal, a shipmate was murdered after ship owners initially refused to pay a $300,000 ransom. "We heard six gunshots, but no one could believe Chen was dead," he said. Later, when the hostages were allowed up on deck, it was covered with blood. [2]

More recently, American sea captain Richard Phillips did not have to wait seven months to escape the clutches of Somali pirates. After his U.S.-flag ship carrying humanitarian aid for Africa was attacked in April, he gave himself up as a hostage so his shipmates could go free. He spent several days in a lifeboat with the pirates before U.S. Navy snipers killed his captors and freed Phillips. [3] Since then the pirates have seized several more ships with dozens of hostages.

The uptick in piracy in the Gulf of Aden has become the face of the lawlessness that engulfs Somalia. Until recently, the chaos had been largely contained within Somalia's borders. But in recent years what began as the occasional attack by local fishermen, angry at foreign vessels vacuuming their coastal waters, has morphed into one of Somalia's biggest sources of revenue, with sophisticated criminal gangs ramping up the hunt for ransoms.

Attacks on commercial ships off Somalia's coast increased from 20 to 111 between 2006 and 2008. Last fall, a vessel was attacked on average once every other day. Though killings have been rare, about 300 seamen and 18 vessels were being held by Somali pirates in late April. Ransoms paid in 2008 alone amounted to between $50 million and $80 million. [4]

The growth of Somali piracy was an unforeseen consequence of the 2006 U.S.-backed Ethiopian invasion of Somalia. The invasion ousted Somalia's governing Islamic Courts Union (ICU), which had effectively stamped out piracy during its brief reign in 2006. "The Islamic Courts, for some reason known only to themselves, decided to take action against maritime piracy," says Pottengal Mukundan, director of the Internation-

al Maritime Bureau. "They made a public announcement saying those guilty of piracy would be punished in 2006. During the summer of 2006, there were no attacks at all."

Since the ICU was ousted, piracy has exploded. Armed with rocket launchers and machine guns, Somalia's buccaneers prowl the seas in small vessels that can range as far as 200 miles off shore. Often they'll approach a boat disguised as fishermen or

French soldiers take suspected Somali pirates into custody on the French warship Le Nivose on May 3, 2009. Attacks on commercial ships increased from 20 in 2006 to 111 in 2008. Last fall, a vessel was attacked on average once every other day.

AFP/Getty Images/Pierre Verdy

traders, then fire weapons at the bridge and attempt to climb aboard using ropes and grappling hooks. Once aboard there is little foreign militaries can do. The pirates quickly take the crew hostage and steam the hijacked ship back to Eyl and other pirate bases along Somalia's Indian Ocean coast to await ransom payments.

The pirate gangs have become highly organized and intertwined with Somalia's various militias. "They have spies," says

Gérard Valin, a vice admiral in the French navy, who led a successful raid on pirates in April 2008 after the payment of a ransom to free a French yacht. "They have people in Djibouti, Nairobi and the Gulf giving them intelligence about the good ships to take. It's a business. They have people for taking ships, and they have people for negotiations."

The millions of dollars flowing into Somali fishing villages from piracy have overwhelmed the local economy. Pirates have built luxurious new homes and support hundreds of others who supply food, weapons and khat leaf, a stimulant popular with the pirate gangs. Ilka Ase Mohamed lost his girlfriend to a pirate who wore a black cowboy hat, drove a Land Cruiser and paid a $50,000 dowry to his girlfriend's mother.

"This man was like a small king," the 23-year-old Mohamed told *The Washington Post*. "He was dressed like a president. So many people attended him. I got so angry, I said, 'Why do they accept this situation? You know this is pirate money!' " [5]

The wave of attacks in late 2008 climaxed with the hijacking of the *Sirius Star*, a Saudi supertanker carrying $100 million worth of crude oil. Since then, foreign navies, which had largely ignored the problem, have rallied to the cause. As of late March as many as 30 warships from 23 countries were patrolling the area in a loose anti-pirate alliance that includes the United States, Iran, India and Pakistan. [6] Still, the problem won't be solved at sea, says Valin. Even with two dozen warships on patrol, he says, it's often difficult to distinguish between a fishing boat and a pirate skiff until the pirates are nearly aboard a commercial vessel, and many countries struggle with how to prosecute pirates picked up in international waters.

What's needed, experts say, is a functioning government on land that will shut down pirate safe havens. That's no easy task for either the newly elected Somali government of Sheikh Sharif Sheikh Ahmed — which controls just a few small areas in southern and central Somalia — or the Puntland regional government, which is the nominal authority over the areas

Somali Piracy Up Sharply

The 114 pirate attacks in the Gulf of Aden and Indian Ocean so far this year represent an 11-fold jump over 2004. This year 29 of the attacks were successful, more than twice the 2007 number.

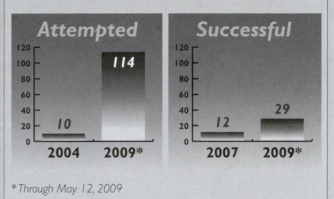

Somali Pirate Attacks, 2004-2009

*Through May 12, 2009

Source: International Maritime Bureau

where most of the pirates operate. Pirate ransom revenues last year were greater than either government's budget, and a U.N. report in December accused the Puntland administrators of complicity with pirate gangs. [7]

[1] "Chinese Sailor Recalls Terror of Somali Kidnapping," Agence France-Presse, Jan. 4, 2009.

[2] *Ibid.*

[3] Josh Meyer, "Snipers kill pirates in dramatic rescue," *Chicago Tribune*, April 13, 2009, p. 1.

[4] "Somalia: Anti-pirate Alliance," *Africa Confidential*, March 20, 2009, p. 8.

[5] Stephanie McCrummen, "Somalia's Godfathers: Ransom-Rich Pirates; Coastal Villagers Find Blessings and Ruin at Hands of Sea Robbers," *The Washington Post*, April 20, 2009, p. A1, www.washingtonpost.com/wp-dyn/content/article/2009/04/19/AR2009041902236.html.

[6] "Somalia: Anti-pirate Alliance," *op. cit.*

[7] "Report of the Monitoring Group on Somalia," United Nations, Dec. 10, 2008, www.un.org/sc/committees/751/mongroup.shtml.

end of those aspirations and of the country's nine-year-old democracy.

The army seized power under Gen. Barre, who quickly moved the government toward communism. On the first anniversary of the coup in 1970, Barre announced that his nation of nomadic herders henceforth would pursue "Scientific Socialism," Barre's own strain of Marxism.

"The Big Mouth," as he was known colloquially, soon established internal-

security services and security courts to prosecute political crimes and "Victory Pioneers," modeled on China's Red Guards, to defend the revolution. [42] Exerting unprecedented political authority over the people, he tried to quell tribalism by prohibiting citizens from referring to their clan affiliations and by building rural schools and clinics. [43]

Meanwhile, Ethiopia's Selassie won a major diplomatic victory after World War II, when he persuaded the U.N.

to unite Eritrea and Ethiopia, dashing the hopes of Eritrea's fledgling independence movement. But by the 1960s, the emperor's reign — backed by the landowners who ruled millions of peasants like medieval serfs — was chafing at the currents of the 20th century. His Amhara-dominated government faced rebellion from Tigrays in Eritrea and Oromos in southern Ethiopia. He also faced war with Somalia, which still sought control of the Ogaden. [44]

By 1973 the imperial regime's denial and botched response to a famine in northern Ethiopia, combined with soaring inflation and pressure from the Somali and Eritrean rebellions, led to a military revolt. The next year, "His Imperial Majesty Haile Selassie I, King of Kings, Lord of Lords, Conquering Lion of the Tribe of Judah, and Elect of God" was ousted. [45]

The new military government — headed by Lt. Col. Mengistu Haile Mariam and calling itself the Derg, the Amharic word for committee — aligned itself with the communist bloc and nationalized all private land, giving each peasant family 10 hectares (25 acres). The aging Selassie mysteriously died the same year. Many Ethiopians believe he was smothered with a pillow by Mengistu himself.

In 1977, the Derg was still struggling to consolidate its rule. To eliminate civilian Marxist rivals, it launched the so-called Red Terror, during which tens of thousands of students, businessmen and intellectuals suspected of disloyalty to the military government were murdered. [46] Meanwhile, with rebellions widening in the southeast and north, Somalia seized the opportunity to invade the Ogaden in hopes of fulfilling the grand dream of a Greater Somalia.

Although the Ogaden War pitted two of the Soviet Union's client states against each other, the U.S.S.R. eventually supported Ethiopia. Reinforced with Cuban troops and Soviet airpower, the Derg's army drove the Somalis out of the Ogaden in early 1978. [47]

Civil Wars

The 1983-1984 famine that would make Ethiopia synonymous with images of emaciated children resulted not just from drought but also from government policies intended to starve rebel-held areas. [48] With the Derg preoccupied with preparations for a lavish 10th anniversary celebration of the

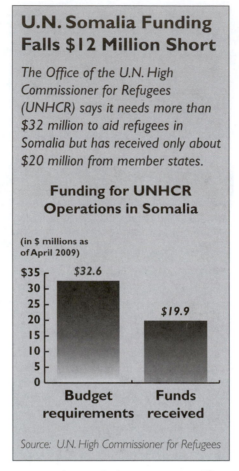

U.N. Somalia Funding Falls $12 Million Short

The Office of the U.N. High Commissioner for Refugees (UNHCR) says it needs more than $32 million to aid refugees in Somalia but has received only about $20 million from member states.

Funding for UNHCR Operations in Somalia

(in $ millions as of April 2009)

Budget requirements: $32.6
Funds received: $19.9

Source: U.N. High Commissioner for Refugees

communist revolution, up to a million Ethiopians died in the famine as the government systematically tried to hide images of starving peasants from the outside world while using aid to buttress government control rather than to alleviate suffering. [49] In an effort to undermine support for the rebels, entire regions of Tigray peasants in the north were forcibly moved to government camps — a policy known as villagization. [50]

Meanwhile, the humiliation of the Ogaden War led to an unsuccessful coup attempt in Somalia against Barre, led by officers from the Darod's Majerteyn sub-clan. From then on Barre maintained power by playing off the clans against each other. After the war, 700,000 Ethiopian Somalis poured across the border into Somalia, swelling the population by up to 20 percent. The collapse of the banana and mango plan-

tations under socialism made Somalia's economy increasingly dependent on foreign aid.

The result was a widening civil war. By 1990, with government control of the countryside collapsing, Barre's enemies referred to him as the "Mayor of Mogadishu." In January 1991 he was chased from Mogadishu by a Habar Gida (a subgroup of the Hawiye clan) militia headed by a former heroin smuggler and police chief, Gen. Muhammad Farah "Aideed," whose nickname means "one who does not take insults lying down." [51] After a long sickness, the Somali state was now dead.

In Ethiopia, Mengistu's demise came the same year. By 1988 the Ethiopian Army was demoralized by the failure to win a military victory or reach political compromise with Isaias Afwerki's Eritrean People's Liberation Front. With Eritrean rebels controlling access to the Red Sea and Zenawi's Tigrayan rebels pushing south into central Ethiopia, Mengistu fled to Zimbabwe, and rebels occupied Asmara and Addis Ababa. [52]

Somalia's Descent

Back in Mogadishu, Barre's 1991 ouster led to an orgy of bloodshed. A period of "ethnic cleansing" ensued, mostly along clan lines. The Darod were especially targeted for their links with the hated Barre. Individual militia groups took control of the port, the airfield and major intersections.

At checkpoints, travelers were asked to recite the names of their ancestors — a Somali ritual that identifies people by clan and sub-clan. Those with the wrong lineage were often shot on the spot. [53] Darod militias retreated south, laying waste to the villages of smaller clans and killing and terrorizing civilians and stealing their grain. The ensuing famine claimed some 300,000; a million more were forced from their homes in search of food.

In reaction, the United States sent 28,000 troops to join 5,000 international peacekeepers under the optimistic banner Operation Restore Hope. [54] Though the mission initially succeeded in delivering aid to tens of thousands, it quickly became bogged down in street battles with militias and efforts to capture Aideed. In October 1993 several U.S. helicopters sent on a mission to arrest two of Aideed's top lieutenants were shot down over Mogadishu. In the ensuing effort to rescue trapped U.S. pilots and commandos, 18 American soldiers were killed and 84 injured in fighting that left hundreds of Somalis dead. Afterwards, the naked bodies of American soldiers were dragged through the streets as residents celebrated.

Immortalized by Mark Bowden's book *Black Hawk Down*, the battle led U.S. forces to withdraw by March 1994 and the remaining U.N. peacekeepers to leave a year later. [55] The stinging humiliation suffered by the U.S. military in Somalia is widely credited with leading to America's hesitancy in 1994 to intervene in a month-long genocidal rampage in Rwanda that left nearly a million people dead. [56]

After the U.S. withdrawal Aideed's militias expanded their control of southern Somalia, allying themselves with Islamists aligned with hard-line Saudi and Egyptian clerics. Aideed declared himself "interim president" but was killed in 1996 in fighting with rival Hawiye militias from the Abgal subclan. [57] Thereafter, the international community largely ignored Somalia until the terrorist attacks on New York and the Pentagon on Sept. 11, 2001, led to a renewed focus on Somalia as a haven for Islamic terrorists. [58]

One-Party Rule

Ethiopia embarked on a new path after 1991. The Derg had been defeated primarily by the separatist Er-

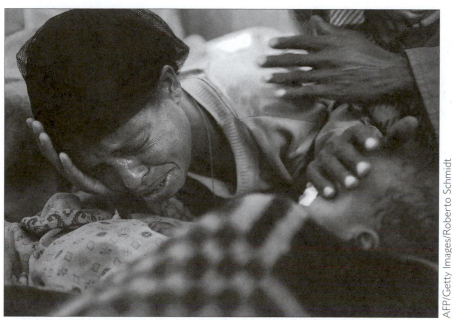

A mother in the Ethiopian town of Kuyera grieves over her sick child at a medical center run by Doctors Without Borders on Sept. 3, 2008. Earlier that day two children in nearby beds had died of malnutrition. Food shortages caused by a 2008 drought left at least 75,000 Ethiopian children under age 5 at risk, according to the U.N.'s Office for the Coordination of Humanitarian Affairs.

itrean People's Liberation Front. Zenawi's Tigray People's Liberation Front (TPLF) claimed power in Addis Ababa and agreed that Eritreans should be allowed a national referendum on independence. By 1993, Eritrea was independent, and Afwerki was in power in Asmara.

To expand his base, Zenawi reconstituted the TPLF as the Ethiopian People's Revolutionary Democratic Front (EPRDF) during the last years of the civil war. The party, still dominated by Tigrayans from the north, became the foundation of a one-party state. Opposition parties faced harassment, intimidation and imprisonment while politically favored businessmen were given control of economic assets. Tension over economic disputes soon emerged between former allies Zenawi and Afwerki: Eritrea raised port fees on its landlocked southern neighbor and destabilized the Ethiopian birr, still used by both countries, by establishing its own currency market. [59]

The friction erupted into warfare in 1998 in the town of Badme. An estimated 70,000 were killed and 750,000 displaced by the fighting before the Organization of African Unity helped arrange a cease-fire in 2000. By then Ethiopian troops had conquered Badme, and a 25-kilometer demilitarized buffer zone had been established inside Eritrean territory, patrolled by U.N. peacekeepers.

After the war, Afwerki quashed dissent in Asmara, arresting those who questioned his war strategy and abolishing the private press. Rule by the increasingly isolated Afwerki has evolved into a personality cult, and the economy has stagnated as military conscription decimated the labor force. Although an independent boundary commission awarded Badme to Eritrea in 2002, Ethiopia has never fully accepted the decision, and Eritrea — lacking both diplomatic support and military equipment — lacked the power to enforce it.

Ethiopia then briefly moved toward democracy. During political campaigning in 2005, the opposition Coalition

The Troubled Horn of Africa

The increasingly harsh government of Ethiopian Prime Minister Meles Zenawi has triggered calls for Western governments to withhold aid from the regime. But in part because Ethiopia has staunchly supported the West's anti-terror campaign, international aid to Ethiopia has grown dramatically in recent years.

for Unity and Democracy (CUD) debated ruling party officials on state television and was allowed to stage large rallies in several cities.

After the election, the ruling party claimed an outright victory in parliament, but the CUD disputed the claim. In ensuing demonstrations, 193 people were killed by government security forces, and 127 top opposition leaders, journalists and human rights activists were jailed. Since then democratic freedoms in Ethiopia have been steadily scaled back. In 2008 local and parliamentary elections, opposition parties managed to win just three of 3.6 million races. [60]

In Somalia, the roots of the country's latest attempt at governance trace to 2004, when the Transitional Federal Government was formed with Ethiopian support under the leadership of President Abdullahi Yusuf, a Darod warlord from the Puntland semi-autonomous region. Yusuf's government was viewed skeptically from the beginning by many Somalis, who saw it as a puppet of Ethiopia. [61]

The fledgling TFG largely stayed in exile in its initial years, and by 2006 all-out war had erupted in Mogadishu between a group of CIA-backed anti-Islamist warlords calling themselves the Alliance for the Restoration of

Peace and Counterterrorism and supporters of the Islamic Courts Union (ICU), a group of Islamists that sought to bring order to the lawless country by settling disputes and bringing criminals to trial under Islamic law. By mid-2006 the alliance, widely despised by ordinary Somalis for its corruption and criminality, was defeated and replaced by the ICU — which ended fighting in much of southern Somalia while instituting a strict form of sharia law. [62]

But the ICU, openly supported by Ethiopia's nemesis Eritrea, laid claim to Ethiopia's Ogaden region. By December 2006 it had succeeded in provoking an Ethiopian invasion. The United States, hoping to capture al Qaeda suspects linked to ICU radicals, gave the Ethiopians intelligence and logistical support, and U.S. Special Forces accompanied Ethiopian troops in the invasion. [63]

Ethiopia's technologically superior army quickly smashed the ICU's militia. But it soon found controlling Mogadishu more difficult than invading it. Within weeks remnants of the ICU's military wing — al-Shabaab — had allied with disaffected local clans to begin a bloody guerrilla campaign against the Ethiopian occupation. Ethiopia sought African Union peacekeeping troops to replace its forces in Mogadishu, but less than a quarter of the 8,000 authorized AU troops arrived in the first year after the Ethiopian invasion. [64]

Meanwhile the TFG under Yusuf's leadership proved both corrupt and inept. Reliant on Ethiopian soldiers for security in Mogadishu, it failed to bring functioning schools or clinics to the areas of southern Somalia nominally under its control. As the insurgency grew in Mogadishu, hundreds of thousands of people fled the fighting for makeshift refugee camps west of the city. Members of the government were accused of looting food aid from World Food Programme trucks. Radio stations that broadcast critical news were shuttered, and journalists were arrested.

Two years after Yusuf returned to Mogadishu, a U.N. report found that his government's central bank and finance ministry appeared to exist "in name only" and that Yusuf kept a printing press inside his presidential compound to print Somali shillings.

Ethiopian efforts to train a Somali security force to bolster the TFG failed dramatically. By October 2008, an estimated 14,000 of the 17,000 troops trained by the Ethiopians had deserted. [65] The Islamists recruited hundreds of the armed deserters by paying them $200 a month and playing on resentment of the Ethiopian occupation. [66]

By late 2008 Islamists and other opposition militias controlled most of southern Somalia, including the key ports of Kismayo and Merka. Disillusioned with Yusuf's failure to make peace with moderate Islamists, Ethiopia gave notice that it would withdraw troops even if that meant the Islamists would reclaim control.

Yusuf resigned in December 2008 after neighboring states threatened to freeze his assets. Ethiopian troops headed for the exit within weeks, opening the door for a new attempt at peace in the Horn of Africa. ∎

CURRENT SITUATION

Fledgling Government

On May 24, a suicide bomber driving a Toyota Land Cruiser exploded a bomb at the gates of a TFG military compound in Mogadishu, killing six soldiers and a civilian. [67] The bombing was just the latest incident in a new spasm of violence between the TFG and Shabaab insurgents that has seen the Islamist militants tighten their grip over southern and central Somalia.

It wasn't supposed to be this way. After Ethiopian troops, widely despised by ordinary Somalis, pulled out of Mogadishu in January, Yusuf was replaced as president of the TFG by Sheikh Ahmed, the moderate Islamist who had chaired the Islamic Courts Union before the Ethiopian invasion and, from exile in Djibouti, had opposed both the occupation and Yusuf's corrupt government. Though 14 previous U.N.-backed Somali governments had failed to bring peace and stability to the country, it was hoped that Ahmed, as a Hawiye clan leader with previous links to some of the insurgent groups' leaders, could make peace with the Hawiye and Islamist militias opposed to the TFG.

Instead, bolstered by as many as 300 foreign fighters and arms from Eritrea, al-Shabaab has rejected Ahmed's overtures and moved from strength to strength, capturing Ahmed's hometown of Jowhar and neighboring Mahaday, cutting government links with central Somalia. [68] Ahmed has been forced to take refuge in a compound in Mogadishu, protected by foreign troops from the African Union. The growing chaos has led the TFG's new prime minister, Omar Abdirashid Ali Sharmarke, to all but rule out peace talks with insurgents.

"I don't think there is a chance to just sit with them and discuss issues with these people," Sharmarke told Reuters in late May. "The only way to deal with them that they can understand is to fight, and we are prepared to eradicate them." [69]

As fighting intensified in May, Ethiopia launched an apparent strike into Somalia, raising the specter of a possible re-invasion should the TFG collapse and al-Shabaab take control. [70] "Ahmed and the new TFG face an increasing challenge from al-Shabaab and an allied organization known as Hizbul Islam," says Shinn, the former ambassador to Ethiopia. "Al-Shabaab, although not centrally controlled, is well financed from outside and relying on a growing number of foreign fighters."

"The euphoria with which Sheikh Sharif's government was greeted has evaporated," says Abdi, of the International Crisis Group. "Things are very difficult. Unless something happens to unlock this logjam, this is just one of those cycles of transitions that will end up in a failure."

The TFG's reliance on 4,000 Ugandan and Burundian troops in Mogadishu — operating under the African Union — also hurts the fledgling government's legitimacy. "As foreigners [the AU troops] are also resented," says Shinn. "They are keeping the port and the airport out of the hands of al-Shabaab and protecting the presidency. The TFG probably could not accomplish this on its own."

Additional outside help seems remote. The U.N. has repeatedly declined requests from African nations to send a force to stabilize the country, while the AU has struggled to find more countries willing to contribute to the force. An uptick in attacks on AU peacekeepers last year has raised fears that the mission could end in a debacle as the U.S.-U.N. mission did 15-years ago.

"The AU peacekeepers haven't kept any peace because there is no peace to keep," says historian Lewis. "They're just useless."

Still, al-Shabaab also faces risks, especially since its brand of Islam is more radical than Somalia's traditional Sufi Islam. Among the moves that have provoked public revulsion: the amputation of the hands of accused thieves, public flogging of criminals and desecration of the graves of Sufi saints. Most dramatically, in October Islamist clerics in Kismayo ordered the public stoning of a young woman who may have been as young as 13 for committing adultery. Human rights

Somalis displaced from their homes in war-torn Mogadishu prepare a meal at the Dayniile camp — one of dozens that surround the Somali capital. The ongoing civil war and poverty have sent more than a million refugees fleeing to neighboring countries or to camps inside Somalia, where they depend on international assistance for food and shelter — aid that is often blocked by violence, theft or piracy.

AFP/Getty Images/Abdirashid Abdulle

groups said the woman, who was killed in a stadium in front of as many as 1,000 onlookers, had been raped. [71] More recently, al-Shabaab's decision to continue its war after Ethiopia withdrew has also tarnished its identity as a liberation movement fighting Ethiopian occupiers.

"In Mogadishu, public disappointment towards al-Shabaab militants is growing," says Faizal Mohammed, a Somali columnist for the Addis Ababa-based *Sub-Saharan Informer.* "Hawiye elders and some religious leaders have criticized al-Shabaab's move to continue the war after the Ethiopian withdrawal and to target AU peacekeepers."

The TFG also received a recent boost when Islamist warlord Yusuf Indahaadde, the former ICU defense minister, decided to support Ahmed and the TFG after Ahmed announced his government would implement Islamic law. [72]

"It will be messy and slow and it will be subject to reversals, but there is no reason why the right coalition of political and religious and business interests could not pull something together," says Menkhaus, the former U.N. official. "This new coalition government, it's the type of government that could work."

Meanwhile, the country continues to be a source of terrorism. On March 15 a suicide bomber allegedly trained in Somalia killed four South Korean tourists in Yemen. Three days later a second bomber attempted to kill a group of Koreans investigating the attack. [73]

Some analysts say the U.S. and Ethiopian intervention in Somalia has worsened the threat of terrorism by radicalizing the Islamists. "The problem has grown into a much bigger, hydra-headed problem because of that policy," says Lefkow, of Human Rights Watch. "That was a very ill-judged strategy on the part of both the Ethiopians and the U.S."

Ethiopia has a different view. "Ethiopia successfully neutralized" the Islamic Courts, says Ethiopian Foreign Minister Seyoum Mesfin. "Today there is only al-Shabaab and a few terrorist groups working as small units without any formidable organization. Their military backbone [and] organizational structure have been completely shattered."

Frazer, the former Bush administration diplomat, says the Ethiopian intervention had little effect on the threat. "When Ethiopia wasn't there, they were opening the country to jihadists," she says. "When Ethiopia was there, they were continuing to do it. After Ethiopia left, the country is still open to jihadists."

Standoff Continues

In February Ethiopian state-run television was filled with images of troops parading through Ethiopian cities, celebrating their withdrawal from Somalia. Though the two-year occupation of Somalia began with the ouster of one anti-Ethiopian Islamist group and ended with a more radical anti-Ethiopian group taking control of much of the country's south, Ethiopia's foreign ministry declared "Mission Accomplished." [74]

"We believe a great victory has been secured," Prime Minister Zenawi said on March 19. But the withdrawing troops have not had much time to rest. Despite official denials from Zenawi's government, Somali residents along the border between the two countries have reported repeated Ethiopian incursions since January. [75] In March the Ogaden National Liberation Front — an Eritrean-backed ethnic Somali separatist group in eastern Ethiopia — claimed it killed 24 Ethiopian troops near the town of Degehebur, not far from the Somalia border. [76]

Meanwhile, the standoff between Ethiopia and Eritrea continues to feed regional instability. Throughout 2008 Eritrea delivered up to $500,000 a month to a faction that was battling both Ethiopian troops and TFG security forces inside Somalia. And Eritrea

Continued on p. 170

At Issue:

Should the West cut aid to Ethiopia over human rights concerns?

BERHANU NEGA
*EXILED FORMER MAYOR, ADDIS ABABA
LEADER OF OPPOSITION GROUP GINBOT 7
PROFESSOR OF ECONOMICS, BUCKNELL
UNIVERSITY*

WRITTEN FOR *CQ GLOBAL RESEARCHER*, MAY 2009

the West's policy toward Ethiopia has been a disaster, and President Barack Obama and European leaders must reconsider their support to its government. Ethiopia received more than $1 billion in U.S. aid last year plus generous support from the United Kingdom and European Union. However, the country's human rights record is among the worst on the continent and getting worse by the day.

The possibility of a peaceful transition to democracy vanished in 2005 after Prime Minister Meles Zenawi's security forces killed 193 innocent civilians for peacefully protesting a stolen election and jailed tens of thousands of democracy activists, including 127 opposition leaders, journalists and civil society activists — including me.

Ethiopia is now a totalitarian police state with a human rights record comparable to that of Robert Mugabe's Zimbabwe. Meles and his inner circle have cowed the parliament, the courts and the press. Human rights groups claim the government has killed civilians in several regions. The government held local elections last year with more than 95 percent of the candidates from the ruling party; passed a restrictive new press law; jailed opposition leader Birtukan Mideksa and banned most human rights, democracy and gender-equality organizations.

Why shore up such a brutal dictatorship? Ethiopia is one of the poorest nations in the world, and Western policy makers say aid helps the poor more than the government. But after 18 years in power, Meles' regime still cannot feed its people: Some 14 million Ethiopians required foreign food aid last year. Donors have little control over how aid is delivered, and the government deliberately withholds foreign food aid to punish villages sympathetic to ethnic-Somali rebels.

The West's aid props up an anti-democratic regime and is ineffective in helping the poor. But proponents say Ethiopia — bordered by war-torn Sudan, a belligerent Eritrea and lawless Somalia — needs aid to remain stable in one of the world's toughest neighborhoods. But that's hard to swallow, given that Ethiopia's disastrous, two-year occupation of southern Somalia ended up ejecting a moderate Islamist government while empowering radicals; its nine-year border dispute with Eritrea remains unresolved; and numerous, armed indigenous groups wage domestic attacks with increasing ferocity.

U.S. and European economic pressure could make Meles' government negotiate a peaceful settlement to the country's explosive political problems.

PATRICK GILKES
ADVISER TO ETHIOPIA'S MINISTRY OF FOREIGN AFFAIRS; AUTHOR, THE DYING LION, CONFLICT IN SOMALIA AND ETHIOPIA; *AND, WITH MARTIN PLAUT,* CONFLICT IN THE HORN: WHY ERITREA AND ETHIOPIA ARE AT WAR

WRITTEN FOR *CQ GLOBAL RESEARCHER*, MAY 2009

activists who call for cuts in foreign aid to Ethiopia are seriously misguided. Ethiopia's government is far from perfect, but those who pressure the U.S. Congress and other Western governments to slash assistance to Ethiopia should remember it has averaged economic growth of 11 percent from 2003 to 2008, nearly double Africa as a whole and comparable to that of the Asian "tiger" economies in the 1990s.

The country launched a five-year Sustainable Development and Poverty Reduction Program in 2006 and is devoting about 60 percent of its federal budget to "pro-poor spending," as defined by the World Bank. This is one of the best rates in Africa.

The government have held defense spending to less than 1.5 percent of gross domestic product, even as it has fought a two-year anti-terrorism engagement in Somalia and strives to deter Eritrean aggression. Ethiopia remains a desperately poor nation, but there have been massive investment and major advances in infrastructure, education and health.

Despite the opposition's failure to take up seats in the first multiparty federal elections in 2005 and ensuing violence, local elections took place last year without incident. Ethiopia's federal structure has produced widespread acceptance of self-rule and meaningful fiscal and political devolution. Ethiopia provides a very clear demonstration of the effective use to which aid can and should be put. These must be developments well worth nurturing.

Much has been done in human rights — despite exaggerated opposition claims and poor research by Human Rights Watch and other groups. This includes major training programs for the judiciary, armed forces and police as well as the recent establishment of a government ombudsman and a Human Rights Commission. The recently enacted law regulating nongovernmental organizations (NGOs) has been controversial, but its critics wildly overstate its ramifications. The goal is protection and transparency for NGO humanitarian and development activity.

Ethiopia's long and close relations with the United States and Europe have been enormously important to development. Amidst international financial crisis and climate change, Ethiopia needs support to ensure development efforts don't falter, as it successfully implements its long-term strategy of democratization and poverty reduction. There's still much to do. This is certainly not the time to interrupt the process or threaten regional stability.

Continued from p. 168

regularly delivers arms and ammunition by small boat to Somali insurgents. It has also supplied arms and funding to the militia of Mohamed Sai'd "Atom," whose Shabaab-affiliated fighters have battled Puntland security forces. Atom's militia was also implicated in the kidnapping of a German aid worker in 2008 and a bombing

Eritrea's support of such groups has hindered its diplomatic efforts to get international enforcement for the Ethiopia-Eritrea Boundary Commission's 2002 decision awarding Badme to Eritrea. [78] With a strong push from Ethiopia, the African Union's Peace and Security Council in May called for international sanctions against Eritrea for its role in arming Somali militants.

in February 2008, the border skirmish could again flare up into all out war.

But many analysts believe such an outcome is unlikely. "Eritrea doesn't have diplomatic might or military strength to challenge the status quo," says Shinn, the former U.S. ambassador to Ethiopia. "It's not in either of their interests to resume that war, and they both know it."

However, both regimes have used the continuing presence of an external threat to sharply reduce democratic freedoms. "The stalemate on the border feeds and in turn is fed by growing authoritarianism in both states," said a June 2008 International Crisis Group report. "The ruling regimes rely on military power and restrictions on civil liberties to retain their dominant positions." [81]

However, it continued, "Both regimes have an interest in keeping the conflict at a low simmer rather than resolving it." ∎

A Somali insurgent holds a rocket-propelled grenade launcher in Mogadishu in January 2009, shortly after Ethiopian troops ended a two-year occupation of parts of Somalia. Some analysts say U.S. support for Ethiopia's 2006 invasion of Somalia radicalized many Somalis and increased the threat of anti-U.S. terrorism from Somalia.

AP Photo/Farah Abdi Warsameh

OUTLOOK

Unresolved Conflicts

that killed 20 Ethiopian migrants waiting for transport to Yemen in the Puntland port of Bossasso. [77]

"The Eritreans, under Isaias, are pursuing the same sort of strategy they followed in winning their independence: setting out to weaken Ethiopia from as many directions as possible," says Connell, the former adviser to the Eritrean government. "This results in steady support for all of Ethiopia's enemies, within Ethiopia's borders and without. Hence the support for Islamists in Somalia, whom you might least expect Eritrea to favor."

Ethiopia also backs proxies. In May 2008 it hosted a conference of Eritrean rebel groups and opposition parties in Addis Ababa. [79] Last August, Ethiopia delivered 3,000 to 5,000 AK-47 assault rifles to the Puntland semi-autonomous government and has provided weapons and training to at least one other anti-Islamist militia in Somalia. [80]

Tens of thousands of troops from the two armies remain dug in across their shared border, sometimes only meters apart. And without U.N. peacekeepers, who were forced to withdraw

Few analysts are optimistic that the Horn of Africa's political and economic status will be vastly improved over the next decade.

For the moment, Ethiopia's future looks the brightest. The government says economic growth averaged 11 percent between 2003 and 2008, bolstered by large inflows of aid and debt forgiveness. Some independent economists say the figure is overstated, and that real growth has been around 7 or 8 percent — still a remarkable figure for a land-locked country with no significant oil or mineral reserves.

But, problems abound. The global financial crisis will undoubtedly slow growth. Exports of coffee, Ethiopia's largest foreign-exchange earner, appear likely to decline for the second consecutive year while hospitals and factories face shortages of key supplies. And with dim prospects for a breakthrough with Eritrea, Ethiopia will probably face continuing conflict on at least three fronts: in Somalia, in the Ogaden and along its northern border with Eritrea.

"The future is impossible to predict so long as this simmering confrontation remains unresolved," says former Eritrean adviser Connell. Ethiopia and Eritrea "have enormous potential for growth, but the conflict between them and attendant repression of rights within each country hold both back."

Ethiopia's government, dominated by ethnic Tigrayan Christians from the northern highlands, remains unpopular with the ethnic Amharas and Oromos from central, southern and western Ethiopia, who together make up nearly two-thirds of the population. And the recent crackdown on opposition leaders, the press and human rights groups casts a pall over upcoming 2010 elections.

"I'm not optimistic that 2010 is going to be a breakthrough," says former U.S. Ambassador Shinn. "The tip-off was the local elections in 2008. I think that's a pity."

The government's failure to improve food self-sufficiency also leaves the ongoing threat of drought and famine, which helped trigger the demise of both the communist Derg regime and the Selassie government. "Ethiopia has a relatively high population growth rate," says Shinn. "If you can't feed your people and you're constantly at the mercy of foreign handouts, you've got to do something about it."

In Eritrea the outlook is decidedly dim. The economically and politically isolated government offers few prospects for improving its citizens' lives. "Eritrea is a one-man dictatorship masquerading as a one-party state," says Connell, who formerly worked for the Afwerki government. "The ruling party is little more than a cabal of Isaias Afwerki

loyalists, whom he plays off against one another to maintain his iron-fisted rule. The closest analog I can imagine is North Korea." Afwerki's repressive rule, he adds, "is far more effective and all-encompassing than that of, say, [President Robert] Mugabe in Zimbabwe."

In April Human Rights Watch accused Eritrea of becoming a "giant prison" and issued a 95-page report detailing government atrocities against dissidents and evangelical Christians. Thousands of Eritreans risk the government's shoot-to-kill policy to flee to neighboring Sudan and Ethiopia each year, the report said. [82]

"The country is hemorrhaging," said an independent analyst, who asked that his name not be used so that he can continue traveling to Eritrea. "It's largely a police state. I don't see how the regime can survive in the long term. The government has control at the moment, but at some point something will give way."

In Somalia, analysts say probably only an Islamist government can reach across clan divisions to bring a semblance of order to the country's south. "It wouldn't surprise me if an Islamist movement took hold," says the historian Lewis. "How severe it will be and how rigorous is up for grabs."

Unfortunately, he continues, "the radical Islamist movement that they have now developed is particularly poorly educated and poorly informed about the world. It's taking the Somalis really back almost to colonial times."

Rebuilding the country after 18 years of civil war will be a long and difficult task.

"The best-case scenario is that [TFG President] Sharif may succeed in bringing in the hardline groups and — after a bumpy five to six years of transition — we may see a moderate Islamist government take control and become a regional player," says Abdi, of the International Crisis Group. "The worst-case scenario is Sharif's government will collapse, and insurgents will

step up their attacks and Ethiopia will invade Somalia again. Somalia is by no means out of the woods."

If the radicals succeed, the threat from terrorism is likely to grow. The recent recruitment of Somali-American jihadis to fight in Somalia raises the question of whether radical Islamists in Somalia might be able to export suicide bombers to Western countries with Somali immigrant communities.

"Would they be able to use U.S. passport holders from places like Minneapolis as sleepers?" asks Menkhaus, the former U.N. official in Somalia. "It's something we need to pay attention to."

The Obama administration should take a more low-key, comprehensive strategy in helping Somalia than the short-term counterterrorism goals followed by the Bush administration, according to Menkhaus. "In fighting terrorism on land and piracy at sea, U.S. national security interests will be better secured if we aligned ourselves more with the interest of most Somalis in better security and effective governance," he writes. "Helping to build the house and using the back door will be much more effective than barging into the front door of a house that has yet to be built." [83]   ∎

Notes

[1] "Somalia: Exodus Continues Despite Lull in Mogadishu Fighting," IRIN News, May 21, 2009, www.irinnews.org/report.aspx?Reportid=84483.
[2] "Escalating Violence Displaces Somalis," U.N. High Commissioner for Refugees, summary of briefing by spokesman Ron Redmond, May 26, 2009, www.unhcr.org/news/NEWS/4a1bbefb2.html. See also "Some 45,000 Somali Civilians Flee Mogadishu in Past Two Weeks," U.N. High Commissioner for Refugees, May 20, 2009, www.unhcr.org/cgi-bin/texis/vtx/news/opendoc.htm?tbl=NEWS&id=4a140e5b2, May 26, 2009.
[3] "Beyond the Fragile Peace Between Ethiopia and Eritrea: Averting New War," International Crisis Group, June 17, 2008, p. 10, www.crisisgroup.org/home/index.cfm?id=5490&l=4.

4 "United Nations Human Development Indices: A Statistical Update 2008," U.N. Development Programme, http://hdr.undp.org/en/statistics.

5 "Consolidated Appeal for Somalia 2009," U.N. Office for the Coordination of Humanitarian Assistance, Nov. 19, 2008, www.relief web.int/rw/dbc.nsf/doc104?OpenForm&rc=1& cc=som. See also "Somalia is Worst Humanitarian Crisis: U.N. Official," Global Policy Forum, Jan. 30, 2008, www.globalpolicy.org/component/content/article/205/39493.html.

6 See "European Parliament resolution of 15 January 2009 on the situation in the Horn of Africa," European Parliament, www.europarl.europa.eu/document/activities/cont/200901/2009 0122ATT46879/20090122ATT46879EN.pdf.

7 For background, see John Felton, "Aiding Refugees," CQ Global Researcher, March 1, 2009, pp. 59-90.

8 Aidan Hartley, Zanzibar Chest (2003), p. 187.

9 "Horn of Africa Media Briefing Note," U.N. Development Programme, Feb. 11, 2009, www.reliefweb.int/rw/rwb.nsf/db900sid/EDIS -7P6MR3?OpenDocument. Note: The U.N. does not have statistics for those in need of emergency aid in Eritrea, which evicted most foreign aid organizations following the 1998-2000 Ethiopia-Eritrea war.

10 Derek Byerlee and David Spielman, "Policies to Promote Cereal Intensification in Ethiopia: A Review of Evidence and Experience," International Food Policy Research Institute, June 2007.

11 "Eritrea," CIA World Fact Book, Central Intelligence Agency, www.cia.gov/library/pub lications/the-world-factbook/geos/er.html.

12 Dina Temple-Raston, "Al Qaeda Media Blitz Has Some on Alert," National Public Radio, April 8, 2009, www.npr.org/templates/story/story.php?storyId=102735818.

13 Lolita C. Baldor, "Terrorists Moving from Afghan Border to Africa," The Associated Press, April 28, 2009, http://abcnews.go.com/Politics/wireStory?id=7445461.

14 Ken Menkhaus, "Somalia After the Ethiopian Occupation: First Steps to End the Conflict and Combat Extremism," Enough Project, www.enoughproject.org/publications/somalia-after-ethiopian-occupation-first-steps-end-conflict-and-combat-extremism.

15 Dan Ephron and Mark Hosenball, "Recruited For Jihad?" Newsweek, Feb. 2, 2009, www.newsweek.com/id/181408.

16 Alex Perry, "Somalia's War Flares Up Again," Time, Nov. 12, 2007, www.time.com/time/world/article/0,8599,1682877,00.html.

17 Scott Johnson, "An Unclenched Fist: Barack Obama Has a Unique Opportunity to Bring Something Resembling Stability to Africa's Horn," Newsweek, Feb. 2, 2009, www.newsweek.com/id/181313.

18 Scott Johnson, "Dilemmas of the Horn," Newsweek, April 21, 2008, www.newsweek.com/id/131836.

19 "Biographies of High Value Terrorist Detainees Transferred to the U.S. Naval Base at Guantánamo Bay," Office of the Director of National Intelligence, Sept. 6, 2006, www.dni.gov/announcements/content/DetaineeBiogra phies.pdf.

20 Lloyd de Vries, "Elusive Al Qaeda Suspect Was Real Deal," CBS News, Jan. 10, 2007, www.cbsnews.com/stories/2007/01/10/world/main2347258.shtml.

21 Alisha Ryu, "US Airstrike in Somalia Targets al-Qaida Suspect," Voice of America, March 3, 2008, www.voanews.com/english/archive/2008-03/2008-03-03-voa15.cfm?CFID= 141624149&CFTOKEN=26521211&jsessionid= de308dbc94966565a9d81e432739512c471d.

22 Hamsa Omar and Jason McLure, "Somali Breakaway Regions Targeted by Suicide Bombers (Update1)," Bloomberg News, Oct. 29, 2008.

23 Jeffrey Gettleman, "The Most Dangerous Place in the World," Foreign Policy, March/April 2009, www.foreignpolicy.com/story/cms.php?story_id=4682.

24 Akwei Thompson, "Somali's New 36-Member Cabinet Larger Than Speculated," Voice of America, Feb. 22, 2009, www.voanews.com/english/Africa/2009-02-22-voa20.cfm, March 14, 2009.

25 For background, see Brian Beary, "Separatist Movements," CQ Global Researcher, April 2008, pp. 85-114.

26 I. M. Lewis, A Modern History of the Somali Nation and State in the Horn of Africa (2002), p. 289.

27 Alisha Ryu, "New Puntland President Faces Stiff Challenges," Voice of America, Jan. 15, 2009, www.voanews.com/english/archive/2009 -01/2009-01-15-voa51.cfm.

28 "Report of the Monitoring Group on Somalia," United Nations, Dec. 10, 2008, www.un.org/sc/committees/751/mongroup.shtml.

29 Jason McLure, "Caught in Ethiopia's War," Newsweek.com, Jan. 22, 2008, www.newsweek.com/id/98033. See also Jeffrey Gettleman, "In Ethiopia, Fear and Cries of Army Brutality," The New York Times, June 18, 2007, and "Collective Punishment: War Crimes and Crimes Against Humanity in the Ogaden Area of Ethiopia's Somali Retion," Human Rights Watch, June 11, 2008, www.hrw.org/en/node/62175/section/1.

30 Jason McLure, "Ethiopian Police Re-arrest Opposition Leader Mideksa," Bloomberg News, Dec. 29, 2008.

31 "Clean Sweep for Ethiopian Party," BBC News, May 19, 2008, http://news.bbc.co.uk/2/hi/africa/7408185.stm. Also see Jason McLure, "Ethiopian Law Curbs Promotion of Rights, Critics Say," Bloomberg News, Jan. 6, 2009, www.bloomberg.com/apps/news?pid=206011 16&sid=ahIahjCUZMz0&refer=africa.

32 "President Isaias Afwerki's Interview with Al-Jazeera Television," Eritrean Ministry of Information, April 24, 2008, www.shabait.com/cgi-bin/staging/exec/view.cgi?archive=17&num=8190.

33 "Somalia: To Move Beyond the Failed State," International Crisis Group, Dec. 23, 2008, p. 26, www.crisisgroup.org/home/index.cfm?id=5836&l=1.

34 Graham Hancock, The Sign and the Seal (1992), pp. 12-13.

35 Harold G. Marcus, A History of Ethiopia (2002), pp. 99-104, 138-142.

About the Author

Jason McLure is a correspondent for Bloomberg News and *Newsweek* based in Addis Ababa, Ethiopia. He previously worked for *Legal Times* in Washington, D.C., and in *Newsweek's* Boston bureau. His reporting has appeared in *The Economist*, *Business Week*, the *British Journalism Review* and *National Law Journal*. His work has been honored by the Washington, D.C., chapter of the Society for Professional Journalists, the Maryland-Delaware-District of Columbia Press Association and the Overseas Press Club of America Foundation. He has a master's degree in journalism from the University of Missouri.

[36] Sebastian O'Kelly, *Amedeo: The True Story of an Italian's War in Abyssinia* (2003).

[37] Marcus, *op. cit.*, pp. 150-152.

[38] Lewis, *op. cit.*, pp. 22-23.

[39] *Ibid.*, p. 48.

[40] *Ibid.*, p. 181.

[41] *Ibid.*, pp. 201-202.

[42] Ayaan Hirsi Ali, *Infidel* (2007), p. 55.

[43] Lewis, *op. cit.*, pp. 210-212, 224.

[44] For a first-person account of the student ferment that led to Haile Selassie's ouster, disillusionment under the succeeding Derg regime and the 1977 Ogaden War, see Nega Mezlekia, *Notes From The Hyena's Belly* (2000).

[45] Marcus, *op. cit.*, pp. 173-178, 180.

[46] Mezlekia, *op. cit.*, p. 295.

[47] John Lewis Gaddis, *The Cold War* (2005), pp. 207-208.

[48] See Robert Kaplan, *Surrender or Starve: Travels in Ethiopia, Sudan, Somalia and Eritrea* (2003).

[49] See Myles F. Harris, *Breakfast in Hell: A Doctor's Eyewitness Account of the Politics of Hunger in Ethiopia* (1987).

[50] Marcus, *op. cit.*, pp. 208-209.

[51] Lewis, *op. cit.*, pp. 245-246, 259-263.

[52] Michela Wrong, *I Didn't Do It For You: How the World Used and Abused a Small African Nation* (2005), pp. 349-352.

[53] Hartley, *op. cit.*, p. 184.

[54] Lewis, *op. cit.*, pp. 264-265, 268-269.

[55] See Mark Bowden, *Black Hawk Down: A Story of Modern War* (1999).

[56] For background, see Sarah Glazer, "Stopping Genocide," *CQ Researcher*, Aug. 27, 2004, pp. 685-708.

[57] Lewis, *op. cit.*, p. 280.

[58] *Ibid.*, pp. 305-306.

[59] Marcus, *op. cit.*, pp. 237, 242, 249-250.

[60] "2008 Human Rights Report: Ethiopia," U.S. Department of State, April 24, 2009, www.state.gov/g/drl/rls/hrrpt/2008/af/119001.htm.

[61] Ken Menkhaus, "Somalia: A Country in Peril, A Policy Nightmare," Enough Project, Sept. 3, 2008, www.enoughproject.org/files/reports/somalia_rep090308.pdf.

[62] *Ibid.*

[63] Gettleman, *op. cit.*

[64] Jason McLure, "Nigeria Needs Helicopters, Tanks to Send Troops to Somalia," Bloomberg News, June 28, 2008.

[65] "Report of the Monitoring Group on Somalia," *op. cit.*

[66] "Somalia: To Move Beyond the Failed State," *op. cit.*

[67] Mustapha Haji Abdinur, "Suicide Attack on Somali Military Camp Kills Seven," Agence France-Presse, May 25, 2009.

[68] Derek Kilner, "Somali Insurgents Take Another Town North of Capital," Voice of America, May 18, 2009, www.voanews.com/english/2009-05-18-voa18.cfm.

[69] Abdiaziz Hassan, "Somali PM: Little Hope of Talks with Insurgents," Reuters, May 21, 2009.

[70] "Ethiopian Forces Return to Somalia: Witnesses," Agence France-Presse, May 19, 2009.

[71] "Stoning Victim 'Begged for Mercy,'" BBC News, Nov. 4, 2008, http://news.bbc.co.uk/2/hi/africa/7708169.stm. See also: "Somali Justice — Islamist Style," BBC News, May 20, 2009, http://news.bbc.co.uk/2/hi/africa/8057179.stm.

[72] "Residents: Islamic Insurgents Seize Somalia Town," The Associated Press, May 20, 2009.

[73] "Man Blows Himself Up in Failed Yemen Attack," Reuters, March 18, 2009, www.reuters.com/article/latestCrisis/idUSLI290474.

[74] Jason McLure, "Ethiopia Quits Somalia, Declares 2-Year 'Mission Accomplished,'" Bloomberg News, Jan. 5, 2009, www.bloomberg.com/apps/news?pid=20601116&sid=aJqblcQ0bUCo.

[75] Abdi Sheikh and Abdi Guled, "Ethiopia Denies Its Troops Enter Somalia," Reuters, Feb. 3, 2009. See also: "Ethiopian Forces Return to Somalia: Witnesses," Agence France-Presse, May 19, 2009.

[76] Ogaden National Liberation Front Military Communique, March 7, 2009.

[77] "Report of the Monitoring Group on Somalia," *op. cit.*, p. 33.

[78] "Beyond the Fragile Peace Between Ethiopia and Eritrea: Averting New War," *op. cit.*

[79] Jason McLure, "Eritrean Group Calls for 'Popular Uprising' Against Government, Bloomberg News, May 8, 2008.

[80] "Report of the Monitoring Group on Somalia," *op. cit.*

[81] "Beyond the Fragile Peace Between Ethiopia and Eritrea: Averting New War," *op. cit.*

[82] "Service for Life: State Repression and Indefinite Conscription in Eritrea," Human Rights Watch, April 16, 2009. See also Jason McLure, "Eritrea a 'Giant Prison,' Human Rights Watch Says (Update 1)," Bloomberg News, April 16, 2009.

[83] Ken Menkhaus, "Beyond Piracy: Next Steps to Stabilize Somalia," Enough Project, www.enoughproject.org/publications/beyond-piracy-next-steps-stabilize-somalia.

FOR MORE INFORMATION

African Union, P.O. Box 3243, Addis Ababa, Ethiopia; (251) 11 551 77 00; www.africa-union.org. Seeks political and economic cooperation among the 53 member nations.

Amnesty International, 1 Easton St., London, WCIX 0DW, United Kingdom; (44) 20 74135500; www.amnesty.org. Advocates for human rights around the globe and publishes periodic reports on abuses.

Council on Foreign Relations, 1779 Massachusetts Ave., N.W., Washington, DC 20036; (202) 518-3400; www.cfr.org. Nonpartisan think tank that offers extensive resources, data and experts on foreign policy issues.

Enough Project, 1225 I St., N.W., Suite 307, Washington, DC 20005; (202) 682-1611; www.enoughproject.org. Lobbies for ending genocide and crimes against humanity.

Human Rights Watch, 350 Fifth Ave., 34th Floor, New York, NY 10118-3299; (212) 290-4700; www.hrw.org. Investigates human rights abuses worldwide with a team of lawyers and researchers.

Institute for Security Studies, P.O. Box 1787, Brooklyn Square, Tshwane (Pretoria) 0075, South Africa; (27) 012 346 9500; www.iss.co.za. African foreign policy think tank that provides a range of views on African issues.

International Crisis Group, 149 Avenue Louise, Level 24, B-1050 Brussels, Belgium; (32) 2 502-9038; www.crisisgroup.org. Provides independent research on international relations and the developing world.

Bibliography

Selected Sources

Books

Ali, Ayaan Hirsi, *Infidel*, Free Press, 2007.
This coming-of-age tale of a Somali girl living in Somalia, Saudi Arabia, Ethiopia, Kenya, the Netherlands and, finally, the United States explores how Somali culture and Islamic codes subordinate women.

Hartley, Aidan, *The Zanzibar Chest*, Harper Perennial, 2003.
A Reuters correspondent's memoir of covering wars in Somalia, Ethiopia and Rwanda in the early 1990s is interlaced with his family's British colonial history in East Africa and Yemen. Highlights include his eyewitness account of entering Addis Ababa in 1991 with Tigrayan rebels for the fall of the communist Derg regime and witnessing the U.S. military's "Black Hawk" assault on Mogadishu.

Lewis, I. M., *A Modern History of the Somali*, James Currey Ltd., 2002.
One of the few Western academics to have spent his career studying Somalia, anthropologist Lewis focuses on how clan identities have shaped Somalis' history.

Marcus, Harold G., *A History of Ethiopia*, University of California Press, 2002.
This brief history begins with the famed fossil of Lucy, a human ancestor who roamed eastern Ethiopia 4 million years ago, and ends shortly after the 1998-2000 Ethiopia-Eritrea war.

Mezlekia, Nega, *Notes from the Hyena's Belly: An Ethiopian Boyhood*, Picador USA, 2000.
An Ethiopian writer's memoir of growing up during the 1970s provides a first-person account of the country's communist revolution and the ethnic tensions between Somalis and Ethiopian highlanders that still shape regional politics.

Wrong, Michela, *I Didn't Do It For You: How the World Used and Abused A Small African Nation*, Harper Perennial, 2005.
Mixing history and travelogue, a British journalist traces Eritrea's four-decade battle for independence after World War II. Wrong shows how the stubborn and resourceful Eritrean resistance becomes a pawn of Cold War powers and documents post-independence disillusionment under the dictatorial regime of former rebel leader Isaias Afwerki.

Articles

Ephron, Dan, and Mark Hosenball, "Recruited for Jihad?" *Newsweek*, Feb. 2, 2009, www.newsweek.com/id/181408.
Two Washington journalists uncover efforts by Somali Islamists to recruit fighters from U.S. refugee communities.

Gettleman, Jeffrey, "In Ethiopia Fear and Cries of Army Brutality," *The New York Times*, June 18, 2007, www.nytimes.com/2007/06/18/world/africa/18ethiopia.html.
The only Western journalist to enter Ethiopia's Somali region without being accompanied by Ethiopian security forces in recent years gives an account of atrocities by Ethiopian soldiers. Gettleman was arrested by the Ethiopian government during the trip.

Gettleman, Jeffrey, "The Most Dangerous Place in the World," *Foreign Policy*, March/April 2009, www.foreignpolicy.com/story/cms.php?story_id=4682.
The New York Times East Africa correspondent gives a short history of how Ethiopia and the United States exacerbated Somalia's civil war between 2005 and 2008.

Perry, Alex, "Somalia's War Flares Up Again," *Time*, Nov. 12, 2007, www.time.com/time/world/article/0,8599,1682877,00.html.
Perry outlines the motivations of the various actors in Somalia's civil war, including the transitional government, Islamist militias, Ethiopia and the United States.

Reports and Studies

"Beyond the Fragile Peace Between Ethiopia and Eritrea: Averting New War," International Crisis Group, June 17, 2008, www.crisisgroup.org/home/index.cfm?id=1229.
The continuing cold war between Ethiopia and Eritrea after their 1998-2000 war is fueling a host of regional conflicts.

"2008 Human Rights Report: Ethiopia," U.S. Department of State, Feb. 25, 2009, www.state.gov/g/drl/rls/hrrpt/2008/af/119001.htm.
Despite its close ties with Ethiopia's government, the U.S. State Department provides one of the most rigorous and detailed reports on human rights violations under Prime Minister Meles Zenawi.

"Report of the Monitoring Group on Somalia," United Nations, Dec. 10, 2008, www.un.org/sc/committees/751/mongroup.shtml.
The U.N. team that monitors Somalia's arms embargo describes the various militias and their links to foreign governments, piracy and other illicit activities.

Menkhaus, Kenneth, "Somalia: A Country in Peril: A Policy Nightmare," Enough Project, Sept. 3, 2008, www.enoughproject.org/files/reports/somalia_rep090308.pdf.
A former U.N. official in Somalia dissects the missteps by Somali regional and international powers that led Somalia to the brink and suggests how to bring peace to the troubled country.

The Next Step:

Additional Articles from Current Periodicals

Development Aid

"UK to Send Further GBP10 Million Aid," _Daily Monitor_ (Ethiopia), June 11, 2008.

The United Kingdom has announced plans to contribute £10 million to Ethiopia in response to a worsening humanitarian situation.

"U.S. Government Promises More Aid," _Somaliland Times_, Sept. 21, 2008.

An American diplomat says the United States plans to provide more development aid to Somaliland if the region shows measurable progress.

Verling, Lúc, "Former Torture Victim Urges EU to Withhold €122M Eritrean Aid," _Irish Times_, April 3, 2009.

A former Eritrean torture victim has urged the international community to withhold a proposed 122 million euro development package to the country.

Malaria

"Ethiopia Made 'Progress' in Malaria Prevention, Says Minister," _ENA_ (Ethiopia), Sept. 2, 2008.

Ethiopia's minister of health says strong national efforts have positioned the country to reduce the burden of malaria and eventually to eliminate it as a public health threat.

"Ethiopia Mortality Rate Due to Malaria Declines By Half — Study Says," _Walta_ (Ethiopia), June 6, 2008.

A new study has revealed that deaths in Ethiopia due to malaria have decreased by 50 percent over the past three years.

McNeil Jr., Donald G., "Plan Tries to Lower Malaria Drug Cost," _The New York Times_, April 17, 2009, p. A12.

International health agencies and European governments have revealed a campaign aiming to reduce the cost of malaria medicine to as low as 20 cents per unit in countries such as Ethiopia.

Piracy

"Piracy Death Penalty Call By Somalia," _Birmingham Post_ (England), April 21, 2009.

The Somali government has called for the death penalty for pirates who attacked a Norwegian tanker in the Gulf of Aden.

Mbitiru, Chege, "There and About — Somali Pirates Face New Offensive," _The Nation_ (Kenya), May 5, 2008.

The United States, Great Britain, France and Panama are considering a resolution that would allow other nations' warships to enter Somali waters in order to combat piracy.

Oloya, Opiyo, "Ensuring Peace in Somalia Will Bring Piracy to an End," _New Vision_ (Uganda), Nov. 25, 2008.

Improving political stability in Somalia is necessary to curb piracy off the country's coast.

Salopek, Paul, "Who's Pirating Whom?" _Chicago Tribune_, Oct. 10, 2008, p. A6.

Somali pirates say their attacks and ransom demands are tough payback for the international community's abuse of Somalia's territorial waters.

Terrorism

"Somali Islamist Leader to Support Govt If Removed From Terror List," _Puntlandpost_ (Somalia), April 6, 2009.

The chairman of a Somali liberation group based in Eritrea has promised to support the new Somali president if the chairman's name is taken off the U.S. list of terror suspects.

"Somalilanders Alarmed That the Increasingly Pro-Al-Shabaab Tone of the BBC's Somali Broadcast Might Influence Some Younger People to Become Terrorists," _Somaliland Times_, Nov. 15, 2008.

Concern is growing in Somaliland that slanted television coverage of terrorists could lead the younger generation to accept and promote terrorism.

"U.S. Officials Warn of Terrorist Recruitment of Somali-Americans," _Thai Press Reports_, March 13, 2009.

U.S. authorities are investigating possible links between Somali terrorist groups and the disappearance of several Somali-American teenagers and young men.

Voices From Abroad:

MIKHAIL VOYTENKO
Chief Editor, Maritime Bulletin-Sovfracht, Russia

'A greater threat than terrorism.'

"In my view, from the point of view of world shipping, this will be a greater threat than terrorism. This is criminal, and the Somali pirates showed that this was possible. I think that very soon they will be joined by others, who are much more experienced and more combat-ready."

Centre TV (Russia), November 2008

AHMEDOU OULD-ABDALLAH
Special Representative to Somalia, United Nations

Help needed for Somalia's government

"It is a long-running conflict. . . . The tragedy in Somalia is the central government has been very weak. We have the beginning of a credible [government]. We have to help it be functional."

States News Service, May 2009

LOUIS MICHEL
Commissioner, Development and Humanitarian Aid European Commission

Europe is committed.

"The challenges in the Horn of Africa are huge and multidimensional. On the strictly humanitarian side, the area has suffered persistent drought in recent years, and more and more people are struggling to survive. Humanitarian aid is an expression of Europe's solidarity with those who are most vulnerable."

Daily Monitor (Ethiopia), August 2008

ZERIHUN RETTA
Ethiopian Ambassador to Ireland

Peace opportunities exist now.

"It is not in the interest of Ethiopia to stay longer in Somalia, and it is ready to withdraw its forces from Somalia at any time. Ethiopian troops are unable to return home without leaving a dangerous vacuum that would result in the annihilation of the window of opportunities created for peace now."

Irish Times, June 2008

NICOLE STRACKE
Security and Terrorism Researcher, Gulf Research Centre, United Arab Emirates

Pirates have created an organized venture.

"Pirates have not really harmed a lot of hostages, and this is likely to change. . . . [P]iracy has developed its own dynamic and now resembles a professional and highly organised business venture, starting from the selection of maritime targets to the final stage of receiving and dispensing the ransom."

Gulf News (United Arab Emirates), May 2009

PAUL MOORCRAFT
Director, Centre for Foreign Policy Analysis England

Comparisons to Afghanistan are fair.

"Although Washington has over-egged the Islamist threat and al-Qa'idah links to the Somali crisis, the comparison with Afghanistan before 9/11 carries some weight. The state-sponsorship of terrorism and piracy is a growing threat."

Business Day (South Africa), December 2008

SOMALI PIRATE
Unidentified

Our tough conditions.

"We are saying we are pirates pushed by hunger, the lack of a government. . . . [T]he solution is that the world should recognize Somalia and help put its government in place."

NTV (Kenya), September 2008

ISAIAS AFWERKI
President, Eritrea

Eritrea's right to defense.

"We don't need any confrontation [between Eritrea and Ethiopia]. We have our right to self-defence. We have been committed to our legal obligations as far as the border is concerned. As I indicated earlier, we will abide by the letter and spirit of the agreement."

U.N. Integrated Regional Information Networks, October 2007

KWESI ANING
Lecturer, Kofi Annan International Peacekeeping Training Centre, Ghana

Recognize Somaliland.

"The lack of recognition ties the hands of the authorities and people of Somaliland, as they cannot effectively and sustainably transact business with the outside world and pursue development goals."

Public Agenda (Ghana), June 2007

Deng Coy Miel/Singapore